Minorities in American Society

Minorities in American Society

FOURTH EDITION

CHARLES F. MARDEN
Rutgers, The State University

GLADYS MEYER
Barnard College, Columbia University

D. VAN NOSTRAND COMPANY
New York   Cincinnati   London   Toronto   Melbourne

D. Van Nostrand Company Regional Offices:
New York   Cincinnati   Millbrae

D. Van Nostrand Company International Offices:
London   Toronto   Melbourne

Library of Congress Catalog Card Number: 72-7764

ISBN: O-442-23460-0

Published by D. Van Nostrand Company
450 West 33rd Street, New York, N.Y. 10001

Published simultaneously in Canada by
Van Nostrand Reinhold Ltd.

10 9 8 7 6 5 4 3 2 1

Acknowledgments

The authors wish to express their appreciation to the following persons who have given, in various ways, generous assistance in the preparation of this new edition: Professor Madeline H. Engel, Lehman College of the City University of New York; Professor Isabella Bick, Stern College, Yeshiva University; Professor Raymond E. Sakumoto, the University of Hawaii; and Miss Barbara Winkler for research and typing. Dr. Marden wishes to acknowledge for the fourth time his gratitude to his wife, Freda W. Marden, for a wide range of contributions from typing and editing to critical comments, and to his son Dr. Philip W. Marden for his helpful contributions.

Preface

The central concern of this Fourth Edition of *Minorities in American Society* remains the same as that of earlier editions—the position of minority groups within the social structure of the United States today. The situations of minorities in America have become obviously and increasingly fluid and dynamic. This new edition reflects the changes and the course of events in dominant-minority relations in the five years since the Third Edition: the revival of ethnic consciousness and identification; the increased polarization of blacks and whites; and the continuing trend toward co-equal pluralism in the United States, to cite only a few examples which are further discussed in the Introduction.

The plan of organization and central features of the book remain essentially the same. Part I (Chapters 1–4) is an introduction to minority problems and situations; Part II (Chapters 5–16) considers the situation of specific minority groups; and Part III (Chapters 17 and 18) discusses social policy and sociological theory. The number of chapters has been reduced by two from the previous edition. Material on religious and cultural minorities has been combined into one chapter, while the chapter on race has been expanded. Part II opens with five chapters on black-white relations, a change in the order of presentation from the previous edition. The black situation is now presented first and at length because of its prominence, and a new chapter, "The Black Challenge," has been added. A new emphasis in this edition is on the increased activity and militancy of minority groups and the effect of this activity on dominant-minority relations in the United States today.

Contents

Minorities
in
American
Society

Introduction

This book was first conceived in the aftermath of World War II in response to a renewed interest in the situation of "minority peoples" of the United States. We had been through a war which heightened awareness of discrimination in American life. In fighting the Nazi ideology, America was forced to look at its own shortcomings. The labor necessities of war had seen the first national effort to eliminate discrimination in employment. The tragic and, to many, unnecessary internment of the Japanese had heightened awareness. The plight of the refugees and the greater involvement of blacks at a better level in the armed forces made it imperative that national attention be focused on minority issues so that the gains might be maintained and the mistakes rectified. In our first edition (1952), most minorities were still members of visible sub-communities with their own internal organization, leadership, and cultural roots. The first edition tried to present minorities primarily through the focus of community.

The 1954 Supreme Court decision outlawing school segregation, together with the Court's other decisions making it clear that imposed segregation always meant inequality, began to undermine a long institutionalized racial system of inequality. This legal decision was strongly resisted in the South. Thus our second edition (1962) perforce gave special attention to the conflicts this changed situation brought about: less attention was given to the minority communities, and at the time integration appeared to be the prospect for the future.

1

The post-war era led to a great development of interest in intergroup relations in the behavioral sciences, particularly those where ethnic or "racial" relations of a dominant-minority form were involved. Much research was undertaken in an attempt to provide a more extensive description and interpretation.[1] Out of this also came suggested social policy by which change could be effected. In consequence, as we approached our third edition (1968) this broader base of available studies called for our giving greater attention to theories of intergroup relations and to the refinements of concepts. Of particular concern in this connection has been a developing challenge to previous theories of assimilation of the non-WASP (White Anglo-Saxon Protestant) ethnic and "racial" groups to American life.[2]

During the 1960s the accelerating momentum of the black challenge to white dominance and the responses of white America to it became a major domestic phenomenon of the decade, and it continues to be of nationwide significance as migration of blacks to all the nation's large metropolitan districts continues apace. Even by the time our 3rd edition (1968) appeared, the increasing militancy of the black challenge pointed to foreboding possibilities which required special attention. As we came to our 4th edition, the large scale rioting of the sixties which had taken white America by surprise had diminished. But in urban communities with a large number, or a large proportion of blacks, polarization between blacks and whites has increased in the past five years, with open interracial conflict frequent enough so that currently it has become a normative aspect of the life of such cities[3] and will remain so for some unpredictable years ahead.

From a broader sociological viewpoint, this current polarization and black militancy has paved the way for the latest significant development in intergroup relations. Crystalizing in this decade is a revival of ethnic consciousness and identification in new forms among most other minorities, and interestingly, among some ethnic components not currently thought of as minorities, e.g., Italian-descended Americans. Psychologically this is manifested by efforts to create a stronger personal pride and self-

[1]One of the most elaborate of such researches is that of Robin Williams, *Strangers Next Door: Ethnic Relations in American Communities* (Englewood Cliffs, N.J.: Prentice Hall, 1964).
[2]The first comprehensive treatment of this new theoretical development is found in Milton M. Gordon, *Assimilation in American Life* (New York: Oxford University Press, 1964).
[3]In 1971 nearly 200 interracial disorders of sufficient dimension to receive attention in the national press occurred.

respect in lineage, e.g., "Black is Beautiful." Culturally there are efforts by racial and ethnic groups to develop some sense of their native roots. These, of course, are not in a pure and scholarly sense self-definitions in terms of African cultures or the Spanish cultures of Spain or Mexico; but rather the group's own derivative variant. This has an integrative effect for the sub-community, although, of course, a divisive effect on the society as a whole to the degree that it handicaps communication. Politically much of the rationale for this sub-community revival is the hope of creating a political base whereby the minority may win benefits for its group on a local or on a national level (state level is not very important except in the South). These benefits are financial aid for development, access to political office, both elective and appointive, and freedom from centralized bureaucratic forms, as for example in community control of schools.

This rapid emergence of sub-ethnic consciousness within the broader identification as equal Americans[4] (with some "extremist" exceptions) has been accompanied by the wide acceptance by minority leadership, by dominant sympathizers, and by some of the rank and file of both groups that *confrontation* and *demonstration* are the most effective weapons for pursuing their interests. This is in part a heritage of a decade of civil rights effort. At its worst it leads to irresponsible violence. But for the majority of those using this tool, there is still the expectation of being able to effect change within the system, provided they are noisy enough and visible enough. Hitherto dominants have tried to make minorities invisible culturally and often ecologically. Now minorities are responding by strengthening and capitalizing on visibility.

One problem which became more acute as we approached the 4th edition was the terminology to be used in referring to certain groups. Groups which hitherto had attached little importance to what they were called, unless it was derogatory, have recently come to attach pride to their collective names. Racial and ethnic terms such as "Chicano" and "black" have in many cases become rallying points and sources of self-identity. However, because this trend is relatively new it has been difficult to decide in some instances on the proper terminology.

[4]The term "Americans" in this text refers to citizens of the United States exclusively. This usage is an unfortunate example of this country's ethnocentrism in that it excludes other peoples living in North America; however we use it here to avoid awkward repetition of the term "citizen of the United States."

Often the most precisely descriptive term is awkward—for example, "citizens of the United States of European ancestry." Up to World War II one could have used for the dominant-ethnic component White Anglo-Saxon Protestants, (WASP). Generally speaking, when we use this term it should be considered more broadly to mean white people of Christian and European lineage who no longer have minority status. In areas where the name bestowed upon the WASP dominants by the minority peoples became common usage by all, we use the current term: Anglo in the southwest and *Haole* for Euro-American-descended whites in Hawaii. Changing circumstances render group names used earlier currently inadequate. Thus former designations such as Spanish-speaking or Latin Americans for peoples deriving from south of the Rio Grande or the Caribbean region are no longer appropriate, e.g., for mainland Puerto Ricans, Cubans, and the large Mexican-descended American ethnic group.

The most difficult—as well as the most delicate—in considering current race relations, is the appropriate name to use for Americans of African descent. The word "Negro" has been by far the most usual name applied for a long time in all formal contexts. The word "colored" was an alternative, even used by Negroes themselves as in the name of the National Association for the Advancement of Colored People. But with the growing development of pride in their ancestry the shift to the term "blacks" has come into widespread use in the national mass media, as well as among the black people themselves, although government documents, including the Census, still use "Negro." Actually, research as to what proportions of the people involved prefer which of these various group names has not been made. We shall therefore use all these terms in varying contexts: for example, in the historical material, Negro; in dealing with the new developments, especially since the early sixties, most often we shall use "black." We use "black," however, with some regrets, because being a "color" name it tends to emphasize the one visible genetic characteristic most commonly used to denote racial differences—differences which, from a scientific viewpoint, are irrelevant bases for evaluating any person. On the other hand, we recognize the need of this group for some other name than "Negro," bestowed on blacks by whites and for so long associated with their derogatory image, in order to develop pride in its identity. "Black is beautiful," and so is yellow, or brown, or white. But some group name denoting cultural qualities of equally high order to those of other American ethnics would be preferable. Among some blacks, the term Afro-American is coming into usage. One faces the fact that the continuity of the original African cultures has been lost, and that for a very large number of black Americans, substantially no vestigial remnants of their African past persist or have been revived. Nevertheless, in the cities with large black populations, there has been an increasing interest in discovering the great achievements of Africa; in identifying with militant African anti-colonialism; and in borrowing styles of dress and of art that are symbolic of the dignity of African heritage.

THE POINT OF VIEW OF THIS BOOK

Recent approaches to the study of minorities have selected various emphases, and recent research has contributed to these selected foci. There are authors who have stressed culture: the richness and right to integrity of variant cultures within the national state. There are psychologically oriented authors who are primarily concerned with attitudinal and perceptive aspects of intergroup relations. Still another approach is comparative, to discover and delineate recurring and perhaps generic problems of dominant-minority relations in a number of national states.

Our concern is to write about the position of minorities within the social structure of the United States today. In a society as dynamic as that of America the situation of minorities is increasingly fluid. Therefore, when we can we will identify trends. Much conflict between dominants and minorities in the last decade has been institutionally focussed. Minorities have increasingly pressed for political and economic incorporation with equality of chances and equality of sanctions. Great gains have been made in this area. But in the end the fundamental issues of dominant-minority relations will depend on how people in communities regard one another and how they associate with one another.

We have chosen *differential visibility* as the basis for the classification of minorities which governs our material. We have emphasized, though not exclusively, *discrimination* as the significant mechanism by which minorities are held in subordinate status. Our substantive material has been drawn, where possible, from *community studies*, as local and regional variations and variation in structure and type of community will affect both dominants and minorities. We have noted changes in public policy which affect communities, as community sentiments in turn affect policy. The process of interaction between dominants and minorities is a *reciprocal* one. Changes in either the behavior of dominants or of minorities will bring about reactive behavior, favorable or unfavorable, in the other group and thus affect the pattern of relationship.

A NOTE ON ORGANIZATION

The purpose of this book and its plan of organization can both be stated by reference to its division into three parts. In Part I, "Some Basic Approaches to Analyzing American Minorities," the main concepts and processes essential for description and analysis of dominant-minority relations are presented. In Part II, "Major Minority Situations in the United States Today," each of the main minority peoples' situations is described and analyzed separately, with more extensive attention to black-white relations because of their critical importance. The schema of treatment of these substantive chapters is twofold: *developmental* and *interactional.* Our emphasis in each situation is upon the interrelation between the dominant and the minority as a particular example of large-scale societal differentiation. Ethno-racial differentiation is widespread in the modern world; only social class difference is more universal, and religious differentiation may rival ethno-racial differentiation in frequency. Whereas in the United States all three of these large-scale population differences exist and often overlap, their interrelations also require attention.

Further complicating analysis of the heterogeneous, ethno-racial population of the United States is the fact that even within the ethno-racial structure there are rank orders of status in which some groups are both a minority, with some groups above them, and in part a dominant, with some groups below.

In broad terms the development of dominant-minority relations usually follow a pattern of three sequences: (1) the establishment of dominance, (2) the maintenance of dominance, and (3) the decline of dominance. The time spans of the three processes may vary widely. For example, it took the European invaders two hundred years to establish dominance over the American Indians, whereas the African slaves were brought here in abject minority status at the outset. In a general way non-British European immigrants went through the complete cycle in not over three generations. The third phase is not to be considered as a complete decline in dominance. It simply reflects the current factual trend—a decrease in the degree of discrimination toward minorities. While we have suggested that in general the non-British European descendants "have made it," it is still to be determined when, if ever, and which of the remaining minorities "will make it."

In Part III we discuss the current theoretical orientation as contrasted with earlier theoretical approaches; provide a synthesized interpretation of dominant-minority relations in terms of the institutional structure of the United States; summarize the social forces influencing the current trends; and discuss social policy and action which might be brought to bear upon the extremely critical problems which now face the nation.

A NOTE TO STUDENTS

These are days when students as well as many other serious-minded Americans are critical of education for what they consider its lack of *relevance* to the social problems of the times. At this introductory point, it is pertinent to define the term, "social problem." Sociologists consider that whether any set of social facts constitute a "problem" or not depends on the value system of the person viewing the facts; and the definition of the problem varies with the person's value system. Both these points can be illustrated this way. To the traditional white Southerner, the rising militancy of Negroes following World War II presented the "problem" of how to keep blacks in their place, or later, how to resist outside pressure in behalf of the minority as long as possible; to the liberally-oriented white the problem has been how to cooperate in advancing the blacks to complete equality.

Many of our readers may be thinking "So what? We know what you describe so meticulously constitutes a serious social problem. Why don't you tell us what to do about it?" Some of our student readers may not be aware of the fact that the behavioral scientists have long argued among themselves as to how much their teaching and writing should be objective—descriptively accurate, analytically sound, and unbiased; or to what extent their work should be geared directly at problem-solving. Sociology in particular in its aim to be, as a science, objective faces the problem that its field deals with basic values about which other people feel deep emotion. We propose to face up to this concern head-on by stating at the outset that we agree with Gunnar Myrdal who in a recent address at Harvard University said, "There can never be and never has been a 'disinterested' research in the social field as there has been in the natural sciences. Valuations are in fact determining our work even if we manage to be unaware of it."[5]

In line with this the value system we shall adopt in this text derives from two beliefs: (1) that democracy is the most desirable form of social organization; and (2) that the welfare of the society as a whole, either the nation, or the local community, takes precedence over the welfare of any special groups within this whole. We shall discuss many social problems throughout the book, as well as at the end. Wherever we do, it is from the above value frame of reference.

[5]Reported by Robert Reinhold, *New York Times*, Nov. 6, 1971, p. 33.

Part I

Some Basic Approaches to Analyzing American Minorities

1 **M**inorities in the United States and in the Modern World

As linguistic, economic, social and cultural drives are integrated into philosophies of action by groups, it will become apparent that the . . . world is being submerged in tribalism and ethnic communities. . . . The crucial thing to note is that we have passed the point of no return, so that we cannot go home again. . . . By creating the most flexible situation we can, we may find the tools and techniques to survive the changes ahead. . . . There will be new tribes and new turf—in our lifetime.*

By and large reality has been conceptualized in terms of the narrow point of view of the small minority of white men who live in Europe and North America. We must abandon (this) partial frame of reference of our oppressors and create new concepts which will release our reality, which is also the reality of the overwhelming majority of men and women on this globe.†

*Vine Deloria, Jr., *We Talk, You Listen* (New York: The Macmillan Co., 1970).
†Lerone Bennett, "The Challenge of Blackness," *Black Paper Series*, Institute of Black World Publications, April, 1970.

MINORITIES IN THE UNITED STATES

Indians

From the earliest settlements in the colonial period until 1871, white Americans increasingly encroached on the land possessed by American Indians resulting in a great decline in the Indian population. Indian-white relations were considered formally, if somewhat fictionally, as contractual relations between sovereign political entities. Tribes were often called "nations." In 1871 Indians became official wards of the United States Government and thus formally, as well as actually, a minority. During the wardship period neither the welfare nor the status of the Indians improved much until 1934, when the broad policy established under the New Deal began helping the Indians improve their economic welfare with maximum possible retention of their tribal identities and cultures. Since then controversy has existed between those white Americans who retain this New Deal approach and those who want to see the tribes liquidated and Indians as individuals put on their own like other Americans. Federal government policy toward Indians in the post-World War II period has vacillated around these two viewpoints with the New Deal approach tending to hold its own on paper but often not adequately implemented. Thus the welfare of all tribal Indians added together is still the lowest of the nation's manifold minorities.

Africans

Since 1619 when the first African slaves were brought to Virgina, African descended people have been systematically discriminated against by formal legalized institutions in the South and informal institutionalized practices in the North. Throughout the entire time (aside from the brief abortive Reconstruction period) they have been denied equality of opportunity. In every way this 12 per cent of our population constitutes the nation's number one minority. The determined effort on their own part, reinforced by various social forces in general during and since World War II, to improve their status and welfare precipitated a national crisis of the most serious dimensions, and it is now obvious that it will still take a considerable time to reach some tolerable accommodation of interests.

Europeans

Even before American Negroes moved from slavery to the status of a minority caste, there began an influx from Europe which was destined to change the character of the United States profoundly. First came the Irish, Scandinavians, and Germans, later the Southern and Eastern Europeans. The customs of these various peoples differed markedly from those of the "natives." The relation of these various peoples to the older residents followed a similar pattern, beginning with indifference, antagonism, and conflict and ending with varying degrees of acceptance.

Once restriction of European immigration went into effect with the Immigration Act of 1924, an important era in United States history came to an end. While there remain some European immigrants who will live out their days never fully assimilated into American life, their children and certainly their grandchildren have been or are being assimilated.

Further interest lies particularly with the descendants of Southern and Eastern European immigrants. There has been a resurgence of pride in their ancestral heritage on the part of subsequent generations and a feeling of ethnic identification and equality with the original WASPs (White Anglo-Saxon Protestants), whose former dominant position now appears less secure.

Asians

Overlapping chronologically with European immigration was that of the Chinese and Japanese who concentrated in West Coast communities. At first they were tolerated with condescension as exploitable labor. But as these people, particularly the Japanese, began to succeed in competition with native whites, further immigration was curtailed by the government. Those who remained here were fixed in a pattern of segregated minority status little altered until the drastic relocation of the West Coast Japanese during World War II. This unique epoch in the history of American minorities, from any long-range view an unfortunate episode, revealed a certain ineptitude and immaturity in the handling of minority group problems. Since the War the economic status of both the Chinese and the Japanese has improved and discrimination against them has markedly declined, particularly in the case of the Japanese.

While evacuation dispersed the Japanese somewhat, many of

the evacuees returned to the West Coast. Of all non-European minorities, the native-born Japanese have achieved the highest welfare and are widely accepted as good Americans, although they are largely still identified also as Japanese. Substantial segments of the Chinese, partly by their own choice, are still considerably insulated in Chinatowns. However small pockets of middle-class Chinese are found scattered in suburban communities. The ebbs and flows of Asian immigration to the mainland United States has been affected by immigration law. Restriction in the early stages kept their number small. But the new immigration act of 1965 opened the doors to a limited number and accounts for the large growth rate of both the Chinese and Japanese, as well as that of the only other sizable Asian American minority, the Filipinos, whose numbers almost doubled in the 1960–1970 decade.

From the Other Americas

Until recently, immigration from other parts of the Americas has been largely from Canada and from nearer areas south of the Rio Grande. British Canadians have never been considered as a minority. However French Canadians largely settling in upper New England experienced much the same process of adjustment as the South-Eastern European minorities. From the Southern Americas in time order came Mexicans and Puerto Ricans.

Mexicans

Following the restriction of European immigration a large influx of Mexicans into the Southwest began. The usual pattern of native-immigrant interaction occurred: welcome as menial laborers, but discriminated against otherwise; acculterated slowly up to World War II, and accelerated since then. In the whole United States persons descended from former or current Mexican national lineage number now some six million, thus being one of the larger minority groups. In the Southwest also there are descendants of the Spanish-speaking people who inhabited the region when the Anglos invaded and subsequently annexed the area. Known as "hispanos" they make up a substantial part of New Mexico's population. While in New Mexico they have never been formally discriminated against, their economic and health conditions for years ranked among the lowest in the nation. In the thinking of dominant Americans outside the Southwest the larger and continuous migration of Mexican nationals has tended to blur the distinctive historical position of these hispanos.

Mexican-descended Americans have been the least upwardly status minded of immigrant groups, but recently they have become more aggressive in protecting their rights, particularly through labor unionization.

Puerto Ricans

A more recent minority situation arises out of the influx of a substantial number of Puerto Ricans to the mainland. At first largely localized in New York City, Puerto Ricans are now spreading across the nation. They have encountered the usual problems of an immigrant group adjusting to a strange cultural environment. As a people with a language difference and varying degrees of physical visibility, they have encountered discrimination and exploitation.

Despite an unknown amount of Negro genetic strain intermingled with Spanish and Indian strains, mainland Puerto Rican immigrants are generally thought of as part of the white population. Because of this and other circumstances, their full acceptance as equals may proceed more rapidly than the currently more acculturated blacks.

The Refugee Groups

While a minor portion of the total immigration to the United States was prompted by either political or religious persecution, numerous international events since 1930 have led thousands of people from various parts of the world to flee their homelands for political reasons. Among those coming to this country have been "refugees" from the Nazis in the thirties; persons displaced in Europe as a result of Russian expansion during and since World War II; and more recently "escapees" from Communist China and Cuba.

The large growth rate of the Chinese American population during the 1960–1970 period includes a substantial number of refugees from Communist China. In many cases these were Chinese, especially students, who, as temporary residents in the country at the time of the Communist take over, were given regular immigrant status and have received citizenship.

A substantial number of anti-Castro Cubans also fled to this country as the new government gained power in 1958. Most settled first in Miami; however many have resettled in other communities. As was the case with many recent Chinese newcomers, the Cuban refugee groups have had a disproportionate number of better-educated and professional people which has facilitated successful adjustment. About one-fourth of Miami's population is now Cuban-descended and they play an influential role in the city's economic life.

As an example of other not generally known-about "refugee" groups, recent attention has focused on Haitians who have been escaping to New York City since the advent of the Duvalier dictatorial regime in 1957. First came the elite, followed by middle-class Haitians, and finally a lower class, each being neatly separated in three different areas of the City to retain the class distinctions intact.[1]

Religious Minorities: Catholics and Jews

Since the United States has been primarily a Protestant nation, residents with non-Protestant backgrounds have generally experienced some degree of minority status. Protestant discrimination against Roman Catholics became a constant phenomenon, although its more overt manifestations have been intermittent. Antipathy toward the Irish was directed as much toward them for being Catholic as for being Irish, partly because of the aggressive leadership of the Irish in American Catholicism. Protestant discrimination against Roman Catholics was strong following the advent of substantial Irish immigration beginning in 1849. Currently Catholic identification, per se, is no longer associated with minority status. The later immigrant groups of predominantly Catholic background—Italians, Poles, Mexicans, and Puerto Ricans—are viewed more as "foreigners" than as Catholics.

The story of Americans of Jewish ancestry presents several unique and in some ways baffling facets for the student of intergroup relations. Broadly speaking, Jews accommodated to American life more quickly and successfully than other non-Protestant European immigrants. But Gentile discrimination against them has been a constant phenomenon at least since the 1880s. The Jews are not a race, nor do they fit the common definition of a nationality. Their identification with a distinctive religion and related

[1]Martha Weinman Lear, "New York's Haitians: Working, Watching, Be' Be Doc," *New York Times Magazine*, October 10, 1971.

cultural elements and their long struggle in the Diaspora to maintain their distinctiveness has given them a persistent collective identity. The status of Jews in the United States today is a subject of much dispute among scholars. With certainty we can state that there is among Gentiles a substantial volume of prejudice against Jews and, perhaps small in total amount but often virulent, anti-Semitic activity; and among Jews there are clearly identifiable sub-communities heavily concentrated in metropolitan areas.

Hawaii's Peoples

Of all the states, Hawaii is so unique in many respects that it is appropriate to put it last. From the democratic value frame of reference it far outdistances all other states in racial tolerance. Various circumstances in the early contacts between the Euro-American invaders and the Polynesian natives of an advanced preliterate kingdom facilitated the easy acquisition by the Euro-Americans first of economic and later of political dominance. A formal and informal pattern of ethnic equality was institutionalized from the start and became the traditional pattern, with the "haoles" (whites) as an upper class and the native Hawaiians as a lower class, aside from their leaders. Since due to their native culture the Hawaiians were unsuited to the humdrum labor necessary for efficient exploitation as workers by the haoles, energetic labor from Asia, first Chinese and then Japanese was imported. Meanwhile the native islanders' culture and population declined. On the other hand, at the outset the formal Western democratic institution of public education and the absence of any formal discrimination resulted in increasing acculturation and occupational mobility of the immigrant Asians. Thus before World War II Hawaii's ethnic relations assumed substantially the usual Western class system except that the line between the classes was also a racial line, with the higher classes white and the lower classes Asian. The aboriginal Hawaiians were scattered on the lower tiers of the class hierarchy, somewhat on the side.

Since World War II the continuing development of the above processes has brought increasing economic and political power to the Chinese and Japanese, tilting the ethnic stratification system toward the co-equal pluralistic form.

A striking illustration of white Hawaii's relative lack of "racism" is the high rate of intermarriage between "haoles" and the non-white groups, as well as between other ethnic groups. In

1969 intermarriage between haoles and non-haoles was close to 20 per cent.

One recent ethnic development in Hawaii is the increase in the haole population due to mainland migration, so that in 1970 for the first time since 1900, the "white" population was noticeably larger than that of the Japanese and had a more balanced class structure—more lower-class whites. Another recent development is an increasing militancy among the ambiguously ranked descendants of the aboriginal Hawaiians, now largely "part Hawaiians."

Size of Minority Populations of the United States

The preceding section indicates that a large part of the current population of the United States involves Americans who either are, or have descended from, peoples who were at some time minority peoples in the status meaning of the term. In general, only those who trace their ancestry to Britain, France before the Louisiana purchase, and Holland prior to the national period have not experienced minority status. The process of assimilation, however, moved most of the European descended peoples into the dominant category. There remains nevertheless a substantial number of people whose racial, ethnic, or religious identification carries with it significant discrimination. In Table 1-1 we endeavor to provide the best available data on the numbers of each of these peoples, their proportion of the total national population, and percentage of growth during the decade 1960–1970. First listed are those American peoples who are counted by the United States Census as "racial." It is well to bear in mind several points about this list. (1) In the 1970 Census racial designation was based on self-identification—that is, each resident specified his race. (2) The overall figure for the Asian peoples includes Hawaii where the interracial situation is greatly different from the mainland states. (3) The high growth rate of the Asian peoples indicated in the past decade is in considerable measure due to changes in immigration law opening wider the doors to other than Europeans. (See Chaps. 3 and 11.)

In the second section of the table are listed those people who are still generally considered "minorities" sociologically on bases other than race. Here the sources as indicated are only the best available estimates, and in Table 1-2 these are included in the total white population by the Census. Because we are concerned with all categories treated by dominants as minorities, we have attempted

TABLE 1-1   ESTIMATED POPULATION OF MINORITY PEOPLES IN THE UNITED STATES IN 1970 AND GROWTH PERCENTAGE FOR THE DECADE 1960–1970

Group	1970 Population rounded per 1000	Percentage of Total Population	Growth Percentage 1960–1970 decade
1 Negro	22,600 (a)	11.1 (a)	19.7
2 American Indian	793 (a)	3.9 (a)	51.4
3 Japanese	591 (a)	2.9 (a)	27.4
4 Chinese	435 (a)	2.1 (a)	83.3
5 Filipino	343 (a)	1.2 (a)	94.9
6 Other (Asians)	720 (ab)	3.6 (a)	230.0
7 Jewish American	6.000 + (b)		
8 Mexican American	5,000 (1969) (c)		
9 Puerto Rican (Mainland)	1,500 + (c)		
10 Cuban	625 (d)		
11 Other Ethnics	xxx		

(a) United States Census, 1970. P. C. (1) - 131, Table 60, p. 293.

(ab) The *Census* footnote includes here Koreans, Hawaiians (aboriginal) Aleuts, Eskimos, Malayans, and Polynesians.

(b) Population estimate for 1970, *American Jewish Yearbook* 1970, p. 354.

(c) U.S. Bureau of the Census, 1971.

(d) *New York Times Yearbook,* 1971, p. 287.

TABLE 1-2   ESTIMATED TOTAL OF THE MINORITY POPULATION OF THE UNITED STATES, 1970

Total Population of the United States	203,212,000
Total Dominant "White" Population (a)	165,000,000
Total Minority "White" Population (a)	13,500,000
Total Minority Non-White Population (b)	24,500,000

(a) From Table I categories 7, 8, 9, 10 are subtracted from 178,000,000 white population as given by the 1970 U.S. Census.

(b) A rough and rounded total of categories 1 through 6 of Table 1-1 the so-called "racial" categories.

a different approach as indicated in Table 1-2 by a process of adding and subtracting from the pertinent figures of Table 1-1.

Table 1-1 shows that Negroes currently comprise slightly over 90 per cent of the total non-white population.[2] The basic tables

[2]Prior to this Census the Negro portion of the total non-white population has been well over 90 per cent. Thus many studies and reports used the white/non-white dichotomy as near enough to reflect black-white comparisons. If the relatively greater growth rate of the non-black portion of the non-white population continues, data using the white/non-white division should be abandoned.

of the Census fail to provide the numbers of peoples who are generally considered minorities in the status as well as numerical sense. Thus in the second part of Table 1-1 we have included four groups and subtracted this total from the Census "white" population to estimate the total proportion of the American population in minority status. Such a procedure, as indicated in Table 1-2 raises the minority total to nearly 20 per cent.

DOMINANT-MINORITY RELATIONS AROUND THE WORLD

The systematic study of intergroup relations, and especially the dominant-minority form, has been most extensively studied in the United States for several reasons. First of all, it has been in this country that the social science of Sociology has developed the farthest. Secondly, the heterogeneous racial and ethnic composition of the United States furnishes the widest field for exploration. But the dominance of the more powerful ethnic component over the less powerful component within the same jurisdiction has had an extensive history throughout much of the world since the fifteenth century. The search for a more general analysis and interpretation of dominant-minority relations as a logical consequence of the dynamics of the modern nationalistic world societies is attested to by the appearance of a number of comparative studies within recent years.

For the above reason before preoccupying ourselves with minority peoples in the United States, we wish to provide a brief summary of similar phenomena in modern world history which will have some value in our later explanation of its widespread occurrence. Obviously, a brief analysis will have to omit many minor aspects of the areas we deal with and leave out some areas altogether.

To a large degree the establishment and maintenance of the dominant-minority pattern of inter-people relations derived from the migration of European peoples to Africa, the Americas, and Southeast Asia. In the earlier years the main purpose of this invasion was economic. Several of the areas invaded were either sparsely inhabited or occupied by peoples who were militarily or technologically less powerful. Thus the invaders were able to establish political control over such portions of these areas as they desired. Following trade, the Europeans began to exploit the agricultural and mineral potentials of the areas. For this they needed manual labor. Where the local inhabitants could be efficiently used for this purpose they were employed, and from this situation arose a colonial system with the relatively small number of Europeans in each area becoming administrators and rulers and, in terms of our interest, a dominant group controlling the natives in subordinate status, using whatever force was necessary. Where the native population were either too few in number or culturally unable to be efficiently utilized, the dominant colonial Europeans imported slaves or sought out other more sophisticated immigrants.

Africa: Sub-Saharan

From the dominant-minority point of view the simplest pattern of the colonial system developed in Sub-Saharan Africa, aside from South Africa. The British, French, Portuguese, and Spanish invaded the coastal areas of equatorial Africa first for trading purposes. Subsequently they pushed inland to develop the agricultural and mineral resources. Due to their vastly greater military power, they were able to establish political control with a small number of resident European political, military, and economic administrators. Native African labor was utilized and systematic dominance based on race was established over the natives. As Banton writes, "By keeping the gulf between the races fairly marked and preserving white prestige, a relatively small group of people has been able to exercise close control."[3] According to Raymond Kennedy, the outstanding characteristics of this system have been the political and economic subordination of the native population; poor development of social services, especially education, for natives; and the color line with its rigid social barriers between the white ruling class and the subject people. Of these, the most important feature for the study of minorities is the last—the color line. Concerning this, Kennedy writes:

> The colonial code that dictates complete social segregation of the races is rationalized either by the commonplace assertion that natives are ignorant or unclean or uninteresting; or by the claim that they do not desire whites to become familiar with them; or by the argument that informality, camaraderie and, most of all, intermarriage would weaken the prestige of the ruling class in the estimation of their subjects. . . .

[3]Michael Banton, "Africa South of the Sahara" in Melvin Tumin, *Comparative Perspectives on Race Relations* (Boston: Little, Brown & Co., 1969), p. 27.

The British colonial code draws the most rigid color of all. Paradoxically, the greatest colonizers in the world are the most provincial in their attitudes toward strange groups and cultures. The British have been in contact for a longer time with more dark peoples than any other western nation, yet they hold aloof from their subjects to an unequalled degree. They refuse to associate freely or make friends with other races, and their exclusiveness had engendered a reciprocal feeling toward them on the part of their colonial peoples. The attitude of the latter varies from indifference to active dislike, but, except in isolated instances, it never approaches friendliness. Natives often express a grudging admiration for the moral rectitude, financial incorruptibility, and legalistic fairness of Britishers, especially government officials, in the colonies; but bonds of mutual friendship and affection are lacking. . . .[4]

Limited European acculturation of some natives took place, but aside from work contacts most natives retained their historic way of life. Because of the small number and the frequently transient residence of the European administrators, miscegenation was so limited that the number of "coloured" was small, which made this area essentially a two-tiered stratification system based on race.[5]

Latin America

In South and Central America the ethnological picture was more complicated. In the highland and Andean areas the Spanish after defeating the Mayas, Incas, and the Aztecs enslaved or peonized the native Indians and utilized those needed as workers in the plantation system. In the lowland areas, especially Brazil, where they were unable to use the natives as desirable workers, the Latins imported African slaves. As in North America, Indian lands were expropriated, their peoples were retired to the hinterlands and were highly decimated. Two processes followed in Latin America which distinguish its ethnoracial history. The Latin Europeans tended to reside on a more permanent basis and continuous

[4]Raymond Kennedy, "The Colonial Crisis and the Future," *The Science of Man in the World Crisis*, ed. Ralph Linton (New York: Columbia University Press, 1945), pp. 318, 320. By permission of the publisher, Columbia University Press.
[5]An ILO African labor survey including thirty-five states and territories south of the Sahara lists a quite small number of "coloureds" aside from the European "settled" states of Southwest Africa, Northern Rhodesia, and Angola. See Tumin, *Comparative Perspectives on Race Relations*, p. 26.

miscegenation produced a mixed racial population, *mestizo*, in the Indian countries, *mulatto* in Brazil and adjoining lowland areas. This mixed component formed an intermediary segment which, while still definitely a minority and only slightly economically better off than the pure blacks, was in a sense socially recognized as having higher status. However Latin American nations after breaking their political ties with the home countries remained a two-class, essentially plantation society until the twentieth century.

The mixing of races over the centuries tended to prevent any such sharp distinction based on race as in colonial Africa and the South of the United States. The process went so far in Mexico that this nation became essentially a mestizo nation. Mexico's only "race" problem concerns the remaining rural pockets of Indians who still live apart from the main society in a traditional life style.

It is the areas where African genetic lineage is still prominent that degrees of color (black African genetic features) are *one* of several factors which influence the social status of a person in the general stratification system. But even here it is generally agreed that "money tends to whiten" and per contra "poverty tends to darken."

In the Caribbean areas, the general historic picture is that various European powers invaded and established colonial dominance. It is here that the small native Indian populations were essentially annihilated (bequeathing some genetic strains), and African slaves and their eventually freed descendants became the working class. Through the years miscegenation produced a proletariat of widely ranging degrees of colors. In Puerto Rico the skin color categories are recognized: white, mulatto, and black. But public opinion insists that while white skin color is preferred it plays a relatively insignificant role in social mobility and is not even important within class. There are, however, some evidences that preoccupation with color is not uncommon in the Islands.[6] (See Chap. 12.)

With the current political freedom of those areas where the socially dominant whites are few in numbers, there is a possible revival of "racism" between the "mulatto" and "black" portions of the population as a form of class struggle based on reputed race identifications.

[6]Melvin Tumin with Arnold Feldman, "Social Class and Skin Color in Puerto Rico," in Tumin, *Comparative Perspectives on Race Relations*, p. 197.

Southeast Asia

In Southeast Asia the invading Europeans established political control to facilitate economic exploitation in their own interest and assumed the dominant-invader subordinate-native minority pattern: English in Burma and Malaysia, French in the Indo-China area, Dutch in Indonesia, and Spanish in the Philippines. In Southeast Asia, however, a new interracial situation emerged. While utilizing native labor, immigrations took place: Indians primarily entered into Burma and Malaya and Chinese to all of Southeast Asia, but in large numbers to Malaysia (especially Singapore) and parts of Indonesia. Except for the Philippines these Southeast Asian societies became stratified tri-racially: the dominant Europeans—the immigrant races—the natives. The intermediate rank position of the immigrant Indians and Chinese arose because they were in general more advanced than the natives in the knowledge and skills suited to technical and supervisory positions. For this reason their immigration was encouraged by the colonial rulers. In fact Europeans favored and protected the immigrants from the animosity of the natives who resented their presence in the higher positions and the resulting favored status.

This situation is of considerable current interest because out of it has developed a "racial" problem which during the 1960s reached serious dimensions. Now that these former colonies are struggling independently to develop viable national sentiment, the position of the immigrant races, especially the Chinese, as numerical minorities is precarious. The most conspicuous example has been in Singapore. In 1948, the Malayan peninsula with Brunei and North Borneo became the Federation of Malaysia. But with 87 per cent of the national population balance Malay and 62 per cent of the urban population Chinese,[7] it is not surprising that the long smouldering Malay hostility toward the Chinese engendered tensions resulting in serious rioting. As a result, Singapore with a roughly three-fourths Chinese population seceded from the Federation. The fact that their ancestral homeland nation is becoming an increasingly powerful force in the world may, at least indirectly, eventually provide some reassurance to the Chinese in the other Southeast Asian nations, though the older generation is economically and ideologically deeply involved with Taiwan.

[7]See Guy Hunter, *South East Asia—Race, Culture, and Nation* (New York: Oxford University Press, 1966), p. 33.

The British Commonwealth

The role of Britain as the greatest colonizer of all has already been mentioned. As the period of colonialism comes to a close, the former British colonies are, in general, better prepared for self rule. This may well account in part for the goodly number of these new nations who freely chose to become members of the British Commonwealth, the most important being India.

Further attention here is limited to the portions of this unique political federation where British people penetrated to the geographically temperate zones which became the new nations of Australia, New Zealand, and with earlier competition from France, our neighbor, Canada.

A major difference in the colonialism in these lands was that British people (as well as the French) settled permanently in these areas and actually worked their homesteads as in our colonial New England. In both Australia and New Zealand, the British found preliterate peoples whom they were able to push out of the way.

New Zealand

The Maori in New Zealand fought back in the nineteenth century to finally lose out in 1870. As in other similar situations, the native population declined, but after becoming essentially wards in New Zealand the indigenous population began to increase again so that currently it comprises some eight per cent of New Zealand's nearly 3,000,000 people. Over 90 per cent of the nation is of British descent. Auckland, the second largest city, with more than 70,000 Maoris is considered to be the biggest Polynesian city in the world. Maoris are stereotyped by the white (pakeha) as inferior and are discriminated against, especially in employment and housing, but in recent years race relations have not been particularly antagonistic. While pakeha-Maori intermarriage is frowned upon by whites, in recent years it has nevertheless been substantial. Thompson in 1963 made the point that "the tendency for those of mixed Maori-pakeha parentage to opt for identification with the Maori group certainly suggests an absence of gross discrimination."[8] The urban-dwelling Maori are highly accultur-

[8]Richard Thompson, "Race Relations in New Zealand" in Tumin, *Comparative Perspectives on Race Relations,* pp. 186–187.

ated to Western society, and their former tribal culture is essentially dying out with the remaining vestiges found in rural, essentially all Maori, villages.

Australia

In Australia, the indigenous population proved no obstacle to British settlers. Many have been integrated into Australian society. Others have persisted in traditional life patterns in arid sections of Australia. The Tasmanian natives, however, did put up a fight which was settled by the complete annihilation of the natives by the British. The policy of limiting immigration to Europeans only has avoided any more "race" problems but has also limited the potential economic development of the nation due to inadequate labor manpower. Advertisements such as "Australia Wants You" have for some time been regularly placed in United States "want ads." However, the rising power of Communist China has caused Australia to reconsider its former superior attitude toward Asians. It has begun to admit small numbers of Japanese and to ally itself with the non-communist Asian nations politically.[9]

Canada

The ethno-racial history of Canada is more complicated. The history of Canadian-Indian relations broadly parallels that of the United States with about the same results in the low status and welfare for Indians under the wardship of the federal government. While, in general, the national policy of Canada has been to keep it a white man's country, it did not prevent some migration of blacks so that in the larger eastern cities and in Nova Scotia there are conspicuous black population pockets. While integrated functionally into the Canadian economy, they occupy an alienated position in the national life.

Of greatest current interest, however, to the student of interpeople relations has been the development in Canada of what we will consider later as a "derived minority situation," specifically the relation of the French Canadians to their British fellow nationals. Here arises a minority situation—or at least so the French

[9]The Southeast Asia Treaty Organization (SEATO) was framed (1955) to resist communist aggression. Members were: Australia, France, Great Britain, New Zealand, Pakistan, Philippines, Thailand, and the United States. Disagreement over the U.S. Vietnam policy has weakened its usefulness.

people think—derived from the eighteenth century victory of one former dominant over the other. Up to this point, it is still true that in the distribution of wealth and class position, English Canadians clearly skew toward the higher positions. How much of this is due to any strictly ethnic discrimination by the English sector and how much to the differences in cultural orientation, remains an unsettled sociological question. The scientifically-oriented cultural values of the largely Protestant English have been an advantage to them in the urban, success-oriented Western culture in contrast to the rural, Catholic, humanistic-oriented cultural heritage of the French. On the other hand, it is clear that there is a strong feeling of superiority on the part of the English toward the French. Whether this bi-ethnic division is a true dominant-minority situation (in Canada as a whole, but certainly not in the province of Quebec), it has been and still continues to be a type of interpeople division which is a distinct national problem periodically creating crises. Following the increasing militancy of the French in recent years, the federal government is now officially bilingual. Time, with its inevitable acculturation between the two ethnic groups, may resolve the problem without the necessity of the French giving up their sub-communal entity in order to achieve coordinate status.

England: The Mother Country

During the nineteenth century and up to the end of World War II in Great Britain itself inter-ethnic relations have not been a significant aspect of British society, in part because it was so highly homogeneous. While there have been residing in London peoples from all parts of the world, the numbers of each ethnic group have been small. As Banton puts it, "in the past English society has been relatively successful in admitting small numbers of newcomers and making Englishmen of them."[10] Up to the current period, the non-British residents were looked upon as *culturally different immigrants* without much thought of color difference, even when clearly visible. But the substantial migration of Jamaican blacks as well as a stepped up immigration of Asian and African commonwealth citizens has caused, in Banton's words, "grounds for thinking that since the middle of the 1950's, the *immigration* perspective has become less appropriate to

[10]Michael Banton, *Race Relations* (New York: Basic Books, Inc., 1967), p. 373.

studies of the British scene and the *racial* one more so."[11] While there is no official discrimination against any non-British group residing in England, there is no question that they are discriminated against, especially in housing and occupation as an official government survey has documented. Despite clear white disapproval there has been a substantial amount of West Indian-white intermarriage. Faced with accelerating white concern at the mounting immigration, the Commonwealth Immigration Act came into effect in 1962 and has reduced immigration. In 1964 there were about 1,000,000 colored people in England, nearly half of whom were West Indians. The limitation now placed on future immigration may very well keep the increasing racist ideology within bounds, enabling Britain to avoid the much greater problems in black-white relations facing the United States.

South Africa

Next to the United States, the Union of South Africa has the most complex interpeople composition of any nation in the world. Compared to the United States, however, its current interracial pattern is far more specifically defined, and may be characterized as highly stable rather than in flux. The racially dominant position of the slightly less than one-fifth of the Union's white population over the four-fifth's who are non-white is firmly entrenched. The white population itself is divided about 6 to 4 between the Afrikaner (Dutch descended) and the English, along with a small Jewish population which is only socially distinctive. In a broad status ranking the English, with higher economic level, rate above the Afrikaners who have, however, since 1948 held political control. As van den Berghe writes:

> The following basic aims and principles of "race policy" have been shared by all South African governments since Union:
> 1. The maintenance of paternalistic White domination.
> 2. Racial segregation and discrimination, wherever there was any threat of equality or competition between Whites and non-Whites.
> 3. The perpetual subjugation of non-Europeans, and particularly Africans, as a politically powerless and economically exploitable group.[12]

[11]*Ibid* p. 384. Italics ours.
[12]From *South Africa* by Pierre L. van den Berghe. © 1965 Wesleyan University, Middletown, Conn. By permission of Wesleyan University Press.

Of the Union's 21,500,000 population (1970), non-whites include 3 per cent Asians (Indian), 10 per cent colored (mixed white-African), and 68 per cent Africans (Bantus). Since it is the Africans who prompt the rigid race-caste system, we shall pass over the other two, except to point out that the operation of the current official *apartheid* system has in no sense improved the slight advantage they formerly had over the Bantus.

South African *apartheid* (apartness) is divided into two main parts: (1) the native area reserve plan and (2) maximum possible segregation of those non-whites who live in white areas. The government emphasizes to the world outside the first point, and has in fact made some gestures toward development of the reserve areas. Since, however, the Bantu Homestead Areas comprise 13 per cent of South Africa's land, it is obvious that the larger part of the 16,000,000 natives will have to continue to reside in and earn their livelihood in white areas. In fact, they are needed to fill the requirements of menial labor below the level of skilled labor. No natives are permitted to belong to unions and when of necessity they are employed in the same level of jobs as whites, are paid much less. The small Bantu middle class gains its living providing professional and other services to the local black population.

Among the numerous practical hardships suffered by Bantus, those living in white areas are being increasingly forced to live in separate sections built on the outskirts of the cities where they must travel long distances to their work. Also natives must have in their possession at all times a pass book on which their officially determined racial status is clearly indicated.

The enforcement of this system, probably the most ingenious rigid racial subordination ever devised short of outright slavery, is an economic burden upon the national economy. Despite this added drain upon the economy, South Africa is a relatively affluent nation with most of its income (beyond that needed to keep the Bantu alive and subordinated) going to the whites. In summarizing the situation in the mid-1960s, we draw upon van den Berghe again.[13]

South Africa is held together in a condition of "static disequilibrium" through a grim mixture of political coercion and economic interdependence. However exploited the Africans are, they depend

[13]For a penetrating analysis of the economic implications of South Africa's racial policy on its economy, see Pierre L. van den Berghe, *South Africa: A Study in Conflict* (Middletown, Conn.: Wesleyan University Press, 1965), Ch. 8, "The Economic System and Its Dysfunction."

for sheer physical survival on wage employment in the money economy. To withdraw one's labor is to face nearly immediate starvation. The price of survival at the minimum subsistence level is exploitation, oppression, and degradation. But 3,000,000 people cannot indefinitely repress the frustration and fury of 13,000,000 people living in their midst. A South African divided itself awaits its impending doom.[14]

While there have been no legal or structural changes in the system since 1965, there has been a small increase in public criticism within the Union by white citizens, especially clergymen, including one white woman member of the South African Parliament.

Jews: In Diaspora and in Israel

The Jewish people for centuries, prior to the establishment of Israel, have lived in scattered groups primarily in all Western-oriented, temperate zone nations. In each locale despite their successful adjustment, Jews as a group have retained a distinctive sub-communal and sub-cultural identity. Being also always a numerical minority they have been in most times in most places discriminated against. Anti-Semitism has been a constant phenomenon in the Western world. Jews have often been described as the universal minority. Discrimination has manifested itself in a wide range of persecution: residential segregation in ghettos, sporadic pogroms, particularly in Eastern Europe, climaxed by the nearly successful Nazi practice of genocide. Since in broad outline the Diaspora phase of Gentile-Jewish relations is well illustrated in the United States and treated in detail in Chapter 16 we will dispense with further elaboration in this comparative world picture.

The latest development concerning Jews of interest to the sociology of dominant-minority relations arises from the establishment of Israel (1948). Here we find an historic reversal with Jews as the dominant people over an Arab minority of about 10 per cent inside the State of Israel. Of further significance has been the development in the relations of the European imigrant Jews (Ashkenazim) and the Jewish immigrants from Arab countries of the Middle East and North Africa (Sephardim) especially from

[14]From *Race and Racism* by Pierre L. van den Berghe. Copyright © 1967 John B. Wiley and Sons, Inc. By permission of John Wiley and Sons, Inc. The population figures are as of 1960.

Morocco, in which the Europeanized Israelis behave as a non-formalized dominant over the "Arabized" Jews. While the super-ordinate status of the European over the non-European Israeli partakes of something of a class hierarchy, the cultural distinction together with the generally darker appearance of the latter give this inter-group relation a dominant-minority form. It is more like our native dominant-South European intergroup relations of earlier days.

Up to this point, this survey of ethnoracial relations has referred to nations with capitalistic systems. We now proceed to consider the two most powerful communist nations, the U.S.S.R. and the Peoples' Republic of China.

Soviet Russia

In Soviet Russia the ruthless destruction of small tribal peoples in Asiatic Russia, the forced acculturation of non-Russian peoples within the Union, the annexation of contiguous Baltic nations against their will, and the indirect forcing of other adjoining nations to operate monolithic communist systems as the price of maintaining an outward form of independence, suggest that given somewhat different opportunities and adequately superior power, Russians are not different from other ethnic groups.

The interpeople situation which has gained the most world-wide attention has been Soviet Russia's treatment of its several million Jews. A communist regime by its very nature cannot tolerate true ethnic pluralism. In the early decades of the regime it appeared that persons of Jewish ancestry would undergo no discrimination if they would give up being Jewish. But the U.S.S.R.'s inability to Sovietize its Jewish people has in recent years re-opened the question. The most that can be said is that the Soviet government does not act as "racist" minded as most capitalistic nations. As long as a Soviet citizen is willing to refrain from voicing in any form whatsoever—even artistically—any opposition to the policies of the day, the color of the skin or their hair texture is apparently irrelevant. However, there is considerable indication that the attitudes of many European Russian persons toward their Asian compatriots is highly condescending and that the carry-over of long standing anti-Semitism is still present in the populace.

The recent change in official Soviet policy to permit limited immigration of its Jews to Israel has implications for sociological theory of intergroup relations. Despite the minority position of

Jews in numerous democratic countries, this highly sophisticated minority has acquired considerable economic and political power in the Western world which the Kremlin found it expedient not to ignore.

Communist China

Within a year of its establishment, the Communist regime of China annexed the independent state of Tibet whose culture was quite distinctive. In 1959 the Chinese military suppressed a revolution by the Tibetan people. The 1972 rapprochement between Red China and the United States may help pave the way to the reannexation of Taiwan, possibly against the majority will of the Taiwanese people who probably will not be consulted.

In concluding this brief picture of the minorities around the world, some of the omissions are footnoted.[15]

DOMINANT-MINORITY RELATIONS: A WIDESPREAD PHENOMENON IN MODERN SOCIETIES

This survey of ethno-racial relations in the modern world lends strong support to the following major proposition:

> That dominant-minority relations have been a universal characteristic of modern world societies whenever two or more peoples meet under the following conditions: 1. that the peoples in the contact situation differ sufficiently in either culture or physiognomic appearance (genetically determined racial features) or both; 2. where one of the meeting peoples is sufficiently more powerful than the other to establish and maintain dominance over the lesser.

The proposition just stated logically raises the question "why?" More definitive answers come from the entire book and

[15]Among other instances omitted are: Rhodesia where in a population of about 5,000,000 five per cent of British-descended whites dominate 94 per cent of blacks and a small colored (mixed) population, much as in South Africa; historically, the total indirect elimination of a small contingent of African slaves from the now reputedly all-white population of Argentina (one of the least known of genocidal phenomena); numerous small groups of still more aboriginal than the historic native peoples still survive in Asia; others like the Etas (Bukarin) of Japan, the Arctic residing Eskimos of Canada, and the Lapps in the northernmost areas of Scandinavian nations; and the now anachronistic colonial dominance over Angola and Mozambique by Portugal.

are dealt with directly in relation to the United States in Chapters 3 and 4. Here we give a brief introductory answer focussed on the early contact situation.

In view of the misconception in the public mind of the terms race and ethnic, perhaps it is well to use the term *people*—defining a people as a large social aggregate whose participants perceive themselves as a group and/or are perceived by other aggregates in the same area as "different" in broad and fundamental ways. What happens when different peoples meet and have to deal with one another? In the literature it often has been argued that the primary stage is one of positive reaction (friendly, curious, economically reciprocal) as with Indians teaching Mayflower passengers how to survive in the wilderness or, as sometimes claimed, in the spontaneous reaction of small children. Whereas such a utopian picture may have been historically sporadically correct under conditions where both groups were equally at the mercy of the environment, this can hardly be claimed for contemporary people or contemporary children in a world of mass communication and high technology. Each individual brings to new contacts the imposed patterns of the society in which he has lived. Therefore, in the meeting of peoples of different appearance or behavior, whatever positive attitudes may be spontaneously present at some level, it is inevitable that these will be modified or negated if confronted with unfriendly avoidance, or competition or aggression, with the resulting psychological correlates of dislike or prejudice. Individuals are motivated to survive, minimize pain, and maximize pleasure. In order to do this they must be in groups. They necessarily internalize group identity and loyalty. In short each *people's self-interest and ethnocentrism* is basically circumscribed to its own group. This inevitably means that some degree of conflict between peoples will arise sooner or later.

Types of Conflict Situations

There are a number of different types of conflict situations. Since *dominant-minority conflict* is the subject of our book, we need not elaborate upon it here, but we will consider briefly a few other types of conflict situations.

INTERDOMINANT CONFLICT   Numerous instances of two (or more) invading peoples who dominate various sections of an area and its native peoples result in conflict between them. Out of this may arise an intermediary dominance of one of these over the other. Examples: English vs. French Canadians; English vs. Afrikaner in South Africa; Protestant vs. Catholic in North Ireland.

INTER-MINORITY CONFLICT   We have treated inter-minority relations as though only two peoples meet in an area. In numerous instances, the United States perhaps being the extreme example, there have been several different peoples interacting in the same areas. Out of this situation often develops a hierarchy of minorities in which higher ranking minorities deal with lower ranking ones in the typical (if diluted) fashion, e.g., Jewish-black relations in the United States.

MISCEGENATION   Miscegenation often creates a substantial mixed racial group which in turn becomes an intermediary minority vis-a-vis dominant and subordinate pure racial groups, as with the *mestizo* population of Mexico, as formerly was true of Cape Coloreds, or of some mulattoes of the old South.

Alternate Results of Conflict

In the early phase of interpeople conflict, three broad types of adjustment may arise.

1. *Elimination of one people by the stronger.* One group may eliminate the other and retain or take the area for itself, ranging from annihilation to pushing the other into smaller and less valuable or desirable portions of the area. Probably complete annihilation did occur in prehistoric times. Close approximations have occurred in historic times,—i.e., the Tasmanians and the American Indians, particularly in the Carribean area. (This does not preclude the survival of some genetic strains of the annihilated through miscegenation). And, more commonly, aboriginal groups have been highly decimated by retiring to less desirable areas but nonetheless retaining their identity under difficulties.

2. *Accommodation* and *Coordinate Pluralism.* Interpeople conflict may be resolved by some political and economic arrangement which brings about some common political and economic unity (functional integration) but where each group retains much of its social and cultural identity. Usually this has involved spatial separation, i.e., the French, German, and Italian sections of Switzerland.

3. *Superordinate-subordinate accommodation* (dominant-minority pattern). In the modern period the most frequent mode of

accommodation developing in the *early* phases of interpeople conflict has been the establishment of dominance by one and subordination of the other. Since it is this pattern of interpeople relations as found in the United States which is the main subject of our book, further analysis of this pattern will be made in the next section.

4. *Assimilation.* We shall see that in *later* phases of interpeople relations the total merging of the dominant and minority, ultimately including genetic amalgamation, frequently has taken place. This then ends the dominant-minority pattern as far as a particular pair of different peoples is concerned. From what has preceded, it should be clear that assimilation as an adjustment in the *earlier* phase of interpeople relations is not possible. Of all the European immigrant peoples coming to the United States after nationhood only the later British immigrants did not undergo a period of minority status.

Suggested Readings

FOR THE UNITED STATES

Barron, Milton L. *Minorities in a Changing World.* New York: Alfred A. Knopf, 1967.
   A book of readings largely dealing with various American minorities. Part II includes minorities in various other societies.
Glazer, Nathan and Patrick Moynihan. *Beyond the Melting Pot.* Cambridge, Mass.: The M.I.T. and Harvard University Press, 1963.
   An analysis of New York City's Negro, Puerto Rican, Irish, Italian and Jewish ethnic groups.
Rose, Arnold and Caroline, eds. *Minority Problems.* New York: Harper and Row, Publishers, 1965.
   Readings including descriptions and analytical articles. Part II contains readings on other parts of the world.

COMPARATIVE STUDIES

Banton, Michael. *Race Relations.* New York: Basic Books, Inc., 1967.
   Deals with theoretical conceptions with descriptive material drawn from many areas of the world.

Mason, Philip. *Patterns of Dominance.* New York and London: Oxford University Press, 1970.
Stresses confrontation between white and non-white, colonialism and racial segregation past and present.

Schermerhorn, R. A. *Comparative Ethnic Relations; A Framework for Theory and Research.* New York: Random House, 1970.
Primarily theoretical, the book draws upon interpeople relations around the world.

Shibutani, Tamotsu and Kian M. Kwan. *Ethnic Stratification: A Comparative Approach.* New York: The Macmillan Company, 1965.
Around a well formulated original schema of analysis of ethnic stratifications, the authors draw widely upon ethno-racial situations the world over.

Tumin, Melvin. *Comparative Perspectives on Race Relations.* Boston: Little, Brown, Co., 1969.
Following an introduction by the author on race relations are articles by special students of ethno-racial relations of many areas of the world.

van den Berghe, Pierre L. *Race and Racism.* New York: John Wiley and Sons, Inc., 1967.
Conceptualizing race relations in two models, Paternalistic and Competitive, the author provides a chapter each on Mexico, Brazil, the United States, and South Africa as bases for final comparative analysis and conclusions.

Wagley, Charles and Marvin Harris. *Minorities in the New World.* New York: Columbia University Press, 1958.
Two anthropologists analyze dominant-minority relations by means of six cases involving American Indians, Negroes, and European immigrants in Brazil, Mexico, Martinique, the United States, and Canada.

2 Introduction to the Sociology of Minorities

Ethno-racial relations[1] are a special dimension of established social relations within any given multi-group society. Thus the situation of minorities is a special focus within the general problems of social analysis. In this chapter we will deal with key *concepts* (the tools of sociology) as they apply to stabilized and to changing dominant-minority patterns. Subsequent chapters will illustrate this analysis as we present the substantive situation of specific minorities.

DEFINITION OF KEY TERMS

What Is Dominant?

The dominant group in a society is one which is able to control power, both economic and political, toward two ends: (1) to protect and advance its own group interest by restricting the opportunities of other ethno-racial groups; and (2) to perpetuate its own ideas of what is "right," "desirable," "good." Like all other peoples, dominants believe the survival of the society depends on "others," to a degree at least, coming to share their values and to behave accordingly. Social science refers to this universal phenomenon as ethnocentrism.

[1] This term is adopted because this form of intergroup relations is variously considered as ethnic relations or race relations with little consistency or precision in the public mind as to the meaning of either term.

Members of the dominant group share a common value system, a common language, and a common history. Dominant norms are historically derived, and their preeminence is established by custom and by law. To the extent that subgroups do not fully share these assumptions, they are restricted, formally or informally, to a greater or lesser degree, from full and equal participation in the full range of the life of the society.

Before the rise of national states, dominant-minority relations existed between kinship groups (tribes, clans, "peoples") or religious groups where varying patterns of subordination or of "tolerance" were to be found. In the modern world the secular state has the military and legal prerogative to determine the protection and participation of the people within its geographic borders, and in many instances, within its extended political hegemony. The state is distinguished from the other great institutions, such as the family and the church, by its "exclusive investment with the final power of coercion."[2] We shall consider a dominant group, then, *as one within a national state whose distinctive culture and/ or physiognomy is established as superior in the society, and which treats differentially or unequally other groups in the society with other cultures or physiognomies in order to maximize its own group interest.*

Minority: A Definition

The anthropologists Charles Wagley and Marvin Harris, in presenting case studies in the Western Hemisphere from materials which, in part, were prepared for UNESCO by social scientists of five countries, have arrived at the following definition of a minority which we have adopted as the fullest and most appropriate:

(1) Minorities are subordinate segments of complex state societies; (2) minorities have special physical or cultural traits which are held in low esteem by the dominant segments of the society; (3) minorities are self-conscious units bound together by the special traits which their members share and by the special disabilities which these bring; (4) membership in a minority is transmitted by a rule of descent which is capable of affiliating succeeding generations even in the absence of readily apparent

[2]Robert M. McIver and Charles H. Page, *Society* (New York: Rhinehart and Company, 1937), p. 436.

physical or cultural traits; (5) minority peoples, by choice or necessity, tend to marry within the group.[3]

This statement gives us five criteria which can be applied to the designation of a group as a minority in a contemporary society. First, to be a member of a minority is not only to be part of a social group vis-a-vis another social group, but to be so within a political unit. Thus the political power groups, as well as the legal structure, will profoundly affect the situation of minorities. Second, attitudes of dominant members toward minorities are bound up with a system of values which devalues certain physical and cultural traits. Third, minorities are conscious of themselves as groups. In some cases members of a minority group deliberately adhere to values which vary from those of the dominant group and which they wish to preserve; sometimes they share disabilities arising from historical attitudes and discrimination. Fourth, one is a member of a minority without choice.

The chief limitation of the definition we have quoted is its failure to stress discrimination. Minority status is an imposed status except for sectarian separatist groups, and has validity only as dominants possess the power and opportunity to sustain it. Similarly we should prefer to state Wagley and Harris's fifth point the other way around. Minority peoples tend by necessity or choice to marry within their group. The minority's resistance to out-marriage may be due to regard for a particular cultural heritage, or to fear that out-marriages will result in unhappiness, or to a combination of these reasons.

Relations of the dominant group to any particular minority must always be understood in a historical dimension. Present attitudes derive from past patterns of interaction, even now when there are changed relations between the dominant group and the minority.

Analyzing Behavioral Differences

The social sciences have been concerned with examining social structure, culture, and personality. Historically the pioneering efforts in the analysis of social structure have been the province of sociologists; comparative cultures have usually been the focus of attention for anthropologists; and psychologists have

[3]Charles Wagley and Marvin Harris, *Minorities in the New World: Six Case Studies* (New York: Columbia University Press, 1958), p. 10.

been concerned with personality. Obviously, all these three areas of behavior are interrelated, and to some extent, especially more recently, anthropologists and psychologists have included social structure within their focus, for it is impossible to deal with the beliefs, language, ceremonies, and other symbolic behavior that distinguish one culture from another without also seeing what the relationships in each society are. In the same way, in the study of personality we must not only consider within what beliefs and rituals a child is brought up and with what quality of emotional interaction, but also where the family is placed in what kind of social system.[4]

In this book our primary focus is on social structure, although where it is appropriate we shall expand our discussion to include some contributions by anthropologists and psychologists. We emphasize social structure in order to focus on the fact that whatever differences have characterized various groups in America, structural disadvantages have existed for certain groups, and they are now being challenged.

What Is Social Structure?

When we use terms such as "the structuring of a situation" we imply a continuity in attitudes, definitions of ourselves and others, and expectations of behavior that extend beyond any particular encounter. Social relations in any stable society take place within a complex fabric of such continuities. They are governed by a set of *beliefs* within each individual or group about themselves and about the way they must act in order to obtain benefits from their action. In sociological theory, we say that beliefs leading to action are *values*. For example, the dominant society in the United States has had a major "belief leading to action," (i.e., to policy) that *work* is good for the character. There are historical roots for this belief deriving from the struggle for power of middle-class merchants and artisans against feudal privilege. Early settlers of the United States had to work to survive. The conditions of settlement in an underdeveloped, underpopulated country reinforced, by experience, the necessity for work in order to have any security. Obviously, on the other hand, many blacks in slave gangs, who could have neither security nor reward from work, did not incorporate this value, whatever they may formerly have had in their lost African culture.

[4]For a somewhat more systematic discussion of these interrelationships see Ch. 18.

Clearly not everyone shares the dominant values however much the attempt is made to instill them by education or enforce them by power. In any multi-group nation like the United States there are also *variant* values.[5] These are values that are integrated into another traditional culture than that of the dominants. For example, Spanish Americans of the Southwestern United States are brought up to view the roles of men and women differently, to consider time more loosely than is necessary for Anglo industrial society, to place family loyalty in priority over job loyalty. Under these circumstances, an individual adhering to variant values may find himself disparaged, misunderstood, and discriminated against by the dominant society.

Both dominant and variant value systems are sets of *official values* designed to maintain continuity, and to give a form for expectations. They are acquired hierarchically: that is to say, from people commanding respect in the community (parents, teachers, textbook heroes, and so forth). *Unofficial values,*[6] on the other hand, are concerned with present interest rather than historical continuity. They are acquired and supported by present experiences which lack hierarchical character. (From the point of view of dominants, these are usually called *deviant values*.) Unofficial values may be of many kinds, but they always contain some elements which are in conflict with official values. They may be values held by an artistic group, a political protest group, or a religious sect. They can even be obsolete values clung to by groups whose interests are suffering in the face of change. Members of minority groups are often attracted to groups that adhere to unofficial values because it may seem harmonious with their present interest to protest or deny official values. This is especially true where a minority person has felt the discriminatory character of the official value system. It may also be a way of minimizing the discomfort of minority identity to form associations with a group not necessarily of one's own heritage trying to escape from or to reform the society. On the one hand they may try to set up a small society of their own as with the many communal experiments today. On the other hand, they may unite around a political philosophy or a political party committed to

[5]Florence Rockwood Kluckohn, "Dominant and Variant Value Orientations," in *Personality in Nature, Society and Culture*, rev. ed. Clyde Kluckohn and Henry Murray with the collaboration of David M. Schneider (New York: Alfred A. Knopf, 1953), pp. 342ff.
[6]Milton L. Barron, *The Juvenile in Delinquent Society* (New York: Alfred A. Knopf, 1954), p. 203.

the overthrow of the existing structure. Upholders of the official system have frequently linked *unofficial* values with "foreign" and sought to mobilize anti-minority sentiment as a weapon against those professing unofficial values. Thus early miners' unions were described as "drunken fighting Irish."

Norms, Roles, Status

In analyzing a stable continuous situation in society in addition to talking about the values of the members of the society we also use other terms to define expectations and differentiations.

Norms are the implicit rules of behavior—that is, the group, *according to its values* defines what actions are approved, or "good," or "taken for granted" (normal). There are norms governing, for example, the conduct of family life, economic life, political behavior, religious participation, and education. When these norms have persisted across generations we speak of them as institutionalized, or a particular configuration establishing some segment of social behavior we call an *institution,* such as marriage as an institution of family life, a contract as an institution of economic life, the state as an institution of political life.

Within these institutionalized patterns individuals carry out their lives. The performance of their functions from day to day is a *role,* and there are expectations (norms) of how roles should be fulfilled: the "loving" mother, the "reliable" workman, the "efficient" secretary are rubrics expressing some aspect of role definition. The failure to carry out the institutional roles in the manner defined by the dominant culture is a major justification offered by dominants for devaluation of minorities: "They don't *do* right." The explicit or implicit definition of roles in the institutions of society ensures continuity and a reasonable degree of order. On the other hand, this very function of continuity often makes for a lag in appropriate or useful adaptation to change.

Status defines the relative position of a person or a group with regard to other persons or groups in the hierarchy of prestige. Honored positions in the society usually go to those who best fulfill significant dominant institutional roles. The overall problems of status are linked with the problem of social class (access to the opportunity structure), or caste (absolute barriers to selective types of social participation). We are interested primarily in the relationships between dominants and minorities with regard to their *relative* status. Though this is, as we shall see, intertwined with questions of social class, it can be considered a separate matter. While some actions unite dominants and minorities on the basis of class interests (as in some labor unions, political parties, etc.), more common in the past, and to a considerable extent in the present, is the alliance of dominants across class lines to keep minorities in subordinate status.

STRUCTURED DOMINANT-MINORITY RELATIONS

For a differentiated ethno-racial structure to exist there must be some perceptible differences among groups in either appearance or behavior which identify them to other members of the society.

Biological Visibility

PHYSICAL TYPE   The traits that are highly valued in American culture are the Caucasoid features. Any variation from the ideal type is held in less esteem in the popular culture. Where differences from the Caucasoid type are perceived, as illustrated by those physical features of the Japanese or the Chinese which distinguish them from the white, we speak of biological visibility.

LINEAGE   Lineage is invisible visibility. We consider it an aspect of biological descent. In cases of severe devaluation of minorities even a small proportion of minority ancestry is enough to designate membership in a minority. "Negroes" who are so completely Caucasoid in their physical features that they cannot be identified by sight are identifiable as Negroes by the general knowledge of their Negro lineage. In periods when dominant elements strongly desire to exclude minorities from privileges and participation and when biological visibility becomes less noticeable, rules of descent have been made official, as in the case of the Jews in Nazi Germany.

What "Race" Is

We will discuss what science has shown us about the origin, tenuous stability, and purity of "racial" traits in a subsequent chapter. At this point we are concerned simply with the various ways people are identified as different in terms of their appearance and behavior. The fact of their difference provides a rationalization for unequal treatment, and in the case of physical differences, this is *racism*.

Ethnicity

Many people avoid the racial issue by stressing cultural differences. *Ethnic* is an increasingly popular term in dealing with the subject of minorities. Often it is used adjectivally as an equivalent of the term *minority*. This is of course inaccurate. *Ethnic* is a term which emphasizes the cultural ethos (values, expectations, symbols) of a group and formerly, quite properly, was limited in reference to groups whose cultural characteristics are their prime distinguishing factor. *Dominants as well as minorities are members of an ethnic group.* An ethnic group, unlike a nationality group, is a population which has preserved visible elements of a tradition without primary reference to former loyalties to a nation-state. The French emigres who came to New Orleans after the French Revolution were a nationality group. The present French-Canadians are an ethnic group. Minority status may strengthen ethnicity, just as ethnicity may contribute to minority status.

Cultural Visibility

LANGUAGE AND NONVERBAL COMMUNICATION The practice of speaking another language in the family or among close associates may serve as a mode of identification in both a derogatory sense for the dominant group, or in a sense of cultural pride for the minority. The language of gesture, facial expression, posture, and emotional tone all express cultural learning and vary from culture to culture. Different societies allow different ways of expressing emotional reactions to joy or pain or trouble, and these reactive patterns also are used to identify minorities in a derogatory way. For example, one study by Zborowski has shown that doctors and nurses with Anglo-Saxon norms of reserve in emotional expression often fail to understand and are impatient with the reactions of patients from non-Anglo-Saxon societies, (crying, complaining, etc.).

DRESS Although there are only a few highly coherent minorities that maintain traditional modes of dress—for instance the Amish, Hassidic Jews, and Navahoes (on the reservation)— dress has in the past been a major symbol of cultural identity. Nationality societies whose members have long since adopted the dominant modes of dress for everyday living, often still wear the traditional "costume" to celebrate patriotic or religious festivals. Modes of hair style and ornamentation may also indicate a particular cultural heritage. Sometimes an insecure group will adopt a mode of dress as part of a struggle for identification, as for example, the Zoot suits that were worn by young Mexican Americans in the early 1940s (see Chapter 11).

INSTITUTIONAL BEHAVIOR   Different ways of behaving in family, economic, political, and religious life often make members of minorities conspicuous. For example, filial obligations and parental authority may make a young person different in his group participation from his schoolfellows. A minority member with different religious practices living in a highly coherent Protestant community may in this sense be visible to his neighbors.

ASSOCIATIONS   An aspect of visibility frequently ignored in the discussion of minorities is what we shall call *associational visibility*. An individual may have no visible traits that would designate him a member of a minority, but he identifies himself by the group with which he generally associates, particularly in his most intimate contacts. While as a means of identification associational visibility is derivative from other bases, it acquires significance through long practice.

OVERLAP OF TRAITS   A minority is sometimes identified only by physiognomic traits, but usually there is an overlap of physiognomic and cultural traits. Sometimes there are only cultural traits which may occur in any of several combinations. Perhaps only two minority groups can easily be fitted into a simple visibility scheme: the immigrants from the north of Europe who differ in ethnic culture without basic religious difference, and contemporary American Negroes, many of whom are distinguished almost solely by their physiognomic features.

A useful clue to arranging minorities in a classification based on visibility may be found by considering the ways in which the dominant-status group has reacted to the visibilities involved. Proceeding in this manner, it can be observed that the dominant groups in the United States have conceived of minority groups in three ways: as "foreigners," as "colored," and as non-believers in the faith of the dominant group. While in most specific situations the dominants look on the minority in some combination of these three ways, in each case it seems possible to accord priority to one. For example, although the great majority of Italians are known to be Catholics, it is that entire configuration of cultural elements which compose the Italian "ethos" which identifies them most prominently. Again, while the Japanese are often thought of as foreigners, it is their physiognomic visibility which comes first to the mind of a person of dominant status when the word "Japanese" is mentioned. The leading element in the consciousness of the dominant in his conception of the Japanese is appearance. In spite of the fact that "color" is one of the less accurate traits to employ in "racial" classifications of mankind, it is consciousness of color which has loomed largest in the white man's concept of the other peoples of the earth. Wherever color difference is associated with other differences in the United States, it has always taken precedence over other factors in retarding assimilation.

Numbers and Concentration as Related to Visibility

A few dispersed individuals or families, whatever their physical or cultural traits, are less likely to be subject to all the disabilities of minority position. They may be viewed with curiosity, tolerated, or ignored. When there are large numbers of a particular minority in a community, however, there is more likely to be a consensus of differential treatment. This is all the more so if they are forced to cluster in a given area of the community, or if they do so from choice. They are then not only visible as individuals, but visible as a segment of the community.

What we are dealing with here, obviously, is peoples who, in one form or another, are perceived as different from one another. If they had encountered one another in the first days of exploration, they might have had only curiosity about each other's differences, even as some very small children do, but in today's world superordinate-subordinate relationships have been established and historically maintained, even if they are now being challenged. Thus there is a customary expected set of attitudes, approved ways of behaving, definitions of self, and differential access to opportunity that have been "structured" over time.

THE ESTABLISHMENT OF DOMINANCE

Differential Power

The establishment of dominance occurs, as we have noted, when one group possesses the superior power to utilize other groups to further its own best interests. This involves establishing its own values and institutions as normative, while those of other groups are regarded as subordinate or inferior. Sometimes this is achieved by military conquest, sometimes through superior technology and/or organization, sometimes through superior numbers. In the case of voluntary migrants, they may have to adapt to the established norms of their new environment and they may find themselves culturally ill-equipped for immediate adjustment. The achievement of dominance nevertheless takes place through the *use of force* or through the *threat of force* which covertly underlie other mechanisms of devaluation. Minorities respond by sporadic conflict, by negotiation, by separatism, and by accommodation.

THE MAINTENANCE OF DOMINANT-MINORITY PATTERNS

Law and Custom

Law and custom replace force to sustain over time the achieved dominance, and the initial definition of subordinate group is expanded to apply to other visible groups that may be added to the population. Force, or the threat of force, however, remains the ultimate sanction for maintaining dominance. It may be legitimately used (law enforcement) to ensure the preservation of established relationships, or, in periods of tension, force may be used in defiance of law.

In stable periods the law has pre-eminence, with *authority* to enforce. Thus political control of the state by adherents to dominant norms will ensure laws upholding these norms. In the creation of policy toward minorities, the state may, for example, grant or deny citizenship, as in America where for a long time it excluded Orientals and defined limited citizenship for the conquered American Indians. Furthermore, the state plays its role in the subjugation of minorities not only through law and policy, but through its system of education. It presents historical models of esteemed behavior: the founding fathers and other "great men." Conversely, only too often, idealized subordinate roles are also presented in the official education: Pocahontas and Uncle Tom become the faithful protectors and upholders of Anglo-Saxon dominance. Public rituals and symbols constantly stimulate or reinvoke sentiments of loyalty, affection, and commitment to dominant values.

From time to time in American history there have been legal restrictions on the right of movement and of assembly. These have applied primarily to Negroes, slave and free before the Civil War, and to white indentured servants as long as the indenture system controlled the labor supply. American-born Japanese were confined in internment camps along with their Japanese-born parents in World War II.

Custom governs the whole web of traditionally appropriate behavior. When dominance is maintained in a relatively unchanging society, custom ensures the continuance of previously defined appropriate ways of interacting. These may even be elaborated into a rigid etiquette which amplifies the fact of dominance in all spheres of life. Probably the extreme example of this is the pattern of relations between whites and Negroes in the more traditional sections of the South. The common understanding of what is expected and allowable between the two groups governs almost every phase of contact.

In the American legal system, resting as it does on English common law, there can never be too wide a gap between enforceable laws and accepted customs. The problem emerges most clearly in the tension between local and state laws and federal laws: while local and state laws cater to the needs and attitudes of the people of a particular region, federal laws legislate for a much broader and varied populace including many who do not share the regional or local patterns. Thus federal and state laws may and often do come into direct conflict.

In order to maintain a stable pattern of dominance, specific patterns of action and attitude are incorporated into the social system and become self-understood or taken for granted on the part of dominants. These attitudes and actions are sustaining processes; they also ensure the restriction of people with other patterns of action or other attitudes from full participation in power and economic opportunity.

Categorical Discrimination

Discrimination—differential and unequal treatment by the dominant of the minority—is an essential feature of the dominant-minority relationship. Discrimination is categorical when it is applied to all members of the minority. For example, Irish immigrants arriving in Boston in pre-Civil War days found signs at places of employment saying "No Irish need apply."

Discrimination may operate in hotels, jobs, social organizations, admissions to schools, colleges, and universities, and so forth, wherever there is categorical exclusion or categorical limitation of numbers. Discrimination may also operate to create unequal rewards for work that is done, in wage differentials, or in access to promotion. It may operate in the sphere of political rights, thus limiting access to the ultimate channel of power or redress. Provisions like the poll tax have effectively deprived many people from their share in the political decision-making process.

POLITICAL DISCRIMINATION Because our Constitution guarantees civil equality to all regardless of race, creed, or national origin, political institutions have become the major focus for efforts to reduce discrimination. On the whole, great strides have been made, and political discrimination persists only in localities and regions where state and local laws obtain. The several problems of political discrimination that remain are generally subsumed under the term "civil rights." Segregation in public education, rights for Indians, access to tax-supported facilities, such as recreation areas, and so forth, are also within the sphere of political discrimination.

ECONOMIC DISCRIMINATION The problem of economic discrimination is more complex, since attempts at regulation by law can in many instances be interpreted as unwarranted interference with the rights of private property. Types of economic discrimination include discrimination in employment, either by announced policy or by private agreement, and also the subtler problem of the promotions and privileges available in certain occupational channels. Another type of economic discrimination is residential discrimination, where informal agreements of property owners exclude some minorities from some residential sections.

The economic sphere has been increasingly invaded by state regulation in the twentieth century, and legislation has barred certain types of economic discrimination in some places. Economic pressure through threat of boycott or unfavorable publicity has lessened discrimination in those sectors of business most vulnerable to such mechanisms: transportation, hotels, and retail stores, for example. Discrimination in trade unions is another type of economic discrimination.

SOCIAL DISCRIMINATION   Discrimination in the private areas of life is not subject to control by law and will be the last to disappear. Most amenable to change, even in defiance of local sentiment on occasion, have been the religious institutions, though this is not occurring without struggle. Country clubs, fraternities, private schools, and other voluntary organizations may set their own rules and will maintain varying degrees of discrimination depending on how strong the in-group feeling of their membership is. The final area through which discrimination can continue to operate longer is in the family and its attitudes, from social invitations through the spectrum of private life to intermarriage. All practices, formal and informal, which limit admission to groups, or situations that are primarily sociable or prestige-defining, are what we shall in conformity with common practice refer to as *social discrimination*, without particular reference to their institutional base.

Segregation

. Segregation is an enforced pattern of settlement, or a pattern in the use of facilities which has the effect of categorically defining inferior status. Formal and informal restrictions may operate to exert these limitations. The dislike of many dominants of entering into close contact with various minorities leads to residential restrictions and/or to segregation in the use of public services. Local law and custom may require a member of a minority group to enter a public building by a separate entrance, to work in industry on a separate floor, to use separate waiting rooms and railroad cars, to attend separate schools. Segregation may be viewed as either ecological or institutional in character. It may be formally established, or formally demanded, but it is usually informally enforced.

Segregated communities almost always represent a poorer

average level of living with respect to quality of housing, public services, health, and education. Thus, in the long run, segregation is a cost to the total community. Where formal and informal residential restriction has kept in inferior conditions of life those people who wished to move out, the situation is analogous to the medieval ghetto and is indeed often referred to as such in sociological writing and popular discussion of minorities. The original use of the term "ghettoizing" in relation to the American subcommunity occurred in Louis Wirth's book, *The Ghetto*.[7] At the time Wirth wrote, the ghetto situations he described held true for many nationality sub-communities in America's cities. Although these have declined in number and size, the problem of segregation is still very real for several of the minority groups.

The Class Structure as a Stabilizing Factor

The American colonies inherited the British class structure based on wealth and occupation, with the significant difference that at its apex there was no hereditary aristocracy. Until the first decade of the nineteenth century class position was demarcated by customary dress, and since, apart from Massachusetts, there was no free public education until the 1830s (and even later in new states) modes of speech also characterized class levels.

The urgent need of the new continent was for unskilled and semi-skilled labor. Immigrants were recruited under the indenture system and subsequently under contract labor and finally as free labor to supply this need in the North, while imported slaves provided the agricultural and domestic labor force for the agrarian South. The vast majority of migrants (voluntary or forced) therefore started low on the class scale. On the other hand, individual improvement in economic circumstances and social status is a historical norm in the American tradition. Discrimination gave "native" Americans a competitive advantage in the upward climb. A Senator from Massachusetts in 1852 described the mechanism clearly:

> That inefficiency of the pure Celtic race furnishes the answer to the question: How much use are the Irish to us in America: The Native American answer is, "none at all." And the Native American policy is to keep them away.
> A profound mistake, I believe. . . . We are here, well organized

[7]Louis Wirth, *The Ghetto* (Chicago: University of Chicago Press, 1928).

and well trained, masters of the soil, the very race before which they yielded everywhere besides. It must be, that when they come in among us, they come to lift us up. As sure as water and oil each finds its level, they will find theirs. So far as they are mere hand-workers, they must sustain the head-workers, or those who have any element of intellectual ability. Their inferiority as a race compels them to go to the bottom; and the consequence is that we are, all of us, the higher lifted because they are here. . . .[8]

Increasingly as larger numbers of "different" peoples came, minorities were forced to seek improved positions within separate subcultural hierarchies. In the caste situation of the antebellum South parallel class structures occurred even more dramatically. Differences of prestige became established between house servants, skilled workmen, and field hands on the plantation, and between Negro craftsmen and unskilled Negro workmen in the cities. Such a parallel hierarchy persisted in much of the South through custom and local ordinance even after the legal position of slaves and freedmen had changed.

The overall class position of minorities, then, from the mid-nineteenth century until after World War II could be described by the following diagram.

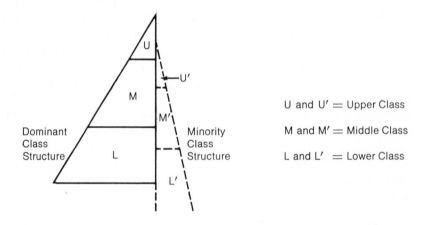

FIGURE 2-1. THE RELATION BETWEEN THE DOMINANT-MINORITY STRUCTURE AND THE CLASS STRUCTURE

[8]Edward Everett, "Letters on Irish Emigration," in *Historical Aspects of the Immigration Problem, Select Documents*, ed. Edith Abbott (Chicago: The University of Chicago Press, 1926), pp. 462–463.

A classic study of stratification in a New England small industrial city elaborates this. Taking ethnic as distinct from "racial" minorities, it was found that in 1933 in "Yankee City" members of an ethnic minority were distributed over several segments of the six-fold class structure. For example, some Italians were found as high as the lower-middle class. They were thought of, however, as Italians and reacted to accordingly. Within each class level to which they rose, the ethnics were thought of as somehow not quite the same as the native members of the same class—that is, until as individuals they became assimilated. If one examines the status of ethnic minorities in the United States, the conclusion seems inescapable that it represents a combination of the horizontal and vertical principles of social differentiation. The test of the existence of a minority is to verify dominant behavior toward it within the same class.[9]

The Rationale of Dominance: Prejudice and Ideology

As persons, members of the dominant segment of the ethno-racial hierarchy are members of numerous other social structures and possess other values—e.g., religions or ethical—which may conflict with their dominant behavior. Thomas Jefferson, although a slave holder, voiced qualms about the slave system. To maintain a self-respecting image of themselves as human beings and to answer criticism of outsiders (or maverick insiders) dominant people need a psychological justification of their dominant behavior. This rationale is accomplished by the development of ethno-racial prejudice, continuously reconditioned in nearly all children reared in dominant status. These prejudices are further reinforced by an alleged intellectual ideology, currently labelled as the doctrine of "racism." That these prejudices are not objectively valid, and that the racist ideology has substantially no scientific truth, as will be discussed later, is not pertinent at this point. As long as they are believed by dominant people they serve a necessary function in order for a hierarchical ethno-racial structure to be maintained.

Whereas segregation and discrimination are *actions* within a

[9]See W. Lloyd Warner and Paul S. Lunt, *The Social Life of a Modern Community* (New Haven: Yale University Press, 1941), Ch. 5, "How The Several Classes Were Discovered," and p. 225, Table 7, "Class and Ethnic Groups."

Although it is now recognized, as theory of stratification has developed, that the "Yankee City" studies are classifications of "status" (prestige) rather than "class" (access to economic positions), we have retained the original terminology.

system of institutional patterns, prejudice is an *attitude* unfavorable to or disparaging of a whole group and its individual members by virtue of their identification with the group. Prejudice may have cultural (value-related) and psychological (satisfaction-related) underpinnings, or both.

PREJUDICE AS FALSE PERCEPTION Sometimes prejudice is the result of a false perception of a minority as learned from the various socializing agents to which children and youth are exposed. It is probable that most dominant-status persons who consciously or unconsciously take the advantage over minorities do so simply as a result of behaving in a customary way, without any personal or intentional hostility and often with limited experience of contact with the minority.

False perceptions are enhanced by *stereotypes*. A stereotype is an oversimplified generalization that emphasizes only selected traits of another group. It tends to evoke a generalized reaction to any member of that group. To some extent stereotypes arise out of the tendency to save time and effort. As one author points out, "It is much easier to have a definite opinion as to the type of creatures women are, and behave accordingly, than to analyze and study each woman anew." What is significant in a stereotype of a minority group is that the selected traits tend to be those that emphasize difference from the dominant norm, and they tend to make up the whole image of an entire group, thus serving as an excuse for differential treatment. The assumption is that these traits are innate and hereditary and therefore that no change in the treatment of the stereotyped minority is warranted. Since newspapers and magazines and other forms of mass communication depend on popular approval for their sales, they often serve as reinforcing agents in the maintenance and continuance of such generalized popular stereotypes. They often help create a stereotype of the dominant groups as well. Minorities often have stereotypes regarding dominants, especially if they have a strong cultural tradition with different values from those of the dominants.

PREJUDICE AS PERSONALITY STRUCTURE Anthropology and psychiatry have called our attention to the fact that some personalities need to feel superior in order to have a secure self-image. In general, as far as we know from research, one can identify this need for dominance with an insecure person who has been brought up by very dominating adults. No community problems may occur if there are other outlets for his need to be superior—if, for example, the person may with cultural approval in turn dominate his children, or his servants, and if no major threat to his way of life occurs. When external circumstances challenge his way of functioning, his livelihood, his personal security, he may need to lay the blame for this at the door of members of the society whom he believes are of lesser worth— "aliens," "trouble-makers," "competitors." This is the person whose prejudices grow out of his *personality needs*. His prejudices develop with regard to any given important social stereotype that impinges on his environment. It may be a "native" in colonial Indonesia, an African in Afrikander South Africa, a Japanese on the West Coast, a Jew in Nazi Germany. Some societies seem to produce fewer of this type of personality, while in other societies this type of personality seems to be more nearly the norm. No culture is composed *entirely* of one type of person or another.

It is these personalities that form the hard core of prejudiced citizens who resist change in the position of minorities and who refuse to surrender their stereotypes of minority groups. Persons who do not have such a personality structure may also have stereotypes which they acquired through learning in their environment, but they can relinquish them when given an opportunity for re-learning. The personality type that needs prejudice to support its precarious self-esteem usually cannot modify it through learning.

PREJUDICE AS PANIC REACTION   A third type of prejudice may be brought into play in situations of generalized anxiety where persons are played upon by propaganda or mob psychology to share attitudes against a minority which they would not have imagined for themselves in a time free of stress and of which they are often later ashamed. The existence of dominant-minority patterns provides an outlet for frustrations which can under some circumstances be mobilized into temporary aggression against a minority.

MINORITY RESPONSES TO RESTRICTIVE PROCESSES OF DOMINANCE

When dominance has been established, dominants also define appropriate responses of minorities to their subordinate position. If the differentiating traits are very marked and the barriers to opportunity for the minority rigid, a pattern of stabilized accommodation will be characteristic since the dominants expect it and the members of the minority have no choice.

Stabilized Accommodation

In stabilized accommodation both dominant and minority groups come to accept that, in essence, a caste system exists. Furthermore, certain modes of behavior or roles are attached to each group. In a stabilized situation, a minority individual acts according to the role assigned him by society. This mode of adaptation is one in which both superior and subordinate positions are taken for granted. Both dominant and minority members accept the same rationalizations for the existing pattern. Both may equally defend it. A high degree of *personal* sympathy and understanding may in some instances develop between dominant and minority individuals under these circumstances, as separateness is clearly understood and both are interdependent parts of an established social system.

The psychological costs of this system are high. For the minority person it may affect his perception of reality. Indeed it was testimony to this effect by psychologists that was taken into consideration by the Supreme Court in the school desegregation issue. A stabilized subordinate position may create difficulty for a member of the subordinate group in handling repressed hostility and inevitable resentment. A variety of devices often develop to help him ease his psychic burden: clowning, intragroup aggression, fantasy, as well as psychological disorder of greater or lesser severity. Even when occasional direct protest occurs it is doomed to failure, not only because of the power of reprisal, but because of the overwhelming difficulty of assessing the situation correctly for success. For the members of the dominant group too, there are greater costs than are often recognized. The need to maintain such a rigid system puts strains on the individual, especially in the period of childhood socialization, and often results in covert envy and sadistic exploitation of the subordinate group.

It is true, however, that some individuals may *choose* an accommodative adaptation even when the barriers against the whole group are not severe enough to maintain this pattern for all members. This will be a matter of temperament, skill, or previous social experience.

Acculturation

Acculturation is one of the sustaining processes whereby minorities are incorporated into the dominant culture. The term, when used to define a process, refers to the changes in individuals (and, if sharing the same experiences, groups of individuals) whose primary learning has been in one culture and who take over traits from another culture. Dominants expect minorities to acculturate, at least to a degree. Since dominants, like all ethnic groups, assume *their* values and social system to be the best, and since some degree of familiarity with the dominant language is assumed essential to reciprocal communication, there is always some pressure for some acculturation even under severe restrictive patterns.

The process of acculturation takes place on two levels, often referred to as "external" and "internal." *External* acculturation is behavioral, in which material culture (refrigerators, cars, telephones, nylon stockings, etc.), everyday language, and secular (work, for example) roles are acquired. Key attitudes and behavior in the private spheres of life remain subcultural if acculturation is only external.

If the cultural element is paramount in differentiating the minority group, the degree of discrimination will vary directly with the degree of external acculturation. This is, however, often perceived with different priorities by dominants and by members of minorities.

While a substantial degree of acculturation is essential for a minority person to play his restricted functional role in the established dominance system, he is not always encouraged to be too ambitious in this respect. The purpose of the dominant system is to facilitate greater opportunity for dominants and lesser opportunity for members of the minority. While, of course, this to some extent applies to the class system (perhaps less so in the United States), the lower-class dominants have many advantages over the lower-class minorities.

The acculturation of many minorities to sufficiently assume their appropriate roles in the system often conflicts with the minority's own cultural system, as may be seen in their adaptation to occupational roles.

Occupational roles are key factors in the acculturation process. Improved occupational positions with the accompanying roles are much sought by minorities and are the point of interaction where much pressure and counter-pressure is exerted. Conflict usually can be resolved only by minority members' learning new role behavior.

Although occupational roles are perhaps the most significant, other institutional roles are important also as focal points in dominant-minority relations. When the Irish entered politics the role of the political leader was defined by them in the light of their political heritage of protest and insurgence, the present necessity of vote-getting, and lack of access to the prerequisites of political leadership available to John Adams conservatives. The immigrant group created a new structure of urban politics and new roles in the ward boss and the local party boss which brought bitter but not always successful opposition.

Family roles as defined by one group may be alien to the other. A Puerto Rican mother may quit her job and apply for public assistance because her daughter has reached puberty and in the cultural framework it is now the mother's duty to stay home and chaperone her daughter. A father, in many European societies, who sees his paternal role as providing for a good marriage for his daughter may be bewildered when a college scholarship committee tells him she is not eligible for scholarship aid as long as her dowry is in the bank.

For the dominants fluent, unaccented language and performance of institutional roles according to dominant norms are the most important. The minority member may on the other hand view the material aspect of acculturation as paramount: the labor-saving device or the big car. Even under the condition of extreme barriers to minority participation in the full range of opportunity in the society, more recognition and respect has usually gone to the more acculturated.

Internal acculturation occurs where the cultural *attitudes* of the dominant culture have been acquired. If there is close congruence between the dominant and minority cultural values, internal acculturation may precede external, as with the North Europeans and to some extent the Japanese. On the whole, however, as our non-northern-European populations have come largely from pre-technological tribal or feudal societies, the other sequence has been more common. Behavior changes first, then dominant norms are internalized and become the assumption from which behavior emanates spontaneously.

The level of acculturation as a mode of adaptation in minority groups is typically generational—that is to say, the child of the immigrant becomes more acculturated than his immigrant parents and thus as a parent himself socializes his children to more of the dominant culture and less of the immigrant culture.

Minorities may, however, *choose stabilized acculturation and resist complete assimilation* as a mode of adaptation. This may be because they value a specific historic tradition of which they are part. Or they may feel that identity with a group that shares the same cultural tradition gives security. Or it may be their assessment that even with total acculturation all barriers to participation in the society will not be lifted for them.

In the past there has been great effort on the part of dominant "civic minded" institutions and groups to aid acculturation. The dominant society has indeed largely succeeded in imposing cultural dominance despite the incorporation of some cultural products of minority peoples: jazz, spaghetti, canoes, etc. A current trend, however, is the revitalization of visible cultural symbols, rituals, and even speech patterns of minority peoples to proudly define for all others their cultural group identity. This is particularly true of groups who have suffered categorical discrimination on the basis of their "racial" appearance, where even complete acculturation has failed to remove all barriers to equal participation. Such groups—blacks, Indians, Asians, Spanish-Americans—find unity in cultural pride and a rooted heritage out of which they seek power blocs to challenge the old stabilized pattern.

The "Vicious Circle"

Once established, the dynamics of dominant-minority relations set in motion a continuous series of reciprocal stimuli and responses which has been frequently called the "vicious circle." Discriminatory practices operate to keep a minority in disadvantaged circumstances which may lead to low standards of living, health, education, and morals. These poor conditions then give support to the dominant group's rationale for discrimination. The discrimination and the low standards mutually "cause" each other. Myrdal points out that,

> If things remain about as they are, or have been, this means that the two forces happen to balance each other. . . . If either of the factors changes, this will cause a change in the other factor, too, and start a process of interaction where the change in one

factor will be continuously supported by the reaction of the other factor. . . .

If, for example, we assume that for some reason white prejudice could be decreased and discrimination mitigated, this is likely to cause a rise in Negro standards, which may decrease white prejudice still a little more, which would again allow Negro standards to rise, and so on through mutual interaction. If, instead, discrimination should become intensified, we should see the vicious circle spiraling downward.[10]

Assimilation

Throughout the period of the stabilization of dominance the expectation of the dominant culture is that "others" will either stay separate or subordinate or will be assimilable. Assimilation as viewed until nearly the close of the nineteenth century expected and allowed for *individuals* at all class levels to become part of the dominant society. At this time it meant that one must be "white," have acculturated externally and internally, speak English like a native (perhaps anglicize one's name), feel identity and loyalty as an American, and subscribe in behavior and feelings to the Protestant ethic. Indeed, in all but the very highest levels of society, the visible manifestation of Protestant affiliation was necessary. At the very top, men of wealth and talent might preserve a separate affiliation if their behavior and values were congruent with those of the dominants. This was more true of individual Jews than of Roman Catholics, except in local hierarchies (like Baltimore and New Orleans) where there had been old Catholic settlement.[11]

This was a possible adaptation for individuals, not for groups. As such it kept alive the expectation of mobility and success for the aspiring, and incorporated talents into the dominant structure. In this sense, *selective, individual assimilation* was a stabilizing factor in the society. The only *group* that was easily and almost totally assimilated in the nineteenth century was the British (not including the Irish).[12]

The attempts to assimilate sizable groups of "others" were first of all not possible in periods where sufficient continuing

[10]Gunnar Myrdal, *An American Dilemma* (New York: Harper & Brothers, 1944), pp. 75–76.
[11]E. Digby Baltzell, *The Protestant Establishment: Aristocracy and Caste in America* (New York: Random House, 1964), p. 73.
[12]Rowland Tappan Berthoff, *British Immigrants in Industrial America, 1790–1950* (Cambridge, Mass.: Harvard University Press, 1953).

migration reinforced and kept alive old cultural attachments. In the second place it would have aroused, and eventually did (1880–1940), so much anxiety and apprehension on the part of segments of the dominant population that barriers which had not existed before were erected against the complete acceptance of "others."[13]

Nevertheless, although discrimination and prejudice increased for three quarters of a century, the dominant society succeeded in imposing *cultural*, if not always institutional, dominance, despite the incorporation of some external, peripheral culture traits from the migrating groups.

The operating concept of assimilation has now largely changed in the second half of the twentieth century, as we shall discuss below; but this could not occur until large, sufficiently acculturated groups had brought great pressure to bear on the dominant segments of the society.

THE DECLINE OF DOMINANCE

The stabilization of dominance may become so embedded in the controls of beliefs, customs, and institutional roles that it can continue virtually unchanged for long periods of time, as with slavery in the South. When the whole society is adapting to general changes it may, for a time at least, undergo even more severe enforcement, as with South Africa today. The twentieth century in America, however, has witnessed the modification and gradual decline (not without struggle) of WASP dominance. This has been made possible through three broad processes: (1) general social changes which, in our national history, have led to (2) modification of the structure of dominance as new needs had to be met, and this in turn has (3) made possible and effective the direct challenge and protest of certain minorities themselves.

General Social Trends Affecting Minorities

INDUSTRIALIZATION   The transition from a predominantly agricultural and merchant to a predominantly industrial nation dominated in the second half of the nineteenth and first quarter of the twentieth century in the United States. This affected

[13]See Baltzell, *The Protestant Establishment*, Ch. V., and John Higham, *Strangers in the Land: Patterns of American Nativism 1860–1925* (New York: Atheneum, 1965).

the recruitment of the growing industrial labor force, the change in the status of workmen, and the attitudes toward immigrants.

As Warner and Low[14] point out with regard to "Yankee City," in the early days of industrialization industrial workers had the status which had existed for free white wage earners under the handicraft system. There was an opportunity for able individuals to rise to supervisory or management positions or eventually to become entrepreneurs, much as the journeyman had once been able to become a master craftsman, setting the standards for his workmen, marketing his product, and being a small merchant capitalist. As industrialization grew and the factory system became the dominant pattern of production, the competition to cut labor costs brought a lower wage standard and a decline not only in the style of life of the industrial worker but in the prestige of his occupational group. Since immigrants contributed largely to this growing labor force, they shared and increased the lowered position of the American industrial workers. As more and more immigrants came, there was a tendency to identify all industrial labor as "foreign," all the more so when tensions grew up around the struggle to form labor unions. A study in the 1940s of a small industry in a midwest community showed that the industrial workers were referred to as "Poles," though in fact 50 per cent of this group were of native American stock.[15]

In dominant-minority relations today, the most significant aspects of the industrialization process are the impact on the South of recent and increasing industrialization and whether or not companies will follow local or national standards of hiring and promotion of minorities; structural changes in the occupational field with advancing technology; the situation of the minority agricultural labor force (mostly Mexican American) in relation to the large corporation farms and vineyards of the Pacific Coast; and the progressive, but by no means universal elimination of discrimination in unions.

URBANIZATION   The growth of our urban, multi-group society has had a significant effect on minority participation. Folk cultures, with their kinship patterns, language, and folk beliefs, have been brought in contact with other cultures, and subjected

---

[14]W. Lloyd Warner and J. O. Low, *The Social System of the Modern Factory* (New Haven: Yale University Press, 1941).
[15]August B. Hollingshead, *Elmtown's Youth* (New York: John Wiley & Sons, 1941).

to the secularizing influence of dominant economic, educational, and legal systems. The institutional balance of folk cultures, where family and religion take precedence, is borne upon by the multi-group urban community, where the dominant institutions are economic and political.

Another aspect of urbanization has been that the size, density, and heterogeneity of cities have made possible segmentation of roles, so that public and private roles need not necessarily overlap. This has aided the acculturation process.

It is significant that over half the population of the United States now lives in metropolitan areas—that is, in a big city or its suburbs. Although suburban patterns of dominant-minority relations vary from the patterns of the central city, the economic dependence of suburbs on the city, as well as other ideological influences emanating from the metropolitan core, has an impact which is being felt more and more.

THE WELFARE STATE   The problems of an industrial society, the urban balance in national politics, the experiences of the great depression of the 1930s and of world wars have led to an increasing centralization and extension of federal power. National responsibility has been accepted for at least a bare minimum guarantee of health and welfare. There has been a growing shift from the ideology of *laissez faire* to what is sometimes called "the reluctant welfare state." Federal legislation from the Social Security Act of 1935 to the civil rights and anti-poverty legislation of the 1960s have to a degree improved the situation of minorities, as ethno-racial/minority groups have had a proportionately higher percentage of "the poor," the "uneducated," the "untrained" (technologically). Federal legislation has made some important inroads on discriminatory ceilings of regional customary practices, whether it is Mississippi and blacks, Texas and Chicanos, California and Asians, or the whole nation and American Indians.

Such limited legislation, though helpful to segments of the minority populations, has not solved the problems of economic security, economic opportunity, or personal dignity of minorities. The response to a continuing devaluation has been, for many members of a minority, the reassessment and affirmation of pre-American cultural heritage to establish their own self-worth, and the attempt to form ethnic political blocs to win access to more equal, rather than minimal, marginal, security and opportunity.

International Pressures

Dominant-minority relations in the United States must now, willy-nilly take cognizance of a world situation. We have had a public policy in this century of exerting our influence to preserve "democracy" and "private enterprise" throughout the world. We are facing the fact that we may have to deal with powerful segments of the world who are not ethno-racially North European, and whose economic organization is not ours. The Asian-African bloc is a wholly new dimension in the world balance and affects the hopes, identities, and aspirations of some minorities who find the barriers of American society too insurmountable. The ideal of a different organization of property attracts others who have seen in other nations more opportunity for the education of the able of whatever class, because a new economic organization has brought about a new and more future-oriented educational system. More opportunity for local participation in decision-making, though encouraged by anti-poverty legislation, is still viewed skeptically in this country by the vested interests of business or labor. Some of the powerless turn toward Cuba, China, Ghana, Algeria as one set of models; or the Soviet Union as a sophisticated, secular, technologically competitive model; or toward an emotional, rather than ideological, model of "homeland"—Israel, West Africa, Indian reservations (a sentiment stressing "peoplehood").

Minorities as groups respond to the total situation which is no longer local, regional, or even national for all (though still for many) in a variety of ways. Some may "make it" in terms of the goals of American society and the approved means of achievement. At the other end of the spectrum some may give up, and some may rebel and look to other models than the discriminating society. (See Chap. 18 for further discussion of alternative adaptations.)

The Modification of Political Dominance

The possibility of modifying the political dominance of "the Protestant Establishment" has meant that the contenders must have sufficient acculturation to be able to use the political processes. It is not surprising that the Irish were the first to take advantage of political channels, for they were English-speaking and had the experience of having been a cultural minority within the

United Kingdom. The urban political machine became an instrument for minorities to obtain local power. For several decades it operated, through its patronage system, as a welfare agent for minorities who supported it. Changes in the welfare structure of the nation have made this function (though not always this practice) obsolete. The machine also opened career channels in politics to minority members. It became an arena for intergroup integration between various national minorities, and subsequently during and after the Depression of the 1930s, a channel for the integration of dominants and minorities. The character of the machine has changed as its functions have changed and as urban politics has been more closely related to the national political structure.

As significant as the legislative structure has been the judicial structure, not only in the composition of the local magistrates' bench, but, particularly in the present, the Supreme Court. Although legal restrictions on minorities have received different adjudication in different periods, according to the composition of the bench and the spirit of the period, the Supreme Court has had the chief responsibility for the definition and interpretation of the rights of minorities, and the federal judiciary the responsibility for implementation of federal legislation on behalf of minorities.

For half a century there have been members of religious or ethnic minorities appointed to the Supreme Court (and in 1967 the first Negro was appointed). Cases are argued before the highest court by lawyers who are members of minorities. The success of one minority in obtaining a favorable ruling emboldens others to use the same (though prolonged) process of redress. After the Supreme Court decision terminating the exclusion of Negroes from juries (a southern regional practice) Mexican Americans were able successfully to use the same channel. Even religious minorities such as the Amish or Jehovah's Witnesses whose beliefs and value system are opposed to participation in secular affairs of the state have modified sufficiently to employ counsel from outside their membership and seek recourse to the courts.[16]

The Challenge to Dominance

Although some challenge to dominance is continually going on, we have suggested that this is small and largely unsuccessful in a period when a nation is stabilizing its institutional patterns,

[16]See Chap. 3 for examples.

or when, as in America, the expanding economy (and, historically, the expanding frontier) creates sufficient hope for individual improvement within the system that the pressure for modification is counteracted by the prospect of new rewards within the status quo. Thus the growing movement against slavery in the early decades of national independence was set back by the development of the "cotton culture" made possible by the cotton gin and the steamboat. For the minorities of European descent, in the period of national expansion the expectation persisted *both* on the part of dominants and of minorities that the immigrants would assimilate and share in the opportunities of the developing country. One must recognize, however, that increasing acculturation brings increasing restlessness with restraints of the dominant society. For many the process was too selective and too slow.

MARGINALITY   In the theory of minority adjustment which assumed that minority groups moved through a series of steps to ultimate assimilation, there were certain groups, as we shall see in subsequent chapters, that were at some time declared "unassimilable." Within this theoretical frame groups were sometimes defined as being in a marginal *stage*.[17] This referred to the fact that the direction of leadership and membership was toward the incorporation of dominant values and goals, emulating even if imperfectly dominant institutional roles, although "visible characteristics" of the minority and discrimination persisted. The group then took on a double identity illustrated by the self-designation of hyphenated status: "I am an Italian-American."[18]

Another way of discussing marginality is to see it as an *individual adaptation* to minority status. Robert K. Merton has defined the marginal person as one whose reference group (the group from which he takes his norms) is different from the group of which he is a member. That is to say, he emulates and strives to be accepted by a group of which he is not yet, or is only peripherally, a member.[19] Viewing marginality this way, it can be said to occur whenever an individual is abandoning the mode of adaptation that has prevailed in the group of which he is a member.

[17]Robert E. Park, *Race and Culture* (Glencoe, Ill.: The Free Press, 1950).
[18]Baltzell refers to this (in *The Protestant Establishment*) as *marginal culture* without any implication of its being a stage in a sequence, pp. 62–70.
[19]Robert K. Merton, *Social Theory and Social Structure* (Glencoe, Ill.: The Free Press), pp. 290–291. In Merton's definition marginality may apply equally to movement between any contiguous groups, as for example, upward or downward mobility between social classes.

This usually makes him, to a greater or lesser degree, an "outsider" to both groups.

Internally the marginal person may suffer from conflict of values and conflict of loyalties. This may operate to make him anxious and to lower his efficiency in fulfilling the roles he is seeking to carry out. His anxiety may even keep him from perceiving the subtler aspects of role behavior in the group toward which he is striving. If he is able to rationalize his striving to the point where he suppresses or disciplines any conflicts in abandoning one group for the other, he risks being regarded as a renegade by the group he strives to leave and as an "operator" by the group he is moving toward.

His problem is often easier if he does not have to carry a double burden of class marginality along with race or culture marginality. Too often, however, there is this double burden as the minority member comes to accept the dominant American norm of class mobility. Since the institutional patterns of a culture are its guarantees of continuance, honored positions in the society go to those who best fulfill significant dominant institutional roles. People who have had prolonged subordination often have no opportunity to perceive or learn these roles, or feel they must reject them because they are impossible. Others cling to roles defined by variant value systems. Yet increasingly there is the rising aspiration for the benefits to be derived from improved positions, which leads to role relearning, role conflict, or role modification. This is where the real personal crises of dominant-minority relations occur.

For Baltzell, the marginal individual (as contrasted with the marginal culture) is the completely acculturated person who is still identified (sometimes by choice, though not necessarily) as a member by descent of a religious, ethnic, or "racial" minority.[20] According to Baltzell's analysis the top elite, nationally, can absorb a modest percentage of marginal men of high talent (bankers, federal judges, etc.) and does so, whereas the levels below, and to a large extent the *local* hierarchies of status, tend to persist in a parallel status structure.

COMPETITION   The marginal *individual* challenges dominance by the successful competition for honorific occupational positions. This is possible in a technological or developing society

[20]Baltzell, *The Protestant Establishment*, pp. 62–70.

so long as particular skills and/or abilities clearly contribute to the needs of the society at the decision-making level.

Where individual competition shows some degree of success, there has been in the past, and may persist, a tightening of *social* barriers against successful persons of minority identification or descent (however tenuous the minority tie.) This may filter down from top levels and become not only social but more general discrimination for people lower on the status scale who fear that their opportunities for moving up are being jeopardized.

THE STRUGGLE FOR POWER   Marginal *groups* who have taken on enough aspects of the dominant culture to share its goals and have some frame for perceiving what means will help them achieve as a group rather than as individuals, express their challenge to dominants in a struggle for legitimate or illegitimate power. This has been illustrated by the degree to which political organization depending on minority support and supporting minority interests in one period captured East Coast city politics and perhaps changed the character of large city politics throughout the nation. For a time city politics was linked with rackets and other nonlegitimate avenues to affluence, often attracting minority ability where legitimate channels were closed through discrimination.[21]

Nonviolent civil rights efforts represent an innovating attempt to achieve legitimate power, in the sense that they exert pressure for the state to modify patterns of discrimination, for channels of economic opportunity to be opened, and for civil participation within the legitimate structure.

At another level people who have neither the confidence in nor knowledge of the legitimate channels will be vulnerable to spontaneous outbreaks of protest. If these become widespread (like riots spreading from city to city) it makes an impact on the Establishment. If this kind of protest is an isolated instance, it is usually ineffective. Sometimes it also retards the efforts of other modes of protest which seek more sophisticatedly to modify existing structures. As a phenomenon of protest it is most often the weapon of the most depressed of the minorities who are under the double pressure of severe discrimination and poverty, as with the Irish in the nineteenth century and the Negroes today.

[21]For a description of this interlocking and its meaning to one minority neighborhood in a large eastern city see William Foote Whyte, *Street Corner Society* (Chicago, Ill.: The University of Chicago Press, 1943).

NATIVISM   Any organized protest effort of any sizable minority group has the effect of creating reactive movements designed to legitimately or illegitimately restrain minorities. Conflict increases polarization of interest and *nativistic* movements on the part of dominants who seek to, and sometimes for a time are able to, increase discrimination and stimulate latent prejudice. The largest number of followers of such movements may themselves be (in the general sense) marginal, economically, socially, or even sometimes ethnically. This situation is likely to emerge and become even stronger if the total society is undergoing confusing changes, such as rapid industrialization or urbanization.

Dominant nativistic movements seek to maintain a particular historical value system and status as expressed in an idealized historical image. Polarization also gives rise to minority nativistic movements which reach for an idealized past as a locus of identification. The marginal character of adherents to such movements is clear as the image of the idealized past which they project is expected to include the benefits of the contemporary society, thus indicating the duality of reference groups. No Zionist sought a biblical society in Israel. Black Muslims have taken a great ethical, progressive and "world" religion as the locus of their identity and combined it with a modern idea of power. The Garvey movement which advocated the return of Negroes to Africa did not envisage return to a tribal society.

The processes of conflict and protest are of course *disjunctive processes:* they disrupt the ongoing social pattern. For those people who have adapted and conformed to the system, disruption in itself is anxiety producing. *Yet no social change occurs without disruption for some* (like the displacement of some people who are used to a neighborhood in order to build better housing for more people). Disjunctive processes are part of the ongoing social experience, and although they are often focal at a particular time they do not preclude simultaneous sustaining processes, or integrative processes which grow out of the new demands on the society.

INTEGRATION   As we pointed out early in this chapter, when minorities have enough power (economic or political), cooperation has been through negotiation in the form of an implied contractual relationship between one group as a group and the other as a group. When individual cooperation between dominants and minorities *on the basis of equality* occurs we have the phenomenon of integration. Thus children within an integrated school may be friends and equals. Neighbors in an integrated neighborhood may cooperate as equal members of a taxpayers group or a community committee or as members of a neighborhood parish. Integration occurs in the equal association of individuals when the minority still identifies itself as a minority. In this way it differs from assimilation.

Protest movements, despite their disjunctive effect on the previously existing social equilibrium may be integrative factors in dominant-minority relations. This may be true *internally* through the opportunity they provide for committed members of both the dominant group and the minorities to come into frequent interaction as they work toward a common goal. They contribute *externally* to the degree they have a successful impact on the social situation. The *internal* integrative effect will be minimized if the majority of the membership of a given movement is either dominant (as with the antislavery movement) or minority (as with the National Congress of American Indians). The *external* effect will be minimized if the movement fails to change institutional patterns, not merely to achieve official abrogation of discrimination. Another limitation to the integrative impact of protest movements is their contemporaneous focus. If in addition to their immediate demands they become ongoing organizations they may lose flexibility in adapting to changing needs of a new generation of membership.

Assimilation in a Pluralistic Society

The history of America has been that of absorbing many peoples. As long as the migration was predominantly northern European it was assumed that all those of Caucasian stock would "disappear" as separate identities. For many this has been true. Coupled with this assumption was the designation of some peoples as "unassimilable." This was particularly a public argument regarding Asiatics on the West Coast, and was used as a platform for limitation of Asiatic migration. At one point, at the turn of the century, there was a variant of the older belief about assimilation: the *melting pot theory*, which claimed that from the merging of the many ethnic heritages a new type of person—the "American" —would evolve. At this time the public mind viewed people whose style of life was American and whose language was English as "assimilated," so long as there were no alien racial characteristics.

In contradistinction to the "melting pot" view was the concept of *cultural pluralism*. The heavy migration of the turn of the century with the resulting urban nationality sub-communities had an impact on political and social thinking within the urban milieu. Social workers, like those of Chicago's Hull House, were concerned with supporting the dignity of cultural heritage of immigrants confused by the impact of the new American environment. Politicians were recognizing subcultural identity in their bids for the "Italian vote" or the "Polish vote." Ethnic groups often controlled one type of operation, one floor in an industry, or one local of a labor union.

The dangers to the state of really diverse value systems within it is real, for to preserve justice and public order there must be a common understanding of norms, of what is a "fair" way of dealing with others. Furthermore, the latent effect of a really established cultural pluralism can lead to the mechanism "divide-and-rule." The maintenance of a total (or largely) separate cultural identity has often had the effect of increasing visibility and discrimination and deterring minorities from challenging their subordinate position. Effective challenge to dominance, as we have tried to show, can only come when at least some institutional acculturation has taken place.

What has happened in America has been that truly separatist communities, by choice, like the Amish, or by force, like the American Indians, have been small groups who kept their cultures intact by geographic and institutional separation. The rest of the groups, in interaction with others, acculturated to a greater or lesser degree as far as *secular* institutional participation was concerned (public schools, politics, jobs), and such pluralism as was retained was traditional religion, festival ritual, food, and other aspects of the personal rather than the public world. Cultural pluralism in the visionary sense of the early decades of the twentieth century proved incongruent to the effective needs both of minorities and of the total society, however humanistically appealing it was as a philosophy.

Stabilized Acculturation and Structural Pluralism

Association in work, in politics, and public life do much to break down "social distance" between disparate groups. The public recognition of the achievement of minority individuals has enhanced the "respectability" of minority descent. As large segments of the ethnic minorities have moved into middle-class occupations and become acculturated to middle-class norms, ethnicity, at least in the large urban multi-group communities, becomes more and more a private matter or a symbolic appeal in some public or political situations. Blue-collar workers, too, are more American than ethnic in their life styles. To some extent this process may be observed also with regard to "racial" minorities if housing patterns permit interracial community contact.

"Respectability" means, then, that at least in the secular spheres of life, to a considerable degree acculturation, at whatever class level, has taken place. It means, furthermore, that minority institutional patterns have modified and become more coherent with dominant norms. Yet within this frame of acculturation there persists, it is argued, a preference for intimate associations with people whose cultural and/or religious and racial heritage is like one's own. We have called this mode of adaptation *stabilized acculturation*. More recently Milton M. Gordon has used the term *structural pluralism*.

> We have chosen to focus on the nature of group life itself in the United States as constituting the social setting in which relationships among persons of differing race, religion, and national origin take place. For these 190 million Americans are not just individuals with psychological characteristics. They belong to groups: primary groups and secondary groups, family groups, social cliques, associations or formal organizations, networks of associations, racial, religious, and national origins groups. And the nature of these groups and their interrelationships has a profound impact upon the way in which people of different ethnic backgrounds regard and relate to one another.
>
> In particular, we have called attention to the nature of the ethnic group itself as a large subsociety, crisscrossed by social class, and continuing in its own primary groups of families, cliques and associations—its own network of organizations and institutions—in other words as a highly structured community within the boundaries of which an individual may, if he wishes, carry out most of his more meaningful life activities from the cradle to the grave. We have pointed to the considerable body of evidence which suggests that the ethnic varieties of Americans, excepting the intellectuals, tend to remain within their own ethnic group and social class for most of their intimate, primary group relationships, interacting with other ethnic and class varieties of Americans largely in impersonal secondary group relationships.

The United States, we have argued, is a multiple melting pot in which acculturation for all groups beyond the first generation of immigrants, without eliminating all value conflict, has been massive and decisive, but in which structural separation on the basis of race and religion—structural pluralism, as we have called it—emerges as the dominant sociological condition.[22]

This is to say that the majority of the members of minority groups in urban America at the present time, if the primary differentiating characteristics have been religious and cultural, and they are second or third generation, are assimilated at the appropriate class level in the spheres of work and political life and in their external life style. In the sphere of sentiment and intimate association, however, there are still strong religious and/or ethnic bonds. (This is equally true of WASPs as an ethnic group.) Gordon makes an exception for the intellectuals as a true interethnic stratum. We pointed out earlier in this chapter Baltzell's observation that at one time, and perhaps re-emerging today, the business and political elite associated as equals within the top echelons, despite differences of descent and affiliation. We might also add that protest movements in many instances create an interethnic associational base. Bohemias, the sections of metropolitan centers where the artists and their satellites congregate, have traditionally been exceptions to the pattern of structural pluralism.

The effect of the clustering of ethnic groups in the manner presented by Gordon has one dysfunction in that it may perpetuate some of the stereotypes of "others" among the different groups. Gans, in his study of an Italian working-class community, suggests that often this stereotyping of neighbors who are Irish, or bosses who are Jewish, is completely without malice.[23] Nevertheless there is always the risk, as Gordon points out, that stereotyping has a direct relation to prejudice and, as we have indicated, in times of general social stress can be used to mobilize insecure people to action against the stereotyped group.

We shall discuss in the chapter on religion and minorities the idea that there is no absolute reason why this kind of pluralism cannot be viable. In a certain sense the image of such a stabilized pattern is Utopian, because it assumes that, as in an ideal mar-

---

[22]Milton M. Gordon, *Assimilation in American Life* (New York: Oxford University Press, 1964), pp. 235–236.
[23]Herbert J. Gans, *The Urban Villagers* (New York: The Free Press, 1962), p. 36.

riage, private sentiments never interfere with the common good. Indeed, however, there has been recognition increasingly that "respectable" differences are allowable. Even with regard to the most visible differences (physiognomic) there is no longer, as there once was, public, national, and academic argument that certain peoples are unassimilable.

Structural pluralism is a solution for a minority group in adjusting to the dominant society which may be held as ideal (and this ideal may be shared by some dominants). For others it may be seen not as ideal but as a transitional reality to be followed by complete incorporation of the dominant values and affiliations including the private spheres of behavior and sentiment.

To see any direction of movement one must relate the mode of adaptation to *possibilities* as well as to goals. Louis Wirth has posited four possible goals for minority groups: secession, pluralism, assimilation, and achievement of dominance.[24] As Wagley and Harris point out, at the present time only two of these alternatives have any significant place in minority aspirations in the Western Hemisphere: pluralism and assimilation.[25]

Amalgamation

Amalgamation is the biological merging of previously distinct "racial" or "subracial" stocks. Amalgamation always takes place to some degree with or without formal approval when members of one group live in constant interaction with members of another. With members of both groups having a similar degree of acculturation and a similar position in the overall status system, cross-marriages begin to take place even in the face of group disapproval. The character of the American family as a nuclear family and the geographic mobility of Americans have facilitated this process. Similarly, there have frequently been cross-marriages at upper-status levels where the frame of reference is international rather than national, as with some intellectual and social elites. And finally, when there is a pattern of severe exploitation and subjugation of the minority by the dominant group, sexual exploitation will be one facet of the configuration.

[24]Louis Wirth, "The Problem of Minority Groups," in *The Science of Man in the World Crisis,* ed. Ralph Linton (New York: The Columbia University Press, 1945), pp. 354-364.
[25]Wagley and Harris, *Minorities in the New World,* p. 286.

Suggested Readings

Countryman, Vernon, ed. *Discrimination and the Law.* Chicago: University of Chicago Press, 1965.
  Papers and discussion on legal aspects of discrimination in employment, education, public accommodations, housing.

Gordon, Milton M. *Assimilation in American Life.* New York: Oxford University Press, 1964.
  An analysis of choices and trends affecting urban minorities.

Hughes, Everett C. *Social Change and Status Protest: An Essay on the Marginal Man.* Indianapolis: The Bobbs-Merrill Reprint Series in the Social Sciences, No. 129.
  A classic, provocative essay.

Kramer, Judith R. *The American Minority Community.* New York: Thomas Y. Crowell Company, Inc., 1970.
  A fresh approach to the situation of American minorities with special focus on the meaning of community.

3 **R**eligious and Cultural Minorities

Differences of religion, "national origin," and "race" have provided the rationalizations throughout America's history for discrimination and aggression by dominants against minorities. In this chapter we will deal first with religious discrimination, and subsequently with dominant-minority relations as they have developed between groups of different *European* national origin. Often there is a popular assumption that European groups have "made it" and there is no longer a "problem." The concept of "race" is of such significance in today's social and political arena that we shall deal with it separately in the next chapter.

At the time of the European settlement of America, apart from the slavery of Africans, religion was the only institutional ground for discrimination. The first steps to modify this were taken with the establishment of the independent nation. Throughout the nineteenth century the focus was more often on alien folkways of people of various "national origins." Often religion and national origin are so intertwined that the same group may be seen at one time from one focus, and at another from the other. This was true of the Irish, where Irish folkways were the target of prejudice long before the "Irish-Catholic" syndrome emerged.

Religious minorities and nationality minority groups are *cultural* structures around central value systems that are to a greater or lesser degree at variance with the dominant value system. In any complex society there is potential intergroup conflict, and institutional conflict, where peoples have differing beliefs affecting specific issues of public policy. The conflict may be simply an adjustive mechanism if the groups have *equal status* and *equal protection*. In the sphere of religious difference this has largely been achieved, though not easily or to the exclusion of continuing potential vulnerability. The situation with some ethnic groups seems to be entering a new phase in a struggle for a similar co-equal pluralism.

THE PROBLEM OF RELIGIOUS MINORITIES

The Colonial Heritage of Religious Discrimination

The American colonies were settled in a period when Europe had not yet resolved the problem of separation of religious identity and national identity. The nations of Europe in consolidating the authority of the state against feudal interests had leaned on the support of religion by designating an "established" church. Countries whose powerful elites were anti-Roman Catholic developed national Protestant churches supported by state funds. European countries that remained Catholic incorporated powerful political roles for members of the Church hierarchy.

The established churches acted as a conservative force, upholding the prerogatives of the joint political religious power structure. They were effective in continuing traditional order. But with the growth of economic enterprise and the entry into economic power of groups not favored by the establishment, both religious and secular, there were further moves of disaffection. These were manifestly (that is, consciously expressed as) religious movements. People found new ways of expressing beliefs and then found themselves deprived of a voice in political affairs. The movements were therefore also latently political. These "dissenters" were eventually offered a solution in migration to the New World. William Penn wrote to his son in 1700 that "it was the Government (of the new colony) which engaged me and those that adventured with me. . . . for being Dissenters, we therefore came that we might enjoy that so far of which would not be allowed us any share at home."[1] Before independence the American colonies were subject to the religio-legal restrictions of the mother country, and there were instances of Catholics and Jews

---

[1]*Papers Relating to Provincial Affairs,* Pennsylvania Archives of History and Biography, 2nd Series, VII. 11.

who were not by birth English, being denied citizenship because of religion.

The Principle of Disestablishment

The Crown colonies tended to be chiefly Anglican (Church of England) in the enfranchised population because of the position of the Governor and the military. Other colonies, however—Pennsylvania, Rhode Island, Maryland, Massachusetts—were "disestablishment" colonies. These latter controlled much of the commerce and had been the most restless with British rule. Thus in the formation of an independent nation the principle of disestablishment prevailed. This meant that there would be no *official* religion, and that no public funds would go for the support of any ecclesiastical body.

The American Constitution in its First Amendment guaranteed that there was to be no state religion, implying thereby no religious requirement for citizenship, franchise, or office holding; there was to be no meddling by the state in private religious practice. The statements were brief and general and have from time to time been annuled by state laws. The separation of church and state, as the principle has come to be called, differentiates between the claims of two bodies of authority.[2] It has been said that Thomas Jefferson was interested in the principle in order to protect the state from the church, and that Roger Williams was interested in it to protect the church from the state.[3]

The guarantee of "freedom of religion" as conceived by the Founding Fathers was of course seen by them as assurance that no particular *Protestant* denomination would be *the* dominant one. Up until 1850 Protestants were the dominant religious group; however, non-Protestants (or at least their elites) were absorbed into the secular life of the nation without any religious discrimination resulting.[4] Dissenters with significant numbers to be conspicuous and differing from the general community norms in

---

[2]A special note should be made of the distinctive position of Friends (Quakers). This body was so prestigious that it retained certain concessions won in colonial times: exemption from legal oaths and exemption from bearing arms. The military exemption has subsequently been extended to other sectarians, notably Mennonites and ultimately such contemporary groups as Jehovah's Witnesses and Black Muslims, but not without struggle.

[3]Earl Raab, *Religious Conflict in America* (Garden City, N.Y.: Anchor Books, Doubleday and Co., 1964), p. 7.

[4]E. Digby Baltzell, *The Protestant Establishment: Aristrocracy and Caste in America* (New York: Random House, 1964), p. 73.

beliefs and practices continued to find solutions in separatist colonies on the frontier. The large body of non-Protestants of European descent did not migrate till after 1850. Non-European religions were ignored. The Black Protestant Church was barely emerging. American Indian religions were not given the dignity of recognition.

To understand the significant deepening and broadening of the guarantee of religious freedom and equality in America it is necessary to consider the nature of religious bodies within the larger social structure.

Religion and the Social Structure

Religion is an internalized commitment to a *value system*. Certain central values are designated as *sacred*—that is not subject to utilitarian or empirical judgment. The "sacred" is something experienced, either by direct revelation or by repeated ritual. Freud sees it as man's confrontation with his powerlessness when he perceives himself in hazardous crises of the life cycle, or of nature's scarcity, or of personal jeopardy and the struggle for survival. The particular content of religious belief is inevitably influenced by the social experience of a particular group in both the past and the present.[5]

Religious bodies differ from one another in their deeper felt orientations that both affect society and are affected by it. They also differ in their use of symbols, ritual, and liturgy, and it is usually these extrinsic features that make one group visible and "foreign" to another. A genuine religious movement that becomes institutionalized and persists over generations (as contrasted with a transitory cult or revitalization movement) has the problem of coming to terms with the secular society. It has the choice of becoming accommodated to the society and its other institutions with their expectations of economic, political, and familial behavior or of being critical of and rejecting secular societal norms. The former pattern is usually called a *church;* the latter a *sect.* A church attempts to be inclusive. Membership is by birth and theology is explicit. The sect is based on a principle of voluntary joining and is exclusive of all who have not shared its experience of regenerative commitment. A sect is apt to be austere and ascetic, at least initially. But persistence over time, especially if

[5]Thomas F. O'Dea, *The Sociology of Religion* (Englewood Cliffs, N.J.: Prentice-Hall, 1966), Ch. 2.

accompanied by prosperity may lead to a lessening of its separatism from the secular world. At this point it becomes a denomination and a church.

Established religious bodies that have worked out (to them) acceptable compromises between their particular theology and "the world" appeal to those classes that are also the most established in the world. In America, the denominations of the Founding Fathers (in the East) or of the pioneer evangelists (in the South and West) with their emphasis on ritual or preaching have become the respectable and honored churches. On the other hand, sects that have sought to relieve stress with the hope of a new messianic coming or through frequent experience of religious enthusiasm, have provided expression to people whose position in the secular opportunity structure is by choice or necessity cut off from worldly success.

The Rise of Religious Discrimination

The resurgence of religion as a rationalization for discrimination and the consolidation of WASP dominance is bound up with other struggles and social changes. Targets for religious discrimination have been Protestant sectarians, non-Protestants, and non-Christians whenever they have been conspicuous in numbers or had highly visible religious practices inimical to dominant mores.

The Struggle for the Protestant Establishment

THE FIRST PHASE: 1789–1850   Until about 1850 Protestant dominance was so sufficiently clear by virtue of numbers, early migration, and economic advantage that members of religious minorities could be incorporated in the secular life of the nation without having religion emerge as a categorical reason for discrimination. This situation was able to persist till roughly the middle of the nineteenth century for several reasons. Conflicts of the period were regional, between the East Coast and the new Middle West. The major power struggles were those of the Eastern commercial classes against the workingmen of the East and the rural settlers of the Middle West. Both sides of the struggle were predominantly Protestant, but in religious terms they represented the established religious groups of the East: Episcopalian, Presbyterian, Congregational, versus the rising sectarian groups of the expanding nation: Methodists, Baptists, Disciples of Christ, etc., later to become the established denominations of the West. These popular evangelical, democratic, sectarian movements whose appeal was to farmers and workers contributed to the success of the Jacksonian revolution (eliminating, as it did, property qualifications for voting, imprisonment for debt, and advancing of free public education). The period was one of lively theological controversy, not unmixed with belief in Divine intervention, Divine mission, a modicum of superstition, and an upstanding conviction of human worth as more significant than doctrinal designation.[6] New forms of religion emerged out of the American experience developing from cult to sect to denomination over the century. Thus discrimination in this period was within the framework of class issues, with religious affiliation secondary. The "peculiar" people among native-born sectarians had the frontier to absorb them at a time when communication with the frontier was technologically limited.

A second factor of importance was that the largest body of non-Protestants did not migrate in great numbers until steamships were the common mode of trans-Atlantic travel. These were the Irish and the German Catholics. Although the Irish had come in a small steady stream since the mid-eighteenth century, the heavy Irish migration began in the 1850s spurred by famine in Ireland, ship companies seeking fares, recruitment of unskilled labor for American industries, and a land tenure system which left large segments of the Irish population landless. Irish labor crews built most of the railroads from the Alleghenies to the Rockies, and were miners in the Appalachian region. Many settled in Eastern cities, in the newer communities of the Middle West, and finally in the far West and California. Germans were much more widely distributed in the opening rural areas of the Middle West. Although many of them were Protestant, Chicago, St. Louis, St. Joseph, and various counties in Illinois, Missouri, Iowa, and Wisconsin had large contingents of German Catholics. Their arrival coincided with the opening of the railroad to Chicago and they dispersed to the West to follow their traditional occupations.

THE RISE OF RELIGIOUS DISCRIMINATION   The end of the nineteenth and the first decades of the twentieth century, however, saw the rise of real discrimination on religious grounds. On the part of the national elite it was first directed against the Jews.

[6]Thomas F. O'Dea, *The Mormons* (Chicago: The University of Chicago Press, 1957). See Chapter I for a summary of the religious ferment of the period.

This temporarily successful effort to protect and consolidate WASP dominance was precipitated by several factors. The first and not the least of these was the displacement of the old commercial upper class by new wealth after the Civil War. First the transportation wealth and subsequently the industrial wealth pushed the old merchant families and their descendants into lesser positions of power. Some of the newly rich validated their social position by intermarriage with the old families. Some old families were clever enough to seize on the new developments. But for most, they were left without economic or political power and retreated into creating structures of social exclusion. One must see this movement against the backdrop of very rapid economic development. (The national income quadrupled between 1870 and 1900, and doubled again by 1914). The displaced patricians were supported in their attempt to create exclusive enclaves in "society" (resorts, elite boarding schools, metropolitan clubs, and country clubs) by the new wealth which aped their parochialism in order to be "in." The result was "restriction" of membership where this had never occurred formally before.

The attitude leading to restriction filtered down to other segments of society. It was embraced by groups facing the heavy migration of Eastern European Jews whose folkways were conspicuously different and who were chiefly small merchants and industrial workers. It affected provincial cities undergoing the pangs of industrialization, affording them a scapegoat offered by the national models.

A phenomenon of this period was the rise of "old stock" associations with their emphasis on descent and date of migration as the criteria for social status.[7]

The rise of the urban political machine, in a number of cities largely in the hands of the Irish, with its patronage system of dispensing jobs or other aid and its frequent collusion with enterprises unacceptable to old Protestant mores, led to the anti-Irish Catholic syndrome. This was the more true as Irish clergy dominated the American Catholic Church at the time, and in some localities the church hierarchy had indirect controls on the local political machine. The response from many Protestants was the revival of the church-state issue.

Anti-Semitic and anti-Catholic feeling was at its height in the 1920s and even in the 1930s as World War I and the Depression

[7]Baltzell, *The Protestant Establishment*, p. 110 and pp. 90ff; 114ff.

made shockingly apparent the shift from a largely rural nation protected by two oceans to an industrial nation with international interdependence. The religious issue in dominant-minority relations has never been so widespread since, although there have been sporadic resurgences. (See Chapter 16 for discussion of recent anti-Semitism.)

MINORITY ADAPTATION TO PROTESTANT DOMINANCE

The Sects—Protestant Revitalization Movements

Religious revitalization movements, with their strong sense of peoplehood and often with messianic hopes, have been prime targets for aggressive action against them in the name of religion. Below we present three examples, which in their sequence can illustrate the slow extension of the guarantee of religious freedom to religious movements outside established churches: the first involved unmitigated brutality; the second was solved by separatism and the flexibility of the religious body; the third by aggressive legal defense.

The Ghost Dance[8] ← begin

> "All Indians must dance, everywhere, keep on dancing. Pretty soon in next spring, Great Spirit come. He bring back all game of every kind . . . All dead Indians come back and live again . . . Whites can't hurt Indians then . . . send word to all Indians to keep dancing and the good time will come. (Wokoya, the Piute Messiah)"

On October 9, 1890 about a year after the forced breakup of the great Sioux reservation Kicking Bear told Sitting Bull of his visit to the Piute Messiah. Kicking Bear had always thought that Christ was a white man like the missionaries, but this man looked like an Indian. "I will teach you how to dance a dance, and I want you to dance it, and when it is over I will talk to you." They had danced late into the night and the next day he talked to them throughout the day. "In the beginning," he said, "God made the earth, and then sent Christ to earth to teach the people, but white

[8]Adapted from Chapter 18 of *Bury My Heart at Wounded Knee* by Dee Brown. Copyright © 1970 by Dee Brown. Reprinted by permission of Holt, Rinehart and Winston, Inc.

men treated him badly, leaving scars on his body, and so he had gone back to heaven. Now he had returned as an Indian, and he was to renew everything as it had been and make it better." Sitting Bull was skeptical, but he was willing to let Kicking Bear teach the dance because many of his people had heard of it. Indeed on almost every Indian reservation the Ghost Dance was spreading like wildfire.

Indian Bureau inspectors and Army officers at Western stations were bewildered and frightened. "A more pernicious system of religion could not have been offered to a people who stood on the threshold of civilization," said Indian agent McLaughlin, a Roman Catholic. At McLaughlin's request Kicking Bear was arrested, but the Secretary of War refused to meet the request to arrest Sitting Bull also. As more arrests occurred on the reservations leaders took their followers to remote places where even as the wintry weather came they continued dancing. On November 20 the Indian Bureau telegraphed a list of "fomentors of disturbances" among the Ghost Dancers to Army headquarters in Chicago. Sitting Bull's name was on the list. Meanwhile troops had already been brought into the nearby Pine Ridge Reservation. A former agent of the Indian Bureau, asked to make recommendations, said "I should let the dance continue. The coming of the troops has frightened the Indians. If the Seventh Day Adventists prepare their ascension robes for the coming of the Savior, the United States Army is not put in motion to stop them. Why should not Indians have the same privilege?"

On December 15, an attempt was made to arrest Sitting Bull, but a crowd of Ghost Dancers intervened. In the scuffle between Ghost Dancers and military police a bullet struck and killed Sitting Bull.

One on the list of "fomenters" was Big Foot who had a camp at Cherry Creek. Demoralized and fleeing Indians from Standing Rock reached him and told of Sitting Bull's death. Big Foot immediately gathered his people and set out for Pine Ridge to seek the protection of the last of the great chiefs, Red Cloud. On the way they were intercepted and taken to the cavalry camp at Wounded Knee. There were 120 men and 230 women and children. They were assigned a camping area and it was surrounded by mounted Hotchkiss guns (range, two miles). Big Foot lay in his tent hemorhaging from tuberculosis. In the night a contingent of the 7th Regiment arrived and took charge (this was Custer's old regiment).

In the morning the Indians were assembled and disarmed. One Indian who was deaf did not understand and held on to his rifle. The Hotchkiss guns opened up. There were 153 known dead Indians, and doubtless more wounded who died that night in the dreadful blizzard that followed.

> "I did not know then how much was ended. When I look back from this high hill of my old age, I can still see the butchered women and children lying heaped and scattered all along the crooked gulch as plain as I saw them with eyes still young. And I can see that something else died there in the bloody mud, and was buried in the blizzard. A people's dream died there. It was a beautiful dream . . . the nation's hoop is broken and scattered. There is no center any longer, and the sacred tree is dead."
>
> (Black Elk)

In dealing with American Indian religious manifestations it was not until 1961 that the "Native American Church" was recognized as a legitimate church in a Supreme Court ruling. This religious sect uses an hallucinatory drug in its ceremonies (peyote). Before 1965 there were some state laws against its use. In the 1966 scare about the widespread use of LSD, making this a federal crime, an exception was made for hallucigenics in the rituals of the Native American Church.[9] Thus after 70 years the harmless expressions of religious hopes, enthusiasms, and visions have been protected. It is probably useful to recognize that even as late as 1960, with the decimation and demoralization of American Indians, the suit in their behalf was made by Anglos (the American Civil Liberties Union), the Indians themselves having had neither incentive nor opportunity to develop a legal cadre of their own. This is changing now.

The Church of Christ of the Latter Day Saints (Mormons)

> "A man of near 60 years of age, living about 7 miles from this place, was taken from his house a few nights since, stripped of his clothing, and his back cut to pieces with a whip, for no other reason than because he was a Mormon, and too old to make a successful resistance."[10]

[9]Peter Nabokov, "The Peyote Road," *The New York Times*, Mar. 9, 1969, Sect. vi, pp. 30–31, 129–132, 134.
[10]News item in The *Quincy* (Illinois) *Whig*, May 30, 1864, cited in *Frederick Hawkins Piercy, Route from Liverpool to Great Salt Lake Valley* (Cambridge, Mass.: Harvard University Press, 1962), pp. 216–217.

Probably there is no instance of religious persecution in American history comparable in scope and severity to that inflicted on the Mormons. Originally a sect, now a world wide church with two and a quarter million members, it was founded in 1830 in upper New York State. The original organization was created by six young men, the oldest thirty-one years of age. The theology, including the principle of continuing revelation, on which the sect was founded, is not germane to our discussion, though it undoubtedly agitated some in the beginning, in a period replete with religious controversy. Joseph Smith, the Mormon prophet, was arrested and imprisoned twice in the first year of the organized body's existence. The young sect was aggressive in missionary activity, attracted converts, sought to incorporate the Indians whom it defined as "the lost tribes of Israel," and projected an ideal community in the (then seen as) Far West near what became Independence, Missouri.

Between 1833 and 1839 some 1,500 Mormons moved to Missouri from New York and from a second settlement in Ohio. A temple was projected and they were initially welcomed by both Indians and white settlers. Shortly after their influx the U.S. Government forbid them to proselytize among Indians. Their economic pattern upset non-Mormon settlers; for Mormons, each man was to own and carry on his own enterprise (farm or business), retaining such part of his earnings necessary to maintain his family; the rest was to go to the church and there were to be no rich or poor. Finally political issues arose. Mormons were anti-slavery and most of their neighbor settlers were pro-slavery. Pitched battles broke out between Mormon and non-Mormon settlers. The militia intervened. Several leaders, including Joseph Smith were court marshalled and were to be executed. The soldier responsible for executing them refused. The entire community was ordered out of Missouri.

They chose a site on the Mississippi River in Illinois about 50 miles above Quincy and founded the town of Navoo (transliterated from the Hebrew, meaning "beautiful"). Here they built a prosperous town and, at last their first temple (reputed to cost a million dollars). They offered religious freedom to all Navoo residents. The jailed Mormon leaders in Missouri escaped. There were repeated efforts to have them extradited. The Governor of Illinois defended them, but local vilification increased. There were clashes. Joseph Smith and two others, somewhat apprehensively, agreed to appear in court in Carthage to answer charges of incitement to riot. The judge continued the case to the next session; they were then charged with treason and put in jail, and on the 27th of June 1839 a mob assassinated them. Joseph Smith was 39 years old.[11]

In the next years, as violent pressure increased against the Navoo community it was decided to move west. The first contingent of Mormons left for beyond the Rockies in February 1846. In the next several years one of the great dramas of American migration took place as Mormons, some in their fourth migration (New York-Ohio; Ohio-Missouri; Missouri-Illinois; Illinois-Utah), as well as new Mormon converts from the docksides and mill centers of England, set out with ox teams or in bands of two or three hundred on foot, pushing handcarts, to "Zion."

Behind they left homes burned, and their temple in Navoo which had been fired by an incendiary. They came to the desert around the great Salt Lake and built a flowering city.

In 1896 Utah became a state. Coincidentally or necessarily, the Mormons annulled their practice of polygamy (theologically, in an Old Testament-based religion polygamy is possible in "spiritual" and ritualistic marriages, with no relevance or implication for cohabitation, as women achieve salvation only through men— a patriarchal theology). Indeed there has always been some controversy within the Mormon Church about the intent or validity of social polygamy, and the practice began to die out naturally as a more settled life developed and the sex balance became more equal.

Mormons today are a strong anti-secular body. They still require two years of "missionary" work (now, accepted by some as social service religiously motivated) from all young people. Able Mormons have given service to the nation in wartime and in peacetime in the same spirit that they give money and time to their church. Despite their world membership they are a particularly American kind of church with a great tradition of the virtues and manifest destiny of the American pioneer experience: the work ethic, social justice, personal responsibility, community mutuality. To some people today they appear conservative, and the risk for rank and file Mormons is that they may ally themselves with others who are conservative about individual property, work, etc. without the sense of communal responsibility that a religious commitment gives.

[11]Charles Samuel Braden, *These Also Believe* (New York: The Macmillan Co., 1949), pp. 421–431.

The Church of Christ of the Latter Day Saints has been flexible, responsible, and non-puritanical. It has shown both the strength to survive and grow and the capacity not to be unduly caught by a rigid set of beliefs, however loved. Theologically, this is a benefit from a doctrine of continuous revelation. Mormons are not now persecuted, not because the "outside" world has become wiser, but because Mormons within their belief system have found a way, more precisely or less so, to maintain their community of identity and commitment *within* the world without totally becoming *of* the world.

The most serious social problem for the Church is the question of American blacks. Despite the history of anti-slavery sentiment, Mormon theological and organizational tradition, though welcoming black-Americans into the Mormon fold, does not allow them into the hierarchical stages of priesthood. In this, the pattern is too much like other institutions of the society which have been "liberal," but unwilling to give black Americans a chance to share decisions and authority within the institutional structure.

There are some splinter groups within the Mormon fraternity, the largest of which is the Reorganized Church of the Latter Day Saints with 156,670 members. They have always claimed that polygamy was undoctrinal. The headquarters of this branch is in Independence, Missouri, which may suggest that this group made an early acculturation to avoid a vulnerable, though vague, position of the original body.

Some eighty per cent of the world's Mormons live in the United States, more than half of these west of the Mississippi. A recent study of a small Mormon community in the Southwest shows the relation to four other cultures of the region and gives some sense of the dilemmas and strengths of an "average" Mormon group in relation to both dominants and other minorities.[12]

Rimrock is a Mormon, unincorporated village in western New Mexico, 38 miles south of U.S. Highway 66. Mormons first came here as missionaries to the Indians in 1870. After an epidemic of smallpox wiped out all but one family, the central church body "called" families from nearby Arizona to renew the community. At present in the Rimrock region there are settlements of Anglo "Texans," Spanish Americans (New Mexico Hispanos), Zuni Indians, and Navaho Indians. In the present hierarchy of the five

[12]Evon Z. Vogt and Ethel M. Albert, eds. *People of Rimrock* (Cambridge, Mass.: Harvard University Press, 1966), especially Chapters 2 and 7.

subgroups in the region, "Texans" and Mormons rank equally and highest. Below them are the Spanish Americans, with Zunis equal or a little higher and Navahos at the bottom of the scale. There has been some Mormon-"Texan" intermarriage. Rimrock Mormons will work for "Texans" and "Texans" for Mormons. Neither will work for Indians and only rarely for Spanish Americans.

Mormons view Indian religion as an apostate degeneration of Ancient Israelite roots and allow Indian converts to retain some participation in Indian ceremonials. Nevertheless they have absorbed some of the dominant attitudes toward Indians as "lazy, dirty" people. They regard Zunis as "better" because they are settled and agricultural, whereas Navahos are nomad. Nevertheless, the Mormon economic system in Rimrock depends on Navahos for labor and more specially for suppliers and customers as the Mormons are the brokers who sell Indian products to the wider market and supply trading post consumer items to Navahos. Recently there has been a revival of missionary activity and there are now 112 Navaho Mormons in Rimrock, two of whom have attained higher positions in the Mormon priestly hierarchy. Many Navahos, however, view Mormon religious profession a "lip-service religion" and charge them with increasing encroachment on Navaho lands and exploitation of Navaho laborers and consumers. Zunis have no economic dependence on Mormons and have largely resisted missionary efforts.

The Jehovah's Witnesses

A more recent militant sect which has become increasingly urban is the Jehovah's Witnesses. As we have said, sectarianism arises out of social and emotional needs that are not met by the Establishment at any given time.

The Jehovah's Witnesses, now with nearly half a million adherents, was founded in 1870 in Allegheny, Pennsylvania, and until 1931 was known by various names. It began as a Bible class. Followers in the United States and abroad now number nearly a million. Charles Taze Russell, its founder, was a member of the Congregational Church and of the YMCA. He was "converted" to the Adventist doctrine, which was fundamentalist and held to the literal interpretation of the prophecies of the book of Revelation that Christ would return to earth and reign for a thousand years. The central task for living men and women, then, in the belief of the Witnesses, is to convince others of the truth they hold, namely, the imminent violent end of this evil world. In order to be among those saved in the millennial reign one must bear witness to Christ in every act—that is all conduct is governed solely by religion. Every Witness is an ordained minister with a duty to preach. All free time must be spent spreading the gospel. The mode of proselytizing is chiefly through published tracts and the magazine, *The Watch Tower*, which are distributed in house-to-house canvassing or on street corners, and engaging the recipients in persuasive discussion. The sect has survived the difficult problems of succession of leadership and is now a tightly knit organization controlled by three corporations, similar to an ecclesiastical autocracy.[13]

A Witness must refuse to obey any law that is contrary to God's law, as derived from fundamentalist theology. On the other hand, Witnesses must obey any laws which do not conflict and must never present the truth through lawless means. Witnesses are expected to bear action against them stoically and not to retaliate. Indeed many rejoice in adversity, which they interpret as foreshadowing an imminent millennium. Witnesses are opposed to all organized religious bodies, as diverting people from the truth, and they are particularly anti-Catholic.

The Witnesses have experienced persecution and violence on the community level and have had many conflicts with the law. The violence against them either in direct outbreak or in illegal arrests was at a peak in 1940, with 335 incidents of mob violence.[14] As they are opposed to military service, 4,300 served prison sentences for violation of the draft laws in World War II. It is estimated that about six to ten thousand Witnesses were sent to concentration camps in Nazi Germany, and other governments abroad have taken action against them.[15]

The Flag Salute Controversy

The Jehovah's Witnesses came into prominence over their long battle to be exempt from saluting the American flag as a public-school requirement. The first flag salute statute was passed in 1898 in New York State. Thirty states and various localities in the remaining states had enacted such statutes by 1938 when the

---

[13]See Herbert Hewitt Stroup, *The Jehovah's Witnesses* (New York: Columbia University Press, 1945), p. 21 for description of corporate organization.
[14]See David R. Manwaring, *Render Unto Caesar: The Flag Salute Controversy* (Chicago: University of Chicago Press, 1962), pp. 169–171, for charts of incidence of violence 1940–1943; and Stroup, pp. 145–149.
[15]Manwaring, *Render Unto Caesar*, p. 30.

American Civil Liberties Union undertook to survey the question. The requirement of the salute was pushed by patriotic organizations and reactionary nationalist groups. Manwaring cites the Ku Klux Klan (in 1925), the D.A.R. (1923) and various fraternal groups.[16]

Before the issue became focused around the Jehovah's Witnesses there had already been incidents of religious objection to the ritual from Mennonites and other sectarians. On September 30, 1935 in a Lynn, Massachusetts high school, Carleton Nicholls, a Witness, refused to salute the flag and was expelled from school. On October 6, Joseph Franklin Rutherford, then President of the Witnesses, delivered a radio address upholding Nicholls' act. The Witnesses employed legal counsel and filed a petition with the State Supreme Court for Nicholls' reinstatement. The court upheld the school.

It was decided not to appeal at the time. Nevertheless, the ground had been broken for litigation. The Witnesses had no prohibition against using the courts; indeed, Rutherford had been a practicing attorney for twenty-seven years before he became president of his sect. Furthermore, as a small and unpopular body, the Witnesses could not resort to political pressure for a change in the statute. The issue became increasingly serious to them as they equated the salute with the Hitler salute at a time when their members were being persecuted in Germany. The first case to reach the Supreme Court on the flag salute issue was that of *Minersville School District* v. *Gobitis* in 1940. The Witnesses were defeated, Justice Frankfurter writing the majority opinion and Justice Stone presenting a dissenting opinion. This was a blow to the Witnesses, especially as they had just before been upheld by the Court on an issue (*Cantwell* v. *Connecticut*) involving distribution of literature and public proselytizing. The liberal press and the religious press (including two Catholic publications), much of the law press, as well as much of the general press were adverse in their criticism of the decision. The decision came just before the wave of violence against the Witnesses in the summer of 1940, and the widespread nature of the outbreaks was generally attributed to the Court decision.[17]

In 1943 the Supreme Court heard the last of the flag salute cases (*West Virginia State Board of Education* v. *Barnette*.) The decision this time was favorable to the Witnesses. Justice Jackson

[16]*Ibid.*, pp. 4–5, 7, 8.
[17]For analysis of the Supreme Court opinions and the reaction to the decision, see Manwaring, *Render Unto Caesar*, Chapters 7 and 8.

wrote the majority opinion. His central point distinguished between state requirements of educational substance such as American history and requirements of ritual.

The Jehovah's Witnesses are well equipped in organization,
legal talent, and funds to carry on a long, hard legal fight. Under
present leadership, and since their success in the courts, some of
the militancy has mitigated, though the dedicated spirit still dominates members. Jehovah's Witnesses have no racial bars, as they
see themselves obligated to save, by incorporation if possible,
every man on earth.

It has been a long struggle to achieve co-equal status for
religious belief systems. The illustrations we have presented of
revitalization movements demonstrate the slow road we have
taken to "protect the church from the state." Since sectarian
movements are always to some degree critical of the secular establishment, they perforce arouse anxiety in some people. Often, too,
anti-sectarian action has masked hidden economic motives: desire
for Indian lands, or envy of Mormon prosperity, for example.

THE ESTABLISHED RELIGIONS AND THE
DECLINE OF DOMINANCE

Since World War II there has been increasing sentiment that the
religions that share the Judeo-Christian tradition are equally "respectable, American" institutions.[18] Whereas this optimistic outlook reflects the fact that an increasingly equal proportion of the
"stable and respectable" middle class belong to the three major
religious bodies, historically both Catholics and Jews have experienced discrimination and aggressive action against them, not
only in individual instances, but categorically as representatives
of their religion.

The Roman Catholics

About 25 per cent of the American population is Roman
Catholic.[19] The problems of Catholics as a minority are bound up

[18]Will Herberg, *Protestant-Catholic-Jew* (Garden City, N.Y.: Doubleday and Co.,
1955).
[19]Claims by religious bodies as to membership may vary depending on whether or
not they count, in Christian churches, all baptized infants, or only adult church
members in good standing. For non-Christian groups, also, there is the question of
affiliation by descent or by present participation. The current estimates on the

with, first, the historic factor that America was settled by Protestant groups that had a heritage of protest against the Church of Rome. Their own group solidarity was maintained, in part, by teaching to successive generations the nature of this protest.

There were both doctrinal and organizational foci for their opposition. Doctrinally all Protestants opposed the primacy and ultimate authority of the Pope. Other doctrinal points of conflict were confession, penance, absolution, and indulgence. For most Protestants from the Reformation on, the Bible became the authority rather than "the Church." Initially, of course, for all, and still for some "fundamentalist" groups, this authority was accepted literally. But since the nineteenth-century development of documentary re-examination of the Bible and its sources, literalism has declined especially among the urban populations, though there is still the heritage of Biblical training (Protestant) versus Church Doctrinal training (Catholic). Some Protestant groups were also opposed to the centralized, bureaucratized structure of the Roman Catholic Church. Large denominations that elect their own leaders have seen the hierarchical appointments of Rome as anti-democratic. For anti-liturgical Protestants the Catholic form of worship with its rituals, vestments, and symbolic participation has seemed pomp and splendor, or idolatry. To a young nation engaged in settlement, with early marriage patterns, the celibate clergy, and the monasteries of monks and nuns wearing strange traditional garments and living in enclosed communities were objects of suspicion and mistrust. Thus in the problems of interreligious relations there were both doctrinal (intrinsic) and customary (extrinsic) areas of devaluation.[20]

The Catholic Church in the nineteenth century was ill-equipped to interpret itself to non-Catholics. Many of the priests were foreign born and many foreign trained. They felt that their primary obligation was to minister to the migrating ethnic populations for whom they made a link with the Catholic heritage of the home country. The fact that the Irish were English-speaking

---

basis of present participation are about 36 per cent for combined Protestant bodies including sectarians; about 25 per cent for Roman Catholics; about 5 per cent for Jews, about 2 per cent for Eastern Orthodox, and .03 per cent for Buddhists, and the remainder nonaffiliated.

[20]In the eighteenth century where there were occasions of Catholic political leadership in Maryland and briefly in New York, there was greater religious tolerance than under Protestants.

See John Tracy Ellis, *American Catholicism* (Chicago: University of Chicago Press, 2nd edition, revised, 1969), p. 19.

gave them an advantage in achieving major influence in the Catholic Church in America, especially in the East.

There were then historical institutional roots for anti-Catholicism which for many people provided an easy rationale on which to focus their distress about other uncertainties and change. The first large migration of the Irish in the 1850s coincided with the nativist Know Nothing Movement which was anti-immigration and anti-Catholic. Later class and labor issues as well as general "anti-foreign" sentiment fanned mistrust of southern and eastern European Catholics as well as of the Irish. How much of nineteenth century anti-Catholicism was primarily a religious issue is hard to estimate. But certainly as late as the first quarter of the twentieth century there were specific hostile acts categorically toward Catholics by the Ku Klux Klan. Job discrimination at middle and upper levels continued till the 1950s. In the growing urban centers of the East and West Coast there was often a link between local Irish politicians and the Church hierarchy. Establishment Protestants, sectarians, and Jews took a dim view of this, and raised afresh the principle of separation of Church and state, in this instance to "protect the state from the church."

Where the church, any church, is the focal center of a socio-religious community recent research suggests that this tends to foster a provincial and authoritarian view of the world.[21] It is these enclaves that most often know the least about other groups, their values, and their customs. They are also probably most vulnerable to distress if general social change impinges on the security of their religious, cultural, and social unity.

One study has found that today status identification is in some instances more important than religious communality, but even in those circumstances where interreligious friendships occur within closed status groups, there may be little sense of the content of belief of other religions than one's own.[22]

The Jewish Religion

Throughout American history until this century Jews were viewed as a religious group and religiously tolerated, though often

[21]Gerhart Lenski, *The Religious Factor* (Garden City, N.Y.: Doubleday and Co., rev. edition for Anchor Books, 1963).
[22]W. Widick Schroeder and Victor A. Oberhaus, *Religion in American Culture: Unity and Diversity in a Midwestern County* (New York: The Free Press of Glencoe, 1964), p. 182.

personally discriminated against in employment, education, and residence, and humiliated or injured. Anti-Semitism is such a complex problem that we discuss it elsewhere at length (Chapter 16). Whereas Catholic doctrine had until this past decade a specific definition of the Jewish responsibility in the death of Christ, it is doubtful if this in itself had much to do with rank and file attitudes of Catholics toward their Jewish neighbors which were, in urban settings, usually cordial. Protestants, as American Protestantism is so much more Biblical than doctrinal, had little quarrel with Jewish religion, though often with what they perceived as Jewish competition. Only in the post-Nazi period have there been any significant acts of violence against synagogues or Jewish religious symbols.

Jews have been strong supporters of the separation of church and state, as indeed were colonial Roman Catholics when they were a small minority, though well placed in terms of social class.[23]

The Negro Church

The Negro Protestant churches in their several branches together represent the most continuously independent institution of black Americans. Since 1816 when the African Methodist Episcopal Church was founded in Philadelphia, the black churches have given a special identity to black Americans: they provided an opportunity for leadership when it was denied in secular spheres; they gave a congregation experience in planning and budgeting money when the larger society gave no such opportunity.[24]

There has been no anti-religious effort against the black churches, *per se*, though there have been strong efforts to integrate black Americans in white establishment churches, especially in the decade following the Supreme Court decision of 1954 which declared enforced segregation, *ipso facto*, discriminatory and unequal.

We include mention of the Black Church here, not because of any overt action against it, but because it is a segment of established religion in America, and shares some of the dilemmas discussed below.

---

[23]Ellis, *American Catholicism*, p. 31.
[24]E. Franklin Frazier, *The Negro Church in America* (Liverpool: The University of Liverpool, 1963; Schocken Paperback edition, 1966), p. 23.

RELIGIOUS FREEDOM, ECUMENISM, AND
RELIGIOUS PLURALISM

Religious freedom seems to be accepted by present day Americans and upheld by the final resources of secular power, as long as the position, or practice, is clearly defined as "religious." There will, of course always be conflict of ideas and institutional policy, but if these are recognized as legitimate and reasonably co-equal they are no different from the disagreements between Republicans and Democrats. They contribute to the creative ferment of an alive society.

Religious bodies themselves still face some dilemmas including: their relation to their particular commitments and beliefs; the role of organized religion for an individual's sense of identity; and their relationship with other religions and secular society. Here we see two trends, as yet unresolved.

The ecumenical movement, initiated by Pope John XXIII, has stimulated much dialogue and attempted rapprochement between religious groups, as have the theological influences of the Jewish theologian, Martin Buber, and the Protestant theologian, Paul Tillich. This effort has certainly made for greater understanding at some leadership and elite levels of co-equal searches for the correct approaches to man, society, and God. Ecumenism may stimulate some community contacts between different religious groups, and some vague thinking that we are "all basically alike and respectable together within the Judeo-Christian ethics." This is a middle-class position, and there are counter movements.

Former "minority" religious institutions are at present less concerned with ecumenism than with the definition of differences. To a degree this constitutes a struggle by religious bodies to preserve their particular interpretation of God and man; and in part a struggle to assure that ecumenism does not violate a church's identity. It is, in one way, an attempt to affirm one's own heritage of belief, which may be modified but not corrupted. Thus we have new affirmations of the historical bases on which Catholics assert their unique part in building America.[25] We have new statements of Jewish theology, pointing out some fundamental differences between Jewish and Christian religion.[26] We have the development

[25]Ellis, *American Catholicism*, Chs. iv and v.
[26]See for example Arthur A. Cohen, *The Myth of the Judeo-Christian Tradition* (New York: Schocken Books, 1971).

now of Black Theology.[27] These appear to be attempts to make explicit the differences germane to a truly co-equal status, not based solely on legal tolerance.

Another problem confronting the established religions is the involvement of some of their adherents in civil protest against state policies. Black clergy took a major role in the early civil rights protests, especially Dr. Martin Luther King. More dramatic, for today, have been the protest actions of Catholic activists, like the Berrigan brothers, against the Vietnam War. Neither of these efforts have been against *people;* the first was against customs and laws; the second was against symbols of the policy of the secular establishment. As we pointed out at the beginning of this chapter, the established churches face the problem of finding and maintaining an appropriate compromise with the secular social structure. Activism in the name of the church against specific state policies creates dilemmas for both the institution of the state and the church.

What we see is, then, both an official and popular acceptance of a plurality of religious values and rituals so long as they are "purely religious." The religious bodies on the other hand are trying to define themselves more specifically in terms of *co-equal* pluralism. And in the issues of social change all are to one degree or another wrestling anew with the problems of the church and the world.

"NATIONAL ORIGINS," ETHNICITY, AND CULTURE

Over forty-five million immigrants have come to the United States since 1820 when the first records were kept. Three quarters of these came from various countries of Europe, and although some returned home, having made some money or been disappointed, most of them stayed. They represented a broad spectrum of differences in language and folkways. It was at first assumed that by at least the second or third generation they would be absorbed into the dominant American culture, and for many throughout the nineteenth century this occurred. In the first decade of the twentieth century America was called "the melting pot" where a fused brand of American was emerging from varying European lines of

[27]James H. Cone, *Liberation, A Black Theology of Liberation* (Philadelphia and New York: J. B. Lippincott Co., 1970).

descent, molded by the American experience, but nevertheless fundamentally WASP. Today we hear a great deal about ethnic pride and witness the formation of ethnic protest groups and ethnic community organizations.

In the rest of this chapter we shall examine the situation of the non-WASP immigrant and the questions that this new trend toward ethnic pluralism raises.

THE GREAT ATLANTIC MIGRATION

Immigration, as the United States of America has known it, has been a peculiarly American institution. One British author has described it as "the greatest folk migration in human history," and "the most persistent and pervasive influence" on the development of the United States.[28] The Great Atlantic Migration opened a continent, built an industrial nation, and was a demonstration of political democracy's capacity to survive religious, national, and racial heterogeneity. The survival of the political institutions on which identification as an American is so strongly based today did not occur without pressures and counter-pressures in meeting the challenge of unity born of heterogeneity.

The European migration has traditionally been broken into three periods before the restrictive legislation of 1924: the colonial, the "old," and the "new" immigration. Although this classification has had an effect on public opinion and on policy, there is no valid reason for it. The reasons for which immigrants came at all periods were similar; the skills they brought and their ability to adapt to the American environment show great consistency, however much groups differed culturally. Some came earlier, some later. The *impact* of immigration, however, varied; and the attitudes toward immigrants varied at different periods of the nation's development.[29]

Except for slaves and transported convicts, migration involved in most instances a *decision* and a risk, which to an extent may have strengthened self-reliance, adaptability, and enterprise. Despite lingering loyalties to distant lands, the experience of migration inevitably worked against traditional values.

[28]Maldwyn Allen Jones, *American Immigration* (Chicago: University of Chicago Press, 1960), p. 1.
[29]*Ibid.*, pp. 4–5.

FIGURE 3-1. TOTAL IMMIGRATION TO THE UNITED STATES BY DECADES*

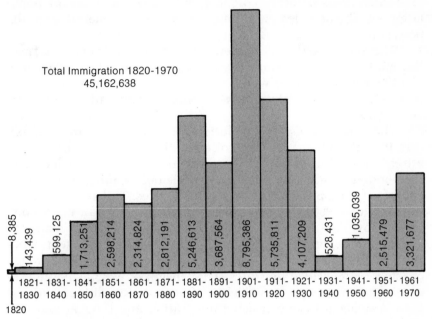

Total Immigration 1820-1970
45,162,638

| 8,385 | 143,439 | 599,125 | 1,713,251 | 2,598,214 | 2,314,824 | 2,812,191 | 5,246,613 | 3,687,564 | 8,795,386 | 5,735,811 | 4,107,209 | 528,431 | 1,035,039 | 2,515,479 | 3,321,677 |

1821- 1831- 1841- 1851- 1861- 1871- 1881- 1891- 1901- 1911- 1921- 1931- 1941- 1951- 1961
1830 1840 1850 1860 1870 1880 1890 1900 1910 1920 1930 1940 1950 1960 1970
1820

Statistical Abstract of the United States, United States Department of Commerce, Bureau of the Census, 92 Ed., 1971, Table 130, p. 89.

Reception of the Immigrants

Public issues related to immigration in the American colonies before the Revolution involved immigrants who lacked visible means of support, those convicted of crimes abroad, and Catholics. The criteria for acceptance had to do with economics, religion, and "moral standing;" there was no nationality criterion, though from time to time the Scotch-Irish, the French, and the Germans briefly encountered hostile attitudes. The attitude toward immigrants could be summed up as "welcome tinged with misgiving."[30]

The power struggle of the Revolutionary and post-Revolutionary period assured the pre-eminence of English political institutions and the English language. The success of the War of Independence united diverse elements behind a leadership stemming from the predominance of Englishmen in the first two

[30]*Ibid.,* p. 40.

generations of settlement. Although only New England and the Tidewater areas of other colonies had a predominance of population of English descent, these were the entrenched and the powerful.

The newcomers, of whatever origin, so far removed from Europe by the three-month voyage, were nevertheless sufficiently identified with the new world to be able to take individual positions—loyalist or revolutionary—without needing to form nationality blocs.[31]

The immediate post-Revolutionary period saw growing concern for the political influence of new migrants: political conservatives feared the growth-by-immigration of the anti-federalists; the popular democratic front was suspicious of the acceptance of emigrés from toppling European aristocracies. The Alien and Sedition Acts of 1798 had "anti-foreign" implications and were accompanied by "anti-foreign" outbreaks. Attempts were made to lengthen the period of residence before enfranchisement from two, to five, to fourteen years, but the longer periods, though enacted, were evaded by states. The tension of establishing a new nation made itself felt. Both the American Revolution and the Civil War acted to improve the integration and the status of the immigrant groups. But the periods of tension preceding and during wars and accompanying economic depressions occasioned outbreaks against "foreigners."

The acculturation and assimilation of the nineteenth-century migrants depended on a number of factors. There was at the time a public policy against grants of land to ethnic groups, although several efforts were made to have such nationality enclaves established in the West. Dispersion greatly affected the rapidity of acculturation. Voluntary concentration on the part of the immigrants slowed their merging with the dominant Anglo-Saxon culture; but repeated nativistic movements also affected attitudes toward these new people. It is important here to distinguish between a passive dislike of foreigners based on ethnocentrism and the more violent mass zenophobia, marked by irrational hysteria, and often inspired by specific political interests.

Early nativism (pre-Civil War) had as its most prominent theme anti-"foreignism." Economic competition was not at this time a *manifest* issue. The Know-Nothing Party, which had its heyday in the two decades before the Civil War, revived the old Federalist efforts to limit office-holding to the native-born, to ex-

[31]*Ibid.*, pp. 53ff.

tend the period for naturalization, and to exclude criminals and paupers. Nativism re-emerged after the unifying interim of the Civil War, particularly on the West Coast. The restrictive acts of 1882–1885 were not an integrated attempt to deal with immigration, but rather a series of unconnected measures favoring special interests. The role of organized labor in "anti-foreign" efforts began to be felt, in California and the Midwest, in mines, and in heavy industries, where new immigrants from Europe were used as strikebreakers or where other groups (such as Orientals) were willing to work for low wages. After the Haymarket bombing of 1886, the tendency to link the terms "foreign" and "radical" gained new impetus.

The nativistic movements of the nineteenth century reflected, in part, the struggles of the newly settled West to achieve a balance of national power; they reflected the unease of the agricultural sector, and of new industry, with the efforts to create a strong labor movement; and they reflected the problems of growing cities. All these factors contributed to the attempts to consolidate the dominance of the Anglo-Saxon Protestant segment of the population. With the 1890 census the frontier was declared closed, and soon thereafter the myth of the frontier as the basic American experience began to take shape. Since most of the post-Civil War immigrants had little relation to the settling of the frontier, the myth helped to devalue latecomers.

THE RESTRICTION OF IMMIGRATION

Immigration restriction is only one facet of the attempt, successful for a time, to ensure the dominance of one segment of the population, a population that bolstered its claim to legitimate privilege and leadership by descent, by language, and by having given, as it were, the *imprimatur* to "American" styles of thought and behavior. The heavy waves of immigration at the turn of the century were needed for growing industry. They were facilitated by better transport and encouraged by persecution or over-population in Europe. They precipitated a consolidation and articulation of the "Establishment" which manifested itself in social and political restrictive measures, despite the beginnings of reform movements and welfare efforts.

THE DILLINGHAM COMMISSION   In 1907, when the nation was experiencing the greatest volume of immigration of all time, the Dillingham Commission was created to study the question of immigration and report to Congress. It was this Commission that coined the concept "old" and "new" immigration. The theme runs through the entire forty-one volumes of the report that the "old" immigration was of a different kind, had dispersed and entered all phases of American life, whereas the "new" immigration had congregated together in such a way that assimilation was impeded. The implication was that these late arrivals constituted pockets of people without American standards, values, or loyalties. In comparing "old" and "new," the Dillingham Commission's report took no account of the longer period of settlement of the "old" immigrant group. Furthermore, it lumped all old and all new into two simple categories without taking into account the vast differences in skill, motivation, and social organization within each category.

The Report came during a period of economic depression and gave support to a growing sentiment in favor of immigration restriction. Indeed, it provided the rationalizations on which the quota system subsequently was enacted. The anxieties of World War I, the increasing status of organized labor (won during the war), the fear of "radical" movements which appeared to be sweeping Europe at the close of the war, the psychological tests for the army which had showed low ratings for Southern Europeans from peasant cultures, all increased the pressure for restriction.

The movement to restrict immigration gained backing from three public groups. The first, and probably most influential, was organized labor. Labor's position was based primarily on the practical consideration that immigrant labor accepted low wages and was generally more tractable, thus retarding union efforts to improve the workers' economic position. A second public favoring restriction was composed of those various individuals scattered throughout the country who attributed many of the nation's ills to the presence of "too many ignorant foreigners." In examining the newspapers and magazines from 1900 to 1930, Woofter found that from 1907 to 1914 there occurred a marked change in public sentiment toward immigration. "The undesirability of certain racial elements" was becoming more persuasive than economic argument against restriction.[32] Finally, there was a growing feeling that the nation could not go on indefinitely trying to assimilate

[32]T. J. Woofter, Jr., *Races and Ethnic Groups in American Life* (New York: McGraw-Hill Book Co., 1933), p. 31.

such large masses of people of different cultures. This point of view is reflected in the report of the United States Immigration Commission in 1911, which recommended restriction on economic, moral, and social grounds. The first congressional act to give expression to these pressures was the measure to bar as immigrants any aliens who were illiterate (a measure passed in 1917 over President Wilson's veto). This kind of test was aimed at curtailing southern and eastern European immigration. Actually, it failed to reduce materially the volume of immigration, and Congress turned to a system of numerical limitation.

The Quota System

Congress first passed the Immigration Act of 1921, the most important aspect of which was that it restricted immigration on a basis primarily numerical—the first time this principle had been applied. The act provided that the number of aliens of any nationality admissible to the United States in any one year be limited to 3 per cent of the number of foreign-born persons of such nationality who were residents of the United States in 1910. The Act did not apply to the Western Hemisphere or to countries otherwise regulated, such as China and Japan. The total yearly quota admissible under this Act was 357,803. The effect, although not the wording, of this law was discriminatory against southern and eastern European nationalities. The quotas set up permitted about 200,000 from the northern and western countries and 155,000 from the others. Since from 1910 to 1914 the average annual immigration from the northern European countries had been less than the quotas allowed, in practice the law did not greatly limit immigration from these areas. But it did greatly restrict southern and eastern European immigration, which had averaged 738,000 annually during the 1910–1914 period.

The Immigration Act of 1921 at its expiration was supplanted by the Immigration Act of 1924. Two different systems of quota apportionment were then set up: one temporary, in order to give the Immigration Commission time to work out proper quotas for the other, the permanent quota allotment. The temporary quota, which was to operate for three years, provided that "the annual quota of any nationality shall be 2 per cent of the number of foreign-born individuals of such nationality resident in continental United States as determined by the United States Census of 1890, but the minimum quota of any nationality shall be 100."

The effect of this Act was to reduce the number of yearly immigrants still further to 164,667 and to discriminate even more strongly against the "newer" immigrant countries. Northern and western Europe were allotted 80 per cent, whereas the southern and eastern nationalities had only 20 per cent of the quota. The permanent provisions of the Act of 1924, which took effect in 1929, reduced the annual quota to 153,774. The law called for the apportionment of the total quota among the countries to which the Act applied according to their relative contribution to the American population as enumerated in 1920. The actual immigration at the time of the passing of the first restriction (1921) as compared with the quotas, for selected countries, demonstrates the effect of the quota system. In 1921 there were 652,364 immigrants from Germany; in 1929 there were 25,957. For Ireland there were 28,435 immigrants in 1921; the quota figure for 1929 was 17,853. For Italy there were 222,260 in 1921; the 1929 quota was 5,802. Several small modifications were made between 1929 and 1952 that represent the changed status of populations in the shifting of national borders or the creation of new nations.[33]

IMMIGRATION SINCE THE ESTABLISHMENT OF RESTRICTION

Although there have been amendments, and two special acts affecting immigration outside the quota system, there has been no fundamental change in the policy of restriction. A review of the immigration situation until the first major amendment in 1952 shows the following.

IMMIGRATION ADJUSTS TO THE QUOTA LIMITS: 1925–1930   During this period practically all European nations utilized their quotas to the full. The fact that the total immigration exceeded the quotas is accounted for by the admission of non-quota immigrants as permitted by the Act of 1924, the largest group of which were the wives, husbands, or minor children of resident immigrants.

IMMIGRATION FAR BELOW THE PERMISSIBLE LIMITS: 1931–1935   The drastic decline in European immigration begin-

[33]Edmund Traverso, *Immigration: A Study in American Values* (Boston: D. C. Heath and Co., 1964), pp. 118–119.

ning with 1930 clearly reflects the economic depression of these years, which made coming to America less attractive to Europeans. In addition, the federal government instructed its consulates abroad to apply rigidly the clauses in the immigration legislation denying entry to persons likely to become public charges.

REFUGEES INCREASE THE TOTALS: 1936–1940   While the rise in European immigration beginning in 1936 may have reflected in part the improved economic conditions in the United States, it was substantially advanced by the arrival of thousands of Europeans who sought asylum from persecution in the expanding Nazi Reich: about 243,000.

WORLD WAR II VIRTUALLY CUTS OFF ALL IMMIGRATION: 1941–1946   Interestingly enough, because of the manpower shortage during the war, the United States imported on temporary visas from Mexico, Canada, and the West Indies some 350,000 laborers.

DISPLACED PERSONS INCREASE IMMIGRATION AFTER 1946   These are Europeans who were rendered homeless through the destruction of the last war or who for various reasons could not with safety resume residence in their pre-war community: 400,000.

CHANGES IN THE IMMIGRATION LAW

The McCarran-Walter Act, 1952

The McCarran-Walter Act did not change the policy of the quota system but involved setting up preferences within the same system. Immigration officials were ordered to give first preferences to persons with skills currently in short supply, and second preference to relatives of persons already in this country. Other provisions of the Act included codifying the entire series of immigration bills and allotting quotas for the first time to Asiatic nations, in most instances 100 per annum (185 for Japan). Immigration had been debated bitterly for the previous five years. The Act was passed over President Truman's veto and reflects the continuance of "nativist" preferences and a fear of possible "subversive" infiltration. The failure to liberalize the approach to immigration on the one hand and the tiny concession to naturalization of Asiatics on the other represents the fundamental unease and inevitable compromises in democratic political action, with a changing world and America's new role within these changes.

The 1952 Act made no real attack on the "national origins" bias of the quota system. It simplified the national origins formula of the 1924 Act by basing the annual quota on a flat one-sixth of one per cent of the population of that origin in the 1920 Census. The total quota was 154,657.

President Truman's veto message[34] sharply criticized the quota system as defined in the Act, describing it as a "discriminatory policy." He cited the quota from Poland, for example, 6,500 as against 138,000 exiled Poles seeking to come here.

The Act of 1965

Sentiment against nationality quotas had been building up, and in the 1960 Presidental campaign both Republicans and Democrats included some statement in their platforms urging modification. On October 3, 1965, further amendments to the immigration law were enacted which, beginning December 1, 1965, were to eliminate over a five-year period of transition "national origins" as a basis for selective entry into the United States. Although only 10 per cent of the total quota may be admitted from any one country in a single year, the principle of preferential nationality has been supplanted by one more equitable.

In the amended law the preference system of granting visas is retained from the 1952 revision with only minor modification to admit more professionals and to allow some adjustments in health requirements. The law defines different classes of immigrants: those eligible for preference visas (relatives, professionals, skilled or unskilled labor in short supply, refugees) who come within the total quota. There are additional places for non-preference immigrants. These, like skilled and unskilled workers (category six) must have certification from the United States Department of Labor. Western hemisphere immigrants enter freely, not as part of the quota, but also must have Labor Department certification. The 1965 amendment, in harmony with its relaxation of discrimination, adds free migration to Western Hemisphere colo-

---

[34]"House Document No. 520," *Congressional Record* (Washington, D.C.: Government Printing Office, 1952), 8225–8228.

nials (largely Caribbean) on the same basis rather than as part of the applications of their mother country. The law still retains from the McCarran-Walter Act exclusion of members of "totalitarian" or "communist" political parties, a requirement often difficult to interpret justly.

The amendments since 1952 have made for greater justice and greater consistency in our immigration policy. They seem to indicate in the preference quotas recognition of the hardship of separated families and the easier adjustment of newcomers if they have family here. Preferential acceptance of scientists and artists certainly enriches America, although this may contribute to the "brain drain" abroad.

Making It: As a Group

Although linguistically different, the Germans, Scandinavians, Swiss, and French Huguenots never suffered the categorical discriminations that most subsequent groups encountered. The more rapid acculturation and social acceptance of these northern Europeans was facilitated by many favorable circumstances. For one thing, they were less visibly different. Their cultures had more affinity to the dominant Anglo-Saxon culture. They were largely Protestant. They were more experienced in democratic political practices. And they possessed a heritage of independent agricultural occupation. The relatively small proportions that settled initially in cities were mainly skilled craftsmen or professionals. That they were "looked down on" and "poked fun at" is illustrated by the following jingle quoted by Smith, directed at members of an immigrant group in Minnesota:

> Swedie, Swedie, stuck in the straw,
> Can't say nuthin' but "Yaw, yaw, yaw,"[35]

But with the acquisition of the English language, without an accent in their children's cases, most north Europeans became accepted Americans. They intermarried (Germans and Scandinavians) in the second generation; in the third they out-married and no longer spoke the language of their forefathers. They shared the Protestant ethic of hard work, improvement of self and land or enterprise, believed in education, and founded colleges. In the

[35]W. C. Smith, *Americans in the Making* (New York: Appleton-Century-Crofts, 1939), p. 149, n. 28.

private spheres of life there was still some intragroup life in which they shared a sense of common heritage and nuances of communication. Like other American white Protestants of north-European descent they maintained some sense of the country of their heritage, some interest in their traditional European roots, but the former "homeland" became, as one writer has called them "ghost nations," no longer experienced as real.[36]

THE IRISH   The considerable number of Irish people who came to the colonies in the eighteenth century appear not to have been thought of as a people apart from the rest, except for a period when they arrived in large numbers. In the nineteenth century they were the first of the great ethnic migrations. They settled primarily in cities and stayed heavily concentrated in the North Atlantic states, except for those employed in mining and the construction of railways and canals. In the three decades before the Civil War they encountered much resistance and discrimination from the "native" population. For one thing, they were Catholic and anti-British. They were rural people who had settled largely in cities and towns. They entered the lower occupational ranks of unskilled work, thus starting with lower-class status at a time when class distinction was becoming more important.

This was America's first confrontation with a peasant culture.[37] The English, Scandinavians, or Germans who came to America in the nineteenth century came from towns or from freehold farming patterns. The Irish had been long exploited by the English landholding system. The unchallenged position of the Catholic Church cemented bonds of identity. A history of famine, a family and inheritance system that led to late marriage and many unmarried men and women, the ambivalent situation of being English-speaking but not part of English-derived institutions, and migration in large numbers put the Irish in a peculiar relationship to dominants. Some welcomed them as a necessary working-class contingent; others engaged in flagrant discrimination. This discrimination is memorialized in an American folksong popular in the music halls of the 1860s.[38]

[36]Nathan Glazer, "Ethnic Groups in America: From National Culture to Ideology" in *Freedom and Control in Modern Society*, eds. Monroe Berger, Theodore Abel, and Charles H. Page (New York: D. Van Nostrand Company, 1954), p. 179.
[37]For a description of Irish peasant social structure and factors leading to emigration, see Conrad M. Arensberg and Solon T. Kimball, *Family and Community in Ireland* (Cambridge, Mass.: Harvard University Press, 1940).
[38]Edith Fowke and Joe Glazer, *Songs of Work and Freedom* (Garden City, N.Y.: Doubleday and Co., 1961), p. 154.

I'm a decent boy just landed from the town of Ballyfad;
I want a situation, and I want it very bad.

I seen employment advertised, "It's just the thing," says I
But the dirty spalpeen ended with "No Irish need apply."

Prior to the great migration in the years 1846–1850, the Irish were distributed throughout the class structure. Glazer and Moynihan, writing on the Irish in New York today, find that this is once more true. In the interim period they were far outstripped by some of the other groups migrating at the same time. Glazer and Moynihan attribute this in part to their Catholicism, which did not impart a strong ethic of individual success, to their immediate involvement and ultimate success in politics, which strengthened attitudes of discrimination against them, and to their high rate of alcoholism.[39]

Father Andrew Greeley, a scholar long involved in ethnic studies, expresses in a popular article his regret that the Irish have opted to show WASPs that they can be "respectable," thereby losing their particular style and flavor, both as Catholics and as political pragmatists. He feels that in the light of their experience they should better have allied themselves with the political aspirations of black and Spanish speaking Americans.[40]

Making It: As an Individual

The first thing he did was anglicize his name: Paul Stanley.

Through the aid of his athletic prowess he had graduated from college and gone to law school while supporting himself working in the law office of a local lawyer of upper middle-class (native) status.

Paul's father and mother had come from Poland when they were children. They had both worked in the shoe factory and had gone to an "Americanization school" to improve their English. They were proud of their home, which they owned outright, kept well painted, and landscaped with cast-off tires, a border of half-buried beer cans, and well-tended garden and lawn. They looked down on their less ambitious neighbors and also the Riverbrookers (lower-lower class people) with "native" status.

[39]Nathan Glazer and Daniel Patrick Moynihan, *Beyond the Melting Pot: The Negroes, Puerto Ricans, Jews, Italians, and Irish of New York City* (Cambridge, Mass.: The M.I.T. Press and Harvard University Press, 1963), p. 254, 256ff.
[40]*New York Times Magazine*, March 14, 1971, pp. 32ff.

Mr. Stanley was very fond and proud of his son, for whom education had opened the door to greater social heights. Their first serious rift came when Paul became interested in Annie Taylor, a Riverbrooker girl; Paul wanted to marry her and eventually did, much to the disappointment of his parents. Annie's family were a typical ne'er-do-well low-class family known to the truant officer. Annie herself was the most ambitious and respectable of the lot and had in school managed to be accepted in "better-class" cliques of girls. Because of all the in-law complications, Annie and Paul ran away to get married, causing a split in Annie's family, who said she had married a "damn foreigner" and a Catholic fellow. Following their marriage, the new Stanleys drew away from both sets of parents, who were not after all the kinds of parents they wanted their new friends to meet. Their new home was in a nonethnic neighborhood.

After graduating from law school Paul had been invited to join the Caribous, made up mostly of Yankees, with only a few Poles. Within a year after his marriage, Paul became a member of the Antlers (higher social rating than the Caribous) and played bridge there several nights a week. He began to neglect his Caribou contacts. The Stanleys were now in a social clique made up of Yankee lower-middle class folks but were not, of course, ever invited to dinner at the home of the still higher-class Antlers whom Paul knew at the club, or ever called on by the nice ladies of Hill Street—upper class. "And anyway," they said, "we're going to see to it that our children have every advantage."[41]

Making It, Marginally

After 1880 until the restriction of immigration the largest migrations were from eastern and southern Europe. Almost all the migrants were of a different religious affiliation than either established or sectarian Protestants. Peasants came from Poland, Hungary, the Ukraine and other parts of modern Russia; Greeks from mountain and island villages; Italians, first from northern Italy and after 1900 in far greater numbers from southern Italy and Sicily; Jews from the little towns of Poland and Russia fleeing a policy of forced assimilation and sporadic concomitant persecution.

By the beginning of the twentieth century the absorption of older immigrants had considerably broadened what could now

---

[41]William Lloyd Warner and P. S. Lunt, *The Social Life of a Modern Community* (New Haven: Yale University Press, 1941). Condensed adaptation by Charles F. Marden of Warner and Lunt, pp. 188–193. By permission.

be called "native," but there is little evidence that this worked to lessen discriminatory attitudes toward the new groups; quite possibly the opposite was true. There was also in the North a new free Negro group whose opportunities for employment were curtailed by the great influx of immigrants. With regard to class, religion, and national culture the new groups were looked down on.

The Ethnic Sub-Community

Wherever immigrants settled in considerable numbers they at first clustered with people from home. Sometimes they even had little sub-sub-communities, where they had discovered neighbors and friends not only from the home country but from the home district, and they brought their district or regional rivalries with them. Then, as now with the Puerto Ricans, they settled in the sections of the city which were least desirable residentially, since this was what was available to them. Then as now, landlords discovered that exorbitant rents could be extracted for little space and poor quality of housing. Families were forced to crowd into single rooms or "old law" tenements, some of whose rooms had no windows. In the evenings, the people spilled out on the street, weather permitting, and gossiped, quarreled, exchanged news from home, shopped from the pushcarts, and insofar as possible recreated the life of the home village.

Generational Conflict and Marginality

The concentration of immigrants in sub-communities intensified the problems of the second generation. What gave security to their elders created conflict for the children of the immigrant growing up in America. Like all other parents, immigrant parents conditioned their children to their accustomed social heritage. The children, as a result of their school experience and the other outside stimuli that their growing knowledge of the English language opened to them, wanted to become Americanized. The children began to perceive that the culture of their parents was not American as defined by the outside dominant native world. Furthermore, the immigrant children learned that the ways of their parents were defined as inferior and that they, too, were socially rejected because of their background. Handlin discusses the fact that a great deal of the generational problem was compounded by the insecurity of the immigrant parents in their own roles. In the new environment a confusion arose as to the old established rights and duties between husband and wife and parents and children. Without the protective cover of well-defined roles, father, mother, son, and daughter faced each other as individuals under the most trying conditions.[42] Some of the difficulties are summed up by Whyte.

> Some ask, "Why can't those people stop being Italians and become Americans like the rest of us?" The answer is that they are blocked in two ways: by their own organized society and by the outside world. Cornerville people want to be good American citizens. I have never heard such moving expressions of love for this country as I have heard in Cornerville. Nevertheless, an organized way of life cannot be changed overnight. As the study of the corner gang shows, people become dependent upon certain routines of action. If they broke away abruptly from these routines, they would feel themselves disloyal and would be left helpless, without support. And, if a man wants to forget that he is an Italian, the society around him does not let him forget it. He is marked as an inferior person—like all other Italians. To bolster his own self-respect he must tell himself and tell others that the Italians are a great people, that their culture is second to none, and that their great men are unsurpassed.[43]

Some of the second generation did become Americans in their incorporation of the American goal of achievement and success. The traditionally sanctioned means to business success were frequently closed to them, however, because of ethnic discrimination and low socioeconomic status. For many, achievement or monetary success could be found in politics or the rackets and, as Daniel Bell has pointed out, both politics and crime in the large urban areas have experienced successive invasions by ethnic groups.[44]

For those individuals who did correctly perceive the expectations and values of the dominant society, the situation in which they found themselves was often marginal. Taking the dominant group as their reference group and incorporating dominant norms and goals, they found themselves at a competitive disadvantage,

---

[42]Oscar Handlin, The Uprooted, (Boston: Little, Brown & Co., 1952) p. 239.
[43]William Foote Whyte, Street Corner Society (Chicago: University of Chicago Press, 1943), p. 274. By permission.
[44]Daniel Bell, "Crime as an American Way of Life," Antioch Review, Summer, 1953. Also in Bell, The End of Ideology (Glencoe, Ill.: The Free Press, 1960).
    See also Ch. 18, for Robert K. Merton's analysis of the responses to available goals and means.

and were often made to feel inferior. Such a person, Chick Morelli, is described by Whyte. He identified with the schools, his teachers, the settlement workers, saved his money, got an education, tried to organize an "improvement" program in his community of "Cornerville," but came to see politics as the only career open to him despite his associations with people outside his sub-community. He even came to believe that Italians themselves were to blame for the discrimination they received, yet he did not successfully establish himself in "native" middle-class society.[45]

Interaction in the American Institutional Structure

The urban political party, the lower ranks of the civil service, and the trade union were each major modes of involving the immigrant in American life.

The involvement of the immigrant in politics is as old as the nation and the early struggles between the propertied and the popular parties. The immigrant vote was marshaled for every election, often with the individual voter understanding the issues only very vaguely at best. The heavy concentration of the Irish in the port cities of the East let them very early play an active role in organizing local politics. As urban centers grew throughout the nineteenth century, "machine" politics developed, seeking local control and party influence in the state and national elections. In the East, and to some extent in other industrial areas, the machine was Democratic and the leadership initially was Irish. The political machine operated on a basis of patronage and personal favors, which aroused the criticism of the "good government" organizations. However, the machine was able to make politics more personal for the immigrant, and therefore more meaningful, than could forces whose approach to civil life was impersonalized and abstract.

Handlin describes machine politics as more characteristic of the second generation than of the immigrants themselves. Since the group that migrated often was too involved in other pressures, did not command the language, and had no history of political participation, it remained apathetic.[46]

During the nineteenth century, the lower civil service jobs in the cities became a channel for the establishment of immigrants and their children. The police force, the fire department, and the

[45]Whyte, *Street Corner Society*, pp. 52–56.
[46]Handlin, *The Uprooted*, Chapter 8.

post office had their lower ranks filled from the new groups. The link between political patronage and the police allowed for a considerable amount of corruption, but it also kept the police of America free of the authoritarian and severe disciplinary attitude found in some of the immigrants' home countries.

The labor movement, too, involved the immigrant in an organizational structure which helped him adapt to the conditions of the new country. Throughout the nineteenth century, factories tended to deploy their labor force in a way that maintained ethnic solidarity, each department or shop having a particular ethnic character. Union locals therefore similarly were largely or exclusively composed of one ethnic group. But in the experience of a strike or in the conduct of union affairs above the shop level, native Americans, British, Irish, German, Welsh, Russian Jewish, Italian, and many others worked together. The major involvement of immigrant workers in unions came in the early twentieth century, but immigrants were prominent in the Workingmen's Party, a labor party before the Civil War, in the Knights of Labor, and in the formation of the American Federation of Labor.

But even with these bridges of contact with the dominant natives, the typical immigrant became only partially acculturated to American life. The pattern of subcommunal segregation described above retarded the process; yet, given the situation as it was, such a response was logical and necessary. Mass immigration was encouraged and tolerated because the rapidly growing industrial society greatly needed cheap labor. Yet, for the most part, the immigrant was not desired as a neighbor, a friend, or a competitor by the dominant natives. Segregation suited perfectly the natives' attitudes and arose in part in response to them. And, temporarily, it met the need of the immigrant for a sense of self-respect, for expressing his accustomed modes of life, for social and emotional security—a sense of *belonging*.

The Peer Group Society[47]

Although the second generation produced some marginal individuals and others who moved out and up, there was always a contingent—smaller or larger—which remained as part of an

---

[47]Herbert J. Gans, *The Urban Villagers: Group and Class in the Life of Italian-Americans* (New York: The Free Press, 1962).

ethnic subsociety. The nationality neighborhoods of the first generation became interethnic as vacancies occurred and low-rent housing was in demand. Herbert J. Gans has studied one such urban neighborhood. The largest ethnic group was Italian, although the neighborhood included Poles, Albanians, Ukrainians, Greeks, and a residue each of elderly Irish and elderly Jews. There were also a scattering of middle-class professionals and students attached to the nearby teaching hospital, artists, gypsies, and groups of single men as well as some of the very poor, with the pattern of broken families and the mild pathologies of the psychologically disabled. Only seven per cent of the population was "American" in background.

Gans gives a picture of the second-generation Italians of today as a "peer group society" in which sociability centers around a gathering of family and friends, occurring several times a week. "One could almost say that the meetings of the group are at the vital center of . . . life, that they are the end for which other everyday activities are a means." The activities of such a group center largely around the exchange of news and gossip. This serves as a mechanism of social control, supplies information and advice, provides entertainment and drama about one's own group that are provided for others through the mass media. This translated "village" social behavior reinforces group identity and interprets selectively the "outside" world. It protects the group from disorganizing influences and substitutes for formal organizations.

Gans sees this tightly woven ethnic society threatened by larger social changes. In the specific instance, the neighborhood he studied had been designated for urban renewal, which would inevitably lead to the ecological dispersion of many of the families. The fact that the younger generation will stay in school longer will lead many of them out of the blue-collar occupational world of their parents. The discontinuance of arranged marriages will, despite the strong family controls, lead to increasing interethnic marriage.[48]

---

[48]Russo in a study of three generations of Italian Americans in New York City notes the increasing rate of out-group marriage. Between the second and third generation there has been a decline in the number out-marrying other than Irish and an increase in Italian-Irish intermarriage, as both groups participate more in the general pattern of American Catholic religious and social organizations.

N. J. Russo, "Three Generations of Italians in New York City: their Religious Acculturation" in S. M. Tomasi and M. H. Engel *The Italian Experience in the United States* (Staten Island, N.Y.: Center for Migration Studies, 1970), pp. 195ff.

The Persistence of Ethnicity

Many social forces are operating to break down the ethnic sub-communities as they have formerly existed, but there are counterforces that are making for a revival of ethnic identity and pride. Andrew Greeley reports on a study of college graduates representing eleven ethnic groups. Data on political, racial, cultural, and artistic attitudes were collated. He concludes from this study that the socialization experience of higher education has not eliminated ethnically linked differences in attitudes and behavior even among groups whose geographic dispositions are similar. He suggests that such differences are likely to persist for a long time to come.[49]

The degree of cultural cohesion of the ethnic minority will vary with degree of ecological separation and the degree of family control. Social structural barriers, especially in the opportunity structure—in type and quality of education available and in access to occupations and to formal associations—affect the degree and desirability of abandonment of the subculture. Finally, individual temperaments may rebel against membership in the sub-community, or may find shelter in retaining it as the focus of their identity.

Today, then, we must say that the older assumption that all European immigrants would assimilate, in the nineteenth-century sense of submerging into the dominant culture, no longer fits. What seems to be happening is an interplay between a changing dominant society and dynamic subcultures. These subcultures bear increasingly less relation to the folkways of the countries from which they were derived, but their members participate with varying selectivity in a life flavored with meaningful elements that are not WASP.

Some of the revival of emphasis on ethnic heritage is part of the overall malaise of a streamlined technological society where there is an increased concern with creating a sense of community: a longing for the warmth, zesty interaction of the "urban villages" that are passing.

Another aspect of the revival of ethnic pride, however, is the confusing and defensive position in which 40 million working-class Americans in the major cities of industrial America find themselves. The status of manual labor has declined, and outside

[49]Andrew Greeley, "A Note on Political and Social Differences Among College Graduates of Different Ethnic Groups," *Sociology of Education*, Winter, 1969, pp. 98–103.

their own sub-community they find little respect for their being butchers, plumbers, automobile workers, or shoemakers. Real wages have not increased, and automation and market reorganization threaten many. These men and their families have also shared the American Dream but as the independent "near poor," little attention or money is available to them for community improvement. So they close in, demand community control, oppose busing and are frightened. Formerly they were called Polaks, Wops, Hunkies; now they are called Pigs and Hard Hats with the same or fiercer contempt. One Polish American has pointed out

> Liberals scapegoat us as racists. Yet there was no racial prejudice in our hearts when we came . . . The elitists who smugly call us racists are the ones who taught us the meaning of the word bigotry . . .
>
> Government is further polarizing people by the creation of myths that black needs are being met. Thus the ethnic worker is fooled into thinking that the blacks are getting everything.
>
> Old prejudices and new fears are ignited and the two groups end up fighting each other for the same jobs and competing so that new schools and recreation centers will be built in their respective communities. What results is angry confrontation for tokens, when there should be an alliance for a whole new Agenda for America. . . .[50]

The new voices of "ethnic" Americans are proof that they are deeply and actively part of American life. Their assumptions are American assumptions, for good or ill, and their creativity is at America's disposal, not just their wage earning labor. The creation of a stable and dynamic society that is religiously pluralistic has largely been achieved. Whether a similar mosaic of peoples can be created depends on how much real respect for variants can be engendered, and on fair and equal access to the opportunities that American society offers. Americans respond easily to pleas of injustice, but many Americans, of all the variant backgrounds, are uneasy with *differences*. The future of America lies no longer in the hands of WASPs, but in the hands of all Americans who may cherish, but must also transcend, their communalities.

---

[50]Barbara Mikulski, "Who Speaks for Ethnic America," *The New York Times*, Sept. 29, 1970.

Suggested Readings

ON RELIGIOUS MINORITY ISSUES

Baltzell, E. Digby. *The Protestant Establishment: Aristocracy and Caste in America.* New York: Random House, 1964.
An account of the consolidation and beginning decline of Protestant dominance.

Braden, Charles Samuel. *These Also Believe: A Study of Modern American Cults and Minority Religious Movements.* New York: The Macmillan Co., 1949.
Thirteen profiles of major American religious movements, with excellent bibliographical material.

Cohen, Arthur A. *The Myth of the Judeo-Christian Tradition.* New York: Schocken Paperback, 1971.
A Jewish theologian challenges the Herberg thesis and fuzzy liberal thought about Jewish-Christian differences of belief.

Cone, James A. *Liberation: A Black Theology of Liberation.* Philadelphia and New York: J. B. Lippincott Co., 1970.
A Black Christian theologian defines the new Black theology.

Ellis, John Tracy. *American Catholicism,* 2nd ed. rev. Chicago: The University of Chicago Press, 1969.
A chronological account of the development of the Catholic Church in America, integrated with the social and political history of critical periods.

Weigel, Gustave, S. J. *Churches in North America.* New York: Schocken Books, 1965.
An excellent presentation of non-Roman Catholic religious bodies in the United States, written for Roman Catholic students "as a bridge to understanding."

ON ETHNIC MINORITIES

Binzen, Peter. *Whitetown U.S.A.* New York: Random House, 1970 (also available as a Vintage Paperback).
A rich study of problems and attitudes in a white working class district of Philadelphia.

Gans, Herbert J. *The Urban Villagers: Group and Class in the Life of Italian-Americans.* New York: The Free Press, 1962.
A provocative analysis of the subculture of blue-collar Italian Americans.

Glazer, Nathan and Moynihan, Daniel Patrick. *Beyond the Melting Pot: The Negroes, Puerto Ricans, Jews, Italians and Irish of New York City.* Cambridge, Mass.: The M.I.T. and Harvard University Press, 1963.
Thoughtful analyses of five populations in a metropolitan environment,

with historical perspective on each group, and interaction between them today,

Handlin, Oscar. *The Uprooted.* Boston: Little, Brown & Co., 1951.
A lively account of the voyage and settlement of America's immigrants, with good discussion of the rewards, trials and adjustments of the transition.

Jones, Maldwyn Allen. *American Immigration.* Chicago: The University of Chicago Press, 1960.
A brilliant reappraisal by an Englishman of the great migration from Europe to America.

Kramer, Judith. *The American Minority Community.* New York: Thomas Y. Crowell Company, 1970.
An exploration of the meaning of minority membership and the bases for a sense of communality in first, second, and third generations.

Warner, W. Lloyd and Srole, Leo. *The Social Systems of American Ethnic Groups.* New Haven: Yale University Press, 1945.
A classic study of ethnic patterns in a small New England manufacturing city.

4   **R**ace and Racism

In dominant-minority relations "race" is a basic category and provides the most obvious cue to visibility or identification. The term is placed here in quotation marks because its meaning and significance in the popular thinking and behavior of dominants are vastly at variance with current scientific thinking. That the beliefs about race which have become established in popular sentiment may well constitute "man's most dangerous myth" was anticipated in the 1880s by a French pro-Aryan writer, Vacher de Lapouge, when he wrote, "I am convinced that in the next century millions of men will cut each other's throats because of one or two degrees more or less of cephalic index."[1]

In the long history of the world men have given many reasons for killing each other in war: envy of another people's good bottom land or of their herds, ambition of chiefs and kings, different religious beliefs, high spirits, revenge. But in all these wars the skulls of the victims on both sides were generally too similar to be distinguished. Nor had the war leaders incited their followers by referring to the shapes of their heads. They might call them the heathen, the barbarians, the heretics, the slayers of women and children, but never our enemy Cephalic Index 82.

It was left for high European civilization to advance such a

---

[1]Vacher de Lapouge, cited by Ruth Benedict, in *Race: Science and Politics*, rev. ed. (New York: The Viking Press, Inc., 1945), p. 3. (The cephalic index is a ratio of skull measurements.)

reason for war and persecution and to invoke it in practice. In other words, racism is a creation of our own time.[2]

The research of the last fifty years, in physical anthropology primarily but also in related fields, has given an entirely new perspective on the physiological groupings of man. There is now consensus in anthropology, biology, psychology, and sociology as to what races are and are not. In 1950, UNESCO published a series of research monographs that represent international scientific agreement on what is known about races. The understanding of the physiological phenomena of "race" has depended on the development of the sciences. In populations without basic scientific orientation the term "race" is connotive of social attitudes derived from historical social ·xperience, the universal ethnocentrism of isolated peoples, or folk superstition. It is therefore important to know clearly what is fact about race as a correction for traditional usages.

WHAT "RACE" IS

Origin of "Races"

To begin with, mankind apparently started out as one race. Since *Homo sapiens* evolved thousands of years before written history, it is not possible to know the racial features of prehistoric man with any exactitude. However, contemporary anthropology generally accepts on the basis of fossil evidence and the logic of evolutionary and genetic principles a monogenetic rather than a polygenetic theory of man's origin. Montagu has put it thus:

> Concerning the origin of the living varieties of man we can say little more than that there is every reason to believe that a single stock gave rise to all of them. All varieties of man belong to the same species and have the same remote ancestry. This is a conclusion to which all the relevant evidence of comparative anatomy, palaeontology, serology, and genetics points. On genetic grounds alone, it is virtually impossible to conceive of the varieties of man as having originated separately as distinct lines from different anthropoid ancestors.[3]

[2]Benedict, *Race: Science and Politics*, p. 3-4, by permission.
[3]M. F. Ashley Montagu, *Man's Most Dangerous Myth: The Fallacy of Race*, 4th ed., rev. and enl. (Cleveland: The World Publishing Co., 1964), p. 83. By permission.

Differentiation of "Races"

Long before written history, the major differentiation of mankind into the main varieties occurred as a result of migration, and of natural selection as it affected the survival of certain variations in their environments. Ever since Linnaeus, the Swedish botanist, started the classification of plant and animal life in the eighteenth century, geneticists and physical anthropologists have been examining the differences in the physical characteristics of man. Linnaeus established four categories of man—*americanus, europaeus, asiaticus,* and *afer.* Since the eighteenth century these categories have been refined so that some discussions include seven major groups with many subgroups. The criteria for grouping depend on such factors as cephalic index, blood type, shape of facial features, degree of body hair, and so forth. Since no group is totally homogeneous in all of these indices, these older categories are now primarily of interest to researchers in the biological sciences and physical anthropology. What the groups of people represent in actuality are societies which through geographic isolation and barriers of social organization have intermarried for thousands of years, bringing into prominence selected dominant biological traits. These are sometimes referred to as "Mendelian populations," a term derived from the geneticist Mendel, who demonstrated the existence of dominant strains and recessive strains in inbreeding and crossbreeding. From this point of view the tall Watusi of Uganda, the pockets of blond Andalusians in Spain, and the Sherpas of Nepal are "Mendelian" populations.

> Such physical traits as the color of the eyes or hair and the pigmentation of the skin do pass through the genes from parents to children. The carriers have been identified and described. We know now that a group of individuals with common characteristics will procreate offspring with the same characteristics. Mankind is composed of a variety of populations which differ among themselves in the frequency of many genes. These Mendelian populations will reproduce themselves across time.[4]

Twentieth-century research has shown that physical type is not only the result of genetic transmission but is dependent on

[4]Oscar Handlin, *Race and Nationality in American Life* (Garden City, N.Y.: Doubleday Anchor Books, Doubleday & Co., Inc., 1957), p. 151. (Reprinted by arrangement with Little, Brown & Co., Boston, Mass.)

other factors as well. Selection affecting physical type can take place because of environment. Before the advent of modern medicine the physical type best suited to survival in geographic regions gradually emerged as dominant, and high infant mortality eliminated variations. Cultural factors such as language over time affect the mouth formation necessary to produce a selected sound. As a contemporary physical anthropologist writes, ". . . culture, which has affected other free-living animals too, has probably affected us more profoundly than it has any others because we created it, we cannot escape it, we have been constantly exposed to it as long as there have been men on earth, and we could not live without it."[5]

Since agreement on categories is basic to thinking and research, most scholars today work within the broad categories Caucasoid, Mongoloid and Negroid. These refer very generally to groups of people with visible physical traits. The designations, however, are matters more of convenience than of accuracy. As Ruth Benedict aptly writes:

> No one doubts that the groups called Caucasoid, Mongoloid, and Negroid each represent a long history of anatomical specialization in different areas of the world; but the greater numbers of individuals cannot be assigned to one or another of these races on the basis even of several . . . [physical] criteria. . . . There are Whites who are darker than some Negroids; dark hair and eyes are common among all races; the same cephalic index is found in groups of the most diverse races; similar hair form is found among ethnic groups as distinct as native Australians and Western Europeans.[6]

Instability of Racial Type

Throughout history great migrations alternating with long periods of endogamous mating created and recreated visible subtypes. The American Indian illustrates the process of subtype development. The ancestors of the Indians came from Asia and possessed general Mongoloid features. Natural selection and thousands of years of isolation, limiting the range or variability to that present in the original migrating groups, perfected a distinctive Indian type.

[5]Carleton S. Coon, *The Living Races of Man* (New York: Alfred A. Knopf, 1965), p. 23.
[6]Ruth Benedict, *Race: Science and Politics*, rev. ed., pp. 45ff.

While throughout all history mixing occurred across main divisions, in the past few centuries the wandering and mixing of peoples has created many new subtypes, involving combinations of traits from the main racial divisions. We may cite the Pitcairn Islanders, of *Mutiny on the Bounty* fame, and the American Negro. The present Hawaiian situation, where the various ethnic groups are intermarrying with increasing freedom, is a most interesting example of racial change going on today.

From the foregoing it can be seen that race is a highly unstable phenomenon. The racial variability of *Homo sapiens* has undergone more or less continuous modification. This changing nature of race makes the idea of a "pure" race meaningless. The greatest homogeneity in "racial" traits is found among small groups of people long isolated from the main currents of human travel and exchange.

All historical evidence makes us accept the inevitability of the crossing of strains wherever peoples come in contact with one another. But biological crossing is not the only modifying factor. In the early part of this century, Franz Boas, conducting an anthropological study of immigrants at the request of the United States Immigration Commission, was the first to show that a supposedly unchangeable index of physical type was mutable. He found that the cephalic indices of immigrants from south and eastern Europe, as compared with their children, altered according to the length of time spent in the American environment. Furthermore, they all altered toward a uniform type more nearly in accord with the measurements of older American stock. Japanese who emigrated to the United States are physically different from their siblings who stayed in Japan. During the last two centuries, Americans of British descent have grown three and a half inches taller than their Revolutionary ancestors, and proportionately heavier. The cephalic index may drop dramatically in a single generation among people who have abandoned cradling.[7]

Race and Physiology

Comparative studies of the physiology of samples of racial groups have shown in some cases significant differences, in others mutability over time, and in others no differences at all. There is much current research on how and why people are different from

[7]Coon, *The Living Races of Man*, Ch. 10.

one another physiologically, and at the present time one can relatively accurately delineate how, but only hypothetically why; although Coon suggests that the "why" answers to the relationship between physical environment and physiological phenomena may not be far away.[8]

In the cluster of traits which make up visible differences the most relevant one to the American popular mind is *skin color*. According to contemporary research skin color depends on the differences in melanin production in the body and on such secondary factors as disintegrated hemoglobin. That is, we know now the biological and physiological factors which make for darker or lighter skin. Coon thinks we are approaching the period where we will know why natural selection favors one or the other in different environments, for example, darker skins among people living in the wet tropics, or why the skin color of American Indians varies regionally. For Indians, skin color is darkest where radiation is at the peak, but in the tropical forests of South America (at high altitude) it is quite light, as is true of the inhabitants of rain forests in Borneo.

Another comparative dimension is immunity to disease. What seems to be apparent is that natural selection and adaptive mechanisms stabilize over time resistances to particular diseases in particular environments. Change in the environment may make people differentially susceptible to new diseases or may weaken resistance patterns to those endemic to their former environment. Coon suggests that malaria, so acutely debilitating to Europeans in Africa and Southeast Asia, and to which "native" populations have developed resistance may actually have preserved these people from the onslaughts of technically superior and better organized Caucasians and Mongolians. He further cites the suggestion that malaria may have increased in these areas in the shift from a hunting-gathering economy to agriculture, which brought about cleared forests, pockets of still water in which mosquitos could breed, kept people anchored to specific places and allowed human and animal excreta to accumulate.[9]

As a final illustration, we refer to "blood," about which so much popular superstition has developed. There are four types of human blood and each type is hereditary. But Caucasians, Mongols, and Negroes have all these blood types. Blood plasma derived from various racial groups was utilized for the wounded in World

[8]*Ibid.*, Chs. 8 and 9.
[9]*Ibid.*, pp. 277–278.

War II irrespective of their race, with no effect on the personality or physiology of the recipients.

Race Crossing

Random observation of people in large metropolitan areas of the United States will readily reveal persons of hybrid characteristics of the main races of mankind whose external features are well proportioned and handsome. An occasional unpleasing-looking hybrid may be noted, but the same can be found among persons who are not hybrids. What science has to say about the effects of race crossing may be approached by first considering some conclusions drawn from specific studies of particular interracial crossings.[10]

POLYNESIAN-WHITE CROSSING   The hybrid descendants of English mutineers and Tahitian women are taller than the average Englishman or Tahitian, and are more vigorous and healthy. They are perfectly alert. The physical type of the descendants is in every way harmonious, with white characteristics predominating.

AUSTRALIAN-WHITE CROSSING   All unprejudiced observers agree that the offspring of aboriginal-white crossings in Australia are of an excellent physical type and that both the aborigines and the hybrids possess considerable mental ability.

HAWAIIAN MIXTURES   In Hawaii there are hundreds of varieties of mixed types, involving native Hawaiians (Polynesians), Japanese, Filipinos, Koreans, Chinese, and whites of many nationalities. The descendents of mixed Hawaiian unions have a much higher fertility rate than other ethnic groups and in height, weight, and other physical characteristics tend to be intermediate between their Hawaiian and non-Hawaiian forebears.

INDIANS-WHITE MIXTURES   Boas showed that the "half-blood" Indian was taller and more fertile than the parental Indian and white stock. Krogman concludes that Seminole Indians of Oklahoma, who are the descendents of a mixture of runaway Creek Indians, Negro slaves, and whites, are on the whole good

---

[10]The examples given are taken from Montagu, *Man's Most Dangerous Myth*, Chapter 8.

physical types, and often beautiful. There is not the slightest evidence of degeneration or disharmony in development.

The verdict of biological and anthropological science is clear and unequivocal: race crossing per se has no deleterious biological consequences. On the contrary, and most disconcerting to the exponents of racism, the preponderance of evidence points to at least an initial biological superiority of the progeny of the first hybrid generation over that of the respective racial parental generation. The phenomenon of "hybrid vigor" well known in plant and animal biology is indicated in many human interracial crossings. Of this the biologist Jennings writes:

> In view of the immense number of genes carried by individuals of each race, and their separate history up to the time of the cross, the relatively few defects that have arisen are almost certain to affect genes of different pairs in the two. Hence when the races cross, the individuals produced will receive a normal gene from one parent or the other in most of their gene pairs; and since the normal gene usually manifests its effect, the offspring of the cross will have fewer gene defects than either of the parents.[11]

> Thus the offspring of diverse races may be expected to be superior in vigor, and presumably in other characteristics. . . . Data on this point are not abundant, but it is possible that hybrid vigor is an important and advantageous feature of race crosses in man.[12]

The merits of race crossing may be argued at the social level, but those who argue against it will find no support from biological science.

WHAT RACE IS NOT

Race and Culture

"Race" as it is used today only emerged as a concept in the late seventeenth and eighteenth centuries. Until this time for Europeans the definition of "others" was Christian vs. non-Christion. As European expansion and imperialism began to develop

[11]H. S. Jennings, *The Biological Basis of Human Nature* (New York: W. W. Norton & Company, 1930), p. 280. By permission.
[12]H. S. Jennings, "The Laws of Heredity and Our Present Knowledge of Human Genetics on the Material Side," in *Scientific Aspects of the Race Problem*, H. S. Jennings et al. (New York: Longmans, Green & Co., 1941), p. 71.

peoples were encountered whose culture, values, and ways of life were different from the known and familiar. Since these people also looked different, there was the naïve assumption that their ways of behaving were related to the way they looked. Thus in the period of imperialist expansion for most people the concepts race and culture became inextricably intertwined. If one recognizes that culture is man's way of adapting to his environment, as we have indicated above, it is more likely that culture affected race than race, culture. The separation of physiognomic adaptations and cultural solutions did not become explicit until the development of the physical and social sciences. For almost three hundred years then, from the seventeenth to the twentieth centuries, there was no factual basis for interpretation of differences, although always there were some sensitive individuals who appreciated other cultures without regard to visible physiognomic differences. As the fact or the spirit of imperialism grew, visible differences became the rationalization of what were really cultural conflicts. The technological superiority of the Europeans and European-descended peoples established dominance over less technologically developed societies and externally rationalized this on the basis of the confusion of race and culture. A European naïvete and ethnocentrism justified dominance in terms of "the white man's burden." As acculturation to the European dominance spread, the racial emphasis became more pronounced as the justification for subordination.

The institutionalization of dominant-subordinate relationships depends on the preservation of norms across generations. But norms are derived from values. Differences in the content and emphasis of values will give a different cast to patterns of subordination. For example, in Brazil, Catholic Christianity was sufficiently in control of the value system in the early period of settlement, that imported Negroes and indigenous Indians were accepted by Europeans and incorporated into the social system according to their education and "ability" if they were Catholic. It is true that as Brazil developed there was cruel exploitation of Indian labor, and Negro slaves coming in the later importations had less access to channels of opportunity. The result has been that lower classes tend to be darker. But in contrast to the North American traditional pattern, Negro or Indian descent has never been *per se* a barrier to entry into economic or social elites. In early Brazil intermarriage was frequent, manumission frequent, the family structure of slaves was protected, and tribal groups were often kept intact. In contrast in North America, the indigenous social structures of African peoples were shattered, sexual exploitation rather than Catholic marriage was more typical, and manumission, although it occurred, was less frequent than in Brazil. One factor in the North American situation was a less unified superordinate religious value system.

Race and Nationality

The tendency to identify race and nation is perhaps the most widely held of all beliefs relating race to culture. It is in Europe, the very region where racialist theories were most earnestly expounded, that the lack of correlation between racial subgroups and national culture is most clearly illustrated. This is notably true of Germany, France, and England, where Nordic, Alpine, and Mediterranean traits have been shown to be harmoniously blended in the citizenry of each nation. Dominian wrote "Northern France is perhaps more Teutonic than southern Germany, while eastern Germany is, in many places, more Slavic than Russia." Hankins points out that within Germany, "a relative purity of Germanic elements along the Baltic and North Seas (but mixed even there with Slavic Poles and Wends) gradually gives way to the southward to an increasing complexity in which Alpine and Mediterranean elements increase."[13]

Since the English were racially mongrelized within the broad Caucasian limits, it follows that the old American stock was correspondingly a mongrel mixture of European varieties. In a study of Americans descended from this English stock, Hrdlicka showed that they ranged widely in skin color, hair color, and eye color, with intermediates predominating over either the alleged Nordic type with fair skin, blue eyes, and blond hair, or the swarthy-complexioned, brunet, Mediterranean type. Altogether, the measurements indicate extensive hybridization in the old American stock.[14]

Social Race

From the foregoing discussion it is apparent that the term "race" as traditionally used has neither descriptive accuracy nor categorical validity. Nevertheless, this traditional concept persists

[13]F. H. Hankins, *The Racial Basis of Civilization* (New York: Alfred A. Knopf, 1926), p. 286.
[14]Alec Hrdlicka, *Old Americans* (Baltimore: The Williams & Wilkins Co., 1925), Chapter 3.

in cultures as a mode, among others, of ranking people socially. This is what Wagley calls "social race."

> "Social race" (i.e., the way in which the members of society classify each other by physical characteristics) is one of a series of values which give individuals rank and determine their social relations.[15]

In analyzing populations in rural Brazil, Wagley found he had to resort to the term "race" for the concept of "social race" because this was the common term not only in the popular vocabulary but also in the collection of census statistics.

> Throughout this report, when the term "race" is used, the authors hold no brief for its validity as a physical or genetic classification. In one sense or another, the term is always used in this volume in a social and cultural sense. It is well known that colour or race data in population statistics reflect the social categories of the census takers, and it is interesting to reflect upon the variety of social definitions of "race" which would inevitably be involved in any census of Brazil. . . . Even our own observations as to the probable "racial" affiliation of an individual or group of people are by necessity "naked eye" judgements certainly coloured by our own social and cultural experiences. Throughout this report, then, we are interested in the social definitions of "race" . . . and in their effects upon the life of the people of the communities studied, while exact physical classification is of little interest for our purpose.[16]

In keeping with Wagley's position, we too shall have to discuss race with the understanding that we are referring only to popular social categories which affect the way in which groups behave toward one another.

Ethnic

In much contemporary writing on intergroup relations, the term "race" has been abandoned and the word "ethnic" substituted. In this book when the term "ethnic" is used in connection with groups which are distinguishable by physiognomic as well

[15]Charles Wagley, ed. *Race and Class in Rural Brazil* (Paris: UNESCO, 1952), p. 14.
[16]*Ibid.*, p. 14. By permission.

as cultural traits, we will be emphasizing the cultural ethos of the group. When the group is referred to as a "race" we will be emphasizing the barriers that are erected against them within the dominant pattern of race attitudes.

RACE AND INTELLIGENCE

With the development of science in the nineteenth century and the infant social sciences toward the end of the century it was inevitable that "scientific" explanations should be offered for the visible differences between peoples. Biologists were still concerned with gross and simple aspects of genetics. Methodology in the social sciences was underdeveloped, largely merely some logical deduction from an unverified assumption with illustrative examples. The entire era was governed in biological and social science by a committment to an evolutionary theory that saw evolution as a straight line from "lower" forms to "higher" forms. Evolution over millions of years in biological forms does show a direction of development from simpler to more complex organisms. Perhaps in the recorded years of human history from stone age to space age, societies have moved from simpler to more complex, but certainly in no straight line, as civilizations in Asia and Africa in times past surpassed the Europeans of the same period both in technology and in complexity of social organization.

The attempt to "scientifically" demonstrate that some peoples genetically have less ability than others emerged in a particular time when it was germane to the interests of particular established social patterns. It was not conscious or deliberate, but an aspect of the cultural assumptions of Europe and America. Since there has been a recent upsurge of the same kind of attempt to validate assumptions about *de facto* situations, the fallacies must be examined. As Baltzell points out in *The Protestant Establishment*,[17] scholarship is inevitably influenced by current ideologies; or as the Polish sociologist, Ossowski has said, "The relation of the state to the sociologist is that of a drunk to a lamppost, it wants support, not light."[18]

[17]E. Digby Baltzell, *The Protestant Establishment* (New York: Random House, 1964), Ch. 4.
[18]Quoted in John Daniels and Vincent Houghton, "Jensen, Eysenick and the Eclipse of the Galton Paradigm" in Ken Richardson, David Spears, Martin Richards, eds., *Race and Intelligence*, (Baltimore: Penguin Books, 1972), pp. 71–72.

The Biological Fallacy

Arthur Jensen, a contemporary American, is the chief exponent of the primacy of gentic differences as an explanation of lower I.Q. scores for blacks as compared with whites.[19] Jensen has used wide comparative data, but in the first place his use of the genetic factor is simplistic and inaccurate. What are genetic, hereditary factors? John Hambley, a British biologist writing in criticism of Jensen and others, describes the biological process.[20]

Genes are the basic particles of heredity. They are located on the chromosomes found at the nucleus of each cell. They occur in pairs, one of each pair being transmitted from each parent. The pairs may contain identical or nonidentical genes. There is a very large number of genes in each organism.

The function of each gene is to produce protein (nutriment). Not all genes are active at any one time. From the moment of conception genes are being switched on and off. It is the interaction and integration of this switching on and off that constitutes development. The shuffling of these units in producing each egg and each sperm allows for tremendous scope for variation. Indeed, with the exception of identical twins, each individual is genetically unique.

Furthermore, genes are in continual interaction with the biological environment from conception on, both nourishing it and reacting to it; it is therefore impossible to predict from the initial gene pool what will be most active at any one time in development. Biology is only on the threshold of knowing what may affect gene activity (nutrition, for example, or hormone stimulation). Environment, biological and social, pre-natal and postnatal, is so complex and the gene pool of an individual so large that variation is constantly taking place at all levels. This is what makes individual adaptability.

Although most biologists agree that there are differences in gene frequency (number of genes) in different "racial" populations, race is here a value-free biological category which bears no relation to IQ which is a social measurement.

---

[19]Arthur R. Jensen, "How Much Can We Boost IQ and Scholastic Achievement?" *Harvard Educational Review*, Vol. 39, No. 1, 1969.
[20]John Hambley, "Diversity: A Developmental Perspective" in *Race and Intelligence*, pp. 114–127.

What Is Intelligence?

Societies have usually recognized "intelligence" as a capacity to learn skills easily and to transfer and apply a specific piece of learning or observation to a new problem containing similarities and variations. This latter quality involves the ability to "conceptualize"—to see relationships between objects, persons, or ideas apart from the individual properties of each. These folk understandings of intelligence are found in all societies, though not necessarily explicit, and not necessarily specifically rewarded.

In complex hierarchical societies, however, those people who can correctly assess object, personal, or idea relationships easily often have particular advantages. Even where there are barriers of class or caste and hereditary privilege, complex societies have to a greater or lesser degree had some channels of opportunity for the "intelligent" if this "intelligence" is channeled in the service of the established social system. In Imperial China the Imperial Civil Service was open to all who could pass the examinations, and often the extended kinship would aid the "brightest male" to have the tutoring necessary to compete. In medieval Europe the Church offered a career channel to the lesser privileged who had "ability."

This, though is a *social* definition of intelligence. There is also the possibility of a *biological* definition. The Swiss biologist, Piaget, who has worked for half a century on the study of cognitive functions in children, emphasizes that "intelligence" is not a set of discrete capacities. Intelligence is an equilibrator in the organism that compensates for external disturbance. It has three functions: it organizes the organism into a whole entity in its interaction with environment; it assimilates and utilizes stimulus from the environment, incorporating it into the growing organism; it accomodates, that is, modifies the internal structures of the organism to suit and make use of the input from the environment. Thus the growth of intelligence is the organization and adaptation of the total organism to the interaction with the environment outside itself.[21] In this view, no separate skills, mathematical or manual, or any mechanistic combination of them is a measure of intelligence.

[21]John Redford and Andrew Burton, "Changing Intelligence," in *Race and Intelligence*, pp. 29–31.

IQ As A Measuring Instrument

Today intelligence is measured throughout Western society by comparative score on standard examinations and/or psychometric tests. The two most widely used tests are the Stanford-Binet and the Wechsler (WISC) tests. These attempt to rate children on an achievement scale according to an average for their age group.

The first dilemma is the content of the tests. Children do not come from a standardized environment. Furthermore as total organisms they have individual reactions to individual experiences which make them see relations differently from what may be expected. For example, an American Indian child of eight, in response to a multiple choice vocabulary question: "This book belongs to me. . . . It is yours, mine, theirs, ours" underlined ours. She came from a common property culture. The Standard-Binet scales were standardized on whites only. Furthermore they have a middle-class bias (e.g. "Why do we like books?" What will a shanty child from Appalachia do with this?)[22] Or consider the middle-class white child of six who, when asked in such a test "Are rocks like eggs?" replied "yes." The weekend before he had been at the sea shore and he and his sister had collected smooth rocks that were egg shaped.

The second dilemma is the condition under which a person takes the test. Black children often do better if the tester is black. Children do better if they are told that they will probably do well. Minority children do better if they believe they are being measured against their own group rather than a national average.[23]

Standardized psychometric tests to a degree serve a social purpose. They are a mode of allocating individuals to slots in a particular social structure. Some experiments are being made to see if "culture free" tests can be designed; in some places the effort is being made to test in small groups with a known and trusted tester. But these are few and far between. Aside from the fact that possibly no such test can measure intelligence, any gross data from them that compares the scores of different populations against a white, middle-class average is misleading. On the one hand it may support the myth of biological inferiorities. On the other it may agitate reformers to bend efforts to homogenize American society (forced or coaxed acculturation). Not only does

[22]Joanna Ryan, "The Illusion of Objectivity," in *Race and Intelligence*, p. 53.
[23]Peter Watson, "Can Racial Discrimination Affect I.Q.?" *Ibid.*, pp. 62–67.

such a policy destroy, for many, the equilibrium between the individual organism and the environment; but it is also a social loss in that it reduces alternatives for the productive interaction of individual growth and social development. A standardized homogeneous society and a standardized measurement of "intelligence" may be an efficient and "fair" way to allocate position in the hierarchy of decision making— a meritocracy, but it may even more seriously impoverish both individuals and the society.

RACISM

The Ideological Dimension

The revival of the biological argument for "white" superiority is a measure of the crisis of our time. When the institutionalized pattern is threatened with change, additional supporting arguments are marshalled to uphold the existing structure. Thus the first arguments about the nature of "races" were based on Biblical Old Testament "authority," and later the beginning of the scientific study of man, which, like all *beginning* scientific endeavor must deal with categories of phenomena and with differences, laid a base for a belief in biological determinism—that is, that ability and behavior are determined by physical type.

The popularity of pseudoscientific Nordic claims stimulated reactively vigorous research and writing which was ultimately to demolish, in intellectual circles, not only Nordic doctrine but all other expressions of racialism. From this exploration has emerged the scientific view of race presented earlier in the chapter. If the elimination of minority discrimination depended solely on "debunking" the racialist doctrine, such discrimination would disappear in a generation. But as the history of racial doctrine suggests, belief in its claims does not rest soley on inadequate knowledge of its objective error but partly in the desire of the dominant to believe it.[24]

The Ideological Factor

When we examine the scientific literature of the seventeenth century with a view to discovering what beliefs were held concerning

[24]See Gerhart Saenger "The Effectiveness of the UNESCO Pamphlet Series on Race," *International Social Science Bulletin*, Vol. VI, No. 3. Dr. Saenger found many resistances to using the UNESCO material in schools and colleges.

the variety of man, we find that it was universally believed that mankind, was comprised of a single species and that it represented a unitary whole. . . . Physical differences were, of course, known to exist between groups of mankind, but what was unfamiliar was the notion that the differences exhibited by such peoples represented anything fundamental.[25]

In all modes of social conflict in the eighteenth and nineteenth centuries "racism" became involved. It was invoked by the nobles of France to justify their superiority to the bourgeoisie, and later espoused by reactionary political theorists throughout nineteenth-century Europe.[26]

The potential power of racism in stimulating group conflict can be further illustrated by its application to two twentieth-century phenomena: the Japanese pan-Asiatic movement and the rise of the Hitler Reich. While it would be oversimplification to explain the aggressive policy pursued by Japan in the twentieth century wholly on the basis of their notion of race superiority, that this notion was prevalent and served a useful purpose in developing morale for aggressive political policies should not be overlooked. According to the Japanese scholar Hirata, "from the fact of the divine descent of the Japanese proceeds their unmeasurable superiority to the natives of other countries in courage and intelligence." While like all tribes and nations, the Japanese were always ethnocentric, the development of distinct "racial pride" as part of the cultural paraphernalia essential to whip up national enthusiasm for military, imperialistic expansion was a part of the great borrowing of Western ideas and knowledge which characterized modern Japan.[27]

One group of writers was the "Aryan" school. From philological research that revealed similarities in the languages of the Persians and Indians and those of the western Indo-Europeans, the Greeks, Romans, Teutons, Celts, and Slav, they concluded that all languages derived from a common source, and they posited a primitive Aryan tribe from which all the later Aryans descended. Considering these languages superior and assuming without question that language and race are related, this school expounded the theory of the "superior Aryan race."

[25]M. F. Ashley Montagu, *Man's Most Dangerous Myth: The Fallacy of Race*, 4th ed., rev. and enl. (Cleveland: The World Publishing Co., 1964), p. 16. By permission.
[26]See Jacques Barzun, *Race: A Study in Superstition*, rev. ed. (New York: Harper & Row, 1965), Chapter 2, "The Nordic Myth."
[27]Willard Price, "Japan's Divine Mission," *The New Republic*, Nov. 17, 1937.

In the Nazi ideology, racism was a dominant theme. It was not, however, a new point of view, but rather the logical culmination of selected strains of political argument throughout the nineteenth century. As Barzun states, "the race-overtones are nothing new and the rearrangement of Tacitus's Nordic myth was peculiar to France only in its details. Hitler showed how readily it applies to the Third Reich."[28] Whereas French writers were debating the superiority of Franks to Romanized Celts and the English were dreaming of Anglo-Saxon encirclement and hegemony of the world, the Nazi's applied the argument against the Jews, who in the century since the establishment of full civil rights for them in Germany had risen in status and made so many contributions to German enterprise and German thought. In the critical period of economic, political, and social reorganization after the defeat in World War I, the Nazi philosophers expounded the notion that the development of an "Aryan" state was the only bulwark against chaos, and that the German nation must be "purified" from the deteriorating "international" influence of the Jewish "race." In practice, the Nazis subjected Jews to persecution and extermination. Once the German Nordic "race" itself was thus purified, the rest of the "race" was to be incorporated into a pan-German state, and Germans in other parts of the world, notably the United States, were to be encouraged to retain their racial purity and to foster Nazi ideas.

Racial doctrine became the support of nationalist rivalries by adding to the cult of nationalism the idea that "our nation (or a dominant segment of it) is a superior race." But, most pertinent to our interest, racism became a strong support of slavery and imperialism.

> Racism did not get its currency in modern thought until it was applied to conflicts within Europe—first to class conflicts and then to national. But it is possible to wonder whether the doctrine would have been proposed at all as explaining these latter conflicts—where, as we have seen, the dogma is so inept—if the basis for it had not been laid in the violent experience of racial prejudice on the frontier.[29]

In the process of establishing their economic hegemony over most of the world and in developing less settled areas under this

[28]Barzun, *Race: A Study in Superstition*, p. 23.
[29]Benedict, *Race: Science and Politics*, p. 111. By permission.

domination to their own greatest advantage, white Europeans, particularly the English—who passed on this tradition to the Americans—developed a caste-like relation to the "natives" of their colonies and, under an even more indisputably inferior status, to the forcefully imported slaves. In fact, it seems clear that in actual time sequence, the white men first exploited native labor and brought in slaves and then expounded a theory of the inferiority of the "colored" peoples to support their *de facto* status.

WHY DOES RACISM PERSIST

The Psychological Dimension

Research has shown us that individuals who are unsure of their valuableness, their importance, or their sexuality are prey to a need to define someone else as inferior, or "less moral" or whatever. If the society offers them candidates in a minority as being either lesser or threatening, they can be rallied to vigorous anti-minority sentiment.[30] Such a person has important needs which might be expressed simply by being derogatory to his children, his wife, or his associates. But it is much easier and less fraught with daily conflict if it can be projected on those the society defines as inferior.

Groups of people, often when threatened with social or economic change over which they have no control, and which is inimical to their present assumptions or future aspirations easily adopt racist attitudes. Sometimes these are focused in competitive access to scarce rewards. For example, a generation ago, under covert quota systems dominants had prime access to institutions of higher education and to professional schools, not to mention greater opportunity for financial aid. In the rectifying of this situation, segments of the dominant population today are expressing increased racial antagonism as their proportion of the anticipated reward is cut down. Declining neighborhoods on the one hand or lily-white suburbs on the other, panic into group racism when visible minorities move into their neighborhoods and threaten to challenge their control of community life and leadership. Sometimes propagandists have deliberately offered a particu-

[30]See Philip Mason, *Race Relations*. (New York: Oxford University Press, 1970), Chapter 4, "Pressures from Within." For a theoretical discussion of this, see Chapter 18 of this text.

lar minority or several minorities as targets to channelize the unrest occasioned by widespread social stress. Thus in World War II there were organized anti-Semitic campaigns; there were riots against Mexican Americans, as well as a predominant racial theme in sentiment and action about the Japanese.

The Social Structural Dimension

Discrimination is structured inequality. It is maintained by customary (covert) or official (overt) barriers to jobs, to equal educational opportunity, to political participation. Legislative changes in the last two decades have removed many official barriers. But the implementation of legislation is still being fought on the community level throughout the nation. Powerful political interests, through patronage, and powerful economic interests, through, for example, apprentice programs, membership policies of organizations, etc., still structure discrimination. This would be less possible, if from the first grades on, the content of education were changed to include and emphasize the whole American experience and the dignity of all Americans. A major bulwark of institutionalized racism is the educational system.[31]

In summary, the doctrine of racism appears to have developed in relation to the colored races as an ideological and moral justification for a system already established and highly useful to white dominants. It has been continued for the same reason.

Race-thinking, to use Barzun's term,[32] is, as he points out, a superstition—literally, an idea that "stands over" facts. Philosophers of racism, (with the aid of other intellectual disciplines) have contributed in the past to "the astonishing enterprise of super-superstition." It has been so pervasive a part of Western thought for some centuries that it has subtly infected us all so that surprising sentiments may be heard to emerge with regard to the French-Algerian conflict, the Arab-Israeli conflict, the inverted racism of "Negritude" in former French Africa, or "Black Power" among American Negroes. The urge to build theories about collectivities in order to mobilize collective hostility is still with us. Any hope for social peace lies in "turning group antagonisms into consciously economic or political struggles by removing their racist covering." There are established channels for dealing

---

[31]Michael B. Kane. *Minorities in Textbooks* (Chicago: Quadrangle Books, Inc., 1970).
[32]Barzun, *Race: A Study in Superstition,* Preface to the second edition, p. x.

with economic and political conflict. There are none for the un-defined group aggressions of the confused, the frightened, the egocentric, the alienated, who subsume groups as identically cap-able or incapable, reliable or treacherous, lovable or hateful.

Suggested Readings

Barzun, Jacques. *Race: A Study in Superstition,* rev. ed., New York: Harper & Row, 1965. Also available in Harper Torchbook edition.
European ideologies of race.

Gossett, Thomas F. *Race: The History of an Idea in America.* Dallas: South-ern Methodist University Press, 1963.
A history of racial attitudes in America by a Southern liberal.

Kane, Michael B. *Minorities in Textbooks.* Chicago: Quadrangle Books, 1970.
Forty-five secondary school texts from major publishers are examined for their treatment of minorities. (American History, World History, Social Problems).

Knowles, Louis L. and Prewitt, Kenneth, eds. *Institutional Racism in America.* Englewood Cliffs, N.J.: Prentice-Hall, Inc., 1969.
An analysis of ways racism is perpetuated politically, educationally, economically, ecologically, and in the administration of justice.

Mason, Philip. *Race Relations.* New York: Oxford University Press, 1970.
A thoughtful analysis of the many dimensions of race relations.

Richardon, Ken, David Spears, and Martin Richards, eds. *Race and Intel-ligence.* Baltimore, Md.: Penguin Books, 1972.
Biologists, psychologists, and sociologists contribute to a review of recent research related to race differences.

Part II

Major Minority Situations in the United States Today

5 **N**egro-White Relations: Demography and Background

Among the various dominant-minority situations in the United States Negro-white relations obviously occupy first place as a social problem and currently as a social problem of the utmost gravity. We therefore devote more attention to this intergroup situation than to the others.

The Negro minority is by far the largest, constituting a little over a tenth of the nation's population. It is the oldest minority, the first Negro slaves having been brought to Jamestown in 1619.[1]

This minority has the lowest status of all ethnic and racial groups. A large portion of the Negro population has a very low standard of living, even though with the emergence of a class structure within the population, the welfare within the group as a whole is at present highly variable. Differing from the other minorities, the continuity between its original African cultural heritage has virtually disappeared through the long years of servitude and caste conditions so that such cultural distinctiveness as Negroes may have is largely derived from the experience of slavery and discrimination.

The two most important factors which explain why Negroes have so long remained a minority are that (1) they are Negroid in their physiognomic characteristics or in their known lineage; and (2) their ancestors were in the vast majority of cases slaves. In

[1]Indian-white relations did not become dominant-minority relations in the true sense until the Indians became wards in 1871.

the first of these chapters devoted to Negro-white relations we shall deal briefly with the period of slavery and its aftermath.

THE GROWTH AND DISTRIBUTION OF THE NEGRO POPULATION

Growth

Table 5-1 shows that the number of Negroes in the United States has increased each decade since 1790. It also shows that broadly the proportion of Negroes to the total population declined from 1880 to 1930, primarily as the result of the great increase in the white population through immigration from Europe. From 1930 to 1970 the percentage of the national population counted as Negro increased slightly from 9.7 to 11.1 per cent; and from 1950 to 1970 the percentage increase of the Negro population was about 8 per cent greater than that of the white population. The fertility rates of Negro women have broadly followed the fluctuations in that of white women, although at a substantially higher level than that of whites.[2] But higher death rates retard their proportional increase. However, it is expected that the per cent rate of Negroes in the total population will increase at about one per cent in the next decade.

Regional Distribution

Through the entire national period up to 1910 the Negro population was highly concentrated in the South—over 90 per cent. Within the region under slavery, Negro migration was of course governed by the owners and traders of slaves. The southern and southwestern expansion of the plantation economy from the upper South was paralleled by a corresponding expansion of the Negro population in these areas. In spite of the freedom for Negroes to move where they desired after the Civil War, very few migrated to the North, and almost none to the West. From 1910 on there has been a marked migration out of the region (slowed down somewhat by the depression decade), so that by 1970 the proportion of the total Negro population in the South had dropped to 53 per cent. Until 1940 this exodus from the South was to the North East and the North Central regions. A small but

[2]Reynolds Farley, *Growth of the Black Population* (Chicago: Markham Publishing Company, 1970), p. 244.

TABLE 5-1   GROWTH OF THE NEGRO POPULATION SINCE 1790*

Census Year	Number of Negroes	Percentage of Total Population	Percentage Increase of Negroes During Decade	Percentage Increase of Whites During Decade
1970	22,530,289	11.1	19.7	11.9
1960	18,871,831	10.5	25.4	17.5
1950	15,044,937	9.9	17.0	14.4
1940	12,865,518	9.8	8.2	7.2
1930	11,891,143	9.7	13.6	15.7
1920	10,463,131	9.9	6.5	15.7
1910	9,827,763	10.7	11.2	21.8
1900	8,333,940	11.6	18.0	21.2
1890	7,488,676	11.9	13.8	27.0
1880	6,580,793	13.1	34.9	29.2
1870	4,880,009	12.7	9.9	24.8
1860	4,441,830	14.1	22.1	37.7
1850	3,638,808	15.7	26.6	37.7
1840	2,873,648	16.8	23.4	34.7
1830	2,328,642	18.1	31.4	33.9
1820	1,771,656	18.4	28.6	34.2
1810	1,377,808	19.0	37.5	36.1
1800	1,002,037	18.9	32.3	35.8
1790	757,208	19.3		

*United States Bureau of Census, Negroes in the United States, 1920–1932, pp. 1–2; Sixteenth Census of United States, Population, Vol. II, p. 19. 1960 Census, P. C. (A2)–1, p. 4. 1970 Census P. C. (1) 3, p. 262.

hitherto unprecedented trend toward the West began in consequence of the labor demands in that region created by World War II. Most of this migration was to California, which led all the other states in the percentage rise in Negro population during the 1951–1960 decade—90 per cent. By 1970 the state had 1,400,143 Negroes. A prime factor accounting for this trend out of the South has been increasing job opportunities outside the region. In their studies the Taubers did not find any clear support for the thesis that among the "push" factors was the desire to escape the southern discriminatory pattern of race relations.[3] However, autobiographies of Negroes do show that this desire was a compelling motive in some instances.[4]

[3]Karl E. and Alma F. Tauber, "The Negro Population in the United States," Chapter 2 of John Davis, ed., The Negro Reference Book (Englewood Cliffs, N.J.: Prentice-Hall, 1966), p. 111.
[4]See for example Richard Wright, Native Son (New York: Harper & Brothers, 1940); and Horace Cayton, Long Lonely Road (New York: The Trident Press, 1965).

Urban Trend: Metropolitan Concentration

The most significant change in the distribution of the Negro population since 1910 has been the shift from rural to urban, more marked than that of the white population and also strikingly concentrated in the larger metropolitan areas as indicated in Table 5-2. As examples, Chicago had a sixteen-fold increase in its per cent Negro from 1910 to 1970; and New York had a ten-fold increase. Washington, D.C. with over 70 per cent Negro approaches

TABLE 5-2   THE TWENTY-FIVE LEADING CITIES IN NEGRO POPULA-TION IN 1970 AND THEIR PER CENT NEGRO, 1910, 1950, 1960, 1970

City	Negro Population, 1970 (In Thousands)	Per Cent Negro Of Total Population			
		1970 (.00)	1960 (.00)	1950 (.00)	1910 (.00)
New York City	1,667	21	14	10	02
Chicago	1,103	33	23	14	02
Detroit	660	44	29	16	*
Philadelphia	654	34	26	18	06
Washington, D.C.	538	71	54	35	29
Los Angeles	504	18	14	9	*
Baltimore	420	46	35	24	15
Houston	317	26	23	21	30
Cleveland	288	38	29	16	*
New Orleans	267	45	37	32	26
Atlanta	255	51	38	37	34
St. Louis	254	41	29	18	06
Memphis	243	39	37	37	40
Dallas	210	25	19	13	*
Newark	207	54	34	17	*
Indianapolis	134	18	21	15	10
Birmingham	126	42	40	40	40
Cincinnati	125	28	22	16	05
Oakland	125	35	23	12	*
Jacksonville	118	22	23	27	51
Kansas City, Mo.	112	22	18	12	10
Milwaukee	105	15	9	3	*
Pittsburgh	105	20	17	12	05
Richmond	105	42	42	32	37
Boston	105	16	10	5	*

All data except the 1910 column taken from the U.S. Census, 1970, P.C. (S1)2, *Negro Population in Selected Places and Counties*, Table 1, Cities with a Negro Population of 50,000 or more by rank 1970, 1960, 1950. 1910 data: U.S. Bureau of Census, *Negro Population, 1790–1915*.

*Leading 1970 cities who had few Negroes in 1910.

being a "Black City." Of the larger Northern cities, Newark, New Jersey, is more than 50 per cent Negro and the population of Detroit is being pushed to that point. Extending the list to all cities with a Negro population of 50,000 or more adds two more Northern cities to the over half Negro population—Gary, Indiana, (52.8 per cent) and Compton, California, (71 per cent).

The list of leading cities does not provide an adequate picture of the degree of concentration. In many places, the Negro areas have pushed out to an adjacent municipality: for example Newark's main Negro area has extended into adjacent East Orange, N.J. which also has a majority Negro population. Again, whereas Los Angeles City has an 18 per cent black population, Los Angeles County has 65 per cent, being greatly affected by the suburban city of Compton with 71 per cent of its 78,000 population being Negro. The extent of concentration can be carried further. Smaller suburban satellite industrial cities near metropolisis often have large proportions of black people; for example, New Brunswick, New Jersey, 35 miles from New York City, has a 24 per cent Negro population.

In general, the leading Southern cities listed in Table 5-2 have had substantial Negro populations for some time. Thus it is not surprising that the percentage of their Negro population does not show much increase and in some cases drops.

The implications of these striking changes in the distribution of the Negro population will be discussed in later chapters. In conclusion here we point out that the national Negro population is expected to increase a little more proportionally than the white population but to remain a definite numerical minority, one important factor in power vulnerability. On the other hand, the exceptionally high urban concentration already has had two effects: (1) providing in some local areas such a substantial number as to give blacks considerable political power; and (2) markedly accentuating interracial tension in such areas.

CHARACTERISTICS OF THE NEGRO PEOPLE

The minority status of Negroes in the United States has rested in large measure on the beliefs developed and sustained in the minds of the white population that being Negroid in racial ancestry means that Negroes are innately inferior in many ways. In our Chapter 4 on race, it was seen that contemporary social science seriously challenges this belief. In the first place, how actually Negroid is the population counted as such in the United States?

The Negro American: A New Genetic Type

The "visibility" of the Negro population is accounted for by the fact that all the members have some genetic lineage from Negro ancestry. In the United States a person is considered a Negro if he has any known Negro lineage, whether he can be identified by his appearance or not. There is no precise data indicating what distribution of the basic Negroid traits are now present in the population known as Negro. The United States Census count in 1920—the last year a distinction between mulatto and black was made—gave the figure of 15.9 per cent for mulattoes, which all students of the question consider a gross undercount. Pettigrew estimates that about one-fourth of the Negro gene pool consists of genes of Caucasian origin.[5]

Most Negroes in the United States show one or more of the basic Negroid traits: dark skin, thick lips, "wooly" hair, and prognathism; in a minor proportion, the evidence of these traits are so faint that one cannot be sure of identifying them; and in a relatively small percentage there is absolutely no somatic evidence of Negro lineage, but either the individuals themselves, or others who know them vouch for some Negro ancestry. The American Negro population of today is, biologically speaking, quite different from that of the original slaves. The processes by which this change has come about will now be described.

Selective Mating Processes

INTERTRIBAL MATING   While knowledge of the ancestry of American Negroes is not too precise, it is considered that most of the present Negro population traces the Negro part of its ancestry back to slaves who originally came from the West Coast of Africa. Since under slavery their mating was not tribally endogamous, the first process was the intermixing of these original tribal variations. This would have produced a new, but African, Negro type if it had not been for the crossing of slaves very early with both Indians and white people.

---

[5]See Thomas Pettigrew, *A Profile of the Negro American* (New York: D. Van Nostrand Company, Inc., 1964), p. 71.

NEGRO-INDIAN CROSSING   Before the nineteenth century there was some intermingling between Indians and Negroes, with the result that some of the admixtures disappeared into the Indian population. Herskovits found 27 per cent of a Negro sample to have some Indian lineage.[6] Additional Indian genetic strains resulted from the increasing importation, in the later periods, of slaves from the West Indies, where "crossing" with Indians had occurred. However, later studies suggest that the amount of Indian admixture in the Negro population is not so high as in Herskovits' sample.[7]

NEGRO-WHITE CROSSING   The population from which the African slaves were recruited already had some admixture of Caucasian genes, as a result of miscegenation with the Portuguese who settled on the Guinea Coast for slave trading purposes and through contact in Europe, whence some slaves were brought to the West Indies.

In the colonies themselves, indications are that the first extensive Negro-white crossing took place between indentured white servants and Negro slaves. As the indentured servant disappeared and the Negro slave system developed, mating between white and colored people continued through the access to Negro slave women which the system gave the white male owners and white men in general.

The next stage came with the Civil War and its aftermath. "The Northern army left an unknown amount of Yankee genes in the Southern Negro people."[8] Under the caste system which supplanted slavery, interracial crossing continued more or less in the same pattern of white male exploitation of Negro women, although the women had somewhat more freedom than under slavery. While evidence is scarce, most writers agree that the amount of miscegenation has declined throughout the twentieth century.

"LIGHT" SELECTION AMONG NEGROES   It was generally acknowledged even by Negro students of race relations that mate selection within the Negro population itself favored those Negroes who were "whiter." The higher status of mulattoes was due not

[6]Melville Herskovits, *The American Negro: A Study in Racial Crossing* (New York: Alfred A. Knopf, 1930).
[7]Pettigrew, *A Profile of the American Negro*, p. 68.
[8]Gunnar Myrdal, *An American Dilemma* (New York: Harper & Brothers, 1944), p. 127.

only to their "lightness" but also to the fact that the dominant whites inclined to favor them. Thus in general mulattoes have had more economic and educational opportunity. This selective mating bias among Negroes had the effect of increasing the distribution of white genetic factors in the Negro population.[9] Here the current increasing pride among blacks in their black identity would be expected to decrease further white contribution to the future Negro gene-pool.

PASSING   By "passing" is meant the successful and permanent assumption of "white" status by a person who knows he has Negro ancestry. In studying the African ancestry of the white population in the United States, Stuckert, using the method of genetic probability tables, estimated that during the years 1941–1950 an average annual mean of 15,500 Negroes passed. There was an annual rate of 1.21 per 1,000 Negro population, and the rate was found to be increasing.[10] The effect of passing is to remove from the Negro population strains which would increase the Caucasian admixture in the Negro population. The process adds some Negroid admixture to the white population, but very little, since the Negroes who pass have few Negroid genes to add, because "passers," when they marry, tend to select either white mates or equally white Negro mixtures.

The Negro American Genotype

The white racist myth has exaggerated the genetic difference between the races when in fact their similarities are far greater. Applied to the Negro American, Glass points out:

> In all, it is unlikely that there are many more than six pairs of genes in which the white race differs characteristically, in the lay sense, from the black. Whites or blacks however, differ among themselves by a larger number than this, a fact which reveals our racial prejudices as biologically absurd. It is only the consistency of the difference, not its magnitude which looms large in our eyes. . . . the chasm between human races and peoples, where it exists, is psychological and sociological; it is not genetic.[11]

[9]For further discussion of this subject, see Otto Klineberg, ed., *Characteristics of the American Negro* (New York: Harper & Brothers, 1944), Pt. V, Ch. 9, "The Future of the Hybrid," by Louis Wirth and Herbert Goldhammer.
[10]Robert P. Stuckert, "African Ancestry of the White American Population," *The Ohio Journal of Science*, May, 1958, pp. 155–160. The main finding of this study was that 28 million "white" persons have some African ancestry.
[11]Bentley Glass, *Genes and the Man* (New York: Teachers College, Columbia University, 1943), pp. 173–174.

Ashley Montagu has summarized the genotype of the American Negro as follows:

> . . . the American Negro represents an amalgam into which have entered the genes of African Negroes, whites of many races and social classes, and some American Indians, and that as far as his physical characteristics are concerned the American Negro represents a successful blending of these three elements into a unique biological type. All his characters are perfectly harmonic, and there is every reason to believe that he represents a perfectly satisfactory biological type. His biological future is definitely bright.[12]

MENTAL CAPACITY   The white racist myth has included the belief in the mental inferiority of Negroes. Scientific studies of this subject have relied on intelligence quotient tests (none of which satisfy behavioral scientists themselves). Most comparative black-white scores show a lower median score for blacks, but also a wide overlapping range in the score distribution. However, the high levels of actual *achievement* already manifested by many Negro Americans belie the notion of categorical inferiority. In a recent symposium article, one participant maintains that I.Q. scores are not socially meaningful. "I.Q. appears to have no *independent* relation to occupational success."[13]

Cultural Characteristics of Negro Americans

All the minorities previously treated started out in this country with distinctive ethnic cultural differences which have been passed on to native-born generations in increasingly diluted form. The situation of Negroes in this respect is considerably different. The sharp impact of slavery went far to destroy the many tribal cultures which the Negroes brought with them. Scholarly controversy prevails among the students of the history of the Negro in the New World concerning the extent to which African culture traits have survived, or to what extent Negro cultural adaptations in the New World were influenced by their aboriginal culture.[14]

A considerable number of scattered, specific cultural traits

---

[12]Ashley Montagu, *Man's Most Dangerous Myth: The Fallacy of Race* (New York: World Publishing Company, 1965), Fourth Edition, Revised and Enlarged, p. 816. By permission of the author and publisher.
[13]David R. Cohen, "Does I.Q. Matter," *Intellectual Digest*, July 1972, p. 37. Italics ours.
[14]A brief introduction to this historical problem is found in Frazier, *The Negro in the United States*, (New York: The Macmillan Co., 1949), Ch. I, "Significance of the African Background." For fuller discussion of the topic, see Melville J. Herskovits, *The Myth of the Negro Past* (New York: Harper & Brothers, 1942).

have been found in specific Negro groups which can be directly traced to African origin. It is significant, however, that more of these have been found among Negro groups in the West Indies. For other, more prevalent aspects of American Negro culture and behavior which present a vague, general similarity to African cultural forms, the continuity of African heritage is highly debatable. For example, was the frequency of common-law marriage in Negro rural life derivative from African customs, or can it be explained by the highly destructive impact of slavery on the stability of Negro family life? Is the predilection of American Negroes for the Baptist denomination, which features total immersion, due to the surviving influence of West African "river cults," as Herskovits speculates, or is it more simply attributable, as Frazier suggests, to the vigorous proselytizing activities of the Baptist denomination.[15]

So far as African heritage is concerned Elkins writes: "No true picture . . . of African culture seems to throw any light at all on origins of what would emerge in American plantation society as the stereotype 'Sambo personality.' " He further concludes that the cultural level and the social organization of the various African societies from which the slaves were obtained "entitles one to argue that they must have had an institutional life at least as sophisticated as Anglo-Saxon England."[16] Thus if Elkins' conclusion is accepted it follows that most of any cultural distinctiveness of the Negro minority in America has developed out of their experience in the United States. Any aggregate of people who are collectively isolated from the mainstream of the broader society in which they reside develop some cultural distinctiveness. Broom and Glenn write "the present state of knowledge does not permit an accurate estimate of the extent to which there is a distinctive Negro American way of life different in kind from that of the surrounding whites."[17] We will return to this topic again in Chapter 9 in connection with the goals of the Negro Revolt. Here we note that in regard to significant aspects of culture, American Negroes are Christians, heavily Protestant, speak English, and that their subcommunity social structure parallels that of the white community.[18] Thus of all American minorities the Negro minority most resembles the WASP prototype.

[15]Frazier, *The Negro in the United States*, pp. 10–18.
[16]Stanley M. Elkins, *Slavery: A Problem in American Institutional and Intellectual Life* (Chicago: The University of Chicago Press, 1959), p. 97.
[17]Leonard Broom and Norvall Glenn, *The Transformation of the American Negro* (New York: Harper & Row, Publishers, 1965), p. 22.
[18]With the possible exception of the family and sex-role differences generally.

Personality Traits of the Negro American

Since the African cultural heritage brought by American Negro slaves was substantially eliminated, it follows that any group personality characteristics which distinguish them from the rest of the population have resulted from the impact of their experience in this country, and from genetic factors as modified by extensive hybridization under slavery and caste. This background discussion will not be concerned with changes which may be in process of development, especially among the young, in consequence of the dramatically changing conditions since the onset of World War II.

Under slavery there emerged a white stereotype of Sambo which Elkins described thus:

> Sambo . . . was docile but irresponsible, loyal, but lazy, humble but chronically given to lying and stealing; his behavvior was full of infantile silliness. . . . His relationship with his master was one of utter dependence and childlike attachment; it was indeed this childlike quality that was the very key to his being. Although the merest hint of Sambo's manhood might fill the Southern breast with scorn, the child "in his place" could be both exasperating and lovable.[19]

The stereotype of the Negro held generally by twentieth-century white Americans ran about as follows: The Negro is lazy, won't work unless he has to, and doesn't know what to do with money when he gets it. He is dirty, smelly, careless in appearance, yet given to flashy dressing. He is much more "sexy" than the white man, and exercises little restraint in sexual expression. He has low mental ability incapable of anything but menial labor. He is naturally religious, but his religion is mostly emotion and superstition. On the other hand, in his simple way, the Negro is a likeable fellow, clever in a childlike way, and has natural abilities as a singer, dancer, and actor which surpass those of most white folks. Obviously, by this time an increasing number of white Americans no longer hold this image of the Negro, and even those who hold it in diluted form are at least rationally forced to exclude the rising number of educated and middle-class Negroes.

Turning to scientific conclusions, regarding Negro-white differences, a summary of research findings follows:

[19]Stanley M. Elkins, *Slavery*, p. 82.

In psychophysical and psychomotor functions, differences appear between whites and Negroes which may not be accounted for by differential environment conditions. However, a tendency is prevalent in the literature to indicate that most differences of this nature may be leveled off when social and economic variables are controlled. . . . In temperament ("personality") studies, Rorschach, T.A.T., PAT., and P-F Studies, differences are found, but again there is insufficient evidence to determine the relative contributions of genetic constitution and experiences. At least in those reactions which indicate responses to a dominant group culture, experience seems to be the major, if not sole determinant. Overall likeness in psychodynamics appears more extensive than differences.[20]

SOCIOPATHIC DEVIANCE   The white Americans' unfavorable view of Negroes was increased by the larger percentage of sociopathic behavior shown in comparative studies. Negroes are disproportionately found on police records, in penal institutions, and have higher recorded illegitimacy rates, intergroup violence, and homicide. While written with reference to crime, the following excerpt is also a good interpretation of the so-called Negro "pathology" in general.

White supremacists are quick to interpret these data as further evidence for their theories of the genetic inferiority of Negroes as a "race." There is, however, no scientific evidence to support such claims. But there are considerable data which indicate that a multiplicity of social factors produce these criminal patterns among Negroes.

One broad set of factors is socio-economic in character. When compared with white Americans, Negroes are concentrated in those social sectors which exhibit high crime rates regardless of race. Thus, Negroes are more often lower class and poor, slum residents of the nation's largest metropolitan areas, victims of severe family disorganization, Southern in origin, young, and unemployed. Note that each of these characteristics is an important social correlate of crime apart from race—and especially for those violations with the highest Negro rates.

The other, closely related set of factors involves the special type of discrimination inflicted upon Negroes. As with other minority groups who find discriminatory barriers blocking their path toward the mainstream of success-oriented America, many

[20]Ralph M. Dreger and Kent S. Miller, "Comparative Psychological Studies of Negroes and Whites in the United States," *Psychological Bulletin*, Sept. 1960, pp. 393–394. By permission.

Negroes turn to crime. Crime may thus be utilized as a means of escape, ego-enhancment, expression of aggression, or upward mobility. The salient feature of Negro Americans is that they have accepted and internalized American culture, but are generally denied the chief rewards and privileges of that culture. High crime rates are but one consequence of this situation.[21]

BACKGROUND: PHASES IN NEGRO-WHITE RELATIONS

The centuries-old interaction between African-descended and white Americans in the United States has followed a more complicated course than that of other minority situations requiring more adaptation of our general three phase schema. Bearing in mind that any attempt to mark off the phases and to date them must be arbitrary since always there is overlap, the following outline will be followed: (1) Slavery: white dominance over Negroes as slaves, 1619–1863; (2) Early reconstruction: decline in white dominance, 1866–1875; (3) Later reconstruction: the re-establishment of white dominance, 1875 to circa 1900; (4) The maintenance of the dominant white Southern biracial system, circa 1900–1954; (5) The establishment and maintenance of white dominance in the North, from World War I to World War II; and (6) The considerable decline in white dominance: in the North after World War II and in the South after May, 1954, and still in process.

The System of Slavery: The Colonial Period

Dominance of white Americans over Negroes was established at the outset from the time the first twenty slaves were bought by Virginia settlers in 1619. However, since there was no precedent in English law at this time, it seems to have been assumed that the status of slaves was similar to that of white indentured servants, with stipulated ways of being manumitted. But early in colonial history, differential treatment of Negroes began. For example, when three bound servants, two white and one Negro, had been brought back to Virginia from Maryland after attempting escape from servitude, the court, having ordered thirty lashes for all three, further ordered that the white servants should serve three years in bondage, but that the Negro should serve his master

[21]Pettigrew, *A Profile of the Negro American*, pp. 155–156.

for the rest of his life.[22] By court actions such as these, the differential status of Negroes evolved into a clear pattern of slavery, which eventually became established by more explicit law. In Virginia the slave status was fixed by a law making all non-Christians who came into the colony as servants from across the seas slaves for the rest of their lives. In 1682 this law was repealed and in its place another substituted "making slaves of all persons of non-Christian nationalities thereafter coming into the colony, whether they came by sea or land and whether or not they had been converted to Christianity after capture."[23]

Although early developing into a fixed institution, Negro slavery grew indispensable only as the plantation system of agriculture became important and more widespread. This system involved the large-scale production of a staple crop for commercial exchange and required cheap labor. At a time when land was either free or cheap, white men wanted to work as independent farmers, not as wage earners. Thus Negro slaves filled the increasing manpower demand. The colony of Georgia, founded in 1735, first prohibited the importation of Negro slaves, but by 1750, as the plantation system began to spread into the new colony, the act was repealed. The number of Negroes in Georgia increased from a reported 349 in 1750 to 15,000 by 1773.[24] The nexus between the plantation economy and slavery is further illustrated by the difference between the two Carolinas. In North Carolina the plantation economy failed to develop on a large scale and so did slavery; in South Carolina, where the plantation system developed on a large scale, "the number of Negroes had become so numerous that it was felt necessary to encourage the importation of white servants to secure the safety of the colony."[25] Finally, in the North, where there was no plantation economy, no large-scale slavery developed. By 1790, when the first federal census was taken, the proportion of free Negroes to those in slavery ranged from the all-free Negro population (5,462) in Massachusetts to other states where a third to a half of the resident Negroes were still slaves.[26]

The introduction of slavery into the colonies came as an extension of the institution already established in the West Indies. The slave trade was carried on largely by the British, although subsequently colonists themselves took a hand in it, especially

[22]Frazier, *The Negro in the United States*, p. 24.
[23]*Ibid.*, p. 26.
[24]*Ibid.*, pp. 32–33.
[25]*Ibid.*, p. 32.
[26]*Ibid.*, p. 34.

New England port merchants.[27] This trade was a highly hazardous and adventuresome occupation. It was not easy to get the slaves or to deliver them since, aside from the problem of holding them by force, great mortality occurred from the usually overcrowded conditions in the "Middle Passage" journeys. However, when things went well, as they obviously often did, the profits were high. Franklin writes, "It was not unusual for a ship carrying 250 slaves to net as much as £7,000 on one voyage. Profits of 100 per cent were not uncommon for Liverpool merchants."[28] Estimates of the number of slaves imported to the colonies and later to the states range from 500,000 to 700,000; and even though further importation was officially prohibited after 1808, Collins estimated that about 270,000 were imported between then and 1860.[29]

The National Period to the Civil War

In spite of the fixed position of slavery in the colonial economy during and for a short period following the Revolutionary War, there were signs that the slavery system might be abolished. Slavery was coming under increasing attack from a moral viewpoint, not only from Northerners but from enlighteend slaveholders such as Washington and Jefferson. The first President desired to see a plan adopted for the abolition of slavery; and Jefferson wrote in his autobiography, "Nothing is more certainly written in the book of fate than that these people are to be free."[30]

The attitude of the public was affected by economic interests as well as moral idealism. Frazier indicates that opposition to slavery was expressed in Delaware, Maryland, and Virginia, where a diversified agriculture was supplanting the production of tobacco, whereas in the lower South, where the production of tobacco, rice, and indigo was still important, there was strong opposition either to suspending the slave trade or to the emancipation of the Negro.[31] In the midst of these conflicting attitudes toward slavery, the Constitution of the new republic compromised on the issue by setting 1808 as the date after which the importation of slaves was to be abolished. The abolition of slavery in many

[27]Maurice R. Davie, *Negroes in American Society* (New York: McGraw-Hill Book Co., 1949), p. 18.
[28]John Hope Franklin, *From Slavery to Freedom* (New York: Alfred A. Knopf, 1947), p. 57.
[29]Winfield H. Collins, *The Domestic Slave Trade of the Southern States* (New York: Broadway Publishing Company, 1904), p. 20.
[30]Myrdal, *An American Dilemma*, p. 85.
[31]Frazier, *The Negro in the United States*, p. 35.

state constitutions in the North and its declining economic significance led many people to share with Jefferson the belief that slavery was on its way out.

But the hopes of those opposed to slavery were destined to be dashed by the invention of the cotton gin. With this invention Southern cotton planters were able to meet the rapidly growing demand of the English market. The expansion of cotton economy increased by leaps and bounds, especially from 1815 on. This development was accompanied by the growth of the slave system and the slave population. (See Table 5–3.)

TABLE 5-3   GROWTH OF THE SLAVE POPULATION IN THE UNITED STATES, 1790–1860*

Census Year	Slave Population	Per cent of Decennial Increase
1790	697,624	—
1800	893,602	28.1
1810	1,191,362	33.3
1820	1,538,022	29.1
1830	2,009,043	30.6
1840	2,487,355	18.8
1850	3,204,313	28.8
1860	3,953,760	23.4

*United States Bureau of the Census, *Negro Population in the United States, 1790–1915* (Washington, D.C., 1918), p. 53.

From 1790 to 1803 the natural increase of the slave population was supplemented by foreign importation of over 100,000 slaves. Although, as Table 5–3 shows, the percentage of increase after 1810 declined, a substantial number of slaves was smuggled in to augment the natural increase. As the plantation system spread south and west away from Maryland, Virginia, and Kentucky, many slaves were bred for sale by their first owners to work in the new areas.[32]

Having built not only its economy but a total society on the foundation of slavery, the South needed rationalizations which would justify it. Thus there began to emerge in the pre-Civil War period learned treatises solemnly concluding that "the Negro" was naturally meant to be a slave and that he was obviously inferior to the white. Many of these treatises invoked Biblical sanction and

[32]*Ibid.*, p. 42.

two of the most scholarly were written by Presbyterian ministers.[33] The growing intellectual support for the established system reached its climax in the words of Chief Justice Taney, who in his famous decision in the Dred Scott case declared, "A Negro has no rights which a white man need respect."[34]

Thus it appeared clear that, far from declining, the slave system during the early nineteenth century in the South grew constantly stronger. This is important to keep in mind as we turn to the reconstruction days. It does much to explain why the Emancipation Proclamation, which freed slaves in the legal sense, did not protect them from the caste barriers that were erected to supplant those of slavery.

The American Slave System: Comparison with Latin America Slave Systems

The degree of authority accorded to the master is affected by many factors, of which the economic role of the slaves and the character of the other institutions in the society are important. The actual exercise of the permitted authority was sometimes influenced by the human qualities of affection, on the one hand, and of aggresiveness and cupidity on the other, qualities which are in part structured by the general culture but which always vary to some extent with individual personalities. Too, the responses of slaves to their condition varied with their cultural level and their personality variables.

In Latin America, where a slave system flourished for many years, law, religion, and the mores of the society made the formal status of slaves considerably different from that of slaves in the British-settled area of South America and in the southern United States.[35]

First, in Latin America, slaves had rights protecting them against many specific abuses from their masters. The power to inflict certain physical punishments upon slaves was limited by

[33]*Ibid.*, pp. 46–47.
[34]*Ibid.*, p. 43. This decision involved a slave who sued for freedom because his master had taken him to Illinois to live for sometime before returning with Scott to Missouri. Scott lost the case because the court ruled that the phrase in the constitution "people of the United States" was not meant to apply to slaves.
[35]Frank Tannenbaum, *Slave and Citizen* (New York: Alfred A. Knopf, 1947), p. 49. Much of material is drawn from this book. However, Marvin Harris in *Patterns of Race in the Americas* (New York: Walker Co., 1964) criticizes Tannenbaum's overemphasis on the actual effect of this formal pattern upon the actual treatment of slaves by Brazilian plantation owners which he found to be similarly brutal to that found in the American South.

law, and slaves could obtain legal redress if the master over-stepped these bounds. Married slaves could not be separated from each other against their will. "The children followed the status of their mother, and the child of a free mother remained free even if she later became a slave."[36] We have seen that the slave had practically no protection by law from the arbitrary exercise of authority by the master. The slave had no property rights. Married partners could be separated from each other, and children from their parents. That they were is attested to in advertisements of the day, such as this:

> NEGROES FOR SALE. A Negro woman, 24 years of age, and her two children, one eight and the other three years old. Said negroes will be sold SEPARATELY, or together, *as desired*. The woman is a good seamstress. She will be sold low for cash, or EXCHANGED FOR GROCERIES. For terms, apply to Matthew Bliss and Co., 1 Front Levee.[37]

Second, the Latin system favored manumission, and a more-or-less steady change from slavery to freedom was going on all the time. "A hundred social devices . . . encouraged the master to release his slave, and the bondsman to achieve freedom on his own acount."[38] The American system operated to prevent manu-mission. While some slaves were freed, as the system grew in strength during the early nineteenth century the pressures against this became greater.

A third contrast is seen in the difference in the status of former slaves once they became free. In Latin America the freed person, whatever his racial lineage, assumed a place equal to that of all others in the civic community. Authorities differ as to whether or not Negro ancestry might have been a handicap in the class status system of Latin America, but there seems little doubt that many Negroes came to occupy high public position and that white-colored intermarriage was never looked upon with the abhorrence that it is looked upon in the United States. Although the position of the Negro freed before general abolition was in some respects higher than that of those still enslaved, the fact that he was still a Negro meant that he was considered an inferior person.

Among the various social forces which Tannenbaum offers in explanation of the contrasts in these two slave systems was the

[36]*Ibid.*
[37]*New Orleans Bee*, quoted in Tannenbaum, *Slave and Citizen*, p. 77. By permission of the publishers, Alfred A. Knopf.
[38]Tannenbaum, *Slave and Citizen*, pp. 53–54.

presence in the Latin-American legal system of Spanish law, with its established precedents of specific definition of slave status, and the absence of any corresponding precedents in British law. He further notes the influence of Catholic doctrine in contrast to the position of Protestantism. Although the Church did not interfere with the institution when the domestic law accepted it, it had early condemned the slave trade and officially prohibited Catholics from participating in it, not too successfully. Still further, the Church considered that slave and master were equal in the sight of God, gave slaves the right to baptism, and insisted that masters bring their slaves to church. This stands in sharp contrast to the total neglect of Negroes by the Episcopal Church in the British West Indies, and to the position of the Protestant denominations in the South of the United States. After 1700 there was no systematic opposition to teaching the Christian doctrine to the Negro slave, but the churches in the South generally made no attack on the institution of slavery itself.

Slavery: Interpersonal Relations

Slavery as a system of human relations cannot be maintained without the use of force. While most slave states passed statutes designed to protect the slave from unnecessary sufferings, in practice, these were seldom enforced. Thus the disciplining of Negroes was left largely to the master or his white overseer, who was restrained only by his own conscience and such group pressure as the white mores of the community brought to bear. When it was felt to be necessary, the masters did inflict corporal punishment and even death on the slaves.

Nevertheless, the relations between the two racial groups came to be ordered by a system of etiquette and ritual which more or less explicitly defined the proper reciprocal behavior whenever members of the two races were together. The actual relations between groups never perfectly coincide with the formal status. White-Negro relations under slavery were sometimes overlaid with a sense of mutual responsibility and reciprocal affections. This was particularly true with house servants who identified themselves with the family, and who were often biologically related to it.

On the other hand, Aptheker documented about 250 slave insurrections and rebellions involving ten or more people.[39] Better

---

[39]Herbert Aptheker, *American Slave Revolts* (New York: Columbia University Press, 1943), p. 162.

known is the fact that many slaves attempted to flee to free territory, some successfully. The odds, however, against either rebellion or escape were so overwhelming that some form of accomodation to the inevitable was the price of survival. Accommodation to slavery required taking on—at least as role playing—all the traits of servility and dependence.

Reconstruction

BRIEF CHALLENGE TO WHITE DOMINANCE   The emancipation of slaves and the end of the Civil War were followed by a brief challenge to white dominance. But emancipation was forced upon the South against its will, of course, and the implication of freedom could be carried through only by a costly, large-scale federal program and the application of considerable pressures upon the South. The problem was twofold: how to implement and guarantee the new political status of Negroes as free men; and how to reconstruct the economy of the South in such a manner that Negroes would have a secure economic position.

The war had wrought enormous material property losses on Southern whites, as well as taking away their slaves. Many of the freed slaves who, both during the war and immediately after it, had flocked to the cities or to the vicinity of Northern army camps found no means of livelihood. In 1865 the Bureau of Refugees, Freedmen, and Abandoned Lands was established to aid in the economic rehabilitation of the freedmen, as well as the property-less whites, and to promote an educational program for the Negroes. The general plan was to furnish land and tools with which the freedmen and landless whites might become self-sustaining farmers.

However, during the seven years of its existence (1865–1872), the Bureau was unable to accomplish its economic objectives. It had woefully inadequate funds for the size of the job. The amnesty granted former Confederates restored to them the land which had already been leased to Negroes, who consequently became landless again. When efforts were made to resettle both white and Negro tenants on public lands in the Gulf areas, inability to raise enough capital and general discouragement with the whole program spelled failure. The desire of the more influential portion of the white South to retain the traditional system of agricultural production and to keep the Negro in his servile place did nothing to help. And the half-hearted support of Northerners contributed to the failure of the government to carry through the program. The lukewarm support was due in part to the usual reluctance to appropriate the rather large funds needed for the task. Northerners, although believing in theoretical freedom for Negroes, were far from advocating that they be accorded full, equal status. The combination of proprietary interest in the South and the traditional white attitudes toward the proper status of Negroes, shared by many Northerners as well as nearly all the white South, conspired to defeat what appears in retrospect to have been a validly conceived plan for the economic rehabilitation of the South.

The same combination of interests and attitudes appeared in opposition to the fulfillment of the other objective in the Northern plan for reconstruction of the South: to make Negroes first-class citizens. Soon after the close of the war, eight Southern states instituted the so-called Black Codes. By various statutes affecting apprenticeship, labor contracts, debts, and vagrancy, these codes went far to reestablish the servile position of Negroes. Frazier cites the following example:

> The Florida code states that if any person of color failed to fulfill the stipulations of a contract into which he entered with a plantation owner or was impudent to the owner, he should be declared a vagrant and be subject to punishment for vagrancy.[40]

When the Republican government of the North realized that the South was in fact nullifying the Emancipation Proclamation, it set about to exert pressure to force acceptance. Through the Fourteenth Amendment to the Constitution, declared effective in 1866, abridgement of the full civic equality of all citizens was declared unlawful, and the supplementary Fifteenth Amendment, effective in 1870, specifically denied the right to abridgement of the voting privilege "on account of race, color, or previous condition of servitude." Still further, Congress passed in 1867 a series of reconstruction acts which called for the temporary governing of the South by military rule until such time as genuinely democratic elections could be held and governments so elected should get under way. In the governments which followed, many Negroes were elected to state assemblies, and twenty were sent to Congress. Some of these Negro officials demonstrated unusual ability.

In these turbulent years the majority of Southerners naturally

[40]Frazier, *The Negro in the United States*, p. 127.

resented the attempt of the "carpetbaggers" to reconstruct their society, aided by their own "scalawags," as the Southerners who cooperated with the Yankee officials were called. They made much of the point that complete civic equality for Negroes would give the colored population control over the South. Actually, in no state were Negroes ever the dominating factor in the government, though in several states they constituted about half the population. The Southern attitude toward the Negro was not reconstructed, as the testimony of Carl Schurz indicates:

> Wherever I go . . . I hear the people talk in such a way as to indicate that they are yet unable to conceive of the Negro as possessing any rights at all. . . . The people boast that when they get freedmen's affairs in their own hands . . . "the niggers will catch hell."
>   The reason of all this is simple and manifest. The whites esteem the blacks their property by natural right, and however much they admit that the individual relations of masters and slaves have been destroyed by the war and by the President's emancipation proclamation, they still have an ingrained feeling that the blacks at large belong to the whites at large.[41]

The next phase of the reconstruction drama opened as the Republican Congress began to weaken. In 1872, the disabilities imposed on the former Confederate leaders, which prevented their participation in political affairs, were removed. The Freedmen's Bureau was abolished, depriving many Negro laborers and tenants of much-needed economic support and moral aid. The climax came when the Civil Rights bill of 1875 was declared unconstitutional. This bill, as Myrdal puts it, "represented the culmination of the Federal reconstruction legislation, was explicit in declaring that all persons . . . should be entitled to the full and equal enjoyment of the accommodations, advantages, facilities, and privileges of inns, public conveyances on land and water, theaters, and other places of public amusement . . . applicable alike to citizens of every race and color, regardless of previous condition of servitude."[42] When the bill was declared unconstitutional, the North seems to have given up.

From 1875 on, the door was open for the unreconstructed

[41]Report of Carl Schurz, Senate Executive Document, No. 2, 39th Congress, 1st Session, cited by W. E. B. DuBois, *Black Reconstruction in America* (New York: Harcourt, Brace & Co., 1936).
[42]Myrdal, *An American Dilemma*, p. 579. By permission.

white Southerners to carry out their own program of reconstruction. The result was the biracial pattern of race relations in which the dominance of white over colored was assured. This social system has remained broadly intact down to the late 1950s. Reconstruction on this biracial basis involved the use of both legal and illegal procedures, since in the white Southern view Negroes had already advanced too far. The illegal phase of the reconstruction was spearheaded by a number of secret societies, of which the Ku Klux Klan is the most widely known. Extralegal activities were supplemented by further Black Code legislation, which segregated Negroes and otherwise accorded them unequal privileges. While it took some years to accomplish the task, the white South succeeded in establishing a color-caste system.

Reconstruction: An Object Lesson

What happened in the reconstruction period is an excellent object lesson in social science. It illustrates the consequences of attempting swift and radical social change without adequate social planning. In hindsight, it is clear that the federal government attempted to accomplish too sweeping objectives in too short a time against too strong a set of opposing forces and with too little public support from the North itself. For example, how could it have been expected that white Southerners, long steeped in the tradition of slavery, could change their complex attitudes and habits concerning Negroes overnight? Again, how could it have been expected that slaves, held to such a low level of literacy and moulded into a servile, dependent personality pattern, could immediately become self-reliant and civically active? Furthermore, how could it have been expected that such a program could be carried on without a greater consensus of Northern opinion to support it? To raise such questions in hindsight and to leave the matter there is obviously unfair to the many intelligent and socially conscious white people, both North and South who set the objectives and tried to carry them out. Neither the theoretical knowledge of human nature and social processes nor the accumulated practice of social engineering had advanced to a point in 1865 to have made success possible. We cite the lesson for its value at the present time.

The United States is now in an extraordinary period of disequilibrium in white-Negro relations, precipitated by the Supreme Court's school desegregation decision. We face this period with a considerably greater body of social theory, techniques, and practices in intergroup relations. In areas of the nation where the attitudes of the dominant group are not too intransigent, some of this knowledge has been usefully applied as will be discussed in later chapters.

Suggested Readings

Aptheker, Herbert. *American Negro Slave Revolts.* New York: Columbia University Press, 1943.
   The most complete history of the subject.
Baughman, E. Earl. *Black Americans: A Psychological Analysis.* New York: Academic Press, 1971.
   A recent interpretation of psychological nature of black Americans based on a survey of research up to 1968.
Berry, Brewton. *Almost White.* New York: Macmillan Co., 1963.
   A study of pockets of people with mixtures of Indian, white, and Negro lineage found in over 200 communities in the Eastern United States occupying anomalous status position.
Elkins, Stanley M. *Slavery: A Problem in American Institutional and Intellectual Life.* Chicago: The University of Chicago Press, 1959.
   An institutional approach to the subject.
Franklin, John Hope. "Brief History of the Negro in the United States," Chapter 1 of the *American Negro Reference Book.* Englewood Cliffs, N.J.: Prentice-Hall, 1966, edited by John P. Davis.
   An outstanding historian of the American Negro summarizes the subject in seventy-five pages.
Myrdal, Gunnar, et. al. *An American Dilemma: The Negro Problem and Modern Democracy.* New York: Harper & Brothers, 1944.
   The most comprehensive assemblage of facts about Negroes in relation to whites in American society. The Swedish writer has presented his own interpretation of the data and researches provided by scores of American scholars. Chapter 7, "Population"; Chapter 8, "Migration"; and Chapter 10, "The Tradition of Slavery," bear on this chapter.
Stampp, Kenneth. *The Peculiar Institution.* New York: Alfred A. Knopf, 1956.
   A scholarly approach to slavery.
Tauber, Karl E. and Alma F. Tauber. *Negroes in Cities.* New York: Atheneum, 1969.
   A thorough description and analysis of residential segregation and neighborhood change.
————. "The Negro Population in the United States." Chapter 2 of *The Negro Reference Book,* ed. John P. Davis. Englewood Cliffs, N.J.: Prentice-Hall, 1966.
   A briefer treatment of the subject.

6 **N**egro-White Relations: The Traditional Southern Pattern

The previous chapter briefly delineated the process by which the white South reestablished dominance in a new pattern of race relations after the abortive attempt to develop racial equality following emancipation and the Civil War. This chapter will describe this system and consider its implications for the South and the nation. By 1910 it had been crystallized and remained essentially intact to World War II. In view of the post-war changes, we employ the past tense generally even though much of this pattern still prevails, especially in the Deep South. The still strong resistance to change in the South is better understood by keeping in mind that most of today's adult white Southerners have been conditioned since birth to the biracial system here described.

The South includes seventeen states and the District of Columbia. The following states are considered border states: Delaware, Kentucky, Maryland, Missouri, Tennessee, Oklahoma, and West Virginia. The term "Deep South" is not so definite geographically. It certainly includes Alabama, Georgia, Louisiana, Mississippi, and South Carolina. Arkansas, Florida, North Carolina, Texas, Virginia, and the District of Columbia account for the rest of the South.[1]

---

[1]To Southerners "Deep South" meant the areas where the plantation economy earlier was extensive and vigorous.

CASTE SYSTEM

In common with many other, although not all, students of minorities, we shall designate this Southern interracial pattern as a caste system. In its ideology and in the institutions which governed race relations, the categorical segregation of the two races in a large number of social relations was clear. Intermarriage was flatly prohibited. While specific identification with a particular occupation, as was characteristic of the traditional Hindu caste system, was not so marked, nevertheless the Southern pattern did not generally permit the performance together of the same tasks by members of the two races. Furthermore, the rising middle class of Negroes in the South was in the main segregated from the white middle class. It was the absence of explicit religious sanctions in support of its biracial system which mainly distinguished the Southern pattern from other caste systems.

The Southern caste system had two main features—segregation and the so-called caste etiquette. The former involved the physical separation of Negroes from whites; the latter included the rules to be followed when interaction must unavoidably take place between one or more members of each race. Both the patterns of segregation and the caste etiquette always symbolized the superordination of the white people and the subordination of the Negroes.

Segregation[2]

Residentially, in rural areas, Negroes were scattered but did not live close to whites except on plantations, where the mansion was separated conspicuously, though often not far, from the Negroes' shacks. In small towns there was a clustering of Negro homes on edges of the community. In Southern cities there were varieties of Negro residential patterns: the back-alley residence plan, as seen in Charleston; the isolated community, as in Tulsa; the one large Negro area with smaller scattered clusters found in many cities. Interestingly enough, Southern whites did not appear to object to having Negro families live near them, as Northern whites did. However, in the South when homes of Negro families

[2]See Charles S. Johnson, *Patterns of Negro Segregation* (New York: Harper & Brothers, 1943), for the fullest single-volume discussion of segregation at the height of the development of the system.

were spatially proximate to those of white families, there was usually some outward manifestation of the superior-inferior status—for example, whites facing the streets and Negroes, the alleys.

A striking example of segregation was in hospitalization. In some places there were isolated wards for Negroes. But more often the hospitals would not admit Negroes, and there were few Negro hospitals. Instances occurred of Negroes in need of emergency operations dying because the nearest hospitals would not admit them.

ECONOMIC SEGREGATION   Segregation in economic life had two main aspects: in employment, and in the role of the Negro as a customer. In regard to employment, the basic principle was that Negroes must not work alongside whites on equal functional terms. For instance, one restaurant might have all Negro waitresses and another across the street all white waitresses, but no restaurant would mix the two. This principle operated to limit Negro employment to occupations which whites did not care to enter. (The one important exception was tenant farming, in which both races engaged but in which they did not work together.) As a result, the most menial and the poorest paid occupations were left for Negroes. When technological improvements came along to make any particular occupation more rewarding, the whites tried to keep the Negroes out, as they did following the introduction of farm tractors and the mechanical cotton picker.

Until 1935 labor unions in the South excluded Negroes from membership, or at most permitted them to organize in separate auxiliary locals. Since the earlier days of the caste period, Negroes had become a majority in certain semiskilled or skilled trades; the development of unions had the effect of driving them from these occupations. The elimination of Negroes as engineers on railroad locomotives and the gradual decline in the number of Negro firemen and brakemen correlated with the rise of the railway workers' union.

The color line was less rigidly drawn against the Negro as a customer in commercial establishments. Two generalizations held largely true. The cheaper the price level of the goods to be sold, the more welcome was the Negro trade. Thus the five-and-ten-cent stores and the chain food stores generally welcomed Negro trade and provided reasonably courteous service, while the more exclusive stores either refused or discouraged Negro patronage through discourtesy. The other general rule was that the more intimate the personal relationship involved in a commercial transaction, the more likely the Negro was to be excluded. In beauty parlor and mortuary services the races were strictly separated. But when the services rendered, though involving considerable interpersonal relationships, were such that the position of the vendor was clearly superior to that of the buyer, as in the case of medical or legal counsel, white professional people often would take Negro clients.

EDUCATION   Seventeen states had entirely separate school systems. No contact at all took place between the teachers or pupils of the two systems except the unavoidable contact of the white superintendent. This separation went far to root firmly in the attitudes and habits of children of both races the practice of race segregation. Negroes were not admitted generally into public libraries in the South, and a Negro had no access to library facilities unless he could get a white friend to take out a book for him. In a few large cities Negro branch libraries were established.

PUBLIC SEGREGATION   Public recreational facilities were generally scarce in the South outside the large cities, and whites did not share those that existed with the Negroes. Negroes were generally excluded from public parks, and only a few cities had parks for Negroes. Except where a special section of a public playground was set aside for them, the colored people were not permitted to use public playgrounds. At one time, a common sign in Southern parks was "Negroes, Soldiers, and Dogs Keep Out."
In hotels and restaurants the segregation was absolute and complete. Outside the larger cities, where some Negro hotels and restaurants existed, it was impossible for Negroes who were traveling to get a meal or lodging unless some Negro family gave them hospitality. In public buildings, such as post offices, and tax offices, Negroes usually waited in line until every white person appearing had been served. Separate toilets for each race was the general rule in public places where both races were admitted. The best-known device of the segregation system was "Jim Crow" transportation. In local transportation, where the vehicles were often not physically partitioned, Negroes had to go to the rear and whites to the front, the dividing line being set on each trip by the proportion of each race aboard. Of this Johnson wrote:

"The operator is empowered to regulate the space occupied by each race in accordance with the respective number of passengers. This system is subject to abuse since it permits the attitude of the operator to become a factor in segregation."[3]

The Code of Race Etiquette

Since Negroes were an important part of the economic life of the South, they could not be totally segregated. To allow for some interpersonal relations there developed an elaborate pattern of racial etiquette,[4] the function of which was to make clear the superordinate caste positions. For example, a white man did not shake hands with a Negro when introduced to him. An exception would be when a white man visited a Negro college or, sometimes, a Negro home. The white person did not address the Negro person as "Mr." or "Mrs.," but rather by his first name or by his last without the courtesy title; the Negro always addressed the white person as "Mister," "Marse," or "Missus," or better still by some such title as "Colonel," which often the white man did not actually possess. Professionally trained Negroes could be addressed as "Professor," "Doctor," or "Reverend." Negro women were never referred to as "ladies," but either as just "women," or, irrespective of age, as "girls." Negro men were expected to doff their hats when they spoke to white men, but the latter were not expected to reciprocate. When Negroes called at white men's homes, they came to the rear door; the white man, of course, always appeared at the front door. Whenever circumstances brought Negroes and white people together at mealtime or on recreational occasions, the races were not expected to sit together at the same table or play together. Thus when a white person visited a colored home, if the Negro hostess wished to provide food for her guest, etiquette prescribed that they not eat together. With the exception of quite young children, Negroes and whites did not ordinarily play together.

Endogamy is the primary principle of caste. Marriage across caste lines was not recognized and was forbidden by law in Southern states. Most adamant of all the taboos was the one against any sort of casual interpersonal relations between a white

[3]*Ibid.*, p. 49.
[4]See Bertram W. Doyle, *The Etiquette of Race Relations in the South* (Chicago: University of Chicago Press, 1937), for a fuller description of the subject.

woman and a Negro man. No one thing was more dangerous to a Negro male than to be in a situation that could be even remotely construed as indicating personal interest in a white female. Negro men understood this and acted accordingly. Brought up to know that the rope or faggot await the Negro accused—falsely or otherwise—of "sexual" interest in a white woman, Negro men in the South, as a general rule, avoided white women.

The Interrelation of Class and Caste

In the South the class system was linked with the caste system in significant ways. In most Southern communities, particularly in cities, class differentiation developed within the Negro caste. Negroes performing higher-ranking functions—ministers, teachers, doctors, farm agents—had achieved a higher-class status within their racial group. The class position of such Negroes was generally recognized by the white people, and they were accorded differential treatment from that accorded the lower-class Negroes. Frequently upper-class whites came to the defense of higher-class Negroes who got into trouble with lower-class whites. Warner and Davis cite the case of a colored professional man who accidentally ran down and killed with his car a drunken lower-class white man. Local bankers offered money for the Negro's defense, and upper-class white women called at his place of business to indicate that they supported him in his difficulty.[5]

This class bond which cut across caste lines prompted upper-class whites on occasion to attend special functions conducted by upper-class Negroes, and at such occasions special courtesies not generally acorded Negroes by caste etiquette might be extended by the whites, such as addressing the Negro women as "Mrs."

This class-differentiated aspect of the caste system operated more to strengthen caste, however, than to undermine it. While it accorded upper-class Negroes some differential privileges, these always fell clearly short of equality; and to receive them upper-class Negroes had to accept caste, at least outwardly. This special relation also served practical purposes in the maintenance of the biracial system. While caste relations are fundamentally antagonistic, they cannot exist without some degree of cooperation. In their function as leaders, the middle- and upper-class Negroes

[5]W. Lloyd Warner and Allison Davis, "A Comparative Study of American Caste," in *Race Relations and the Race Problem*, ed., Edgar T. Thompson (Durham: Duke University Press, 1939), p. 243.

were expected to exert their influence to control the Negro masses to preserve order.[6]

METHODS OF ENFORCING CASTE

The methods employed for sustaining this caste pattern of race relations in the South may be conveniently treated under the headings of legal methods, illegal force and intimidation, and custom. Bearing in mind that at many points these three methods of social control reinforce each other, we shall discuss each separately.

Legal Methods

Specific local and state laws required segregation of the two races in many of the categories of interaction noted above. Southern state supreme courts upheld these laws, and for a long time the Supreme Court of the United States upheld Southern segregation laws in the cases reaching it. One important exception concerns housing segregation by state or municipal law. In 1915, a Louisville, Kentucky, city ordinance forbidding Negroes to reside in certain areas was declared unconstitutional by the United States Supreme Court.[7] It further ruled that the segregated public facilities and services provided Negroes should be equal to those provided for whites. As we shall presently indicate, every description of the facilities for Negroes in the South documented the fact that Negroes did not have equal public facilities, in spite of this interpretation of the Constitution. Segregation continued to be upheld by local law.

DENIAL OF VOTING   Between 1890 and 1910, eleven Southern states adopted special requirements for voting designed to deny Negroes the franchise. One was the poll tax, requiring the citizen to pay a special tax of a dollar or two for the privilege of voting. While not a large sum, by various other devices it was made to serve its purpose. Sometimes the tax was retroactive—

---

[6]These class-linked relations should not be confused with the intergroup relations which are in substance nonconformity to caste. There have been, of course, throughout the whole period considered, a few white people here and there, more particularly in cities, who did not believe in caste and who, with due deference to the personal costs of nonconformity, have participated in informal mixed gatherings on a plane of social equality.
[7]See Johnson, *Patterns of Negro Segregation*, p. 175.

that is to say, in order to vote in any one year, poll tax receipts for a number of years had to be shown if asked for by the election official. An arrearage of, say, $10 was effective in keeping a Negro from voting.

Negroes were barred from voting in the Democratic primary with the excuse that any political party may restrict its membership. Before 1941 the United States Supreme Court in decisions concerning these white primary regulations failed to overrule the specific laws in this connection. Other qualifications for voting left opportunity for discrimination through their administration. For example, educational tests were sometimes stipulated. By asking Negro applicants for registration questions concerning government which they could not possibly answer, officials could keep them off the list. Or such devices as giving the Negroes only a day for registration when the white officials were not available were further employed.

Illegal Violence and Intimidation

Not all segregation and race etiquette, however, was upheld by law. The part of it not so covered was reinforced by intimidation and extralegal violence. The Negro who violated the customary etiquette found himself brought to order by whites by abusive language and warnings. If he persisted in violation or if the breach was considered particularly heinous from the dominant caste's viewpoint, he might be physically maltreated or even lynched. If the violations appeared to be in any sense en masse, a whole Negro street or area might be destroyed by white groups as a way of "teaching the nigger to keep his place." The authors of the book *Deep South* write:

> In fact, it is considered entirely correct for the white person to resort directly to physical attack upon the Negro. Thus, if a Negro curses a white, the white may knock the Negro down; and the failure to do so may even be considered as a failure in duty as a white. . . .
>
> It is a common belief of many whites that Negroes will respond only to violent methods. In accordance with the theory of the "animal-like" nature of the Negro, they believe that the formal punishments of fines and imprisonments fail to act as deterrents to crime.[8]

[8]Allison Davis, Burleigh Gardner, and Mary R. Gardner, *Deep South* (Chicago: University of Chicago Press, 1941), pp. 45–46. By permission.

A planter puts the traditional Southern white viewpoint thus:

> The best thing is not to take these young bucks into the court house for some small crime but to give them a paddling. That does them more good than a jail sentence. If I catch a Negro stealing a hog or some chickens, what is the use of taking him into court? He would get a fine or a jail sentence and unless I pay him out he will lie up in jail, and when he gets out he will keep on stealing.[9]

As a result of this traditional support of intimidation and violence, law itself was caste-patterned, applying very unequally to the two races. When any altercation occurred involving a white and a Negro, the Negro was usually presumed to be wrong. The word of a white person was ordinarily taken against that of a Negro, even when many whites knew that the white person was lying. Furthermore, the law failed to protect the Negro against extralegal violence on the part of whites. It was generally impossible to get anybody to testify that he had any knowledge about illegal acts of violence perpetrated against Negroes. As a result, lynching after lynching occurred in the South. Even those reported in the national press, where the fact of lynching was incontrovertible, seldom resulted in indictments and trials. Negroes were carefully kept off juries in the South. However, Federal Supreme Court reversals of Negro convictions where the defense argued successfully that Negroes in the communities involved were purposely not called to jury duty began to break this caste practice to a degree.[10] For a long time the only chance for some measure of justice for the Negroes was if they had a white protector who would intercede for them. Frequently an employer would say a good word for his Negro employee and get the case dismissed or the sentence lightened.

White Southerners at times resorted to intimidation and violence for the purpose of preventing Negroes from voting. Davie furnishes the following example: "There are numerous instances of Negroes who attempted to register or vote being driven away, beaten up, or killed. More generally the opposition took the form of intimidation. For example, a Negro went to the registration booth in his county and asked if he could register. The white official replied: 'Oh, yes, you can register, but I want to tell you

[9]*Ibid.*, p. 46.
[10]Myrdal, *An American Dilemma* (New York: Harper & Brothers, 1944), p. 549.

something. Some God-damn niggers are going to get killed about this voting business yet.' " In Dennison, Texas, in the fall of 1932, handbills were scattered throughout the town reading as follows:

NIGGER!
The white people do not want you to vote Saturday.
Do not make the Ku Klux Klan take a hand.
Do you remember what happened two years ago, May 9?
George Hughes was burned to death, the county courthouse destroyed. . . . For good reason.

Riots on election day in which both whites and Negroes were killed occurred in various sections of the South.[11]

Custom

The casual traveler in the South would not have noticed the intimidation we have mentioned. He saw for the most part an orderly pattern of segregation and race etiquette. On the surface he saw no resentment. But, although indications of intimidation were not present each day, no Negro brought up in the South was unaware of the threat of violence. Negro children were taught by their earliest experience with white people to conform to the established pattern. Negro parents had to punish the rebellious inclinations of their children who naïvely approached white persons as equal human beings.[12] And the white children in the South were, of course, conditioned to assume all the appropriate attitudes and behavior patterns of the dominant caste. Any tendency to really like Negro children had to be sternly disciplined to make sure that they were not treated as equals. Thus the Southern caste pattern was supported by the conditioning and custom of the Southerners of both races to assume the reciprocal social roles required to keep it intact—the white to be arrogant, exploitative, superior; the Negro to be submissive, exploited, and inferior. Most of the time this combination of implicit intimidation and habituation worked quite successfully. The Negro who occasionally threw caution to the wind and rebelled against the pattern was dealt with summarily. The white person whose conscience occasionally

[11]By permission from *Negroes in American Society*, by M. R. Davie. Copyright 1949. McGraw-Hill Book Co., p. 266.
[12]See Calvin C. Hernton, *Sex and Racism in America* (Garden City, N.Y.: Doubleday and Company, 1965), pp. 53–58, for personal testimony.

pricked him submerged his inclination under the pressure of public sentiment.

EFFECTS OF THE CASTE SYSTEM

In discussing the effects of the race caste system as it operated in the South we will consider its effect on personality and behavior, on the welfare of the Negro, on social organization in Southern communities, and on the political and economic development of the region.

Effects on White Personality

The value of treating the social structure as an independent variable and the normative behavior of the people reared in it as the dependent variable is well illustrated by considering how being reared in the Southern biracial system affected the personality of the white Southerner. One of the earliest and best-known field studies of the Southern racial system was that of John Dollard of a cotton community.[13] Dollard analyzed the gains accruing to white people under the caste system which were in turn "losses" to the Negroes. First was the economic gain, enabling white people to exploit Negroes as workers and consumers. A typical year for the Negro tenant farmer ran as follows: After the cotton had been sold and the Negro had paid his debts, he was broke. The landlord advanced him "furnish" to carry him through the next harvest. The charges for this "furnish" were not regulated and the accounting was typically in the landlord's hands. While this exploitative advantage was not always completely utilized, it was difficult for the Negro to get justice if his accounting differed from that of the landlord.

Second, Dollard mentions the "sexual gain." The system gave white men exploitative sexual opportunity with Negro women, while any sexual advances of Negro men toward white women were absolutely tabooed and infractions often punished by death. The white caste ideology considered Negro women sexually promiscuous and therefore the numerous white males who took this advantage felt little guilt whether they used force, or otherwise

[13]John Dollard, *Caste and Class in a Southern Town* (New Haven: Yale University Press, 1937).

made it economically or socially advantageous for Negro women to submit.

The third gain Dollard saw accruing to the white caste was "ego" gratification. The daily expressions of superiority toward all Negroes which the whites could indulge and the responses of submissiveness by the Negroes bolstered the self-esteem of the whites, especially those among the less privileged ranks.

The normative white Southerner was a person who assumed the superordinate role toward Negroes which involved considerable ambivalence. The role called for "bullying" and exploiting Negroes and for treating with patronizing kindness those Negroes who acted in the appropriate subordinate role. It also called for unwavering defense of the system—ideological and behavioral. There were two types of deviant white Southerners: those who carried the superordinate role too far, who were over-bullyish and exploitative, lost repute but not status and were not otherwise punished for such behavior, even though it was often illegal. The other deviant type of white Southerner was rare, one who openly called for and occasionally participated in some organized attempt to challenge the established system.

Lillian Smith, depicts the effect of the system on white Southerners. In *Killers of the Dream* she describes her own childhood experience when her parents had taken into their family an apparently white child living with a Negro family only to return the child again to its adopted parents when it was discovered that in fact the child had Negro lineage. Miss Smith wrote as follows:

> Something was wrong with a world that tells you love is good and people are important and then forces you to deny love and to humiliate people. I knew, though I would not for years confess it aloud, that in trying to shut the Negro race away from us, we have shut ourselves away from so many good, creative, honest, deeply human things in life. I began to understand slowly at first but more clearly as the years passed, that the *warped, distorted frame we have put around every Negro child from birth is around every white child also.* Each is on a different side of the frame but each is pinioned there. And I knew that what cruelly shapes and cripples the personality of one is as cruelly shaping and crippling the personality of the other. I began to see that though we may, as we acquire new knowledge, live through new experiences, examine old memories, gain the strength to tear the frame from us, yet we are stunted and warped and *in our lifetime cannot grow straight again* any more than can a tree, put in a

steel-like twisting frame when young, grow tall and straight when the frame is torn away at maturity.[14]

Effects upon Negro Behavior and Personality

Dollard's study essentially covers the range of possible personality and behavioral adjustments of Negroes to the inevitable frustrations of being brought up in such a system.[15] However, in line with more recent theoretical analysis we distinguish between the normative type of adjustment and the more deviant adjustments. The normative adjustment was to accept the role assigned to a Negro under the system—to be docile, servile, and to adhere to the rules of etiquette and segregation. This type of behavior was sometimes accompanied by an internalization of the white stereotype of the Negro; and in other instances was merely *role playing* of necessity in order to get along better under the system. This tendency of most Southern Negroes most of the time to act normatively under the system furnished the basis for one of the major elements in the race ideology of the white Southerner, namely that on the whole "their" Negroes were content with the system. The fact that Negroes seldom openly manifested hatred for white people should not be interpreted to indicate that they do not cherish such a feeling inwardly. Warner and Davis wrote that "Anyone who believes that the hostile statements uttered by Southern whites toward Negroes are extreme should be allowed to hear those uttered by Negroes, even Negro children and adolescents toward whites."[16]

Deviant responses as adjustments to the frustrations of caste were numerous.[17] (1) *Ritualistic.* Certain Negroes whose circumstances and/or ability permitted strove to achieve higher status within the Negro community, for example as professionals, civil servants, through pursuing the goals of the white value system. Ironically, the very existence of the segregation system afforded this opportunity and this higher status of such Negroes was recognized by whites, as well as by Negroes, as long as they did not challenge the system. (2) *Retreatist.* Escape from the frustrations

[14]Reprinted from *Killers of the Dream* by Lillian Smith. By permission of W. W. Norton & Co., Inc. Copyright 1949, 1961 by Lillian Smith.
[15]See Dollard, *Caste and Class in a Southern Town*, Ch. 12.
[16]Lloyd Warner and Allison Davis, "A Comparative Study of American Caste," in Edgar T. Thompson, ed., *Race Relations and the Race Problem*, p. 237.
[17]The terms used in our schema here are closely related to the meaning given them in Robert Merton's classic exposition in "Social Structure and Anomie," in *Social Theory and Social Structure* (Glencoe, Ill.: The Free Press, 1957), pp. 130–160.

of caste by retreating from the tension took several forms. (a) *Hedonism.* Enjoying as fully as possible those pleasures not denied by caste. Here one may distinguish those activities closer to the normal responses of all mankind such as taking an unexcused day off from work to go fishing and losing a day's exploitative pay, or casual sexual activity; and those responses more personally disorganizing such as drinking, drugs, and the other so-called vices.[18] (b) *Intragroup aggression.* Another way of coping with frustration is to fight other Negroes. There is much data on homicide among Negroes.[19] (3) *Rebellion.* Some (but, under the caste system, few) Negroes responded to systematic discrimination by attacking either white persons or the system. The first were almost always impulsive acts since all Southern-bred Negroes knew it would lead to violent reprisal. The second was deliberate, for example, participation in some planned activity usually by a group asking for some improvement in welfare. Sometimes if carried on with due deference such a response met with success.

While the life of Southern American Negroes under these established patterns of dominance was not a total vale of tears, there is ample empirical material to show that coping with the frustrations of caste left deep psychic scars.

Mark of Oppression

Many years ago Herbert A. Miller referred to the high prevalence among minorities of the attitudes of fear, hatred, resentment, jealousy, suspicion, and revenge—which he labeled the "oppression psychosis." The essential point made by Miller has been substantiated by research, even though the term "psychosis" may be applicable only to those more intensely affected by discrimination. Kardiner and Ovesey, after studying twenty-five Negro males by personality tests and psychoanalytic techniques, concluded as follows:

> On the whole we must be satisfied that the conclusions derived from the three different experimental approaches—the psychodynamic analysis, the Rorschach test, and the T.A.T.—are essen-

[18]See Harry Bredemeier and Jackson Toby, *Social Problems In America: Costs and Casualties in an Acquisitive Society* (New York and London: John Wiley & Sons, 1960), Chapters 7 and 8.
[19]While homicide is, of course, active in a sense, we place this under retreatism because it is taking out one's aggression on the wrong category of persons.

tially the same. The major features of the Negro personality emerge from each with remarkable consistency. These include the fear of relatedness, suspicion, mistrust, the enormous problem of the control of aggression, the denial mechanism, the tendency to dissipate the tension of a provocative situation by reducing it to something simpler, or to something entirely different. All these maneuvers are in the interest of not meeting reality head on. . . . The defects in adaptation are not of mysterious or racial origin but owe their existence entirely to the arduous emotional conditions under which the Negro in America is obliged to live.[20]

Karon studied a small but rigorously selected sample of Northern and Southern Negroes and Northern whites, employing the Tompkins-Horn Picture Arrangement Test. His findings were that caste sanctions have an effect on the personality structure of Negroes born and reared in the South in eleven characteristics, six of which are related to the problem of handling aggression. This research rejects the formerly oft-stated hypothesis that the Southern Negro, because he lives in a consistent interracial system, is not disturbed by caste sanctions, in contrast to the Northern Negro, who lives in a more ambiguous racial situation. Karon's findings show a consistent relationship between the severity of the caste sanctions and the appearance of these disturbed traits. Rural Southern Negroes are "worse off" than the urban Southern Negroes; Northern Negroes born in the South are worse off than those born in the North.[21]

Dreger and Miller in their review of studies up to 1960 conclude that "On the basis of the evidence available it does appear that Negroes more frequently (than whites) experience psychiatric difficulties, particularly of a severe nature."[22]

The Welfare of the Negroes in the South

In practically all indices of welfare, the Negro population continued through the first half of the twentieth century to rank well below that of the white population. Since this has been so

[20]Abram Kardiner and Lionel Ovesey, *The Mark of Oppression* (New York: W. W. Norton & Company, 1951), pp. 337–338. By permission.
[21]Bertram A. Karon, *The Negro Personality* (New York: Springer Publishing Company, 1958), pp. 169–175.
[22]Ralph M. Dreger and Kent S. Miller, "Comparative Psychological Studies of Negroes and Whites in the United States," *Psychological Bulletin*, Sept., 1960, p. 392. See Horace R. Cayton, *The Long Lonely Road* (New York: The Trident Press, 1963), for a dramatic personal illustration.

amply demonstrated we will simply summarize the main points.[23]

Negroes were highly concentrated in the lowest occupational levels with a small percentage scattered in middle levels. Average family incomes were about one-third that of white families. Negroes were paid less for the same type of work at all levels. Negro housing was of poorer quality than that of whites. Comparative studies show markedly disparate health for Negroes and higher death rates. Associated with this was the lack of medical services, particularly hospitalization directly due to segregation.

Comparing the educational level of the Negro population in the South in 1930 with its level at the time of emancipation indicates tremendous strides. In 1870, 81.4 per cent of Negroes were illiterate; in 1930, this figure had been reduced to 16.3 per cent.[24] Comparing the educational facilities for Negroes with those of white persons in the South at any given time, however, reveals gross disparities. During the year 1939–1940, the Southern states spent $55.69 per white child in average daily attendance in schools as against only $18.82 for each Negro child.[25] At the higher educational levels the differential opportunity of Negroes was even more striking. In 1933–1934 only 19 per cent of the Negro children of high-school age were in high schools, as compared with 55 per cent of the white children of the same age.[26] Education of Negroes at the college level in the South before 1890 was exceptionally limited, and the schools available were supported largely by private contributions, chiefly from Northern religious denominational sources. In 1890 an amendment to the original Morrill Act adopted in 1862 required that federal funds be divided fairly between the white and the Negro institutions in states having the dual system. Subsequently, seventeen land-grant agricultural and mechanical colleges for Negroes were established, receiving some of their support from federal funds under this Act. But wide disparities continued to exist in both the quantity and the quality of Negro higher educational institutions in the South.

---

[23]See Gunnar Myrdal, *An American Dilemma*, Ch. 16; Maurice Davie, *Negroes in American Society* (New York: McGraw-Hill Co., 1949), Chs. 5, 6, 10, 11, and 12; and E. Franklin Frazier, *The Negro in the United States*, rev. ed. (New York: The Macmillan Company, 1957), Part 5.
[24]Davie, *Negroes in American Society*, p. 139.
[25]See Frazier, *The Negro in the United States*, p. 437.
[26]*Ibid.*, p. 436.

THE IMPACT OF THE CASTE SYSTEM ON THE SOUTH

Tension and Violence

Despite the facade of a smoothly operating biracial system, racial tension was constantly present in the region in those local communities with sizeable Negro populations. It is inevitable that where constant tension exists, violence will sporadically occur. Making some allowance for the tendency of novelists to dramatize, the writings of Southern novelists, as Erskine Caldwell, for example, suggest that interpersonal violence in which individual white Southerners maltreated individual Negro people was more or less an everyday occurrence. On a larger scale and more sporadically, the two characteristic modes of expression of this violence have been lynchings and riots.

LYNCHING   In American history there were many lynchings of white people as well as blacks. From 1892 on, Negro lynchings greatly exceeded those of whites. With minor fluctuations, the numerical trend was sharply downward from the peak decade of 1892–1901 during which 1124 Negro lynchings were recorded.[27] The trend was sharply downward so that for the years 1952–1958 only four lynchings were recorded.

Lynchings occurred mostly in small towns in rural areas. The accusations made against persons lynched ranged widely from homicide to merely boastful remarks. A special study by Arthur Raper of nearly a hundred lynchings convinced the writer that a third of the victims were falsely accused.[28] Myrdal suggests that the conditions related to lynching were poverty, the fear that the Negro was "getting out of place," and the general boredom of life in small communities in the South.[29] While in total volume of physical harm done to Negroes under the caste system, lynching looms small, Myrdal found it to have a "psychological importance out of all proportion to its small frequency." In analyzing the effects of lynching Myrdal has this to say:

> The effects of lynchings are far reaching. In the locality where it
> has happened and in a wide region surrounding it, the relations

[27]Tuskegee Institute started recording lynchings of both whites and blacks in 1892 and continued from then on.
[28]See Arthur Raper, *The Tragedy of Lynching* (Chapel Hill: University of North Carolina Press, 1933).
[29]See Myrdal, *An American Dilemma*, pp. 560–562 for discussion of lynching.

between the two groups deteriorate. The Negroes are terror stricken and sullen. The whites are anxious and are likely to show the assertiveness and suspicion of persons with bad, but hardened consciences. Some whites are afraid of Negro retaliation or emigration. Every visitor to such a community must notice the antagonism and mutual lack of confidence between the two groups.[30]

Knowledge of a lynching had adverse effects throughout the nation, evoking brutalized feelings among some whites, twinging the consciences of others, and, for a time at least, raising the level of interracial tension in all racially mixed places.

This discussion of lynching should not be concluded without mentioning that many white Southerners deplored lynching, whatever their degree of commitment may have been to the caste system, in general. The organization of the Association of Southern Women for the Prevention of Lynching in Atlanta in 1930 is one example.

RACIAL RIOTS   Under the Southern race system, racial rioting largely took the form of mob action by whites directed at defenseless Negro areas, stimulated usually by rumors of Negro assaults on whites. Franklin writes: "In the new century (1900) a veritable epidemic of race riots broke out and before the end of the first decade there had been at least half a dozen major racial upheavals."[31] While some of them took place in the North, they may be interpreted as one of numerous devices for sustaining the color line.

Political Effects

The South as a region has had a political development which differs from that in the rest of the country. (1) The proportion of people who participate in politics has been markedly smaller than in the rest of the nation. We have already referred to the virtual disfranchisement of Negroes. Bunche estimated that in eight Southern states, the so-called Deep South, never more than 80,000 to 90,000 Negro votes had been cast in general elections up to 1940, and only a handful in the primaries, the elections that really count.[32] The proportion of the white electorate which participated

[30]*Ibid.*, p. 564. By permission of the publishers, Harper and Row.
[31]John Hope Franklin, and the Editors of Time-Life Books, *Black Americans: An Illustrated History* (New York, 1970), p. 92.
[32]Ralph J. Bunche, "The Negro in the Political Life in the United States," *Journal of Negro Education*, July, 1941, 567–584.

in politics was also decidedly less than in the rest of the nation. In 1940 only 28 per cent of the adult population of twelve Southern states went to the polls, in contrast with 53 per cent for the rest of the country. (2) The South for all practical purposes has had a one-party system, the Democratic party. The primary contests in this party constituted in essence the final decision. (3) From this it followed that political opposition was more confined than elsewhere to rivalries between factions and personalities in which the basic issues contested in the nation as a whole were not debated. Since the Democratic party in the South represented traditional and conservative influence in the national Congress, the same kind of liberal political pressures which had arisen elsewhere in the nation, representing broadly liberal and human welfare interests as opposed to conservative and propertied interests, had not manifested themselves in any marked degree in the South. Since wide exercise of the franchise, a two (or more) party system, and the vigorous debate of new ways to further the democratic ideal are signs of a healthy democracy, the democratic political process in the South may properly be regarded as having been retarded.

To what extent are these distinctive developments in Southern politics attributable to the effect of its system of race relations? Since we adhere to the general principle that the causal factors in such complex social phenomena are always multiple and interact with one another, we shall not suggest that the system of race relations is all-determinative. Nevertheless, the interrelationship between the phenomena of race relations and these political developments is highly impressive. The elaborate devices to limit the electorate arose primarily as a way of preventing Negroes from exercising active citizenship. Once established, these political phenomena furthered the politicoeconomic interests of the middle and upper classes of the white South in opposition to those of the lower-class whites. The failure of the latter group to generate more effective political expression of its interests is in considerable measure related to its preoccupation with "keeping the Negro in his place."[33]

Effect on the Economy of the South

Rupert Vance, an outstanding student of the Southern region, described the South's position (1930) in the national economy in

[33]See Lillian Smith, *Killers of the Dream*, pp. 154–168.

these terms: "The statistical indices of wealth, education, cultural achievement, health, law and order reduced to a per capita basis combine in every instance to give the Southern states the lowest rankings in the Union."[34] After a careful appraisal of the natural resources of the region, Vance concluded that it was not lack of adequate natural resources which accounted for the South's relative poverty. He found the chief explanation in the manner in which the Southern economy had been organized.

After the Civil War, Southern economic reconstruction called for carrying on the plantation agricultural economy, with chief emphasis on cotton production. Since this economy required cheap labor, the caste system developed in part as a means of guaranteeing the continued employment of Negroes in their accustomed role at subsistence wages. Furthermore, in order to hold its place competitively in a national economy generally more efficient than its own, the South was forced to exploit the soil to the point of diminishing returns. In this way, a cycle of reciprocal forces was established which operated to retard the economic development of the region. The relatively inefficient economy could provide only subsistence wages for the laborers involved. Their marginal income in turn retarded the regional demand for goods which would have favored the development of industrial enterprise. Furthermore, the marginal economy was unable to produce enough to furnish the capital needed for industrial development. This capital had to be furnished, therefore, from outside the region, which meant that part of the gains were drained from the region itself. In order to get this capital, the South offered the inducement primarily of cheap labor costs, which still further aggravated the low standard of living, extending it to a wider segment of its white population. While the expanding industrial economy offered some opportunity to transfer Negroes from farm work to city work, the caste system prevented their employment in other than the lowest-paying capacities.

Clearly, many factors are involved in interpreting the cycle just described. Nevertheless, the influence of the caste system is apparent at every turn. As Vance has written: "The South holds the Negro back; the Negro holds the South back; and both point in recrimination."[35]

[34]Rupert B. Vance, *Human Geography of the South* (Chapel Hill: University of North Carolina Press, 1932), p. 442. By permission.
[35]*Ibid.*, p. 43.

Variation in the Southern Pattern

The foregoing description has disregarded variations in order to indicate the general Southern pattern. Some significant rural-urban contrasts, however, should be noted. The city environment permitted some relief to Negroes from the omnipresent impact of caste through the opportunity it afforded to build a separate community structure. At least within this area, Negroes could live their own lives.[36] Compared with the smaller places, there was less actual personal interaction between the members of the two races in the city. Since traditionally the caste system carried with it much direct personal dependence of individual Negroes on particular white people, through which conformity to the mandates of caste could be closely scrutinized, the greater drawing apart of the two races in the Southern cities placed the control of caste on a more impersonal basis.

The Border States

The major variation in the Southern pattern of race relations is seen by considering the border states. In none of these was the "white primary" to be found; among them, only Oklahoma had "Jim Crow" streetcars. In these states the code of etiquette was frequently less explicit and less binding. However, in all of them intermarriage between Negroes and whites was prohibited by law, and the segregation of Negroes in schools remained up to 1954.[37]

The pattern of race relations in Washington, D.C., is naturally of particular significance, not only because it is the capital but because it is visited by foreign officials of all other nations. On the one hand, Washington, as part of the Southern area, reflected in many ways the Southern attitude and behavior in Negro-white relations. On the other hand, the influence of the federal government imposed certain exceptions to the traditional Southern pattern. Thus Negroes were not "Jim Crowed" in District transportation; they had equal access to all institutions and services directly operated as federal government property. Before World War II, the national government employed a limited number of Negroes

[36]One of the authors was told by a Negro physician in a Louisiana city that the members of his family went "down town" as seldom as possible because they so profoundly disliked the caste requirements.
[37]See Myrdal, *An American Dilemma*, p. 1072, Table 1, for a checklist of the various features of the caste system for each Southern state.

in higher-ranking occupations, qualified by the tendency to place them in special assignments dealing with Negro problems. But generally, Washington in the period before World War II presented substantially the same picture as other border cities. School segregation, for example, prevailed, and Negroes were denied the use of general restaurant and amusement facilities in the city.

Changes in the Southern Pattern

Between 1880 and World War II race relations in the South revealed changes that went rather rapidly in one direction and rather slowly in another. As we have seen, most of the gains made by Negroes following Emancipation were lost by the establishment of the caste system. On the other hand, the welfare of Negroes improved somewhat along with the general national trend, even though at all times with wide discrepancies with the welfare of the whites. Circumstances operating to improve Negro welfare were the opportunity presented by World War I for Negroes to find employment in the North, the tendency of the federal government to require more equitable use of federal funds for Negroes, especially during the depression years of the 1930s, and the beginnings of some breakdown of segregation in labor unions in the mid-1930s.

The earnest efforts of a small group of Southern white liberals in behalf of Negroes deserve recognition as an influence in keeping the Southern pattern slightly unfrozen. The group comprised a few writers, journalists, educators, and some club women, whom Myrdal described as "mostly a fraternity of individuals with independent minds, usually living in, and adjusting to, an uncongenial social surrounding."[38] Because for the most part they possessed high social prestige either through their lineage from Southern aristocracy or through the national pre-eminence they had acquired in professional fields, their espousal of the Negro's cause was tolerated. Their first efforts were directed at striving for equal justice, particularly against lynching, and gaining for the Negro a fairer share of public monies spent for education, health, and other aspects of welfare. They were unable to challenge the system of segregation itself. The Southern liberals were not able to influence political life to any marked extent, and their influence was largely confined to the higher social and educational levels of

[38]*Ibid.*, p. 467.

Southern society. The main organization through which Southern liberalism found expression was the Commission on Interracial Cooperation, founded in 1919. In Myrdal's judgment its most far-reaching effect is *"to have rendered interracial work socially respectable in the conservative South."*[39]

Finally, we consider the effect of Negro leadership and organization on the course of Southern race relations during the caste period. Under slavery the organized activities of Negroes in their own behalf consisted, as we have seen, largely of abortive slave revolts. The outstanding leader among Negroes in the nineteenth-century was Frederick Douglass. Following emancipation, which he had urged upon Lincoln, he worked to secure full equality for the Negroes, but saw the fight lost during the Southern reconstruction. Organized movements among Negroes subsequently divided into "protest" or "accommodative" patterns. The former, which Douglass espoused, aimed to secure full equality for Negroes; the latter aimed to secure the betterment of conditions without challenging the institution of caste itself. During the early twentieth century the protest type of activity was almost exclusively confined to Negroes in the North, which we shall consider in Chapter 7. In the South the unquestioned spokesman for the Negroes was Booker T. Washington, who is generally considered a leader of the accommodative type, though some of his biographers think the extent of his compromising has been overstressed, particularly in view of the circumstances which he faced. Rose summarizes the role which Washington played and the philosophy behind it:

> It is wrong to characterize Washington as an all-out accommodating leader. He never relinquished the right to full equality in all respects as the ultimate goal. But for the time being he was prepared to give up social and political equality, even to soft-pedal and protest against inequalities in justice. He was also willing to flatter the Southern whites and be harsh toward the Negroes—if the Negroes were allowed to work undisturbed with their white friends for education and business. But neither in education nor in business did he assault inequalities. In both fields he accepted the white doctrine of the Negroes "place." In education he pleaded mainly for vocational training. Through thrift, skill, and industry the Negroes were gradually to improve so much that later the discussion could again be taken up concerning their rights. This was Washington's philosophy.[40]

[39]*Ibid.*, p. 847. Italics in original.
[40]Arnold Rose, *The Negro in America* (New York: Harper & Brothers, 1948), p. 240. By permission.

However one views the relative merits of the protest as against the accommodative program of action, beyond question Washington had the greatest influence of any single Negro on the development of Negro welfare during his time. His influence was most concretely evidenced in the development of Tuskegee Institute, over which he presided for many years.

Suggested Readings

Chalmers, David M. *Hooded Americanism: The First Century of the Ku Klux Klan.* New York: Doubleday & Co., 1965.
A full-length and scholarly history of this well-known "nativistic" organization.

Davis, Allison, and Dollard, John. *Children of Bondage.* Washington, D.C.: American Council on Education, 1940.
An intensive study of eight Negro adolescents in the Deep South indicating the effects of the Southern pattern on the Negro personality.

Lewinson, Paul. *Race, Class and Party: A History of Negro Suffrage and White Politics.* New York: Grosset and Dunlap, Universal Library Edition, 1965.
A pioneer historical study of the interrelation of race and class in Southern political life from slave days to 1930.

Lewis, Hylan. *Blackways of Kent.* Chapel Hill: University of North Carolina Press, 1955.
A comprehensive and intimate account of the life of Negroes in a typical biracial community of the Piedmont area.

Meier, August. *Negro Thought in America 1880–1915.* Ann Arbor, Michigan: The University of Michigan Press, 1966.
Analyzes the racial ideologies of Negro leaders in the age of Booker T. Washington.

Pettigrew, Thomas P. *A Profile of the Negro American.* New York: Van Nostrand Co., 1964.
Chapter 1, "The Role and Its Burdens," and Chapter 2, "Reactions to Oppression," examine the impact of white domination on the Negro personality.

Rohrer, John H., and Edmonson, Munro S. *The Eighth Generation: Cultures and Personalities of New Orleans Negroes.* New York: Harper & Brothers, 1960.
An intensive follow-up study of the subjects of Davis and Dollard's study of the children of bondage who as adults comprise the eighth generation of New Orleans Negroes.

7   **T**he Pattern of Northern Dominance

While there were Negroes in the North from colonial days, the first great migration from the South and the metropolitan concentration lead us to focus this chapter on the pattern of Negro-white relations which developed in the North between the two wars.

In the North, Negroes were discriminated against substantially everywhere, but not in as many aspects of life nor so intensely as in the South. The welfare of the Negro in the North was the lowest of all large minorities, but the relatively higher general standard of living in the North was reflected in the higher standards of Northern Negroes as compared with those of Southern Negroes.

A basic difference between the Northern and Southern situation has been the absence in the North of such precise institutionalization of the minority position of Negroes as the Southern caste pattern involved. In the South, caste relations were well defined in law and in the regional mores; and control mechanisms for maintaining the system had become standardized through years of practice. In the North the discrimination and segregation which did exist lacked such explicit sanction in the mores; also lacking were such established control devices for holding the Negro in minority status. For Southern white people in general the attitudes and values of the caste system were an integral part of their personalities; and for Southern Negroes the reciprocal attitudes and behavior patterns were deeply structured in their personalities. Caste was an intrinsic part of the Southern social structure and daily touched the lives of the people of both races. In the North the segregated position of Negroes was only a fragmentary aspect of Northern community life, and many white people, even in communities with sizable Negro populations, were scarcely aware of its presence.

The many contrasting circumstances in the two regional situations accounting for this basic difference can be stated only briefly in this overview. The North did not have the tradition of slavery, having abolished slavery decades before Emancipation. And in no Northern community did the number of Negroes approach a majority. Thus, while Negroes were highly useful to the economy of the North, their labor was never considered essential to Northern economic life, as in the South, especially as long as European immigration furnished cheap labor. The concentration of Negroes in the larger cities of the North, where their residential segregation resembled that of other ethnic and racial minorities, made their position appear less sharply in contrast to the dominant white community than in the South, where Negroes were the only considerable minority.

THE ESTABLISHMENT AND MAINTENANCE OF DOMINANCE

The Pattern of Discrimination

A close-up view of the general pattern of Negro-white relations in the North may be obtained from the comprehensive study of Chicago made by Drake and Cayton. In essence their book, *Black Metropolis*, typifies the Northern situation. Much of the material was gathered for this volume in the 1930s, though some of it refers to the impact of World War II.[1] Since 1940 there have been enough changes in the situation in Chicago, as well as elsewhere in the North, to prompt the use of the past tense in this chapter. Much of the description which follows, however, is still applicable in this day.

RESIDENTIAL SEGREGATION   Negroes in Chicago were highly concentrated in residence; 337,000—90 per cent of all— lived in the Black Belt. [174] The difference between this and other

[1] St. Clair Drake and Horace R. Cayton, *Black Metropolis* (New York: Harcourt, Brace & Co., 1945). Page numbers of future references to this work in this chapter will be bracketed and placed in the text.

ethnic colonies found in cities was that while the others tended to break up in time, the Negro area became increasingly concentrated. The particular area was on the lower South Side, long considered by Chicago planning boards a "blighted area." The extent of congestion is indicated by the fact that Negroes were living 90,000 to the square mile, as compared with 20,000 in neighboring white apartment house areas. [204] This high degree of spatial segregation "is primarily the result of white people's attitudes toward having Negroes as neighbors. Because some white Chicagoans do not wish colored neighbors, formal and informal controls are used to isolate the latter within congested all-Negro neighborhoods." [174]

The real force of the measures to contain the Negro area began when the mass migration took place. "It was only after 1915, when 65,000 migrants came into the city within five years, that resistance became organized." [177] Property-owners associations began to take active steps to forestall sale and rent of property to Negroes outside the Black Belt. "A wave of violence flared up, and between July 1917 and March 1921 fifty-eight homes were bombed. . . . The victims of the bombings were Negro families that had moved into white neighborhoods, as well as Negro and white real-estate men who sold or rented property to them." [178] The major device for controlling the Negro community was the restrictive covenant—an agreement between property owners within a certain district not to rent or sell to Negroes. Attempts to upset restrictive covenants legally were for a long time unsuccessful. However, in 1917 the Supreme Court (245 U.S. 60) ruled that a municipal zoning ordinance which segregated Negroes and whites was unconstitutional, but it was not until 1948 that the highest tribunal declared that restrictive covenants in private housing transactions could not be upheld by law (334 U.S. 1–1948).

OCCUPATIONAL DISCRIMINATION   Discrimination in jobs was seen in the tendency to deny Negroes jobs when white people were out of work. Drake and Cayton state that in 1940, *"while Negroes made up only 8 per cent of the available workers, they constituted 22 per cent of the unemployed. . . .* Almost half of the Negro domestic servants, a third of the semiskilled workers, and a fourth of the unskilled were unemployed in 1935." [217] Negroes were substantially barred from numerous pursuits. "The job ceiling for Negroes . . . [tended] to be drawn just above the level of semiskilled jobs, with the skilled, clerical, managerial, and supervisory positions reserved for white workers." [262] Again Negroes had not consistently held their competitive position in certain occupational fields. For example, during the depression Negroes lost out to whites in restaurants and hotel jobs. If a restaurant wanted to employ white waitresses, there could not be any Negroes in a similar capacity.

As small compensation for these inequities, Negroes had a substantial monopoly in the two occupations of Pullman porter and redcap, where "the earnings and the prospects of advancement are dependent upon cheerful and, if necessary, ingratiating service. . . . Even very well-educated Negroes did not scorn such jobs." [237]

The low economic position of Negroes was in part explainable by their relative lack of skills and training for higher ranking jobs, and by the tendency of Southern Negroes to flock to the North in numbers in excess of the job opportunities available to them. But in considerable measure it was due to racial discrimination: to the tendency of white workers to refuse to work alongside Negroes and of employers to assume that this was always so; to the tendency of white customers to resent being waited on by Negroes, except in the most servile services, and of employers to assume the universality of this reaction by white clients; and to the tendency to consider the Negro as somehow different, "not quite one of us," and therefore inferior.

SOCIAL DISCRIMINATION   In contrast to the South, Negroes in Chicago were not segregated in their utilization of many public facilities. Public parks, public transportation facilities, stores, and public toilets were open to them. However, the more intimate the situation, the more doubtful the acceptance of Negroes on equal terms. In theaters, restaurants, and particularly swimming places, Negroes were discouraged by every possible means from associating with whites. In the Midwest metropolis, bathing beaches and swimming pools were among the primary tension points. The Negro press reported:

POLICE OBJECT TO MIXING OF RACES
ON BEACH; ARREST 18.
SAY THEY ARE TRYING
TO PREVENT RACE RIOT. [105]

While the color line was seldom drawn in theaters or at large public gatherings, in recreation situations that emphasized active participation as distinct from merely looking on, Negroes were barred; and in all situations where men and women participated together, there was a rigid line. Whatever may have been their ultimate hope, Negroes themselves put less stress on the desirability of achieving equality in this more intimate sphere than in others. This difference in the relative importance attached to social equality by the two races was favorable to facilitating adjustment in Negro-white relations in the North.

CIVIC "EQUALITY"   In marked contrast to the South was the civic "equality" accorded Northern Negroes. However, the term "equality" is here placed in quotes because what Negroes had in Chicago and elsewhere in the North was limited by the framework of dominant-group attitudes toward minority groups. It is hard to prove that a teacher "looks down" on Negroes, or that a juror will not believe Negro testimony when it contradicts that of a white person. But one cannot study the events without being convinced that equality was qualified by prejudice.

Drake and Clayton wrote that "To Negro migrants, fresh from the South, Midwest Metropolis presents a novel experience—a substantial measure of equality before the law. Here, they can expect a reasonably fair trial in the courts, with a choice of colored or white counsel. There are no lynchings." [108–109] Negroes had full political rights. Even though they were thought of as a minority group, their right to vote and participate in political organization was not denied. What this opportunity to be a citizen meant to Negroes is described as follows:

> Politics became an important, perhaps the most important, method by which the Negro sought to change his status. It was often the only avenue open for struggle against caste tendencies. This struggle invested his political behavior, even when corrupt, with an importance and a dignity that similar behavior could not command in any other portion of the population. [343]

As a result of their political activities, Negroes made substantial gains in Chicago.

> Within a decade after the Great Migration, Black Metropolis had elected two Negro aldermen, one State Senator, four State Representatives, a city judge, and a Congressman. . . . Wielding such political power, Negro politicians have been in a position to demand appointive positions for a few hundred individuals and equitable treatment in the courts for the masses (as well as dubi-

ous "benefits" from the great Chicago enterprise of "fixing" and "rigging" everything from traffic tickets to gambling dens). They have also been able to expose and check discrimination in the administration of the civil service laws and in the enforcement of the Civil Rights Law. They have created, among influential white politicians of all parties, an awareness of the Negro's desire for equal opportunity. [109–110]

The minority status of Negroes was reflected, however, in politics as in all other phases of our lives. Of this Drake and Cayton write:

The color line in politics is also reflected in the types of political plums that go to Negro politicians and their henchmen. The big contracts and the heavy graft are reserved for whites. Negroes get the petty "cuts" from gambling and vice protection. In fact, a tradition has developed that Negroes will not demand big political rewards. . . . Political leaders in Midwest Metropolis, balancing the pressures of ethnic, economic, and religious blocs, are forced to grant some of the demands of Negroes, and Negro politicians shrewdly demand all that they think the traffic will bear. [111]

EDUCATION   Curiously, in view of their exhaustive coverage of Negro life in Chicago, Drake and Cayton wrote very little about education. For the North in general during this period, Myrdal, however, noted the following:

There is little school segregation required by law in the Northern and Western states: Arizona requires it in elementary schools and makes it permissive in secondary schools; Kansas, Wyoming, Indiana, and New Mexico make school segregation permissive in the elementary grades and sometimes also in the secondary grades. Some communities in the southern parts of New Jersey, Indiana, Pennsylvania, Ohio and Illinois use organized pressure contrary to law to segregate Negroes in at least the elementary grades. In practically all other areas of the North there is partial segregation on a voluntary basis, caused by residential segregation aided by the gerrymandering of school districts and the system of "permits." The segregation is fairly complete for elementary schools, except where Negroes form only a small proportion of the population, but there is much less segregation in secondary schools. In few cases—if any—is this segregation accompanied by discrimination, however, except that form of discrimination which inevitably arises out of isolation. In fact there is probably more discrimination in the mixed schools than in the segregated ones in the North; frequently Negroes in mixed schools are kept out of swimming, dancing, and other athletics, and out of social clubs. There are, however, some Negro teachers in mixed schools in many Northern cities, and Negroes sit on the boards of education in a few big Northern cities.[2]

The opportunity for Negroes to acquire higher education in the North was less than for secondary schools. Northern state universities did not prohibit Negro enrollments, but the vast majority of the private institutions either categorically did not accept Negroes or accepted only a "token" Negro or two. Myrdal concludes that there was no serious restriction on higher education of Negroes in the North, supporting his view by pointing out that only four Negro colleges, all of these established before the Civil War, were located in the North. However, it is pertinent to note that before 1940 a large number of Northern Negroes had gone South to attend Negro colleges—3,000, for example, in 1938–1939.[3] They may have done this because these colleges were less expensive or because they received scholarships. However, it is also possible that they had the feeling that they would face a number of unpleasant discriminations in Northern colleges. Caliver writes that Negro students "seldom lived on campus and in general, they seemed not to belong in the same way that white students felt themselves a part of the university."[4] Discrimination in higher education was likewise seen in the fact that before World War II not more than five white colleges had a Negro on their faculties.

Methods of Maintaining Dominance

Generally speaking, segregation outside the South was not supported by law. A few non-Southern states banned intermarriage; and certain local communities officially segregated Negroes in schools, but such laws were usually overridden by court decisions. In some communities the police attempted to keep Negroes out of certain public areas, such as beaches, but these actions were

[2]Myrdal, *An American Dilemma* (New York: Harper & Brothers, 1944), p. 633. By permission of the publishers.
[3]Ambrose Caliver, *United States Office of Education, National Survey of Higher Education of Negroes*, Vol. IV (Washington, D.C.: Government Printing Office, 1942–1943), p. 13.
[4]*Ibid.*

nowhere legally supported. Subterfuges, like making the commercial recreational place a "club," were sometimes successful. In a left-handed way law-enforcing agencies frequently supported segregation by refusing to arrest whites who molested Negroes.

Segregation was upheld by common practice—practices by whites to keep Negroes within the bounds of minority status and the reciprocal practices of Negroes to accept this status. While Negroes bitterly resented this, to have some peace of mind, they put up with discrimination most of the time. The fact, however, that these practices were of doubtful legality meant that Negroes could challenge civic discrimination on occasion, and by this means kept the pattern of relationships unfrozen. Sporadic gains here and there were made. Generally, when Negroes pressed cases of discrimination involving civil rights they won them. But, of course, since legal vindication is a costly process, such cases were not numerous.

As in the South, the Northern pattern was supported by the prevalence of the "racial ideology" which looked upon Negroes in the mass as inferior. There was, however, a wider variation in racial attitudes and beliefs in the North. What in comparison appears clearest in that Northern attitudes were not crystallized into any uniform public opinion. As Drake and Cayton wrote: "In the South, every white man feels impelled to protect every white family, clique, and church from 'Negro contamination.' In Midwest Metropolis, each person is concerned only with his own." [119]

Variations in the Northern Pattern

In minor aspects the picture of Chicago's Negro community and its relation to the larger community is affected by its particular locale; but less extensive studies of other large cities indicate that *Black Metropolis* was typical of Negro-white relations in the metropolitan areas of the North, where the far larger proportion of the Northern Negro population lived.[5] Variations in the Northern pattern were in the main related to three situations.

RECENCY OF MIGRATION   The status of Negroes in Northern cities varied with the extent to which a given city shared in the Great Migration. Generally the status of Negroes in the North as

[5]See for example, Robert A. Warner, *New Haven Negroes* (New Haven: Yale University Press, 1940).

a whole declined in the years attending this migration. Further-more, the occurrence of the depression of the 1930s, during which so large a proportion of Negroes were on relief, retarded improvement in welfare. Even in New England, which did not greatly share in the Great Migration, the traditional tolerance toward Negroes declined. Frazier writes, "The increase in the Negro population [of Boston] during and following World War I accentuated race consciousness among Negroes as well as whites."[6]

Confirmation of the principle that animosity to a minority rises with the sudden influx of a new group into a particular area comes from a study of the situation in the Northwestern communities to which Negroes migrated during World War II.[7] Before 1940, Negroes comprised less than 0.5 per cent of the population covered in this study; by 1945 the Negro population had increased 300 per cent. The very small and inconspicuous group of Negroes living in the area before this recent migration "had learned gradually to adjust themselves to white patterns, and whites had in turn more or less come to accept this small Negro minority as a natural part of the population." However, "with the appearance of new faces, unfamiliar with the community's mores, tensions began to be apparent."[8] Contributing to the tension was the fact that the white "newcomers" to these localities came from areas with more discriminatory patterns, and they translated their usual attitudes into behavior in the new situation. Furthermore, the change in white attitudes was resented by the old-time Negro families, whose status deteriorated in the face of the general rise of antagonism toward Negroes, producing friction within the local Negro group. Insofar as social policy can be brought to bear on future adjustment of Negro-white relations, these Northern and Western experiences point toward discouraging a large influx of Negroes over a short period of time into any one community.

THE SMALLER CITY VERSUS THE METROPOLIS   Since the major portion of the Northern migration went to the large cities, little attention had been given to Negroes in the smaller cities. In Muncie, Indiana, the Lynds found in 1929 that "the sense of racial separateness appears in widely diverse groups." Negroes were not permitted in the Y.M.C.A., for example. "News

[6]E. Franklin Frazier, *The Negro in the United States* (New York: The Macmillan Co., 1949), p. 254.
[7]T. H. Kennedy, "Racial Tensions Among Negroes in the Intermountain Northwest," *Phylon*, 1946, 7: pp. 358–364.
[8]*Ibid.*, p. 360.

of the Negroes is given separately in the papers under the title 'In Colored Circles.' "[9] In 1935, in their post-depression study of the same city, the authors found Negroes had better leadership and organization but that they "occupy a more exposed position . . . than before the depression."[10] In smaller communities, Negroes were further handicapped because their numbers were inadequate to furnish for themselves a complete, separate community life.

INFLUENCE OF THE SOUTHERN PATTERN ON THE NORTH   In concluding the discussion of variables in the Northern scene, it is pertinent to note two influences of the Southern pattern on the North and West. First, the migration of white Southern workers to the North which, when recent and in substantial numbers, tended to disturb the pattern of toleration of Negroes in many Northern communities. This was notable as a factor in the tense Detroit situation of World War II. Second, in those Northern states bordering on a state with a Southern pattern, variation in race relations from south to north was noticeable. In New Jersey, for instance, before state government policies inaugurated in the 1940s, school segregation was more pronounced in the southern than in the northern portion of the state. The part of Illinois which dips down into the South still showed strong Southern caste influence.

All these variations make it clear that throughout the North white Americans normatively were unwilling to accord Negroes real equality.[11]

IMPACT OF THE NORTHERN RACIAL PATTERN ON NORTHERN COMMUNITIES

The pattern of Negro-white relations just described affected the life of those Northern communities with any substantial Negro population in many ways.

[9]Robert S. and Helen M. Lynd, *Middletown* (New York: Harcourt, Brace & Co., 1929), p. 479, footnote 1.
[10]Robert S. and Helen M. Lynd, *Middletown in Transition* (New York: Harcourt, Brace & Co., 1937), p. 465.
[11]A notable exception to the rigid line of discrimination in the North has recently appeared from a field study by George K. Hesslink, published as *Black Neighbors: Negroes in a Northern Rural Community* (Indianapolis: Bobbs-Merrill, 1967). Hesslink uncovered a Michigan village in which Negro descendants of pre-Civil War fugitive slaves interacted with whites on a mutually equitable basis from the early years. The study is significant because it underscores the different pattern of interracial relations in a smaller community not steeped in traditions of interracial hostility but which is now faced with the potentially disruptive effects of migration and social change.

The Negro Ghetto: A Blighted Area

The formation of separate sub-communities of Negroes fitted easily into the pattern of Northern city life where other ethnic sub-communities were no new phenomenon. But as time went on, the other ethnic colonies tended, first to move out of their original "slum" location, and later to disappear through a considerable assimilation of subsequent generations. However the Negro sub-community persisted and grew, creating serious problems in such cities. Resistance to admitting Negroes into new areas resulted in fantastic overcrowding. In Detroit in 1939 Negro rates for over-crowding were twice those of whites.[12] When finally the walls of the black ghetto burst, infiltration of Negroes into other dilapi-dated areas began. However, when some Negroes did get a foot-hold, whites began to move out and more Negroes moved in, until the new block, or section, came to be generally Negro.

It has been demonstrated that all slum areas, regardless of who lives in them, although highly profitable to particular special interests, are an economic drain on the community at large and unvaryingly yield a disproportionate share of the social patholo-gies—delinquency, crime, high disease rates. That the presence of a Negro ghetto in a Northern community is no exception has been amply demonstrated by many studies of such areas.[13]

Tension and Violence

The presence of segregated Negro areas was a constant source of interractial tension and sporadic interracial violence. In 1919, riots occurred in at least 26 American cities. Interracial violence tends to arise in non-work situations where whites and Negroes may meet. One such circumstance occurs when Negroes begin to move into a new area, as in Detroit in 1942 where one of the worst riots (prior to the 60s) occurred. Of this Myrdal writes:

> . . . [I]n trying to move into a government defense housing project built for them in Detroit, Negroes were set upon by white civilians and police. The project was built at the border between Negro and white neighborhoods but had been planned for Negroes. En-couraged by the vacillation of the federal government and the friendliness of the Detroit police (many of whom are Southern

[12]Robert Weaver, *The Negro Ghetto* (New York: Harcourt, Brace and Co., 1948), p. 115.
[13]See Robert Weaver, *The Negro Ghetto*; E. Franklin Frazier, *The Negro in the United States*, Part IV; and Gunnar Myrdal, *The American Dilemma*, Ch. 14.

born) and stimulated by the backing of a United States congress-man and such organizations as the Ku Klux Klan, white residents of the neighborhood and other parts of the city staged protest demonstrations against the Negro housing project, which led to the riot.[14]

Public recreational areas are another stimulus to violence as in the "Belle Isle Riot," also in Detroit near a recreational park.[15] Foreshadowing the 1960 riots was the Harlem Riot of 1935 where an outbreak of violence occurred in the Negro area itself where some 10,000 slum dwellers smashed windows, hurled bricks, and looted stores, choosing those of white merchants.[16]

Ambiguity of the Northern Pattern

In contrast to the South, the Northern pattern was more am-biguous which created an additional problem for the Southern born Negroes and the children they reared. The Negro was in many ways freer to do things he could not do in the South, but was frequently at a loss to know just how much freer. He could go to this restaurant, but that one refused him service. He could play on the school team, but he could not go to the dances. And, while treating him like a minority person, the Northern practice at the same time held the Negro more accountable to behave ac-cording to the general norms of the community. Petty thievery was almost expected of the Negro by the white Southerner, and was dealt with as one ordinarily deals with it in the case of chil-dren. But the Northerners put him in jail for it. "Illegitimacy" in the South (often occurring within stable monogamic unions) was laughed off by Southern whites as "natural for darkies," but in the North it frequently brought investigation by a white welfare worker.

Finally, while the South held out no prospect to the Negro of ever rising above the confines of caste (allowing only for some upward class mobility within caste), the Northern situation, ill defined and perplexing as it was, was sufficiently fluid to encour-age Negro aspirations. But since Northern white attitudes were by no means ready for the full step, Negroes' hopes were fre-

[14]Myrdal, *An American Dilemma*, p. 568. By permission of the publishers, Harper & Brothers.
[15]See Alfred M. Lee and Norman D. Humphrey, *Race Riot* (New York: the Dryden Press, 1943) for a full account and analysis.
[16]Roi Ottley, *Black Odyssey* (New York: Charles Scribner's Sons, 1948), p. 258.

quently raised too high, only to be dashed. The relatively better education offered the Negro in the North encouraged him to prepare himself for occupations, employment in which he would subsequently be denied. His desire for better housing, and often the means to pay for it, was raised only to be frustrated by restrictive covenants. He was at the same time encouraged to develop higher cultural interests and refused a seat in a theater. Thus the lack of clear definitions of expected Negro behavior and the uncertainties and fluidity characterizing their relations with whites placed considerable strain on Negro personality.

OPPORTUNITY TO CHALLENGE DOMINANCE

In spite of the disorganizing effect of the none-too-well defined situation of the Negro and of the very considerable discrimination against him, compared with the South, the North afforded two advantages: the opportunity for individual Negroes to reach higher levels of success, and the greater opportunity to work effectively to advance the race.

Rise of Negro Middle Class

In the North the class structure was more elaborated than in the South. The social class structure of "Black Metropolis" is described as follows by Drake and Cayton:

The process of differentiation among Negroes in Bronzeville has given rise to a loose system of social classes which allows for mobility upward and downward. This class structure operates as a system of social controls by which the higher-status groups "protect" their way of life, but admit "strainers" and "strivers" who can make the grade. Individuals and organizations on the higher-status levels become models for imitation and also serve as an incentive toward social mobility. . . . At the top are uppers, oriented predominantly around "Society" and Race Leadership, and with a small group of Gentlemen Racketeers who have gained some status as Race Leaders but who are not accepted socially. Below them is the middle class with four "centers of orientation" —church, social club, "racial advancement" (including *individual* advancement), and "policy." At the bottom is the lower class with a large "disorganized segment," but also with a "church-centered" group and a small group of "secular respectables" interested in "getting ahead." Underlying the whole structure is the "under-world" of the Black Ghetto. [710-712]

A few individual Negroes in the North had gained fame and fortune in areas competitive with white people: Joe Louis and, even earlier, Jack Johnson in prizefighting; Roland Hayes and Paul Robeson in concert singing; Paul Lawrence Dunbar, Countee Cullen, James Weldon Johnson in literature. The theme which the artists emphasized was often related to Negro life and problems.

For most of the Negroes who achieved higher social and economic status, it was the very separation of the Negro community that provided most of this opportunity. It created a monopoly for those businesses which involved intimate contact with the person of the Negro, such as hairdressing, restaurants, and funeral service.

In professional service, however, where the relationship to the client is less personal, aspiring Negroes, when they managed to hurdle the difficulty of acquiring professional training, were in competition with white professionals for the trade of the Negro population while being generally barred from competition for the white trade. Negro physicians were handicapped by the lack of hospitals for their patients, and frequently were not permitted to treat their patients in general hospitals. Of the 1,063 Negro lawyers in the entire nation in 1940 two-thirds were in the North with less than one-fourth of the Negro population. In the North the ministry of Negro churches was the leading professional opportunity. Teaching offered much less opportunity since, contrary to the South where only Negro teachers could teach Negro children, white teachers taught schools of any racial composition.

Aside from these opportunities Negroes were conspicuously under-represented in business, even compared with other racial minorities, such as Chinese and Japanese.

One of the largest of all Negro businesses was insurance. "For the year 1945, the 44 member companies of the National Negro Insurance Association reported nearly 4,000,000 policies in force, largely health and accident policies."[17] This opportunity arose because general insurance companies were reluctant to underwrite Negro policies on the same actuarial basis as those of whites because of the wide differentials in health and mortality rates between the two races.

Another higher occupational opportunity arose from the nec-

[17]Frazier, *The Negro in the United States*, p. 401.

essity of integrating Negroes somehow into the civic life of the whole community. Thus some Negroes held positions as liaison agents representing their people in community-wide activity. The not-too-active participation of Negroes in Northern politics offered some opportunity in party politics with occasional appointment to public positions, as reward or through civil service.

Finally, it is inevitable that among a people so situated there should arise an "underworld," often abetted and patronized by whites, and affording opportunity for some Negroes to achieve financial, if not status, reward.

Thus the Northern scene afforded Negroes qualified opportunity for getting ahead and accounted for the growing upper and middle class in the Northern Negro communities. The values and modes of life among the middle-class Negroes were similar to those in the white middle class. Drake and Cayton put it thus:

> The whole atmosphere of middle-class life is one of tension, particularly at upper-middle-class level, or among people on the way up, but not yet secure in their position. The drive to get ahead, to "lay a little something by," to prepare for the education of children, and at the same time keep up "front" by wearing the right kind of clothes, having a "nice home," and belonging to the proper organizations—the pursuit of these goals brings into being definite social types which Bronzeville calls "strivers," and "strainers." With limited incomes, the problem of striking a balance between the conspicuous consumption necessary to maintain status, and long-range goals like buying property and educating children, becomes a difficult one. During the depression years particularly, Bronzeville's middle-class families faced a continuous crisis. [667–668]

This opportunity for the more educated and ambitious Negroes in the North to rise to higher status presented something of a dilemma regarding their attitudes toward advancing the race. Frazier pointed out that segregation protects certain Negro professionals to some extent from competition with whites in corresponding occupations—a competition which was keener and which he felt many of the Negro professionals could not meet successfully.[18] It was clear that a rapid breakdown of the segregated pattern would create much insecurity for the Negro middle class, and it is reasonable to hypothesize that, unconsciously at

[18]See E. Franklin Frazier, *The Black Bourgeoisie* (Glencoe, Ill.: The Free Press, 1957), for fuller treatment of the rise of the Negro middle class.

least, this would temper the vigor of the participation of its members in desegregation movements.[19] On the other hand, esteem among Negroes, as well as other minorities, was to be bestowed on those who championed the advancement of the race.

Organization of the Negro Challenge

We have seen that even under slavery as well as under Southern caste, some Negroes actively protested against their minority status. In the North in the early twentieth century Negro efforts to advance the race embraced a wider range of activities.

REVITALIZATION MOVEMENTS   Of the movements aimed at revitalization most important despite its failure was the "Back to Africa" movement led by Marcus Garvey. A West Indian full-blooded Negro, Garvey arrived in Harlem in 1916 for the purpose of getting help in his efforts to improve the condition of Jamaican Negroes. Coming to the conclusion that Negroes in the United States could never become assimilated into the general white society, he organized the Universal Improvement Association, the broad aim of which was to establish an African Republic where American Negroes could live. Garvey was imprisoned in 1925, accused of using the mails to defraud in connection with the financing of his movement. Many white commentators felt that he had been ill-advised by associates, not realizing that he had broken the law. While the movement continued in various forms it had dwindled away by the time of his death in 1940.

Assessing Garvey's work, Cronon finds no tangible gain resulting from the movement, but on the other hand writes: "Garvey's work was important because more than any other single leader he helped to give Negroes everywhere reborn feeling and a new awareness of individual worth."[20] As such it foreshadowed the spirit of the current black challenge.[21]

"Glamor" personalities, such as Duke Ellington, Paul Robeson, and Marian Anderson, often functioned as Negro leaders, not

[19]This point is illustrated in the later school desegregation crisis. Many Negro teachers in the South viewed with anxiety the possible loss of jobs or demotion in administrative rank as a consequence of school integration

[20]Edmund D. Cronon, *Black Moses: The Story of Marcus Garvey and the Universal Negro Improvement Association* (Madison, Wis.: The University of Wisconsin Press, 1955), p. 222.

[21]The other most publicized popular movement was a cult formed by Father Divine (George Baker). This charismatic leader established a cult practicing a doctrine of love among all people. Cultists who joined his "heaven" turned over their posses-

so much because of their actual civil rights activities but because of the fame and fortune they achieved in the white man's world. Comparatively "glamorous" white people do not necessarily play a civic leadership role. In the case of Negroes, however, a sort of "race" leadership is thrust upon them by the barriers they broke in achieving recognition, whether or not they were inclined to achieve a leadership role.

THE NEGRO INTELLIGENTSIA   The 1920s saw the emergence of a group of Negro intellectuals whose purpose was to enhance the self-respect of Negroes by glorifying the great accomplishments of Negroes past and present. Prominent among the leaders of this movement were W. E. B. DuBois, editor of *The Crisis;* Charles S. Johnson, editor of *Opportunity;* Alain Locke, editor of the volume *The New Negro;* and Carter G. Woodson, who had organized The Association for the Study of Negro Life and History in 1915 and began the publication of *The Journal of Negro History.* This movement had much moral support and financial aid from liberal-minded white people.

ACTIVIST ORGANIZATIONS   The first effort to organize a movement among Negroes in protest against their minority status was launched in 1905, when twenty-nine Negro intellectuals met at Niagara Falls and planned the formation of a national organization to challenge all forms of segregation and discrimination. Such a bold program was opposed by Booker T. Washington and thus in a way challenged his accommodative leadership. Although the organization itself ceased to be effective after 1915, it prepared the way for the formation of the National Association for the Advancement of Colored People (NAACP), through which in part the spirit of the Niagara movement lived on.

Following the Great Migration and World War I, some younger Negro leaders in the 1920s, of whom A. Philip Randolph, president of the Brotherhood of Sleeping Car Porters, was to become the most influential, saw the Negro's greatest hope in alignment with the postwar Socialist movements. It is clear, however, from the relative failure of urban radical movements that the

---

sions and lived under his security. While it lasted he took care of his followers. See Hadley Cantril, *Psychology of Social Movements* (New York: John Wiley & Sons, 1941), Chapter 5, "The Kingdom of Father Divine," for an interpretation of this movement.

majority of Negroes aligned themselves politically with the major parties. Generally it appears that they merged with the New Deal element of the Democratic Party with only an occasional convert to Communism.[22] As we shall see in our account of the trends since 1940, the protest activity continued to gain ascendancy over the accommodative approach.

The first two organizations that have continued to be the most influential in working for the improvement of Negro welfare and status are the National Association for the Advancement of Colored People and the Urban League. These two organizations were not exclusively Negro but interracial, with substantial white membership. While they have operated in the South with considerable difficulty, they originated in the North and received greater support in this region.

The NAACP was formed in 1909 following a severe race riot in Springfield, Illinois, the previous year. It was started on white people's initiative, but its active workers have usually been Negroes. The long-run objective of the Association has always been to win full equality for the Negro as an American citizen. Its specific activities have been in the field of civil liberties, constantly fighting legal cases of discrimination, such as anti-lynching legislation, the abolition of poll taxes, and so on. The strategy of its approach has been practical and opportunistic. The Association did not conduct an omnibus legal campaign against the Southern caste pattern but selected strategically important cases in specific fields of discrimination. It saved many Negroes from unequal court treatment; prevented the extradition of Negroes from North to South for trial; and helped establish the precedents which led to inclusion of Negroes on juries—to select only a few of its many legal successes.

The Urban League was founded in 1910, also on white initiative. It arose primarily to help the recent Negro migrants adjust to Northern city life. It became a general social welfare agency performing various welfare services: health work, recreational work, delinquency prevention, and acting as an informal employment agency for Negroes. In contrast to the NAACP, the Urban League had used informal and educational methods in pursuing this goal rather than a legal approach.

[22]See Wilson Record, *The Negro and the Communist Party* (Durham, North Carolina: University of North Carolina Press, 1951), for a full treatment of the topic. The author finds membership of American Negroes in the Communist Party to have been inconsequential and doubts that up to 1950 it ever exceeded 8,000.

One great weakness of both these organizations was their lack of support from the Negro masses. This was due in part to the generally low educational and economic status of the Negro masses and the widespread prevalence among Negroes of a resigned and hopeless attitude as far as cracking the color line was concerned. Lack of mass support was also due to the fact that, as in all class structures, the interests of the Negro middle class and the Negro lower class were not identical in all respects.

Race Relations: A Regional Issue

Before turning to consider the trend since World War II, during which great changes in Negro-white relations have occurred, it is pertinent to emphasize that the very existence of regional attitudes and practices as disparate as those portrayed in the past two chapters had been a perennial source of regional conflict affecting the unity of the nation. The slavery issue threatened national unity until the close of the Civil War. From 1880 to World War I, the North in general tended to leave the Negro problem, as far as it was thought of as such, to the South. The Great Migration to the North brought the problem home. The discriminatory pattern that developed appeared at first to suggest a moving of the region closer to that of the South. However, more Northern people began to feel that the prevailing pattern of race relations could not permanently endure in a political democracy and began to work for change. In short, there emerged a definition of black-white relations as a *national* problem. This emerging new definition of the race problem received considerable impetus from the New Deal. In the operation of large-scale relief and in other government-planned projects, the tendency was toward providing Negroes a fairer share. Here and there Negroes were placed in new situations alongside whites. The number of Northern organized groups, especially religious groups, that became interested in democratizing race relations grew.

While these new trends were developing in the North, there was no perceptible indication of the South's readiness to accept this redefinition of the race problem or to basically alter its traditional biracial system. Thus the approach of World War II found a long-standing regional issue assuming new dimensions, more sharply focused by the greater influence of the North—as the predominant center of national opinion-making—in the formation of national policy.

The Impact of World War II

We find it difficult to assess the effect of World War II on the patterns of Negro-white relations in both the North and the South. Such a major national crisis necessarily required some alteration in the established patterns. But in both regions, the broad trend immediately following the war was to resume the previous patterns. It was some ten or more years later that the Black Challenge to white dominance crystalized into a sustained movement. However, the carry-over of new wartime experience in interracial contact for many persons both white and black reinforced other social forces which made the 1960s a ripe time for the Black Challenge.

Negro Job Opportunities

The main effect of the war grew out of the labor shortages which afforded Negro men and women new opportunities for employment, more steadily, and at higher wages with a consequent rise in the standard of living.[23] Some change in status occurred in the employment area. In many war jobs Negroes worked alongside whites on equal terms and were increasingly accepted into labor unions, to a limited extent even in the South, on an integrated basis.[24]

However, even under the urgency of war, acceptance of Negroes was not easy. Employers were reluctant to hire Negroes and white workers showed resistance to accepting them as co-workers.[25] In order to overcome as much as possible of this resistance President Roosevelt issued an executive order in 1941 establishing the Fair Employment Practices Commission, which aimed to require all government agencies and all private firms with government contracts not to discriminate on the basis of race or national origin. While this Commission had neither legislative sanction nor much real power of enforcement, substantial gains in the number of Negroes employed followed its establishment.[26]

Aside from these economic gains, the line of segregation held substantially the same. Even the National Capitol Housing Author-

[23]See Robert C. Weaver, *Negro Labor a National Problem* (New York: Harcourt, Brace and Co., 1946).
[24]See Drake and Cayton, *Black Metropolis*, pp. 309–310, for the Chicago picture during World War II.
[25]See Herbert R. Northrup, *Organized Labor and the Negro* (New York: Harper & Brothers, 1944), for an account of this subject.
[26]See *Fair Employment Practices Commission, Final Report, June 28, 1946* (Washington, D.C., 1947).

ity bowed to the prevailing housing pattern in building low-rent housing units.[27] In other more intimate areas of social relations, substantially no change took place.

The Armed Services

The armed services practiced a policy of segregation. In the Army, Negroes were assigned to colored units, most of which were in supply services where the tasks were largely menial labor. A few thousand Negro officers were trained and placed over Negro troops, frequently under the command of a white captain. In army posts, separate recreational rooms were maintained, and nearly all communities which any considerable number of soldiers frequented—North as well as South—restricted colored troops to the Negro areas and set up separate USO's. For the most part, Negro units were kept out of combat. According to Rose, "In Europe there were some efforts made to keep Negroes from fraternizing with the civilian population, when no such bar was set up against the white troops."[28]

The policy of segregating Negro troops reflected the wishes of the white troops. A survey of the attitudes of servicemen made in March, 1943, revealed that about 80 per cent of the white troops preferred to have the two groups separated in PX's, service clubs, and military units.[29] While over 90 per cent of the Southern white respondents approved segregation it is significant that over 70 per cent of the Northern white troops likewise indicated approval. The Negro respondents showed far more opposition to being segregated, as would also be expected, but the detailed findings provide significant indication of how Negroes viewed their situation generally. Of the Negro sample, 37 per cent disapproved separation in military units; 36 per cent approved; 17 per cent thought it made no difference; and 10 per cent were undecided. Comments by some of the antisegregation Negro soldiers emphasized primarily the democratic principle involved, for example: "Separate outfits shows that the Army continues segregation and discrimination. Is this the Democracy we are told we are fighting for?" The 36 per cent of Negro soldiers who approved of segregation did so on the basis of expediency, on a realistic appraisal of

[27]See *Segregation in Washington, A Report of the National Committee on Segregation in Washington* (Chicago, 1948).
[28]Arnold Rose, *The Negro in America* (New York: Harper & Brothers, 1948), p. 138.
[29]Samuel A. Stouffer, et al., *The American Soldier*, Vol. 1 (Princeton: Princeton University Press, 1949), pp. 566–570.

white prejudice. Among the reasons given by Negroes for taking the pro-segregation viewpoint were a fear of interracial friction—"A white soldier would call a colored soldier 'nigger' and it would be a fight"; a desire to withdraw from the situation of not being wanted—"so long as there are so many prejudiced white people, it would be too unpleasant"; a desire to prove that Negro groups can match the achievements of white groups; and finally, a desire to associate with those who understand one another—"I had rather be with my own color. Then I know where I stand."

Some experiments in desegregated units were conducted toward the war's end without any important difficulties—paving the way for the postwar integrated policy which was to come.[30]

In spite of segregation policy and practice, the total impact of experiences in the armed services had effects disturbing to the traditional pattern of caste relations. More objectively measurable was the introduction of colored servicemen to new standards of welfare—in diet, health, and sanitation; and the increased training in many new skills, some of which could be useful in peacetime. A measure of the Negro soldiers' feeling about the value of their army training is seen in their answers to the direct question on this where 61 per cent replied it would help them, compared with 39 per cent who so replied among the whites.[31]

Less tangible but perhaps in the long run more significant was the impact of service experience on the attitudes of GI's of both races. Northern-born Negro servicemen trained in the South came face to face with the stricter Southern caste system. Southern Negro GI's stationed in the North experienced some measure of unaccustomed freedom. In Europe many Negro GI's found white people wishing to accept them like any other American soldier. Equally disturbing to traditional attitudes and habits was the impact of war service on many white Southerners. This is most dramatically illustrated in Margaret Halsey's account of her experiences operating a servicemen's center in a large Northern city.[32]

---

[30]See Charles Dollard and Donald Young, "In the Armed Forces," *Survey Graphic*, Jan. 1947, p. 68.
[31]Stouffer, *The American Soldier*, p. 537.
[32]Margaret Halsey, *Color Blind* (New York: Simon and Schuster, 1946).

Suggested Readings

Fishel, Leslie H., Jr. *The Negro American: A Documentary History.* Glenville, Illinois: Scott, Foresman and Company, 1967.
Chapter 10, "Reaction and Renaissance" is composed of readings pertinent to this chapter.

Lee, Frank F. *Negro and White in Connecticut Town.* New York: Bookman Associates, 1961.
A study of race relations in a small town emphasizing the techniques of social control.

Locke, Alain. *The New Negro.* New York: Albert and Charles Boni, 1925.
One of the first books surveying the literary and artistic contributions of the Negroes to American culture.

Osofsky, Gilbert. *Harlem: The Making of the Ghetto.* New York: Harper & Row, 1966.
An outstanding history of Negro New York, 1890–1930.

Spear, Allan H. *Black Chicago.* Chicago: The University of Chicago Press, 1967.
A historical study of the making of a ghetto in Chicago from 1890 to 1920.

Waskow, Arthur I. *From Race Riot to Sit-In: 1919 and the 1960's,* Garden City, New York: Doubleday Company, Anchor Books, 1966.
The first half of this volume describes and analyzes the major race riots of 1919 in the light of their origins, the riot process, and how they were dealt with.

8 Changing Black-White Relations: A National Crisis

In this chapter attention turns to the black-white relations occuring from the end of World War II to the beginning of the full-scale Black Challenge which has brought the racial situation to a crisis. Since the beginning of this development was in the South, this region is dealt with first. In the 1960s the focus of the crisis shifted to the North in line with the large-scale black migration. Thus black-white relations, so long thought of as a regional problem, became a major national domestic issue. We shall also attempt to assess the main changes in black welfare and status through the 1960 decade, leaving analysis of the "Black Challenge" as a movement and the white response to it to the following chapter.

Prologue to the Black Challenge

Following World War II the pattern of black-white relations tended to resume much of its pre-war character. In the South, substantially no change at all occurred until the crisis which was precipitated by the Supreme Court's school desegregation mandate in 1954 which, in the Deep South, was successfully resisted until the 1960s. The tempo of interracial tension and violence rose as Southern blacks sought to have the successive court rulings outlawing local public accommodations enforced.

The North approved of the courts' rulings on school desegregation and other public forms of discrimination, and was generally critical of the South's resistance. But it should not be over-looked that what the South was being ordered to do was what had long been practiced in the North. However, because of the flexibility of the Northern racial pattern, other forms of Northern discrimination were being challenged by individual blacks or local groups oftimes successful and oftimes not. This sort of piecemeal process was whittling away at discrimination in public and civic discrimination in the absence of any broad challenge. The separation of the races spatially and socially remained intact. But the increasing flow of Southern blacks to the great metropolitan centers created problems in housing, employment, and welfare, and aggravated racial tensions.

As background for analyzing the Black Challenge which is before the nation, attention is directed to broad social forces in the society which bore on the black-white situation.

THE EFFECT OF SOCIAL FORCES

Economic, Technological, and Ecological Trends

The expanding economy offered some new jobs for Negroes and some at higher levels for qualified Negroes. This was considerably offset by a decrease in demand for unskilled workers brought about by technological changes leading to large-scale unemployment. The nation in general became increasingly more affluent. In this Negroes shared but disproportionally to whites. Their concentration in larger centers gave them increased localized political power, but aggravated slum conditions, and increased racial tension. Theoretically "rationalization" of the economic system favors job placement on the basis of achieved qualifications rather than ascribed status; and the keener competition for profit turns attention to the rising purchasing power of the Negro population. But long-standing racial mores impeded these logical trends.

Political and Governmental Trends

The traditional basis of democratic governmental institutions pressed for more equality for Negroes as reflected in court decisions, civil rights legislation, and governmental administration particularly at the federal level and, outside the South, at some state and local levels. The growing Negro vote influenced office-seekers to promise improvements and prompted office-holders to pay attention to Negro requests. The general trend toward the "welfare state" helped to sustain the welfare of the many poorly paid and unemployed Negroes. Provision of this aid, however, reinforced a traditional concept among whites that Negroes won't work and are glad to live on relief. Finally, increasing sensitivity to adverse world opinion of the United States' racial system favored both official and voluntary action to offer more equality.

Cultural Trends

The general increase in educational facilities was shared by Negroes if unevenly and spottily, aside from the whole matter of desegregation, and had some effect on debunking the myth of innate Negro inferiority. The increasing dissemination of social science findings was creating a younger generation of white adults who at the intellectual level were more aware of the errors of the doctrine of racism and more conscious of the damaging consequences to American society of the persistence of the traditional intergroup pattern. All these influences favoring the decline in discrimination prompted the leading organized religions to reassess the implications of their practices in regard to the race question.

The Elaboration of Mass Media

In the post-war period there was an elaboration of the mass media. The leading American newspapers and magazines gave racial news wide coverage and tended to editorialize in favor of the American Creed. Television, however, is the medium that has the most powerful influence on both blacks and whites. Witnessing the jeering faces of white mothers as Negro students entered hitherto white schools might have been a powerful stimulus for the cause of racial justice. Likewise the televising of civil rights activities may have aroused in witnessing blacks the desire to participate in the movement themselves.

Since the net effect of the operation of these social forces was to improve the welfare and to a limited extent the status of Negroes, it tended to raise the aspirations of Negroes still further and to spur more concerted direct action by Negroes and those whites committed to the Negro cause.

World Opinion

The adverse world opinion of the United States for its discrimination against blacks influenced official and voluntary action toward its elimination. Not well recognized as yet was the incubating conception of the "Third World" to be composed of the non-white peoples against the two white worlds of communism and the capitalist West.[1]

I. THE CHANGING SOUTH

Before 1954

In the South following World War II the pre-war pattern of race relations was continued with some minor exceptions.

In the area of civil rights, the following developments may be noted: an increase in Negro voting—595,000 Negroes were on the voting rolls in 1947 and 1,008,614 in 1953;[2] some increase in Negro jury service prompted by a growing disposition of the federal courts to overturn convictions where the failure to call Negroes into service was attested; some beginnings of arresting and trying white people for crimes of violence against Negroes; the appointment of some Negro police officers to cover Negro areas. No precipitate rise in violence toward Negroes was apparent, although the virtual disappearance of lynching was somewhat offset by a rise in the bombing of Negro homes—more than forty being reported for a year and a half period during 1951 to 1952.[3] While there was some reactivation of racist organizations, such as the Ku Klux Klan, white public opinion against such extremists was evidenced by the outlawing of masked gatherings in some Southern cities.

In education, two significant developments in the post-war years were (1) a partial breach in the pattern of segregation in higher education at the graduate level. Estimates indicate more than 200 Negroes enrolled in hitherto exclusively white graduate schools in 1951, and (2) a trend toward greater equalization of the segregated Negro school system as compared to the white system. A special study of public school education in 1952 found that con-

[1]See Ronald Segal, *The Race War* (New York: The Viking Press, 1967), Chapter 1.
[2]Margaret Price, *The Negro and the Ballot* (Atlanta: The Southern Regional Council, 1959), p. 9.
[3]"Blight, Bigotry, and Bombs," *The New South* (Atlanta, Ga.: Southern Regional Council, July, 1952).

siderable improvement had been made but that much more progress would be needed before the real equalization of the Negro schools would be achieved.[4] These improvements were prompted in the hope that they might influence the impending Supreme Court Decision not to order desegregation.

Thus on the surface in the main the Southern biracial system remained intact, then came the Supreme Court decision outlawing segregation.

The Supreme Court School Desegregation Decision: May 17, 1954

This decision concerned five separate cases, which the court consolidated since the same legal question was involved in each of them. In each case Negro children through their legal representatives had sought admission to white public schools, had been denied this right by local courts, and eventually had appealed the unfavorable decisions to the Supreme Court of the United States. The National Association for the Advancement of Colored People took charge of the case, directed by Thurgood Marshall, later to become a Supreme Court justice himself. The core of the decision is found in the following excerpts:

> We conclude that in the field of public education the doctrine of "separate but equal" has no place. Separate educational facilities are inherently unequal. Therefore, we hold that the plaintiffs and others similarly situated for whom the actions have been brought are, by reason of the segregation complained of, deprived of the equal protection of the laws guaranteed by the Fourteenth Amendment. . . .
>
> Segregation of white and colored children in public schools has a detrimental effect upon the colored children. The impact is greater when it has the sanction of law; for the policy of separating the races is usually interpreted as denoting the inferiority of the Negro group. A sense of inferiority affects the motivation of the child to learn. Segregation, with the sanction of the law, therefore has a tendency to retard the educational and mental development of Negro children and to deprive them of some of the benefits they would receive in a racially integrated school system. . . .

[4]Truman M. Pierce, and others, *White and Negro Schools in the South* (Englewood Cliffs, N.J.: Prentice-Hall, 1955), p. 292. See pp. 291–292 for summary.

Whatever may have been the extent of psychological knowledge at the time of Plessy vs. Ferguson, this finding is amply supported by modern authority. Any language in Plessy vs. Ferguson contrary to this finding is rejected.[5]

The way the Court handled these cases indicated awareness of strong negative reactions and that enforcement would be beset with special difficulties. The decision was unanimous and read by Chief Justice Earl Warren. The Court postponed its implementing order until May 31, 1955, when it ordered compliance "with all deliberate speed." This phraseology indicated that the Supreme Court did not expect affected states to integrate all schools at once, but that some reasonable plan for eventual complete integration should be made and a beginning announced. It was left to district federal courts to decide whether a particular plan presented in its area was designed to accomplish really complete integration in a reasonable time.

It is essential to emphasize that the implications of the school decision went far beyond the matter of schools alone. It appeared that the reasoning presented in supporting the decision had general application—in effect the court was saying that all state-imposed racial segregation was unconstitutional. By stating that it was reversing *Plessy* v. *Ferguson* (1896), which held that segregation in public transportation was legal provided the facilities were equal, the Court seemed to imply this general application. Subsequent decisions by various courts within the federal system in widely divergent fields further supported this interpretation. In short, the school desegregation decision appeared to undermine the entire legal, or *de jure*, basis of public racial discrimination throughout the United States. Obviously, for the South this legal situation was bound to create a crisis of a profoundly critical nature. Since we wish to discuss the Southern crisis in these broader terms, we will at this point summarize the main facts concerning school desegregation and later discuss the crisis period in broader terms.

---

[5]347 U.S. 483. The number 1 case was *Brown, et al.* v. *Board of Education of Topeka, Kansas.* Three other cases were linked together with *Brown, et al.*: *Briggs* v. *Elliott* (South Carolina); *Davis* v. *County School Board of Prince Edward County, Virginia; Gebhart* v. *Belton* (Delaware). A separate decision in *Bolling* v. *Sharpe,* 347, U.S. 497, to the same effect was read following *Brown, et al.* This case concerned segregation of public schools in the District of Columbia and therefore involved the federal government directly.

School Desegregation in the Southern Region

The most striking fact was the slow pace of desegregation. (1) The District of Columbia was the only area to desegregate all its school immediately following the decision. (2) Substantial integration in the border states occurred in the first few years so that by the school year 1960–1961 almost half (49 per cent) of Negro pupils in those states combined were in school with whites. (3) In seven of the eleven Southern states, a very few school districts desegregated before 1960 and even up to 1965 the percentage of Negro pupils in school with whites was five per cent or below.[6] Most desegregation up to 1964 took the "token" form—that is, admitting only a few Negroes into a white school and calling it "desegregated." (4) Before 1960, no public school desegregation at all had taken place in Lousiana, Georgia, Alabama, and Mississippi. The first break in these states came in New Orleans where in November 1960, under court order the Orleans Parish School Board admitted three pupils to one elementary school and one to another. The first sharp increase in the Deep South came as a result of pressure brought by the U.S. Department of Health, Education, and Welfare requiring all school districts to submit "affidavits of compliance" with the court order as a requirement for receiving federal funds. This new policy had considerable effect but even by 1967, only 15.9 per cent of all Negro pupils were in school with whites.[7]

It was not until the school years 1970–1972 that the South, especially in city areas, began in earnest to desegregate on a widespread scale, and in some cases even to use bussing for this purpose, accomplished with little tension.[8]

School desegregation in the South had other difficulties. "Tokenism" slows up integration since the few Negro students, if not openly abused—as some of the first to enter were—are not socially accepted and therefore often Negro students selected have hesitated to enter; those who did enter sometimes withdrew. Moreover, where desegregation took place with considerable Negro enrollment, resegregation, or decided imbalance, occurs through

[6]These seven states listed in order of first district desegregation were Texas, Arkansas, Tennessee, North Carolina, Florida, South Carolina, and Virginia.
[7]See *Statistical Summary of School Segregation-Desegregation in the Southern and Border States*, 1966–1967, published by Southern Education Reporting Services, Nashville, Tennessee, p. 2.
[8]See James T. Wooten, *The New York Times*, August 29, 1971, p. 45.

the withdrawal of white students.[9] Finally, there is the matter of *de jure* vs. *de facto* desegregation. The school board of a particular district might officially desegregate but in some areas within the district there might be no Negroes or no whites, so that while the district was counted as a desegregated district, the proportion of Negro students in school with whites might or might not be high. The housing segregation of Negroes in large cities plus the "flight to the suburbs" of whites (similar to the Northern situation) made this distinction between *de jure* and *de facto* significant.

The potentially adverse consequences of school desegregation for Negro teachers was recognized from the very start of the process. In 1966–1967, at least 41,403 Negro teachers in the South were reported to be serving on desegregated faculties, out of a total of 113,557.[10]

THE SOUTHERN CRISIS

The school case decision of 1954 precipitated a crisis for the South, especially the Deep South. Since the implications of the decision were, from the Southern point of view, revolutionary, it is not surprising that what followed was a bitter, continuous struggle between those committed to traditional continuity and those intent on basic change in the Southern interracial system.

Following the school desegregation decision, tension and conflict between the races rose sharply. Biracial relations in most communities were polarized between active Negro groups and reactionary white groups, pitted against each other on the desegregation issue. Moderate white leadership was unable to exert influence; liberals faced extraordinary reprisals.[11] Effective communication between the white and Negro communities broke down. The issue had become the abolition or survival of the segregation system itself.

[9]In 1960 in Orchard Villa School, Dade County, Florida, the admission of even a few Negro students brought white student withdrawals. At the end of the school year the school was all Negro.
[10]"Statistical Summary of School Segregation-Desegregation in Southern and Border States, 1966–1967," *Southern Education Reporting Service* (April, 1967), p. 2.
[11]We define a segregationist as one who believes that retention of the biracial system is the most important thing to the South; a moderate as one who believes in segregation but gives many other things priority over this issue and who is therefor willing to compromise on the race issue; a liberal as the white Southerner who believes that desegregation in varyng degrees of rapidity is desirable, whether or not he is able to do anything about it.

The interracial struggle has followed a course which we will describe in the following phases: (1) Southern whites viewed the situation as a crisis and the prevailing segment reacted accordingly with strong resistance. (2) Negroes challenged further areas of segregation with considerable success. (3) Further extra-regional pressures were brought upon the South with reference to other forms of segregation: from Congress in the form of Civil Rights legislation which led to increasing intervention by the federal government, and from voluntary groups, such as the "Freedom Riders." (4) Under the impact of all these pressures, the resistance movement began to weaken and reluctant compliance with desegregation orders increased.

White Resistance

A measure of the unreadiness of the white South to accept desegregation can be gained from public opinion polls. On the school issue itself, the extent of Southern white disapproval is indicated by a Gallup Poll in 1954 which found 71 per cent of its Southern white sample disapproving the school decision, as compared with 30 per cent outside the South.[12] Southern white support for the traditional system is further attested in another poll, where the respondents were requested to choose between "keeping the races apart," and "bringing them together" as the best solution to the Negro-white problem. Nearly three-fourths of the Southern white respondents were for segregation while only about one-sixth favored integration.

In such an attitudinal climate it is not surprising that tension increased. A report found 530 cases of violence, reprisal, and intimidation from 1955–1958.[13]

ORGANIZED RESISTANCE: WHITE CITIZENS COUNCILS Of the various groups opposing desegregation, the most prominent was the White Citizens Council movement. Originating in Mississippi it spread to other states. Members included people of high status and power which may explain why its activities were non-violent. Besides influencing state legislation, the Council's chief

[12]Data furnished by American Institute of Public Opinion, Princeton, New Jersey, which has conducted polls on the question of desegregation since 1954.
[13]"Intimidations, Reprisal, and Violence in the South's Racial Crisis," published by the Southeastern Office, American Friends Service Committee, Department of Racial and Cultural Relations, National Council of Churches of Christ in the United States of America; and the Southern Regional Council, 1959.

activity was to apply economic pressure on both Negroes and whites who participated openly in desegregation. The effectiveness of this was illustrated by the eviction by white landlords of Negro tenants from their farms in two counties of Tennessee (1960). The reason given for this action was that because of mechanical improvements the Negroes were no longer needed. But the evicted tenants included Negroes who had been active in attempting to register to vote. A federal district court order stopped these evictions.

SUCCESS OF WHITE RESISTANCE   In addition to its success in delaying public school desegregation, the white resistance movement was effective in two other areas: (1) A pre-1954 trend toward integration of Negroes in college was slowed down[14] and (2) Efforts to limit further extension of the voting franchise to Negroes took place. A Florida study shows that most of the postwar Negro registration took place by 1950. The author commented that: "Increasing tension over the segregation issue is making it more difficult for officials and candidates in the South to maintain a moderate position on this (the voting) issue, or seek Negro support on other issues."[15]

The predominance of the resistance elements of the white South over moderates seems clear to 1960. The upsetting of a moderate white Southern Congressman, Brook Hays, of Little Rock in 1958 by a write-in vote suggests why other Southern politicians who may have privately held moderate views did not outwardly oppose the resistance movement.

Negro Reaction to the Crisis

To many white Americans the most surprising consequence of the Southern situation was the reaction of Negroes. This arose because of the wide discrepancy between the way the white people thought the Negro felt and the way the Negro actually felt. As a consequence of the social distance between the two groups, whites seldom learn much of the Negro's feelings. This was further aggravated by the tendency of Negroes in conversation with white people to conceal their real feelings. Finally the misinterpretation

[14]United States Commission on Civil Rights, *Report on Racial Discrimination in Higher Education*, 1961, as reported in *The New York Times*, January 16, 1961.
[15]H. D. Price, *The Negro and Southern Politics: A Chapter of Florida History* (New York: New York University Press, 1957), p. 106.

on the part of whites was largely a matter of wishful thinking. Many believed what they wanted to believe, which helped to justify the situation.

It is easily understandable that induration to minority status prevented many Negroes from active participation in the desegregation movement. Fighting for their rights was fraught with danger and the experience of integration itself was often uncomfortable. But this was not the prevailing mood in Negro response.

The Supreme Court's decision in the school cases raised the level of aspiration of American Negroes to new heights. For the first time since the Southern Reconstruction, younger Negroes began to feel that first-class citizenship was a possibility within their own lifetime. For an increasing number of American Negroes, "Uncle Tom" was now dead.[16] This prevailing mood has been demonstrated in various protest movements.

THE MONTGOMERY BUS PROTEST   "Jim Crow" laws as applied to public transportation have always been a major source of irritation to the colored minority. Aside from the principle involved, they have been a practical inconvenience, heightened by the fact that Negroes use public transportation more than whites. The practice promotes inefficiency and is costly. It is therefore not surprising that a Negro challenge on this point should be one of the next steps.

As is often the case in such a situation, the precise time and the particular place resulted from a fortuitous incident, in this instance in Montgomery, Alabama, in 1955.[17]

On December 1, 1955, a Negro woman refused to "move back" on a crowded bus so that a white woman could have her seat. For this the bus driver had her arrested. The Negro community of Montgomery reacted by organizing a boycott of the buses. The Negroes walked or arranged car pools. The movement was led by the Montgomery Improvement Asociation, formed for the purpose. The leader of the organization was the hitherto unknown Reverend Martin Luther King, Jr., who, as a result of his role in the protest movement, emerged as a nationally recognized Negro

[16]The name "Uncle Tom" has long been used among Negroes to designate those Negro leaders who have placated whites by not challenging the segregation system, thus strengthening the accommodative relationship while hindering attempts at social change.
[17]See L. D. Reddick, *Crusader Without Violence: A Biography of Martin Luther King, Jr.* (New York: Harper & Brothers, 1959). Chs. 8, 9, and 10, give an account of the Montgomery bus protest movement.

leader. A remarkable development in this affair was the practically unanimous and well-disciplined cooperation of the Negroes of the city. At the outset, the M.I.A. made the modest demand for a "first come, first served" procedure in bus seating, the Negroes to start from the rear, the whites from the front. Since this did not challenge the Jim Crow principle directly, the National Association for the Advancement of Colored People would not lend its assistance. However, when this modest demand was rejected, the M.I.A. adopted the NAACP viewpoint, calling for complete integration, and received the national organization's support.

The bus boycott continued for many months at great loss to the local bus companies, while a legal case was carried finally to the United States Supreme Court. On November 14, 1956, this Court upheld a previous district court decision declaring the transportation segregation laws of the State of Alagama unconstitutional. On December 21, 1956, integrated buses rolled down the streets of Montgomery for the first time, with Dr. King and other M.I.A. leaders sitting up front.

Other Negro Protest Activity: "Sit-Ins" and "Freedom Riders"

Other challenges involved "sit-ins" directed at the taboo against Negroes eating in public restaurants with whites. In 1960 Negro students in Rock Hill, South Carolina sat down at a local store lunch counter and were refused service. This movement spread despite much abuse from white Southerners and frequent arrests. However, it led to rioting. Within a year most Southern branch stores of national corporations served Negro customers on the same basis as whites.

In May, 1961 a group of Northerners of both races decided to test the extent of Southern compliance with the court ruling that segregation in public facilities involving interstate commerce was illegal. As the riders proceeded farther South they met increasing resistance culminating in a riot in Montgomery which led Attorney General Robert F. Kennedy to send in federal marshals to abate the tension. Despite a federal request to let matters "cool off," similar rides took place, meeting with varying degrees of resistance.

The striking aspects of these protest activities were the use of the non-violent techniques by the protesters and their discipline in this regard. News and television portrayals of incidents involved usually showed the whites in a most unfavorable light as compared with the protesters.[18]

Further Federal Pressures: The Courts and Administration

FEDERAL ACTION ON VOTING While the federal courts were continuing to issue orders of desegregation, the Congress of the United States made no supplementary moves to further the desegregation process until 1957, when the first Civil Rights Act for many years was passed.[19] Its main provisions were (1) to authorize the establishment of a Commission of Civil Rights, whose duties were: to study the entire problem, including specifically denials of the right to vote; to collect information concerning legal developments denying equal protection of the laws; and to appraise the laws and policies of the federal government with respect to equal protection, (2) to empower the Attorney General to seek court injunctions against interference with the voting rights of any individual, and (3) to establish a Civil Rights Division in the Department of Justice. But as the long effective resistance to school desegregation shows, court ruling and laws depend upon their administrative implementation. State governments of the Deep South did nothing to implement them. Only Southern federal district courts and efforts of the federal government to intervene were effective, although at times these attempts were hampered by Southern Congressman as well as by the varying attitudes of the presidents.

ON VOTING The Commission found that in 1956 only about 25 per cent of the nearly five million Negroes of voting age as of the 1950 Census were registered, in contrast to 60 per cent of voting-age whites. Five months elapsed after this report appeared before any complaints were filed, first from Alabama and Louisiana. In the hearings held, ample proof of discrimination was found despite the refusal of local authorities to testify. But the Commission found that the federal government faced difficulties in prosecuting violations. "The history of voting in the United States shows, and the experience of this commission has con-

[18]The Congress of Racial Equality (CORE) had trained some student protesters in non-violent activity.
[19]Students of the realities of politics and government in the United States will know that the Southern Congressional representation has special means at its command to block any legislation dealing with racial discrimination—for example, chairmanships of key congressional committees acquired through seniority.

firmed, that where there is a will and opportunity to discriminate against certain potential voters, ways to discriminate will be found."[20]

Reluctant Compliance

From roughly 1960 on Southern white reaction took the form of reluctant minimum compliance to federal law, delaying as long as possible. Gradually, the threat by a Negro organization to take cases to court or of federal intervention spurred some white authorities to institute "voluntary" desegregation.

Certain consequences of the increased tension and conflict which affected the region adversely, strengthened the trend toward compliance:[21] (1) Unfavorable economic effects were felt. The South lost national conventions because the cities were unable to guarantee non-discriminatory treatment of Negro members. Certain businesses otherwise disposed to locate in the South were waiting until the racial atmosphere cleared. (2) The education of whites as well as Negroes became seriously disturbed. Southern universities lost many faculty members and found difficulties recruiting new ones. (3) Southern politicians with aspirations for public office have found that the segregationist label, necessary for election in the South, is often a disqualifying mark outside the region.

SOUTHERN BLACK REACTION TO LIMITED GAINS

The Gains

Along with the nation and black Americans generally, the welfare of Southern blacks has improved. But wide disparities between their welfare and that of whites remain. While in some indicants the differential welfare may have slightly closed, in the main they have not. Some illustrations are these:

"Poverty among Negroes in the South is about three times more prevalent than in the rest of the country."[22]

[20]"With Liberty and Justice for All," an abridgement of the *Report of the United States Civil Rights Commission*, 1959, p. 88.
[21]See *The Price We Pay*, prepared by Barbara Patterson and other staff members of the Southern Regional Council and the Anti-Defamation League, for extensive examples of the various costs of discrimination, particularly to the South.
[22]Andrew R. Brimmer, "The Negro in the National Economy," Ch. 5 in John P. Davis, *The Negro American Reference Book* (Englewood Cliffs, N.J.: Prentice-Hall, 1966), p. 263.

Health has improved but the seven to eight year lower life expectancy as compared with whites still remains.[23]

There are far more blacks attending the formerly all-white state universities.[24]

Against subtle discrimination practices by unions, some upward mobility has occurred in occupational but not in the clerical fields.[25]

In public accommodations, blacks have gained but customary habituation tends to cause blacks often not to assert their rights.

Marked gains have occurred in the administration of equal justice. The white man pleading guilty of shooting James Meredith in June 1966, while Meredith was making a protest march, was sentenced to three years in prison. This was the highest sentence given a white assailant of blacks up to this time.

A landmark in the history of Mississippi justice occurred in October 1967, when an all-white Neshoba County jury presided over by a Mississippi-born Federal judge, found seven out of fifteen white Mississippians guilty of participating in a plot which had resulted in the death of three civil rights workers in 1964. One of the convicted defendants was the chief deputy sheriff of the county. At first the jury reported itself deadlocked but were "persuaded" by the judge to try again to reach a verdict.

Political Participation

In its long run implications, the most significant gain for Southern blacks was, and continues to be, increasing participation in the political arena.

"During the 1960s black Americans in the South made remarkable gains in their struggle for the right to participate meaningfully in the political process. Registration of blacks has more than doubled [reaching about 4 million in 1972]. The number of black elected officials increased six-fold. [But] there are still more than two million Southern blacks not registered."[26]

In the year 1970, the number of Southern black elected offi-

[23]See William Payne, "There is Hunger Here," *U.S. Civil Rghts Digest*, 1969, pp. 34–40.

[24]In 1971 the per cent of black enrollment in the University of Mississippi was 3.5; in the University of Alabama, 3.7; and in the University of South Carolina, 5.1.

[25]See Herbert Hill, "The Pattern of Job Discrimination Against Negroes" in *Minority Problems*, eds. Arnold M. and Caroline B. Rose (New York: Harper and Row, 1965), pp. 153–155.

[26]Data supplied by the Voter Education Project, Atlanta, Georgia, as of early summer, 1972.

cials had reached over 650, including fifteen members of the Georgia Legislature one of whom, Julian Bond—who when first elected was refused seating until a court ordered his admission—has acquired a national reputation. One indication of the effect of this black political participation has been the tendency for Southern white candidates for office to ignore the race issue.

Interracial Tension and Violence

It is inevitable that in a period of heightened tension, violence will increase. Despite the efforts of Dr. Martin Luther King, Jr. to lead the protest movements with the non-violent technique, from 1955 through June, 1966, 108 persons are known to have been killed in race-related incidents.[27] Six of the thirty-one riots reported up to mid-August for the year 1967 were in Southern cities.[28]

Assessment of the Current Southern Situation

Now that black-white relations have become a national problem, focused in metropolitan areas, there are increasing similarities in all regions. Since the pace of change resulting from the Black Challenge has slowed down, it appears that the assessment of the Southern situation made by Blumer in the mid 1960s, with some qualifications, is still broadly applicable.

It is a serious mistake, however, to regard the achievement by Negroes of civil rights, as presently defined, as equivalent to removing the color line. . . . The contested area of civil rights is, as previously stated, but the outer band of the color line. Inside of it lies the crucial area of economic subordination and opportunity restriction—an area of debarment of Negroes which is exceedingly tough because it is highly complicated by private and quasi-private property rights, managerial rights, and organizational rights. Still further inside of the color line are the varied circles of private association from which the Negro is grossly excluded. Thus, the successful achievement of civil rights merely peels off, so to speak, the outer layer of the color line. By itself, it does not alter significantly the social positions of the two racial groups. It raises somewhat the position of the Negro on the dominance-

[27]"Violence," New South, November, 1965, and a 1966 supplement, Southern Regional Council, Atlanta, Georgia.
[28]Time, August 11, 1967, "Riot Toll: 1967 and Before," p. 11.

subordination axis but leaves this axis of relationship essentially intact.[29]

The main qualifications stem from the increasing political power of Southern blacks. As we have noted, Southern politicians already play down the race issue. But more broadly, in the past few years, the moderate and liberal white Southerners have been able to challenge the power of the traditional white Southern racists, for example in the election of Reuben Askew as Governor of Florida. In short, in the urban areas of the South, white Southerners are becoming adjusted to accepting the civic rights of blacks and to interact with blacks on a formally equal basis in regard to public matters.[30]

In conclusion, it is essential not to overrate black progress obtained via the political route. Registration to vote does not mean that all registrants will vote, as was indicated by the overwhelming defeat of Charles Evers, the black mayor of Fayette, Mississippi, in his recent campaign for governor of that state. As with American voters in general apathy plays a part; but also the long ingrained fear of reprisals affects black participation, particularly in smaller communities.

II. THE CRISIS IN THE NORTH[31]

In describing and analyzing the black community it is most essential to keep in mind that by the 1950s it had become far more elaborated in the socioeconomic levels, and as will be shown, became increasingly so in the 1960s. Because for so long, and still, the oftcalled black "masses" were so numerically predominant, it is their image which constitutes the stereotype of "blacks" among most white people.

[29]Herbert Blumer, "The Future of the Color Line," Ch. 15 in John C. McKinney and Edgar T. Thompson, eds., *The South in Continuity and Change* (Durham, N.C.: Duke University Press, 1965), pp. 329–330.
[30]Even so die-hard a segregationist as George Wallace, who made a symbolic gesture of defiance of federal law by confronting the federal marshal escorting the first black student to be admitted into Alabama State University, no longer talks about "Segregation Forever." In his brief 1972 campaign for the Democratic nomination for president, his main race-related issue was opposition to "bussing" school children, which has considerable appeal nationwide.
[31]"North" is used here as a convenient short word for those parts of the nation outside the South. More precisely it refers to the urbanized areas with a major metropolis as the core and satellite areas in their vicinities, as indicated in Chapter 5, Table 5–1.

The Ecological Pattern

In Grodzins study of Pittsburgh in the mid 1950s he found Negroes highly concentrated and made the following prediction which is still broadly accurate. "The picture for the future is clear enough: Large non-white concentrations (in a few cases numerical majorities) in the principal cities; large white majorities, with scattered Negro enclaves in their suburbs."[32]

In large cities with substantial Negro populations, the residential distribution of Negro people tends to follow this pattern: (1) There is a main Negro area—Harlem, for example—not far from the central business district, where a large part of the population dwells and major businesses and recreational enterprises catering to Negroes are located. (2) There are other smaller pockets of almost exclusive Negro residents, typically sections becoming less desirable for residence. (3) There are some mixed white-Negro areas in the inner core of the metropolitan area where the white people are of lower economic level. (4) Where Negroes have moved to the suburbs, the areas involved tend to become all Negro.

The process by which Negro residential segregation comes about is roughly as follows. Start with a sizable compact Negro area with population growing by births and even more by migration from the South. White resistance makes any movement directly outward or jumping to other low-rent areas difficult. However, some vacancies do occur in these other areas as upwardly-mobile non-Negro families move out. One or two Negro families thus manage to get a new block or section. Whites, having tried first to prevent this "invasion" and failed, now react in panic and begin to move out rapidly. More Negroes move in, and the section becomes all Negro.[33]

To a large extent, the movement outward constitutes a spreading of the slums, with all the concomitants typically associated with slums: low income, substandard dwellings (for which blacks have to pay disproportionately higher rents), overcrowding, and higher rates of sociopathic behavior. Whether the movement takes the form of pushing out to the contiguous areas or jumping into new sections, the areas become all black. In consequence, the

[32]Morton Grodzins, *The Metropolitan Area as a Racial Problem* (Pittsburgh: University of Pittsburgh Press, 1958).
[33]See "Where Shall We Live?" *Report of the Commission on Race and Housing* (Berkeley and Los Angeles: University of California Press, 1958), Ch. 2.

black community remains separate from the white and, except for work contacts, black social isolation from whites is increased and most of the ghetto inhabitants "live, eat, shop, work, play and die in a completely Negro world."[34]

The Social Organization and Culture of the Black Ghettos

The larger portion of the population of black ghettos consists of migrants from the South and their children. Whatever elements of stable social organization or cultural norms the migrants may have brought with them were, in any case, not adaptable to their new environment. Thus new ways of life had to be developed more or less ad hoc. This meant necessarily weak social organization as reflected most extremely in the life of young blacks, and in weak family life. The large number of fatherless families attests to the weakness of black family life. A 1971 report shows 56 per cent of the *black poor* (not the overall black median) live in families headed by mothers as compared with 30 per cent among the *white poor*.[35] Earlier Moynihan concluded "it's probable that not much more than one third of Negro youth reach 18 years having lived all their lives with both their parents."[36] He further sees the main problem in the position of the Negro male which boils down to his insecure position as a worker, poorly paid, or unemployed, engendering a feeling of despair at not being able to fulfill family responsibilities.[37] Recorded rates of illegitimate births in the black population have run about ten times that of the recorded white illegitimate births.[38]

In addition to a weak family structure, and no doubt related to it, the ghetto area generally has weak community organization. Liebow, on the basis of his in-depth study of a small sample of

---

[34]*Ibid.*, p. 11. We think "work" should not have been included.
[35]U.S. Census, "Characteristics of the Low-Income Population: 1971" (P–60, No. 82).
[36]Daniel P. Moynihan "Employment, Income and the Ordeal of the Negro Family" in Talcott Parsons and Kenneth Clark *The Negro American* (Boston: Houghton Mifflin Co., 1966) p. 150.
[37]*Ibid.*, pp. 148–150.
[38]We are not unmindful of the criticism of Moynihan's analysis of Negro family life as indicated by the appearance of *The Moynihan Report and the Politics of Controversy*, eds. Lee Rainwater and William Yancey (Cambridge: The M.I.T. Press, 1967). The data, however, are clear. It should be borne in mind, however, that the weak family organization among blacks occurs in a total American society which shows much family instability. Also, there are indications of high premarital pregnancies in the white population but they are more often followed by marriage than in the case of blacks. That a considerable number of slum-dwelling blacks manage to live more conventional (as whites define) family life is clearly the case.

young adults in Washington, D.C., finds that "this streetcorner world does not at all fit the traditional characterization of the lower-class neighborhood as a tightly knit community whose members share the feeling 'we are all in this together.' "[39] As to a distinctive culture, the same author writes: "nor does it seem profitable . . . to look at it [streetcorner society] as a self-supporting ongoing social system with its own distinctive 'design for living,' principles of organization, and system of values."[40] Following up the same theme the author writes:

> "No doubt, each generation does provide role models for each succeeding one. Of much greater importance for the possibilities of change, however, is the fact that many similarities between the lower-class Negro father and son (or mother and daughter) do not result from "cultural transmission" but from the fact that the son goes out and independently experiences the same failures, in the same areas, and for much the same reasons as his father. What appears as a dynamic self-sustaining cultural process is, in part at least, a relatively simple piece of social machinery which turns out, in rather mechanical fashion, independently produced look-alikes."[41]

Economic Welfare

Major problems for black ghetto residents include low economic welfare and income, narrow occupational distribution, and high rates of unemployment. As to income, the comparative per cent of all white and black persons living below the poverty line in 1959 was 55 for non-whites and 18 for whites;[42] in 1971 the relative rates were about 31 per cent for blacks and for whites, 10 per cent. Comparative per family incomes for 1971 show a median black family income to be about 60 per cent of the median of white families. The differential gap between the racial groups is not appreciably closing.[43] Comparative unemployment rates between whites and non-whites showed a high degree of consistency from 1954 through 1968, the non-white rate being double that of

[39]Elliot Liebow, *Tally's Corner: A Study of Negro Streetcorner Men* (Boston: Little, Brown & Company) p. 219.
[40]*Ibid.*
[41]*Ibid.*, p. 223.
[42]See William L. Henderson and Larry C. Ledebur, *Economic Disparity* (New York: The Free Press), p. 331.
[43]See "Characteristics of the Low-Income Population: 1971," U.S. Census Bureau (P–60, No. 82), 1971.

the white rate.[44] The data on income and unemployment would naturally be expected to be reflected in occupational distribution, as Table 8-1 shows.

TABLE 8-1   EMPLOYMENT BY OCCUPATION,[a] 1967, AND CHANGE, 1960–1967 (Numbers in Thousands)

| | Employed, 1967 | | Change, 1960–1967[a] | | | |
| | | | Number | | Percentage | |
	Non-white	White	Non-white	White	Non-white	White
Total	8,011	66,361	970	6,721	14	11
Professional and technical	592	9,287	263	2,141	80	30
Managers, officials, etc.	209	7,286	31	396	17	6
Clerical	899	11,434	391	2,158	77	23
Sales	138	4,387	25	99	22	2
Craftsmen and foremen	617	9,228	203	1,083	49	13
Operatives	1,882	12,002	465	1,434	33	14
Service workers, except private household	1,519	6,037	287	1,136	23	23
Private household workers	835	934	−169	−278	−17	−23
Nonfarm laborers	899	2,634	−70	−61	−7	−2
Farmers and farmworkers	423	3,131	−453	−1,389	−52	−31

[a]The 1967 data pertain to persons 16 years of age and over, while in 1960 the age cutoff was 14 years. Since 14–15-year-olds make up less than 2 per cent of total non-white employment, it can be assumed that they have almost no effect on the 1960–1967 occupational change.
Source: U.S. Department of Labor, Bureau of Labor Statistics.

Taking the occupational levels—operators, service workers, and private household workers—roughly reflecting an approximate substandard income in urban areas, shows that the disparate ratio of blacks is wide, even making allowance for the shift from the rural areas to city occupations.

The Higher Socioeconomic Levels of the Black Community

During the post-war period, the percentage of black Americans in the higher socioeconomic levels has increased greatly, as indicated by percentage change from 1960–1966 in Table 8-1.

THE LOWER CLASS   There has been for sometime, and in the past decade increasingly so, a segment of the black population

[44]Henderson and Ledebur, *Economic Disparity*, p. 330.

which holds relatively stable jobs including what is generally categorized as lower-middle class, roughly reflected in Table 8-1 by craftsman and foreman, and in parts of the clerical and sales segments. In a recent study focused on the black middle class, Kronus finds noticeable differences between the blue collar segment and the white collar group.[45] Along with their lower occupations, income, and education go a different life style. While their family patterns and consumer practices are similar, this author finds less interest in politics and interracial concern, and less interaction with the white community.[46] Their family patterns did not differ.

THE BLACK MIDDLE CLASS   In summary of the black middle class, Kronus finds that "In terms of life style and consumption patterns, they appeared to live within their means, to take life seriously, and to accept their responsibilities to family, work, and community."[47] Aside from work interaction with whites and frequent co-associations in the general community civic matters, the black middle class has little association with whites. Liberal white people who seek to establish friendly social relations usually find blacks polite, but suspicious of their intentions, and reluctant to reciprocate.[48] A major frustration for middle-class blacks is their difficulty in finding housing suited to their life style which they can afford, simply because they are black. Ever since Frazier's *Black Bourgeoisie*, numerous writers have called attention to their fundamental dilemma. In a limited sense the black middle class has "made it," and to identify too actively with advancing the race can well jeopardize their present position; on the other hand, not to do so causes lack of respect and ill-feeling among the less successful blacks.

THE ELITE   As we have seen, there has been throughout this century a small group of substantially wealthy blacks whose wealth was gained almost exclusively from services rendered to black people but, as Kronus states, the last fifteen years have produced a larger and more distinct black elite about which he further writes:

[45]Sidney Kronus, *The Black Middle Class* (Columbus, Ohio: Charles E. Merrill Co., 1971).
[46]*Ibid.*, pp. 60–61.
[47]*Ibid.*, pp. 38–39.
[48]See Lois Mark Stalvey, *The Education of a WASP* (New York: William Morrow and Co., 1970) for a most penetrating description of white attempts to accept blacks as social equals.

The elite is no longer composed only of a handful of successful entrepreneurs and sports and entertainment figures, but it includes an expanding number of executives, educators, and government employees, both elected and appointed, who are integrated into the commercial and political mainstream of American life. This movement may be considered by some as "tokenism," but if it is, it is a degree of tokenism never before witnessed, even during Reconstruction.[49]

The implications about "tokenism" are well illustrated by the appointment of Dr. Leon Sullivan, a former black minister, to the Board of Directors of General Motors in 1971. Well aware that his appointment was in a sense tokenism, Dr. Sullivan stated that: "Blacks account for 14 per cent of GM's personnel, but they own only twelve of the company's 13,600 dealerships. If I am going to stay on the board, they are going to have many more black dealers, and black salesmen."[50]

Housing Discrimination

While polls through the 1960s show that a majority of Northern whites say they would not object to Negroes as neighbors, there are many indications that when faced with the actual situation, large numbers do not behave accordingly. Through the 1960s, little change occurred in breaking down racial residential segregation of blacks.[51] Much of the concentration of lower-class Negroes in less desirable housing occurred because of their low income and because few whites sought such areas. Attempts by public housing authorities to furnish new housing, or to subsidize in part private business, outside the black areas—now called "scatter-site housing"—met with strong resistance because according to federal law, such housing must be "open housing" (racially).[52]

WHITE BELIEFS: MYTH OR FACT   What are the main reasons—beliefs, fears, rationalizations—given by white people for rejecting Negroes as neighbors?
(1) *Deteriorating Property Values*   The belief is widespread

[49]Kronus, *The Black Middle Class*, p. 136. By permission of Charles E. Merrill Company.
[50]Franklyn Peterson, "Black Capitalism in the Black," *New York Sunday News*, Oct. 10, 1971.
[51]"Crisis of Color, '66," *Newsweek*, Aug. 22, 1966, p. 28.
[52]A recent attempt by New York City to locate a high rise apartment complex on a "run down" section of otherwise high-class Forest Hills was a continuing source of local community dispute in 1971 and 1972.

that entrance of Negroes into an area inevitably causes property values to decline. This belief does not objectively imply any personal prejudice.

(2) *Negro "Bad" Housekeeping and Disorderly Behavior* These two closely related beliefs held by whites are part of the long-held stereotype of Negroes as inferior people. They serve as logical reasons for not wanting Negroes as neighbors. Whites who hold these beliefs fear deterioration of the physical appearance and moral climate of their neighborhood.

(3) *Interracial Conflict* Whites express the fear that there will be interracial conflict in which their own safety will be endangered.

(4) *Fear of Inundation* It is commonly believed that once any Negro family moves into their block, others will follow and the neighborhood will become all Negro. As we shall see, it is this belief which stands as the last barrier to developing racially mixed residential areas.

(5) *Fear of Loss of Status* A revealing illustration of this feeling is seen in this incident:

> A white woman, commenting on a Negro family's purchase of a house a few doors away, observed that it was a "fine" family, the husband was a surgeon, and she had no personal objection to them whatever. But, she added, people driving by see the little boy playing on the sidewalk. "How are they to know he is a doctor's son?"[53]

From various studies of race and housing during the 1960s the following conclusions emerged: (1) Where whites do not move out en masse, there is often little effect on property values, aside from those which might have taken place because of the changing situation of the areas as a whole. (2) It is after the area begins to reach a point of all-Negro occupancy that the less desirable consequences of overcrowding and downgrading of the area begin to set in. The first Negroes to take advantage of a vacancy in the white area tend to be similar in income, education, habits, and manners to their white neighbors. (3) Interracial conflict is more frequent on the borders of Negro-white areas and at the beginning of the entrance of Negroes in new neighborhoods.[54]

[53]*Report of the Commission on Race and Housing*, p. 18.
[54]See these studies all published by the University of California Press (Berkeley and Los Angeles), Nathan Glazer and Davis McEntire, *Studies in Housing and Minority Groups*, 1959; Davis McEntire, *Residence and Race*, 1960; and Luigi Laurenti, *Property Values and Race*, 1960.

While there are numerous other variables affecting minority housing, Glazer and McEntire state that it is likely that color alone plays a dynamic role in the situation.[55]

Methods of Segregating Blacks in Housing

The direct process by which blacks were kept from moving into white areas involved the real estate and financial businesses. Some realtors would not handle such transaction or there was the reverse phenomenon, "block busting": when one or two Negro families managed to move into a white neighborhood, realtors were known to have encouraged whites to sell and move quickly before the "inevitable decline in property values" began, and from then on showed the properties for sale only to Negroes. For realtors this was a highly profitable business.[56]

In general, mortage lending institutions were unwilling for a long time to finance black home purchasing, and even as increasing legal pressures were brought to bear, still showed considerable reluctance.[57]

Even those whites who claim to be willing to live in an integrated neighborhood do not mean one which is largely black. The crucial point in planning mixed racial areas is to avoid the "tipping" point which should be well below 50 per cent black. Since to set "quotas" is now illegal, "benign quotas" must be voluntary. Often black residents themselves try to discourage further black purchases in the area.[58]

URBAN REDEVELOPMENT AND NEGRO HOUSING   The housing segregation of Negroes (in varying situations, of other minorities) is inextricably interrelated with metropolitan planning. For example, both the erection of low-cost housing developments and higher-class apartments on the fringes of the slums require the displacement of present occupants, who are frequently Negroes. In any building financed by federal funds, suitable relocation of displaced residents is supposed, by law, to be accomplished before new buildings can start, but when the present

---

[55]Glazer and McEntire, *Studies in Housing and Minority Groups*, p. 10.
[56]See George and Eunice Grier, *Equality and Beyond: Housing Segregation and the Goals of the Great Society* (Chicago: Quadrangle Books, 1966), pp. 34–35.
[57]*Ibid.*
[58]Dan W. Dodson, "Can Intergroup Quotas Be Benign?" *Journal of Intergroup Relations*, Autumn, 1960. Reprinted in Earl Raab, *American Race Relations Today* (Garden City, N.Y.: Doubleday and Co., 1962), pp. 125–134.

occupants are Negroes, finding a new residence is a difficult task. Thus either new developments are delayed or the displaced Negro residents face great hardship.

The Extent of Black-White "Neighborhoods"

Recently for the first time, a systematic study of "neighborhoods" including both blacks and whites has been completed.[59] The general conclusion of this study is as follows:

> Thus, 81 per cent of the nation's households remain in segregated neighborhoods, while roughly 10 per cent are in integrated neighborhoods where Negroes represent only 3 per cent or less of the neighborhood population. To put it another way, *only 4 per cent of the households in the United States are located in integrated neighborhoods that are more than 10 per cent Negro.*
>
> It is probable that a substantial number of white residents in the integrated neighborhoods we studied, because they are in the overwhelming majority, have no social or community-based contact with the few Negroes who live in their neighborhoods. It is even possible that most white residents in some of our integrated neighborhoods are unaware of the presence of any Negroes.[60]

We added the italics in the above summary to emphasize the point that as of 1967 the "tipping point" following which resegregation may be expected is indeed quite low. The report is based in fact on "mixed" neighborhoods in which there is apparent movement of some families of both races into the area, thus eliminating neighborhoods where black resegregation is on the way.

FUTURE PROSPECTS   The Bradburn team makes the following prediction as to the future:

> The proportion of Negro households in open and moderately integrated neighborhoods will rise slowly with little fuss being made. In northern and western substantially integrated neighborhoods, there will be a more rapid increase in the Negro population, but some of these neighborhoods will become resegregated. More white segregated neighborhoods will get their first Negro families, and

[59]Norman Bradburn, Samuel Sudman, and Galen L. Gockel with the assistance of Joseph R. Noel, *Side by Side: Integrated Neighborhoods in America* (Chicago: Quadrangle Book Co., 1971). Based on a national opinion research monograph, *Racial Integration in American Neighborhoods: A Comparative Survey* (NORC Report No. 111-B). The data were acquired in 1967.
[60]*Side by Side.* p. 62. Italics ours. By permission of Quadrangle Books, Inc.

in most cases there will be no major reactions. Where there are strong reactions, the neighborhood will probably become a changing or Negro segregated one. Most white segregated neighborhoods, however, will remain segregated for the foreseeable future.[61]

In interpreting their prediction of a quite modest increase in *mixed neighborhoods*, it should be clearly understood that this term refers solely to the fact that a few black *households* are found there. The accounts which are provided in their in-depth study of six communities out of their sample show that the first black entrants met with serious opposition; and that after the area settled down to stable integration (of less than five per cent black) the blacks were treated with indifference or cooly and in no sense socially integrated. From their admittedly (and now regretted) limited probing of black respondents the authors can only predict without the important variable of what blacks themselves are likely to do. Such limited information as they acquired indicated that blacks who moved into white neighborhoods did so in order to have a more desirable place to live, not to "mix with whites."[62]

Northern Schools and "Desegregation"

The Supreme Court school decision had less immediate impact on the North because with some few exceptions segregated schooling for Negroes as an *official* policy had been abandoned wherever it existed. Nevertheless, the decision prompted review of school districting and assignment practices. Since there was much *de facto* school desegregation arising out of housing segregation, many smaller Northern communities made changes in pupil assignments to correct "racial imbalance." Some of these changes required "bussing" some students of both races out of their neighborhoods, with considerable opposition from many parents of both races.[63]

School desegregation in the inner metropolitan areas created enormous problems which have become almost impossible.[64]

In New York City by 1966 the percentage of students who were black was 29.3 and of Puerto Ricans, 20.9; and for the six

[61]*Side by Side.* p. 192.
[62]See *Side by Side*, Ch. 2 "Neighborhood Profiles."
[63]Princeton, N.J., a spatially compact community went the whole way, assigning all students for specified grades to the same school.
[64]See Nathan Glazer, "Is Integration Possible in the New York City Schools?" *Journal of Intergroup Relations*, Autumn, 1960.

year period to 1966 white enrollment had dropped 17 per cent. Metropolitan areas with much larger numbers of Negroes in their population than New York had even greater problems. It is an ironical fact that although the 1954 school desegregation order was originally directed at the South, in the Northern urban areas there is now more *de facto* school segregation than in the South.

At the turn of the 1970 decade, two significant problems in school integration developed. The first grew out of the inability to provide racial balance within the political boundaries of cities with large black populations. Some official efforts are now being made to get suburban cities to permit the assignment of pupils in black districts into predominantly white schools. Also, the reverse is happening. Some smaller communities, mostly white, which have already combined their high school students into one school and where the black enrollments are increasing, now wish to withdraw.[65] The second development has been to raise the "bussing" issue into the political arena at the highest levels. A recent call by President Nixon for a moratorium on bussing brought confusion into the whole picture.

From the viewpoint of social science there are two objectives which unavoidably clash in certain situations: the desirability of better quality education for blacks; and the desirability of increasing interaction of black and white children. On the first matter, the tentative conclusion of social science is that for black children to attend a predominantly middle-class school improves their educational achievement, especially at the higher grade level where the achievement climate set by their middle-class white peers is effective.[66] For the beneficial effect to be maintained, the black ratio of students should be relatively small. Black students in classrooms less than half white achieve no more than those in all-black classrooms.[67]

Discrimination in Law Enforcement and Justice

In the American society, it has long been clear that law and justice have been differentially enforced and administered with

[65]In 1972 the U.S. Supreme Court denied a Virginia community the right to remove their students from the consolidated school.
[66]J. S. Coleman, et al., *Equality of Educational Opportunity* (Washington D.C., U.S. Government, 1967). Actually Coleman concludes that for lower-class students, irrespective of race, to attend schools where middle-class students set the climate is beneficial, but even more so for blacks.
[67]Thomas Pettigrew, *Racially Separate or Together* (New York: McGraw-Hill Book Co., 1971), p. 63.

some degree of inequality related to class status and power, systematically documented by Robert L. Sutherland, in *White Collar Crime* twenty years ago. This being true with respect to class, it is bound to be the case with reference to minorities who lack power. In the South we have seen that it was openly institutionalized. Outside that region it simply became recognized practice, focused more around police action than in the courts.

Given the total situation in Negro-white relations it is inevitable that the police will to some extent discriminate against Negroes. This total situation includes these factors: (1) White people discriminate against Negroes generally. (2) While in democratic theory the administration of justice is equal, in practice it is differentially administered with some degree of inequality related to status. This being generally true even in regard to class status, it is even more bound to be the case where dominant-minority status prevails. Dominant-status people are not apt to be deeply concerned about discriminatory police treatment of minority people, and police practice reflects in the long run the attitudes of the dominants. (3) Generally, white police not only share white prejudice but are, because of recruitment from lower-ranking status levels, apt to be drawn from the segments of the white population where the salience of white prejudice is highest. (4) Negro policemen, as Negroes, are less secure and under pressure to conform to white police practice.[68]

The Negro slum dweller's image of the policeman is not that of a protector but of a punisher. Representing white law in which most Negroes have experienced or witnessed discrimination, the policeman is viewed with hostility. The police and Negroes hold reciprocal hostile images of each other: the police look upon the Negro masses as inclined to be lawbreakers; the Negro masses view white police as prejudiced. Thus it is inevitable that mutual distrust will continue to exist as long as the white community generally treats Negroes as a minority.

The foregoing can stand without special reference to the Black Revolt. But the revolt has given it increasing significance for at least two reasons. The revolt inevitably heightens the salience of the conflict and the increasing polarization of white versus Negro as "enemies." It is not too difficult to understand that many

[68]See Nicholas Alex, *Black in Blue: A Study of the Negro Policeman*, (New York: Appleton-Century-Crofts, 1969).

Negroes in such a conflict situation view *any* arrest of a Negro as a discriminatory act even when the arrest is obviously valid. Furthermore, the revolt situation increases the occasion for police-Negro conflict. Both from a strictly legal view and from a police administrative view the boundary line between a legally proper "protest" activity and an illegal one is not always easy to draw. To this may be added the tendency of court interpretations to be currently more fluid and unpredictable, which adds to the perplexity of police authorities.

The continuation of police and military brutality is still widely alleged by black people, particularly the more militant black groups, with varying degrees of factual support. There are, however, many communities where special efforts have been made to train policemen to deal with individual black persons with more understanding and to act with more restraint in dealing with black protests and confrontations. Also juries, even when all-white, have shown a tendency to acquit black defendants when their guilt is not established. In this process of change, that this is sometimes not perfect is understandable.[69]

Integration in Government and in the Armed Services

Government at both the federal and local levels has been a major factor in attempting to improve (as yet not too successfully) the economic welfare of ghetto blacks and in fostering integration by employing blacks, and in higher status positions. While at first this started by appointing to many government agencies a black liaison officer between the agency and the black community, it has begun to go beyond this. For example, Thurgood Marshall was named to the United States Supreme Court by President Lyndon Johnson. The concentration of blacks in metropolitan areas accounts for there being twelve black Congressmen in 1972. Edward Brook's election as Senator from Massachusetts could not have occurred without substantial white votes.

THE ARMED SERVICES The order of President Harry Truman in 1948 to integrate the Armed Services was completed

[69]In 1970, the Jackson State killing of four blacks by white militia appears to be one. It is not overlooked by blacks that the Kent State killings of white students in the same year, also related to student protests, caused more unfavorable criticism from the American public than the Jackson State episode.

well before the Vietnam fighting. This integration was ordered against the advice of most military authorities and against the wishes of a majority of white soldiers. Experience has shown its functional value from the viewpoint of military efficiency.

Integration in the armed services has also had significant consequences in the interracial field. The earlier opposition of white soldiers to military integration showed a marked drop between 1943 and 1951.[70] It is most interesting that attitudes of white soldiers in mixed units consistently reveal more approval of desegregation than white troops in all-white units. "Yet the fact remains that the general pattern of day-to-day relationships *off the job* is usually one of mutual racial exclusiveness."[71] This raises doubt as to whether comradeship in the "foxhole" will carry over when white soldiers return to civilian life.

The attitudes of blacks in the Armed Services is mixed, but in general it is favorable. Blacks are drafted proportionately in excess of whites, probably due to the greater legitimate reasons for deferment on the part of white young men. On the other hand, the reenlistment rate of blacks is high. Obviously the military offers the blacks a secure job; their first experience of equal association with whites; and in cases of promotions provide the experience of "commanding" whites. In Vietnam a larger proportion of blacks have been in combat units.[72] Moskos considers it "probable that military experience contributes to an activist posture on the part of Negro servicemen returning to civilian life."[73] He also finds it more than coincidence that the founders of the Deacons for Defense, a para-military group organized in 1964 to counter Ku Klux Klan terrorism, were all veterans of Korea or World War II. While there have been numerous incidences of physical conflict between black and white troops off-duty, in this respect they mirror the currently normative situation between young black and young white males since the onset of the Black Challenge to dominance.

---

[70]Samuel A. Stouffer, et al., "The Negro Soldier" in *The American Soldier*, p. 586. O. R. C.
[71]Charles C. Moskos, Jr., "Racial Integration in the Armed Services," *American Journal of Sociology*, 72, September, 1966. The entire article covers pp. 132–148.
[72]Some black leaders view this as a part of a subtle genocidal effort on the part of whites. See below p. 270.
[73]Moskos, p. 146.

Suggested Readings

ON THE SOUTH

Blumer, Herbert. "The Future of the Color Line," Ch. 15, in John C. McKinney and Edgar T. Thompson, eds., *The South in Continuity and Change.* Durham, N.C.: Duke University Press, 1965.
A penetrating and hard-hitting analysis of the Southern racial scene.

Coles, Robert. "It's the Same but It's Different" in Talcott Parsons and Kenneth B. Clark, eds., *The Negro American.* Boston: Houghton, Mifflin Co., 1966.
A psychiatrist provides an insightful interpretation of how Southern black children learn to cope with their subordinate position.

Dietsch, Robert W. "Some Progress, More Myth: The New, New South." *The Nation* (May 17, 1971), pp. 615–618.
Describes ways in which many Southern schools maintain segregation inside officially desegregated schools.

Griffin, John Howard. *Black Like Me.* New York: Signet Books, The New American Library, 1960.
The story of the experiences of a white Northerner who altered his physical appearance and travelled through the South as a "black" man.

Sarratt, Reed. *The Ordeal of Desegregation: The First Decade.* New York: Harper & Row, 1966.
Traces the various public reactions to the Southern school desegregation process and the causes of slow progress; projects the probable future in this movement.

Silver, James W. *Mississippi: The Closed Society.* New York: Harcourt, Brace and World, 1962.
An historian analyzes what sort of society the bi-racial system made Mississippi.

ON THE NORTH

Bradburn, Samuel S., Galen Gockel, Seymour Sudman with the assistance of Joseph R. Noel. *Side by Side.* Chicago: Quadrangle Books Co., 1971.
The most comprehensive attempt to estimate the number of neighborhoods in the United States where black Americans reside among whites.

Clark, Kenneth B. *Dark Ghetto.* New York: Harper & Row, 1965.
A penetrating analysis of the social dynamics of the ghetto and the psychological effects on the inhabitants, as revealed in Harlem and other New York ghetto areas.

Glazer, Nathan and Daniel P. Moynihan. *Beyond the Melting Pot.* Cambridge: The M.I.T. Press and Harvard University Press, 1963.

Chapter 1 provides a description and analysis of the Negroes of New York as one of the metropolis's five large ethnic components.

Goldsmith, Marcel L., ed. *Black Americans and White Racism.* New York: Holt, Rinehart and Winston, 1970.
Readings largely composed of specific research articles on a wide range of topics.

Levy, Frank. *Northern Schools and Civil Rights.* Chicago: Markham Publishing Co., 1971.
Focuses on hte attempts in Massachusetts to implement this state's Racial Imbalance Act, but also deals with the Northeast in general.

Liebow, Elliot, with a forward by Hylan Lewis. *Tally's Corner.* Boston: Little, Brown and Company, 1967.
An insightful study of Negro streetcorner men based on close contact observation of black young men in Washington, D.C.

Pinkney, Alphonso. *Black Americans.* Englewood Cliffs, N.J.: Prentice-Hall Inc., 1969.
A short treatment of Black Americans over the entire period.

Stalvey, Lois. *The Education of a WASP.* New York: William Morrow and Co., 1970.
A penetrating personal history of a white liberal woman's experience actively attempting to develop close friendly relations with blacks.

9   The Black Challenge

A question many white Americans have raised in recent years grows out of two developments in the field of black-white relations from World War II to 1970: (1) As seen in Chapter 8 black Americans as a group made very substantial gains in civil rights and moderate gains in welfare-income, health, and education, although the gap between black and white has not been substantially closed. (2) On the other hand from the early 1960s to the present, blacks have mounted a substantial challenge to their position with varying degrees of aggressive action. This has prompted white Americans to ask why after such gains have occurred blacks should become increasingly aggressive. A broad answer lies in sociological propositions set forth at least twenty-five years ago.

> Conflict is especially likely in periods of rapid change in levels of living. The probability of conflict is increased insofar as the changes have a differential impact on various groups.
>
> Among the members of any dominant group the greatest incidence of open conflict behavior toward a given minority will be found among those classes which are most vulnerable to competition from the minority.[1]

[1] Robin Williams, Jr., *The Reduction of Inter-Group Tensions* (New York: Social Science Research Council, Bulletin 57, 1947), pp. 58–59.

These propositions have been amplified in later sociological theory by the concept "relative deprivation." This concept means that the person's sense of frustration is relative to the welfare and status of others about him. A further distinction was noted by Runciman between "egoist" and "fraternalistic" relative depriva- tion—that is whether one compares his own personal situation with others belonging to his group, or whether he compares the position of his group with others in the society. This distinction is especially pertinent to dominant-minority relations.[2] The indivi- dual black college graduate with a white collar job may feel less deprived than his unemployed brother; but when he finds it im- possible to locate a home in a neighborhood commensurate with his socioeconomic position, he becomes aware of the deprived position of his group. This distinction contributes to understand- ing why the Black Challenge, as with other popular uprisings, is not generally led by the most objectively deprived members of their group.[3]

As Chapter 8 pointed out, the post-war period was in a sense "ripe" for blacks to mount a sustained challenge. But, as will later be indicated, white America was not prepared for it. In a broad sense the ultimate aim of most black Americans is to achieve a position individually and/or collectively in which they have *complete equality of opportunity* and *exactly the same free- dom as all other Americans*.[4] The main differences among them focus around the integrationist-separatist axis. It seems helpful to set forth first in conceptual terms the various alternatives the integrationist-separatist axis present. These are as follows:

1. *Integrated Assimilation*. This process involves the continu- ation of integration into the economy, polity, and civic life of the existing American public structure; and hopefully also integration into primary group life. The process should ultimately reach a point where black identification as a basis for societal differen- tiation would disappear.

2. *Pluralistic Assimilation*. This process involves the retain- ing of black group identity which would be primarily (a) struc- tural, that is, retaining a black sub-community in the primary aspects of life with integration into the secondary, or public,

---

[2]W. G. Runciman, *Relative Deprivation and Social Justice* (London: Rutledge and Keegan Paul, 1966).
[3]See Thomas Pettigrew, *Racially Separate or Together*, Ch. 7, "Why Black Unrest in the 1960's" (New York: McGraw-Hill Book Company, 1967) for extensive dis- cussion of this topic.
[4]See Whitney Young, "To Be Equal" (New York: McGraw-Hill Company, 1964)

aspects of the larger community; or (b) cultural and structural, involving not only face-to-face associational ties but also possessing a culture in varying degrees distinctive from that of the more general society and of the other subethnic groups. This situation would become somewhat analagous to the current Jewish subcommunity.[5]

3. *Separation.* This envisages varying degrees of maximizing the separation of blacks from whites and the maximum black group autonomy possible at various levels. The theoretical possibilities are: (1) leaving America and establishing a new community;[6] (2) setting off a sizable geographic part of the United States to be substantially all-black with federated association with the rest of the country—broadly similar to the overseas divisions of the French Union, or Jamaica, as a part of the British Commonwealth; (3) forming separate sections within larger white political subdivisions with maximum possible self-support and maximum possible local governmental autonomy.

THE BLACK CHALLENGE AS A MOVEMENT

The Black Challenge to dominance has created a basic reversal in the interactive process in black-white relations. Before, racial interaction involved black adjustment to white dominance and acceptance of any concessions granted by whites to them; since the movement got under way, blacks have taken the initiative to change their situation and whites face the problem of how to adjust to the black action.

The Black Movement has greatly polarized the relations between the races with more group self-consciousness on both sides. It has increased the salience of the conflict and raised it to the level of a major national domestic issue. The Kerner Report described the situation as follows:

> This is our basic conclusion: Our nation is now moving toward two societies, one black and one white, separate and unequal.[7]

[5]See Milton Gordon, *Assimilation in American Life* (New York: Oxford Press, 1964), Chs. 6 and 7.
[6]In a paper read by Charles P. Loomis at the annual convention of the American Sociological Association, in San Francisco, California, August 28, 1967, Dr. Loomis suggested this solution but further suggested finding some place in the less populated areas of South America for this purpose, an "Israel," for those Negroes who want "out" of the United States.
[7]*Report of the National Advisory Commission on Civil Disorders* (New York: Bantam Books, 1968), p. 1.

The movement is a large mixture of individual and collective black actions. Some are unorganized, sporadic and spontaneous; some planned and organized. It is highly diffuse with no centralized command; and the various challenging entities differ as to the exact definition of the goal, and correlatively, differ as to the methods to be pursued. Perhaps one may say that the unifying theme is the subjective mood of nearly all black Americans expressed by "We shall overcome" and "Right on!"

The Civil Rights Movement

As a sustained movement, the first thrust was to strike at the most vulnerable point in white American racism—the inconsistency between its written constitution, particularly in the Bill of Rights, and the flagrant failure to apply it to blacks. Beginning with the courts, followed considerably later by legislation in some states and by Congressional action, one by one all forms of public discrimination were outlawed on paper, culminating last in the outlawing of discrimination in housing in 1968.[8] But, as grossly illustrated in the South, court edicts and legislative acts are only effective to the degree that the administrative agencies enforce them. As indicated in the Southern resistance to school desegregation and other court decisions, effective administration at the local level and the reluctance of the federal government to bring pressure made blacks realize that other more aggressive action was needed.

Protests and Demonstrations

NON-VIOLENT RESISTANCE   The first forms of confrontation were protest and demonstrations using passive resistance as in the Montgomery bus boycott, the sit-ins, Freedom Riders, and James Meredith's March in Mississippi. This passive resistance phase grew out of the influence of Dr. Martin Luther King, Jr.'s philosophy. The first step away from this technique was passive civil disobedience as illustrated by Dr. King's defying a court order in Birmingham which resulted in his arrest and the repression by white officials of protest activities. Dr. King's efforts to spread the non-violent protest movement to wider areas were

---

[8]Law H.R. 2516, PL 90-2-84. See *Congressional Quarterly Almanac*, Vol. XXIV, 1968.

not successful and were tragically terminated in Memphis by his assassination. The organization which grew out of Dr. King's Montgomery triumph, The Southern Christian Leadership Conference, continues and still represents the strictest non-violent approach but as an organization has less influence. Its leaders, Dr. Ralph Abernathy and Coretta S. King, have considerable personal influence.[9]

Two other organizations using non-violent demonstration technique were The Congress of Racial Equality (CORE) and The Student Non-Violent Coordinating Committee (SNCC).

THE CONGRESS OF RACIAL EQUALITY CORE antedates the Negro Revolt, having been founded in 1942 in Chicago by people who felt that direct action and demonstrations were needed to supplement the previous sorts of challenge to white dominance. It used the "sit-in" technique in a Chicago restaurant in 1943 and in Palisades Amusement Park, New Jersey, in 1947–1948, successfully effecting desegregation. But it was not until the Negro Revolt began in earnest that CORE became a major civil rights organization. We have previously cited its "freedom riders" action in the South; the organization has continued direct action demonstrations ever since. CORE has not always been able to control its more militant chapters, as in the case of the somewhat unsuccessful "stall-in" to keep people from the New York World's Fair in April, 1964.[10] It has been the most interracial in membership of all the organizations.

THE STUDENT NON-VIOLENT COORDINATING COMMITTEE SNCC (or "Snick" as it is often referred to) was organized in 1960 to coordinate the activities of numerous college student groups of both races on behalf of civil rights. Its direct action protests, sit-ins, and demonstrations, were successful in desegregating hundreds of segregated facilities in Southern cities.[11] SNCC has carried on more sustained activities of education and voter registration. It has more successfully identified with the rank and file of Southern Negroes than the other organizations. Many of its members, white and black, have been jailed. As Clark puts it,

[9]Both were listed among the 100 most influential black Americans by *Ebony*. See issue of May 1972, pp. 77–84.
[10]Kenneth Clark, *The Negro American* (Boston: Houghton Mifflin Co., 1966), p. 609.
[11]C. Eric Lincoln, *The American Negro Reference Book*, p. 472.

"SNCC has not overtly repudiated King's philosophy of non-violence, but it does not root its own acceptance of this strategy in love of the enemy.[12]

As we pass to a new mood in the Black Movement, assessment of passive resistance is in order. In the past at particular times and places, it had considerable value. Any more militant technique used prior to the 1960s in the South would have been severely repressed, as the suppression of a Birmingham riot showed. But passive resistance is more effective when the minority, as in India, is overwhelming in numbers. When used by small groups, it requires special training to keep the protestors non-violent against official rough handling. Furthermore, such a technique runs counter to American culture, in which aggressive individual and collective competition to get ahead with the least interference of the state to limit this competitive drive has been a dominant theme. American history is replete with instances where conflict arising from the pursuit of this cultural norm has transcended the legal rules of the game, from the lawless frontier through strife in labor's struggle to unionize, and in other sporadic uprisings.[13]

In the sixties the Black Movement took on a more militant tone. A symbolic marking of the turning point was the March on Washington on August 28, 1963. Initiated by A. Philip Randolph and organized by Bayard Rustin, some 250,000 Americans held a day-long protest before the Lincoln Memorial, perhaps the largest single demonstration in the nation's history. All Negro organizations (aside from the "separatist" groups) were represented, with a number of white supporting organizations and individual sympathizers joining them. Despite the fears of many Washingtonians, the occasion was extremely orderly. The march symbolized the readiness of black Americans (except the Separatists), however else divided, to continuously pursue the Black Challenge.

Unorganized Violence

Given the ghetto conditions, the changing mood of Black Americans, and the sharper polarization of black-white relations as a conflict situation, it would be expected that increasing interracial violence would occur. Vandalism and robbery, accompanied often by physical violence on the part of the ghetto youth, have

---

[12]Kenneth Clark, *The Negro American* p. 616.
[13]See Ovid Demarius, *America the Violent* (New York: Cowles Book Co., 1970) for an account of violence in American history.

become a normal aspect of inner city life. Interracial conflict is also quite common between young male groups of both races in situations where they meet, for example, in integrated schools or in public recreational areas. While such violent episodes are not part of the organized black action, they heighten the tension in race relations.

RIOTS   The most destructive and publicized form of unorganized violence was rioting within the ghettos themselves. Riots with interracial implications are no new phenomenon. Grimshaw identified thirty-three major interracial disturbances in the United States between 1900–1949.[14] But the sixties witnessed an unparalleled number of riots with a substantial number of deaths and injuries, and enormous property losses. From 1964 to midsummer of 1967 there were fifty-eight cities in which large scale rioting occurred in ghettos with 141 killed, close to 5,000 reported injured, and vast property damage.[15]

While the basic causes of rioting are rooted in a long history of white racism with its prejudice and discrimination, the Kerner Commission found other central factors in disorders: "disadvantaged conditions, intensive and pervasive grievances, a series of tension heightening incidents, all culminating in the eruption of disorders at the hands of youthful, politically aware activists."[16]

Our special interest is the relation of rioting to the general movement. Writing during a period of comparative lull in massive riots, it appears that the Kerner Commission served a limited purpose—focusing the attention of white people on black ghetto conditions. In a somewhat similar manner, the 1970–1972 outbreak of prison riots, using the technique of holding custodial hostages, have focused attention upon the deplorable conditions of most penal institutions in which blacks constitute a disproportionate number of inmates. Thus, in a sense then, the unorganized rioting served a useful purpose to the movement despite its costs to blacks and to the community. It is of interest to note that, in general, mass rioting has not often been repeated in the same cities, reflecting a feeling that more of the same will not serve a useful purpose.

[14]Allen D. Grimshaw, "A Study in Violence" (Doctoral Dissertation, University of Pennsylvania, 1959), pp. 178–180. For a fuller treatment and analysis see Grimshaw, *Racial Violence in the United States* (Chicago: Aldine Publishing Co., 1969).
[15]See *Time*, August 11, 1967, p. 11.
[16]*Report of the National Advisory Commission on Civil Disorders*, p. 10.

Revolutionary Activists

It is axiomatic that among oppressed groups in the modern world some will reach the conclusion that their oppression will never be removed under the existing politico-economic system; and that the solution of their problem lies in bringing about a new system. Several movements among blacks with this revolutionary orientation have arisen such as the Revolutionary Action Movement (RAMS).[17] A crucial dilemma among black revolutionaries is whether to work for a separate Black Revolution, or to join forces with whites who also have a revolutionary orientation. Considering the numerical minority position of blacks, the former course seems unlikely to make much headway.[18] Among the black revolutionary organizations who to some degree work with non-black activist groups is the Black Panthers.

THE BLACK PANTHERS   The Black Panthers was organized in 1966. Its members had no faith that the present American system would ever accord blacks equality, and were avowedly revolutionary of the separatist type. In their statements they disavow the use of violence except in self-defense. But they have engaged in confrontation likely to provoke police violence, leading to "shoot outs" between police and the Panthers. On one such occasion in Oakland, California a policeman was killed and Huey Newton, the Black Panthers' leader, was convicted of manslaughter, and spent nearly three years in prison.[19] The Panthers have fostered or supported other groups in various welfare and confrontation activities in the black community. In several subsequent trials of other Black Panthers in other cities, juries failed to convict, apparently because the prosecution case often rested largely on the testimony of law enforcement agents planted inside the movement. Even though the Panthers have worked largely among blacks, it claims to be for all the oppressed peoples of the world, as suggested in the following summary of its philosophy by Bobby Seale:

[17]See "Revolutionary Nationalism" in John H. Bracey, Jr., August Meier, and Elliott Rudwick, eds. *Black Nationalism in America* (Indianapolis and New York: The Bobbs-Merrill Co., Inc., 1970), pp. 504–556.
[18]See Lewis M. Killian, *The Negro Revolution: Possible or Impossible?* (New York: Random House, 1968) for an extensive treatment of the black revolutionary dilemma.
[19]After a long appeal case, the State Supreme Court of California reversed the conviction and two retrials ended in deadlocked juries.

We need to establish a system based on the goal of absolute equality, of all people, and this must be established on the principle of *from* each and every person, both male and female, according to their ability, and *to* each and every person, according to their needs. We see establishing socialism in the society as a means by which we begin to remove the oppressive social obstacles, and hope to build a society where some day a man and a woman can relate to each other totally on the basis of natural attraction.[20]

Currently the movement appears inactive following extraordinary efforts by federal officials to repress it, climaxed by a "shoot out," according to official account, where leader Fred Hampton was killed in his own apartment while in bed.

Separatists

By separatists is meant those black activists who have concluded that white Americans will never accept blacks as equals in the United States, and therefore see no hope but to try to maximize the degree of their separation from whites. The theme of separation has a long history among blacks in the United States.[21]

THE BLACK MUSLIMS   Among contemporary black activist organizations, the Black Muslims is the largest and most clearly separatist of all black American organizations. While founded in Detroit in 1930, its continuity and development dates from 1934 when Elijah Muhammed (born in Georgia as Elijah Poole) became and has remained its leader to date. Since the organization is highly secretive, the size of the membership is not known. While it has some eighty temples located in cities with large black ghettos its membership country-wide embraces only a small proportion of even the ghetto residing blacks.

The movement is a racial-religious sect. Its membership is recruited from the poorest and most disorganized elements of the black ghettos who develop a strong personal discipline and devote much time to the cause. The philosophy is completely racist, proclaiming the superiority of the black man over the white. It stereotypes the white race generically as devils; and believes that there is no such thing as a "good" white man. To Muslims, Christianity is anathema. To quote its leader, "The white man has 'given

[20]Bobby Seale, *Seize the Time: The Study of the Black Panther Party.* © 1970 Random House, Inc. Reprinted by permission of the publisher.
[21]See Bracey, Meier, Rudwick, eds., *Black Nationalism in America.*

you Jesus' while he has robbed you blind."[22] The movement itself
is organized as a religion, "The Nation of Islam in the West," and
carries on religious meetings and rituals resembling Moham-
medanism, but has no formal association with Islam.

The Muslim position on violence is ambivalent. On the one
hand, its philosophy is based on total hatred of the white man. On
the other hand, having to live in a white society, the members are
enjoined to obey white laws and work diligently when employed
by whites, and are commanded not to be aggressive toward whites
unless attacked.[23] This ambivalence toward the use of violence
may, as Lincoln observed, serve the function of "providing outlets
short of violence, for the aggressive feelings aroused in its members" toward whites.[24] In their policy statement, the Muslims have
asked that some area in the United States be given over to them
by themselves as a sort of bi-national section of America.[25] More
realistically, the movement has become the wealthiest black organization by starting from the tithing practice among its members and shrewdly investing its capital, making possible the
operation of many small business enterprises, all-black operated,
with considerable success.

In any direct way, the Black Muslims have remained aloof
and, until recently, unrelated to the rest of the black activists, but
it has provided continuity to the Black Nationalist idea; and in
many particular parts of its program, such as its "Black Capitalism," resembles other activist practices. Recently it has cooperated with other separatist groups.

It is significant to note that the most astute minister of the
Black Muslims, Malcolm X, broke from the movement to form
the Organization of African-American Unity because of his feeling
that it was not wholly necessary to avoid cooperation with white
people. The change in his feeling developed in part from his
acceptance on an equal basis while traveling in Mohammedan
North Africa. His assassination prevented this new development,
but as a legacy he left an outstanding book of his life.[26]

[22]*Mr. Muhammad Speaks,* May 2, 1959. (A newspaper published by the movement).
[23]The killing of a New York policeman who entered a mosque on police business
in the summer of 1972 is illustrative. It has been a standing practice that all persons entering a mosque are routinely "frisked."
[24]C. Eric Lincoln, *The Black Muslims in America* (Boston: The Beacon Press, 1961).
See pp. 248–253 for a fuller discussion of the functions and dysfunctions of this
movement for American society.
[25]See "Elijah Muhammed: What Do the Muslims Want" in *Black Nationalism in
America,* pp. 415–417.
[26]*The Autobiography of Malcolm X.* With an introduction by M. S. Handler (New
York: Grove Press, 1965).

Integration

Remaining closest to the idea of direct assimilation of blacks into the main American society approach were the earlier established agencies. The NAACP besides continuing its legal efforts to gain enforcement of laws, assisted in the political registration of blacks and in helping to get more blacks educated for law, much needed in the South. The Urban League, while Whitney Young was its director, carried out as one of its main projects the operation of a "job bank" for employers to use for filling new openings with qualified blacks. This project is credited with placing some 60,000 blacks in suitable positions in mostly white controlled enterprises. The A. Philip Randolph Institute, directed by Bayard Rustin, focuses on black poverty as the central issue and works toward the integration of blacks with American unions. These organizations have made more pragmatic contributions to the direct integration of blacks into the main stream of American society.

Pluralistic Assimilation

Another alternative for black action is pluralistic assimilation, limited either in the structural sense or combined with a definitive cultural distinctiveness. Actually the present situation is pluralistic accomodation on an unequal basis, imposed on blacks by whites. The difference is that those blacks who belong in this category now do not desire gradual total integration but want to retain ethno-racial distinctiveness. To what extent the pluralists think of pluralistic assimilation as a temporary stage leading to complete assimilation, or a more desirable mode of permanent adjustment, is not clear. But either way the pluralists generally agree that to achieve sub-ethnoraciality on an equal basis will require strengthening the sense of black unity, developing pride in their ethno-racial identity, and mobilizing their collective power to obtain equal opportunity and respect for their subidentity.

The more ardent pluralists oppose in theory any more association with whites than is necessary to perform their functions in the public-economic arena. However, moderate pluralists leave open to individual personal choice—when available—either to pass over into the main (which is to them white) stream of community life, or not. In practical terms the integrationists too may settle for personal option but object to being pressured into the choice by other blacks. But in any case, this pluralistic trend is based on the increasing conviction that if blacks are to improve their position, they have to bring it about themselves. As a slogan to symbolize this conviction the term "Black Power" arose.

Black Power

This term has been so widely and ambiguously used both by its proponents and the white media that some interpreters consider it as a symbolic term to unify the maximum number of all black activists—an "umbrella" term. It can however be viewed as the dynamic part of the structural-pluralistic approach which is suggested by the following from Stokely Carmichael and Charles V. Hamilton, leading proponents:

> It is a call for black people in this country to unite, to recognize their heritage, to build a sense of community. It is a call for black people to begin to define their own goals, to lead their own organizations, and to support those organizations. It is a call to reject institutions and values of this society.
> The concept of Black Power rests on a fundamental premise: *Before a group can enter the open society, it must first close ranks.* By this we mean that group solidarity is necessary before a group can operate effectively from a bargaining position of strength in a pluralistic society.[27]

In attempting to crystallize the Black Movement under the banner of Black Power and to reach agreement on specific goals to promote it, the first National Conference on Black Power was held in Newark, New Jersey in July, 1967, which Alphonso Pinkney summarized as follows:

> This conference was attended by more than 1,000 black delegates from 42 cities in 36 states. They represented a broad cross section of black leaders, ranging from the militant black nationalists to employees of government agencies. One of the most significant aspects of the conference was its bringing together for the first time a wide assembly of black people who met in workshop sessions to define the concept of Black Power and who agreed to implement its components. When the conference ended, a series of resolutions had been passed, including the following: (1) the

[27]Stokely Carmichael and Charles V. Hamilton, *Black Power: The Politics of Liberation in America.* © 1967 Stokely Carmichael and Charles Hamilton. Reprinted by permission of Alfred A. Knopf, Inc.

establishment of black financial institutions such as credit unions and nonprofit cooperatives, (2) the establishment of black universities, (3) selective purchasing and boycotting of white merchants in black communities, (4) the demand for a guaranteed annual income for all people, (5) a boycott by black athletes of international Olympic competition and professional boxing, in response to the stripping of the world heavyweight boxing title from Muhammad Ali, (6) boycotts of Negro churches which are not committed to the "black revolution," (7) boycotts of Negro publications accepting advertisements for hair straighteners and bleaching creams.[28]

The wide range covered in the resolutions noted above with two exceptions—selective boycotting and guaranteed income for *all* Americans—leads away from integration; and in two points it aims to bring pressure on black integrationists to act in accord with the Black Power view of black churches and certain black businesses.

Two of the most concrete manifestations flowing from the Black Power movement are "black capitalism" and black politics.

Black Capitalism

Black Capitalism is a movement to encourage the maximum development of separate economic enterprises all owned and controlled by black people and serving mainly black people.

From the economic viewpoint, Black Capitalism has dubious merit. Dr. Andrew Brimmer, the single black governor on the Federal Reserve Board argues strongly against it. Among the reasons he advances is that "the attempt to expand small scale, Negro owned business is running against a strong national trend."[29] This is seen particularly in the great increase in supermarket branches which greatly outsell small neighborhood food stores, and which offer lower prices. Brimmer observed that in 1968 "a self-employed male in retail trade earned only 63.8 per cent of the earnings of a salaried manager.[30]

Ironically, the limited integration of blacks into the public segment of life has decreased the number of black enterprises by

[28]Alphonso Pinkney, *Black Americans* © 1969. Reprinted by permission of Prentice-Hall, Inc., Englewood Cliffs, New Jersey.
[29]Andrew F. Brimmer, as quoted by George R. Metcalf in *Up from Within: Today's New Black Leaders* (New York: McGraw-Hill Co., 1971), p. 282.
[30]*Ibid.*, p. 283

opening the opportunity for blacks to be accomodated in the general (and white) owned public facilities.

While the federal government, and some financial institutions, have given this idea limited support, black business operations to date have not shown much promise, as Seder and Burrell have indicated.

> The vast majority of black enterprises are still small retail and personal-service establishments—grocery stores, barbershops, luncheonettes, dry-cleaning stores, gas stations. Only a handful of black entrepreneurs have managed to make their way in finance, manufacturing, contracting or wholesaling. And even in the retail and service fields, there are very few establishments of any size. A study published in 1969 in New York City purported to show that more than half of the stores in Harlem were black-owned. However, the survey was taken on sections of Seventh and Eighth avenues, where only small stores are located. The important shopping areas in New York's black community are 116th Street, 125th Street and 135th Street in Harlem, and Fulton Street, Broadway and Nostrand and Pitkin avenues in Brooklyn. Practically all of the larger stores and theatres on these major shopping thoroughfares are white-owned.[31]

Increasing ownership and control of business enterprise would no doubt bolster black pride. But there are other ways in which their low economic condition can be raised by the use of black economic power. One is selective boycotting of stores which fail to hire blacks and to upgrade them in functional position. This technique was employed with considerable success by the Reverend Frank Sullivan in Philadelphia in 1967. Picketing in orderly fashion is a use of black economic power; such devices have the important advantage of being completely in line with procedures now recognized as legitimate for all Americans.

The goal of pluralistic ethno-racial structural identity raises a fundamental dilemma. The main basis of cohesion is a common *racial* visibility or heritage which means emphasizing the very factors which social scientists generally agree are an irrelevant basis for social differentiation, except as dominants have chosen to make it so. To some it appears as racism in reverse. Recognition of this by many black intellectuals and activist-oriented black

[31]John Seder and Berkeley Burrell, *Getting It Together: Black Business Men in America* (New York: Harcourt Brace Jovanovich, 1971), p. 213. By permission.

students has led to efforts toward emphasizing a distinctive black culture.

As a turning point in distinguishing *cultural pluralism* from *separatism*, the following is helpful:

> Cultural nationalism contends that black people—in the United States or throughout the world—have a culture, style of life, cosmology, approach to the problems of existence, and aesthetic values distinct from that of white Americans in particular and white Europeans or Westerners in general. Mild forms of cultural nationalism say merely that the Afro-American subculture is one of many subcultures that make up a pluralistic American society.[32]

Culturalism Pluralism

There are a number of possibilities on which black American culture is, or may be, based: (1) on African cultural heritage; (2) on creative developments from 350 years of American white dominance; (3) or the development of a new subculture, possibly related to twentieth-century Pan Africanism.

THE AFRICAN HERITAGE   The black American Pluralists have pressed for a more accurate teaching of the history of the Negro throughout time, including the great African civilizations of the past.[33] But from the sixteenth century on much of the history of Africa is tragic, including slave exportation and colonialism. Essentially what this fact of the great empires demonstrates is the myth of innate genetic superiority of Caucasians, as we pointed out in Chapter 4. The pulverization of tribal heritages was so thorough under slavery that the continuity of American Negroes with African culture had been virtually lost. Thus while it may develop some sense of race pride to recall the glorious empires, certainly any subculture of the American Negroes living in twentieth-century urban-industrial society is not to be based on adaptive survivals of either the empires or tribalism.

[32]From *Black Nationalism in America*, edited by John H. Bracey, Jr., August Meier, and Elliott Rudwick, copyright © 1970 by The Bobbs-Merrill Company, Inc., reprinted by permission of the publisher. Two of the three editors take the milder position.
[33]See Daniel Chou and Elliot Skinner, *A Glorious Age in Africa* (Garden City, N.Y.: Doubleday and Co., 1960), who state that "at the heights of their power, the great earlier kingdoms of West Africa, Ghana, Mali, and Senegal compared favorably with their contemporary counterparts in Europe and Asia." (p. 116)

UNIQUE MINORITY EXPERIENCE OF AMERICAN NE-
GROES   It was inevitable that the enforced segregation of the
Negro people and the constant humiliating frustration in white-
Negro contacts would develop some distinctive patterned ways of
behavior. But much of these, as we have indicated, (see p. 179) are
either skillful constructive ways of adapting to the inevitability of
minority status, or escapist hedonism.

A "NEW" AMERICAN BLACK CULTURE   Turning to the
possible development of a new, distinctive black American culture,
one finds perplexing questions. Since the preceding discussion
appears to rule out distinctive elements in the public culture, any
such developments would necessarily be limited to forms of primary group relations and to the expressive areas of culture. To date,
external manifestations are seen in relatively superficial manner.
Bayard Rustin has frequently expressed his feelings that it is a
mistake for black Americans to think that soul food, adaptive
African hair styles, black music, art, and drama, and learning
Swahili are the way out for the large masses of black people who
lack the necessities of life.[34]

The most creative development in black American culture has
been in the arts, particularly in music. The major forms of music
developed by Negroes have been the spirituals and the special
form of "gospel" singing traditional in Negro churches. Apparently the only aspect of American Negro music which suggest
African survivals is the antiphonal form found by LeRoi Jones
(now Imamu Barake) in the "blues," and by Zelma George in
gospel music.[35] Considering the arts more broadly, Marion E.
Brown finds that in literature, entertainment, and the fine arts,
Negro artists show much white artistic influence.[36] In the field of
letters Negro poets and writers have concentrated on "racial
themes," largely the plight of American Negroes.[37]

This brief review suggests that the distinctive aspects in the
artistic field have been based on Negro heritage as a minority in
the United States. This does not, however, preclude further original development in the arts reflecting the current more militant
mood.

[34]See Bayard Rustin, *Down the Line, Collected Writings of Bayard Rustin* with an
introduction by C. Van Woodward. (Chicago: Quadrangle Press, 1971).
[35]LeRoi Jones, Chapter 21 and Zelma George, Chapter 20 in *The American Negro
Reference Book*.
[36]*The American Negro Reference Book*, Ch. 22.
[37]Arna Bontemps, *The American Negro Reference Book*, Chapter 25.

From a field study in a Washington, D.C. black ghetto area, Hannerz found the concept "soul" as expressing what blacks in Northern ghettos mean by "Negroness."[38] The author indicates he finds it hard to define the concept "soul." As used in Northern ghettos, "it stands for what is 'the essence of Negroness', and, it should be added, this 'Negroness' refers to the kind of Negro with which the urban slum dweller is most familiar—people like himself. The question whether a middle-class, white-collar suburban Negro also has 'soul' is often met with consternation" [p. 482]. Again Hannerz writes: "It is very clear that what is 'soul' is not only different from what is not 'soul' (particularly what is mainstream middle-class American); it is also superior" [p. 483]. "If one asks a young man what a 'soul brother' is, the answer is usually something like 'someone who's hip, someone who knows what he's doing' " [p. 483].

In attempting to locate objective phenomena associated with this subjective symbol, the author mentions the following: "soul food"— i.e. chitterlings, hog maw, black-eyed peas and other edibles typical of poor man's food in the rural South; "soul" music—progressive jazz and rock-and-roll [pp. 483–484]; and "unstable personal relationships, in particular between the sexes," [pp. 485–486] reflected in the young male preoccupation with seduction and broken families headed by women.

BLACK STUDENTS   It would be expected that black students who were increasingly being admitted to predominantly white colleges and universities would play a significant role in the black movement and begin cultivating a more distinctive new black American subculture. While the exact proportion of black students who came to be considered activists is not known, this segment assumed leadership on the campus. According to Edwards, 1966 marked a turning point among black activist students.[39] Before this they had engaged in the general civil rights movement and earlier protest activities in the outside community; since then they have been turning attention inward to the college and campus, promoting black liberation. Their main demands centered around the establishment of black studies as a major

[38]Ulf Hannerz, "The Rhetoric of Soul: Identification in Negro Society," *Race*, IX, 4, (1968), pp. 453–465. As included in *The Making of Black America*, Volume II, *The Black Community in Modern America*, August Meir and Elliott Rudwick, eds. (New York: Atheneum, 1969), pp. 481–492. Subsequent references to this work will be bracketed and placed in the text.
[39]Harry Edwards, *Black Students* (New York: The Free Press, 1970), p. 61.

curriculum and gaining separate facilities for black students, in housing and separate centers for social and cultural activities, in order to intensify their sense of black identity.

In a narrower sense, the desire for maximum separation within the campus is due to needing some time to get more accustomed to the new experience of associating with whites in an equal "peer" situation, and related to the prejudiced reactions from many white students. But in a broader sense, promoting both campus separation and black studies programs were forms of "laboratory" training for leadership roles in the liberation movement in the black community. In this activity, confrontations rather than protest became a usual technique. These confrontations have involved forceful means such as occupying buildings and closing them for use, and holding college administrators hostage in order to force acceptance of their demands.

The campus proved to be a safer place for these activities than in the outside community. In general, outside the South, college administrators as well as many faculty members attempted to be understanding and sympathetic toward black students; and also, in general, the college preferred to deal with these confrontations by themselves without the aid of outside law enforcement agencies. There was considerable outside criticism of the college authorities for acting, as many whites felt, in too lenient a manner. But as would be expected, such confrontations are occasionally bound to get so unruly that outside security forces had to be called in to restore order, and they are likely to deal with the "confronters" in a more rough-handed manner.

BLACK STUDIES   Black studies courses focus upon treating black-white history in terms of white oppression; in the social sciences, emphasis is on communicative skills and techniques to foster black liberation, and the study of black cultures in Africa and other areas. Their purpose is clearly not directed toward promoting integration. The curriculum is designed to prepare black students for leadership in the black community. While some white students do take individual courses in the black studies curriculum, they are not particularly wanted and, therefore, the courses function less to stimulate greater white student interest in cooperating with blacks in the common national interest than they might. Black students majoring in black studies are required to take general courses which may facilitate their occupational career in the white society.

To what extent a new black American culture may emerge out of this orientation is a question that should by no means be dismissed. There is a large amount of room in American society to develop "designs for living" which place greater emphasis on how to live rather than on how to make a living.[40]

Black Political Power

A highly significant—possibly the most significant—development to advance the position of black Americans has been the rapid rise in the number of blacks who hold public office. In 1967 there were about 650 blacks who had been elected to public office. By 1971 there were over 1600 distributed in 41 states.[41] The elective offices ranged in prestige and influence from Sheriff Lucius Amerson of Macon County Alabama[42] to United States Senator Edward Brooke of Massachusetts.

Analysis of the types of situations in which blacks hold public office are most easily related to the numbers and percentages of blacks in the various electoral subdivisions: where blacks comprise a substantial majority of the political units' population, and where they total a substantial numerical majority.

BLACK MAJORITY ELECTORATES   In the United States at present, black majority political electorates have been found in a few large cities and, in the South, in small towns where the flow of population toward cities has left a black majority.

Of large cities, Gary, Indiana's black Mayor Richard Hatcher is an example. The spreading by blacks out from large city ghettos into adjacent suburban municipalities until they reach substantial majorities is illustrated in New Jersey. In 1972 there were five black mayors of relatively small cities located in suburban sections of Newark and of the Philadelphia-Camden metropolitan area. In contrast in the South was the election of Charles Evers as Mayor of Fayette, Mississippi in 1969, carrying with him an all-black board of aldermen.

Another type of substantial black majority electorate comprises districts within large cities of sufficient size to be allotted representatives to Congress, and in more instances representatives

[40]See Harry Edwards, *Black Students*, Appendix on sample Black Studies Curricula.
[41]See Mervyn M. Dymally, ed. *The Black Politician: His Struggle for Power* (Belmont, California: Duxbury Press, 1971), Preface.
[42]See a printing of a speech delivered by Mr. Amerson at Tuskegee, Alabama, January 1, 1969, in *The Black Politician*, pp. 6–10.

to state legislatures. In 1972 there were twelve black Congressmen in the House of Representatives and a number of state legislators, generally representing electorate districts in the large metropolitan areas, for example, New York, Chicago, Philadelphia, and Cleveland.

LARGE BLACK MINORITY ELECTORATES   City politics is sometimes non-partisan, but even when partisan there are frequently more independent parties or candidates competing for office.[43] Also there are often particular circumstances which make a particular incumbent running for re-election particularly weak as the election approaches. Such situations open up the possibility of minority status candidates to win.

The election of Carl Stokes in 1967 as Mayor of Cleveland was the first major city election of a black Mayor. It could not have taken place without a substantial number of white votes. His opponent, Seth Taft, had high WASP status. While Cleveland was at least two-thirds white, it had a Democratic majority, and Stokes had won his party's nomination with considerable difficulty. But as contrasted with Newark's Mayor Kenneth Gibson and Gary's Mayor Richard Hatcher, Stokes was less clearly identified with the grass roots of the black community, and, therefore, was more palatable to whites.[44]

From his observations as a journalist after studying a number of the important black politicians, Whittemore reached the conclusion that the more acceptable a black politician is to whites the less effective he can be in using his office to help blacks; and that the less black identified the black politician is the better his chances are for high political office.[45]

The election of Kenneth Gibson as black mayor of Newark is a border line instance. At the time, Newark's black population was just around the 50 per cent mark (with Puerto Ricans comprising around 10 per cent of the 50 per cent white population). But his opponent, as a well-entrenched incumbent, was at the time on trial on corruption charges (subsequently found guilty) and under his administration the city's political image was extremely low. Thus, about one-sixth of Newark's whites voted for Gibson,

---

[43]Mayor John Lindsay of New York was re-elected as an independent candidate against Republican and Democratic opponents by less than forty per cent of the vote cast.
[44]L. H. Whittemore, *Together* (New York: William Morrow & Company, Inc., 1971). pp. 305–306.
[45]*Ibid.*, p. 307.

a black, who was a professional man of apparent integrity. Unlike former Mayor Stokes and Senator Brooke who, as Whittemore puts it, "overcame" their blackness, Gibson identified, and has continued to do so, with pride in his racial visibility and in short maintained grass roots connections.[46]

SIGNIFICANCE OF BLACK POLITICAL POWER   The increasing political acceptance of black Americans by other Americans is an example of functional, or instrumental, integration and does not involve social integration. However, associating with whites on a social basis has never been a matter of high priority for the majority of blacks and, with the current pluralistic orientation, may well have still lower priority.

This greater integration of black Americans in the political arena has occurred simultaneously with increasing tension, conflict, and polarization in this interracial sphere which lends support to the militant "Black Power" approach. In terms of common national interest, it is an approach which may be and on the whole has been pursued without resort to violence.

The use of Black Power in politics has turned out to be, in many ways, a promising avenue for blacks to move toward equality; and a means of providing a limited measure of black-white cooperation in the midst of an otherwise highly divisive situation.

For blacks, these political gains give an increasing role in the decision-making area of politics as well as in government. The selection of black State Senator Basil Paterson of New York as vice-chairman of George McGovern's campaign for president, following soon after his own candidacy for Lieutenant Governor of New York State on the Democratic ticket, is an example. Even though a small minority in the state legislatures, where either of the two white parties need a few extra votes, black legislators are in a position to bargain for something they want. This leads to a larger generalization: *the use of group power in this way is neither white nor black but thoroughly American.*

The use of Black Power in politics has had a more unifying effect upon the wide range of factions in the Black Movement than any other activist effort. Julian Bond, black member of the Alabama legislature, maintains that only those who openly identify with the black community will succeed in holding its support. Since it is unfeasible for blacks to form a separate political party,

[46]*Ibid.*, pp. 306–308, 311.

except at the local level, black legislators in either party can act in accordance with their party *except* on race-related issues. There Bond insists they must always vote "black."

The gains made by blacks in politics, however, present problems. The cities where they have gained political control are in a process of decay. However much this exercise of power may enhance black pride, the cities cannot by themselves embark on the extensive urban renewal programs requiring large amounts of money, currently available only from the federal government.[47]

Reaction of the Black Population to the Black Movement

This review of the Black Movement has concentrated on those actively engaged in it, which does not necessarily indicate how the total black population itself feels about the issues involved. Gary Marx provided the most extensive review of studies of black opinions as of 1967. While there is considerable variation in the numbers responding to similar questions in various cities, Marx's discussion appears to permit the following generalizations: (1) Greater support for moderate organization and leaders than the opposite. (2) Disapproval of violence as a means to their goals, although some of this disapproval was on the basis of strategy rather than principle. (3) Approval of protest activities of the sort least likely to provoke violence, e.g. picketing. (4) A majority opinion that blacks had made substantial gains in the past decade or so, but that the progress has been too slow. (5) A majority favoring integration as distinct from pluralism, but also believing in strengthening black institutions and developing pride in blackness. (6) Concern over inadequate police protection in their areas and of police brutality in handling black arrests.[48]

WHITE RESPONSES TO THE BLACK CHALLENGE

How has white America responded to the Black Challenge? As a base from which to start we will use Paul B. Sheatsley's assessment of white sentiment as of the early sixties after the challenge had started but before it had reached its peak in mass rioting and

---

[47]See Fred J. Cooke, *The New York Times Magazine*, July, 25, 1971, p. 7 for an article on the plight of Newark, N. J.
[48]See Gary Marx, *Protest and Prejudice* (New York: Harper Torch Books, Harper and Row, 1967), Ch. 8 "Civil Rights and Tolerance." The generalized statements are our own drawn from his review of the data.

violence accompanying confrontations. Sheatsley's assessment is based on analyzing the findings of polls taken up to this time.

> Certainly there is no evidence that the majority of American whites eagerly look forward to integration. Most are more comfortable in a segregated society, and they would prefer that the demonstrators slow down or go away while things are worked out gradually. But most of them know also that racial discrimination is morally wrong and recognize the legitimacy of the Negro protest. Our survey data persuasively argue that where there is little or no protest against segregation and discrimination, or where these have the sanction of law, racial attitudes conform to the existing situation. But when attention is kept focused on racial injustice and when acts of discrimination become contrary to the law of the land, racial attitudes change. Conversely, there is no persuasive evidence thus far that either demonstration and other forms of direct action, or legal sanctions applied by government, create a backlash effect and foster segregationist sentiment. On the contrary, they may simply demonstrate, ever more conclusively, that it is more costly to oppose integration than to bring it about. The mass of white Americans have shown in many ways that they do not want a racist government and that they will not follow racist leaders. Rather, they are engaged in the painful task of adjusting to an integrated society. It will not be easy for most, but one cannot at this late date doubt the basic commitment. In their hearts they know that the American Negro is right.[49]

Analysis of white reactions to the accelerated Black Challenge will be treated under the following headings: repression; token concession; acceptance; and cooperation. It must be kept in mind that any typology cannot account for the many individual shadings in between each category. Furthermore, it assumes that those falling into each type act consistently with reference to the race issue. However, most white Americans have a generalized attitudinal and behavioral orientation toward blacks and how the white-controlled system should deal with it.

Repression

In a broad and historical sense, it may be said the white-controlled system is repressive, and that in this sense all white

[49]Paul B. Sheatsley, "White Attitudes Toward the Negro," in *The Negro American*, Talcott Parsons and Kenneth B. Clark, eds. (Boston: Houghton Mifflin, 1966), pp. 322–323.

Americans, except those actively cooperating to change it, share personal responsibility. Here, however, we limit the term to that segment of whites who still act to suppress any further advance in the status of blacks and for whom this belief has high priority.

Most students of American racism agree that in the nation as a whole not more than 10 per cent believe in actively repressing by all legal (and sometimes condoning illegal) means any further equality of opportunity for blacks, although the percentage is higher in the South. Indications of their relatively small proportions are found in voting patterns. Perhaps the clearest is the vote for George Wallace in the 1968 presidential election. Outside the South, where repression had so long been normative, Wallace received 8 per cent of the votes. Pettigrew's analysis of the Wallace supporters indicates that those elements of the white population who felt relatively deprived voted for him, and they showed strong anti-Negro sentiments. It was also found that those classified as anti-Negro in the sample were found to be two-and-a-half times more likely to agree that the "police should shoot to kill" to prevent looting during a riot.[50]

That repression of blacks in a far more violent form may eventually be America's way of solving its racial crisis has been cogently argued with extensive documentation by Samuel F. Yette in a book with the sub-title *The Issue of Black Survival in America*. The gist of his case is found in this paragraph:

> The obsolescence of Blacks in America and their will to survive nobly—demand and fight for their rights—provide some with an adequate rationale for black extinction. Legal sanctions for the systematic invasions of black sanctuaries—homes, schools, and establishments—were signed into law before Congress adjourned for the fall, 1970, elections. But, in America, as in Asia, these essentially military measures bespoke the failure of insincere or basically unsound efforts to help black people.[51]

By obsolescence of blacks Yette refers to the fact that large numbers of the black masses are not now needed as workers as a result of technological changes which make obsolete the only sort of jobs which many of them are prepared to take. But though not needed, the increased determination of the black masses to fight

[50]Thomas F. Pettigrew, *Racially Separate or Together*, p. 243. An extensive analysis based on a sample of voters in Boston, Cleveland, and Gary, Indiana. A more intensive analysis was made in Gary.
[51]Samuel F. Yette, *The Choice: The Issue of Black Survival in America* (New York: G. P. Putnam's Sons, 1971), p. 31. © 1971 Samuel F. Yette. Reprinted by permission of the publisher.

to survive and their increasing militancy, Yette argues, may precipitate uprisings which will require legal sanctions for more repressive acts. Yette considers the laws passed by Congress since
1968 giving stronger powers to law enforcement agencies a sign
of a trend in the repressive direction.[52] He further refers to plans
proposed by some Congressmen and the military to cope with
possible larger-scale uprisings using martial law, and for such
procedures as internment camps.

Yette further refers to indirect forms of repression. While he
does give considerable credit to President Johnson for pushing
through civil rights legislation and setting up the Office of Economic Opportunity (OEO) and to Sargent Shriver for trying hard
to make it work, he found that by 1970 these efforts had been
slowed down due to lack of local community support and cooperation. Similarly the various anti-poverty programs were bogged
down by lack of adequate financing and by local white resentment of the cost. Such behavior, he argues, indicates that there
is strong sentiment not to reduce the poverty and disease, which
cuts down the size of the black population [even though the
black population is, in fact, increasing at a higher rate than the
white population]. Yette even further construes efforts to encourage blacks to use birth control and sterilization as a means
of controlling the growth of the black population.[53]

Token Concession

Illustrations of this category are found among whites who do
not want blacks to achieve full equality but face in a practical
sense the need to appease the black by some concessions in order
to limit interracial disorders. The term "tokenism" arose first during the Southern resistance to school desegregation, in that instance not only to appease militant blacks but to satisfy pressures
from the federal government to comply. By accepting a few blacks
into some white schools, it could for a while maintain it had com-
plied to government ruling. The overt manifestations of token
concessions more often come from those in authoritative positions, not only in government but in the economic sphere. This is
illustrated by businesses and unions which, in order to comply

[52]See Chapter 6, "The Laws: A Legal Police State" in Yette, *The Choice*, for an
extensive discussion.
[53]Yette does not indicate that such measures are part of a general trend in the
entire American society and is therefore not discriminatory. Nor does he indicate
that although the black fertility rates are declining, those of whites are declining
more.

with non-discriminatory law or to avoid the threat of a black confrontation, hire or admit a black or two as a concession. Currently there are more signs of a broader non-discriminatory policy to hire blacks, to train them, and to place them in higher ranking positions.

Passive Acceptance

A large portion of white Americans fall into a category which has no strong prejudice against blacks achieving more equality. They do not act to place obstacles in the way of either governmental promotion of programs designed to aid blacks or resent having a black employed to work along side them. There are limits to passive acceptance. Such whites will voice criticism of violent activity and support police action to deal with it. They are likely not well enough informed to know that the authorities may act in a discriminatory manner. They also resent confrontations which cause them great inconvenience. In general, they do not want to associate with blacks socially, nor to have them as neighbors. Included in this category are those who move when it appears that their neighborhood is due to receive any substantial number of black residents. Passive acceptors are not greatly disturbed if one "respectable" black family moves in near them or likely to lend support to those white neighbors who try to harrass this "intruding" black family. These white Americans do not view the rising gain of blacks as a matter of great concern to them personally, and they do not view the black problem as a major domestic issue.

An aspect of white reaction to the disorder produced by the present racial tensions appears not to have been crossed—namely, the factor of white fear. Many white Americans who would not have been classified among the more prejudiced, or anti-Negro, may become so as a result of increasing black pressures on their community. Even whites sympathetic with the Black Challenge often hesitate to send their children to integrated schools where the interracial conflict is frequent.

Cooperation

WHITE LIBERALS Our conception of this category is broader than that acceptable to the black activist. We conceive this to include those whites who believe in the total equality of all blacks. In mildest form here are the "liberals" (much despised by black activists). In action, liberals have expounded their views in public—orally and in writings; have joined interracial organizations; and have attempted to treat blacks as equal human beings, not as "blacks." Unconsciously, their efforts may seem to have patronizing undertones to blacks. Since they are total liberals, not just on the race issue, they do not condone violence, although they are more understanding of why black activists find this necessary in self-defense. Like all human beings liberals have personal problems—their own and their families interests—which they are often unwilling to jeopardize to promote the black cause. More of them are found in the higher educational brackets and in the academic circles, especially the behavioral scientists. Politically, it appears they are more frequently found among Democrats than among Republicans in the North.[54]

The opportunity for liberals to be useful in aiding the black cause is affected by the broad racial atmosphere at any given time and place. We noted the Southern liberals' inability to be helpful during the strong Southern resistance period of 1954–1960; increasingly during the 1960s they have shown more influence in that region. In the North, they could get a better hearing during the Kennedy-Johnson Administration, than in the Nixon Administration which finds it politically expedient to woo the South and the anti-school bussing sentiment in the North. But the white liberal finds that the strong current tendency for blacks to push their cause on their own tends to limit his usefulness. While the black activists do not disdain liberal support, they make it clear that it is to be on the sidelines and not involved in decision-making policy.

WHITE RADICALS   We refer here to those whites who feel that the total social structure, particularly in its economic aspects, should be basically changed—usually to socialism. The small number of Americans who hold this view also want it accomplished by non-forceful means—usually distinguished from communism by the term "democratic socialism." Of all the black movements, the Black Panthers in their philosophy, at least, hold the same view (see p. 255) which furnishes a basis for white radical cooperation with the Panthers.

---

[54]See Thomas Pettigrew, *Racially Separate or Together*, Chapter 10, "The Social Psychology of the Wallace Phenomenon."

WHITE POSITIVISM   This refers to that small number of white Americans who not only think that blacks should gain complete equality for their own sake but believe that it is essential for liberating whites, morally and ethically. It is represented by our earlier quotation from Lillian Smith (see p. 178). Specific illustrations are white parents who desire to have their children have black children not only as schoolmates but also as playmates; and by Lois Stalvey's efforts to associate with blacks as equals, not only to help blacks, but to help herself achieve a self-respecting image.[55] We shall return to this theme in our final chapter.

SUMMARY ASSESSMENT OF BLACK-WHITE RELATIONS

From 1954 to the early 1970s, black Americans made more advances toward equality than in the entire twentieth century preceding 1954. The greatest gain was in the decline of discrimination in political and economic areas and in publicly-operated facilities. But the degree of decline in discrimination was limited by various forms of white resistance and inadequate law enforcement; blacks were disillusioned and black activist groups mounted a challenge which led to much racial conflict.

The black movements aimed at developing a greater sense of unity and a positive image of their black identity. The development of this distinctive subethnicity sharpened the polarization between black and white as opposing segments in the national population. The main division within the black movement concerns whether the aim of the movement should be toward total integration or toward consolidating a distinctive sub-community and culture—frequently considered "nationalistic" by some.[56] The more militant black activists insist upon the right to defend themselves by whatever means necessary against discriminatory treatment. There has been a noticeable development of more hostile anti-white attitudes among black American youth, a more critical attitude toward the values and institutions of white American society, and a greater desire to associate primarily with blacks even in instances where the choice to associate with whites as equals is presented.

[55]Lois Stalvey, *The Education of a Wasp.*
[56]See Charles V. Hamilton, "The Nationalist vs. the Integrationist," *New York Times Magazine,* October 1, 1972 for a recent discussion of this issue among black leaders.

At the turn of the 1970 decade, the momentum of the Black Challenge reached something of a plateau. This may be due in part to a feeling that too much pressure might provoke white repression, or to the effects of indecisiveness over the separatist-integrationist goal within the movement. In the meantime, more effort is being made to see what results may be obtained in using black power in politics.

For the immediate future, we may expect an increasing amount of employment of blacks and, for those who manage to acquire more education, at higher-level positions; an increasing participation in civic life; and more decision making by blacks in areas where they substantially predominate. On the other hand, the material gains made by blacks have been largely limited to the smaller percentage of the group who are acquiring stable working-class and middle-class status. Despite numerous experiments attempting to improve the material situation of slum-dwelling and isolated rural blacks, the amount of gain is not impressive and certainly nowhere near what is needed. Thus, in the great urban ghettos festering frustration and bitterness continue.

White Americans have in the main accepted the equal rights of black Americans in public (instrumental) life, with varying degrees of enthusiasm and reluctance. However, whites continue to be reluctant to associate with blacks as social equals. We agree with Hacker that the socialization of today's white youth through their parents and the informal aspects of racially-mixed schools affords little reason "to believe that oncoming generations of white Americans will display more tolerance than did their parents."[57] If this judgment is correct, we may look forward to constant tension and intermittent open conflict in situations where a sizeable group of blacks are in contact with whites.

Suggested Readings

Bailey, Ronald W., ed. *Black Business Enterprise*. New York: Basic Books, 1971.
   Twenty-six readings by authors dealing with black capitalism in a broad historical and contemporary perspective.

[57]Andrew Hacker, *The End of the American Era* (New York: Atheneum, 1971), p. 122.

Billingsly, Andrew. *Black Families in White America.* Englewood Cliffs, N.J., Prentice-Hall, 1968.
Presents the viewpoint that the so-called matricentric family in the black ghetto is a viable and constructive development in black culture.

Bond, Julian. *A Time to Speak, A Time to Act.* New York: Simon and Schuster, 1972.
The Black Movement in politics is reviewed by an outstanding young black leader.

Cruse, Harold. *The Crisis of the Black Intellectual.* New York: William Morrow, 1967.
Deals with the dilemma facing the black intellectual whose position identifies him with the scientific and humanistic world transcending race and nation, and his feeling of obligation to identify with the black American.

Edwards, Harry. *Black Students.* New York: The Free Press, 1970.
Delineates a typology of black students on the radical-conformist axis and traces the activities of the black student movement in terms of the general black activism.

Greely, Andrew M. *Why Can't They Be Like Us.* New York: E. P. Dutton and Company, 1971.
A study of the attitudes of white ethnic groups toward Negro Americans by a sociologist.

Seale, Bobby. *Seize the Time.* New York: Random House, 1970.
A well organized presentation of the story of the Black Panthers by one of its main leaders.

Stalvey, Lois Mark. *The Education of a WASP.* New York: William Morrow, 1970.
A gripping account of the operation of white racism in specific situations faced by a white middle-class woman who tried to oppose this racism in her own community.

Young, Richard P., ed. *Roots of Rebellion.* New York: Harper and Row, 1970.
A well-selected book of readings on the evolution of black politics and protest since World War II.

10 **A**merican Indians

The vital difference between Indians in their individualism and the traditional individualism of Anglo-Saxon America is that the two understandings of man are built on entirely different premises. White America speaks of individualism on an economic basis. Indians speak of individualism on a social basis. While the rest of America is devoted to private property, Indians prefer to hold their lands in tribal estate, sharing the resources in common with each other. Where Americans conform to social norms of behavior and set up strata for social recognition, Indians have a free-flowing concept of social prestige that acts as a leveling device against the building of social pyramids.*

For nearly three hundred years as the tide of Europeans spread across the continent, white-Indian relations were frought with recurring conflict. Settlers spread, reduced the forest cover, preempted the prairie. The great buffalo herds were exterminated. The sacred Black Hills of South Dakota fell prey to gold prospectors and U.S. military power. The Governor of Colorado, in 1880, succeeded in sweeping the state clean of Indians—Cheyenne, Ara-

*Vine Deloria, Jr., *We Talk, You Listen* (New York: The Macmillan Co., 1970), p. 170.

paho, Kiowa, Comanche, Jacarilla and Ute—to be resettled in arid areas of Utah that Mormons didn't want.[1]

> If one prepares charts showing comparative population statistics for the various colonies, it is possible to see that white success in arms occurred most conspicuously when the white population curve going up crossed that of the Indian going down. This point was reached in the seventeenth century in New England and Virginia, and progressively later in the other colonies and in the later states of the Federal Union. It is well to remember that the U.S. Army was subduing the last vestiges of Indian power late in the nineteenth century only shortly before being called upon to deal with Spain and later Germany.[2]

White America has shown an ideological ambivalence about Indians. On the one hand there is romanticization of Pocahontas, and of Uncas, "the last of the Mohicans" in Cooper's novel. An Indian head in war bonnet graces our coinage. Of all minorities, Indians have had the longest established government bureau, charged with aiding Indians. Indian "blood" in the genetic heritage of whites has not been devalued as with other "racial" minorities. But until very recently these native Americans have been severely devalued by contiguous white populations; myths of their former "savagery" and their present laziness and drunkenness have persisted, and they have been allowed to become the most economically and educationally handicapped segment of the American population.[3]

Numbers and Concentration

Estimates of the number of Indians in 1492 in the area which is now the United States range from 700,000 to 1,000,000. By the time Indians became wards of the government in 1871, the population had been reduced to less than half a million. It is generally

[1]Dee Brown, *Bury My Heart at Wounded Knee* (New York: Holt, Rinehart and Winston, 1970,) p. 380.
[2]Wilcomb E. Washburn, ed., *The Indian and the White Man* (Garden City, N.Y.: Doubleday and Co., Anchor Books, 1964), p. 220.
[3]In 1949 the American Council on Education in a study of textbook presentations of American Indians found only two themes: cruel, bloodthirsty savages, or noble high-minded sons of nature. There was no presentation of Indians as people, no discussion of cultural characteristics of the wide variety of Indian life past or present. See Michael B. Kane, *Minorities in Textbooks* (Chicago: Quadrangle Books, 1970), p. 112; and also Chris Cavender, *An Unbalanced Perspective: Two Minnesotan Textbooks Examined by an American Indian* (Minneapolis: University of Minnesota Press, 1970).

agreed that under the early reservation system the population declined still further, reaching its lowest around 1900. Table 10-1 records the Indian population of the United States from 1890 to the present.

TABLE 10-1   INDIAN POPULATION OF THE UNITED STATES*

1890	248,253
1920	244,437
1940	333,369
1960	523,591
1970	792,730

*United States Census data for the specified years.

Census figures are often considered an underestimate, due in part to inadequate recording, and also due to differences in identifying persons of mixed descent: Indian-white and Indian-Negro. Nevertheless the figures in Table 10-1 suggest to some extent an improvement in conditions for Indians, picking up by 1940. Although Indians are still rated the poorest minority in the United States, changes in policy and in the extension of health services have at least reversed the genocidal trend of the turn the century.

Distribution of the Indian Population

There are people classified by the census as Indian in nearly every state in the Union. Regionally the largest concentration of Indian population is in the Southwest—mainly in Arizona and New Mexico—where about one-fifth of Indians live. The next largest concentration is in Oklahoma, a former Indian territory now containing about 10 per cent of the Indians of the United States. In the South there are scattered groups in Texas, Louisiana, Mississippi, Alabama, Florida, South Carolina, and Virginia; the Cherokee tribes of North Carolina outnumber all other groups combined in the Southern region. In the Northeast the largest numbers are in upper New York State, but there are scattered groups in Maine, Massachusetts, Connecticut, New Jersey, Pennsylvania, Delaware, and Maryland. In the North Central states there are substantial reservations in Minnesota, South Dakota, and North Dakota, with smaller groups in Nebraska, Wisconsin, and Michigan. There is an intermittent scattering throughout California and the Northwestern states.

More than half of American Indians lived on reservations in 1968, but there has been an increasing number who are living as farmers or townsmen. The federal effort of the late 1950s and early 1960s to encourage tribes to dissolve, a policy now abandoned, reduced the reservation populations to a degree. Federal efforts to relocate Indians off the reservations in urban industrial centers lured many, but there have been many who returned, and as of 1972, as will be discussed later, this policy is also being modified.

TABLE 10-2   INDIANS AND ALASKAN NATIVE POPULATION*

	1950	1960	1968
On or near reservations	315,000	365,000	403,000
Outside Federal Programs	106,000	187,000	247,000
Terminated Tribes	—	8,600	4,400
Relocated through Federal Programs	—	40,087	133,337

*National Congress of American Indians, *Sentinel,* Vol. 13, No. 1, p. 9.

Biological and Cultural Characteristics

Anthropologists believe that the Indian peoples migrated to the Western Hemisphere from Asia, but in the 18,000 years that they have inhabited North and South America they have developed a physiognomic type distinguishable from Asiatic peoples. They are brown in skin color, have straight black hair, little facial or body hair. Head shape and nasal index vary widely.[4] Pure-bred Indians are usually distinguishable in their physical appearance even when acculturated to the dominant society.

For many Indians there is also high cultural visibility. This has been reinforced by United States policy which has created the pattern of reservations, and, in the past and to an extent still, by the mistrust Indians feel for dominants in view of their history.[5]

[4]A. L. Kroeber, *Anthropolgy* (New York: Harcourt, Brace and Co., 1948), pp. 136–137.
[5]The mistrust may vary according to the particular history of a given Indian community. A student of Dr. Meyer's who had worked summers on both the Papago and the Ute reservations found a more open attitude among Papagos which she ascribed to their long relatively benign relations to whites since the days of the first Spanish missionaries; the Utes on the other hand had experienced acute conflict with whites. When under the Indian Reorganization Act tribes were allowed to incorporate so that they could borrow money from the government for economic and social programs, the Navaho initially refused, feeling this was just another trick to give the white man access to their lands and resources.

Indigenous Indian cultures, including language, vary widely and are either highly discrete, or loosely related according to the geographic location and historical economic base. Notwithstanding the difficulties of generalizing about such widely varying cultures, certain broad characteristics of Indian societies may be noted, with some reference to their contrast with the cultures of the white invaders. The characteristic features we shall discuss here apply to the Indian people before 1871 when they became wards of the government.

1. The Indian cultures were all preliterate. Thus knowledge and mores were inculcated through the spoken word and the teaching of youth by the elders.

2. While all preliterate societies appear small in contrast with modern societies, Indian societies north of the Rio Grande tended to be small even in the perspective of primitive societies. Tribal relationships were almost entirely personal, and the Indians lacked experience with those secondary, impersonal, formalized relationships characteristic of large-scale complex societies.

3. The Indian economies were primarily hunting and gathering, with fishing in certain areas. In what is now the United States, hoe agriculture was practiced among the Eastern tribes and the Southwest, where maize growing was prevalent. When hoe agriculture was practiced, it was usual for the women to perform the gardening tasks.[6]

4. While individuals sometimes owned items of personal adornment and had property rights to certain songs and crests, property with economic value usually belonged to extended kin or tribal groups. It was inconceivable that any individual member of the group should lack necessities as long as they were available to anyone else.

5. Class distinctions were generally less marked than in preliterate societies in other areas, and where they did exist the material standard of living did not vary greatly from commoner to noble.[7] Too, individual power was greatly limited. Thus in comparing the position of chief among four widely contrasting North American tribes, Goldenweiser writes, "in no case is he [the chief] permitted to exercise actual control over the actions of his people —barring such drastic situations as war or other temporary ex-

---

[6]Robert H. Lowie, *Primitive Society* (New York: Liveright Publishing Corporation, 1947), p. 75.
[7]See Harold E. Driver, *Indians of North America* (Chicago: The University of Chicago Press, 1961), Ch. 19, "Rank and Social Classes."

ploits—and . . . in his daily life he is scarcely distinguishable from any of his subjects.[8]

The Indian Concept of Land and Resources

Like all subsistence societies the Indians were concerned with the conservation of the resources that were their life. Before the coming of white settlers they thought of the land as boundless, with enough for all. Indeed, the colonists initially thought the same. Benjamin Franklin testified before Parliament in 1765 about "those vast forests beyond the Alleghenies not likely to be inhabited in any time to come." Parts of their accustomed terrain had religious and sacred significance to the Indians. The sacred Blue Lake has just been restored to the Taos Indians of New Mexico (1972). The sacred Black Hills of South Dakota were lost to the ten Sioux nations forever. To non-agricultural Indians the common heritage of mankind — the earth — was to be held inviolate.

Indian voices have spoken this way:

In 1625 some of the colonists asked Samoset to give them 12,000 additional acres of land. Samoset knew that land came from the Great Spirit and is as endless as the sky and belonged to no man.[9]

Of the 3,700,000 buffalo destroyed between 1872 through 1874, only 150,000 were killed by Indians.[10]

The Indians killed only enough animals to supply their needs for winter—stripping the meat carefully to dry in the sun, storing marrow and fat on skins, treating the sinews for bow strings and thread, making spoons and cups of the horns, weaving the hair into ropes and belts, curing the hides for tepee covers, clothing and mocassins.[11]

I have heard that you intend to settle us on a reservation near the mountains. I don't want to settle. I love to roam over the prairies. There I feel free and happy, but when we settle down we grow pale and die. . . . Has the white man become a child

[8]Alexander Goldenweiser, *Early Civilization* (New York: Alfred A. Knopf, 1922), p. 120.
[9]From *Bury My Heart at Wounded Knee* by Dee Brown. Copyright © 1970 by Dee Brown. Reprinted by permission of Holt, Rinehart and Winston, Inc.
[10]*Ibid.*, p. 265.
[11]*Ibid.*, p. 269.

that he should recklessly kill and not eat? When the red men slay game they do so that they may eat and not starve. (Santana, Chief of the Kiowas)[12]

The earth was created by the assistance of the sun, and it should be left as it was. . . . The country was made without lines of demarkation, and it is no man's business to divide it. . . . The earth and myself are of one mind. . . . I never said the land was mine to do with as I chose. (Chief Joseph of the Nez Perces)[13]

One does not sell the earth upon which the people walk. (Tashunka Kiko "Crazy Horse")[14]

You ask me to plow the ground. . . . Shall I take a knife and tear my mother's bosom? Then when I die she will not take me to her bosom to rest. You ask me to cut grass and make hay and sell it, and be rich like white men but how dare I cut my mother's hair? (Wowoka, the Piute Messiah)[15]

THE ESTABLISHMENT OF DOMINANCE

Period of Community Diplomacy: 1607–1778

During the colonial period each local English or Dutch settlement dealt with the Indians by whatever means seemed best to it.[16] In Virginia the first settlement, which was founded in 1607, lay within the territory of the Powhatan Confederacy, whose chieftain, Waukunsenecaw, left the small white group in peace. When a new wave of settlers appeared, however, his successor, Opechancanough, fought to drive them out. But in 1644 he was decisively beaten.[17] In Massachusetts, peace prevailed between the Indians and the white men for more than ten years, in part because of an illness which heavily depopulated the tribes nearest the shores. Again, however, as the white settlers became more numerous and began to press westward, many tribes grew hostile. While in some

[12]*Ibid.*, p. 241.
[13]*Ibid.*, p. 316.
[14]*Ibid.*, p. 273.
[15]Paul Radin, *The Story of the American Indian*, p. 368. By permission of the Liveright Publishing Corporation, New York.
[16]The Dutch established the policy of buying land from the Indians, as in the famous purchase of Manhattan Island for a purported $24. The Quakers in Pennsylvania developed a friendly policy toward the Indians and tended, in the early days at least, to fulfill with scrupulous honesty the bargains they made.
[17]John Collier, *Indians of the Americas* (New York: Mentor Books, The New American Library of World Literature, 1947), p. 114.

cases Indian resistance was temporarily successful, the ultimate outcome was always white victory. The technological superiority of Europeans acted here, as elsewhere throughout the era of colonial expansion, to subjugate indigenous peoples. There was friendly trade and barter when whites needed Indians. When whites "needed" Indian lands there was conflict. For most Europeans this was their first encounter with a preliterate culture and they had no orientation which would enable them to understand the customs and social structure that Indians had developed as their adaptation to environment. During the French and Indian Wars the French made alliance with Indians in their common goal of driving out the English settlers, and this increased fear and antagonism in the colonial era.

In 1754 the British Crown formulated a policy for dealing with the Indians which took jurisdiction away from the individual colonies or border groups. Under this policy, "the tribes were independent nations, under the protection of the Crown; Indian lands were inalienable except through voluntary surrender to the Crown; and any attempt by an individual or group, subject to the Crown, or by a foreign state, to buy or seize lands from Indians, was illegal."[18] The attempt of the British Government to carry out this policy amidst innumerable local violations increased the antagonism of the colonists, especially those in the border area, toward the Crown. Thus the Indians indirectly contributed to the final issue of the American Revolution.

Period of Control by Treaties: 1778–1871

The policy of the British Crown was in essence taken over by the new American Government. For the first hundred years the relation of the Indian tribes to the federal government was characterized by treaties, nominally negotiated by the government with so-called sovereign Indian nations. Yet whenever the Indians failed to agree with what the government wanted, they were met with military force. Frequently special local groups moved against the Indians quite independently of the national government, as when the Georgia Legislature passed an act confiscating all Cherokee land and declaring Cherokee tribal laws invalid within the state. Persistently when the white people rode roughshod over their own treaties, the Indians fought back, and a number of

[18]*Ibid.*, pp. 116–117.

Indian wars of considerable dimension took place east of the Mississippi. The Seminole War in Florida and the Black Hawk War in the Illinois Territory, in which Lincoln fought, were among the more famous. The final outcome east of the Mississippi was that most of the Indian tribes were forced into the newly established Indian Territory (now the state of Oklahoma). The exceptions were a few small, relatively harmless bands in Main, New York, Virginia, and Florida, and a considerable number of Cherokees in North Carolina, who put up so much resistance that they were let alone in the wilds of the Smoky Mountain Region.

West of the Mississippi, much of the story of Indian-white relations centers around, first, the situation in California following the gold rush and, second, the subjugation of the Plains Indians throughout the vast Midwest. In California the white men in search of gold forced the Indians out of any area they wanted. From 1851 on, the federal government negotiated treaties with many local tribes by which the Indians agreed to surrender more than half of California. These treaties, because of frontier political pressure, were never ratified by the Senate, and the government subsequently sold to white people much of the land pledged to the Indians.

The subjugation of the Plains Indians beginning about 1870 is described by Collier:

> First there was military assault, on slight pretexts or no pretexts at all, and the government exploited tribal rivalries in order that Indians should kill Indians. The limited and disciplinary war customs of the Plains turned into total warfare, aimed at annihilation, with the United States Army as the driving power. The tribes were finally beaten, however, not through overwhelming numbers or superior armament (though these existed) but through starvation after the whites had destroyed the buffalo. . . . That revelry of slaughter, which had no sportsmanship in it, was recognized as a war measure against the Indians and was deliberately encouraged.[19]

The great Indian wars west of the Mississippi were in large measure resistance to reservation life. People were being removed from the land they loved, their freedom of movement restricted, and usually the reservation land was arid terrain that whites did not want.

[19]John Collier, *Indians of the Americas*, p. 133, by permission.

If the Texans had kept out of my country there might have been peace. But that which you say we must live on is too small. The Texans have taken away the places where the grass grew thickest and the timber was best. Had we kept that we might have done the things you ask. But it is too late. (Ten Bears of the Yamaparika Comanches)[20]

It was not until 1915, with the Ute War that the last of Indian conflict subsided. But the symbolic end was the massacre at Wounded Knee nineteen years—a generation—after the passing of the Reservation Act (see Chapter 3 for account of Wounded Knee). The tribes had been decimated by war and starvation, and now a half century of demoralization and alienation was about to begin.

Reservation Period: First Phase—Forced Assimilation

In 1871, Congress decreed that no Indian tribe "shall be acknowledged or recognized as an independent nation, tribe or power, with whom the United States may contract by treaty,"[21] thus marking the beginning of a definitely new phase in Indian-white relations. The Indians were now wards of the federal government, a unique status for any minority group in the United States. The policy and practices of the Indian Office from this time on were aimed at weakening the tribal organization of the Indians, destroying their culture, and forcing the assimilation of Indians as individuals into the normative American way of life. After several years of public and Congressional debate, a new land policy was adopted with the passage of the famous Dawes Act in 1887. This legislation empowered the President to divide the lands of any tribe by giving allotted individual portions to family heads or other individuals. But the plots so allotted were to be held in trust for twenty-five years, after which they were to become the unrestricted property of each owner. In the meantime they could not be sold. The object of this program was to force each Indian breadwinner to become a self-supporting individual by working his own land. In the meantime the Indians were to be supported directly by the government.

The Dawes Act was the result of crusading efforts on the part

[20]Dee Brown, *Bury My Heart at Wounded Knee*, p. 242.
[21]Ray Allen Billington, *Westward Expansion* (New York: The Macmillan Co., 1949), p. 668. Ch. 32, "The Indian Barrier," pp. 651–670, describes the history of Indian white relations from 1860 to 1887.

of aroused public opinion about the extreme exploitation and decimation of the Indians. It represented a move of the American conscience, but an extremely naïve move, within the ideology of its period. Understanding nothing of Indian social organization, nor recognizing the problems of a nontechnological people, despite the good intentions of crusaders[22] and Congressmen, the land allotment policy was disastrous to the Indians. They lacked the technical knowledge needed to make their holdings pay. They lacked credit to acquire materials (seed and tools) to operate the land. The division of land through inheritance was inimical to most tribes who held land as common property. Under these circumstances they were prey to whites who leased land allotments at below value (ranchers, for example, would lease contiguous allotments for grazing beef cattle for the urban market), and to squatters who impinged on Indian property that was not fenced or cultivated. Over the entire period in which the allotment policy was in effect (1887–1914), the lands held by the Indians were reduced (largely by squatter occupation) from 138 million acres to 47 million acres.[23]

Another phase of the policy of forced assimilation concerned the educational program. Indian children at school age were taken out of their tribal homes and placed in boarding schools, where the use of Indian languages and the practice of Indian ways, such as dress and hair styles, were forbidden. The curricula of the schools were largely that of the white schools, without any adaptation to the particular needs of the Indians. In Macgregor's opinion, whatever practical training the Indian children obtained either for making a living or making better homes was gained from the labor they performed to help support the school.[24]

The first period of reservation policy, until the Reorganization Act of 1934 not only failed to understand cultural differences, and the slow rate of cultural change, especially for segregated groups as was *per se* characteristic of reservations, it further fell short of its objective because of inefficient administration. The Indian

[22]See Helen Hunt Jackson, *A Century of Dishonor*, which first appeared in 1881 (New York: Harper & Brothers). It has now been reissued by Harper & Row as a Harper Torchbook (1965). Mrs. Jackson is also known for her novel, *Ramona*, which deals with the sad fate of California Indians. She has been sometimes called the Harriet Beecher Stowe of the Indian cause. In her view wardship and the Allotment Act were great steps forward for the protection and integration of Indians.
[23]Ward Shepard, "Land Problems of an Expanding Indian Population," in Oliver La Farge, ed., *The Changing Indian* (Norman: University of Oklahoma Press, 1942), p. 11.
[24]Gordon Macgregor, "Indian Education in Relation to the Social and Economic Background of the Reservation," in *The Changing Indian*, pp. 116–127.

Service, particularly in its earlier years, was not conspicuous for the high standards of its personnel. Nor was a particular interest in Indians and their welfare a prerequisite for employment in the Service. Furthermore, the appropriations granted it were inadequate. Even when well-intentioned officials attempted to carry out some sort of policy, they were beset with powerful pressures from special interests to twist the policy to the latter's advantage.

During the 1920s constant pressures were brought to bear by certain vested white interests to enact legislation which would have expropriated further the rights of Indians to their resources. These efforts were defeated and as one result of the publicity attending the hearings in this connection, a comprehensive study of the problems of the administration of Indian affairs was undertaken (1927) by a private agency, the Institute for Government Research, at the request of Secretary of the Interior, Hubert Work. The findings of this study, usually known as the Merriam Survey, went far to create a more favorable government attitude toward the Indians.[25]

Perhaps the demoralization was the greatest for the Plains Indians who fought so long and bitterly against confinement to reservations. The Sioux were relegated to reservations (Rosebud in South Dakota, Standing Rock in North Dakota, and Pine Ridge in Nebraska are the leading ones.) They had been a mobile, hunting culture ranging over a wide terrain. They did not have the social organization or patterns of childhood training to adapt to village life. Everett Hagan who visited the Dakota (the indigenous name for the Sioux) reservations as late as 1961 attested to the enduring despair of these peoples.[26] Hagen stated that "at first the reservations (for these warlike Indians) were essentially concentration camps." In the case of the Sioux the aggressiveness fostered in children and the strict self-control necessary to survival in a hunting culture was symbolized and compensated for in a central tribal ceremony: the Sun Dance. Since this ceremony involved self-inflicted pain, on the one hand, the orgiastic release, on the other, it was forbidden by the new masters. "The whites, moved by their own values, unwittingly removed the last vestige of meaning from lives whose external base had already been

[25]Institute for Government Research, *The Problem of Indian Administration* (Baltimore: The Johns Hopkins Press, 1928).
[26]Everett E. Hagen, *On the Theory of Social Change* (Homewood, Ill.: The Dorsey Press, 1962), pp. 481–484. See Ch. 19 for a case study of the Sioux on the reservations.

destroyed." The result was demoralization, cultism, and eventually apathy. Hagen observed that the inhabitants of the reservation seemed to be suffering from a malaise "more pervasive than malnutrition and more pentrating than cold . . . as ghosts walking about, withdrawn, passive, lifeless. . . ."

Reservation Period: Second Phase—the "New Deal"

The phrase, "New Deal," coined to characterize the early years of Franklin D. Roosevelt's administration, was peculiarly apt with reference to Indian affairs. While the time was ripe in 1933 for reorganization of Indian policy, the sweeping character of the changes undertaken at this time was in considerable measure due to a long-standing sympathetic interest in Indians of the new Secretary of the Interior, Harold I. Ickes, and to the appointment of John Collier as Commissioner of the Bureau of Indian Affairs.

Behind the efforts which culminated in the passage of the Indian Reorganization Act, sponsored by Senator Burton Wheeler of Montana, was a new philosophy concerning Indians held by the new Commissioner and strongly supported by the new federal administration. In essence, this philosophy aimed at integrating Indians into the national life as Indians, making Indian groups self-sustaining while also retaining as much of their tribal culture and group identification as was consistent with life in a modern civilized nation. Collier not only admired the Indians as persons but felt that much of their culture should be preserved, that there was a place for Indians in a multigroup democratic society. He expressed his philosophy thus:

> The new Indian policy . . . seeks to reinstate the Indians as normally functioning units, individual and group, into the life of the world. It makes them equal in the management of their own affairs and the direction of their own lives.
> On the purely cultural side, only sheer fanaticism would decide the further destruction of Indian languages, crafts, poetry, music, ritual, philosophy, and religion. These possessions have a significance and a beauty which grew patiently through endless generations of a people immersed in the life of nature, filled with imaginative and ethical insight into the core of being. . . .[27]

[27]From Report of House of Representatives Subcommittee on Appropriations for the Interior Department, 1934.

The point of view of the new commissioner was reflected in the Indian Reorganization Act passed by Congress in 1934, the chief provisions of which are as follows:

1. With certain qualifications, Indian societies were to be empowered to undertake political, economic, and administrative self-government.
2. Land allotment was to be stopped, and under certain conditions, additional lands could be added to current holdings.
3. A system of agricultural and industrial credit was to be established, and the needed funds were authorized.
4. An Indian Civil Service was to be established and provisions for the training of Indians themselves in administration and the professions were called for.

The Reorganization Act called for the acceptance of its provisions by each tribe individually, determined on the basis of a referendum using secret ballot. Those who voted to accept could organize under it for self-government and could organize themselves as a federal corporation to conduct economic enterprise.

The Indian Reorganization Act was a major shift in government philosophy and policy. Its implementation was slower than hoped, in part due to the enormous pressures on the government occasioned by World War II. It was not until the end of the 1940s that achievements anticipated for a decade earlier began to emerge.

The task envisioned at the passage of the Act was enormous. Memories, preserved in oral tradition, were long. Retreatism, apathy, and the devaluing attitude of whites in the regions surrounding the reservations had taken a high toll. In a study published in 1947, the anthropoligists Kluckhon and Leighton described the dilemmas of the Navaho:

> Different sets of Navahos (depending partly upon age, schooling, location of residence with respect to non-Navaho contacts, and other factors) have shown different major responses to the insecurities, deprivations and frustrations of the immediate past and especially to the "between two worlds" problem. . . . Some focus their energies upon trying to be as like whites as possible. Some find relief in becoming followers of vocal leaders. Others dissipate much hostility in factional quarrels or scatter their aggression in family fights, in phantasies about witchcraft or in attacking "witches," in verbal and other indirect hostilities toward whites, or they turn their aggression inward with resultant fits

of depression. The culturally patterned releases in humor and in "joking relationships" with certain relatives continue to play some part. The central response of certain individuals is in flight—either in actual physical withdrawal or in the escape of narcotics, alcohol, and sex. Still others turn to intensified participation in rites of the native religion and to new cults (e.g., peyote). Partial solutions are achieved by a few individuals by rigid compartmentalization of their lives and by various rationalizations.[28]

Those who have set themselves to follow the white man's trail find themselves—as have representatives of other minority groups—in a (rationally) odd dilemma. While as youngsters they are rewarded by school teachers and others for behaving like whites, as adults they are punished for having acquired skills that make them competitors of their white contemporaries. The more intelligent ones had, by early maturity, realized that their education would bring them into conflict with or isolation from their own unschooled relatives. But the experience of being turned on by their white mentors comes as a painful surprise. They find they are seldom received on terms of social equality, even by those whose standards of living, dress, and manners they have succeeded in copying almost perfectly. They learn that they must always (save within the Indian Service) expect to work for a salary at least one grade lower than that which a white person of comparable training and experience receives. They overhear remarks by those same groups of whites who had goaded them to give up "those ignorant Indian ways." "You can never trust these school boys." "Give me a 'long hair' every time. They may be dumb but they are honest and they work hard." "Educated Indians are neither fish nor fowl. They give me the creeps." Rejected by the white world they have made so many emotional sacrifices to enter, some attempt a bitter retreat to the Navaho world. Others, in sour disillusionment, abandon all moral codes. Still others achieve a working (but flat and empty) adjustment.

Navahos are well aware of the difficulty of their situation. Surrounded by powerful pressures to change, they know that indifference and withdrawal can no longer serve as effective responses. They are conscious of the need to develop some compromise with white civilization. But doubt as to the best form of compromise makes them angry and anxious. Thus suspicion and hostility are becoming a major emotional tone of their relationships with whites.[29]

[28]The above analysis is a classic illustration of Robert K. Merton's paradigm of possible adaptations to competitive goals and means. For a discussion of this theorem see Ch. 18.
[29]Clyde Kluckhon and Dorothea Leighton, *The Navaho* (Cambridge: Harvard University Press, 1947), pp. 113–115. By permission.

Progress Under the Indian Reorganization Act

The new deal for the Indians nevertheless meant considerable strides in economic rehabilitation, increasing tribal self-government, and a slow but steady rise in the welfare of Indians as a whole. By 1948 a total of seventy-three tribes had received charters of incorporation, which meant that with the economic assistance of the government and the technical advice and approval of the Indian Service these groups improved their economic welfare and gained experience in helping themselves. Some tribes through loans have been able to purchase additional lands or to put hitherto unused acreage into effective use. One major problem has been to prevent too great a depletion of Indian land resources because of the desire of many Indians to sell their land to non-Indians or to lease it without adequate safeguards against deterioration. Marked increases in the requests by Indians, some with individual holdings, to sell their lands were reported by the Bureau in 1948 and 1949.[30]

By 1948 a total of ninety-three tribes had adopted written constitutions and had begun to assume larger political self-government. Typically there is a Tribal Council which suggests measures of administration and approves or rejects proposals of the Agency staff. It has considerable control of the tribal finances and appoints a Tribal Court of Indian Judges, which tries all cases of criminal law except those involving the ten most serious offenses, over which the Federal court retains jurisdiction. Nevertheless, the great gap between tribal legal and political practices and those of the white democracy could not be closed at once. For example, it was the practice of both the Navaho and the Papago to decide important matters by face-to-face meetings of all concerned in which the issues were discussed until unanimity was reached, in contrast with the system of majority decision under white democracy. It was clear that the goal of self-government had to be approached by degrees.

Although Congress enacted a law in 1924 making all Indians citizens, seven states barred Indians from voting until about 1940, either by discriminatory laws or interpretations of laws. Following 1940, five of these states began to allow Indians to vote by not enforcing these statutes. Court decisions in Arizona and New Mexico in 1948 opened the door to full voting privileges for In-

[30]*Annual Report of Secretary of the Interior*, 1948, pp. 369–392.

dians, and since then Indians there have generally had the right to vote.

Education for Indian children has been continually improving. From 1950 to 1960 the number of Indian children enrolled in schools increased from 26,716 to 133,316; over the same period the percentage of Indian children attending public schools, rather than the federally operated schools for Indian pupils alone, increased from 50 per cent to 63.5 per cent. It is of special interest to discover that in 1959 some twenty-five tribes themselves provided scholarships in higher education totalling about $500,000.[31]

Later Trends in Official Policy

A considerable reversal in the Indian policy and program occurred in the 1950s. Efforts to speed up the process of liquidating the government's responsibility to the Indians took the forms which may be designated as "relocation" and "termination."

TERMINATION   The termination policy stemmed from a resolution by Congress passed on August 1, 1953, which stated in part:

> . . . [I]t is the policy of Congress, as rapidly as possible, to make the Indians within the terriitorial limits of the United States subject to the same laws and entitled to the same privileges and responsibilities as are applicable to other citizens of the United States, to end their status as wards of the United States, and to grant them all the rights and prerogatives pertaining to American citizenship. . . .[32]

Following passage of this resolution, efforts were made to order or to persuade tribes to request termination of their relation to the federal government. This would have meant in many instances dissolution of tribal organizations and the division of tribal assets among the several members. In view of the lack of acculturation of most Indians to the normative American way of life, especially to the norms of economic self-reliance, termination might well have resulted in the demoralization and pauperization of the Indians of many tribes. Alarmed at this prospect, friends of the Indians protested the policy and it was revised. Indian groups were not to be pressured to terminate unless they themselves

---

[31]*Annual Report of the Secretary of Interior,* 1960, p. 97.
[32]House Concurrent Resolution 108, 83rd Congress, 1st Session.

wanted it and were developed to a point where they could carry on their own affairs. Thus in fact only a few tribes were actually terminated, the most important being the Klamaths of Oregon and the Menomines of Wisconsin, both owners of large tracts of valuable timber.

The results of termination have not benefited the Menomines or the government. "Termination itself costs the government nearly $3 million. And now a once profitable business operation, which supported this tribe for nearly a century, looks to be on the edge of collapse."[33] The shift from a common property culture to individual ownership has created legal problems, involved Indians with banks and lawyers, forced them into dealing with county and state structures with which they are unfamiliar. Ridgeway predicts that "the tribe is likely to be slowly extinguished, the Indians either moving down to the cities or dying in the woods. The old reservation seems fated to become a state park." Menomines today see termination as just one more hoax of the white government. Brandon sees the effort to force termination as an aspect of "McCarthyism" and quotes the late Felix S. Cohen, the principal government expert on Indian legal affairs: "Like the miner's canary, the Indian marks the shift from fresh air to poison gas in our political atmosphere; and our treatment of Indians, even more than our treatment of other minorities, reflects the rise and fall of our democratic faith."[34]

When wholesale termination was anticipated, a special federal commission was set up to clear up unpaid Indian treaty claims and claims of past fraudulence. Although some claims have been clearly exaggeratedly unrealizable, by 1961, out of 800 claims, twenty-one, totalling some $40 million had been paid.

Termination has now been officially abandoned as a policy.

RELOCATION   In 1952 the Bureau of Indian Affairs started what was called the Voluntary Relocation Program, under which reservation Indians, either individually or in family groups, who desired to move to industrial centers for permanent employment and settlement were offered financial and other assistance to enable them to relocate. A reason for adopting this program was the fact that most Indian tribal lands were inadequate to permit viable economies with a rapidly growing population.

The early days of the relocation program were not very suc-

[33]James Ridgeway, "The Lost Indians," *The New Republic,* December 4, 1965, p. 20.
[34]William Brandon, *The American Heritage Book of the Indians,* (New York: Simon and Shuster, 1961), p. 369.

cessful and worked great hardship; expenses were paid to move from the reservation, but there was no aid for the Indian to return if he found the urban experience unsuitable or unbearable. One-fourth to one-third of relocated Indians had returned to the reservations by 1965.

Life in the city has often been difficult and puzzling for relo-catees who moved from wardship status on the reservation to the hazards and monetary pitfalls of urban society. Accustomed to depend on government doles for commodities, health services, etc. many have been ill-prepared for the confusion of alternatives available in an individualistic money economy. Those who re-mained in the city are those who have most successfully con-formed to white standards, at least in the economic sphere.[35]

To assist migration the Bureau of Indian Affairs has offered two programs: a direct employment program and an adult voca-tional trainee program. Between 1952–1968 over 100,000 Indians participated in these programs. A study made by the Bureau of a sampling of these participants to determine success in adjusting to life off the reservation found that successful migration was closely related to higher educational level. Indians who had par-ticipated in the Bureau training programs earned more than migrating Indians who had not. Nevertheless, budget limitations have prevented these programs from assisting enough applicants to markedly reduce the level of surplus labor on the reservations.[36]

A study of Indians in Los Angeles, which in 1966 had 25,000 Indians, suggests that tribal differences are correlated with suc-cessful urban adaptation. Indians from agricultural tribes like the Navaho tend to have weak adaptations; plains Indians moderate, and the highest success is from the Five Civilized Tribes. The author of the survey felt that the expansion of a distinctly urban pan-Indian culture and ideology was a significant aid to many city Indians.[37]

A University of Minnesota report on Indians in Minneapolis stresses housing as a principle problem, due to lack of income and overcrowding. It also emphasizes the lack of coordination of all agencies, public and private, offering services to Indians.[38] Another report from the same Center emphasizes the helplessness felt by

[35]Joan Ablon, "American Indian Relocation: Problems of Dependency and Manage-ment in the City," *Phylon*, Winter 1965, pp. 362–371.
[36]Alan Sorkin, "Some Aspects of American Indian Migration," *Social Forces*, De-cember 1969, pp. 243–250.
[37]J. Price, "The Migration and Adaptation of Indians to Los Angeles," *Human Organization*, Summer 1968, pp. 168–175.
[38]Fred Berger, *The Minnesota Indian in Minneapolis*, Training Center for Commu-nity Programs, University of Minnesota, September, 1970.

agency personnel in dealing with cross-cultural difficulties between Indians and whites. There is a lack of in-depth understanding by agency personnel, an inadequate understanding of agencies by Indians themselves, and structural rigidities in agencies that are frustrating and impeding to employees attempting to provide adequate service. This paper finds agency personnel to have predominantly positive attitudes toward Indian youth and predominantly negative attitudes toward older Indians.[39]

In a comparison of Samoans and American Indians settling in West Coast cities, it was found that the Samoans' positive self-image was a factor in successful adaptation.[40]

The success of urban adjustment then seems to depend on educational level, degree of preparation for migration, the historical social organization of the particular tribe, and the Indians' own self-image. Cities absorbing an Indian labor force need agency personnel more acquainted with Indian values and customs, more housing, more job training, and job-upgrading programs.

As with any program of this sort, the results vary with the attitudes and efficiency of the officials operating the program at local levels. Many Indian leaders, as well as such friends of the Indians as The Association on American Indian Affairs, favor this program in principle. This latter organization feels that the program could be improved by (1) making it clear that relocation opportunities are available to those Indians who really want it without any undue pressures being exerted; (2) improving liaison with local community agencies in the cities of relocation in order to facilitate the adjustment of the resettled Indians; and (3) not stressing the point of permanence of relocation.

Even if substantial numbers of relocated Indians do return to the reservations, the experience will have been educational and the returned members may contribute to the improvement of tribal conditions through their increased acculturation. The main concern of the friends of the Indians is, however, that the relocation program shall not be viewed as a "solution" of the Indian problem, that its operation shall not deflect effort from the more basic problems of aiding the reservation Indians to develop viable economies, to work out their own problems and to be free to determine how much of their traditional cultural heritages they wish to retain.

[39]Arthur M. Harkins and Richard G. Woods, *Attitudes of Minneapolis Agency Personnel toward Urban Indians*, Training Center for Community Programs, University of Minnesota, December, 1968.
[40]Joan Ablon, "Retention of Cultural Values and Differential Urban Adaptation," *Social Forces*, March 1971, pp. 385–392.

Reservation Development

Early in the Kennedy Administration Congress adopted the Area Redevelopment Act which was to be administered by the Department of Commerce. It provided for loans, grants, and technical assistance to areas designated as depressed and underdeveloped. Various Indian reservations were classified as eligible for assistance under the Act.

One of the first proposals submitted was the Navajo.[41]

In October 1961 participation in the Area Redevelopment program was authorized by the Tribal Council "at a duly called meeting, at Window Rock, Arizona, at which a quorum was present, and . . . [the proposal] was passed by a vote of 56 in favor and 0 opposed. . . ."[42] An overall development program was designed jointly by Indian Bureau advisors and Tribal representatives. This document is a little case study in development since the bleak picture of the Navajos presented by Kluckhon and Leighton in the 1940s.

> The Navajo Indian Country, including the Reservation and adjacent lands used and occupied by Navajos, embraces nearly 16 million acres. . . . The topography varies from mountains 11,000 feet high with clear streams and stands of timber, to semi-desert lands at 4,500 feet elevation. The climate for the most part is semi-arid and suited primarily for grazing. The land is used principally for grazing small subsistence flocks of sheep and goats under herd, as well as cattle and horses.
>
> Individual income is very low on a per capita basis.[43] Major sources of income are: *off reservation:* railroad work, farm labor, seasonal harvesting; *on reservation:* State, Federal and Tribal payrolls, welfare and surplus commodities, livestock, agriculture, Tribal public works programs.
>
> There are (1961) approximately 90,000 Navajos in the area, with an estimated labor force of 15,000 to 20,000.
>
> The Navajo Tribe is a distinct political entity, having territorial boundaries within which it exercises a dependent sovereignty subject only to treaty provisions and to the plenary power of the Congress, and within this sphere has and exercises the power of regulating its internal and social relations. The Navajo Tribal Council is the governing body. . . . The Chairman and Vice

[41]Navajo is the name given to the Dinetah people by the Spaniards. The tribe itself still retains the Spanish spelling, but most Anglos write it as it sounds: Navaho.
[42]*Looking Forward: Navajo Overall Economic Development Program*, Transmitted January 4, 1962.
[43]Average (mean) annual income for 1970 is given as $700. John Upton Terrell, *The Navajos* (New York: Harper and Row, 1970), p. 316.

Chairman are the Executive Branch. . . . The Council, the Chairman, and the Vice Chairman are elected for four-year terms by the vote of the people.

The main income to the tribe, to date, has come from bonuses and royalties accruing from uranium, oil, gas and construction materials such as sand and gravel. With the exception of surface use for farming, grazing, and individual business purposes, all income from Tribal lands reverts directly to the Tribal treasury and not to individual Navajo people. This income, though it aggregates many millions of dollars has never been sufficient to warrant individual distribution. Consequently, the Navajo Tribe has utilized tribal funds for the support of programs which benefit members of the tribe in common.

The proposal then lists 16 categories of projects undertaken by the Tribal Council. The proposal itself is for the collection of critical data for planning: Population Census, including skill, aptitude, income, education, etc.; potential for development of recreation areas; utilities studies; forest development; occupational training and retraining; mineral potential.

Each one of the above points rests not only on development of the *physical* resources, but equally important, on comprehensive knowledge of the *human* resource, its aptitudes and its aspirations. Every proposed Overall Economic Development project is spiced with the salt and pepper of physical and human resource amalgamation.

Reservation development has proceeded considerably since this early Navaho proposal. Today Navahos operate a number of new enterprises including their own telephone system. The Pine Ridge Sioux have set up their own construction company so that off-reservation white contractors are no longer needed to build reservation housing, roads, and public works. The Standing Rock Sioux have submitted a plan for 15 enterprises including a bank, a motel, a shopping center, and a cattle ranching operation. There is a bill pending in Congress to allow Indians to contract for the control of services now operated by the Bureau of Indian Affairs.[44]

Those Indian leaders who have been pressing for a focus on reservation development recognize that development will not solve, at least for some time to come, the whole problem of Indian poverty. But they also see the failure of relocation even when ostensibly well programmed.

[44]*The New York Times,* January 9, 1972, p. 56.

Trudy Felix Brightman, an Indian in San Francisco, says the BIA brought her there for training as a dental technician, couldn't find her a job and finally sent her to work as a clothes presser. Most of her friends, she says, left the dental training course only to wind up in factories.[45]

It is their belief however that upgrading on the reservation, breaking the dependency and apathy, will make possible voluntary moves to off-reservation employment less demoralizing.

UNRESOLVED PROBLEMS, UNMET NEEDS

Despite a brightening picture, prolonged and severe damage takes a long time to repair. The National Congress of American Indians reported on Indian employment and income for 1968:

Employment: The Indian labor force was seen as about 120,000—30 per cent of the total Indian population (as of 1960). Almost half are chronically unemployed as compared with total nonwhite unemployment of 7.5 per cent. Half of working Indians were underemployed in seasonal or temporary jobs.

Income: Ten per cent of Indian families had incomes of $5,000 a year or higher; 74 per cent of family incomes are below $3,000. Half the working force had wages below $2,000 a year.[46]

Education: Indians with no school experience were reported as 10.4 per cent in 1968, as compared with 2.3 per cent for the national average and 4.1 per cent for Negroes. Comparisons for students completing school through eighth grade only, show 37.4 per cent for Indians as compared with a national average of 31.5 per cent (figures for Appalachia are 68 per cent). The national average for students completing 12th grade was 24.6 per cent for Indians 12.4 per cent.[47]

In 1970 a study of Indian education in 14 states made for the U.S. Office of Education reported 63 per cent of Indian students in public schools, 31 per cent in schools operated by the Bureau of Indian Affairs and 6 per cent in mission schools. It further reported a rapid increase in the number of Indian college students: 8,000, or 12 per cent of the college age group. This increase has been made possible by increased scholarships through Indian tribal organizations and federal funds.[48]

[45]*The Wall Street Journal,* March 8, 1970, pp. 1, 19.
[46]NCAI *Sentinel,* Spring, 1968, Vol. 13, No. 1. p. 12.
[47]*Ibid.,* p. 15.
[48]*The New York Times,* Dec. 20, 1970, p. 38.

The Office of Education report recommended that more authority and responsibility for the education of Indian children be placed in the hands of Indians. Indians in the South have in some cases resisted bussing of their children. There seem to be mixed motives: they do not want their children so far from home; they do not want them to go to predominantly black schools; they argue that few black or white children are bussed to predominantly Indians schools; and the younger militants are concerned with "a preservation of the cultural heritage." Some of these pockets of surviving Indians are not acknowledged as tribes by the Indian Bureau and have no benefit from Bureau funds.[49]

TREATY RIGHTS One of the most publicized controversies over treaty rights persisted from 1963 to 1969—that of the Northwest Indians against abrogation of their fishing rights. These are small tribes whose livelihood is dependent on fishing, indeed more than livelihood—their "way of life." The confrontation was but one link in a long chain of encroachment that most Indian tribes have experienced as the interests of whites, whether for commerce or sport, have whittled away at Indian resources. In this instance, however, Indians used all means at hand to resist. Despite the fact that the United States Court of Appeals had upheld their treaty rights, arrests of Indian fishermen continued. Protest "fish-ins" were the first step, initiated by the newly formed Survival of American Indians Association. The National Indian Youth Council took up the cause and organized a demonstration at the state capitol in Olympia, Washington. Actor Marlon Brando (who is part Indian) came to lend his support, and was arrested, but released. The demonstration had national media coverage.

The following year Dick Gregory participated in a series of protest fish-ins on behalf of the Survival of American Indians Association. He was arrested, convicted, and served a jail sentence. Demonstrations continued. The American Civil Liberties Union entered the case, and shortly thereafter the Department of Justice announced that at the request of a tribe it would defend Indian fishermen.

On May 27, 1968 the United States Supreme Court upheld the rights of two of the tribes (Nisquallys and Puyallups.)[50]

[49]*The New York Times*, Sept. 13, 1970, p. 78.
[50]American Friends Service Committee, *Uncommon Controversy: Fishing Rights of the Muckleshoot, Puyallup and Nisqually Indians* (Seattle, University of Washington Press, 1970), Ch. 5.

THE URBAN INDIANS   It is estimated that now somewhere between 35 per cent and 40 per cent of Indians live in cities. The largest concentrations are in Los Angeles, Chicago, Minneapolis, Milwaukee, Phoenix, Albuquerque, Tulsa, Oklahoma City, Seattle, and New York.[51] They tend to have the poorest housing, a high rate of school drop out, and marginal jobs. In many instances there is no residential clustering and they live in isolation and often bewilderment. There has been an attempt to organize urban Indians into a nationwide organization, and to establish Indian centers in major cities. In some instances there has been an attempt to take over unused government buildings for Indian residential centers. The most publicized was the occupation of the abandoned federal prison, Alcatraz, in San Francisco Bay which Indians held for 19 months before they were evicted. In Milwaukee they have successfully occupied and now negotiated for permanently an abandoned Coast Guard station on Lake Michigan. Similar efforts in Chicago have failed. They are too small a percentge of population to have much effect on local governments. As off-reservation Indians they are not eligible for education and health benefits provided for Indians by the federal government.

INDIANS AND THE INDIAN BUREAU   There has been great unevenness in the administration of Indian affairs not only because of vacillating policy, but because of the uneven efficacy of the Indian Bureau in carrying out its trust. Personnel in the field agencies have varied at different periods and in different places. Since they are in the field they have the greatest opportunity for developing understanding of Indians and often they are concerned friends of the Indians. There has, however, been much criticism by Indians of the regional offices and of the central bureaucracy in Washington.

Recently there have been struggles in the top echelons of the Bureau between old line accomodative leadership and a more vigorous leadership. In 1971 there was an attempt to downgrade the Commissioner, Louis R. Bruce, a Mohawk-Sioux, and other progressives who surrounded him were transferred to regional posts. This precipitated a revolt and a demand that the Bureau be removed from the Department of the Interior and be directly responsible to the White House. A group of Indians, led by Peter MacDonald, Chairman of the Navaho Tribal Council, barricaded themselves in the Bureau and were forcibly ejected by the police.

[51]*The New York Times,* February 10, 1972, p. 1.

This forced a shake up and Mr. Bruce's policies and leadership were restored. Mr. Bruce has opposed urban relocation and favored increased reservation development programs.[52]

At a news conference January 12, 1972 the Secretary of the Interior, Rogers B. Morton, announced a "re-direction of policy." There are five points in the new program:

1. Accelerated reservation-by-reservation development programs.
2. Redirection of the employment assistance program to train Indians for on-reservation needed development skills.
3. Resources protection to be carried on by a new Indian Water rights from public and private encroachment.
   Rights Office, charged with protecting Indian land and water
4. Road construction.
5. More tribal control of education programs: the plan is for on-reservation high schools and junior colleges, as well as the substitution of day schools for boarding schools for elementary school children, this last contingent on developing roads so that school buses can operate.[53]

INDIAN PRESSURE GROUPS   Although a number of Indian organizations have developed since World War II around specific issues or in special regions, the only one large enough and with a large enough treasury to maintain a lobby in Washington is the National Congress of American Indians. It held its 28th annual conference in November, 1971. Made up of representation from reservation tribes, it nevertheless feels it should speak for all Indians, Alaskan Eskimos, and Aleuts. It is also weighing how to include representation of urban Indians.

Urban Indians have a national organization of their own with younger, more militant leadership—the American Indian Movement (AIM) which claims it represents 25,000 urban Indians. There is also a younger movement among reservation Indians, the National Indian Youth Council. These two groups have been active in protests and demonstrations and have carried these tactics to meetings of the National Congress of American Indians, possibly with some effect on the direction of policy of the older body.[54] This is still an open question.

INDIANS AND THEIR NEIGHBORS   The American Friends Service Task Force concluded its report on the Fishing Rights Controversy with this point:

[52]*The New York Times*, Jan. 9, 1972, pp. 1, 56.
[53]*The New York Times*, January 13, 1972, p. 35.
[54]*The New York Times*, Nov. 16, 1971.

The real issue is the attitude of the whole society toward difference. The Indians look at fishing rights differently and they fish
in different ways. Difference is nearly intolerable in a society
which expects conformity in behavior and outlook—one which
tends to equate equal treatment with identical treatment, acceptable behavior with conforming behavior, integration with assimilation. . . . Hostility rises from the threat presented by differences,
not by danger to the fish.[55]

Suggested Readings

American Friends Service Committee. *Uncommon Controversy: Fishing
Rights of the Muckleshoot, Puyallup and Nisqually Indians.* Seattle: The
University of Washington Press, 1970.
A full and careful analysis of Indian fishing rights facing abrogation
under pressure from the sportsmen's lobby and industry.

Brown, Dee. *Bury My Heart at Wounded Knee: An Indian History of the
American West.* New York: Holt, Rinehart and Winston, 1970.
An eloquent documentary, essential for correcting perspective on the
westward movement.

Deloria, Vine, Jr. *We Talk, You Listen: New Tribes, New Turf.* New York: The
Macmillan Company, 1970.
A rousing polemic for a new pluralism by an Indian activist.

Driver, Harold E. *Indians of North America.* Chicago: University of Chicago
Press, 1961.
A comprehensive comparative description of Native American cultures.

Howard, John R., ed. *Awakening Minorities: American Indians, Mexican
Americans, Puerto Ricans.* 2nd edition. New Brunswick, N.J.: Trans-
action Books, 1972.
A small reader with particularly good selections on American Indians.

Spicer, Edward H., ed. *Human Problems and Technical Change: A Casebook.*
New York: The Russell Sage Foundation, 1952.
Cases 1, 6, 10, 11 and 12 analyze attempts and results of innovation in
several Indian societies.

Terrell, John Upton. *The Navajos: The Past and Present of a Great People.*
New York: Harper & Row, 1970.
A good account of one tribe, especially illustrating the effects of vas-
cillating government policy.

[55]AFSC, *Uncommon Controversy: Fishing Rights,* p. 191.

11 **M**exican Americans —La Raza

The Mexican is pictured on the one hand as the peon, who hat in hand holds the reins for John Wayne in the movies, or is the Frito Bandito on T.V. On the other hand, he is the glamorous hidalgo, *the ambassador of good will for the city of San Diego, and a participant in the Rose Bowl Parade. Between the fanciful extremes of the peon and the hidalgo is La Raza. Probably the most telling observation ever to be printed about us came from the pages of Newsweek (May 23, 1966): "We're the best kept secret in America."*

I would like to say here today that the secret is now out. We are fast becoming America's most promising human catalyst for the creation of a democratic society where cultural heritage and language assets are prime instruments in the acceptance of human diversity as a major national goal. Armando M. Rodriquez, Director of the Office for Spanish-speaking American Affairs, U.S. Dept. of Health, Education, and Welfare

There were approximately 9 million persons of Spanish origin in the United States in March 1971, including over 5 million[1] who were of Mexican descent. Today 80 per cent of Mexican Americans live in urban communities. The largest concentrations are in the

[1]U.S. Bureau of the Census, *Current Population Reports*, Series P-20, No. 224, March 1971.

five southwestern sections of California, Arizona, New Mexico, Colorado, and Texas, though there has been some steady spread to the northern Middlewest: Illinois, Minnesota, Iowa, Wisconsin, Ohio. It is a young, growing population. Eighty-five per cent are native born and 50 per cent are third generation.[2]

PATTERNS OF MIGRATION

The greatest proportion of Mexican Americans have migrated since the annexation of the territories of the Southwest. Trends in immigration have largely been affected by the "pull" of employment opportunities, and the "push" of adverse economic or political conditions in Mexico. As with other groups, immigration declined sharply during the Depression. Then the great demands for manpower during World War II precipitated a rise which reached a peak about 1953. Until the enforcement of immigration restriction after 1929, Mexicans crossed the border freely. The majority came from the rural folk culture of Mexico, to some extent deviants from a feudal social system which viewed economic advancement of the individual as unworthy.[3] A minority came from more sophisticated strata in the hope of improving their financial position. Still others came as refugees from the political upheavals of Mexico.

Wetbacks

The enforcement of immigration restrictions led to the growth of illegal migration, with people popularly designated as "wetbacks." These people crossed the Rio Grande in large numbers.

[2]The precise figures for this rapidly growing population are difficult to arrive at. The 1930 Census attempted to enumerate the Spanish-speaking people of the Southwest under the heading "Mexican," defining this group as people born in Mexico or children of people born in Mexico. This eliminated the older hispano population of the Southwest. In 1940 the census dropped this category, but attempted to determine the size of the Spanish-speaking and other foreign language groups by a five per cent sample of "what language other than English was spoken in your home." This sample was relatively accurate for large cities, but not for small cities and rural areas. In 1960 a sample was taken in five states of people with Spanish surname, but this of course failed to include those who had anglicized their names or women who had intermarried. The current population reports asked the respondents to identify their ethnic descent. Since the actual count is slightly lower for people of Mexican descent than in the 1960 Census we may possibly assume that there has been an increase in assimilation. Nevertheless the Latin Americans: Mexican, Puerto Rican, Cuban, and Central American together, make up the second largest minority in the United States.
[3]William Madsen, *The Mexican-Americans of South Texas* (New York: Holt, Rinehart and Winston, 1964), p. 24.

Illegal ferry services were maintained at designated points along the river. The crossing was made at night on flatboats or rafts. Single men often swam the river pushing a log, holding their clothing above water. This type of illegal entry was hazardous and often unsuccessful. The border patrol returned thousands, but though most of the wetbacks came with the intention of working only for the crop picking season, some stayed on once they were here.

> Alfredo is a tall, handsome man in his fifties who proudly calls himself a Texan. He freely admits to his friends that he entered the United States as a wetback. "My determination to stay was great," he said, "fourteen times they caught me and threw me out but here I am."[4]

Braceros

Braceros came legally to the United States as agricultural labor under contract with the Mexican government. Many of them liked the United States and decided to stay. The statute admitting this type of seasonal labor was allowed to expire at the end of 1964 and braceros are no longer admitted to the country.[5]

THE ESTABLISHMENT OF DOMINANCE

Spanish-speaking people have been in the Southwest for over 350 years. Some of the villages north of Santa Fe, New Mexico, were founded in 1598. A century later Spanish settlements were made in Texas, and almost two centuries later, in California. In each of these three areas, distinctive Spanish cultures developed. Another influence was the relation of the Spanish to the many different Indian groups with which they came in contact. "Until about the middle of the nineteenth century, the *californios*, the *nuevo mexicanos*, and the *texanos* went their separate cultural ways, held together only slightly by, at first, the slender ties of Spain, and later, briefly, by the uncertain and flimsy bonds of independent Mexico."[6]

[4]*Ibid.*, p. 25.
[5]See Celia S. Heller, *Mexican American Youth: Forgotten Youth At the Crossroads* (New York: Random House, 1966), p. 11, for analysis of this statute, public law 78, and its termination.
[6]We are indebted to Prof. George I. Sanchez, of the University of Texas, for supplying "Spanish-speaking People in the Southwest—A Brief Historical Review" (mimeographed), which has been drawn upon in this section.

From the turn of the eighteenth century to the Mexican-American War, intergroup relations ranged from individual friendships to competition, antagonism, and, in many instances, violent conflict rising out of ethnic and racial distinctions. The Mexican society was sharply divided between upper-class property owners and peons. The invader-immigrant Anglos as individuals often competed and sometimes came in conflict with the upper-class Mexicans for economic gain; however, there were many who cooperated with the ruling Mexican elements and through intermarriage became part of Mexican society. Both upper-class Mexicans and Americans considered the peons an inferior, servile class. With the increasing infiltration of Americans, however, relations between Mexican and American became more antagonistic. In Texas, where by 1836 Americans far outnumbered Mexicans, this antagonism expressed itself in a successful revolution resulting in the formation of the Republic of Texas.

By the Treaty of Guadalupe Hidalgo, terminating the Mexican-American War, all the Mexican territory north of the Rio Grande became part of the United States. From this point on, American influence became dominant over Spanish-Mexican; some upper-class Mexicans attempted to join American society; the poorer and illiterate Mexicans became a distinct ethnic minority, notwithstanding the fact that they had become citizens of the United States. The antagonistic character of Anglo-Mexican relations is reflected in the terms "gringo" and "greaser," which each group came to apply to the members of the other, with contemptuous implications. In popular usage before the conquest, "gringo" referred to any foreigner who spoke Spanish with an accent. The term "greaser" referred to a native Mexican or a native Spanish American, and was originally applied disdainfully by the Americans of the Southwestern United States to Mexicans.

Given this situation against the setting of the "trigger-fingered" frontier, it was not surprising that violence should frequently arise. Paul S. Taylor in his study of a border community testified to many instances of violence from both groups. He cites the comment of a local official: "Undoubtedly robberies and murders by Mexicans have continually been perpetrated in Texas, but in retaliation Americans have committed terrible outrages upon citizens of Mexican origin."[7]

In 1914 when diplomatic relations between Mexico and the United States were temporarily severed the Mexican Americans of

[7]Paul S. Taylor, *An American Mexican Frontier* (Chapel Hill: University of North Carolina Press, 1934), p. 65.

South Texas were frequently identified with "the enemy." As
Madsen reports

> A wall of fear grew between Anglo and Latin communities. Re-
> calling this period, a Mexican-American said, "All our people were
> afraid. And here we were in our own country but the Anglos
> thought we were not from here."[8]

Dominance was achieved by military aggression and by Anglo-
American astuteness in seizing economic advantage. After the
annexation of Texas land speculators were able to buy up land
confiscated for unpaid taxes. In 1877, a 3,027-acre original Mexican
land grant whose Mexican American owner was in tax arrears was
sold by the sheriff to an Anglo for fifteen dollars. The boom in
land speculation continued until 1930.[9]

Differentiation

PHYSICAL DIFFERENCES   The "racial" composition of the
population of Mexico has been in this century approximately 10
per cent white, 60 per cent mestizo (mixed Indian and white) and
30 per cent Indian.[10] Since the immigrants to the United States
have been more numerous from the latter two population elements, especially the mestizo, it is not surprising that the results
of the United States Census of 1930, enumerating the Mexican
stock by racial designation as "white" and "colored" for the first
and only time, showed less than 5 per cent as "white," 65,968 out
of 1,422,533 total Mexican stock listed.[11] This considerable admixture of Indian traits does not have any significance in relation to
behavior capacities or traits, since there is no evidence that Indians are inferior in innate capacity. The mestizo cultures are
more Latin American than Indian. The Indian strain does, however, give the Mexican American group a darker appearance. In the
earlier days, this color visibility affected Anglo attitudes toward
Mexicans. Writing about race consciousness in 1930, Gamio stated,

> The darkest-skinned Mexican experiences almost the same restric-
> tions as the Negro, while a person of medium-dark skin can enter

---

[8]Madsen, *The Mexican-Americans of South Texas*, p. 9.
[9]*Ibid.*, p. 56.
[10]Maurice R. Davie, *World Immigration* (New York: The Macmillan Co., 1936), p.
215. Also *Encyclopedia Americana*, 1960, p. 472.
[11]United States Census, 1930, *Population*, Vol. 2, pp. 27, 34.

a second-class lunchroom frequented also by Americans of the poorer class, but will not be admitted to a high-class restaurant. A Mexican of light-brown skin as a rule will not be admitted to a high-class hotel, while a white cultured Mexican will be freely admitted to the same hotel, especially if he speaks English fluently.[12]

Thus Mexican Americans are not a homogeneous group in appearance, but are often identifiable. To the extent that they are predominantly now American born, they are also showing some physical changes, as have the children of other immigrants to the United States: increase in stature, hand length, and nasal index.[13]

Madsen quotes an uneducated Anglo (about 1960) as saying: "The Meskin's not a white man, but he's a hell of a lot whiter than a nigger."[14] A study of a California city of about the same date finds similar comparative attitudes on the part of dominants toward Mexican Americans and Negroes.[15] Madsen also points out that the South Texans whom he studied will only let the term "white" be used for an Anglo. He quotes one anglicized Mexican American as follows:

I think like an Anglo and I act like an Anglo but I'll never look like an Anglo. Just looking at me, no one could tell if I am an American or one of those blasted Mexicans from across the river. It's hell to look like a foreigner in your own country.[16]

CULTURAL DIFFERENCES   The value system of the Mexican Americans has been traditionally associated with the concept of *La Raza* (the race). In the sense this term is used it is nineteenth-century and has no relation to the racialism of North Europeans and American WASPs. Just as the French speak of themselves as a race, so *La Raza* is a cultural concept. It applies to all Latin Americans who are united by cultural and spiritual bonds. It implies that God has planned a great destiny for this people, though it never may be attained because of the individual sins of its members. In other words it is a concept of peoplehood and of

[12]Manuel Gamio, *Mexican Immigration to the United States* (Chicago: University of Chicago Press, 1930), p. 53. By permission.
[13]Marcus S. Goldstein, *Demographic and Bodily Changes in Descendants of Mexican Immigrants* (Austin: University of Texas, Institute of Latin American Studies, 1943).
[14]Madsen, *The Mexican-Americans of South Texas*, p. 11.
[15]Alphonso Pinkney, "Prejudice Toward Mexican and Negro Americans: A Comparison," *Phylon* (First Quarter, 1963), pp. 355 ff.
[16]Madsen, *The Mexican-Americans of South Texas*, p. 8.

destiny, creating deep psychic bonds. One can see the same phenomenon among Jews and, in the early periods of American history, nordic Americans. The central character of the value system
of *La Raza*, however, reflects in the Mexican Americans the long
history of feudalism from Spain, oppression in Mexico, and discrimination in the United States. For most of the older generation
it is a Catholicized fatalism.

Acceptance and appreciation of things as they are, says
Madsen, constitute the primary values of *La Raza*. He quotes an
expression of the world view of the Mexican American:

> We are not very important in the universe. We are here because
> God sent us and we must leave when God calls us. God has given
> us a good way to live and we should try to see the beauty of His
> commands. We often fail for many are weak but we should try.
> There is much suffering but we should accept it for it comes
> from God. Life is sad but beautiful.[17]

Because God controls events the Anglo orientation to and planning for the future is alien to the true member of *La Raza*. For
him, honor, to behave like "a whole man," to maintain dignity and
courtesy, to show respect and to fulfill his obligations to the family of his birth as to the one he founds, these are the core values.

RELIGION   Religion and culture are closely intertwined in
the average Mexican American household. The presence of a family altar in the house symbolizes the family-centeredness of the
culture as much as it does the religious faith.[18] However, as Ruth
Tuck points out, Mexican Catholicism is not church-centered and
she found in *Descanso* that men rarely went to church.[19] Conservative Mexican Americans may still name their sons Jesus, which
seems peculiar and even sacriligious to Anglo Protestants. "We
live with God while the Anglos lock Him in to Heaven."[20]

LANGUAGE   The principal language for Mexican Americans,
whether first, second, or third generation, is some variant of

---

[17]*Ibid.*, p. 17.
[18]Madsen seems to indicate that the family altar is less conspicuous as one goes up
the status scale of Mexican American society. It ceases to be in the living room
and may rather be in the mother's bedroom, *Ibid.*, pp. 35–41.
[19]Ruth D. Tuck, *Not With the Fist* (New York: Harcourt, Brace and Co., 1946),
p. 153.
[20]Madsen, p. 7.

Spanish. This is often a local dialect intermixed with hispanisized English words, and there is considerable variation: from "Tex-Mex" to the Spanish spoken by the hispanos of New Mexico to that of the largely generational dialect, *Pachuco*, spoken by Mexican American urban youth.[21]

The greatest deficiency in the English of Mexican Americans is in informal English. Often they hesitate to speak English at all if they do not know it well as to do so might be discourteous. They do not encourage Anglos to speak Spanish to them. Heller suggests that they may perceive the imperfect Spanish of an Anglo as "talking down" to them. Also, they seem to be embarrassed for the Anglo for his poor Spanish.

Spanish is spoken in the home as long as one identifies with the Mexican American community. Some parents speak some English to their children "so that it won't be so hard for them in school," and upper-class Mexican Americans pride themselves on perfect Spanish and English.

INSTITUTIONAL ROLES   Next to family roles, "manliness," (*machismo*) is the most important community ideal. To be a "whole man" involves a high degree of individuality, yet this is within the family framework as every Mexican American male is expected to represent his family with honor at all times. The manly role makes him sensitive to any authority or competition which would darken his public image with threat of devaluation or failure. According to Madsen, "ideally the Latin male acknowledges only the authority of his father and God. In case of conflict between these two sources of authority he should side with his father. No proper father, however, would act counter to God's will for such behavior would make him less of a man.[22]

This sensitive pride leads the Mexican American to avoid associations that threaten him: to be punctilious about indebtedness, to avoid accepting charity, to occasionally seek personal revenge, to feel that the obligations of affiliation with formal organizations weakens his independence.

Great value is put on male sexual virility with the resulting double standard of sexual morality. Girls are carefully guarded by their mothers and brothers, and wives by their husbands. The approved roles for women are within the household and the family. The Mexican American wife is expected to show her husband

[21]Celia S. Heller, *Mexican American Youth*, pp. 29–30, 59–62.
[22]Madsen, p. 18.

absolute respect. Her fulfilment is in helping her husband achieve his goals as he sees fit.

Father and mother alike share the task of teaching children how to conduct themselves. Proper relations to others in Mexican American society involve patterns of respect and formal courtesy. An "educated" person is one who has been well trained as a social being.

> As long as a Latin conforms to the rules of proper conduct, he is entitled to his own beliefs. One may resent another's actions but not another's opinions or interpretations. The view is expressed in the Mexican American saying, *Cada abeza es un mundo* (Each head is a world unto itself). A person may think as he pleases but he should not try to impose his ideas on anybody else. These concepts of propriety are a major factor in the hostility felt toward missionaries and public health workers who are trying to change Mexican American beliefs. A distinguished Latin citizen voiced his opinion on what he called "brain washing," "Americans have abandoned geographic imperialism, but to them mental imperialism is a wide open field."[23]

The cultural profile as drawn above must not be taken as a stereotype. It is useful for people who do not share the traditional Spanish culture in its North American variant to see some of the core historical attitudes. But it is important to remember that today these attitudes may be held flexibly. Catholicized fatalism has been an adaptation of exploited peasantry of more than one European cultural tradition. It will only persist—the fatalism—if similar situations of closed opportunity and devaluation persist in the environment. That there is more hope and that for many this is changing to a different kind of ethnic pride will be apparent in the subsequent discussion in this chapter. Nevertheless, core elements remain.

In a recent study of children's attitudes in a low-income Mexican American neighborhood ("barrio") in Houston, Texas, the authors concluded that:

> Training in helping, in discipline, and in respect for others all occur early. Most children have numerous relatives who take active interest in them. . . . Most Barrio fathers do command respect, and most Barrio households where there are school age children do have fathers, both legally and functionally. . . .

[23]*Ibid.*, p. 21.

In the larger study of which this child study is a part, our research group has learned that the mood of the Mexican American community of Houston tends to be expansive and optimistic. Anglo prejudice is lessening, the Spanish language is more accepted, things Mexican are gaining popularity. . . . Certainly the Mexican Americans now take considerable pride in their ethnic heritage.

It is our impression that the values of the Barrio children are on the whole conducive to modest success in contemporary urban society. It seems likely that their life chances are better in this respect than those of the Negro children we interviewed.[24]

ANGLO–MEXICAN AMERICAN RELATIONS

In broad outline, the process of adjustment of the Mexican immigrant group follows the pattern delineated for European immigrant groups. For the initial period, the studies of Paul Taylor in four different areas of the Southwest are the most extensive.[25]

Mexican immigrants in the Southwest found employment in unskilled occupations, chiefly as agricultural laborers. Their wages, in common with agricultural labor generally, were low—usually lower than that paid any Anglos employed in the same work. Employers often maintained that this differential was justified because Anglo laborers were more productive than Mexicans. These Mexican laborers were slow to become unionized. Earlier efforts at organization, opposed strongly by the agricultural employers, were generally unsuccessful. While by the late 1920s an increasing number of the Mexicans were buying or building homes of their own, they did not buy farm land for themselves, and they showed little interest in sharecropping. Few opportunities existed for Mexicans in higher-ranking occupations, both because they were not equipped to fill them and because of the discrimination against their employment in occupations involving Anglo fellow workers or serving Anglo trade. Some Mexican clerks were em-

---

[24]Mary Ellen Goodman and Alma Beman, "Child's-Eye-Views of Life in an Urban Barrio" in Nathaniel L. Wagner and Marsha J. Haug, eds., *Chicanos: Social and Psychological Perspectives* (St. Louis: The C. V. Mosby Company, 1971), pp. 118–119.
[25]Paul S. Taylor, *Mexican Labor in the United States* (Berkeley: University of California Press, Publication in Economics, Vol. 6, 1928). In this volume are included three monographs: No. 1 on Imperial Valley, California; No. 2 on the Valley of South Platte, Colorado; and No. 5 on Dimmit County, South Texas. While Taylor, an economist, was primarily interested in the labor situations of the Mexicans, his field of inquiry embraced the general pattern of social relations between the Anglos and Mexicans.

ployed in low-priced stores for the purpose of encouraging Mexican trade.

The housing of the more settled Mexicans was of the lowest standard; and that of Mexicans employed in agriculture of a nondescript variety, sometimes haymows or improvised shelters in the woods. In spite of these poor economic conditions, Mexicans were not often on relief rolls, partly because of their tradition of mutual aid. Nor did Taylor find their criminal arrests more than proportionate.

Spatial Segregation

In towns and cities with any sizable Mexican American population there are still today the residential enclaves where the majority of this ethnic group are concentrated. Mexican Americans refer to them as "colonia" and dominants as "Mextown" or "little Mexico." In 1954 John H. Burma estimated that about three-fourths of all the Mexican Americans in the United States lived in *colonia*.[26]

Discrimination

Whereas there were few legal restrictions against Mexican Americans except in some counties, in subtle ways they were "kept in their place." The pattern of discrimination was summed up in an extensive study of Texas communities conducted during the war years.

> *Economic Discrimination.* (1) Unfair employment practices forcing low economic status upon the majority of Latin Americans. (2) Discrimination exercised by both management and Labor unions in the admission and upgrading of Latin Americans. (3) Exploitation in agriculture. (4) Demand of growers for cheap labor carried to the extreme of favoring illegal seasonal influx workers, thereby denying employment opportunities to resident workers.
>
> *Inequitable Educational Opportunities.* (1) Arbitrary segregation in public schools. (2) Inability of working children to attend schools. (3) Lack of interest of school administrators in enrolling Latin American children and encouraging attendance. (4) Improperly trained teachers and inferior buildings and equipment.

[26]John H. Burma, *Spanish-Speaking Groups in the United States* (Durham: The Duke University Press, 1954), p. 88.

Social and Civic Inequalities. (1) Refusal of service in some public places of business and amusement. (2) Denial of the right to vote in some counties. (3) Denial of the right to rent or own real estate in many cities. (4) Denial of the right to serve on juries in some counties. (5) Terrorism on the part of law-enforcement officers and others.[27]

While there are Mexican Americans who can honestly say they have never encountered any of the cruder forms of discrimination and others who experience them only infrequently, still "it is safe to say that the entire population . . . is aware of barriers against it."[28]

An extremely successful man [Mexican], said: "I don't know why it is, but I've had to fight ever since I first crossed the threshold of a public school. Even now, I seldom sit down in a restaurant without expecting the waiter to come up and say, 'Sorry, we can't serve you.' I'm careful to go where I know such things won't happen, but I still half expect them."[29]

Many Mexican Americans were formerly discouraged from contemplating political action because of discrimination in various places through the poll tax and the disqualification of Mexican Americans for voting in Democratic primaries. In the 1940s Ernesto Galarza complained that

Mexicans are a political non-entity in the U.S. . . . They keep clear of political obligations and therefore do not take advantage of political opportunities. . . . Therefore all pleas to the state governor, the President of the United States, the legislature or Congress must be based on considerations of high human sentiment. In the American political system, however, such sentiments have always been found to fare much better when supported by precinct organization and votes in the ballot box.[30]

Dominant Attitudes Toward Mexican Americans

As is characteristic of dominant groups, southwestern Anglos tended to play down the extent of their discrimination and to

[27]Pauline R. Kibbe, *Latin-Americans in Texas* (Albuquerque: University of New Mexico Press, 1946), pp. 271–272.
[28]Ruth D. Tuck, *Not With the Fist*, p. 52.
[29]*Ibid.*
[30]Ernesto Galarza, "The Mexican American: A National Concern," *Common Ground,* 9 (Summer 1949), pp. 27–38.

rationalize what could not be denied by invoking an unfavorable stereotype of the Mexican American. Tuck put it thus:

> There is nothing Descanso [Anglos] will deny more stoutly than any intention of keeping its Mexican-Americans disadvantaged in order to derive an economic gain from their position. That is why it resents the words caste or semicaste being applied to its practices. Descanso argues, rather, that the bulk of its Mexican-Americans are so low in type that they could not profit by advantage. It seems rather odd to prove this point by making sure that they have continued inferior advantage, but Descanso sees no hint of a vicious circle in this procedure. The "low type" of Mexican, says Descanso, is getting about what he deserves. If he encounters segregated schooling, segregation in use of public facilities, unequal employment opportunities, unequal pay for equal work, or prejudiced law enforcement and justice—what of it? Descanso does not see that, in making these and a thousand other decisions, it is casting a vote that amends, not only the rights and liberties of a certain group, but the very nature of its democratic procedure. Descanso would not think of revising a certain historic document so that it guaranteed life, liberty, and the pursuit of happiness somewhat more to "high types" than to "low types." No, says Descanso, we are just making a few social distinctions, several million of which cannot possibly affect a democracy. You have to recognize, argues Descanso, that some people are just born inferior, generation after generation. As the leader of a church study group put it, "there are always hewers of wood and drawers of water."[31]

The "Zoot Suit" Riot of 1943

One of the severest outbreaks against Mexican Americans occurred during the Second World War at a time when Mexico was our ally. It was the first of a series of riots that summer which in part reflected the tension of a country at war.

> The anti-Mexican riots in Los Angeles ranged from June 3, 1943, until June 9. This was wartime; a nearby naval base made Los Angeles the messa for sailors' leaves. The riots were touched off on June 3 by two incidents. Some servicemen walking through a deteriorated street in a Mexican section of the city were beaten up by a gang of Mexican boys. In a nearby precinct on the same evening some Mexican boys returning from a "club" conference

[31]Tuck, *Not With the Fist*, pp. 53–54. By permission of the publishers.

at the police station on how to avoid gang strife were beaten up by a gang of non-Mexican boys. It does not seem as if the two incidents were connected. The police took no immediate action, but then after their regular duty was over, a so-called "vengeance squad" set out to clean up the gang that had attacked the sailors. They found no one to arrest, but great newspaper publicity was given to the incidents and to the policemen who had made the fruitless raid.

The following night about 200 sailors hired a fleet of 20 taxi-cabs and cruised the Mexican quarter. The Mexican adolescent boys had a fad of wearing long, draped jackets (zoot suits). Four times the taxicab brigade stopped when it sighted a Mexican boy in a zoot suit and beat up the boys, leaving them lying on the pavement. There was no mobilization of police. One police car did intercept the caravan, and nine sailors were taken into custody, but no charges were preferred against them. In the morning papers the war news was pushed off the front page with stories of the night before on a triumphal note of the sailor's move to clean up "zoot-suited roughnecks." The third night, June 5, scores of sailors, soldiers, and marines marched through the Mexican quarter, four abreast, stopping and threatening anyone wearing zoot suits. No sailors were arrested, either by the police, the shore patrol, or the Military Police, although twenty-seven Mexican boys were arrested. In various bars Mexicans were beaten up or their jackets torn off and ripped up. The police announced that any Mexicans involved in rioting would be arrested.

On the night of June 6 six carloads of sailors cruised through the area, beating up teenage Mexicans and wrecking establish-ments. The police came after them in mopping-up operations and arrested the boys who had been beaten up. In the morning forty-four severely beaten Mexican boys were under arrest.

Whipped up by the press, which warned that the Mexicans were about to riot with broken bottles as weapons and would beat sailors' brains out with hammers, the excitement erupted and two days of really serious rioting occurred, involving soldiers, sailors, and civilians, who invaded motion picture houses, stopped trolley cars, and beat up the Mexicans they found, as well as a few Filipinos and Negroes. At midnight on June 7 the military authorities declared Los Angeles out of bounds for military per-sonnel. The order immediately slowed down the riot. On June 8 the mayor stated that "sooner or later it will blow over," and the chief of police announced the situation "cleared up." However, rioting went on for two more days. Editorials and statements to the press lamented the fact that the servicemen were called off before they were able to complete the job. The district attorney of an outlying county stated that "zoot suits are an open indication of subversive character." And the Los Angeles City Council adopted a resolution making the wearing of zoot suits a misdemeanor.[32]

The role of the police is to be understood only if one presumes that their refraining from interference was deliberate and related to an entirely different matter. At the time of the riots a police officer was on trial in the courts for charges of brutality. Shortly after the riots, according to Carey McWilliams, a Hollywood police captain told a motion picture director that the police had touched off the riots to give a break to their colleague in demonstrating the necessity for harsh police methods. As a matter of fact, the charges against the officer were dismissed a month later.

The use of the stereotyped image of the zoot suit appeared in all the publicity and what was simply an adolescent fad was linked in the minds of the readers with the characterizations "gang," "roughneck," "subversive," and so forth. The press and the radio leaped on the bandwagon and were largely responsible in their unanimity for inflaming the population.

The tone of the press clearly deflects the war psychology and the support of servicemen. The servicemen themselves were young men away from home, uprooted from the normal community controls in the anonymous and sex-segregated climate of military life. Many of them engaged in actions that would have been unthinkable in their home environment.

Writing of the problem of Mexican American youth gangs in Los Angeles just after the riots, George I. Sanchez commented:[33]

The seed for the pachucos[34] was sown a decade or more ago by unintelligent educational measures, by discriminatory social and economic practices, by provincial smugness and self assigned "racial" superiority. . . .

When the pachuco "crime wave" broke last year, I communicated with the Office of War Information: "I understand that a grand jury is looking into the Mexican American problem in Los Angeles and that there seems to be considerable misunderstand-

[32]Carey McWilliams, *North From Mexico*, (Philadelphia: J. B. Lippencott, 1949), pp. 244–253. Adapted by the authors.
[33]George I. Sanchez, "Pachucos in the Making" in Wayne Moquin and Charles Van Doren, eds. *A Documentary History of the Mexican Americans* (New York: Praeger Publishers, Inc., 1971; Bantam edition, 1972), pp. 410–411. The original article was published in *Common Ground*, Autumn, 1943.
[34]Pachuco is a youth dialect and a self designation given by these young people to themselves. The word probably stems from a place name in Mexico, possibly associated with place of origin of leaders or members.

ing as to the causes of gang activities of Mexican youth in that area. I hear also that much ado is being made about "Aztec forebears", "blood lust" and similar claptrap in interpreting the behavior of these citizens. It would be indeed unfortunate if this grand jury investigation were to go off on a tangent, witchhunting in anthropological antecedents for causes which, in reality, lie right under the noses of the public service agencies in Los Angeles.

Organizational Patterns

Before World War II Mexican Americans were weak in organizational structure. Tuck describes the situation in Descanso.

> The proliferation of societies, clubs, and associations which distinguishes American life has not yet intruded on the *colonia*. The number of kin of each family is extensive enough to provide a wide circle of friends. There is one large men's organization, the Confederation of Mexican Societies, a council of four mutual insurance groups, whose chief activity is to celebrate two Mexican national holidays. It rather vaguely acts for the "economic, moral, and cultural improvement of the Mexican people." Its constitution specifically restricts any civic activity which is political in nature. From time to time, other organizations had arisen which were more definitely political; however, "most of them have had brief, fitful lives."[35]

The effect of World War II was not, however, only negative to Mexican Americans. The agencies of the federal government brought pressures to bear on employment and on local areas during the war to improve the positions of minorities. The Fair Employment Practices Commission did make for less discrimination in jobs for the duration of the war. Through the Office of the Coordinator of Inter-American Affairs committees were formed to improve relations between Anglos and Mexican Americans. Even more important, this office set up local community service clubs to "stimulate grass roots democracy." Many communities succeeded in special local programs for better recreational facilities, return of dropouts to schools, health surveys, and other local issues. Such ameliorative measures certainly stimulated many individuals and communities so that there was some net gain. But at best this was only a potential underpinning for more lively participation and real voice for the future.

[35]Tuck, *Not With the Fist,* p. 160.

A NEW FERMENT

Immediately following World War II many veterans began to take active roles in community leadership. Some were able to buy better homes, continue education under the G.I. bill, and often obtain better employment. Some were able to be elected or appointed to public office. In Los Angeles, four years after the zoot suit riots the first Mexican American since 1881 was elected to a municipal office.[36]

One of the oldest "civic" organizations, LULAC, the League of United Latin-American Citizens founded in 1929, began in the fifties and sixties to shift from a "betterment" type of organization to a more specifically politically oriented organization. It is moderate, as might be expected of a membership made up of older and more established segments of the Mexican American community, but it has been active in pressing reforms and bringing grievances before state and federal officials. MAPA, the Mexican American Political Association and the Political Association of Spanish-speaking Organizations, PASO, have been more directly political, concerned with equal employment, voter registration, and the election of Mexican Americans to office.

Mexican Americans Go to Court

Of what is probably the greatest significance, overt segregation of Mexican children in the public schools has been eliminated to all intents and purposes. The federal court cases in California, Arizona, and Texas—both those that came to trial and those which did not—have made it abundantly clear that American children of Mexican descent cannot be segregated in the public schools. Even where school authorities have sought to use pseudo-pedagogical reasons for separating "Anglos" from "Latins" the courts have either condemned the practices or have made it patent that the proof of the pudding would be in the eating, thus discouraging the use of subterfuges to cover up "racial" segregation. This break-through in school cases has served as precedent for the attack on segregation in other public services, with widespread success. In all areas there still remain many fronts on

[36]See Beatrice W. Griffith, "Viva Roybal—Viva America," *Common Ground* (Autumn, 1949) for a description of the candidate and of the mobilization of the Mexican American community for the election in which 15,000 new voters were registered.

which the civil liberties battle will have to be fought. Recalcitrant communities (rather, recalcitrant government boards) will seek "legal" ways to perpetuate segregation—in education the devices will include "neighborhood schools," "free choice" in the selection of a school, "ability grouping," "special" provision for migrant children, and the like. Most of these subterfuges will be the subject not of court action but of political action, as has been demonstrated already in a number of communities.

In the area of civil liberties, the *Pete Hernández Case* (Supreme Court of the United States, No. 406, October Term, 1953) has not drawn the attention it deserves, for it is significant not only for Spanish-Mexicans in the United States but for all groups that are treated as a class apart. This case, about a "Mexican" who was tried and sentenced by a jury in a county where "Mexicans" had never served on juries, was carried on up to the Supreme Court of the United States by lawyers of Mexican descent who were financed entirely by funds raised by people of Mexican descent. The unanimous judgment of the Court, written by the Chief Justice, finding for the plaintiff, included the following:

> Throughout our history differences in race and color have defined easily identifiable groups which have at times required the aid of the courts in securing equal treatment under the laws. But community prejudices are not static, and from time to time other differences from the community norm may define other groups which need the same protection. Whether such a group exists within a community is a question of fact. When the existence of a distinct class is demonstrated, and it is further shown that the laws, as written or as applied, single out that class for different treatment not based on some reasonable classification, the guarantees of the Constitution have been violated. The Fourteenth Amendment is not directed solely against discrimination due to a "two-class theory"—that is, based upon differences between "white" and Negro.

This far-reaching decision, handed down two weeks before the *Brown v. Board of Education* (segregation of Negroes) case, laid down a principle on which the Americans of Mexican descent (as well as others) can rely for protection against discrimination and the mistreatment of their class in every area of official public endeavor. The Hernandez case served another cause of equal importance: it gave heart to the "Mexican" leadership,(a leadership whose sights had been raised with their victory in the previous Mendez and Delgado (school segregation) cases.[37]

[37]From an unpublished summary prepared for the authors by George I. Sanchez, University of Texas.

Union Organization

In the 1940s and 50s there were sporadic attempts to organize by Mexican Americans. In 1944 the CIO International Union of Mine, Mill and Smelter Workers succeeded before the War Labor Board in eliminating discriminatory wage rates. But the critical problem for many Mexican Americans is that of low wages for agricultural labor. Although there had been an attempt to organize grape pickers in California in the 1930s these efforts were defeated.

Efforts to organize 1,500 farm workers, seeking a $1.25 minimum wage, in the lower Rio Grande Valley in the sixties received national attention and created conflict with the Roman Catholic Bishop of Texas who disciplined a priest active in organization efforts.

Cesar Chavez: A Non-violent Militant[38]

The entire nation now knows the name of this gentle, diminutive man. All know he is a profound Christian, a follower of Ghandi in his deep commitment to non-violence and in his use of fasts and boycotts as well as strikes as tactics in the struggle for benefits for Mexican American agricultural workers. Sometimes he is called "the Chicano Messiah."

Chavez' first major thrust was to organize grape pickers on ranches supplying the corporate wine industries. In Delano, California he cooperated with a striking Filipino organization and together, by June, 1966 after the longest farm strike in California history, they had won a contract with Shenley giving a minimum wage of $1.75 an hour.

Chavez had attempted to keep his union independent, but when threatened by another grower's invitation to the Teamsters Union, Chavez and the Filipino organization merged (August 1966) becoming the United Farm Workers Organizing Committee, AFL-CIO. The big wineries were a logical first target, as they were nationally advertised and vulnerable to adverse publicity. By September 1968 nearly all the *name* brands had signed contracts (Gallo, Christian Brothers, Almaden, Paul Masson).

Apart from the rival Teamsters, the major threat to California pickers were "green card" workers. These were Mexicans with permanent visas as resident aliens—a measure to circumvent the

[38]Peter Matthiessen, *Sal Si Puedes: Cesar Chavez and the New American Revolution* (New York: Dell Publishing Co., 1969).

discontinuance of the bracero program and to meet farm labor shortages. Green card holders were not supposed to work in fields where a strike had been called, but enforcement was lax.

Table grapes became a target when a subsidiary of one corporation which had a union contract permitted non-union growers to use its label. This led to first a state-wide boycott on table grapes in support of striking grape pickers. Then as California grapes appeared on Eastern markets labeled "Arizona grapes" the boycott became nationwide.

The Defense Department in 1967 bought six times as many grapes to send to Vietnam as it had bought before the strike began. Green card labor was imported and temporary injunctions were obtained permitting use of green card workers on the grounds that the labor clause was unconstitutional.

Chavez' workers then dispersed across the country in a massive effort to spread the boycott. By January 1969 only one chain in New York still sold grapes; stevedores in England, Sweden, Norway, and Finland refused to unload California grapes. By July 1970 the big growers signed. One issue which delayed contract agreement was the union's firm stand against the use of DDT.

Fruit is a large (usually corporate) farm industry in California. Seven per cent of the growers employ 75 per cent of the workers. Wages have averaged $1,500 a year. The UFWOC contracts contain no-strike clauses for the duration of the contract with stringent immediate binding mediation and court action in the event of violation. They also provide better wages, establish grievance and arbitration procedures, make provision for job security, overtime pay, rest periods, jointly administered health benefit plans, certain holidays and vacations with pay, health and safety protections on the job (including field toilets), etc. Dues to UFWOC are $3.50 per month.

The current efforts are to obtain contracts with the big lettuce growers, and again the tactic of boycott is being used. Senator Edward Kennedy, addressing the Democratic National Convention in 1972, opened his speech to nominate McGovern with the words, "Fellow lettuce boycotters."

The Chicano Movement

As in all human groups there are divergences of interest, of judgment, of goals. The Mexican Americans have experienced, like other segments of America, the emergence of a militant youth movement (not all are young, but the leadership is comparatively so) who designate themselves Chicanos. Although the initial emergence was among Mexican Americans, Chicanos include all Latin Americans in their concept of La Raza. The movement, like other militant protest movements, creates a strong bond of identity among its members. It values new roles for women, and reminds its members of roles played by women in the Mexican Revolution and in the grape strikes.

Although Chicanos have consciously or unconsciously taken over some of the pattern of militant blacks, like militant blacks they stand for community control of their own institutions (for example against bussing), and identify to a stronger or weaker degree with a "third world" political stance. They see their relation to other ethnic activists as coalition on specific common issues. They recognize the reality of black urban strength as necessitating making appropriate common cause. One of their strongest stands is for a rapprochement with American Indians.

In terms of "self-development" of Spanish neighborhoods they advocate pooled community funds, cooperatives, credit unions, and the like. Naturally not all Mexican Americans respond to such a program, and one Mexican American denounced the movement in the House of Representatives.[39]

One spokesman for this movement speaks eloquently of his new found identity:

> Chicano is a beautiful word. Chicano describes a beautiful people. Chicano has a power of its own. Chicano is a unique confluence of histories, cultures, languages and traditions. . . .
>
> Chicano has the ring of pachuco slang, of shortening a word, which is typical of our Mexican American experience. It also echoes the harsher sounds of our native ancestors of the Mexican Valley, but is softened by the rounded vowel-endings of our Spanish forebears. It is the perfect word to characterize the mezcla that is la raza. It portrays the fact that we have come to psychological terms with circumstances that might otherwise cause emotional and social breakdowns among our people if we only straddle two cultures and do not absorb them.
>
> Chicano is a very special word. Chicano is a unique people. Chicano is a prophecy of a new day and a new world.[40]

[39]Moquin and Van Doren eds., *A Documentary History of the Mexican Americans,* pp. 463–470
[40]Armando B. Rendon, *Chicano Manifesto* (New York: The Macmillan Company, 1971), p. 325.

HISPANOS: A VARIANT

As we have noted, included in the population of the Southwest are those Spanish-speaking people who are descended from Spanish-Mexican lineage indigenous to the area at the time of the annexation, some of whose ancestry goes back to the sixteenth century. In view of the general statistical confusion concerning Americans of Latin ancestry, their numbers and proportion are difficult to establish. It is clear, however, that in New Mexico and southern Colorado a large proportion of the Spanish-speaking people derive from this hispano lineage as distinct from migrant Mexican lineage; in Texas and Southern California the situation is roughly reversed.

Hispanos in New Mexico

Hispanos comprise about half the population of the state. There are several counties where they number more than 80 per cent of the population. Both Spanish and English are official languages in the state. Compared with the obvious minority status of immigrant Mexicans in other Southwestern states, hispanos do not appear at first to be a minority at all. They are all citizens, and no efforts are made by Anglos to deny them civic privileges. All over New Mexico there are hispanos who participate actively in politics, and in counties where they predominate heavily they frequently run the government. Free and equal access to all public places is accorded all ethnic and racial elements—the Indians and the relatively few immigrant Mexicans, as well as the hispanos. In the entire Southwest region, New Mexico exhibits the least "racial" intolerance. The reason for New Mexico's distinctiveness in this connection appears to lie in the fact that through a long part of the state's history as United States territory, Anglos were a distinct numerical minority, and that, therefore, a pattern of racial tolerance was developed at the outset of Anglo-hispano contact which has been strengthened by tradition. But beneath the surface of this substantial intergroup harmony lie subtle discriminations against the Spanish-speaking people of middle-class status and until recently the pitifully low welfare status of the lower-class hispanos.

The Hispanos of Rimrock[41]

Spanish *conquistadores* and other travelers, officials, and priests passed through this area from 1540 to the annexation. The present hispano settlement, however, descends from migrants from eastern New Mexico who settled in the region in the 1860s. They were scattered and relatively prosperous ranchers. Their largest village, Atrisco was founded in 1882. Since the 1920s Atrisco's population has declined so that in 1950 it had only 89 residents. The other cultural groups in Rimrock are Indians (Zuni and Navaho), Mormons who came in the 1870s, and Texans who came in three small waves beginning at the turn of the century and ending in the thirties.

Anglo-hispano relations in Rimrock have been characterized by the acquisition of dominance by the Texans, not without conflict and abrasion of feeling at various times. Before migration the Texans had known Spanish Americans only in the depressed position of field labor. Mexicans were considered as Negroes. The migrants were distressed to discover that their children would have to attend school in a hispano village, and that many county officials were "Mex." On the other hand, the hispanos were initially tolerant of the newcomers, many of whom they pitied because they were so poor.

Friction began when Texans began to fence land and acquire title to acreage that had been traditionally open range. The first outbreak of hostility occurred in 1934 when a Spanish American teacher, the son of one of the most respected families in Atrisco, was assigned to the newly constructed Homestead school in the Texan village. In the first weeks of school the windows were broken at night and signs appeared: "We Don't Want Any Chile Pickers for Teachers." Finally the schoolhouse was burned down. It is now the consensus of both groups that the fire was started by a Texan extremist.

By 1938 the high school was shifted from Atrisco to Homestead and a few years later the grade school in Atrisco was closed so that hispano children had to go to school in Homestead.

Another serious conflict occurred in 1947. It started with a fight between a Texan and a hispano at a dance; the fighting spread and continued for several days. This outbreak (nicknamed

[41]Evan Z. Vogt and Ethel M. Albert, *People of Rimrock: A Study of Values in Five Cultures* (Cambridge, Mass: Harvard University Press, 1966). The Mormons of Rimrock are discussed in Chapter 3.

"The Spanish American War") has not been forgotten by either group. The antagonism between the groups remains, and such relations as there are between them are sustained by the pattern of employee-employer relations (hispanos always employed by Texans, never the reverse), pupil-teacher, storekeeper, and the tenuous associations at public dance places. Three couples in the Rimrock area represent Anglo-hispano intermarriage. One couple moved away. Both groups talk a great deal about the other two couples (two daughters of the former *patrón* of Atrisco each married a Texan). Texans tend to call the children half-breeds; hispanos refer to them as coyotes, meaning unpredictable—that is, impossible to say how they will turn out. The children are being raised as Catholics and one Texan husband has converted to Catholicism.

Rural Hispanos of Northern New Mexico

Relatively isolated for generations rural hispanos preserve a folk culture and community life based on subsistence agriculture. They have not so much been discriminated against in the usual dominant-minority sense, as neglected.

From an account of a county superintendant of schools we get a picture of these people as they seemed in 1931 before the impact of change.

Here is a typical mountain community, entirely occupied by Spanish-Americans, a gentle, industrious, and intelligent people, brown eyed and sun-tanned. The houses are flat roofed, and are plastered with adobe of warm brown color which conforms to the earth around. Wherever possible, space has been cleared for gardens and little farms. . . . The men and women work together . . . children have been working at the side of the father since they were old enough to work. . . . I have been lenient about school attendance in the fall of the year since they must bring their children into the work in order to save their crops. . . . I mention this in an effort to get across a vital point. . . . If we could, for example, in New Mexico include in our rural school curriculum the old arts such as dyeing, blanket weaving, tin work, needle work and wood carving, employing experts in these lines from the community, and give credits in the schools for this work . . . we might perpetuate something of lasting educational value for the people.[42]

[42]Adelina Otero in Moquin and Van Doren, eds., *A Documentary History of the Mexican Americans*, pp. 368–370. Original article in *Survey Graphic*, May 1, 1931.

But changes have come to a degree. Military service during and since World War II has drawn off young men, and many have subsequently sought a future in the colonia of towns and cities where they often start at the bottom as newcomers replacing those that have moved up and out. State and federal programs in health and agriculture have planted slow germinating seeds of change.

Rural hispanos, while helped considerably by job opportunities opened through federal spending for defense projects (especially in central New Mexico—up ond down the Rio Grande Valley), and by the rising level of prosperity of the nation in recent years, remain a somewhat disadvantaged population in terms of welfare status. Their incomes are lower, their health status less good, their education less complete than those of their urban counterparts. Selective migration has resulted in high proportions of the very young and the very old in some rural areas with the consequent need for institutionalized Anglo-type educational, health, and welfare services. The old hispano culture has proved remarkably resistant—Spanish is still the preferred language in the homes of many rural families—but it is gradually being eroded by the intrusions of Anglo technologies and Anglo institutions. The discovery of uranium and other new and valuable minerals and the increased exploitation of oil and gas resources have brought boom conditions and urban-type employment to some rural areas; but in the core area of hispano culture, the upper Rio Grande Valley, the rate of change, though steady, is slow, and there is much in the life of the area now that would be familiar to one who knew the area a quarter of a century ago.[43]

Tijerina's Republic of San Joaquin del Rio de Chama

A symptom of the circumstances of these northern depressed, rural hispanos is the revitalization or nativist movement of the Federal Alliance of Land Grants, which claimed millions of acres to which titles are held from original Mexican land grants valid before annexation. This group, led by Reies Tijerina ("king tiger") wished to establish a separate hispano state. To dramatize their cause members of this group marched to Santa Fe in the summer of 1966. In October they held a great rally in the National Forest in the foothills of the Rockies. The membership is estimated to be about 20,000.

[43]Lyle Saunders made these observations for the authors. See also, Lyle Saunders, *Cultural Difference and Medical Care: The Case of the Spanish Speaking People of the Southwest* (New York: Russell Sage Foundation, 1954), pp. 285–288.

The governor of New Mexico met with leaders of the movement and felt there was little threat to stability and order from the group. The Santa Fe District Attorney, however, (who has a Spanish surname, but it is not clear whether he is hispano or Mexican American) is an active member of the American Legion and saw the movement as "communist," "subversive," and believed it had a great cache in the mountains of rifles and machine guns. Therefore in 1967 when an annual meeting of the Alliance was scheduled, again in the northern picnic preserves of the National Forest, he arrested several of the leaders and confiscated the membership lists. In retaliation fifteen Alliance members swept down on the hamlet of Tierra Amarilla and attempted to present a warrant for a citizen's arrest of the District Attorney. A fight ensued in which two policemen were wounded and a reporter taken as hostage by the Alliance members. The governor, who was out of state and may have been misinformed, panicked and called the National Guard. Two tanks were sent up into the hills, and after a five-day search in which fifty people, including women and children, were held for two days without food, water, or sanitary facilities, Tijerina was arrested. He was acquitted, but subsequently arrested again and sentenced to two years in prison on charges of assault stemming from the original incident.

Tijerina has sometimes been called the Chicano Don Quixote. His movement promised a "return" to justice, faith, salvation as expressed in the traditional pastoral life of the past.[44]

The publicity surrounding the Alliance brought support and eventually competition from the national Chicano movement. In 1969 Tijerina broke with the Alliance and with the national movement.

LA RAZA: A RENAISSANCE

Change has begun and is accelerating in the Mexican American's sense of himself and of his potential in the United States. The quiet *dignitad* of the hispano farmer in his high New Mexico valley, or the resignation of the Texas melon picker are being infused with a broader and more contemporary sense of themselves and their people. The veteran returning from Vietnam (where the casualty rate for soldiers with Spanish surnames is nearly double

[44]Peter Nabokov, *Tijerina and the Courthouse Raid* (Albuquerque, N.M.: The University of New Mexico Press, 1969).

the proportion of Mexican American young men in the draftee pool);[45] the emergence of barrio newspapers concerned with issues (Steiner lists the names and addresses of twenty-six);[46] the organizer for *La Causa* (Chavez' movement); or the *Alliance de los Pueblos Libres*—all speak to him of La Raza, his heritage, his opportunity: vote! go to court! demonstrate! organize! build!

La Raza embraces a broad spectrum of opinion. Some spokesmen think of it as including all people of Spanish descent in the United States; others think it includes not just the U.S. but the whole Western Hemisphere; but probably most, operationally at least, think of it as the Mexican American. There are fewer disputes about goals than there are about means. The most militant pitch their strength for broad changes in American thought, sentiment, and social structure. The more conservative see opening opportunity for steady, if not dramatic, advances. There is developing a new quality of identity and of community, insuring that Mexican Americans can no longer be "the forgotten people."

Suggested Readings

Heller, Celia S. *Mexican American Youth: Forgotten Youth at the Crossroads.* New York: Random House, 1966.
Conflicts and opportunity expectations of Mexican American youth in Los Angeles.

Matthiessen, Peter. *Sal Si Puedas: Cesar Chavez and the New American Revolution.* New York: Dell Publishing Co., 1969.
A lively account of Chavez and play-by-play record of the United Farm Workers Organizing Committee.

McWilliams, Carey. *North From Mexico.* Philadelphia: J. B. Lippincott, 1949.
A now classic review of relations between Anglo Americans and Americans of Mexican descent until the late 1940s. About to be re-issued.

Moquin, Wayne and Charles Van Doren, eds. *A Documentary History of the Mexican Americans.* New York: Praeger Publishers, Inc., 1971.
A rich source book on history and contemporary trends.

Steiner, Stan. *La Raza: The Mexican Americans.* New York: Harper and Row, Inc., 1969.

[45]Moquin and Van Doren, eds., *A Documentary History of the Mexican Americans,* pp. 480–483.
[46]Stan Steiner, *La Raza: The Mexican Americans* (New York: Harper and Row, 1969), pp. 404–406.

A highly readable overview of the situation of Mexican Americans today, with a bias toward the Chicano movement.

Wagner, Nathaniel N. and Marsha J Haug. *Chicanos: Social and Psychological Perspectives.* St. Louis: The C. V. Moseby Company, 1971. An excellent compilation of recent research.

12   Puerto Ricans on the Mainland

The 1971 estimates of current population indicate that the 1,450,000 Puerto Ricans living on the mainland are the second largest "Spanish-speaking" minority in the United States. (There are over half a million Cubans, of which the largest concentration is in Dade County, Florida; about half a million Central and South Americans; and over a million "other Spanish" from Europe and Asia). Puerto Ricans are chiefly found in metropolitan areas, with nearly two-thirds in New York State, chiefly in New York City. They are a young and rapidly growing population.

At the close of the Spanish-American War Puerto Rico became a United States dependency, and Puerto Ricans became citizens of the United States. A modest migration began to New York City, which was the continental port for most ship passage from the island. In 1910 there were 500 people of Puerto Rican birth in New York. By 1930 the number had risen to 45,000, by 1940 to 70,000. The group included some professional people and small business men, but the overwhelming majority were unskilled workers. A few settled in Brooklyn, but most settled in the East Harlem section of Manhattan, forming a sub-community bordered on the north by Negro Harlem and on the east by an Italian settlement and a declining population of Jews. This section of the city is called *El Barrio* by the Puerto Ricans and Spanish Harlem by the rest of New Yorkers.

Puerto Ricans have free migration as citizens; the initial upswing in migration was undoubtedly precipitated by the restriction on European immigration and propelled by the miserable conditions on the island from which they came.

PUERTO RICO AND THE UNITED STATES

Before 1932 the federal government assumed a laissez-faire attitude toward the island's economy, with the result that American investment in the development of Puerto Rico came from mainland private capital. The extent of absentee interest in the Puerto Rican economy was summarized in 1930 as follows:

> . . . Sugar is 60 per cent absentee-controlled; fruit is 31 per cent, or more; public utilities, 50 per cent; and steamship lines, approximately 100 per cent. There is no important source of wealth that is not partially in the hands of outsiders, and in some instances, such as steamships, outsiders control the entire business. Any estimate of Porto Rico dependence on absentees which places the total at less than 60 per cent of the island's wealth is certainly too low. Not all of the industries belong to absentees, but those which do not are so indebted to continental banks as to be virtually in their possession. Not all of the good land is in the hands of outsiders, but a large portion of it is, and much of the remainder is heavily mortgaged. And finally, there is that type of dependence on absentees which Porto Rico suffers, because of her long dependence on a monopolizing mother country, the necessity of importing vast quantities of food, clothing, machinery, chemicals and drugs. The control of the absentee is all but complete and with the aid of the Coastwise Shipping Act and the American Tariff bids fair to absorb all of the profitable enterprise.[1]

Under Franklin D. Roosevelt's early administrations, governmental effort at reorienting the Puerto Rican economy with more regard for the welfare of the islanders themselves was undertaken. The Puerto Rican Relief Administration was succeeded by the Puerto Rican Reconstruction Administration, which undertook irrigation projects, new highways, new schools, new houses and other development efforts. In 1942 Pattee said "There is little doubt that the present administration . . . postpones, at least, a collapse in Puerto Rican economy."[2]

[1]W. Bailey Diffie and Justine Whitfield Diffie, *Porto Rico: A Broken Pledge* (New York: The Vanguard Press, 1931), pp. 135–136. By permission.
[2]Richard Pattee, "The Puerto Ricans," *Annals of the American Academy of Political and Social Sciences*, Sept. 1942, 223:52.

"The Puerto Rico Reconstruction Administration . . . made definite progress but did not achieve that complete reform that was so desperately needed."[3] An indigenous reform program developed from the emergence of a new political party on the island, the Partido Popular Democrato. By somewhat faltering steps, democratic political institutions have been established, with increasing degrees of self-government permitted. On November 2, 1948, Puerto Rico elected its own governor for the first time. Except for the Presidential appointment of the auditor and Supreme Court justices, and for the power of the United States Congress to annul any law passed by the Insular Legislature (something which has not yet been done), Puerto Rico has attained complete self-government.

Early Conditions

Despite aid from the federal government conditions had not markedly improved. Although the death rate dropped, the birth rate remained one of the highest in the world. In 1898, 83 per cent of the population was illiterate. By 1940 it was only 31 per cent, but policies had shifted back and forth as to which language, English or Spanish, was to be taught at what levels. This wavering led to a reduced effectiveness of education. Neither English nor the Spanish cultural heritage were adequately transmitted. The island suffered heavily during the Depression because of the major dependence on the cash crop of sugar.[4]

Operation Bootstrap

Under self-government Puerto Rico launched "Operation Bootstrap," a development program to raise the levels of living on the island. In twenty years these efforts of the Puerto Rican government raised the per capita income on the island 307 per cent. The program concentrated on two areas of economic improvement. The first was diversification of agriculture. Many of the large sugar areas have been made available for smaller landowners under the "500 acre law," which had been on the books since 1900 but was not enforced. Many new crops were introduced.

[3]*Ibid.*, p. 52.
[4]Nathan Glazer and Daniel Patrick Moynihan, *Beyond the Melting Pot: The Negroes, Puerto Ricans, Jews, Italians, and Irish of New York City* (Cambridge, Mass.: The Harvard and M.I.T. Press, 1963), pp. 87, 88.

The second effort was to encourage industry. By February, 1960, some 600 new factories had been established, creating jobs for 45,000 people. The government aided in the training of personnel by building factories for rent at reasonable rates, and by other measures. In 1956 the income from manufacturing surpassed the income from agriculture for the first time. Puerto Rico has surpassed every Latin American country in increase in per capita income. The social aspects of Operation Bootstrap have included a major public health effort and marked achievements in education. Although Spanish is the primary language, English is a required subject from the first grade on. Now almost the only illiterates are older people. The number of school rooms, teachers, and pupils has more than doubled; higher education has tripled; extension services in education have been developed; and the Division of Community Education has become a focus of interest and training for workers from many countries engaged in development programs.

Despite these advances, in 1958–1959 unemployment on the island averaged 90,000—14 per cent of the labor force. A large proportion of this has been and is being drained off into the labor market of the continental United States.[5]

The complex population problem has been met by Puerto Rico's government through free birth control clinics; the operation for the sterilization of women was made cheap and easy. This policy was bitterly opposed by the Roman Catholic hierarchy, but the opposition had the effect of publicizing the program. By 1950 the birth rate had begun to decline.[6]

Nevertheless, industrialization eliminated jobs as well as creating them. Perhaps even more the experience of Puerto Rico G.I.'s (65,000 in World War II and 43,000 in the Korean War) aroused aspiration for a new standard of material comfort.[7]

The Post-World War II Migration

The Puerto Rican migration has been the heaviest foreign language migration to the Atlantic states since World War I. Up to 1947 and 1948, a large proportion of the Puerto Ricans who came to the continent were contracted for agricultural and domestic

---

[5]Clarence Senior, *Strangers—Then Neighbors: From Pilgrims to Puerto Ricans* (New York: Freedom Books, 1961), pp. 55–59.
[6]Glazer and Moynihan, *Beyond the Melting Pot*, p. 98.
[7]*Ibid.*, p. 96.

labor. There was much unethical traffic in human beings until the island legislature enacted legislation to control and correct the situation. Offices of the Commonwealth of Puerto Rico, set up to assist migrants, were established in New York and Chicago. At present the Migration Division of the Department of Labor of the Commonwealth of Puerto Rico maintains offices in San Juan and in twelve mainland cities. The division's personnel work in approximately one hundred mainland towns and cities each year. Cooperation has also been established between the Puerto Rico Employment Service and the United States Employment Service. Since Puerto Ricans are citizens, job orders from American industry pass through the United States Employment Service to the Puerto Rico Employment Service when qualified local workers are not available. Employers may recruit labor in Puerto Rico directly only with the approval of the Puerto Rican government, and only when a legitimate order is cleared through regular United States Employment Service channels.

In 1948 the Columbia University study[8] of Puerto Ricans in New York City found that 85 per cent of the immigrants had quit jobs in Puerto Rico to come to the United States. What they sought was not so much any job but a *better* job. The data on age of immigrants also suggest that the principal motive for migration has been economic.

Other benefits, too, are sought. Education is thought by many to be better on the mainland, and the ultimate opportunity for improved status is encouraging. There are some for whom life in the home village has become unsatisfactory because of social situations. On the mainland, health and security benefits are easily available. Then there is the glamor of New York. And there are kinship ties to those who have already migrated.

One aspect of the Puerto Rican migration is the ease and frequency with which the migrants may return to Puerto Rico. Although it was also a feature of some of the older migrations to have a proportion of migrants who viewed their sojourn in the United States as a way to improve their economic circumstances, after which they would return home, for Puerto Ricans, because of the nearness to the island and their citizenship status, there is more turnover in population. There is also a considerable amount of seasonal labor, principally for agricultural work. Those who do establish permanent residence and intend to become part of main-

[8]C. Wright Mills, Clarence Senior, and Rose Kohn Goldsen, *The Puerto Rican Journey* (New York: Harper & Brothers, 1950).

land life still keep ties in the island and take frequent vacations "at home" when they can afford it.

Senior reports that 40 to 45 per cent of the new arrivals speak English, but many are timid about speaking it with strangers. In 1957, a survey found that 63 per cent of the Puerto Rican families living in New York City speak English at home. Those who come from rural areas experience more difficulty in the cities than those who have had urban experience. Those who come from mountainous areas tend to be individualistic, while those from cane plantations are more accustomed to cooperative group actions.[9]

Puerto Rican labor is vital to the economic future of some American industries. The Harvard University study of the New York metropolitan region points out:

> The rate of Puerto Rican migration to New York is one of the factors that determine how long and how successfully the New York metropolitan region will retain industries which are under competitive pressure from other areas.
>
> To the extent that some of these industries have hung on in the area they have depended upon recently arrived Puerto Rican workers, who have entered the job market of the New York area at the rate of about 13,000 each year. But the New York area is beginning to lose its unique position. . . . [T]his stream of migration is now spreading to other mainland areas as well, and the spread promises to accelerate.[10]

Population

Puerto Rican population figures are probably not precisely accurate. The nearness of the island makes for a good deal of moving back and forth, especially in times of low employment or other frustrations on the mainland. The most important trend, at present, has been the spreading out of Puerto Ricans. Although the largest number are still in New York State they have now joined the labor forces of other states as well.

The Census Bureau's count of 1,379,043 first- and second-generation Puerto Ricans was less than its estimates in its Current Population Survey samplings, which had been 1,450,000 as of March, 1971, and 1,454,000 as of November, 1969. The samplings

[9]Clarence Senior, *Strangers—Then Neighbors: From Pilgrims to Puerto Ricans* (New York: Freedom Books, 1961), pp. 63–64.
[10]Cited by Senior. *Ibid.*, p. 65. Recently it has been queried whether or not Negroes at least in the past decade could have supplied this labor.

are based on participants' identification of their origin, rather than birth or parentage.

TABLE 12-1   HEAVIEST POPULATION BY STATE*

State	1970	1960
New York	872,471	642,622
New Jersey	135,676	55,351
Illinois	87,515	36,081
California	46,078	28,108
Pennsylvania	44,535	21,206
Connecticut	38,144	15,247
Massachusetts	24,394	5,217
Ohio	20,918	13,940

*State-by-State census figures reported in the *New York Times*, July 9, 1972, p. 49.

VISIBILITY

"Racial" Visibility

The Puerto Ricans at the time of annexation by the United States, had adopted and adapted Spanish institutions and Spanish culture to form their own variant of Latin American civilization. Into the composition of the population had gone white, Negro, and Indian strains. The social structure was that of a plantation economy in which a small upper class, chiefly of landed proprietors, was distinguished from a peasantry, some of it on plantations, some in mountain villages.

Since the abolition of slavery in the island there has been no civic and public discrimination in Puerto Rico because of race. None of the forms of interracial conflict or violence which have been found on the mainland has occurred. This formal absence of discrimination is similar to other patterns in Latin cultures in the Western hemisphere. Furthermore, the population of Puerto Rico presents so wide a range of combinations of physiognomic features that a pattern of dominant-minority relations based on "race" would be difficult to maintain.

Although Puerto Rico is often cited for its absence of prejudice based on "color" visibility, and intermarriage between people of different racial heritages has long been recognized, there is some consciousness of differences. Taken together with the factors of wealth and education, color may affect status. "Whites"

—very light-skinned people—are at the top if they also have wealth and education. Very dark-skinned people are at the bottom unless they have wealth and education. They are then sometimes designated as "trigueno" (brunet) as a circumvention for the term "Negro," or they borrow the French usage, "a man of color." "Indios" are an intermediary group; "grifo" designates the light-skinned, kinky-haired individual.

Padilla has made a chart which shows the differences in the way in which biological visibility is perceived by mainlanders, by other Puerto Ricans, and by individuals with regard to themselves.[11]

References (Mainlanders)	References of Ingroup (Hispanos)	References of Individuals Describing Self
White	White	White
	Trigueno Hispano	Hispano
	Grifo	Trigueno
	Intermediates*	
Puerto Rican or	Negro	De Color (of color)
Mixed	Trigueno	Trigueno
	Indio	Hispano
	Grifo	Indio
	Hispano	
Negro	Negro	De Color
	Trigueno	Trigueno
	Indio	Hispano
	Grifo	Indio
	Hispano	

*A category to include the numerous racial terms used by Puerto Ricans, used by C. Wright Mills, Clarence Senior, and Rose Kohn Goldsen, in *The Puerto Rican Journey.*

This chart shows us that no individual in the group of migrants studied designates himself a Negro. Neither will he call himself Grifo. The hispano group, however, may call him either of these, with implied derogation. When appearance is predominantly "white," the outgroup, mainlanders, may accept the individual as white where both hispano individuals and the hispano group will make some differentiation.

[11]Elena Padilla, *Up From Puerto Rico* (New York: Columbia University Press, 1958), pp. 47–48.

Color is clearly a problem for mainland Puerto Ricans. Mainland attitudes have produced ambivalent attitudes. On the island the greater differential was class rather than color. Furthermore when the earlier migration of Puerto Ricans came there were better relations with the Negroes than with the Italians who were contiguous to *El Barrio*. Italian youth were hostile to Puerto Rican youth and Negro youth more accepting.[12] Yet there is the memory of the fact that during World War II, army camps on the island segregated Puerto Rican troops, and the Navy would not take Puerto Ricans.[13] Puerto Ricans, unless very dark and with Negroid features are listed as white in New York City.[14] The proportion of "colored" in the Puerto Rican population drops from census to census (4 per cent in 1960).[15] Father Fitzpatrick, Professor of Sociology at Fordham University, made a study of Puerto Rican marriages in six Catholic parishes. He found, in the late 1950s, that 25 per cent of the marriages of Puerto Ricans in these widely varying parishes involved people of different color.[16]

Cultural Visibility

Cultural visibility is especially marked among new migrants. Even without hearing the rapid Spanish chatter which goes on in the streets of New York, lower-class Puerto Ricans can usually be identified by their dress, especially the women. Styles favor bright colors. Movement is free, swinging, and graceful. In old-fashioned Puerto Rican families little girls' ears are pierced in babyhood and toddlers will wear earrings. Young men often affect bright jackets and shirts.

The value system of Puerto Ricans shares much with other Spanish cultures. The importance of *dignitad* (self-possession, pride) is paramount in the conception of the ideal person. The culture and social system are male-dominated, with strong emphasis on proving masculinity. A man must be, ideally, stable and strong, sexually virile, honest and reliable in work, aggressive in combat, and sensitive to honor. He is logical and can reason.

[12]Glazer and Moynihan, *Beyond the Melting Pot*, p. 93.
[13]Maxine W. Gordon, "Cultural Aspects of Puerto Rico's Race Problem," *American Sociological Review*, June, 1950, p. 382.
[14]Estimates list 90 per cent of Puerto Ricans in New York City as white. *The New York Times*, March 6, 1972, p. 22.
[15]Glazer and Moynihan, *Beyond the Melting Pot*, p. 91 and 134.
[16]Joseph P. Fitzpatrick, "The Adjustment of Puerto Ricans to New York City," *Journal of Intergroup Relations* (Winter, 1959–1960), pp. 43–52.

Women, on the other hand, are frail, illogical, and easily deluded. Therefore women must be guarded and accompanied by the responsible males of the family.

The human condition is such, in the value scheme, that man is buffeted by many forces. Fatalism underlies much of the thinking, operating sometimes to lower individual aspirations, or quite usually to explain failure and disappointment. Time is infinite. Hurry robs one of dignity; thus commitments within time have wide latitude. Gaiety is valued, singing and dancing enjoyed by all. Emotional expressiveness in word and gesture are the norm. Puerto Ricans sometimes refer to dominants on the mainland as "the cold people."

These values are carried out in the institutional patterns. Within the island social structure the family and the extended kinship form the dominant institutional configuration. Obligations of kinship are strong, as are those of village ties, which for rural families have been the *locus* of the extended family. Male virility is honored by the evidence of many children. Girls are watched over by their mothers before marriage and women by their husbands and mothers-in-law after marriage. The marriage age is early in rural Puerto Rico, often soon after the onset of puberty. "Consensual marriage," like the common-law marriage of the mainland's rural colonial heritage, is acceptable whether or not it is ever formally sanctioned by church or state.

Most Puerto Ricans are Roman Catholic. For many this is a nominal identification with only a tenuous discipline exercised by the affiliation. In New York City, a minority of Puerto Ricans, perhaps 20 per cent, have been attracted to Protestant Evangelical groups. Store-front churches have sprung up, and the Pentecostal Holiness sect and Jehovah's Witnesses have been successful proselytizers. Some of the poorest stratum have embraced various Asiatic and Caribbean cults.

Puerto Ricans come from a society which until recently had very marked stratification, with little chance for mobility. In migration the old criteria of status are weakened, though not destroyed. However, a new precedence is given to the united, stable family ("familia unida"). A family of this sort usually consists of several biologically related nuclear families which recognize mutual obligations toward each other. In the new environment it is the symbol of stability and respectability. Income, occupation, and level of education affect a person's status, as do occupational position and familial connections in Puerto Rico before migration.[17]

PATTERNS OF DOMINANCE

Spatial Distribution

In New York City, where more than half of the Puerto Ricans on the mainland live, the old sub-community, *El Barrio*, south and east of Harlem has overflowed to many other parts of the city. There are concentrations of Puerto Ricans in Brooklyn and the South Bronx, but they still make up about a third of the population of Manhattan, creating different patterns of neighborhood relationships in different situations. Thus on Manhattan's West Side the avenues have large middle-class and upper middle-class apartment houses occupied by "continental whites," while the side streets are filled with Puerto Rican families crowded into converted former private residences that have been abandoned as single-family dwellings in the changing pattern of city and suburban living. Here social class as well as cultural barriers create social distance, and often tension, between mainlanders and migrants.

In New York's Lower East Side, housing conditions are often not as bad for the migrants because of extensive urban renewal in this district. Furthermore because of its historic role as an immigrant neighborhood, the Lower East Side is one of the best-serviced and most intercultural sub-communities in New York City.

Many of the longer established Puerto Rican families are, like other New Yorkers, going to the suburbs, and to the less crowded boroughs of the city.

Raymond A. Glazier of the Community Council of Greater New York has said that the Puerto Rican population in nearby New York suburban counties more than doubled in the decade.[18]

Poorer Puerto Ricans in the central city make up the most deprived segment of metropolitan New York. Although median income has risen for Puerto Rican families in the last decade the gap between their income and the median for all families has widened. In 1959 median family income for Puerto Ricans was

[17]Padilla, *Up From Puerto Rico*, Ch. 2.
[18]*New York Times*, July 9, 1972, p. 49.

$3,811, or $2,280 below the median for all families. In 1970 income for Puerto Rican families had risen to a median of $5,575, but it was $4,107 below that of all families—twice as big a gap as that between Negroes and all families in New York.[19]

TABLE 12-2   POPULATION INCREASE 1960–1970, NEW YORK SUBURBAN AREAS

| Area | 1970 | Increase from 1960 | |
		Number	Per Cent
New York City	811,843	199,269	32.5
Nassau	7,224	3,025	72.0
Suffolk	17,179	9,839	134.0
Westchester	5,715	2,610	84.1
Rockland	3,814	1,602	72.4

Discrimination

No other place in the United States, probably, gives as much lip service to the ideal of nondiscrimination against religious, ethnic, or racial minorities as does New York. Nevertheless, there is much discrimination through evasion of laws and in the areas of daily living not covered by special codes against it.

Since Puerto Ricans form such a large part of New York's unskilled labor force, they have found employment readily in the lowest paying jobs. Discrimination at the lower levels of the occupational structure seems to be linked with the factors of the language handicap, union policies, and traditional "corners" on certain types of employment that have been held by some other ethnic group. The old-line unions in the building trades and on the waterfront have succeeded fairly well in keeping out Puerto Ricans. However, other unions—in the garment trade, the hotel workers and the retail and department store union—have had anti-discrimination policies. Union control of a shop's choice of workers through hiring halls has sometimes been used to break the hold of a particular ethnic group on a shop by forcing mixed crews on the employers. In the white-collar field, public employment is, for Puerto Ricans as for earlier immigrant groups, the chief channel of access.

There have been issues both in education and in health about

[19]*The New York Times,* July 19, 1972, p. 41.

licensing professionals trained in Puerto Rico for positions in schools or hospitals. The Department of Welfare in New York City has accepted training at the University of Puerto Rico for its Spanish-speaking workers, but the Department of Health and the Board of Education have resisted. This might be considered a very mild aspect of discrimination but does express a rigidity in the face of generic competence in needed areas.

Political discrimination is primarily linked with the question of English language literacy. Some Puerto Ricans feel there is discrimination in the courts, since the procedure of American courts deprives them of a chance to plead their cause with emotion, gesture, and Latin eloquence.

Discrimination in good housing continues in many parts of the city. Eagle, in a study of the housing of Puerto Ricans in New York City, was surprised to find so few Puerto Ricans feeling themselves discriminated against. To the question, "Do you think you can live anywhere in the city if you have the money to pay the rent, 87 per cent answered "Yes," and only 5 per cent stated that they felt they had actually experienced discrimination in seeking housing. A partial clue to this apparent unawareness of discrimination lies in the fact that the great majority of Puerto Ricans can afford to seek housing only in the less desirable dwellings. The same study found that while only 3 per cent of those who had lived in the city three years or less complained of discrimination, 10 per cent of those who had lived in New York longer voiced such a complaint.[20]

The Hispanic Community

Some writers have argued that because of the neglect by Spain, the extreme poverty of most islanders until well into the twentieth century, and the inter-mixture of other Caribbean influences, Puerto Rican folk culture is both less rich than other peasant cultures and less Spanish than that of other Latin Americans.[21]

Puerto Ricans have not benefited as the Mexican Americans have from having an older Spanish-speaking tradition to build on in America, or an elite to perpetuate the idea of *La Raza*. Never-

[20]Morris Eagle, "The Puerto Ricans in New York City," in Studies in Housing and Minority Groups, eds. Nathan Glazer and Davis McEntire (Berkeley and Los Angeles: The University of California Press, 1959), pp. 166–167
[21]Glazer and Moynihan, *Beyond the Melting Pot*, p. 88.

theless, they are pridefully conscious of their Spanish heritage. They usually refer to themselves (if they are the migrating generation) as hispanos or latinos, linking themselves with other Western Hemisphere Spanish cultural groups.

> The Hispano group includes Puerto Ricans, their descendants who may or may not be Spanish-speaking individuals, and also Spanish-speaking persons from Latin America and Spain. . . . Sources of solidarity and bonds of understandings among Hispanos are partly derived from the historic common general cultural traditions of the peoples who are considered Hispanos. But, partly, too, they are a reaction to the position of the group as a minority in New York.[22]

Puerto Ricans gain on several counts from this sense of identity. It clearly differentiates them from American Negroes and is seen as protection from the threat of the racial attitudes of mainlanders. Among other Spanish-speaking people, Puerto Ricans gain status by being American citizens. According to Padilla, members of other groups of Spanish cultural origin often claim to be Puerto Rican when they are not.[23] Identity born of language and culture is consciously reinforced by symbolic and ceremonial efforts. Rand describes a Columbus Day celebration in which wreaths were laid at the statue of "the Spanish Columbus" in Central Park (as distinguished from the other statue of the presumably Italian Columbus in Columbus Circle). One placard at this demonstration read

WE DO NOT KNOW WHERE
HE WAS BORN BUT WE DO KNOW
HIM AS A CITIZEN OF SPAIN
AND AS THE ADMIRAL
OF THE SPANISH EXPEDITION
IN WHICH THE NEW WORLD
WAS FOUNDED[24]

There are losses also from this sense of identity, for it is not strong enough to solve all the problems confronting Puerto Ricans in New York. The young person of Puerto Rican descent is subjected not only to conflicts of values and behavior patterns that persist in modified and transformed modes between hispano and mainland culture, but he must seek status and approval both with-

[22]Padilla, *Up From Puerto Rico*, pp. 47–48.
[23]*Ibid.*, p. 11.
[24]Rand, *The Puerto Ricans*, p. 158.

in and outside the hispano group. Furthermore, the dominant culture presents no uniform set of standards in the variety of status and ethnic traditions in metropolitan New York.[25]

Obstacles to Acculturation

There are a number of areas that become focal points of attention in adjustments between traditional acceptable ways of the island and the dominant norms of the mainland. Adjustment has been eased to some extent by the fact that the people of the older urban migration were familiar with public education, wage systems, large hospitals, mass communication, and the electoral process. New migrants have increasingly had experience with these forms as a result of the development of the island. Rand mentions an informant in Chicago who felt that the Puerto Ricans had an advantage over the Mexicans in that city because of the longer exposure, in the island, to certain key structures of mainland society, as well as to entrepreneurial values.[26]

The most obvious problem of acculturation is language. Employers complain of a labor force with which they can communicate only through one or two bilingual members, and they are not sure whether or not directions are being communicated accurately. The Employment Service finds trouble placing workers with little English.[27] The problem for the schools is acute, since hundreds of children enter the public school system with little or no English. The language problem cannot be divorced, however, from the central cultural value of *dignitad*. Many Puerto Ricans understand more English than mainlanders realize, but their pride prevents them from speaking English if they do not speak it well.

The problem of punctuality is acute for the migrants from rural background, who have not had the experience of industrial society, and for women who have been confined to a limited sphere of activity.

Since the family is the dominant institution in the island culture, it is in family patterns and roles that many adjustments are required. Consensual marriage is not recognized in New York State, which outlawed, by statute, common-law marriage nearly half a century ago. Thus the mother of children born in a consensual marriage is ineligible for welfare benefits which might

[25]Padilla, *Up From Puerto Rico*, pp. 88 ff.
[26]Rand, *The Puerto Ricans*, p. 144.
[27]*Ibid.*, pp. 142 ff.

accrue to her on the disability, death, or desertion of a husband in a registered marriage. The custom of early marriage comes in conflict with the New York State age of consent, which is sixteen with parents' permission and eighteen without. The role of women in traditional hispano culture is often at variance with the expectations for women in institutional structures. Independent participation in church and school activities may be denied a Puerto Rican woman by a conservative husband or by the extended kinship group. One finds the phenomenon of a husband having to take a leave of absence from his work to take his wife and children to the clinic, "since she could not go alone." Yet, because New York City is the center for the needle trades, and needlwork has been a traditional skill among the women, many Puerto Ricans have found employment in the factories of the garment district and in the sewing rooms of custom dress shops. Often a woman in the garment industry can earn more money than the men of her family, a fact which creates conflict of roles within the family.

The American ideal of the nuclear family, if adhered to, often can neither provide security nor assure authority. Roles of parents and children become confused without the support of kinship and hispano community approval. Nevertheless, Puerto Ricans are criticized by mainlanders for kinship obligations that take precedence over work or school commitments.

Economically, Puerto Rican acculturation is retarded by the low skill level characteristic of many migrants. According to Rand, there has been some evidence that some Puerto Ricans have not accepted the possibility of moving on to more highly skilled jobs, and are content to remain at the level they have learned.[28]

In politics Puerto Ricans have been handicapped by the requirement for voters to pass literacy tests in English. Since most Puerto Ricans in New York read the Spanish daily papers, many people feel that literacy tests should be given in Spanish if, as it is claimed, the issue is literacy and not literacy-in-English. The participation of Puerto Ricans in city politics has been relatively slight, although it has increased in the last decade. Since the political machine has not the coherent power it had in the beginning of the century when the immigrant vote was wooed, there have only been sporadic efforts to reach the Puerto Ricans, and this usually by a factional group of one or another political party. On the whole, Puerto Ricans have not benefited in New York politics.

[28]*Ibid.*, p. 145.

The role of the church, functioning primarily as it does in the sphere of personal belief and loyalty, and in welfare, is a point of conflict for the migrant in two areas. In education, parochial schools in New York City have not had the space or staff to accept the non-English-speaking child. Many middle-class Puerto Ricans, or those who are conservative, prefer parochial education, especially for the upper grades. They feel that discipline is better, that respect for the teacher is maintained, and they approve of the segregation of the sexes. It is the feeling of organizations concerned with public education in New York that Puerto Rican children with language or disciplinary problems are "dumped" on the public schools, that the best group is syphoned off to the parochial schools, thereby helping to maintain a derogatory image of Puerto Ricans and driving more middle-class families among the mainlanders to use private schools or to move to the suburbs. The second area of conflict within the institutional pattern of religion is that of family planning. Because the marriage age is low and because there are cultural values related to fertility, many young families find themselves with numerous children before they are thirty. We have noted that the government of Puerto Rico has had a public policy of fostering family limitation, but this is contrary to the established doctrine of the Roman Catholic Church. On the mainland, health and welfare agencies, reform groups, and often the hispano mothers themselves are interested in smaller-sized families, especially in the situations of low income and poor housing.[29]

"Eastville"

"Eastville" is not "El Barrio Latino." It is an interethnic slum, not a homogeneous nationality sub-community.

> Regardless of how long they have been melting in the pot, the people of Eastville are seldom identified as just plain Americans. They are designated "Hungarians," "Puerto Ricans," "American Negroes," "American Indians," "East Indians," "Russians," "Italians," "Chinese"—and all of these group labels are conceived as indicating something about the personal, social and biological traits of various group members. It makes little difference in this categorizing whether the individuals were born or have lived all their lives in this country if they still possess characteristics—

[29]*Ibid.*, p. 83.

real or assumed—in physical appearance, in styles of wearing apparel, in knowledge of another language than English, and in their names, that allow them to be distinguished from "real Americans." The term "American" is used, as a rule, with reference to outsiders who do not live in the neighborhood and who, although they may themselves be members of ethnic groups, do not meet the criteria that suggest to Eastvillers membership in any particular group with which they are familiar.[30]

In "Eastville" there are ties of neighborhood that cut across ethnic lines and other identifications that are ethnic.

Among Eastvillers there are levels on which feelings of neighborhood solidarity bind members of all ethnic groups together. By the process of discrimination and dislike people get involved in relationships of conflict, and by common understandings and participation in common activities sentiments of solidarity develop. Both the positive feelings and the negative ones work together to shape the social body that is the neighborhood. The idea that the neighborhood is a bad place in which to live is a shared one among Eastvillers. So, too, is their attitude toward discrimination by outsiders against them. . . .

On the other hand, it is difficult to organize programs of social action in Eastville when ethnic group barriers are ignored or when the sources of loyalty within an ethnic group are not recognized. Beneath the intergroup tensions and conflicts among ethnic groups are working interpersonal relationships among individuals, which override ethnic affiliation.[31]

Although there is neighborliness and often mutual helpfulness, the urban slum neighborhod lacks the homogeneity and long residence of the village.

First and last names are seldom known or recognized in Eastville. People are identified according to whatever characteristic they are best known by in the neighborhood—the man from Italy, the lady who owns the candy store, the woman from Ponce. . . .[32]

Housing is a problem in "Eastville," although the overcrowding is not comparable to that in some districts where there are whole families in one room. The 1950 census reported an average

[30]Padilla, *Up From Puerto Rico,* pp. 1–2. By permission.
[31]*Ibid.,* pp. 11–12. By permission.
[32]*Ibid.,* p. 12.

of three persons per room for "Eastville." Apartments are self-contained units which include a bathroom (sometimes with the tub in the kitchen). Some are "old law" (pre-1911) tenements with windows only in the front and back rooms and airshafts for the intervening rooms. Rents in the middle 1950s, at the time of Padilla's study, ranged from $14 to $80 a month, with "under the table" fees from $800 to $1,500 "for the key." Utilities are extra. The entire area is rat-infested; repairs in electric installations, plumbing, and plaster must usually be undertaken by tenants themselves, as complaints are consistently ignored by the absentee landlords. When weather permits, much of the life of the neighborhood goes on on the street.

> Strewn with garbage though they are, the streets and alleys are notable for the number of people of every conceivable ethnic group who spend a considerable part of their time there to get away from their apartments. Day and night the juke boxes in the candy stores deluge the streets with the tunes of the latest records of the season, and it is not strange to see youngsters or young adults dancing by themselves inside the stores or on the sidewalks to rock 'n' roll rhythms by the Velvets or to Xavier Cugat's mambos and meringues. Others watch and then try the ones they like under the tutelage of those who know the steps and proper motions for the dances. Noise of music and of words in Yiddish, Spanish, Italian and English, barking dogs, movement of people, cars' horns, are interwoven in a polyphonic soundtrack which records the pace of the neighborhood. Only very cold weather or news echoed through the grapevine that gang fights are scheduled, keep people off the streets. Otherwise the streets, the sidewalks, the stores, and the bars are filled with people meeting, chatting, and relaxing.[33]

Living in the midst of people who have conscious ties to ethnic groups, hispanos have continued the pattern of vesting individuals with ethnic identity. The principal ethnic groups recognized by hispanos in "Eastville" are Cubans, Americans, American Negroes, Italians, and Jews. Of these, Americans and Italians are the most highly rated. Jews, Cubans, and American Negroes are, as a rule, less favored, especially the two latter groups.[34]

> An undisputed American, or someone who is American and nothing else, is conceived as having a name that cannot be identified

[33]*Ibid.*, p. 9. By permission.
[34]*Ibid.*, p. 89.

with or traced to a foreign origin; as being reddish and white in complexion, tall, blond, and blue eyed; as doing professional work; and as not knowing Spanish or having an accent when speaking it. He does not understand the Hispano people. Americans are nice, honest, beautiful and funny. Should one or more of these traits be missing, the individual is suspected of not being a "real American," but something else instead.[35]

THE DECLINE OF DOMINANCE?

There was a period in which many social scientists felt that the Puerto Rican population would be split between the "lighter" and darker Puerto Ricans, with the latter sharing whatever possibilities were in store for American Negroes. This kind of split has not occurred. What has happened instead seems to be a division within the Puerto Rican community between the mobile and the very poor.

The mobile choose as their models the earlier immigration and expect that they, too, by the third generation will be absorbed into the mainstream of American life. Such a point of view is expressed in the organization *Aspira*, devoted to working with students and parents to understand and take advantage of educational and vocational opportunities.[36]

There is some justification for this hope. Both the 1950 and 1960 censuses have shown an increasing shift upward in the occupations of second-generation Puerto Ricans.[37]

In 1960 there were 4,000 independent small businesses owned by Puerto Ricans in New York City.[38] This is a large figure and attests to the entrepreneurial skill of a segment of the Puerto Rican population. On the other hand, considering the trends of the American economy, the future of small business is precarious.

One could probably assume that the expectation of the mobile group to blend into American society would be fulfilled with diminishing prejudice and discrimination were it not for the large number of poor Puerto Ricans. Their visibility and their share in the desperate problems of urban blight might possibly precipitate more discriminatory behavior toward all Puerto Ricans.

As we have already indicated, the poor segment of the Puerto

[35]*Ibid.*, p. 90. By permission.
[36]*Ibid.*, p. 128; see also *The New York Times*, May 26, 1967, p. 49.
[37]*Ibid.*, pp. 115–116.
[38]*Ibid.*, p. 112.

Ricans is large and at the bottom of the heap in the urban centers where Puerto Ricans are concentrated in large numbers. They migrated into an America that was a welfare state. They have large families. They have the usual disabilities of the poor. They create many problems for the educational system, the health departments, the welfare departments. They are a headache to city governments and an embarrassment to middle-class America. Nor do they have the claim to the American conscience that has been sometimes an effective weapon of the Negro.

Puerto Rican Welfare

More intelligent effort has been made to meet the problems of the Puerto Rican migration than was possible with the older European migrations. The structures of labor and welfare in the United States have changed. The development of the social sciences has made more knowledge available to influence planning. The position of Puerto Rico as a United States dependency facilitates coordination between the island and the mainland.

The Migration Division of the Office of the Commonwealth of Puerto Rico works both on the island and in its offices in the United States to aid the adjustment process. Each week twenty-nine radio stations throughout the island carry a program, "Guide to the Traveler," based on the experience of previous migrants. By 1960 there were thirty-five committees on migrant orientation in cities and towns in Puerto Rico. Television, radio, newspapers, and printed leaflets are urging knowledge of English, giving information about climate and clothing, the documents needed for schools, the need for driver's licenses, and warning about installment buying and many other topics.

In New York the Migration Division has organized a campaign to urge the newcomer to go to night school. The Spanish-language press and Spanish-language radio carry these appeals, and there are thousands of leaflets distributed by clergy, social workers, health stations, settlements, and banks.[39]

Some progress is being made on the housing problem through efforts at urban renewal. New York City has a program of low-cost, subsidized housing in areas where there have been particularly bad slum dwellings. Renewal of the side streets between middle-class housing is beginning, and clergy, social agencies, and political clubs have aided in bringing negligent landlords to court.

[39]Senior, *Strangers—Then Neighbors*, p. 62.

The school system, where it is practicable, has attempted to draw zone lines so that the ethnic balance of a school's population will not exceed one-third Puerto Rican. The problem is aggravated, however, by the principle of homogeneous grouping, which syphons off the better students into separate classes. Since the number of Puerto Ricans who have qualified for these classes is still not large, the other classes have disproportionately more Puerto Ricans. The Board Education has been experimenting with "culture-free" intelligence tests and with special programs for the gifted of less privileged background. There are about a hundred Spanish-speaking Substitute Auxiliary teachers assigned to schools in the city. The efforts of Negro parents and Negro organizations for improved schools and for revised testing have benefited Puerto Ricans also.

The public welfare agencies, the private nonsectarian welfare agencies, various Protestant denominations, and Catholic parishes and religious orders have given thought and effort to meeting the needs of the new migrant group.

Padilla gives an account of one "welfare" family in "Eastville":

Mr. Rios was injured in an industrial accident in 1953. This later involved orthopedic surgery. Workmen's Compensation was paid for a short period and for the subsequent surgery, but after the discontinuance Mr. Rios continued to suffer pain, and with his injured arm could not find a job. A visiting nurse suggested the family should seek help from the Department of Public Welfare—"go on welfare," and she herself made the contact for the family. The case with the Compensation Board was reopened and Mr. Rios now receives $18 a week from this agency. Mrs. Rios and the three children have supplemental aid from the Department of Welfare. Mr. Rios has been attending night school, has finished grammar school and is now in junior high school. He still has pain and receives treatment from both public and private clinics. He still consults lawyers in the hope of getting indemnification for his injury. In the last seven years the rent has been doubled.

The Rios family have been in New York for twenty years. They belong to a store front church, and the children have been to the church camp summers, although when the daughter reached puberty, her parents no longer allowed her to go to camp. The children are not allowed to play on the streets, though the boys are often "given permission" to go to the park. The children are doing well in school. Mrs. Rios earns a little money by caring for the children of working mothers in her home. Mr. Rios hopes when he "has completed his education" to be able to get a job so they can get off welfare. He is 45 years old.[40]

Mr. Rios represents the kind of need for which the welfare system was devised: the possibility of maintaining the thin line between despair and self-respect. On the other hand, the welfare system, being nationwide and bureaucratic cannot change flexibly, and it is significant that the landlord can raise the rent without the delays and counterpressure of a city administration or Congress. Furthermore, Mr. Rios lives in "Eastville," which is not as isolated or neglected as *El Barrio*.

The Puerto Rican Underclass

"Underclass" is a term now common for the very poor in cities. For the Puerto Ricans of New York, these are mostly found in the tenements of East Harlem. As the mobile move out, the poorest newcomers come in. Much of the housing is still "old law" (pre-1911): half a floor of an old private residence or a four- or five-story tenement, with the toilet in the outside hall for the use of the whole floor, a tub in the kitchen, two of the rooms with air shafts instead of windows, and rats. Garbage collections in these poor districts of New York is twice a week, whereas in middle-class residential sections it is every day.[41]

The anthropologist Oscar Lewis has given us a vivid portrait of a migrant to *El Barrio*.[42] Soledad, whose mother migrated to San Juan from rural poverty in Puerto Rico, brought her children up in a San Juan slum. Soledad came to the continental United States because one of her brothers had come. She came with her children and worked briefly as an agricultural laborer in New Jersey. She then wound up in *El Barrio* where she knew some people from San Juan. A woman not without strength and primitive intelligence, Soledad is a true product of "the culture of poverty."[43] She is confused, full of antagonism when confronted with the bureaucracy of the welfare department, the health clinic, the school system. Her colorful argot, her unstable relations to men, her overprotective yet harsh dealings with her children, her

[40]Padilla, *Up From Puerto Rico*, pp. 134–141, adapted by the authors.
[41]Prof. Meyer found this to be true when working as a field supervisor for a study for the U.S. Dept. of Health, Education, and Welfare in 1965.
[42]Oscar Lewis, *La Vida: A Puerto Rican Family in the Culture of Poverty—San Juan and New York* (New York: Random House, 1965), pp. 127–245.
[43]For a discussion of the concept "the culture of poverty" see *Ibid.*, pp. xlv–lii.

general personal disorganization (by any middle-class standard) still show a woman struggling against odds: some private clinging to bastardized religious beliefs; some great strength in enduring and fighting.

Lewis's *La Vida* has offended many Puerto Ricans, as they fear it will contribute to a derogatory stereotype of them as a group. But Soledad (the name means solitude—"alienation") is not a hereditary national culture. She is of the culture of the most depressed of the urban poor. Without understanding Soledad one cannot understand why the only riot in New York City in 1967— that summer of desperate riots across the country—was in *El Barrio*. As one writer expressed it, "Some of the nation's most intensive community project work had been insufficient to counter the feeling of separation and rejection which had so long afflicted the Spanish-speaking ghetto."[44] To New York it was startling to have Spanish Americans riot. Furthermore the riot, compared with others of the summer (Detroit, Newark, Cincinnati, New Haven) was not as destructive or as prolonged.

Organizations Among the Puerto Ricans

Puerto Ricans have been active in forming organizations. As with other minorities, some of these represent the more established segments of the Puerto Rican community in the United States. On the other hand there is also the emergence of a militant anti-establishment group.

There is one Spanish daily newspaper in New York City. In addition to carrying the usual type of copy it offers itself now as the informant about night classes, the P.T.A., presents itself as the champion of the Spanish-speaking population against the police and other agents of authority who "do not understand the Spanish people." The paper was not founded by Puerto Ricans, but certainly the present journal acts as a force to unify the sense of identity of all the Latin American community.

Labor unions, some with locals almost 100 per cent Puerto Rican serve also as adaptive institutions. A 1959 survey found that 63 per cent of the New York Spanish-speaking households surveyed had one or more union members. These may not have been all Puerto Rican households, as Glazer and Moynihan point out that Mexicans and Cubans appear on the executive board of a

[44]*The New Yorker*, August 5, 1967, pp. 19–23.

major union, along with two Puerto Ricans, though the majority of the labor force in this local was Puerto Rican. The authors imply that Puerto Ricans have not yet achieved competitive leadership positions in proportion to their numbers.[45]

In Manhattan there has been an ongoing struggle for political leadership among the Puerto Ricans. In the Bronx a borough leader has clearly emerged. The Puerto Rican vote has risen to nearly a quarter of a million registered voters in New York City.

A number of indigenous organizations have developed. The Spanish Merchants Association has 200 Puerto Rican members. The Puerto Rican Civil Service Employees Association is thirty-five years old, owns its own building, and has established a successful credit union. The Spanish Club of the New York City Police Department has 250 members, mostly Puerto Rican. The Association of Puerto Rican Social Workers has more than 1,000 members. There are organizations of lawyers, ministers, teachers, nurses, electricians, barbers, bar owners, taxi owners and drivers, and baseball umpires. The Council of Puerto Rican and Spanish-American Organizations of Greater New York now includes fifty-four civic, social, cultural, religious, and fraternal organizations. The Federation of Puerto Rican Organizations of New Jersey has thirty member groups.

The Young Lords Party

Puerto Ricans also have their young militants that are organized in the Young Lords Party. It was initiated by a group of students and members of a gang that had turned political under the influence of militant youth movements among other minorities. It was organized in 1969. It is Third World in orientation. It has been primarily interested in Barrio improvement: cleaning up streets, demonstrating for better services; and in the development of identity.[46] In its account of Puerto Rican history it stresses the large admixture of black slave population brought into Puerto Rico by the Spaniards, chiefly from the Yoruba tribe of West Africa. In this emphasis it attempts to counteract lower status feelings of dark Puerto Ricans as well as to declare its alliance with other Third World[47] groups: American blacks, Amer-

---

[45]Glazer and Moynihan, *Beyond the Melting Pot*, p. 102.
[46]*Palante*, (New York: McGraw-Hill Book Co., 1971).
[47]We are using the term Third World here in its strict political sense of radicals who embrace a Maoist philosophy. The majority of these are of Asian or African descent, but there are also white radicals who see this as a viable political philosophy and are welcome in the coalition.

ican whites, and Spanish-speaking Americans. (There is no discussion, however, of working with the more militant Mexican American organizations. This may be a regional matter as they do see an alliance with some Cubans, and possibly Mexican Americans in New York City of whom there are a few.) There are branches of the Young Lords Party in New York, Philadelphia, Bridgeport, and in two cities in Puerto Rico. They favor independence of Puerto Rico. One of their programs attained nation-wide attention. This was the breakfast program for school children. They have also been very active in involving women and in an attempt to change the image of the docile woman subordinate to her husband or father.

The future of the Puerto Rican minority is bound up with many factors: the development of the island, the dispersion of Puerto Ricans on the mainland, the opportunity for advancement, the consciousness of themselves as a cultural minority, and the future position of racially visible people in the continental United States.

The amazing development of the island economy, if it continues at the present rapid rate, may change the pattern of migration. The development of the island may reduce the available cheap labor force by a considerable amount, especially if the Puerto Rican efforts toward population control begin to show effects. The preparation of migrants can be expected to improve also. Nevertheless, for some time to come, opportunities in the continental United States will outstrip those in Puerto Rico, and the remoter rural areas may still be a source of supply for the mainland labor force, and these rural people are the ones who will have the severest problems of adaptations to mainland urban life.

The future of the island politically is also a factor influencing both the increase or decrease in migration, as well as the feelings within the Puerto Rican group already settled in the United States. Various groups on the island have at one time or another favored either independence or statehood. Independence would at the very least create new problems, and perhaps new emphases, in the development of the island. Statehood would also slow development efforts, since Puerto Rico would then be subject to federal taxation, from which it is now exempt. The former Governor, Muñoz Marin, sees great cultural as well as economic benefits in the present relationship, which allows self-government within "a commonwealth of the American political system." He foresees a future in which Puerto Rico will carry its share of the federal financial burden, and he poses the question of whether eventually a new relationship may not be defined which is neither statehood nor independence. The political future of Puerto Rico, however, is also bound up with other developments in Latin America and the Caribbean, as well as with American policy.

Opportunity for advancement seems to be promising for Puerto Ricans as compared with most early twentieth-century immigrant groups. According to David W. Barry, Executive Secretary of the New York City Mission Society,

> No previous immigrant group so quickly numbered among its members so many policemen, welfare workers, teachers and social workers, office workers and independent business men, and even doctors and lawyers—after barely a dozen years in New York. And the signs of the future are in the substantial enrollment of young Puerto Ricans in the city's colleges and universities.[48]

Whether Puerto Ricans will assimilate, or whether their identity as a cultural minority will be strengthened will be influenced by larger trends in the United States. Some Mexican American leaders include Puerto Ricans in their definition of La Raza, though we find, as yet, no Puerto Rican movement that makes this definition. Efforts at legislation to open equal opportunity by establishing quotas toward "racial and ethnic balance" in employment, education, etc. do strengthen the sense of ethnic identity, at least for the present. Nevertheless it is clear that many Puerto Rican professionals and businessmen are taking their place in the main stream of American life. The future of the dark complected Puerto Rican is more ambiguous as it is inevitably bound up with the future of race attitudes.

Suggested Readings

Abramson, Michael. *Palante: The Young Lords Party.* New York: The McGraw-Hill Book Company, 1971.
A vivid account of Puerto Rican militant youth, with splendid photographs.

[48]Quoted in Senior, *Strangers—Then Neighbors,* p. 67.

Glazer, Nathan and Moynihan, Daniel Patrick. *Beyond the Melting Pot: The Negroes, Puerto Ricans, Jews, Italians and Irish of New York City.* Cambridge, Massachusetts: The M.I.T. Press and the Harvard University Press, 1963.
An informative summary.

Handlin, Oscar. *The Newcomers: Negroes and Puerto Ricans in a Changing Metropolis.* Cambridge, Mass.: Harvard University Press, 1959.
A part of the New York Metropolitan Region Study. The new migrants' problems appraised in the light of the history of the New York City labor force.

Lewis, Oscar. *La Vida: A Puerto Rican Family in the Culture of Poverty—San Juan and New York.* New York: Random House, 1965.
Part II, "Soledad," describes a day with the poorest stratum of Spanish Harlem.

Padilla, Elana. *Up From Puerto Rico.* New York: Columbia University Press, 1958.
A social anthropologist describes and analyzes the daily living of Puerto Ricans in one New York neighborhood.

Senior, Clarence. *Strangers—Then Neighbors: From Pilgrims to Puerto Ricans.* New York: Freedom Books, 1961.
An up-to-date summary of facts about Puerto Ricans on the mainland, with an excellent bibliography.

13   Chinese Americans

Kindness in the father, filial piety in the son, gentility in the elder brother, humility and respect in the younger brother, good behavior in the husband, obedience in the wife, benevolence in the ruler and loyalty in the ministers—these ten are the human duties.   Confucius: Third Discourse*

Tsekung asked, "Is there a single word that can serve as a principle of conduct for life"? Confucius replied, "perhaps the word reciprocity will do." Confucian Aphorium*

The sovereign is careful at the inception of all things. A difference of a hundredth or a thousandth of an inch at the start results in a divergence of a thousand miles at the end.   Confucius: First Discourse*

Events that happen are not put away in books. That would not be fair. Only a few folk have leisure to read, and history belongs to everyone. It flows in every mother's milk and is digested by every babe. Thus it becomes part of everyone's experience to use when needed. That which happens is not past. It is all part of our now.   Chinese rickshaw runner.**

*Lin Yutang, ed. and trans., *The Wisdom of Confucius* (The Modern Library), pp. 235, 186, 215.
**Nora Waln, *The House of Exile* (Boston: Little, Brown and Co., 1933), p. 53.

China's is one of the oldest cultures in recorded history. It is indeed timeless, for the Chinese language has no tenses, so that one only knows from the context of a statement whether it refers to the past or the present. For centuries China was a feudal, hierarchical society bound by reciprocal obligations within the extended kinship, according to age, sex and birth order; and between classes according to traditional roles and responsibilities.

When the first Chinese came to the United States early in the nineteenth century they were more culturally visible than "racially," though they were early defined as a racial group in harmony with the racial attitudes of European-descended people.

The real migration began after 1850 when Chinese labor was sought for mines and railroads. Most of them stayed west of the Rockies in this period. Immigration increased till 1882 when the first of a series of exclusion acts barred any further heavy migration. In 1924 they were definitively excluded under the immigra-

TABLE 13-1   CHINESE IMMIGRATION TO THE UNITED STATES AND POPULATION OF CHINESE ANCESTRY AS RECORDED BY CENSUS

Year	Total Admitted*	Total Recorded**	Per Cent Increase or Decrease
1820 to 1830	3	——	—
1831 to 1840	8	——	—
1841 to 1850	35	758	—
1851 to 1860	41,397	34,933	—
1861 to 1870	64,301	63,199	80.9
1871 to 1880	123,201	105,465	66.9
1881 to 1890	61,711	107,488	1.9
1891 to 1900	14,799	88,869	−16.4
1901 to 1910	20,605	71,531	−20.4
1911 to 1920	21,278	61,639	−13.8
1921 to 1930	29,907	74,594	21.6
1931 to 1940	4,928	77,504	3.4
1941 to 1950	16,709	117,140† (150,005††)	51.8
1951 to 1960	9,657	190,095† (237,292††)	62.3 (58.2††)
1961 to 1970	96,062	(435,062††)	(54.5††)
TOTAL	504,601		

*Annual Report of Immigration and Naturalization Service, Washington.
**United States Census for each decade.
†Includes mainland United States without Hawaii.
††Includes Hawaii.

tion law for a generation. Many of those who came in the nineteenth century did not expect to stay permanently. Others obtained citizenship before the first exclusion act. Still others, of course, eventually were American born, so that there are some fourth generation families today. Some became permanent residents as registered aliens. And always there was a trickle of illegal entries. In the safe harbor of the Chinatowns they could rarely be apprehended. Today, under the provisions of the Act of 1965 long-time residents who entered illegally may regularize their status and apply for citizenship in the regular way, but some are still fearful of doing so, having lived many years under the fear of deportation.

CHINESE IMMIGRATION TO THE UNITED STATES

The Chinese Exclusion Act drastically curtailed, though it did not completely eliminate, further immigration after 1882. During several decades the number of Chinese returning to China exceeded the number of arrivals. "From 1908, when records of departures began, to 1930, while 48,482 Chinese immigrant aliens were admitted, 72,796 departed, thus showing a net loss."[1] Normal natural increase was prevented by the disproportion of the sexes. In 1910 there were 1,430 males to every 100 Chinese females; in 1920, 695.5; and in 1940, 258.3. Finally, because of exclusion there had been an undue proportion of elderly Chinese in the population which accounted for a relatively high death rate for the group. Thus the Chinese population declined from a peak of 107,488 in 1890 to a low of 61,639 in 1920. From 1921 to 1940 the Chinese in America increased but slightly, to a 77,504 total in 1940.

The 1940–1950 decade showed an increase of 51.8 per cent in the Chinese population. Part of this may reflect a more accurate census count gained through the use of Chinese recorders for the first time. But it is a question if even this measure succeeded in getting all the resident aliens counted, since many avoid official contacts because of illegalities in their status—fraudulent claims to derivative citizenship, "jumping ship" by seamen, crossing borders without detection, and "smuggling." Much of the increase actually occurred in the postwar years, when an unprecedented

[1]Maurice R. Davie, *World Immigration* (New York: The Macmillan Co., 1936), pp. 315–316.

number of female immigrants admitted under the War Brides Act helped bring the sex ratio of this population to 1.89. (In 1890 there had been 27 Chinese males to every 1 Chinese female.)

Most of the Chinese who came in the nineteenth century were poor villagers. Within the pattern of the Chinese family system the men came, leaving their wives and children, if they had them, within the shelter of the kinship circle in China. Many of them came as contract laborers, especially for railroad construction. They made no particular effort to settle in agriculture, perhaps because American agriculture was alien to their patterns of cultivation at home. Some returned to China for a time, or several times, to invest their earnings in a strip of land in the home village, to pay the bride price for a wife, or to contribute to the joint family purse. Others saw as their goal small entrepreneurial enterprises in America, where they were free from the "squeeze" of officialdom or the limitations of the class system. Obviously as the Chinese population increased, merchants came also to the principal centers to maintain the supply of familiar Chinese goods. Many of these merchant families were related through organizations of merchants or through family ties to others in other cities of America. They became the power structure of the Chinese subcommunities of the large cities. In smaller centers in the West there was more opportunity for migrating laborers to rise to the position of small merchants.

Sojourners

This term applies to the Chinese who have lived in this country with the idea of making enough money to return to the homeland to live. Siu describes this category thus:[2] "The Chinese sojourners maintain a psychological and social separateness from the larger society and insulate themselves against the full impact of the dominant societies' values, norms, attitudes, and behavior patterns." With this attitude, the sojourner lives a dual existence "which contributes to his sense of non-belongingness in both societies, a fact that is seldom admitted by the sojourner." It is this psychological orientation which marks a Chinese as a sojourner whether foreign or native-born, irrespective of his class position, or whether the time ever comes that he feels affluent enough to return to his homeland.

[2]Paul C. Siu, "The Sojourner," *American Journal of Sociology*, July, 1952, pp. 34–44.

Students and Intellectuals

From 1847, when an American missionary brought three Chinese boys to study at an American academy, to 1954, some 18,000 Chinese nationals have studied in the United States. Most American institutions of higher learning have trained some Chinese nationals. The peak of Chinese student enrollment came in 1949, at 3,916. Since most of this student group have come from the upper strata of Chinese society, their relations with dominant people have been different from those of other Chinese.

The "Slot Racket"

Unique to the Chinese in the United States has been the so-called slot racket. A section of the 1870 citizenship law passed by Congress recognized the right to confer citizenship on Americans born abroad. Chinese residents in this country have made much use of this law to secure entry of others, especially relations with the same surnames. As we have seen, many male Chinese immigrants returned to China from time to time for protracted visits to their families abroad and conceived children there. In countless instances, "sons never born" were reported, thus creating a "slot" on the family tree. Those "slots" enabled people to claim derivative citizenship and enter the United States. Persons claiming derivative citizenship, if born before 1934, were eligible for admission to this country if they could prove that their fathers or grandfathers resided in the United States at one time. The "racket" aspect has been in the selling of these "slots" by legitimate claimants. Arrangements are made to sell the "slots" through Hong Kong brokers for prices ranging from $2,500 to $6,000.[3]

The above considerations explain why there was such a high percentage increase in the census figures for the Chinese population on the American mainland from 1950 to 1960 (62.3 per cent). In addition to more accurate counting, some Chinese students stranded in the country by the Chinese revolution who were given permanent entry, the large number of relatives of Chinese American nationals, and refugees from the mainland of China—mostly merchants and scholars—all swelled the total. For example, of the 5,722 immigrant aliens from China admitted for the 1959 period, 1,348 were wives of American citizens.[4]

The new immigration law has benefited the Chinese under the

[3]*Time*, January 20, 1958, p. 17.
[4]*Annual Report of the Immigration and Naturalization Service*, Washington, D.C., 1959, p. 17, Table 6.

preferences for skills, relatives, and refugees. Many of the Chinese becoming citizens under these provisions already had been granted permanent residence in the United States.

The American Chinese population is highly urbanized. By 1950, as many as 94 per cent were officially counted in cities of various sizes, and according to Lee only 1 per cent could be said to have really rural residence.[5] The trend has been toward concentration in a few large cities. In addition to San Francisco, with the largest Chinatown in the nation, enough Chinese to form a local "colony" are found in Chicago, Detroit, Los Angeles, Brooklyn, New York, Boston, Washington, D.C., Dallas, Philadelphia. The most interesting recent change in the geographical distribution of the American Chinese population has been the southward movement. In 1950 there were 10,432 in the South. While this was still a small percentage of the then 117,629 national total, it represented an increase over 1940 of 112.5 per cent. Of this Lee writes:

> The southern movement gathered momentum during the depression, when the South surpassed all other regions in attracting families who owned and operated general merchandise, food, and service establishments. The Chinese function as middlemen in a multi-racial society where the social relations between the whites and Negroes are strained and hostile. They also play this role in the Southwest, where Mexicans and American Indians are numerous and the Chinese cater to all groups. This is similar to the position the Chinese occupy in South-East Asia, the Caribbean, and elsewhere.[6]

It is of interest to find that in 1940, a hundred years after the Chinese immigration started, for the first time the American-born Chinese exceeded the foreign-born Chinese population. The exceptional tendency for Chinese immigrants to return to their homeland and the long period in which the group had had an excessively high male preponderance account for the delay.

THE ESTABLISHMENT OF DOMINANCE

Visibility

To the Westerners settling the Pacific Coast and the Rocky Mountain area, the Chinese appeared particularly alien. Although

[5] Rose Hum Lee, *The Chinese in the United States* (Hong Kong: Hong Kong University Press, 1960), p. 38. Distributed in the United States by the Oxford University Press.
[6] *Ibid.*, p. 39.

the China trade had been active for some decades, few of these "pioneers" had ever seen an Asiatic. They were immediately subject to derogating attitudes as a "race."

Actually, however, what struck Anglo-Americans, were cultural characteristics, more than racial. The peculiarities of the Chinese language, with its high sing-song intonation and its ideographic writing, bore no relation to any spoken or written language they had known. The men, who were in preponderance and hence most visible, still dressed according to the old-style Chinese custom: long queues, felt slippers, cotton blouses, and little round hats. They were also ridiculed because they accepted domestic work at a time when there were few women available to do it. This did not fit American ideas of a masculine role.

Religiously, none of the nineteenth-century migrants were Christian, although soon the Protestants and subsequently in the twentieth century, the Catholics, began to proselytize among the new migrants.

Discrimination

The discovery of gold in California was a magnet for the first Chinese as it was for many Americans. The Chinese have developed mining all over Southeast Asia, and the pattern for overseas enterprise for the son of a joint family is centuries old. Perhaps much of the peculiarly violent and rough treatment accorded these first Chinese immigrants can be understood when it is remembered that Chinese-native-white interaction first took place in the especially lawless setting of the frontier. Opposition arose to the Chinese as gold miners because they were industrious and persevering, often taking on mining locations that whites considered worthless and making them pay. Thus began the cry that the Chinese depressed the wages and the standard of living of whites, an allegation that was to dog the Chinese as they subsequently became laborers in all the occupations available—as railroad construction workers, as farm laborers, and in varieties of kinds of service for households. In the initial settlement of the Pacific Coast among the settlers going West men far outnumbered women, and the Chinese seized opportunities as cooks, launderers, and other household servants. They filled an acute labor need for a time, but even then were ridiculed for their foreign dress, accents, and customs. They were systematically excluded from white collar and professional occupations. This persisted till World War

II. Although there were some merchants engaged in large international trade, the chief activity of the entrepreneurs was confined to supplying the needs of the resident Chinese.

Acts discriminating against the Chinese were first passed in California in the 1850s and again in the 1880s. Opposition to the Chinese was manifested also in city ordinances that attempted to reach the Chinese indirectly. For example Maurice Davie reported in 1936 that, "San Francisco had a laundry ordinance imposing a license fee as follows: on laundries using a one-horse vehicle, $2 per quarter; two horses, $4 per quarter; no vehicle, $15 per quarter. The Chinese laundries commonly used no vehicle. It was made a misdemeanor for any person on the sidewalks to carry baskets suspended on a pole across the shoulders—a typical Chinese practice."

Frequently the Chinese were exposed to violence, especially in periods of hard times. As a result of the panic of 1873, riots occurred during which the Chinese were robbed, beaten, and murdered by hoodlums who made the Chinese the scapegoats for the ills of the times. Eyewitness accounts report that "it was a common sight in San Francisco and other cities to see the Chinese pelted with stones or mud, beaten or kicked, having vegetables or laundry stolen from their baskets, and even having the queues cut." It was also reported that their washhouses were set afire, and when they tried to escape from burning houses they were beaten and sometimes compelled to die in the flames. The police afforded little protection against these outrageous attacks and the victims did not retaliate. The Chinese government, however, demanded an indemnity, which was paid by the United States government.

Agitation for the exclusion of the Chinese rose throughout the 1870s. At first, there was little support in Congress as most people east of the Rockies had not encountered many Chinese, if any, and the Southern states were watching to see whether, after Emancipation, they might not need to replace Negro labor with Chinese. With the collapse of Reconstruction, the Southerners in Congress supported the Californians, and the Chinese Exclusion Act was passed in 1882, suspending all Chinese immigration for ten years. This was repeated for another ten years in 1892; and in 1902 suspension of Chinese immigration was extended indefinitely. This remained the status of Chinese until 1943, when, under the pressure of the war situation, China was added to the quota immigrant nations and allotted 105 annual entries.

The exclusion of the Chinese by federal legislation is a clear illustration of Congress yielding to the specific will of one of its individual states in the absence of any general national demand. McWilliams has noted the following factors in the situation which help explain it: (1) all but one of some eight anti-Chinese measures passed by Congress were passed on the eve of national elections and for avowed political purposes; (2) the interrelationship of the Southern attitude toward the Negro and the California attitude toward the Oriental prompted Southern representatives to side with California on a *quid pro quo* basis; (3) there was no real knowledge of the Chinese on the part of white Americans throughout the nation, and they failed to recognize the issue as related to national interest.[7]

MINORITY ADAPTATIONS TO DOMINANCE

The Chinese reaction to conflict with dominants was one of passivity and withdrawal. They sought niches in which they would be inconspicuously tolerated.

Occupations

The Chinese moved primarily out of rural areas, and developed occupations that either served their own group (such as restaurants, bakeries, small businesses), or served outside the community in positions where there was a labor shortage (such as in laundries, domestic service, etc.).

Residence

Like other minorities, the Chinese clustered in special sections. This was, in part, natural and voluntary because of their cultural ties, but it was maintained as a result of discrimination because other housing was not open to them. Chinatowns have spread to all the major cities in the United States where there is any sizable population.[8]

These Chinatowns became worlds of their own, with their

[7]See Carey McWilliams, *Brothers Under the Skin* (Boston: Little, Brown & Co., 1943), pp. 87–96, for an extensive account and interpretation of the legislation against the Chinese.
[8]There are no Chinatowns in cities under 50,000, nor in states with very small Chinese populations. D. Y. Yuan, "Voluntary Segregation: A Study of New York Chinatown," *Phylon*, Autumn, 1963.

own system of organization. In the end, they did harm to the public image of the Chinese, as they seemed to be alien and mysterious places. They were, indeed, in former times, not only residential sub-communities, but centers of illegal activities.

Old San Francisco Chinatown: The Anti-Chinese Stereotype

The largest Chinatown in the United States has always been in San Francisco, for many years the most powerful in the network of associational relationships for Chinese in America. Many activities, illegal in America, merely reproduced acceptable behavior in old China. For example, opium has always been smoked in China since the British introduced it in the nineteenth century. It is not surprising, therefore, that a great deal of the narcotics smuggling of former times was located in Chinatown and fortunes were made from the drug traffic. Opium smuggling and opium consumption was at its height in the 1880s, and has gradually declined since then.[9] Then, too, there was active prostitution, since apart from the well-to-do merchants, very few Chinese brought wives, and the predominant immigrant population was male. The Chinese were great gamblers, and gambling houses were part of the Chinese picture. The existence of these illegal activities helped create a stereotyped image of the Chinese, which probably reached its height in the fictitious character of the nefarious Dr. Fu Manchu.

San Francisco was also headquarters for some of the major "tongs." These are merchant associations and in former times there were often violent outbreaks as they attempted to control a particular street or territory. The national press often played up these "tong wars."

The slot racket had seriously disorganizing consequences in the American Chinese community: (1) It added an illegal activity. In addition to "paper" families, many Chinese men had wives in China whom they could not or would not bring to this country. In time these men remarried here, thus victimizing native-born girls and their offspring. (2) It increased the tendency for the Chinese to fail to cooperate with American authorities. Even innocent resident Chinese who might have wanted to expose the perpetrators were likely to fear to do so. (3) The "slotted" residents led a dual life, fearful of exposure which might lead to deporta-

[9]Leong Gor Yun, *Chinatown Inside Out* (New York: Barrows Mussey Inc., 1936), p. 216.

tion. (4) It helped perpetuate the tongs, because many slotted individuals relied on them to protect their false status or that of their "illegal" families in the United States. The attention given to these factors by the police and the press obscured the fact that thousands of Chinese lived out their lives in Chinatown in an orderly and structured fashion.

The Social Structure of the Sub-community: New York Chinatown

New York City has the second largest Chinatown in the United States. An examination of it will delineate the social structure of the immigrant Chinese community as it has been preserved in Chinatowns throughout the nation. New York can also illustrate the changes and the problems that confront members of this sub-community. New York City Chinatown is the nodal center for the 100,000 Chinese in the Metropolitan area.

Chinatown serves social, economic, cultural, and political functions. Socially, Chinatown is indispensable for Chinese, as such a high proportion have no nuclear family life. (There are many single males, living alone, scattered through the Metropolitan area and having no social contact with their local neighborhoods.) Economically, Chinatown is an entrepot for the redistribution of Chinese goods, especially foods for the great Chinese restaurant industry. Culturally, it supports five Chinese newspapers, three Chinese schools, book stores, printing houses, and Chinese movie theaters. Politically, it houses the headquarters of all political and social organizations. Today Chinatown has about 100 voluntary organizations. These make up the network of the power structure of Chinatown at whose apex is the Chinese Consolidated Benevolent Association.

The stated purpose of the Chinese Consolidated Benevolent Association is to maintain a Chinese school, to keep order, to do charitable work, and to supervise immigration and other activities of Chinese residents. It was registered in 1911 with the Peking Imperial Court as the supervisory organization for overseas Chinese. It was responsible not to the government of China, but to the great families of China for their overseas kin. In the 1920s it was registered in New York State as a charity organization. It has been, in the past and for the older generation, the "supreme" organization. Its present situation is that of authority for the older generation. This means, however, there is still considerable authority because of the Chinese age-grading system. However, it is being challenged by the younger Chinese who have formed such organizations as The Chinese Democratic Club and the Chinese Junior Chamber of Commerce.

Family Associations

The simplest form of organization in Chinatown is the family association. These are societies of people bearing the same surname. They do not need to be blood relations. Generally, there will be two or three family associations in each Chinatown that are the most powerful. Not all family names have enough people to support an organization, in which case a few of the weaker families will make a combined group. However, these combinations are not at random. They find some justification for association in Chinese history or literature. The family association is subdivided into a smaller group called a *fong* which is organized according to the village from which the immigrants came. The family associations have social and economic functions. They find jobs, provide capital, finance education, adjudicate disputes among members, provide housing, contacts, and so on. The social functions (mostly held on Sundays) are also important for the dispersed, isolated members of the family group.

Territorial Associations

Most of the Chinese in New York Chinatown are from Kuangtung Province (the Province of Canton). Within this territory there are associations of people from four counties who speak variants of the same Cantonese dialect. Then there are the Haka-speaking people who have an association, and there are several smaller groups from Eastern provinces and one for the Northern Mandarin-speaking Chinese. The territorial associations form the intermediate power structure. The most powerful of them alternate in providing the President of the Chinese Consolidated Benevolent Association (for a two-year term). They have social functions, especially for the older people, but they do not have jurisdiction in disputes. This is the prerogative of the family associations.

The Merchant Associations

In New York the two major Associations represent each of the two major business streets, Mott Street and Pell Street. They also to a degree control dispersed businesses outside of Chinatown. Their major purpose is to limit competition and assure thereby a reasonable livelihood for each of their merchants. Their control outside of Chinatown is declining.

Changing Chinatown

The structure of Chinatown was first challenged a generation ago with the organization of the Laundry Alliance in 1933. Until this time the Chinatown power structure controlled the lives of the little people with the pattern of gentlemanly "face" and power structure "favor" and a considerable amount of official "squeeze" in the best style of Chinese officialdom. It is probable that the laundrymen would never have had the boldness to organize—so humble was their position in the hierarchy—had not outside circumstances threatened their very existence. The large American laundries instituted a systematic campaign against the Chinese laundries, displaying placards showing Chinese laundrymen spitting on white shirts. The Chinese Consul-General protested and with the aid of city police succeeded in having most of the placards removed. The Chinese Consolidated Benevolent Association assessed each laundryman a dollar as an "anti-placard" fee. In March of 1933 there was a proposed city ordinance to license public laundries with a $25 fee and a $1,000 security bond required. The liberal *Chinese Journal* took up the cause of the laundrymen. The CCB, through the editor's prodding, had to take some action, but it was concerned with keeping control. However, an able leader, Louis Wing, emerged from among the laundrymen and with the help of the editor of the *Chinese Journal* in space rented from the Roman Catholic Church on Mott Street, an organization was formed that became an independent, self-determining body. There were many struggles to bypass the Chinatown power structure, and at one point the *Chinese Journal* was boycotted, but both the Alliance and the *Journal* survived. The organization grew, it cooperated with the efforts for improved conditions of other organizations of service trades and by 1935 moved its headquarters outside Chinatown.[10] Its trucks may be seen all over New York today.

During the 1930s and 1940s there was a considerable exodus from Chinatown. The younger, the better educated, in the better occupational positions tended to go to newer sections of metropolitan New York. Chinatown in the early 1950s was left with an

[10]Leong, *Chinatown Inside Out*, Ch. 5, pp. 85–106.

older, poorer, less well-educated general population, which for the oldest generation contained a sharp cleavage between the power elite and stranded sojourners. Many of the American-born second generation are more conservative than the newest immigrants, as Chinatown has managed to preserve a pattern of behavior that disappeared in China decades ago. The teenagers of the third generation are often in open conflict as they seek to emulate American behavior patterns.

Cattell describes many barriers that aggravate the situation of many Chinatown families. There is unfamiliarity with and cultural resistance to using the health and welfare services available. Yet there is a high incidence of illness and of mental illness. In a sample study of 105 cases (1958–1960) the highest percentages were infective diseases and nutritional diseases.[11] These reflect some of the principal problems of Chinatown: low income and bad housing.

Of the 2,323 Chinese families living in Chinatown in 1950, 37 per cent had incomes of less than $3,000, and 55 per cent had less than $4,000. The New York State Housing Survey of 1950 reported that more than 30 per cent of the dwelling units did not contain flush toilets; 48 per cent had no bathtub or shower; 40 per cent lacked hot water; 71 per cent did not have central heating.[12]

Although some improvements in housing have been made, the 1970 Census reports that for the four census tracts that include the old heart of Chinatown, and where the proportion of Chinese residents is highest, there are still 1,100 dwelling units lacking some or all plumbing. There are 471 dwelling units without kitchens. In 35 blocks occupied by dwellings live 26,755 persons; 1,678 of these are children under five, and over 1,000 are over seventy-five, two-thirds of these men. The average size of dwelling units is three rooms (median 3.1; mode 3).[13]

Chinatown suffers from the deterioration of all old urban neighborhoods. Behind the facade of its shops and restaurants that are so attractive to tourists is a poverty ridden, overcrowded ethnic slum.

Not all Chinese live in Chinatown. Like other population

[11]Stuart H. Cattell, *Health, Welfare and Social Organization in Chinatown, New York City.* A Report Prepared for the Chinatown Public Health Nursing Demonstration of the Department of Public Affairs, Community Service Society of New York, August 1962, p. 52. (Mimeographed.)
[12]D. Y. Yuan, "Chinatown and Beyond: The Chinese Population in Metropolitan New York," *Phylon.* Fourth Quarter, Winter, 1966, pp. 324–325.
[13]United States Census, 1970. New York County. Table P-1, General Characteristics of the Population and Table H-1, Occupancy, Utilization, Financial Characteristics of Housing Units.

groups rising younger people and older wealthier people are seeking the suburbs. A study of two Chinese American clubs shows us something of the pattern of friendship, community participation, and sense of identity of these Chinese.

The Chinese of Long Island[14]

Miss Kuo studied two social clubs: *The Circle* and *The Center on Long Island*. These serve a dispersed membership in various suburbs within commuting distance of New York City. The families live in Anglo neighborhoods and represent the same socioeconomic status as their neighbors. The informants report no incidents of hostility. Miss Kuo attributes this in part to the fact that they are dispersed rather than heavily concentrated. Furthermore she emphasizes three other factors that gain them acceptance: they maintain an appropriate style of life consistent with their neighbors; their children are well behaved and often achieve high academic status in school; they are courteous in their attitudes and behavior toward their neighbors.

The Circle is a women's club of about 70 members. It is composed of a young group (average age 30) of American-born Chinese who are teachers, social workers, and white-collar workers. Their husbands have occupations that are skilled, professional, or business. Miss Kuo estimates their average annual income for the family to be about $10,000. Some of these women are college educated. This club has a typical American cast. It provides social events for adults, teenagers, and children; it raises scholarship funds for able young Chinese Americans.

Most of the members of *The Circle* did not grow up in Chinatown. English is the first language for them, though many can speak Chinese to elders or relatives in Chinatown. Most of their parents were skilled workers. In their homes, only English is spoken. They share the American dream of mobility, have aspirations for their children, and have frequent contacts and some friendships with other Americans.

We see this group of American Chinese, then, to be like any other mobile descendents of immigrants in their values and their behavior. Their need to form a "circle," however, suggests that on the one hand they are aware of themselves as a distinct minority and find pleasure and security in associations with people of their own ethnic background and similar socioeconomic level.

[14]Chia Ling Kuo, "The Chinese on Long Island: A Pilot Study," *Phylon*, Autumn, 1970. By permission of the author.

The Center has about a hundred members, men and their wives of a more successful stratum. They are a more recent migration, persons who came from China to the United States for advanced training and could not return after the fall of the Nationalist government. They are of upper-middle class and upper-class origin in China and have maintained or improved their status in America. (This organization does not include the most elite of the New York Chinese such as Pei, the architect, or Tsai, the eminent member of the New York Stock Exchange.) Nevertheless they are engineers, professors, managers and owners of small factories, consultants, and accountants.

The Center consciously works to further Chinese-American cultural relations. The programs are designed on the one hand to widen the membership's knowledge and appreciation of American culture, and on the other hand, to acquaint the American-born children and the non-Chinese community with Chinese art, philosophy, drama, and the classical Chinese language.

According to Miss Kuo this group is unevenly acculturated. Those who were upper class in origin, or who were raised in the large coastal cities of China, or who were raised in Christian high schools and universities are the most acculturated because of early and constant exposure to Western culture in China. Those who belong to only one or none of these categories are still in the process of acculturation. Most of the men associate with non-Chinese at work. They are active in local civic organizations. Eighty per cent of the women are active in church groups. In their daily life they live like other Americans of similar economic status. Since they are a more highly trained group than the young members of *The Circle* they are in a higher income bracket, have larger and better furnished homes, celebrate American New Year with open house for their neighbors, take up tennis, swimming, dancing. They feel they have not encountered prejudice, but they are more ethnocentric in their attempts to preserve for their children and communicate to the non-Chinese community their regard for scholastic achievement, filial piety, harmony, and compromise in human relations as presented in Confucian ethics. Although these families speak English at home, and their children, who go to private schools and Ivy League colleges do not speak Chinese, their children are more familiar with Chinese history and culture than the children of the American-born group studied.

Miss Kuo concludes that the Chinese on Long Island are partially integrated into American life through formal group participation; that those with high technical skills are structurally assimilated regardless of degree of acculturation; and the Chinese desire for complete assimilation is real despite the fact that at present they will seek primary-group contacts among themselves.

THE NEW MIGRATION

When the immigration law was modified in 1965 to eliminate nationality quotas there was an immediate upsurge of Chinese immigration, principally from the port of Hong Kong. Some of these were well-off and had capital and/or family assistance to establish themselves well in the United States. Others were wives and children of men already here, often long here. Still others had spent some time in the refugee camps of Hong Kong and were hoping after a second migration to find some way to independence. Some were unattached youth.

The impact of the 1965 changes in the immigration law can be seen from the following table.

TABLE 13-2   CHINESE ANNUAL IMMIGRATION, 1961–1970

	China Born*	Hong Kong Born**
1960–1961	3,213	
1961–1962	4,017	
1962–1963	4,658	
1963–1964	5,009	
1964–1965	4,057	717
1965–1966	13,736	4,072
1966–1967	19,741	5,355
1967–1968	12,738	3,696
1968–1969	15,440	5,453
1969–1970	14,093	

*Annual Reports of Immigrational and Naturalization Service, Washington, D.C.
**Figures from Bay Area Social Planning Council, Oakland, California, February 1971, "Chinese Newcomers in San Francisco."

Beginning February 1971 the first Chinese refugees were admitted under the "conditional entrant" program. A total of 10,200 visa numbers are reserved for Eastern hemisphere countries under the seventh preference category of the revised immigration law for certain political refugees or refugees from catastrophic natural calamity. How much this will effect an increase in entrance of Chinese will depend on economic conditions in Hong Kong, particularly, and other areas of Chinese dispersion, and on economic conditions in the United States, especially in San Francisco, New York, and Los Angeles.

Family to the Chinese means clan, so that clan members of the same surname, through the family associations were able to assist migration under preference quotas for relatives. Many of the early migrants immediately after the change of the law (1966–1967) came with high hopes and great myths about the golden land of opportunity. But if they did not speak English they of necessity settled in the Chinatowns of the large cities. As the influx continued exaggerated estimates of the numbers circulated. In San Francisco it was claimed that they were coming in at the rate of 8,000 annually, though subsequent research placed the number at 2,500 to 3,000.[15] The occasion for these rumours was, of course, the pressure of new population on the already inadequate resources of these urban sub-communities: housing, employment, and schools which not only had new population problems, but also language problems. Language was, of course also a barrier to adults seeking employment outside Chinese enterprises. A phenomenon of earlier European migrations emerged: the exploitation of newcomers by their own ethnic group. For a time and still to some extent employers took advantage of the language handicap and unfamiliarity with America to pay seriously substandard wages. Government action has brought considerable improvement.

There have also been difficulties for youth, particularly the older unattached youth. Gangs have formed. For a time most of the gang fights were between overseas-born and American-born youths. In New York, in 1972 more trouble arose on the interethnic front as Chinese and Puerto Rican youths crowded each other. Chinese culture is age-graded and when these youths fail to show respect and good behavior their sponsors, and even their parents if they have them, wash their hands of them.[16]

CHINATOWN FACES THE FUTURE

The older leadership in America's Chinatowns have been confused and anxious at the changes that confront them. By both

[15]Bay Area Social Planning Council, "Chinese Newcomers in San Francisco," February, 1971, (offset) p. 63.
[16]For a comparison see Pei-Ngor Chen, "The Chinese Community in Los Angeles," *Social Casework*, Vol. 51, No. 10, Dec. 1970.

choice and necessity the Chinese sub-community was for decades an enclosed society that "took care of its own." Only occasional Anglo social agencies have provided services, though some fringe settlement houses and some churches have been active with a small proportion of Chinatown residents. Now, however, the problems are too severe for the old structures to be effective. The family associations are declining in strength as younger more successful members move out into the larger American world. Most of the affluent whose businesses are located in Chinatown do not live there. The Anglo type of community organization is alien. A middle-age leadership potential exists, but is viewed skeptically and sabotaged by the older traditionalists. Students, both moderate and radical try "to do something" for Chinatown, but these are of necessity shoestring efforts.

Politically the older leadership is strongly emotionally, and often financially, tied to Taiwan. There has been strong anti-mainland-China propaganda. The new relation of the United States to China heightens anxiety among members of the old power structure. Nevertheless they are changing slowly in their community involvement. Whether they will change fast enough to retain leadership in the next decade is a moot question. They are after all upheld by their far flung associations, family and merchant, that tie together the interests of the overseas Chinese from Singapore to Capetown to Berlin to London and to the Western hemisphere. For the present they cannot be bypassed, and this keeps efforts for indigenous community development fractured and retarded. The Chinese are not a large enough minority, numerically, to have much leverage for public funds from the limited pool available to aid deteriorating central cities.

Interethnic Relations

On the whole the Chinese are cautious about people who are foreign to them. Even those who came originally from poor peasantry are aware of the greatness of Chinese civilization and draw pride from this. Good conduct, hard work, and controlled behavior are the ideals for interpersonal relations. For this reason they often devalue people from more expressive cultures. In New York the least liked by the Chinese are the Puerto Ricans, but this is also exacerbated by competition for jobs and housing as overcrowded Chinatown has had to spill over into surrounding areas. There is some unease about black militancy, though often friendliness toward blacks. Chinese, however, are opposed to bussing and do not want school integration.

For the Chinese who have moved away from Chinatown the future is reasonably open. For a generation now there has been little discrimination for qualified white-collar or professional personnel. On a neighborhood level they are still perhaps not very well incorporated and many still seek their friends and buy their groceries on Sunday in Chinatown.

In a ranking of acceptable social associates, Anglos in a small California city found Chinese more acceptable than Japanese, Mexican, or Negroes, but less acceptable than Jews or American Indians.[17]

The decade of the 1970s should bring considerable change for the Chinese American minority, especially in the large Chinatowns. In San Francisco there have been excellent planning studies and hearings before the State Labor Department on minimum wage violations. In New York there is greater voter registration. A Chinatown Foundation has been set up as a vehicle to receive funds for special projects, the first being a state-financed language center. The International Ladies Garment Workers Union is also teaching English to workers in the unionized shops of Chinatown's expanding garment industry. A youth group has set up an information center, is developing programs in the arts, and is taping the history of Chinatown as remembered by the older residents. Some of the newer approaches to community problems are beginning to be developed with increasing participation of Chinese as paraprofessionals or as volunteers. Yet the problems will persist because of the steady migration unless there is a wider and stronger involvement of the better-established Chinese, and this may depend upon the outcome of the present struggles for leadership.

Suggested Readings

Barth, Gunther. *Bitter Strength: A History of the Chinese in the United States, 1850–1870*. Cambridge, Mass.: Harvard University Press, 1964.

[17]Robin M. Williams, Jr., *Strangers Next Door* (Englewood Cliffs, N.J.: Prentice-Hall, Inc.), p. 72.

A vivid account of the life conditions and work conditions of Chinese in the U.S. in the period of heaviest nineteenth-century migration, with excellent source materials.

Hsu, Francis L. K. *Under the Ancestors' Shadow: Chinese Culture and Personality.* New York: Columbia University Press, 1948.
An anthropological study of a West China town; a rich analysis of the role of tradition and accomodations to the present (1937).

Lee, Rose Hum. *The Chinese in the United States of America.* Hong Kong: Hong Kong University Press, 1960. Distributed in the United States by Oxford University Press, New York.
The most comprehensive and informative single volume on the Chinese in the United States.

McWilliams, Carey. *Brothers Under the Skin.* Boston: Little, Brown and Co., 1943.
A summary of dominant actions against Chinese, especially on the West coast.

14 The Japanese in the United States Mainland[1]

In recent years, most writing about Japanese Americans describes their position in terms of a "success story" and with a substantial basis in fact as this chapter will show. As an introduction, it is instructive to compare their experience in mainland United States with the Chinese. Like the Chinese on the mainland, the Japanese settled on the West Coast but in a more stable period in that region's history. Thus, disregarding for the moment the special indignities they suffered as racially kin to an enemy nation in World War II, they were spared much of the physical violence perpetrated on the Chinese in more lawless frontier days.

Although most of the Chinese remained on the West Coast, a considerable number scattered in cities throughout the northern part of the country. But up to the time of their relocation the Japanese remained more highly concentrated in the Pacific Coast states. While the Chinese reacted to native opposition with extreme passivity, the Japanese were less tractable. They held their ground, refusing to disperse like the Chinese, and made ingenious adaptations to the various economic discriminations inflicted on them, such as having an alien father buy land in the name of his native-born son. Consequently, while the native population came to think of the Chinese in stereotype A—the inferior, humble, and ignorant, who could be condescendingly tolerated—the Japanese

[1]We confine this chapter to the mainland Japanese and disregard the Japanese in Hawaii because there are too many differences in the situation to deal with them both in the same chapter.

came to be treated according to stereotype B—the aggressive, cunning, and conspiratorial, requiring other means by dominants to keep them "in their place."

While the Japanese, like the Chinese, retained a greater interest in their homeland, they were not as "sojourner" oriented as the Chinese. Most of the Japanese immigrants expected to stay. This is one reason why the Japanese population in the United States (see Table 14-2) shows an almost steady rise while up to 1930, as we have seen, that of the Chinese showed years of decline. Finally, both groups suffered from the humiliation of severe legislative discrimination, culminating in drastic restrictive immigration. The manner, however, of handling the federal restrictions was noticeably more diplomatic in the case of the Japanese, a contrast attributable to the greater power of the Japanese government, able to protest more effectively against discriminatory treatment of their nationals in this country than the Chinese.

JAPANESE POPULATION TRENDS

For over 200 years, from 1638 to 1868, Japanese citizens were forbidden to go abroad, and foreigners, with few exceptions, were forbidden to enter Japan. The first to go out from the Land of the Rising Sun were students sent to gain knowledge from the rest of the world. Soon after, a limited number of laborers were permitted to leave. But it was the agreement signed by the Japanese government and certain Hawaiian sugar plantation owners in 1885 by which Japanese contract laborers were permitted to go to Hawaii that set emigration into momentum. From then until 1924 there was considerable Japanese migration to Asiatic Russia (302,946), to Hawaii (238,758), to the United States (196,543), and to China (105,258); and, in more limited numbers, to Canada, Brazil, the Philippines, Peru, Korea, and Australia. Considering the enormous rate of population growth in Japan during these decades and the consequent population pressure, this modest amount of emigration is surprising. Failure to emigrate in larger numbers to areas of the world settled by Europeans was due in part to the unfriendly manner with which the Japanese were received and to legal restrictions imposed. The special circumstances leading to substantial Japanese immigration to Hawaii are discussed in Chapter 15.

With overlapping in the 1881–1890 decade, Japanese immigration to continental United States takes on where Chinese immigration falls off. Tables 14-1 and 14-2, show the number of Japanese immigrants admitted from 1861–1970 and the total Japanese population, at the decennial years.

TABLE 14-1   JAPANESE IMMIGRATION TO THE UNITED STATES*

1961–1970	39,128
1951–1960	46,250
1941–1950	1,555
1931–1940	1,948
1921–1930	33,462
1911–1920	83,837
1901–1910	129,797
1891–1900	25,942
1881–1890	2,270
1871–1880	149
1861–1870	186

*Immigration Reports of the Immigration and Naturalization Service: Immigration, by country, by decades, Table 4.

The increase in the Japanese population from 1880 to 1910 was due largely to immigration itself, since the great preponderance of the newcomers were male. After the agitation on the West Coast for restricting Japanese immigration, President Theodore Roosevelt negotiated directly with the Japanese government, and the so-called Gentleman's Agreement was made in 1907. It provided that Japan would not issue passports for the continental United States unless the persons were coming to resume a formerly acquired domicile, to join a parent, husband, or child, or to resume control of a farming enterprise which they had left. This agreement did not completely close the door to Japanese immigration, and the growth of population was due partly to that continued, though greatly diminished, immigration. More significant, however, is the fact that many immigrants after 1907 were women, frequently "picture brides." By 1930 the sex ratio among the Japanese on the mainland had declined to 143.3 males for every 100 females—much more normal than that of the Chinese. The only decennial decline in Japanese population occurred in the 1930–1940 decade, when the number of returning homeland immigrants (8,000) exceeded the new immigrants (2,000) entering. This trend apparently continued up to the time of Pearl Harbor, since the estimated population in 1942 was only 122,000.

As Table 14-2 shows, the population of Americans of Japanese descent on the mainland has continued to increase, reaching 373,983 in 1970.[2] The surprising mainland increase in the 1950–1970 decades cannot be accounted for by births or by the allocation to Japan of an annual quota of 185 for the first time under the McCarran-Walter Immigration Act in 1952. It is largely due to the admission of wives of male American citizens, Oriental or Caucasian. From 1961 to 1965, of the 19,126 Japanese immigrants admitted to the country, 13,601, or 68 per cent, were wives of American citizens.[3] The mainland population was further raised by substantial migration from Hawaii to the mainland.

TABLE 14-2   JAPANESE POPULATION IN MAINLAND UNITED STATES*

Census Year	Number	Decade	Percentage Rate of Increase
1970	373,983*	1960–70	43.4*
1960	260,887*	1950–60	83.3*
1950	141,768	1940–50	11.6
1940	126,947	1930–40	−13.1
1930	138,834	1920–30	25.1
1920	111,010	1910–20	53.8
1910	72,157	1900–10	196.6
1900	24,326	1890–00	1,093.0
1890	2,039	1880–90	1,277.7
1880	148	1870–80	169.1
1870	55	1860–70	
1860	0		

*Source: *United States Census,* Population Characteristics By Race of Non-White Population. Based on mainland figures subtracting Hawaii. Including Hawaii the Japanese population was 591,290 in 1970 and 464,332 in 1960. Before 1950 the Hawaiian population was not included in the total but listed under a separate table of the population of the territories. The percentage rates of increase for the total U.S. Japanese population including Hawaii for 1960–1970 decade was 27.4 per cent; for the 1950–1960 decade, 27.2 per cent.

The high concentration on the West Coast has remained only slightly diminished up to the present. In 1940, 88 per cent of the then 127,000 mainland Japanese resided in this region. California alone had 83 per cent, and most of these were in the Los Angeles area. Outside the West Coast, only New York and Chicago had substantial Japanese sub-communities. The New York sub-com-

[2]Figure obtained by subtracting the Japanese in Hawaii in 1970 (217,307) from the total Japanese population of the United States (591,290). See note in Table 14-2.
[3]Annual Reports of Immigration and Naturalization Service.

munity had, at the outbreak of World War II, declined from an earlier peak of 5,000 to 2,000.[4]

In 1970 64 per cent of the mainland population was still on the West Coast. Adding Hawaii's Japanese, only 20 per cent of the total national Japanese population is outside the West. Chicago was the main non-Western city where the Japanese community permanently gained in size from the relocation of internees.

THE ESTABLISHMENT OF DOMINANCE

The Characteristics of the Immigrant Japanese

The Japanese immigrants were Mongoloid in "racial type" and therefore easily identifiable as different by white Americans, even though not always distinguishable physiognomically from other Asians.

The culture in which the Japanese immigrants had been reared differed more markedly from that of America than the culture of the European immigrants; yet in some aspects it prepared the Japanese for more successful adjustment to life in this country. Before the period of Japanese immigration, Japan had begun transforming itself from a semifeudal into a modern industrial nation. Thus its culture was a mixture of the traditional and the new. Basic in its traditional culture was the intricate set of mores which defined the strong obligation of the individual to the group, to the family, to those of superior class, and to the state. The authoritarian character of Japanese social organization produced markedly obedient and self-effacing personality traits. The strong sense of subordination of the individual to the welfare of the group was reflected in the solidarity of Japanese sub-communities in this country. Deriving also from long tradition was the intricate pattern of etiquette and ritual which prescribed the proper way of behaving in every situation. To conform punctiliously to these elaborate social rituals was a major drive in the Japanese personality, accounting for the reputation for courtesy and good manners which the nineteenth-century Japanese acquired.

The ferment of rapid change had begun in earnest at the beginning of the Meiji Era (1868–1912). The conscious policy of

[4]Bradford Smith, *Americans from Japan* (Philadelphia: J. B. Lippincott Co., 1948), p. 336.

the ruling elite was to transform Japan into an industrial nation with Western technological methods under a centralized government. To the already great skill in farming, necessitated by population pressure and little tillable acreage, new scientific agricultural methods were added. Public education was developed to a high level. The development of scientific medicine and programs of public health were encouraged. While it is difficult to know how much all these new influences affected the mass of the Japanese people, nevertheless, in the willingness to learn and to experiment in matters technological and economic, the Japanese did surpass not only all other Asians but many European immigrant groups.

Native Reaction to the Japanese

The West Coast region to which the Japanese first came was greatly undersettled and provided economic opportunity for population growth and economic development with many menial jobs to be filled. The Japanese were therefore welcomed by the natives in the capacity of laborers. At first Japanese were employed in domestic service. As their numbers increased, some engaged in a wide variety of menial jobs and others began to operate small shops. Since their numbers were small and the jobs they took did not affect the employment opportunities of white American workers, little opposition was felt. Beginning about 1890, however, antagonism began to be displayed by members of labor unions. In that year Japanese cobblers were attacked by members of the shoemakers' union. In 1892, a Japanese restaurant in San Francisco was attacked by members of the local cooks' and waiters' union.[5] From then on, anti-Japanese activity grew steadily in California, rising to a climax in the famous School Board Affair in 1906, when the San Francisco Board of Education passed a resolution requiring the segregation of all Oriental children in one school. At the time there were ninety-three Japanese attending twenty-three different public schools of San Francisco. The resolution brought protest from the Japanese government and precipitated a crisis between the Imperial Government and that of the United States, which led to the signing of the Gentleman's Agreement in 1907.

The rising antagonism toward the Japanese in the cities led

---

[5]Yamato Ichihashi, *Japanese in the United States* (Stanford: Stanford University Press, 1932), pp. 229–230.

them to turn to agriculture.[6] They started out as farm laborers and by the late 1890s outnumbered the Chinese laborers. By 1909 they constituted a large part of the farm labor force in the Western states. It was natural for the Japanese to turn to agriculture. They brought with them knowledge of intensive cultivation of the soil superior to that of many American native farmers. It was likewise natural that more and more of them should aspire to operate farms themselves. By 1909 there were 6,000 Japanese operating farms, the greater number by far as tenants.[7] They experimented with small-scale farming, finally concentrating on fruits and vegetables. They were adaptable, thrifty, and industrious, and the number of Japanese-operated farms increased until 1920.[8]

The success of the Japanese in moving from laborer to entrepreneur, even though on a small scale and usually involving the payment of rent to white owners, led to opposition from white farmers, culminating in the passage in California of the first alien land holding act in 1913. Under this legislation, aliens ineligible for citizenship could lease agricultural land for periods not to exceed three years but could not own it. When it was discovered that the Japanese were buying stock in land-owning corporations and acquiring land in the name of their native-born children, further pressure resulted in a new act, which in substance prohibited the leasing of land by any method by Japanese foreign-born. Similar laws were passed by other Western states, and their constitutionality was upheld by the United States Supreme Court in a test case in 1923. From then on the role of the Japanese in agriculture declined, and return to the cities increased. Nevertheless, at the time of Pearl Harbor they controlled large segments of California's berry and vegetable crops.

THE STABILIZATION OF DOMINANCE

Adjustment of the Japanese as a Minority: The Issei[9]

As with all immigrant groups, the Japanese reacted to minority status by forming separate sub-communities which were a mixture of Old World traits and accommodative institutions. On

[6]*Ibid.*, see Chs. 11, 12, 13, for an account of the progress of the Japanese in American agriculture.
[7]*Ibid.*, p. 178.
[8]*Ibid.*, p. 193.
[9]For convenience, we use the Japanese designation *Issei* for the foreign born; *Nisei*, for the first American born; and *Sansei* for the second and later genera-

the West Coast the main little Tokyo's were in San Francisco, Los Angeles, and Seattle. For the latter, Miyamoto made an extensive study at the end of the 1930s from which we draw.[10]

> The traditional heritage was most clearly seen in continuance of the patriarchal Japanese family, with its extreme emphasis on male authority and filial obligations. In recreation likewise, their play life tended "to revolve about activities that are essentially Japanese in character." The two Japanese daily newspapers in Seattle in 1935 were heavily devoted to activities of the homeland, and few of the foreign-born Japanese read American papers.
>
> Among the accommodative institutions were the economic "pools," the *Tanamoshi*. While 31 per cent of the Japanese were in domestic service and 45 per cent in the trades, there were a substantial number operating small mercantile establishments of their own. But few could accumulate enough capital for these ventures; it required the help of friends and relatives for the start. Often kinfolk formed pools from which various members could draw in initiating new enterprises. Seattle's Japanese had a local branch of the Japanese Chamber of Commerce (*Ken-Jin*) which served social and charitable functions, as well as acting as an agency of social control throughout the Japanese community and representing it in its relations to the larger community.
>
> The high value which Japanese placed on education served to accelerate acculteration. While most of the immigrants themselves lacked higher education, they encouraged their children not only to continue school but also to excel in their studies. Strong parental discipline reinforced the authority of the school. Between 1930 and 1937 in the nine Seattle high schools fifteen Japanese students were either valedictorians or salutatorians of their classes.
>
> In religion, it is somewhat striking to note that 1,200 Seattle Japanese belonged to Christian churches in 1936, more than belonged to all the Japanese religious groups combined. Miyamoto suggests that the many practical services rendered by the mission churches encouraged Japanese membership.

The American-Born Japanese: The Nisei

The increasing acculturation of the Nisei developed cleavages in the closely integrated and self-sufficient Japanese community

---

tions of native born. In addition, the term *Kibei* is used for those American-born who were sent to Japan for their more advanced education. Hereafter these terms will not be italicized.
[10]Shataro Frank Miyamoto, *Social Solidarity among the Japanese in Seattle*, University of Washington Publications in the Social Sciences, Vol. 11, No. 2 (Dec. 1939), pp. 57–130.

life. Cultural conflict similar to that noted in the European groups produced similar strains in family life. The younger Japanese considered their parents "too Japanesy" and began to defy their attempts to discipline them according to the traditional family pattern. The children became interested in American sports, desired freedom in their out-of-school life, and wanted to dress in the fashion of their white schoolmates. For the parents this Americanization brought much sorrow. They could not understand that this desire on the part of their children to act like Americans was dictated by the wish to be accepted as Americans.

The typical conflict between generations among immigrant groups was made more intense for the Japanese by the unusual age distribution of their population. Wide disparity in the sex ratio of the Issei resulted in a great preponderance of males in the older generation. The second generation was proportionately small, and not until the third generation was a more balanced sex ratio present. "As late as 1940, only 27,000 of the 80,00 Nisei were over twenty-one."[11] Many Japanese parents sent their children to Japan to be educated. In 1942 it was estimated that at least 25,000 United States citizens of Japanese ancestry had been educated in schools in Japan. Among these kibei, as they were designated, were the Japanese considered most probably disloyal in sentiment at the time of Pearl Harbor.

As with the Chinese, the conflict of the generations, typical in immigrant patterns, had a different sequel from that of the European nationalities. Anxious as the Nisei were to become Americans and forget Japan, they found that, despite their acculturation, the native community looked upon them as "Japs" because of their "racial" visibility. They continued to be discriminated against in three areas—employment, public places, and social contacts.

In employment the educated Nisei had three choices. He could accept prejudice for what it was, and assume the inferior tasks of houseboy, dishwasher, migratory laborer, cannery hand—just what the dominant group expected of him as an inferior. He could go to Japan and forsake America. Or, if he tried, he could sometimes get a job at a higher level, though far below his actual qualifications.

Many barbershops, restaurants, and hotels refused service to Orientals. Several large coastal cities had restrictive covenants which kept the Japanese out of attractive neighborhoods. And there was discrimination in the social sphere.

[11]Bradford Smith, *Americans from Japan,* p. 245.

The fear of rebuffs, the constant horror of being humiliated in public, made the Nisei draw together in a tight circle, even at college. . . . [Such] organizations only perpetuated their difficulties. They formed noticeable groups on campus. "There's a barrier between Nisei and the other students," said one. "You can feel it. They never feel easy with each other."

Hostility in the social sphere did not as a rule become noticeable until adolescence. The fear of "miscegenation," the old superstitions about racial "hybrids," the fear that friendship might be construed as having a sexual intent introduced at the courting age, a stiffening of attitudes, yet the Nisei were quite as set against intermarriage as the Caucasians, their own fears and superstitions as deeply rooted.[12]

EVACUATION AND RELOCATION: A CASE HISTORY IN WHITE AMERICAN DOMINANT BEHAVIOR

The stabilized accommodation of the Issei-Nisei generations was rudely shattered by Pearl Harbor. On February 19, 1942, the Army was given authority to establish military zones from which any persons, citizens or aliens, might be evacuated and excluded. All Japanese people were ordered to leave the West Coast. This action was the most unprecedented single national action against a large group of people in American history. Analysis of its causes provides insight into the dynamics of dominant-minority relations in the United States. (We shall return to this after carrying forward an account of what happened to the Japanese after February 19.)

At first the Japanese were given time to remove themselves. A few did leave, but soon discovered that they were not wanted elsewhere. A report from the *Los Angeles Times*, March 24, 1942, reads, "Japanese evacuees moving inland from California in a great mass migration will be put in concentration camps if they enter Nevada, Governor E. P. Carville warned tonight." Therefore the Japanese were ordered to stay where they were pending their mass evacuation under military supervision. A new federal agency, The War Relocation Authority, was established to plan for the supervision of the Japanese under detention. Between then and August 8, all West Coast Japanese (over 110,000) were transferred to ten hastily built centers in the Rocky Mountain states and in Arkansas.

[12]*Ibid.*, p. 250. By permission.

In addition to the shocklike psychological effect and the bitterness which evacuation engendered, the Japanese faced enormous economic losses. While the government took steps to protect the material property owned by the Japanese, the guarantees appeared so uncertain that many sold their effects—under the circumstances, of course, at a loss. A business enterprise and a crop in the field could not be "frozen." They had to be disposed of for whatever they would bring at hurried sale or lease, or be abandoned.

Life in the Settlement Centers

The War Relocation Authority faced a unique problem in American history. The policy of the WRA was to organize the community life with maximum self-control by the Japanese. All the evidence indicates that the personnel were highly sympathetic to the Japanese, an attitude criticized by the same elements of the white population that had clamored for evacuation. As was almost inevitable under such circumstances, a number of rebellious activities followed. Of these the most serious was a strike by some evacuees at Poston Center, Arizona, arising out of a feeling that two alleged attackers of a white official had been unfairly punished. In consequence of incidents of this nature, Tule Lake Center, California, became a segregation camp where active malcontents from all other centers were placed and controlled under strict discipline.

Resettlement

The other branch of the WRA's operation was engaged through regional offices throughout the nation in trying to find employment for the Nisei outside the center. The WRA also assumed responsibility for helping the resettler adjust to his new community, as well as to his job. One of its hardest tasks in this connection was to find a place for him to live. Its activities beginning in the spring of 1943 included the resettlement of a few Japanese particularly in the Midwest and the Mountain States. Lack of extensive resettlement in the East was due to Army opposition. Most of those leaving the camps were young adult Nisei who, when they became successfully resettled, often sent for relatives to join them. In the large metropolitan centers it was fairly easy to place Japanese in a wide range of menial and semitechnical jobs. It was difficult to place them in industries with war contracts or in positions calling for contact with the public. Frequent opposition from unions arose. Among the reasons often given for not hiring the Japanese were distrust of their loyalty, the fact that other employers would resent it, that customers would resent it, and that "my son is in the Pacific." Many of the resettlers left their jobs because of their interest in finding work where they could acquire new skills.[13]

Up to January 1, 1945, the date after which evacuees were permitted to return to the West Coast, the WRA had resettled 31,625 Japanese in other parts of the country. Interestingly enough, when the opportunity came, the vast majority of the evacuees returned to their former communities. Since the date for terminating the WRA had been set, their choice had to be quick and the WRA was no longer able to give them individual assistance.

Analysis

As we have noted, the evacuation of all persons of Japanese ancestry from the West Coast and their subsequent internment was a government action without precedent in American history, involving constitutional issues of grave significance. The Supreme Court of the United States upheld the constitutionality of evacuation in wartime,[14] although strong dissents were written by a minority of the justices. However, in retrospect, the whole incident appears to have been a serious error in judgment. For this reason some analysis of the circumstances which led to the steps taken is highly pertinent to the study of dominant-minority relations. The central question is this: To what extent was the decision for evacuation and internment of the Japanese arrived at as a logical necessity for national security, or to what extent was the decision made in response to regional pressures unrelated to security?

THE MILITARY'S JUDGMENT   Since the Western Defense Command of the United States Army was responsible for the decision, it is appropriate to consider first the case which it presented to justify its role in evacuation as presented in its final report.[15]

[13]The authors are indebted to Gordon Berryman, a former employee of the WRA, for sharing these insights into the resettlement process.
[14]*Koramatsu* v. *United States*, 323, U.S. 214. The decision came after the internment was over.
[15]"Need for Military Control and for Evacuation," *Final Report, Japanese Evacuation from the West Coast* (Washington, D.C.: Government Printing Office, 1943), pp. 7–19.

This document referred to as fact some illegal signaling from shore to sea on the West Coast, although it presented no specific proof that Japanese were involved. It cited the result of one spot raid made by the Federal Bureau of Investigation on Japanese homes in which "more than 60,000 rounds of ammunition, and many rifles, shotguns, and maps of all kinds" were found. Such articles, as well as some others, had been declared contraband for enemy aliens. To what extent they were possessed by enemy aliens or by American citizens of Japanese ancestry and to what extent the articles found were evidence of conspiracy is not stated. The report indicated that in three instances in which Japanese submarines shelled West Coast areas, the particular spots chosen were the very ones most out of range of American coastal batteries at the time. It assumed that the Japanese Navy must have had "inside" information, although no evidence was presented to connect West Coast Japanese with this knowledge. The above is in substance the entire case made regarding acts of sabotage or espionage.

Much more of the case presented by the Western Defense Command concerning the security menace of the Japanese was based on the fact that the Japanese were in a position to do much damage and on the assumption that many of them would take such opportunities. The military authorities were much impressed by the residence distribution of the Japanese, which seemed too singularly adjacent to strategic points to be fully coincidental. Surprisingly enough for a military document, the report rested much of its case on sociological argument. Reference was made to "ties of race" as well as strong bonds of common traditional culture that made the Japanese a tightly-knit group. Major emphasis was placed on the considerable number of Japanese associations on the West Coast whose purposes and activities reflected great interest in the ancestral homeland and in some instances involved contributions in behalf of Japan's war with China. Finally, the report stressed and statistically verified the fact that a considerable number of the American-born Japanese had been educated in Japan and subsequently returned to live in the States. The military authorities conceded that many Japanese living in the country were loyal but felt that the task of screening the loyal from the disloyal presented too great a problem and therefore the only safe course was to evacuate everybody of Japanese ancestry.

The sociological observations just noted comprised facts about the Japanese in the United States well known to many people on the West Coast. The Japanese had been the subject of much detailed study by Pacific Coast social scientists long before Pearl Harbor. These students could have greatly assisted the military in making valid interpretations of Japanese society on the West Coast. Of this, Grodzins writes, "as later research has shown military officers did not in a single instance rely on the large mass of scientific materials that had been gathered about American Japanese by such men as Steiner, Park, Strong, Bogardus, and Bailey."[16]

Espionage and sabotage are inevitable concomitants of war. It is reasonable to suppose that some of the enemy aliens would be engaged in the task, though it is also logical to suppose that among the enemy agents would be some who were not Japanese at all. Even in the absence of much specific proof of disloyal behavior on the part of Japanese Americans, the general logic of the situation clearly called for special vigilance over this group by the agents of the Justice Department and prompt action against any particular individuals on reasonable suspicion. With such a policy, actually already in practice before evacuation orders, few Americans, and perhaps even few Americans of Japanese ancestry, would have quarreled. This was, indeed, the policy advocated by the Justice Department. As late as January 12, 1942, Attorney General Biddle said, "Wholesale internment, without hearing and irrespective of the merits of individual cases, is the long and costly way around, as the British discovered by painful experience; for by that method not only are guiltless aliens themselves demoralized, but the nation is deprived of a valuable source of labor supply at a time when every available man must be at work."[17]

The case submitted was highly unimpressive as a justification for such drastic action as mass evacuation. How then is the evacuation to be explained? We turn now to examine a number of factors in the situation.

PRESSURE GROUPS   Grodzins stresses the influence of pressure groups: "The most active proponents of mass evacuation were certain agricultural and business groups, chambers of commerce, the American Legion, the California Joint Immigration Committee, and the Native Sons and Daughters of the Golden West."[18] The list

[16]Morton Grodzins, *Americans Betrayed: Politics and the Japanese Evacuation* (Chicago: University of Chicago Press, 1949), p. 305.
[17]Alexander H. Leighton, *The Governing of Men* (Princeton University Press, 1945), p. 17.
[18]Grodzins, *Americans Betrayed*, p. 17.

of pressure groups can be divided into those with economic motivation for getting rid of the Japanese and those with a nativist, anti-foreign orientation. The following excerpt from a resolution adopted by an Oregon American Legion Post illustrates the sort of pressure that was exerted:

> [that] this is no time for namby-pamby pussyfooting. . . . that it is not the time for consideration of minute constitutional rights of those enemies but that it is time for vigorous, whole-hearted, and concerted action . . . toward the removal of all enemy aliens and citizens of enemy alien extraction from all areas along the coast and that only those be permitted to return that are able to secure special permit for that purpose.[19]

Ten Broeck and his associates[20] place greater responsibility on the commanding officer and his superiors, and on the people of the West Coast generally, among whom there was widespread fear caused by the war and Japan's early military successes.

In summary, we suggest that the evacuation resulted from the interaction of a series of factors: (1) the well-established pattern of dominant-minority relations, long nurtured throughout the history of the relations between native Americans and the Japanese on the West Coast; (2) the crisis of war, engendering fear of those racially identified with an enemy nation; (3) a situation ripe for special groups antagonistic to the Japanese to exploit; (4) the failure of liberal West Coast native Americans to bring sufficient counter-pressure; (5) the position of authority of a commanding officer with unsophisticated sociological judgment; and (6) the fact that higher federal officials had to make a decision while beset with the enormous burdens of conducting a war.

THE HAWAIIAN CONTRAST   It is instructive to conclude the discussion of the evacuation episode with a brief account of a contrasting situation in Hawaii.

At the outbreak of war with Japan, persons of Japanese ancestry comprised about a third of Hawaii's population. Following Pearl Harbor, rumors arose of espionage activities on the part of some island Japanese. Both the military and the insular authorities, failing to find specific evidence, placed their official weight

[19]*Ibid.*, p. 42. By permission.
[20]Jacobus Ten Broeck, Edward N. Barnhart, and Floyd W. Matson, *Prejudice, War, and the Constitution* (Berkeley and Los Angeles: University of California Press, 1954).

on the side of allaying the rumors and indicating their confidence in the loyalty of the Hawaiian Japanese as a group. Limited restrictions were imposed on the alien Japanese, and a few Japanese whose records before the war rendered them suspicious were interned. But some elements of the insular population who, fearful of the possible dangers from the Japanese, called for firmer action. As Lind indicates, there was an increase in public demonstrations against Japanese persons, apparently more from the Filipinos in Hawaii than from the white or other ethnic elements.[21] Nevertheless, the authorities held firm to their policy of vigilance over the Japanese and arrest of only those who acted in a suspicious manner. Fear of the Japanese subsided, and their relations to the rest of the archipelago's population resumed, in the main, their pre-war character. The soundness of the official judgment that the Japanese in general constituted no serious security threat to Hawaii was borne out by future events. Subsequent hearings on the charges of subversive activity by local Japanese brought forth emphatic denials from the War Department, the Federal Bureau of Investigation, and from various insular authorities.[22] On the whole, it can be said that the Japanese were cooperative in accepting the mild restrictions, continued their economic role in Hawaiian production, and ultimately made contributions to the armed services. "The final count of Hawaiian war casualties revealed that 80 per cent of those killed and 88 per cent of those wounded throughout the war were of Japanese ancestry.[23]

How can we account for the strikingly different policies adopted in Hawaii and on the West Coast? Contrary to what one might at first think, the much greater proportion of Japanese in the islands operated against a policy of internment. To have interned one-third of the population would have been a costly process. Furthermore, the removal of the Japanese from the labor force would have drastically reduced the productive capacity of Hawaii just when a maximum increase in production was essential to the war effort.

Underlying the more favorable treatments of the Japanese were certain facets of the general pattern of intergroup relations in Hawaii, which are discussed in more detail in Chapter 15. Here we briefly call attention to two factors which stand in sharp contrast to the West Coast situation. First, a less discriminatory pat-

[21]Andrew Lind, *Hawaii's Japanese* (Princeton University Press, 1948), pp. 56–61.
[22]*Ibid.*, pp. 38–47.
[23]*Ibid.*, p. 126.

tern of intergroup relations prevailed in Hawaii. Tradition frowned on any public or explicit color discrimination. Second, the economic position of the Japanese in Hawaii had developed few antagonisms based on competition. While by 1940 the Japanese as a group had moved far from their earlier role as plantation workers toward various city occupations, this transition had not yet brought them into much direct competition for jobs with the dominant white population.

The Effects of Evacuation

The short-range effects of the evacuation and temporary resettlement on the national welfare were costly indeed. Particularly segments of the West Coast population, as we have seen, made substantial gains out of removal of the Japanese. For these gains, the nation paid a heavy price. The removal of the Japanese retarded the war effort. While eventually many Japanese did find useful work during the war, they would have contributed more if they had remained where they were. In fact, there were so many high-paying opportunities in California created by the manpower shortage that many Mexicans and Negroes migrated there. The whole process of evacuation, the operation of the centers, and the effort of the WRA to relocate the evacuees cost time, money, and energy which could have been used to more constructive purpose.

The effect of the evacuation on the prestige of the United States in world opinion is difficult to appraise. Because of their imperialist activities in Asia, the Japanese abroad were much hated by many other Asian peoples. Nevertheless, the way in which the Japanese in this country were dealt with in contrast to the treatment of Germans and Italians reflected our color bias, and cannot have raised our moral stock with nonwhite people in general.

THE DECLINE OF DOMINANCE

Following the end of the evacuation order on January 1, 1945, the Japanese were free to go where they wanted. As we have seen, many returned to the West Coast. In 1960, the number of Japanese in the states of California, Washington, and Oregon accounted for 69 per cent of the mainland Japanese population. Since in 1940 as many as 88 per cent were concentrated on the West Coast, the difference reflects the dispersive effect of evacuation. The Los Angeles–Long Beach area, with 81,204 in 1960, had about one-third of all the Japanese on the mainland.

Economic Readjustment

Bloom and Riemer estimated the economic loss of the Japanese at $367,500,000, if income losses were added to all other losses: forced sale of their assets, loss of business goodwill, and other losses attendant on their rapid removal.[24] A sample survey of 206 Japanese American families found the median loss per family to be $9,870 at the 1941 value of the dollar.[25]

Some small part of this loss was compensated under an Act of Congress in July, 1948 (Public Law, 886, H. R. 2999), which empowered the Attorney General to reimburse any person not to exceed $2,500 for "damage to or loss of real or personal property . . . that is a reasonable and natural consequence of the evacuation." Claims had to be filed within eighteen months, and any claims for loss of anticipated profits or earnings were excluded. Evacuees filed 24,064 claims. By March 1, 1956, all but 1,936 had been adjusted and paid. Delayed settlements involved claims in excess of the original $2,500 limit. In 1956, Congress amended the act to permit settlement up to $100,000. Settling these claims involved the difficulty of proving the losses and few Japanese had obtained documentary proof of sale in anticipation of such indemnity. The last claim was settled in November, 1965; two of the original plaintiffs had died.[26]

The evacuation undermined the occupational position of the Japanese and forced readjustment upon return at lower socioeconomic levels. Few farmers could re-establish themselves, and produce dealers were far fewer than before the war. Many went into contract gardening, which provided a measure of the independence they formerly enjoyed. The great shortage of housing available for the Japanese increased the number of boarding and rooming houses where the Japanese who did have homes added to their income by charging high prices to fellow Japanese. The housing shortage also increased the number of returnees who went into domestic service, which often provided housing. In general, the pattern of employment for the returnees involved a shift from

[24]Leonard Bloom and Ruth Riemer, *Removal and Return* (Berkeley: University of California Press, 1949), pp. 202–204.
[25]*Ibid.*, p. 144.
[26]William Petersen, "Success Story: Japanese-American Style," *New York Times Magazine*, January 9, 1966, p. 33.

being either independently employed or working for other Japanese to working for non-Japanese employers.

Reaction of Dominant Americans

On the West Coast, knowledge that the Japanese were coming back evoked reaction from racist-minded groups that had been instrumental in causing their evacuation. The American Legion, Veterans of the Foreign Wars, Native Sons of the Golden West, the California Farm Bureau all protested. New "Ban the Jap" committees sprang up. A number of newspapers ran scare headlines which made many Californians uneasy. "Hood River had jumped the gun by erasing the names of its sixteen Nisei soldiers from the honor roll" [subsequently restored].[27] In the first half of 1945 more than thirty serious incidents occurred throughout California.

This time, however, there was a second set of reactions, which had been missing before. Many individuals and groups demanded that the Japanese be given fair play and became active in insisting that they get it. The Fresno Fair Play Committee organized to file eviction suits in behalf of those Japanese unable to move back into their former homes. When machinists of the San Francisco Municipal Railway threatened to strike in protest against the employment of a Nisei, Mayor Roger Lapham averted the strike by going to the shop in person and explaining to the men why the Nisei was entitled to the job. Churches up and down the Coast were focal points of support for the Nisei. This second reaction finally won out.

> The pressure of public opinion all over the country put California on the defensive. It came to a point where the civic pride of the several communities was challenged and race baiting lost favor. At the beginning of 1945 the West Coast papers had been four to one against the Japanese. A year later they were four to one in favor of fair and equal treatment.[28]

The Challenge to Dominance

The American Japanese have as a group made little active challenge to the minority status accorded them. As we have seen, as individuals the majority have been diligent and alert to take the opportunities not denied them to improve their welfare and to

[27]Bradford Smith, *Americans from Japan*, p. 346.
[28]*Ibid.*, p. 349. By permission.

rise in class status. While evacuation came as a shock, as a whole, they put up with it with unusual grace.[29] Mainland Japanese Americans have not been as active in politics as some other minorities and thus have not made maximum use of political pressure to improve their status, although a few Japanese have been elected to state offices in California from areas of heavy ethnic concentration.[30]

Various court decisions invalidating laws and practices which had discriminated against both the Japanese and the Chinese were handed down in 1948–1950. These included a California law which had prohibited fishing licenses to persons ineligible for citizenship; a California Supreme Court decision revoking the law against interracial marriage;[31] and decisions which reversed previous laws which had prevented foreign born Asians from renting or owning farm land.

The one important organization which acted in part to defend the interests of the Japanese against discrimination was the Japanese American Citizens League formed by the Nisei (succeeding the Issei Japanese Association). As time solved many of their ethnic group's problems JACL broadened its interests to include general community affairs, much like the Anti-Defamation League of Jewish Americans. This change facilitated the acculturative process.

THE RISE OF THE JAPANESE

Following this rapid change from the carry-over of native war time hostility against the Japanese toward friendly acceptance, their status has shown a rapid rise. Ironically, the abrupt break in their previous accommodation due to internment appears to have accelerated the process.[32] Leadership was transferred to the Nisei. During internment the Nisei often earned more money than the Issei working in the vicinity of camps, and the relocation of

[29]See Dorothy S. Thomas and Richard S. Nishimoto, *The Spoilage: Japanese American Evacuation and Resettlement* (Berkeley and Los Angeles: University of California Press, 1946.) An intensive study of those Japanese who became bitter enough to renounce their citizenship.
[30]Harry H. L. Kitano, *The Japanese Americans* (Englewood Cliffs, N.J.: Prentice Hall, Inc., 1969), p. 134. The first Japanese American, Norman Y. Mineta, to be elected mayor of a major mainland city, San Jose, California, took office in 1970. His election apparently had no connection with his race as only three per cent of San Jose's population was Japanese. *The New York Times*, Oct. 19, 1971.
[31]Later a decision of the United States Supreme Court declared any state laws against racial intermarriage illegal.
[32]Kitano, *The Japanese Americans*, p. 49.

many in Eastern cities hastened their acculturation to American life. A government survey reported "the institution of arranged marriages is very nearly out of the picture as far as Nisei are concerned.[33] Community managed schools were not reopened. The number of Japanese language newspapers was fewer than before the war.

Japanese Americans, 1970s: Success and Model

Japanese Americans are not only a successful ethno-racial group but are sometimes referred to as the "model American minority" (Kitano, p. 146).[34] While it is clear they are successful, one may still query whether they are still a "minority" in any other sense than numerical. Both their success and "model" Americanism will be developed under the following topics: (1) their high welfare; (2) their low rate of sociopathic deviance; (3) their development of a self-sustaining and well organized sub-communality and identity in no way conflicting with their Americanism; and (4) the decline in white discrimination.

WELFARE   Educational achievement in terms of school years completed shows Japanese far ahead of all other nonwhite groups, and considerably ahead of the total white population (Petersen pp. 114–116). The group has a lower death rate than the white population of the nation (Petersen, pp. 147–148). In income the Japanese ranked first among all nonwhite groups in California in 1960 (Kitano, p. 48), and they had a lower rate of unemployment (Petersen p. 132). "Mental disease is not a major problem for the Japanese" (Kitano, p. 125).

SOCIOPATHIC DEVIANCE: CRIME, DELINQUENCY, AND SUICIDE   Concerning crime, Kitano concludes, "First, the overall rate of crime is very low, and secondly, the trend for the Japanese adult is toward even lower rates. While non-Japanese rates continue to rise, the Japanese rates show a steady drop. . . ." (Kitano, p. 118). He likewise finds the same true with reference to juvenile delinquency (p. 119). Suicide rates among the Japanese Americans

---

[33]*People in Motion: The Postwar Adjustment of the Evacuated Japanese,* United States Department of Interior Publication (Washington, D.C.: Government Printing Office), p. 168.
[34]Our first reference to Harry H. L. Kitano, *Japanese Americans* contains full citation on p. 400. We shall use extensively both this and William Petersen, *Japanese Americans* (New York: Random House, 1971) and will immediately cite the author and the pages in parentheses rather than footnote.

are no higher than among majority Americans. This is especially interesting in view of the belief that in the traditional Japanese culture suicide, instead of being a sin as in Western culture, is not only proper but expected under certain selective circumstances. Kitano appears to doubt that it is socially acceptable in the present Japanese American culture at any rate (p. 100).

The Japanese American Sub-Community

Most Issei measure their success in terms of the success of their children, the Nisei, who despite the usual generational culture conflict have succeeded in developing a Japanese American sub-structure—organizational and cultural—often too American for their parents and too "Japanese" for their American peers. The network of organizations is designed on American models. "Family attitudes . . . are American, yet the sophisticated observer would notice a subtle lack of verbal exchange, a faintly "Japanese" climate here. The college professor, used to giving seminars to Caucasians, would tear his hair at the docile silence of a group of Nisei, yet the cheering and fighting at the Nisei basketball game is as rowdy as at any American game" (Kitano, p. 140).

This Japanese American sub-community is like most ethno-racial sub-communities—class differentiated—but class distinctions are far less effected. The gardener, the C.P.A., and the dentist may make up a threesome at golf. . . . The fairly affluent middle class engage in community service and for leisure often play golf and "take Las Vegas weekends" (Kitano, p. 141).

The smaller proportion of Nisei who have not obtained the typical middle-class status in their more menial occupations interact more with non-Japanese, but even they have not in general incorporated the way of life of other lower-class populations with whom they mingle.

While there are definitely local Japanese sub-communities, they are not spatially compact. But neither is the population randomly scattered. Outside of one main area, others usually live side-by-side in small pockets here and there.

Decline in Discrimination

It is unquestionably clear that white American discrimination against Japanese Americans on the mainland has markedly declined in recent years. Petersen finds it difficult to find data on discrimination other than that based on personal anecdotes (Petersen, pp. 116–117). In housing, a study made in 1956 in San Francisco found that 39 per cent of the sample said they had been discriminated against in seeking better homes against 56 per cent who said they had not been, often because they had not tried.[35] But ten years later Kitano summed up that "Housing is not a major problem for the Japanese" (p. 138). Occasional covert discrimination is found.

OUTMARRIAGE   The fact that intermarriage between mainland Japanese Americans and white Americans is small is questionable evidence of white racial discrimination because Japanese in-group pressure to marry within their own group continues to be strong. Kitano gives an estimate (p. 133) of 25,000 "War Brides" —Japanese women married to American G.I.'s as of 1960. One may well doubt that there were 25,000 additional Japanese-white marriages in the mainland at the same time. However, as the increasing number of Nisei and Sansei move upward, the numbers of suitable marital partners within their own class position will become inadequate and Japanese out-group marriages will increase. It seems clear that most white Americans are not disturbed about this particular interracial marriage.

SUMMARY OF ASSIMILATION OF MAINLAND JAPANESE

The current position of Japanese Americans with reference to assimilation is summarized by Kitano in Tables 14-3 and 14-4. Table 14-3 indicates that assimilation is still primarily cultural. Since it appears that white Americans no longer place obstacles to full assimilation, it may be suggested that the extent to which the Japanese on the mainland remain a distinctive ethno-racial subgroup is largely a matter of their own choice.[36] Table 14-4 indicates that mainland Japanese who live outside the West Coast area are less in-group isolated than the far larger proportion residing in that area. But the future belongs to the Sansei.

SANSEI   As yet, little systematic research on the Sansei is available, in part because they are a young group. Both Peterson and Kitano rely on observations highly weighted toward college

[35]Harry H. L. Kitano, "Housing of the Japanese-Americans in the San Francisco Bay Area," in Nathan Glazer and Davis McEntire, *Studies in Housing and Minority Groups* (Berkeley and Los Angeles: Univ. of California Press, 1960), p. 183.
[36]Perhaps the option to retain ethnic identity will be reinforced by the fact that this is generally the trend at present among many other non-Wasp groups.

TABLE 14-3   GORDON'S PARADIGM OF ASSIMILATION,* APPLIED TO
SELECTED JAPANESE GROUPS

Group	Type of Assimilation			
	Cultural	Structural	Marital	Identi-ficational
Issei	No	No	No	No
Nisei	Yes	No	No	No
Sansei	Yes	No	No	Partly
Kibei	Partly	No	No	No
Recent immigrants (1954 on) Issei	No	No	No	No
War Brides (married to non-Japanese)	Partly	Yes	Yes	Partly
Kai-sha, Students, and Visitors	No	Partly (by social class and by area)	No	No

*Milton M. Gordon, *Assimilation in American Life* (New York: Oxford University Press, 1964). See p. 76.
    Source: Harry H. F. Kitano, *Japanese Americans,* Appendix Table 11. Prentice-Hall, Inc., Englewood Cliffs, New Jersey, 1969.

TABLE 14-4   DEGREE OF JAPANESE ASSIMILATION BY AREA AND
TYPE

Area	Type of Assimilation				
	Cultural	Social-Marital	Occupa-tional	Housing	Political
California (West Coast)	Yes	No	Partly	Party	Beginning
Chicago (Midwest)	Yes	Beginning	Yes*	Yes*	No
New York-New England	Yes	Partly	Yes*	Yes*	No
Hawaii	Yes	Partly	Yes*	Yes*	Yes

*Substantially yes.
    Source: Harry H. F. Kitano, *Japanese Americans,* Appendix Table 12. © 1969. Reprinted by permission of the publisher, Prentice-Hall, Inc., Englewood Cliffs, New Jersey.

students who are nevertheless likely to be influential in determining the future course of American Japanese. Being a second or more native born generation, they are more acculturated. They have adopted forms of organization on the American model: Little

Leagues, fraternities, etc.; intermarriage is increasing though most prefer to marry Sansei; and "their education is job oriented" (Kitano, p. 142). Peterson observes that while "a sizable proportion of the Berkeley student body was involved in the riots of the 1960's" . . . (p. 142), few Japanese students were included. There are some indications that deviant behavior is increasing, though it is far less among them than the national average (Petersen, p. 208). Ironically, it may be that the further acculturation of the Japanese Americans will require moving *down* toward the more typical "norms" of many other American groups.

Earlier reference was made to the Japanese as a "model" ethno-racial group. But Kitano reminds us that this judgement is made from a majority viewpoint. The model is conservative. They have strongly adhered to the Puritan ethic both in its economic and sexual implications (at least behaviorally).

> Japanese Americans are good because they conform—they don't "make waves"—they work hard and are quiet and docile. . . . But, ideally members of the ethnic community should share in any evaluation of their adjustment.[37]

The author further points out that more individuality and originality and broader participation in the larger community life might well be more emphasized in their future development.

Japanese Americans and Racism

The most important contribution of the saga of mainland Japanese to a theory of intergroup relations concerns the concept of race and racism. The long held idea that race difference is an insurmountable barrier to assimilation has been substantially refuted by the Japanese in the United States. But "racism" is as much based on a syndrome of mythical beliefs in the minds of most dominants as it is founded upon measurable physical difference. That it can either be manufactured or developed to high salience when it suits the purpose of a powerful dominant has, ironically, been demonstrated in this century at the expense of the most "successful" minorities: mainland Japanese Americans and Jewish-Germans during World War II.

---

[37]Kitano, *The Japanese Americans.* By permission of the publisher, Prentice-Hall Inc., p. 146.

Suggested Readings

Caudhill, William and George De Vos. "Achievement, Culture, and Personality: The Case of Japanese Americans," *American Anthropologist,* 1956, 1102–1126.
An outstanding study of the Chicago Japanese in the 1950s.

Daniels, Roger. *The Politics of Prejudice: The Anti-Japanese Movement in California and the Struggle for Japanese Exclusion.* New York: Atheneum, 1970.
An historical study of the anti-Japanese movement from 1861 to the Japanese restrictive provisions of the Immigration Act of 1924.

Kitano, Harry H. L. "Japanese-American Crime and Delinquency," *The Journal of Psychology,* 1967, pp. 253–263.
A study of deviant behavior among Japanese Americans.

Kitigawa, Daisuke. *Issei and Nisei: The Internment Years.* New York: The Seabury Press, 1967.
A hard-hitting study of the internment years by a former Christian Japanese clergyman.

Ten Broeck, Jacobus, Edward N. Barnhart, and Floyd W. Matson. *Prejudice, War and the Constitution.* Berkeley and Los Angeles: University of California Press, 1954.
A scholarly account of the Japanese evacuation during World War II with special emphasis on legal aspects.

Thomas, Dorothy S. *The Salvage.* Berkeley: The University of California Press, 1962.
A scholarly account of the internment and restoration of the internees to normal community life.

Thomas, Dorothy S. and Richard S. Nishimoto. *The Spoilage: Japanese-American Evacuation and Resettlement.* Berkeley and Los Angeles: University of California Press, 1946.
An intensive study of those Japanese who became bitter enough about evacuation to renounce their citizenship.

15   The Peoples of Hawaii

Intergroup relations in Hawaii are so very different from any other state that to follow our usual scheme of treating American minority situations is difficult. With less than a million total population, Hawaii has the most heterogeneous ethno-racial composition of any state. Although the dominant status of the white people of Euro-American background over the peoples of Oriental origin was well established when Hawaii became American territory, intergroup relations have continuously been distinguished by the absence of any legal or public discrimination. Non-official discrimination, however, by the white residents against both the native Hawaiians and the successive immigrant groups has been evident. The absence of formal discrimination has led many writers and students to picture Hawaii as a paradise of interracial relations; the informal discrimination has led others to view it less favorably.

Ethno-racial Composition of Hawaii

Table 15-1 presents the official differentiation of Hawaii's population by ethno-racial components. However, the extensive interracial marriage which has taken place over the years makes the official tables highly artificial. Recognition of this was made in the 1970 Census when the distinction between Hawaiians and part-Hawaiians was finally given up. A large part of the 9.2 per cent of the state's population listed in the 1970 Census as

TABLE 15-1   POPULATION OF HAWAII BY ETHNIC COMPONENTS AT SPECIFIED INTERVALS AND BY PER CENT OF TOTAL, 1970

	1853[1]	1884[1]	1900[1]	1920[1]	1950[1]	1960[2]	1970[4]	1970 % of Total
Hawaiian	70,036	40,414	29,799	23,723	12,245	11,294	71,375[6]	9.2
Part Hawaiian	983	4,218	9,857	18,027	73,845	91,169		38.7
Caucasian	1,687	16,579	26,819	49,140	114,793	202,230	298,160	
Portuguese	87	9,967	18,272	27,002				
Other Caucasian	1,600	6,612	8,547	19,708				
Chinese	364	18,254	25,767	23,507	32,376	38,197	52,039	6.7
Japanese		116	61,111	109,274	184,598	203,455	217,307	28.2
Korean				4,950	7,030		8,656	1.1
Filipino	5			21,031	61,062	69,070	93,915	12.2
Puerto Rican				5,602	9,551			
Negro			233	348	2,651	4,953	7,573	0.9
All Other	62	1,397	648	310	1,618	12,305[3]	18,410[5]	2.4
Total	73,137	80,578	154,234	255,912	499,769	632,772	768,561	100.0

[1] See Andrew Lind, Hawaii's People (Honolulu: University of Hawaii Press, 1967), p. 28 for the data through 1950.

[2] U.S. Census, 1960, for 1960 Population by Race, Final Report (P C 2)—C, p. 254.

[3] The Negro components is subtracted from the above U.S. Census table "All Other" category, leaving the "All Other" largely Korean.

[4] "Population Summary for Hawaii, 1972," Statistical Report 87, Department of Planning and Economic Development, State of Hawaii.

[5] "All Other" for 1970 enclude Aleut, Eskimo, Malayan, Micronesian, Polynesian, etc.

[6] In the 1970 Census, for the first time, no differentiation was made between Hawaiian and Part Hawaiian.

"Hawaiian" had been formerly designated as part-Hawaiian (see page 408). The difficulty of ethno-racial classification was further reflected in the 1970 Census by the use of the category "Ethnic Stock" and the notation that persons of mixed ancestry are classified by race of father. A considerable portion of the citizens of Hawaii either identify themselves or are labeled by others as belonging in one of the ethno-racial groups listed in Table 15-1. But one is well-advised to look upon them as distinctively identifiable culturally, with an indeterminable amount of genetic lineage traceable to the people for which the labels originally stood.

Throughout the chapter, we will use the term *haole* (how-lee). The native meaning of this word is "stranger" and it was first applied to the Euro-American invaders. It is now used to mean any "white" or Caucasian person.

The actual figures given in Table 15-1 by decades are not strictly comparable since changes in the basis of classification have occurred over the years. The changes are reasonably clear, however. (1) Between the time of the first white contact in 1778 to about 1850, there were only small numbers of haoles residing in the Islands, with an essentially homogeneous native Hawaiian population. (2) From about 1850 to 1930, successive waves of immigrant peoples—Chinese, Japanese, Filipinos—came to the territory. At various times other ethnics entered Hawaii in response to the demand for plantation labor. Portuguese, Puerto Ricans, and Koreans arrived in sufficient numbers to be classified as separate groups in earlier population tables. There have been, in addition, Spaniards, Germans, Islanders from scattered areas of the Pacific, and Russians.[1] (3) During this period the native Hawaiian population declined. Out-marriage of Hawaiians with other ethnics was so extensive that by 1930 the "Part-Hawaiian" began to exceed the pure-Hawaiian category. (4) During this period also the Japanese came to a position of numerical predominance among all the ethnics. (5) By 1940 the proportions of the ethnic components were showing a tendency to stabilize. (6) Since World War II the proportion of the Caucasian population has been increasing. Whereas in 1950 the Japanese comprised about 37 per cent and the Caucasians 25, by 1970 the latter had jumped to 39 per cent and the Japanese made up only 28. However, a substantial part of the haole population growth is accounted for by military dependents (not counting military per-

[1]See Andrew Lind, *An Island Community* (Chicago: University of Chicago Press, 1938), p. 194.

sonnel itself) and thus the influence on Hawaiian civic life of the haoles is probably somewhat less than that of the Japanese. Contributing to the loss of first place by the Japanese has been a net loss in their island and mainland interchange—estimated for the 1950–1960 decade at 17,300.[2]

The story of ethnic intergroup relations in Hawaii will be divided into three periods: (1) the period of European invasion and the decline of the aboriginal Hawaiian civilization, from 1778 to about 1850, when the immigration of Asiatic people began; (2) the period of haole dominance over both the Hawaiians and the other subsequent immigrant peoples from 1850 to World War II; (3) the period of declining haole dominance, which characterizes the years since World War II.

THE ESTABLISHMENT OF HAOLE DOMINANCE

The Decline of the Hawaiians

At the time of the first white contact with Hawaii in 1778, the Islands were inhabited by a people of Polynesian origin and physiognomic features, who had brown skin, black hair, and were considered handsome by Caucasians.

Their society, though preliterate, was highly elaborated. Early estimates of the native population in 1778 placed the number at about 300,000, but contemporary scholars believe it to have been far less. The early explorers saw only the settlements near the coast and based their estimates of the total population on the assumption that the interior was just as densely populated. It became known that the island of Hawaii, for example, partly covered by bare lava, was quite sparsely populated. The Hawaiians had developed a distinctive way of life suitable to themselves and with sufficient resources available to sustain them. Within a century after the coming of the white man, this civilization was virtually destroyed. The population declined almost to the point of extinction and the small group of white newcomers supplanted the natives as the controlling element in this insular community.

Except for missionaries, the few Euro-Americans who came to Hawaii before the middle of the nineteenth century were motivated almost entirely by economic interests. First confining them-

[2]Components of Change in the Civilian Population by Ethnic Group and Military Dependency, for Hawaii 1950–1960. Estimated by the Department of Planning and Research of Hawaii.

selves to trading, the whites gradually became interested in cattle raising and rice growing—introduced first by the Chinese—and finally in sugar growing, destined to become the economic foundation of the future Hawaii. Thus the haoles sought and gained permanent tenure of more and more valuable lands.

The reactions of the Hawaiians to the haoles were compounded chiefly of awe and friendliness, which aided the haoles in gaining their immediate ends. Their technological superiority evoked native admiration and helped establish haole prestige. As Burrows writes, "They (the natives) seem to have made the generalization that because the foreigners were superior to them in certain points of technology, they were superior in everything."[3] Although some native groups did oppose the haoles as they encroached on their land, in general, encroachment was accomplished peacefully. In 1845 an act was passed prohibiting aliens from acquiring title to land.[4] Like the Indians on the mainland, however, when this act was repealed in 1850, native Hawaiians often sold their land for ready cash.

During the period here under review and beyond it, the native Hawaiian population declined at a staggering rate. In 1950 only about 12,000 pure Hawaiians were recorded.

Adams has summarized the causes for this phenomenal population decline: (1) the sanguinary wars which continued for seventeen years after Captain Cook's first visit; (2) the introduction by foreigners of diseases new and highly fatal to the natives; (3) the hardship and exposure incident to new relations with foreigners, such as cutting and carrying candlewood, service on whaling ships, and the contributions of foodstuffs required for trade; (4) the serious disorganization of production through trade and contacts with the foreigners; (5) the disruption of the old moral order; and (6) the inability of a primitive people to meet the requirements of the new situation promptly.[5] In short, it is clear that this rapid decimation of the Hawaiian population was influenced by haole infiltration, even though haoles as a group or as individuals did not directly contribute to it nor desire it.

In this early period a pattern of interracial relations began to emerge quite contrary to those established by north Euro-Ameri-

[3] Edwin G. Burrows, *Hawaiian Americans* (New Haven: Yale University Press, 1947), p. 17.
[4] *Ibid.*, p. 40. At that time, land was owned by the king. In 1848, a division of the land gave some of it to the people.
[5] Romanzo Adams, *Interracial Marriage in Hawaii* (New York: The Macmillan Co., 1939), p. 7.

cans in their imperialist expansion elsewhere. The number of white people in Hawaii was quite small. They came from various nations and no one nation had gained ascendancy. Hawaiian political autonomy, although influenced by white intrigue, was maintained. The power situation called for treating Hawaiians with due respect and with at least formal equality. Furthermore, the white population was predominantly male, and thus many of those who remained married Hawaiian women. Intermarriage was further facilitated by the freedom regarding marriage within the loosely organized native Hawaiian system.[6] Thus many conditions in the early situation conspired against the drawing of a color line by the white people. Haole prestige, obvious even in the early days, was based more on social-economic power than on race consciousness. For the study of dominant-minority relations, this is the most significant development in the early period.

In the latter half of the nineteenth century, white people established a firm control over Hawaiian society. Nationalistic rivalries among the whites from imperialist nations were resolved in favor of the Americans. Agitation in the islands for annexation to the United States then arose, ultimately producing a revolution and formation of a provisional government favorable to annexation. Official transfer of sovereignty from the Republic of Hawaii to the United States occurred on August 12, 1898.

Economic Dominance

Control over the Hawaiian economy by haoles had been substantially accomplished through the concentration of control over the elaborated plantation system and its auxiliary financial and shipping enterprises. This control was vested substantially in five corporations.

[The Big Five] act in the capacity of factors or agents for all but three of the sugar companies operating in Hawaii, and have substantial stock holdings in these companies. Together, the Big Five control about 96 per cent of island sugar production. Largest of these agencies is American Factors, Ltd., which was formed in 1918 to take over the business of the German firm of H. Hackfeld & Company, and which in 1945 represented nine plantations responsible for 30.8 per cent of the total sugar produced. The others are C. Brewer & Company, Ltd., with 23.5 per cent; Alexander &

[6]*Ibid.*, pp. 46–48.

Baldwin, with 20.8 per cent; Castle & Cook, Ltd., with 14.5 per cent; and Theo. H. Davis & Company, Ltd., with 6.9 per cent. The agency system is less used in the pineapple industry, although some of the Big Five have an interest in that industry. The Big Five have holdings in other important enterprises such as public utilities, docks, shipping companies, banks, hotels, department stores, and affiliated concerns. Power is held not only through direct stock ownership but through financing and supply contracts, through holding companies, through complicated land-leasing systems, through control over transportation agencies, through personal interfamily relationships, through trusteeships, and through a web of interlocking directorates.[7]

This great economic development in Hawaii under Euro-American corporate direction would not have been possible without an additional labor supply. Because of native population decline there were not enough Hawaiians. Furthermore, the natives did not make good plantation workers. Burrows writes, "The whole idea of steady work for wages was so foreign to their old culture that it had no value to appeal to them. . . . When an Hawaiian was hired to work on the plantations, he would work, as a rule, only until he had enough money to buy what he wanted at the moment, and to give his friends a good time.[8] The labor problem was solved by the importation, either under contract or by active persuasion, of a succession of immigrants from various parts of Asia and elsewhere. The order of succession of these ethnic groups is seen in Table 15–1—the Chinese, the Portuguese, the Japanese, and, considerably later, the Puerto Ricans and Filipinos.

This process of immigration developed into a pattern. The need was for cheap and tractable labor. Each new ethnic group would at first serve as plantation workers. As its members became better adjusted to island life, some, growing discontented with their menial lot, would desert the fields for the city or return home. Thus the planters needed replacements. As the numbers of any one ethnic group increased, characteristic antagonism arose, first showing itself among competing workers. The planters' strategy was to try new ethnic sources in order to allay public antagonism against any one group. Furthering this course of action

[7]Ralph S. Kuykendall and A. Grove Day, *Hawaii: A History* (New York: Prentice-Hall, Inc., 1948), pp. 271–272. By permission.
[8]Burrows, *Hawaiian Americans*, pp. 41–43. By permission of the publishers, Yale University Press.

was the fact that the longer any group of workers stayed in Hawaii, the less tractable they became.

While the growth of a strong labor movement in Hawaii is a recent development, there was some organization among workers and some attempted strikes in the early nineteenth century. An ethnically divided working group, however, was not likely to develop strong labor solidarity.

> Early in the century, the policy of denying to Orientals membership in the skilled trades unions smashed all hopes for effective organization, for a "one-nationality" union arouses prejudice and may be crippled by competing workers from another national or racial group, who will work for lower wages or even act as strikebreakers. Discrimination has been charged; it was once a common saying in Hawaii that there are three kinds of payment for the same kind of work—what *haoles* pay *haoles*, what *haoles* pay Orientals, and what Orientals pay Orientals. Racial loyalties have conflicted with labor-group loyalties, although racial antagonism in Hawaii has never been acute. Language difficulties and differences in culture and outlook have further divided allegiances to working-class ideals.[9]

Although after annexation contract labor became illegal, the planters still managed to locate and control the inflow of the additional labor supply needed.

Political Dominance

Wherever the economic control of an area is highly concentrated in relatively few hands, the same economic interests in large measure control the politics and government. While it is true that under American rule all the formal democratic institutions of the American governmental system were established, most students of Hawaii agree that the Big Five controlled the political life of the Islands from annexation to World War II. Illustrative are the remarks of Barber:

> Moreover, they [the Big Five] are represented indirectly in the political affairs of the Territory, members of the legislature being linked with the Big Five, either through former association (or as in the case of the Speaker of the lower House, through being

[9]Kuykendall and Day, *Hawaii*, p. 275.

legal counsel for the sugar industry), or through the bonds of kinship.[10]

Although the non-haole groups combined constituted a numerical majority, they did not until about 1930 begin to challenge haole political domination. Although the Japanese were by far the largest of the ethnic groups, "it was not until 1930 that a number of Japanese-American candidates appeared in the primaries."[11] It will be recalled that federal law made foreign-born Orientals ineligible for citizenship.

Intergroup Relations

The pattern of intergroup relations in Hawaii before World War II involved haole social dominance over and discrimination against the non-haole ethnic groups. However, the reality of the formal, institutionalized pattern of racial equality in Hawaii is attested by practically all writers on Hawaii. From the start there have been no Jim Crow laws; no segregation in schooling; no laws against intermarriage. However, beneath the surface there was evidence of prejudice and discrimination in which race consciousness was a predominant factor. Burrows writes:

> . . . throughout their school years the Hawaiian born of Oriental stock have become more and more American. The process was favored by an atmosphere kindlier toward their race, and more tolerant of racial and cultural differences, than that of the American mainland. But when they got out of school, and set out to win their way toward prosperity, as good Americans are expected to do, they met with a rude shock. They found that the tolerance and friendliness among races, for which Hawaii has been justly celebrated, prevailed only within limits, and at a price. The price demanded by the dominant haoles—never in so many words, but nevertheless insistent—has been cheerful acceptance by other peoples of a subordinate place.[12]

Referring to haole relations with the Japanese, Bradford Smith cites instances of occupational and social discrimination.

[10]From *Hawaii, Restless Ramparts,* by Joseph Barber, Jr., copyright 1941, used by special permission of the publishers, The Bobbs-Merrill Company, Inc., p. 46.
[11]Bradford Smith, *Americans from Japan* (Philadelphia: J B. Lippincott Co., 1948), p. 166.
[12]Burrows, *Hawaiian Americans,* p. 85. By permission of the publishers, Yale University Press.

Discrimination appears in social life as well as in business. . . .
The principal of a Honolulu school told me that in sixteen years
as a teacher . . . he had come to know only three or four haoles
well enough to enter their homes, and all of them were from the
mainland. Even in the faculty lunch rooms racial lines hold in
the table groups.

Social considerations also affect advancement in jobs. A plantation manager wanted to appoint a Nisei chief electrician. If he
did, the Nisei and his family would move into a house in the
supervisor's area and his wife would have to be invited to social
affairs with the other supervisors' wives. The ladies refused to do
this. So the man was not appointed.[13]

The dominance of the haoles over the other ethnic groups
was in considerable measure a function of their class position.
The upper class was composed almost entirely of haoles. Most
other haoles were in the middle class. The smaller number of
lower-class haoles were, or were descended from, sailors or other
occasional travelers who decided to stay there, some of whom
belonged in the "beachcomber" category. In occupational upgrading and in wage rates within the same job levels, non-haoles were
discriminated against. How much this discrimination was based
on "race consciousness" is a difficult question. Judged by comparison with Euro-Americans on the mainland United States, the
haoles certainly showed less negative reaction to "color," as the
frequency of haole out-marriage indicates (see Table 15-2). Before annexation, Hawaii classified its residents on the basis of
nationality rather than race. After annexation the territorial government did classify Euro-Americans as Caucasian, and the offspring of a mixed marriage was classified as belonging to the
non-Caucasian parent's group. In a plantation community where
the differentiation of haoles as the upper class was strongly
marked, Norbeck found the distinction between the haoles and
the Japanese and the Filipinos to be more often thought of as
cultural rather than racial.[14]

Status distinctions developed among the non-haole groups
themselves. The main Hawaiian gradient was haole-Chinese-Jap-
anese-Filipinos. Native Hawaiians were interspersed but generally
toward the bottom. Puerto Ricans and Portuguese also had a
generally low status. In a study of the race preference of the Japanese in Hawaii, Matsuoka found the first preference to be their

[13]Bradford Smith, *Americans from Japan*, p. 166.
[14]Edward Norbeck, *Pineapple Town* (Berkeley and Los Angeles: University of
California Press, 1959), p. 118.

own kind, followed by Caucasians, Chinese, White-Hawaiians, Korean, Hawaiian, Portuguese, Filipino, Puerto Rican in order. "In general, preference depends not on physiognomy but on socioeconomic status."[15] Within the non-haole groups, status differences had significance. Among the Hawaiians, the families descended from chiefs were superior to the commoners; among the Chinese, the Punti were superior to the Hakka; and the "regular" Japanese considered themselves above the Okinawans.

Non-Haole Reaction to Haole Dominance

How did non-haoles react to haole dominance? Burrows analyzed three types of reaction by the minorities to the stress and frustration engendered by minority status: aggressiveness, withdrawal, and cooperation.[16]

AGGRESSION   This had not been characteristic of any of the groups except the Hawaiians at the two periods of their maximum stress: around 1830, when the haoles were rapidly assuming dominance, and in the period of the 1880s, when haoles assumed control of the government. The only form of aggression at all common among the minorities was the mildest one of grumbling.

WITHDRAWAL   The extreme forms of withdrawal were more frequent among Hawaiians than among Orientals: reactions manifested in happy-go-lucky apathy, drinking extensively, and taking life easy—going fishing and strumming the ukulele. Extreme withdrawal was manifested in religious reversion, either in the revival of traditional Hawaiian rites and practices or the embracing of new cults.

According to Burrows, "recreation reversion" gained ground during the last generation [circa 1947] in pronounced forms. This mildest form of withdrawal was illustrated by revival of interest in the traditional culture of the non-haoles' native lands: among the Hawaiians, the revival of ancient pageantry, the hula, and folklore; among the Chinese, the revival of Chinese drama and music; among the Japanese, the revival of Japanese art. While the withdrawal response was more common than aggression, it was still confined to a minority of the persons involved.

---

[15]Jitsuichi Matsuoka, "Race Preference in Hawaii," *American Journal of Sociology*, 1935–1936, pp. 635–641.
[16]Burrows, *Hawaiian Americans*, Part II.

COOPERATION   Cooperation was the main reaction to haole dominance. For the most part, it involved passive conformity to the demands placed on the non-haoles by the haoles. Less often it took the form of asceticism, where the individual meticulously avoids all that is forbidden and drives himself to do his full duty.[17]

Acculturation of the Non-Haole Peoples

Despite these reactions, acculturation of the minority ethnic groups went on. The children of immigrant Orientals were being acculturated rapidly to the haole way of life. All the native-born were educated in public schools of the American type. "By 1940, approximately 65 per cent of the American citizens of Japanese ancestry over the age of twenty-five had completed eight or more years of American schooling as compared with only 30 per cent in the entire population of the Territory."[18] The public-school system encouraged all its pupils to conceive of themselves as full-fledged members of a free and democratic society. As the native-born came of age, which did not occur before 1920 in any considerable number except for the Chinese and Hawaiians, they began to participate more actively in political life. Illustrative of the American orientation of the native-born Japanese, is Bradford Smith's comment on Nisei reaction to Issei attitudes toward Japan's informal war against China after 1931. "The Nisei resented the partisanship of their parents. They resented anything which set them apart from other young Americans. They resented the contributions to Japanese militarism. Family arguments grew bitter, family relations more strained."[19]

Like the Chinese earlier, the enterprising Japanese moved from agricultural work into the cities, and began upward occupational mobility. "By 1930 the Japanese were operating 49 per cent of the retail stores in Hawaii and provided 43 per cent of the salesmen. . . . Fifteen per cent of the Japanese gainfully employed in 1940 were in preferred professional, proprietary, and managerial occupations as compared with 13.7 per cent of the total population."[20]

[17]*Ibid.*, pp. 167–198.
[18]Andrew Lind, *Hawaii's Japanese* (Princeton, N.J.: Princeton University Press, 1946), p. 18. By permission of the publishers, Princeton University Press.
[19]Bradford Smith, *Americans from Japan*, p. 147.
[20]Lind, *Hawaii's Japanese*, pp. 17–18. By permission of the Publishers, Princeton University Press.

Let us conclude our examination of Hawaii's ethnic relations marked by haole dominance by noting those developments which generated social forces leading to the period marked by the rise of the non-haoles.

In the relatively short span of less than 200 years, Hawaii changed from an aboriginal, self-sustaining, isolated, stone-age culture to a modern, urbanized, commercial, industrial community linked closely to international trade. In the early part of this process there was a dichotomized, semi-feudalistic type of society, with an upper-class haole component and the natives (with due deference to the native rulers) and the immigrants as lower class. In the dominant haole value system capitalism, political democracy, and Christianity were basic. These values generated social forces that resulted in the rise in status and power of the Asian ethnic groups. Among the noneconomic developments which contributed to this change were: (1) the maintenance of political control by native Hawaiians for over a century following discovery; (2) the development of a free and integrated public-school system; (3) the introduction of American political concepts with constitutional guarantees of equality of all before the law; and (4) the missionary influence.

HAWAII'S CHANGING ETHNIC PATTERN

Since 1940 certain broad trends in the development of Hawaii have produced changes in the relations of Hawaii's ethno-racial peoples. (1) World War II had a marked impact on Hawaii and its people. (2) Agriculture continued to operate on the large-scale plantation system and the ownership of agricultural land is still concentrated in a few hands—largely in the "Big Five;"[21] (3) The decline in the needed manpower in agriculture led to urbanization which has been highly concentrated in one area. In 1970, about 82 per cent of the state's population resided in the city and county of Honolulu.

Several governmental and political changes have occurred. (4) Political control, long Republican and haole, in the early 1950s changed to Democratic party control in which the Japanese played a major role. (5) The changed political picture together with the increased military expenditures and statehood (1958)

[21]Frederick Simpich, *The Anatomy of Hawaii* (New York: Coward, McCann, and Geoghegan, Inc., 1971), Chapter 4, "The Land."

greatly increased the proportion of people employed by the federal and state government.

(6) The population has grown about 50 per cent since 1950, affected by the increase in military dependents and migration from the mainland of more haoles. For the first time in the Island's history the haole component is about 40 per cent of the population. (7) The state has become increasingly affluent, in which the phenomenal rise of tourism has played a large part in addition to factors mentioned above.

World War II

World War II marked a turning point in Hawaiian intergroup relations. The circumstances of war introduced new tensions, which were of a temporary nature. However, the war further accelerated certain trends that had begun in the period of haole dominance. The exigencies of war brought to the islands an influx of mainland civilian workers and military personnel not accustomed to Hawaii's pattern of race relations. Lind points out that

> As early as 1940 the mounting tide of defense workers, which was to more than double the size of the civilian population of Caucasian ancestry in Hawaii within six years, had begun to make its impact upon the sensitive balance of race relations within the territory. Despite the fairly frequent instances of "shacking up" with local girls, the defense workers generally were highly critical of the free and easy association of the various racial groups in the Islands. Most of them came with fixed ideas, derived from experience with the Negro in the South or with the Oriental and the Filipino on the West Coast. Although living in Hawaii, the psychological barriers they brought with them, along with the limitations imposed by their occupations and their segregated residence, prevented most of them from really becoming "at home" in Hawaii.[22]

Acculturation of the Non-Haole Peoples

In 1970, approximately 90 per cent of Hawaii's citizens were native American born. Having all been educated in American schools they are literate in the English language and 75 per cent consider English their "mother tongue."

[22]Andrew W. Lind, "Recent Trends in Hawaiian Race Relations," *Race Relations*, Vol. V, Numbers 3 and 4 (Dec. 1947, Jan. 1948), p. 60. By permission of the publishers, Fisk University.

Economic Acculturation

OCCUPATIONAL DISTRIBUTION   Each immigrant group started out as plantation laborers and then gradually moved urbanward, first into menial occupations. By mid-century, all immigrant groups were present in all levels of the occupational status scale, roughly in proportion to the time order of their arrival —Chinese, Portuguese, Japanese, and Filipinos. This process has continued so that the distribution of the non-haole occupational levels gets closer to that of the haoles. For example in 1960 the percentage of the first comers, the Chinese, in professional occupations was almost equal to that of the haoles.[23] At the same time some of the latecomer Filipinos had just begun to enter the professions. Simpich states that in the 1960s they were advancing rapidly.[24]

INCOME   A 1964–1966 sample survey on Oahu indicated that the annual median family income by ethnic stock of the father was $9,372 for the Chinese, $8,777 for the Japanese, and $7,246 for the Haole. When the incomes of the military groups were eliminated from the haole total, the haole civilian groups dropped to $5,287 per family which was lower than that of the pure Hawaiians who had a median family income of $5,593.[25] In short, it is clear that taken as groups in general the various ethnic groups are approaching similarity with two exceptions—the Hawaiians (part or "pure") and the Portuguese. While the Filipinos still remain lower, they have been catching up. Since the upper-level haoles are among the wealthiest it appears that the range of distribution of income among the haoles is wider than among other groups.

UNIONIZATION   Further economic acculturation is seen in the great success of the unionization of labor. As later comers are more concentrated in the lower-occupational ranks, the Filipinos have played a considerable role in unionization. But in any case the "divide and rule" technique of business ownership no longer works. The greater proportion of the Chinese in civil service jobs came because, as first comers, they could qualify on examinations.

[23]Andrew Lind, *Hawaii: The Last of the Magic Isles* (London and New York: Oxford University Press, 1969), © 1969 the Institute of Race Relations, London.
[24]Simpich, *The Anatomy of Hawaii*, p. 46.
[25]Andrew Lind, *Hawaii*, p. 64. Survey conducted by the Hawaiian Department of Health.

Political Acculturation

JAPANESE CHALLENGE The largely Republican, haole control of territorial politics was first lost in 1954 when the Democrats gained control of the legislature and the Japanese became its largest single ethnic component. The rise of the Democratic party in Hawaii was significantly related to the effective participation of the Japanese as shown by Sakumoto in a study of the votes in selected areas of Honolulu in ten key elections in the 1960s. The findings were as follows:

> The ethnic factor was most prominent in areas of concentrations particularly of Caucasians and Japanese. Generally speaking, voters in areas of Japanese concentration tended to support Democratic candidates and those in Caucasian areas tended to support Republican candidates; and this relationship was more pronounced where the opponents were Democrats of Japanese extraction and Republicans of Caucasian background.[26]

More broadly, the same author concludes, "The role of the other ethnic factors in the future, we suspect, will revolve around the Japanese/Democratic—Caucasian/Republican axis.[27]

STATEHOOD Hawaii's admission to statehood in 1958 was a reflection of the national civil rights movement; its failure to be admitted before was an example of mainland racial prejudice. The active role of the Japanese bore immediate fruit. Three of the state's members of Congress as of 1972 are Japanese: the charismatic Senator Daniel Inomyu, the vivacious Congresswoman Patsy Mink, and the generally popular Spark Matsunaga. Senator Hiram Fong, Republican of Chinese lineage, completes Hawaii's roster. However it is somewhat puzzling that on the whole this non-white representation has not been conspicuously active on behalf of minorities on the mainland. A hypothesis might be that the Japanese and Chinese Hawaiians no longer consider themselves as minorities—certainly with much justification.

To sum up the acculturation process of the immigrant-descended Asians, there seems no question but that they share the major values of American culture: ambition to improve their

[26]Raymond E. Sakumoto, "Voting Preferences in a Multi-Ethnic Electorate." Paper prepared for the Pacific Sociological Association Conference, March 31, 1967, at Long Beach, California.
[27]Ibid., p. 9.

individual material wealth through equal competition; desire for higher educational achievement; and belief in the political democracy. In short, they are thoroughly American, illustrated by the fact that of those who move away from Hawaii, most migrate to the American mainland.

ASSIMILATION

The degree of acculturation in Hawaii indicates that the various ethno-racial components are functionally integrated into the common public sector of Hawaiian society—its economy, its polity, and its civic life. This section will assess the degree to which assimilation is still on the basis of ethno-racial subcommunality and identity; and the extent to which this involves dominant-minority or coordinate equality between ethnic groups. Since extensive intermarriage has taken place among all the ethnic peoples for years, we start with this.

Interracial Marriage

Table 15-2 shows the steadily rising rates of interracial marriage from 1913 to 1965. The data for 1965–1969 show a tendency for the intermarriage rate to level off. In fact following 1966 (rate 37.6) the next three years show a drop to the 33 per cent range. The variations in out-marriages of various groups reflect two modes. Of the larger resident groups, the Hawaiian and the haole groups out-marry most, although very recent data show a marked drop in the haole rate. The high out-marriage of the Filipinos and Puerto Ricans reflects the high male preponderance. It is obvious that just as the official ethnic population figures are highly artificial so also are the official out-marriage rates. Substantial numbers of the brides and grooms listed under specific categories are themselves from mixed marriages. Lind illustrates the point by quoting a university coed in 1966 who wrote of herself:

> Just who should I tell you that I am. . . . Two of my grandparents were immigrant laborers from Japan, one of whose sons most unfilially married the daughter of a Chinese wedded to a part-Hawaiian lass of God-only-knows-how-many sailor strains. According to your census enumerators I am part-Hawaiian. . . .[28]

[28]Lind: *Hawaii*, p. 120, by permission.

TABLE 15-2   INTERRACIAL MARRIAGES AS PERCENTAGE OF ALL MARRIAGES, 1912–1969

% Out-marriages

		1912–1916*	1920–1930*	1930–1940	1940 1949†	1950–1959††	1960–1964††	1965 1969††
Hawaiian	Grooms	19.4	33.3	55.2	66.3	78.9	85.9	85.7
	Brides	39.9	52.1	62.7	77.2	81.5	85.4	92.7
Part-Hawaiian	Grooms	52.1	38.8	41.0	36.9	41.3	47.0	56.4
	Brides	66.2	57.7	57.9	64.2	58.4	56.8	56.5
Caucasian	Grooms	17.3	24.3	22.4	33.8	37.4	35.1	24.3
	Brides	11.7	13.8	10.7	10.2	16.4	21.1	19.3
Chinese	Grooms	41.7	24.8	28.0	31.2	43.6	54.8	61.1
	Brides	5.7	15.7	28.5	38.0	45.2	56.6	65.4
Japanese	Grooms	0.5	2.7	4.3	4.3	8.7	15.7	28.0
	Brides	0.2	3.1	6.3	16.9	19.1	25.4	30.3
Korean	Grooms	26.4	17.6	23.5	49.0	70.3	77.1	73.0
	Brides	0.0	4.9	39.0	66.7	74.5	80.1	83.6
Filipino	Grooms	21.8	25.6	37.5	42.0	44.5	51.2	50.0
	Brides	2.8	1.0	4.0	21.0	35.8	47.5	51.1
Puerto Rican	Grooms	24.4	18.6	29.8	39.5	51.3	65.0	74.0
	Brides	26.4	39.7	42.8	50.3	60.5	67.2	73.5
Total		11.5	19.2	22.8	28.6	32.8	37.6	35.0

*Derived from Romanzo Adams, *Interracial Marriage in Hawaii*, pp. 336–9.

†Bureau of Vital Statistics, 1 July 1940–30 June 1948 and calendar year 1949.

††Bureau of Health Statistics, calendar years 1950–69.

Source: Romanzo Adams, *Interracial Marriage in Hawaii* (New York, Macmillan Co., 1937), pp. 336–9; *Annual Reports of the Bureau of Vital Statistics* (Honolulu, 1943–9); *Annual Reports, Department of Health Statistical Supplements* (Honolulu, 1950–69).

This indicates that ethno-racial designation is in part a matter of which ethnic group the couple chooses to identify with, probably in most cases that of the father. The one exception seems to be an official designation of anyone admitting or suspected of having a Polynesian ancestor to be labelled part-Hawaiian.

Ethnic Group Identity

It is no longer the case, as in earlier days, that the class and racial stratification system tend to fuse. The educational, income, and occupational range of all the main ethno-racial components indicate what Gordon called "eth-class" system.[29] Second, there is little racial residential segregation. Of this Lind writes: "It is possible, for example, to designate areas of Honolulu where each of the five largest ethnic groups—Japanese, Caucasian, Hawaiian, Chinese, and Filipinos . . . is more heavily represented than any other. . . . However, all five of these groups had some residents in all but one of the census tracts in 1960."[30] As a specific illustration, Lind further refers to a former upper-middle-class and exclusively haole residential area which now has owner occupants distributed as follows: five of Japanese ancestry, five haoles, two Portuguese, one Chinese, one Filipino, and four racially mixed.[31]

ETHNO-RACIAL ORGANIZATIONS There are racially-oriented (not necessarily exclusively so) clubs, a major function of which is to celebrate their traditional holidays and ceremonials, much like the mainland Irish St. Patrick's Day parade. There are recreational and civic clubs based somewhat on ethnic descent. Furthermore there are ethnic religious congregations, some based on Buddhism, and many of various Christian denominations. "But Buddhism has changed in the Hawaiian atmosphere, more often adopting English hymns similar to those of Christianity, and introducing pews, candles, and pulpits."[32]

Decline in Discrimination

Ethno-racial discrimination has been formally illegal, and tradition has long made it bad manners to express racial slurs

[29]Gordon, *Assimilation in American Life*, p. 51. Defined as "a sub-society created by the interaction of the vertical stratification of ethnicity with the horizontal stratifications of social class."
[30]Lind, *Hawaii*, pp. 108–109.
[31]*Ibid.*, p. 109.
[32]Kolarz, Walter, "The Melting Pot in the Pacific," *Social Process in Hawaii*, 1955, 19: pp. 23–26.

publicly. Earlier, both discrimination and prejudice were revealed most markedly in Hawaii when one by one, the immigrant groups, after having moved from plantation to city began to push upward occupationally and outward from their "ghettos." Even the earlier coming ethnics already entering higher status manifested prejudice toward the next comers; and still more, large ethnic minorities showed prejudice toward lower-status subgroups of their own ethnic lineage.

However, our discussion above of the upward socioeconomic mobility of the immigrant Asians, of housing dispersal, and extensive intermarriage support the overall claim that Hawaii's racial situation is one of the best in the world. A 1967 newspaper survey on race relations began its report as follows:

> Hawaii has subtle racial discrimination in housing, business, in religion and in relationships with the Armed Forces, accordng to members of all ethnic groups surveyed by the *Advertizer*. But economic pressure is breaking down the barriers in business and housing, most of the participants in the survey agreed. . . . The Pacific Club's ban on Oriental members and Governor Burns' refusal to join because of that was the subject of stories and comments. So were old racial barriers in the plush housing of Kahala.[33]

In short, what has happened in Hawaii since 1950 has been a decline in ethnic discrimination and prejudice, but Lind observes for this state what has happened generally throughout the nation —a greater public awareness of discrimination but open discussion of the prejudice still has not taken place.[34]

PLURALISTIC ASSIMILATION   Our whole discussion of the rise of the non-haoles indicates that in the main, Hawaii has now reached assimilation on the basis of structural ethno-racial pluralism. This broad generalization, however, applies best with reference to the adjustment of the main immigrant minorities.

Recent Non-White Immigrants

In the past two decades there has been a scattered influx of Polynesian and Eskimo immigrants into Hawaii. While the numbers of "all others" are still small—the 17,000 in 1970 is much

[33]"Our Race Relations," *Honolulu Advertizer* (Sept. 16, 1967).
[34]Lind, *Hawaii*, p. 99.

larger than in 1950. So far there has been little sociological study of what's happening to these people. However the state inter-marriage data for each of the years 1965–1969 list Samoans as a separate category which suggests that they comprise the largest group of "all others." Also the data for this five year period record 375 Samoan grooms, 223 of whom married Samoan brides, sug-gesting that they are now a "visible" ethnic component. But if Hawaii continues to grow and require a larger number of workers at menial jobs, these new ethnic components may increase. Even the Filipinos are now moving so rapidly upward that some new-comers willing to be on the bottom of the economic scale for a time at least, will be needed.

Negroes

The presence of a small number of Negroes in Hawaii might serve as a further test of the society's racial tolerance. A few hun-dred Negroes lived in the territory before World War II. They were often referred to as *Haol-ellele*—black haoles. The present 7,500 Negroes include former servicemen who chose to remain there after the war. Hawaii's blacks moved more or less directly into occupations above the lowest levels. While Smith Street in Hono-lulu is considered something of a Negro area, the blacks are scat-tered in other areas appropriate to their economic status. However, there are some indications that Negroes are thought of as less desirable neighbors by other Hawaiian ethnics. A study of ethnic preferences of landlords found more prejudice against Negroes as tenants than of any other ethnic group.[35] In the final test of racial tolerance—intermarriage—it is noteworthy to indi-cate that in the period 1965–1969 out of 580 Negro grooms 89 married Caucasian brides (15.3 per cent), and out of 375 brides, 28 married Caucasian grooms (7.4 per cent).[36] Neither the local chapters of the NAACP nor the Urban League have been very active, presumably because there is little for them to do. To sum up, it appears that mild manifestations of prejudice against blacks by both white and yellow Hawaiians exist, but not enough to greatly affect the Islands' reputation for racial tolerance. How-ever, the Negro component is small and there are no indications

[35]Harry V. Ball and Douglas S. Yamamura, "Ethnic Discrimination and the Market Place: A Study of Landlords Preferences in a Polyethnic Community," *American Sociological Review*, 1950, pp. 687–694.
[36]Data derived from the detailed yearly charts of the Hawaiian State Department of Health Annual Reports for 1965–1969.

that it will increase greatly in size. Based on mainland experiences, a better test would be a substantial increase in the numbers of black mainland migrants in a short period of time.

The Changing Position of the Haoles

The rise of the Asian-descended peoples of Hawaii has qualified the power position of the haoles particularly in politics and government. This raises the question as to whether haoles are any longer a dominant group as they clearly were up to World War II. To assess their position requires examining the internal structure of the haole component. Greatest prestige accrues to descendants of the nineteenth century Euro-Americans—the *Kamaainas,* some of whose forebears were members of the earlier Hawaiian aristocracy. Control of much of the land and the larger businesses is still largely held by some of this group together with other haoles who are associated with them. But this control is being somewhat constricted and corporate enterprise is now more widely shared. The Big Five is increasing its enterprise abroad."[37] However about half of the privately owned land in Hawaii is owned by five estates established by the original owners whose trustees show variable degrees of social responsibility and strictly private economic self interest. In Simpich's extensive discussion of the ownership and control of both agriculture and other economic enterprise, the wide number of names mentioned are almost exclusively Euro-American names. One exception refers to the Bishop Estate whose income was willed for the purpose of educating Hawaiian children by a Hawaiian Princess who married a haole. The Trustees of the Estate are appointed by the Hawaiian Supreme Court. One Chinese Hawaiian has been appointed, and recently the appointment of a wealthy Japanese Trustee has been the focus of a new "nativistic" movement among some of those considered Hawaiian.

The above discussion suggests part of the answer to the question of haole dominance. A small selective number of upper-class haoles dominates the economy but it appears as much a matter of the sociology of class as of ethnic differentiation. For a fuller answer it is necessary to turn to the lower-status haoles.

The greater balancing of the haole class structure with an increasing participation of lower status and the "beachcomber" segments has had the effect of lowering the prestigious image of

[37]Simpich, *The Anatomy of Hawaii,* Ch. 5, "Merchant Street."

haoles as a whole. Many of the more successful and conventional non-haoles look down upon and show prejudice toward many of the haoles. In short, white visibility as such now no longer automatically carries with it superior status.

The impact of the current haole influence upon politics will depend on the extent to which the now widely class-ranging haoles tend to act politically as an ethnic block or incline to identify with their actual class interest.

The presence in Hawaii at any given time of two large aggregates of mainland people—the tourists and the military personnel and their descendents—requires assessment.

THE MILITARY   Hawaii has had a military establishment ever since annexation in 1898, the size of which was overwhelming during the World War II years, and which has remained at substantial numbers in the years since. Most of the military personnel and their dependents living there have been mainlanders. Romanzo Adams regarded this as a serious threat to the benign race mores of the territory even before Pearl Harbor.[38] Military establishments generally are isolated from the larger community about them, and at the officer level, status conscious. As everywhere, homeless enlisted men seek association with local girls and some intergroup tension emerges. Lind's appraisal of this phenomenon in Hawaii is that on the one hand, bearing in mind the economic gain which the military brings to the Islands, "Islanders have sometimes compromised with their local code of racial equality," and on the other hand, service personnel have often adjusted to local mores—even to the point of marrying non-haoles and permanently residing in Hawaii.[39] Simpich maintains that the military authorities remain aloof from Hawaiian affairs other than those directly involving their work.[40]

TOURISTS   The influx of thousands of tourists to Hawaii each year inevitably has some influence on the Islands' race relations. The tourist, like the military personnel, often holds mainland racial attitudes; but, contrary to the military, can better afford to express these attitudes freely. As Lind writes, "Theoretically, therefore, the tourists afford a sort of pipeline for the intro-

[38]Romanzo Adams, "The Unorthodox Race Doctrine of Hawaii," in *Race and Culture Contacts*, E. B. Reuter, ed. (New York: McGraw-Hill, 1934), p. 159.
[39]A. W. Lind, in Jitsuichi Matsuoka and Preston Valien, *Race Relations: Problems and Theory* (Chapel Hill, N.C.: Univ. of North Carolina Press, 1961), p. 76.
[40]Simpich, *The Anatomy of Hawaii*, p. 270.

duction of mainland conceptions of race relations, and the Islanders economically dependent upon their patronage, notably taxi drivers and hotel operators, tend to 'play up' these imported ideas."[41] He further observes that the tourist in search of new experience and in an uninhibited vacation mood often discards his usual prejudices for the time being at least.

The Hawaiians

Ending the discussion of ethnic-racial peoples in Hawaii with a consideration of the group which in terms of pure native lineage is nearly extinct may seem unusual. But two considerations suggest it.[42] First, it is vestiges of native culture which give Hawaii its main cultural flavor, however genuine or superficial these vestiges may be, symbolized by the word "Aloha." Second, within the Hawaiian group has developed one of the newest manifestations of ethnic "nativism" with organized efforts to revive pride in ancestry and to protect and improve the position of the Hawaiians (mostly mixed bloods) who personally identify with the Hawaiian subgroup.

The perpetuation of the more superficial aspects of the native culture—dances, native foods, etc. disturbs no one. Actually, the nativisms are exploited by the tourist business which employs extensively persons of Hawaiian ancestry as "entertainers and tour guides, presumably because of the 'spontaneity of their aloha' and their cheerful relaxing dispositions [for the] deception of gullible tourists. . . ."[43]

But to revive the more fundamental aspects of Aloha creates a dilemma. As Lind puts it: "How to reconcile the dominant emphasis on the 'success' psychology of the West with the central values of mutuality and sharing in the Hawaiian tradition is, however, a dilemma to which no satisfactory solution has yet to be found."[44]

THE BISHOP ESTATE AFFAIR   Recent efforts among the "nativist"-oriented Hawaiian group to protect and advance their interests have focused upon the Bishop Estate affair.

[41]Lind, in Matsuoka and Valien, pp. 73–74.
[42]It is of interest to note that the only ethnic subgroup to which Lind in *Hawaii* devotes a separate chapter is the Hawaiians, Ch. 4, "Folk People in an Industrialized World."
[43]Lind, *Hawaii*, p. 77.
[44]*Ibid.*, p. 80.

The estate was established by the will of a native princess, who married a haole named Bishop, for the purpose of providing education for Hawaiian children which has been interpreted by the trustees as meaning children of native-Hawaiian ancestry.[45] Recent attempts to force selling some of the Estate's land to outsiders and to remove the restrictions limiting estate-operated schools to only Hawaiian children have been vigorously opposed by "nativistic" Hawaiians. Their discontent was further inflamed by the appointment of a trustee of Japanese origin in 1971. The opposition was not so much against the person chosen, as directed at the failure to appoint an Hawaiian. An ad hoc committee of Hawaiians has prepared a series of complaints to the state government which includes a demand that three of the five trustees of the estate should be of some Hawaiian lineage.[46]

Summary

From annexation as a territory by the United States to 1940, intergroup relations assumed a form of polyethnic stratification in which haoles were dominant and the other ethnics were minorities. The ethnic stratification system was considerably fused with the class system. Since World War II, Hawaii has moved toward a coordinate ethno-racial pluralistic form of assimilation. The composition of the subethnic group is based upon some degree of option on the part of the legion of persons who have mixed racial lineage. This ethnic pluralism is however more structural than cultural. Identification with and association with members of the same ethnic groups in primary (personal) as distinct from secondary (impersonal) relations, rather than behavior and attitude related to their ancestral heritage, are what provides their subethnic unity. The current "nativistic" revival among a segment of the ten per cent or less of the state's population which is considered Hawaiian does not appear likely to disturb Hawaii's general ethno-racial pattern. Hawaii's *peoples* may not for a considerable time become Hawaii's *people* in the *ethno-racial* sense, but they are already "all American" in the *nationality* sense.

[45]According to Simpich, *The Anatomy of Hawaii*, p. 127, the Bishop Estate owns 10 per cent of all the privately held land in Hawaii with an income of close to eight million dollars in 1970.
[46]We gratefully acknowledge reports from several meetings where Hawaiian nativist groups have voiced a militant stance, sent us by Professor Raymond E. Sakumoto of the University of Hawaii.

The major current factor which has potential for altering interpeople relations is the recent greater proportion of the haole population. However, the long established and institutionalized democracy in which "racism" has low salience and the continuing intermarriage of haoles with non-white Hawaiians, even if at a somewhat lower rate, points toward the continuance of Hawaii's reputation for intergroup tolerance.

Suggested Readings

Adams, Romanzo. *Interracial Marriage in Hawaii.* New York: The Macmillan Co., 1937.
    While primarily concerned with intermarriage, the book contains much material on intergroup relations in Hawaii from the beginning of Euro-American contact to the mid-1930s.
Ball, Harry V. and Douglas S. Yamamura. "Ethnic Discrimination and the Market Place," *American Sociological Review,* 1960, pp. 687–694.
    The findings of research designed to determine the extent of ethnic discrimination in Honolulu as indicated by landlord preferences for or rejection of tenants on the basis of their ethnicity.
Lind, Andrew. *Hawaii's Japanese.* Princeton: Princeton University Press, 1948.
    Useful for comparing the Japanese experience in Hawaii during World War II and its aftermath with the Japanese American experience on the mainland.
Miller, Norman and Daniel W. Tuttle, Jr. "Hawaii: The Aloha State" in *Politics in the American West.* Salt Lake City: University of Utah Press, 1969, pp. 152–179.
    Analyzes the ethno-racial composition of Hawaii's legislature.
Norbeck, Edward. *Pineapple Town.* Berkeley and Los Angeles: University of California Press, 1959.
    An anthropological study of a pineapple plantation community in Hawaii.
Samuels, Frederick. "Color Sensitivity among Honolulu's Haoles and Japanese," *Race,* Vol. II, 203–12.
    Finds Japanese Hawaiians closer to Euro-American ethnic component than to "darker" people.
Tumin, Wallace, "New Hawaiian Economy Causes Minority Unrest," *New York Times* (August 13, 1972), pp. 1, 36.
    Problems related to descendants of aboriginals and control of rural lands.

16　Jewish-Gentile Relations

The situation of the Jews in various times and places has encompassed every aspect of dominant-minority relations. The history of the Jews in the ancient world included the experience of being a colonially conquered people. Early in the Christian era they were driven out of their homeland. In this period, usually referred to as the Diaspora, or "Dispersion," and in the succeeding eighteen centuries, they were dispersed throughout the whole civilized world. The persistence of segregated colonies of Jews created a pattern of cultural minorities.

The particular historical developments of the twentieth century have added other dimensions to the position of Jews as a minority. When the National Socialist Party undid for Germany all the gains made in western European social thought since the Age of Enlightenment and exterminated six million Jews, the bonds of identity of Jews throughout the world, which had loosened under two centuries of improved civil status, were reestablished and intensified. The founding of the state of Israel has given many Jews a Jewish political identity and affected the feelings of Jews in other countries.

One cannot consider Jewish-Gentile relations without this historical perspective. It accounts for the fact that Jews have been identified, and have identified themselves at various times and in various places, as a religious minority, an ethnic minority, and a "racial" minority.

The rationale for devoting a special chapter to the Jews as a minority, rather than seeing them simply as members of an established religious group, is this very complexity of identity. The Jews have a long history of stabilized minority status in which they have served important functions in the dominant society and incorporated the goals of the dominant society. Jews have attenuated visibility, if any. (Some sectarian religious Jews have high cultural visibility, but this is a small minority.) Yet Jews think of themselves as Jews, and they have, however loose, bonds with other Jews. To an extent this is due to "the self will that creates unity"; and to an extent it is the result of "the will of others which imposes unity where hardly any is felt."[1]

THE PROBLEM OF JEWISH IDENTITY

American Jews in the twentieth century have been concerned with the question "Who is a Jew?" Barron cites the frequency with which this has been discussed in general and in Jewish periodicals and other publications, as well as how difficult the problem of definition has been for the Israeli government.[2]

Are the Jews a Race?

In Chapter 4 we discussed the fact that "race" as used popularly is a social and not a scientific category. We pointed out that present genetic theory accepts only the fact that certain genetic traits are reinforced by isolation and in-marriage. There seems to be little evidence that Jews were ever totally biologically separated from the surrounding peoples. Even initially in Palestine it is probable that the strong prohibitions against outmarriage were a defense against a considerable intermixture. The goal was preserving the religion, not purity of descent, except as this is characteristic of all tribal peoples.

As the Jews dispersed, the people with whom intermixture occurred became progressively more differentiated in physiognomic features. The Ashkenazim, especially, who were dispersed through northern Europe and from whom most American Jews are descended, are a blending of Nordic and Alpine with eastern

---

[1]Nathan Glazer and Daniel Patrick Moynihan, *Beyond the Melting Pot: The Negroes, Puerto Ricans, Jews, Italians and Irish of New York City,* (Cambridge Mass.: The M.I.T. and Harvard University Press, 1963), p. 139.
[2]Milton L. Barron, "Ethnic Anomie," in Milton L. Barron ed., *Minorities in a Changing World* (New York: Alfred A. Knopf, 1967), p. 26, and note 14.

Mediterranean traits.[3] The other main branch of Jews, the Sephardim, lived long in Spain and the Mediterranean region and through in-marriage tended to develop a degree of physical distinctiveness from other Jews. People of this appearance are often referred to as the "classic" Jewish type, but they are often indistinguishable from other Mediterranean peoples. "The wide range of variation between Jewish populations in their physical characteristics and the diversity of the gene frequencies in their blood groups render any unified racial classification for them a contradiction in terms."[4]

Shapiro, who has examined all the research, anthropological and medical, on the biological traits of Jews, makes the following comment:

> I suppose that one of the reasons, aside from political and cultural ones, that incline many people to accept readily the notion that the Jews are a distinct race, is the fact that some Jews are recognizably different in appearance from the surrounding population. That some are not to be identified in this way is overlooked and the tendency, naturally enough, is to extend to all the stereotype of a part. This process occurs in so many other situations it is scarcely surprising that it does here too.[5]

Are American Jews an Ethnic Group?

It is the fashion today to define any minority as an "ethnic group." As we pointed out in Chapter 2, the term *ethnic* refers to shared culture patterns which are a primary focus of group identification. Many Latin Americans, for example, have a strong sense of cultural foci which are different from those of the United States. There is no overall cultural ethos that distinguishes American Jews from other Americans. To examine this question for American Jews one must consider country of origin, status of Jews in the country from which they migrated, degree of open opportunity in the United States at the time and place of immigration, size and clustering of the migrating group.

In the seventeenth century Sephardic Jews came to the American colonies. This group of Jews originated in the Mediterranean

---

[3]Carleton S. Coon, "Have the Jews a Racial Identity?" eds. Isacque Graeber and Steuart Henderson Britt, *Jews in a Gentile World* (New York: The Macmillan Co., 1942), p. 33.
[4]Harry L. Shapiro, *The Jewish People: A Biological History* (Paris: UNESCO, 1960), pp. 74–75.
[5]*Ibid.*

countries, particularly Spain, and dispersed after the Spanish Inquisition to northern Europe and presently to other parts of the world. Those who came to the United States formed a literate, Orthodox elite. Today they still maintain an elegant, modified orthodoxy, if they are the descendants of the early migration. Secularly they are totally assimilated. They have intermarried with descendants of later migrations, as well as with American Protestants.[6]

In the twentieth century there has been a small migration of Balkan Sephardic Jews who tend to live in clustered pockets of eastern cities. They, however, represent a folk variant of other late migrating village Jews.

The eighteenth and nineteenth centuries saw a considerable migration of Western European Jews, who came at a time of open opportunity, and many of whom had been considerably assimilated into the national cultures of Western Europe from which they migrated. Until the last two decades of the nineteenth century there was real opportunity in rapidly developing America, with little overt discrimination in the large cities, although there were anti-Semitic incidents in the South and the West. The successful German Jewish families maintained close relations with one another, however, intermarried with one another, spoke German at home, and established their pattern of life on the model of the stable, cultured merchant wealth of Europe.[7] These families were, on the whole, strongly behind the movement for Reform Judaism; some were involved in the founding of the Ethical Culture Society, were members of social clubs, felt themselves a true part of American life by the third generation, and were traumatized by the anti-Semitism of the end of the century. They could not in any sense be called an "ethnic" group, although they were forced into a stronger sense of Jewish identity just at the point where they were becoming most American (as contrasted with European).

The largest migration of Jews came between 1880 and 1924. These were primarily from Eastern Europe where they had largely lived in segregated villages or ghettoes of small cities. Most of them were poor and started life in America as skilled and semi-skilled workers or small entrepreneurs. Because of the enforced segregation under which most of them had lived in Europe, they

[6]Steven Birmingham, *The Grandees* (New York: Harper and Row Publishers, Inc., 1971).
[7]Stephen Birmingham, *"Our Crowd": The Great Jewish Families of New York* (New York: Harper & Row, 1967).

maintained a folk orthodoxy in religion which so dominated the daily lives of the villages that it gave this group a cultural uniqueness.[8] Glazer and Moynihan point out that as this was the largest migration of Jews to America it has colored Jewish behavior in many parts of the United States and contributed to the larger culture some of its culturally idiomatic language usages, food, etc.[9] This group of Eastern Jews might have been correctly defined as an ethnic group in the first generation, but today its third-generation descendants have only the most superficial cultural vestiges, if any, and are American "in thought, word, and deed." Partly this is the more true as the group has been economically mobile and the third generation, like other ambitious young Americans, is concerned with status and relatively oblivious to discrimination, actual or potential.[10]

Jews as a Religious Group

Jews are divided by their religious affiliation into three groups: Orthodox, Reform, and Conservative. Orthodox Jews keep as closely as possible to the Mosaic Law and its Talmudic elaboration. This means that they observe their Sabbath (Saturday) as a day of absolute abstention from the work of the other six days. For example, they refrain on the Sabbath from using transportation, from cooking, and from secular reading. Orthodox Jews keep the traditional dietary laws, which include prohibitions of particular kinds of foods and ritualistic regulations concerning the preparation of food. Within Orthodoxy there are some sects, the largest of which is the Hassidic, that are distinguished by their dress, hair style, and the character of worship. Orthodoxy is characteristic chiefly of the Spanish-Portuguese elite and the older generations of the Eastern European immigrants. In recent decades it has had a revival among Jewish intellectuals.

Reform Judaism is an outgrowth of the philosophy of Enlightenment as it affected Jews primarily in Germany. The Reform movement attempted to adapt Jewish religious life to the dominant Protestant model without losing the essential characteristics

[8]See Mark Zborowski and Elizabeth Herzog, *Life Is With People* (New York: International Universities Press, 1952). Two anthropologists have sensitively reconstructed the life of these Jewish villages: a way of life that was destroyed totally by the Nazi conquest of Eastern Europe.
[9]Glazer and Moynihan, *Beyond the Melting Pot*, pp. 141–142.
[10]Judith R. Kramer and Seymour Levantman, *Children of the Gilded Ghetto* (New Haven: Yale University Press, 1961).

of Judaism. This means that it is altered legally and ritualistically, leaving theology unchanged. Some Reform Jews adapt to the dominant culture in observance of Sunday as the Sabbath, and have incorporated in their temple services such modifications as organ music, mixed choirs, and the unsegregated seating of women. The Reform movement in the United States has its main center in Cincinnati and has grown among the German Jewish population. Despite some inroads from Conservative Judaism, it is still the dominant pattern for Midwestern and Southern Jews.

Conservative Judaism represents a compromise and is in part a protest against the extreme modification initiated by the Reform Jewish movement. Less rigid than Orthodox Judaism, it has nevertheless retained much of the liturgical emphasis of Orthodoxy and some of the social practices that preserve the distinctiveness of the Jewish community. Conservative Judaism has often been the comfortable solution for the second and third generation descendants of Orthodox Jews in America.

As with other groups in the United States Jews have a large segment who are secularized, some to the degree of being completely non-religious, while others form a tenuous formal relationship to religion. This is probably most characteristic of metropolitan areas where religious affiliation is not visible and among salaried professionals where the career provides out-group contacts and a secular focus on the task to be performed (business bureaucracies, academic bureaucracies, civil service, etc.). Glazer and Moynihan believe that only a minority of New York City Jews belong to synagogues.[11] The rate of conversion to Christianity is claimed to be small, and probably this is correct with regard to baptism and formal affiliation with Christian churches. But it would be difficult to assess how many have sought anonymity in membership in sectarian religious groups (Quakers, Christian Scientists, etc.) where baptism is not required and is therefore not considered to constitute a betrayal of one's heritage.

The Jews Are a Minority

As we have seen the Jews are not a "race," nor can American Jews be subsumed as an ethnic group. Neither are all people who designate themselves as Jewish members of one or another of the denominations of Judaism. Yet the interplay of historic forces has

[11]Glazer and Moynihan, *Beyond the Melting Pot*, p. 142.

created a centripetal bond which both operates against total assimilation and creates security and varying degrees of mutuality for its members. To be a minority which does not have its sense of identity rooted in strong subcultural values, or in religion, and which competes successfully and seeks admission to full participation in the larger secular society, puts the group in a particularly vulnerable position.[12] Throughout the history of the Jews, economic success and the beginning of social integration have been followed by policies and actions against Jews.[13]

The problems of marginality and ambiguous status for Jews reveal much that is generic to dominant-minority relations, not only in the United States but throughout the world (for example, where developing nations have merchant-minority populations of Indians or Chinese). On the negative side, the burden of tension and alienation for people who are part of both groups can be very great.

THE AMERICAN JEWS

Size and Distribution of the Population

About three per cent of the American population is Jewish. The five and a half million Jews are about the same number as a decade ago. Their proportion to the rest of the population is gradually declining as the higher reproduction rate of other segments, such as the Spanish-speaking populations, increase.

Approximately 75 per cent of the American Jewish population live in large metropolitan areas: Baltimore, Boston, Chicago, Cincinnati, Cleveland, Detroit, Los Angeles, Miami, New York City, Newark, Philadelphia, Pittsburgh, St. Louis, and San Francisco. Nearly half of the Jews in the United States live in the New York

[12]See for example Merton's discussion of in-group virtues that become out-group vices in Robert K. Merton, "The Self-fulfilling Prophecy," *Social Theory and Social Structure* Rev. ed. (Glencoe, Ill.: The Free Press, 1957), p. 426.
[13]Contrast for example the situation of Jews and Gypsies. The Gypsies are as old a minority, originally an Asian religious sect. They were and have remained fundamentally tribal; they have dispersed throughout the whole world of Europe and the Americas. They have had only marginal economic relations with the dominant societies within which they are located and have resisted acculturative or welfare efforts from dominants. Perhaps a major difference lies in the fact that they have no great tradition of literacy and have not contributed to the foundations and development of Western European thought and ethic. Usually they have been able to maintain a tolerated (if devalued) status in their environment, although the racialist doctrines of Nazi Germany classified them as "non-Aryan" and sent them to extermination camps.

metropolitan area (the city and its suburbs). About one-third of the white, non-Puerto Rican population of New York City proper is Jewish.

One stereotype of the Jews has described them as an urban people, and indeed since the decline of feudalism in Europe this has largely been true for Western European Jews. But such a stereotype has implied that they had no roots in the feudal agricultural world. Contemporary research is beginning to discover that there have been a variety of historical ecological *loci* for Jews: they have been landowners, village craftsmen, administrators for feudal estates, and so on. Jews suffered as scapegoats in the transition and uprooting that characterized the collapse of feudalism and the beginning of the modern era. Many of them sought the cities free of feudal control. In this country, however, relatively few moved into agricultural life until the twentieth century, when intensive farming (poultry and dairy farming) opened a channel of opportunity more coherent with the European agricultural practices they had known than isolated open-country farming of the American expanding West.

There was greater opportunity for Jews in the larger cities as the migration on the whole coincided with urban growth in the United States; there was also the possibility of association with other Jews, which provided a sense of community, made available marriage partners for sons and daughters, and allowed them to fulfill the historic obligation of a good Jew: community responsibility. For second- and third-generation Jews, and indeed for some first-generation migrants, this sense of obligation has extended beyond the "Jewish community" to a responsibility for the welfare of the larger community of which they were a part.

For the majority of Jews in America who are urban and middle class, there has been positive interaction with dominants, and any differences are differences of nuance and of opportunity. It is true that there are some Jews who can and do live out their lives in an ecological cluster which allows them association only with their own "eth-class."[14] But even here, public education, higher education, and work experience are changing the pattern for young people. We would hypothesize that the degree of definable difference in behavior varies with one or more of the following factors: age as related to recency of migration, socioeconomic

[14]The term is one coined by Milton Gordon in *Assimilation in American Life: The Role of Race, Religion and National Origins* (New York: Oxford University Press, 1964).

status, degree of Jewish traditional religious identification, and ecological clustering.

Jewish Institutional and Organizational Patterns

THE JEWISH FAMILY   The cohesiveness of the family is one of the strongest characteristics of the Jewish group. This derives in part from the emphasis in Jewish religion on marriage and family life, as well as adaptations of this tradition in such a practice as early (and, in former times, arranged) marriage, and in part from the mutual aid and protection of the extended kinship. Jewish families on the whole live in the nuclear pattern, keeping in closer touch with their relatives, visiting more frequently, and being more willing to aid a promising relative than is characteristic of the dominant pattern.[15] Among the older generation of eastern European Jews, there is the beloved stereotype of the Jewish mother who will sacrifice everything for her family.

Male and female roles are sharply defined, even though American Jews encourage the education of women and their participation in community affairs. Authority in the family is in the hands of the men. For religious Jews, it is important to have sons, since certain rituals can be carried out only by males. Even where this religious emphasis is no longer stressed, the high valuation of sons seems to persist.

The family not only has had important traditional religious functions to fulfill, it has also been a bulwark for joint economic endeavor. Glazer and Moynihan point out how often Jewish enterprises involve fathers and sons or groups of brothers.[16] There are many such business partnerships, and there are family associations which form investment pools. (This latter is characteristic of the traditional Chinese family system, of many European bourgeois families, but has not been a characteristic of WASP families in America except at the top financial levels since the imposition of income taxes.)

One of the indices in the past of complete assimilation has been intermarriage between members of the minority and dom-

[15]Stanley R. Brav, *Jewish Family Solidarity: Myth or Fact.* (Vicksburg, Miss.: Nogales Press, 1940).
[16]Glazer and Moynihan, *Beyond the Melting Pot*, p. 154. See also Birmingham, *Our Crowd*, for the involvement of brothers, sons, and sons-in-law in the founding of the great German Jewish fortunes of nineteenth-century America. (Family trees showing descendants and intermarriages are on the end papers of this volume.)

inants. Because Jews have been with each generation more acculturated to American attitudes and mores there has been an increase of intermarriage. In the past where Jews were sharing the nineteenth-century rewards of the country's rapid development there was a modest degree of intermarriage perhaps in part because there were insufficient marriage partners for Jewish young people, and perhaps in part because the climate was one of euphoria with regard to lack of discrimination against Jews.

A recent study summarized the facts about Jews who intermarry compared with those who in-marry.[17]

1. Jews who intermarry are more likely to have a history of broken homes and lack of contact with the extended family. Jewish men are more favorably disposed toward intermarriage. Intermarrying Jews marry later. Oldest children are least likely to intermarry and youngest children and only children the most likely.

2. Jews living in rural areas and small towns are more likely to intermarry than Jews living in cities. Children of recent residents are more likely to intermarry than children of long-established residents. Jews living in new communities are more likely to intermarry than Jews living in older communities. Reform and unaffiliated Jews are more likely to intermarry than Conservative and Orthodox Jews.

3. Intermarriage seems to appeal to Jews whose socioeconomic positions place them at the periphery of the Jewish community, or outside it. Intermarriage, therefore, is more frequent among the highly upward-mobile members of the salaried professions; Jewish professors and government experts are more likely to intermarry than physicians, dentists, lawyers, business owners. Intermarriage also is more frequent with downward mobility. Small town Jewish craftsmen, foremen, or other blue collar workers are more likely to intermarry.

The preponderance of intermarriage is Jewish husbands and Gentile wives (the reverse of the nineteenth-century pattern). Intermarriage rates vary enormously from community to community and little is accomplished in discussing an average national rate. Factors such as size and length of establishment of the Jewish community, comparative opportunity for status, economic success, and freedom of association between the Jewish community and the Gentile world must be considered.

[17]Lewis A. Berman, *Jews and Intermarriage: A Study in Personality and Culture* (New York: Thomas Yoseloff, 1968), Ch. 14, pp. 547–560.

In a study of "Lakeville," an upper-middle-class midwestern suburb, only 50 per cent of the sample said they would feel *very unhappy* if their child were to marry a non-Jew. This score is for families who also rate low on a scale favoring integration. In other words, people with a strong group consciousness are the most opposed to intermarriage.

> I want her to stay within our group, just as I did and my husband did. It's a different culture, and a lot of things are involved.[18]

However, when presented with the choice for their children of a loved Gentile as compared with an unloved Jew, 85 per cent chose a Gentile. For the generations close to migration preference for a Jewish marriage is strong enough to choose a lower-occupational status in preference to an equal- or upper-status out-marriage. However, only one per cent of the families interviewed said they would reject their child if the child out-married. Ninety-three per cent said they would try to build a meaningful relationship with the Gentile person.[19]

OCCUPATIONS   Accurate estimates of the occupational distribution of Jews are difficult to make, since they must be compiled from studies of different localities, where the job classifications are often not comparable. Some data, however, can give an indication of the character of the Jewish labor force.

According to Seligman, it appears that a smaller proportion of the total Jewish population is part of the labor force than is true of the general population. It is suggested that this may be related to such factors as the longer period of schooling for Jewish children, or to the emphasis on the domestic role of women.[20]

The Jewish male labor force in most of the communities for which we have data appears to be higher in proportion to the general population in the employer and self-employed class. Classifications by industry indicate a concentration in the wholesale and retail trades. Although it is a popular belief that Jews are found most frequently in the professions, community studies which provide occupational information show the manufacturing

[18]Marshall Sklare and Joseph Greenblum, *Jewish Identity on the Suburban Frontier* (New York: Basic Books, 1967), pp. 308–309.
[19]*Ibid.*, p. 315.
[20]Ben B. Seligman, et al., "Some Aspects of Jewish Demography" in Marshall Sklare, ed., *The Jews: Social Patterns of an American Group* (Glencoe, Ill.: The Free Press, 1958), pp. 70–78.

(proprietary and managerial) group greater than the professional in most cases. If we consider the nationwide pattern of Jewish occupations, the exclusive occupational emphasis of Jews on the professions seems to be less than has been generally believed. "In more recent years proprietorship has been of first rank in virtually all the Jewish population studies included here, with clerical occupations second and professional work in third position."[21]

Jews as a group have a higher average age than the rest of the population. Since the older age groups in this country have a higher proportion of professionals, semiprofessionals, proprietors, managers, and officials, this is a factor which must be taken into account in considering the proportions of the Jewish labor force in these categories. In the female labor force in 1950 the Jewish urban population approached the proportions found in the general labor force.

Although in the nineteenth and early twentieth century there were prominent Jewish families in finance and industry, there has since been a dispersion. Jewish business fortunes have come from clothing manufacture, merchandizing, and the entertainment field. Since the late 1930s an even wider diversification has taken place to include a range of light manufacturing, real estate, and building.[22]

The Jewish businessman, from the small storekeeper to the newer manufacturer in electronics, has had to find those sectors of the economy which were not preempted by white Protestants. As a historic minority Jews have been alert to these opportunities. The strong family system has enabled them to mobilize capital (even if in small sums);[23] even in the culture market of publishing, movies, television, theatre, music, and architecture, both as producers and consumers they have been interested more in the new than in the old and traditional.[24]

The proportion of working-class Jews is declining, although the institutions within the labor world which they created survive. There is, as is to be expected, a higher proportion of Jews in working-class and lower-middle-class occupations in cities like New York where there is such a large Jewish population. In cities where they are perhaps five per cent of the population they are more apt to be in middle- and upper-middle-class occupations.

[21]*Ibid.*, p. 73.
[22]Glazer and Moynihan, *Beyond the Melting Pot*, p. 151.
[23]*Ibid.*, p. 154.
[24]*Ibid.*, p. 174.

A study by Herbert Bienstock, Regional Director of the Bureau of Labor Statistics, based on 1967 data, showed 74.9 per cent of Jewish high school students hoping to enter professional and technical jobs, whereas only 20 per cent of their fathers had such jobs in 1964. Because of a projected slow rise in professional and technical jobs, the federal analyst urged Jewish organizations to counsel Jewish youths to consider craft skills where the demand and consequent security may be greater. He also suggested Jewish organizations might provide capital to enable young Jews to develop a trend toward self-employment in accounting, contract services, law, etc.[25]

THE JEWS IN AMERICAN POLITICS   Throughout the nineteenth century Jews could and did participate in any political organization to which their interests inclined them. During the Civil War, Jews were among the partisans of both the North and the South, and within both major parties. The number of Jews before 1880 was so small that they were viewed and viewed themselves as individual voters rather than as group representatives. Western European Jews who participated in European politics at all after restrictions on political participation were removed, adhered chiefly to the moderate democratic movements of the times. Much of the same spirit permeated Jewish political positions, whatever the party affiliation, in the United States. In this period they tended to recoil from all extreme movements, such as the radical Abolitionist movement or the Know-Nothing Party.[26]

After 1880, however, the immigrants from eastern Europe were strongly influenced by radical intellectuals, and for a period Jewish workers and their leaders formed the backbone of the Anarchist and Socialist movements in this country. Partly this was due to an over-reaction after the suppression of political liberty they had experienced under the Tsarist government. "When the Jewish intellectual came to the United States, he was suddenly given an opportunity to theorize openly and to his heart's content. He took full advantage of it: for many years, the Lower East Side [in New York City] was one big radical debating society."[27]

Jews have not only been a voting bloc whose liberal voting pattern has been of great persistence, but, where as in New York City

[25]*The New York Times*, June 25, 1972, p. 27.
[26]Werner Cohn, "The Politics of American Jews," in Sklare, ed., *The Jews: Social Patterns of an American Group*, p. 619–620.
[27]*Ibid.*, p. 629.

there have been large numbers of Jews, there have been the usual urban political careers. Glazer and Moynihan think the Jewish vote is largely ideological and rarely is influenced by whether or not the candidate is Jewish. They give a series of examples where the Jews of New York have preferred a liberal Catholic or Protestant over a conservative or "party machine" Jew.[28]

JEWISH ORGANIZATIONS   Possibly the Jewish minority is the most highly organized of any group in the United States. The organizations fall into four categories: welfare, fraternal, aid to Israel, anti-discrimination.

The welfare organizations are the oldest. Within the tradition that Jews are responsible for their own people, there were by the beginning of this century agencies to aid migration and agencies in each community to aid families in need, children in trouble, educational foundations, hospitals, and clinics. Jewish welfare agencies have been in the forefront in developing high professional levels of practice and in pioneering new services in health and welfare. Today, although still supported by Jewish funds in a national federation, many agencies have become non-sectarian in the clients whom they serve.

The fraternal organizations have mobilized volunteer services of men and women to help meet local community needs, though the organizations are national, with local chapters.

Aid to Israel is carried on by a number of groups with different ideologies and different degrees of commitment to Israel, though a very high percentage of Jews at least buy Israel bonds to help provide the capital for development of the country. "Lakeville" Jews were interviewed as to their degree of support for Israel. Ninety-one per cent approved of raising money for Israel, 63 per cent thought Jews should influence U.S. foreign policy with regard to Israel. Less than a third (31 per cent) belonged to Zionist organizations. Only 14 per cent would give Israeli financial need priority over local Jewish causes. Only 1 per cent would encourage their children to emigrate to Israel or consider emigrating themselves. On the other hand nearly 15 per cent of Lakeville's Jewish families would feel no personal sense of loss if Israel were to be destroyed, and a little over a fourth, however they feel about Israel's survival, feel that the existence of Israel has had a harmful effect on Jewish status and security in the United States.[29]

[28]Glazer and Moynihan, *Beyond the Melting Pot*, pp. 166–171.
[29]Marshall Sklare and Joseph Greenblum, *Jewish Identity*, pp. 226–228.

These figures can remind us that there is no such thing as *the* Jewish position on any issue, even one so closely related to the survival of Jews throughout the world.

The anti-discrimination efforts of Jewish organizations have included data gathering and research, publication, and participation in public hearings from grassroots to the congressional level. Here, too, the data gathering is not limited to Jews, but is concerned with broader aspects of discrimination as it affects all minorities.

Sklare and Greenblum found in "Lakeville" that the highest rate of activity in Jewish organizations was among those who had some degree of religious commitment, though they found no significant difference between strongly observant and mildly religious individuals in the support of Jewish organizations. Furthermore they suggest that for some who are non-religious, organizational participation provides a secular alternative mode of identification with the Jewish community.[30]

THE JEWISH COMMUNITY

Wherever any considerable number of Jewish people reside in an American community there has developed a separate Jewish substructure, usually called the "Jewish community," which has a characteristic relation to the larger Gentile community. Sometimes these are actual ecological communities that have developed through residential discrimination or self-clustering; in other cases residence is dispersed, and the network of social and organizational relationships constitutes the Jewish community. There have been many studies of Jewish communities in different parts of the United States. Over 200 communities are affiliated with the Council of Jewish Federations and Welfare Funds, many of which have been studied from one point of view or another.[31]

A large percentage of American Jews have middle-class status and, like the rest of the American urban middle class, Jews are moving to the suburbs. Let us study briefly the origin and growth of a typical suburban Jewish community.[32]

---

[30]*Ibid.*, p. 261.
[31]See Sklare, *The Jews: Social Patterns of an American Group,* for articles based on the reports of many of these studies.
[32]Herbert J. Gans, "The Origin and Growth of a Jewish Community in the Suburbs: A Study of the Jews of Park Forest," in Sklare, pp. 205 ff.

The Jewish Community of Park Forest

Park Forest is a post-World War II planned community south of Chicago. The men of the community were earning from $4,000 to $10,000 a year in 1949, when the study was made. Among 1,800 families, about 25 per cent of them Catholic, the Jewish community numbered just under 150 families. Of these, about 20 (15 of them mixed marriages) rejected all relationships with the formal Jewish community.[33] The Jewish group was made up of young, highly educated, second-generation Jews of Eastern European parentage, most of whom had achieved or were likely to achieve with continued prosperity middle-class income status.[34] Park Forest Jews lived like other Park Foresters. They wore the same fashions, ate the same food except on special occasions, and participated with other Park Foresters in the culture of the "young moderns." The Jewish families were scattered, with rarely two Jewish families in adjacent houses.

Soon after these young Jewish families arrived they aligned themselves in a number of cliques, which in a remarkably short time formed a network through which news and gossip could be communicated. Gans points out that "The Jews form a cohesive in-group and tend to behave differently toward a member of the in-group than toward a non-Jew, in many cases reserving the intimacy of friendship for the former."[35] He then describes the process by which Jews attempted to recognize other Jews. They were aided in this by a Protestant minister who conducted a religious survey and informed interested Jews who the other Jews in their neighborhood were.[36] Although there was no automatic progression from recognition to acquaintance to friendship, in many cases the desire to associate with other Jews was implied from the first. In general it was a matter of only four to eight weeks before people said they had friends whom they saw regularly.

Sociability patterns did not become exclusively Jewish, but in about half the cases it was pointed out that "best friends" were Jewish. This was defended on the ground that sociability as a primary leisure activity should permit relaxation and self-expression, which was more likely when Jews associated with Jews.

[33]*Ibid.*, p. 206.
[34]*Ibid.*, p. 209.
[35]*Ibid.*, p. 210.
[36]*Ibid.*, p. 212.

The development of the formal community began with the organization of a B'nai B'rith lodge and a chapter of the National Council of Jewish Women. Attendance and active participation in the Council of Jewish Women was soon greater than in B'nai B'rith, reflecting, according to Gans, the women's greater desire for Jewish companionship.[37] Nearly a year after the new suburb of Park Forest had been occupied, some of the leaders in B'nai B'rith met one evening to discuss setting up a Sunday school, which was to be part of a synagogue, either Reform or Conservative. The women in the Council, however, refused to help form a congregation and insisted that all they needed at the time was a Sunday school. Thus began four months of discussion, argument, and conflict.

> In other groups such conflicts can often be explained in terms of power struggles between two socio-economic strata or ideological factions. In the Jewish community, however, they may signify conflicts between groups representing different stages in the ethnic adjustment to American life. . . . In Park Forest, where almost everyone is native born and acculturated to a large and similar extent, the history of the conflict over the Sunday school may be explained as the ascendency of a new type of formal Jewish community, the *child-oriented* one. This contrasts with the traditional Jewish community, which may be described as adult-oriented.[38]

The child-oriented group was successful in creating a school with a historical approach to Judaism rather than a liturgical and theological one. The Sunday school thus became an institution through which to transmit norms of ethnic culture and symbols of identification, whereas the home and family were regulated according to secular, middle-class behavior patterns. Some parents, in expressing their reasons for choosing this kind of Sunday school, pointed out that a Jewish child should know how to identify himself in relation to his Catholic and Protestant playmates. A number wanted their children to know the Jewish tradition so that they could later make a choice as to whether or not they wished to remain Jewish. Others saw Sunday school as providing a defense against later psychological hardships arising out of the minority position of Jews. And some parents were concerned about the fact that, although they selected their intimate friends

[37]*Ibid.*, p. 213. However, it should be pointed out that this greater organizational activity of women is a general suburban pattern.
[38]*Ibid.*, p. 215.

from among the Jewish group, their children chose playmates without regard to ethnic or religious origin. Although a synagogue was not yet established at the time of Gans' study, there was already considerable discussion of one. The reasons for wanting a synagogue were not entirely religious. For many it was to be a symbol of group respectability or of Jewish solidarity.[39]

This suburban community of young Americans reveals facets of Jewish acculturation which contrast with the Jewish sub-communities of a generation earlier. Perhaps this is best shown in the adaptations made in the Park Forest congregation finally established in 1951. The congregation was designated as "Eastern European Reform." It combined a permissive attitude toward practices in the home which involve the sacrifice of secular pleasures (food restrictions and so forth), Conservative ceremonies, Hebrew reading, and responsive singing. The temple kitchen was not kosher but did not serve pork. The rabbi, who was from Eastern European background, had been trained as an Orthodox rabbi but later had changed to Reform. A lecture series on secular Jewish topics attracted good attendance. Otherwise, large attendance occurred mainly on the high holy days.

The example of Park Forest shows that there is a reality to the concept of "the Jewish Community" which is bound up with sentiment, preferences, feelings of security, and also with organizational patterns. The Jews are probably the most highly organized of any minority group. There are welfare organizations that are remarkably efficient in helping Jews in many dimensions of need, from the most objective to the most personal; there are organizations from conservative and moderate to militant concerned with improving the opportunity and public image of Jews; there are organizations concerned with helping the State of Israel; there are organizations who are unconcerned with or covertly anti-Israel. All these appeal to the common responsibility of all Jews for other Jews. Many of them have broadened to espouse the situation and needs of other minorities as well as Jews. There are also several major labor unions which in the past have been largely Jewish in membership and still retain Jewish leadership, as well as cultural and benefit societies for the Jewish working class.

The status structure within the Jewish community once was marked by sharp divisions of prestige, paralleling the nineteenth-century criteria of prestige in the dominant society: date of migra-

[39]*Ibid.*, pp. 224–225.

tion, wealth, country of origin. Status differentiation has become more blurred today: this is partially due to the mobility of the descendents of the later migrants, partially due to greater Jewish solidarity evoked by the anti-Semitism of the twentieth century in Europe and America.

GENTILE ATTITUDES TOWARD JEWS

The history of Jewish-gentile relations is so old, has been so fluctuating, and has been clouded by so much dramatic, desperate, and barbaric action against Jews, even in our own time, that we have little real data about ordinary contacts. Nevertheless, some research can contribute preliminary insights.

Robin Williams and associates, of Cornell University, studied attitudes toward minorities in small cities in four regions of the United States. He and his team asked WASPs whether they had reservations about having various minority members as neighbors, work associates, members of organizations they belonged to. Those objecting to Jews were very small percentages.[40]

TABLE 16-1   REGIONAL ATTITUDES TOWARD JEWS

Those Objecting	Northeast	High Ethnic Industrial Town	Small Southern City
As neighbors	2%	6%	3%
As work associates	3%	−4%	5%
As organizational members	2%	−4%	8%

There are only two important figures in this: high ethnic communities don't want "outsiders" as neighbors, though they are more than willing to have them as work associates and in organizations (assumedly secular, i.e. labor or civic). The small Southern city doesn't mind neighbors as much as it minds work associates and organizational membership. Is it afraid of competitive leadership and strength? The study hazards no explanation.

Williams found Jews in small cities bi-cultural, rather than

[40]Robin Williams, Jr., *Strangers Next Door* © 1969. Table 16-1 reprinted by permission of Prentice-Hall, Inc., Englewood Cliffs, N. J.

marginal, having strong feelings of Jewish identity and high levels of activity in both formal and informal community activities. Overwhelmingly, he says, Jews feel themselves accepted without discrimination. This self-image, however, is not fully in accord with the conceptions held by gentile *leaders* in the small communities. About 80 per cent of these subscribe to prejudicial stereotypes of Jews. "Those who had close Jewish acquaintances regarded them as 'different'; 'not the Brooklyn type'." Nevertheless he found that those who had repeated close contact and personal association often altered their image and evaluation of Jews more generally.[41]

Williams broke down his WASP informant sample according to a model of stereotyped attitudes to separate bigots from tolerants. In a sample of those classified as bigots the question was asked: "Which of the following groups are most threatening: Jews, Negroes, foreign born, Catholics, labor unions, big business?" Forty-five per cent of the sample ranked Jews as the most threatening. (The next highest ranking was labor unions, and the lowest was Catholics).[42] It seems obvious from this finding that the fear and resentment here is that of threat to an established set of assumptions on which status rests in the face of new competitors. Whether individual Jews were in fact competing is irrelevant—they were seen as a risingly successful "other."

The real upsurge in feeling against Jews as economic competitors appears to have started after 1900, reaching a high peak at the outbreak of World War I. In Severson's study of discriminatory want ads, one finds that beginning in 1911 "ads requesting 'Christians only' or 'Gentiles only' appeared at the rate of 0.3 per 1,000, rose to 4 per cent in 1921, to 8.8 in 1923, to 13.3 in 1926; averaged 11 per cent from 1927 to 1931; dropped to 4.8 per cent in 1931, and then rose to 9.4 per cent in 1937."[43] Severson's thesis is that it was not immigration per se, or cultural conflict, which developed this latent prejudice but rather "that the particular exigency of the occasion was the coming into the clerical labor market, particularly of girls into typing and stenography, of second-generation East European immigrants. The situation could be compared today with discrimination in the employment of Negroes in white-collar occupations. When a minority begins to move up in the

---

[41]*Ibid.*, p. 304.
[42]*Ibid.*, p. 106.
[43]A. L. Severson, "Nationality and Religion in Newspaper Ads," *American Journal of Sociology*, January 1939, p. 545.

competitive areas which affect the broad base of American middle-class security, a more widespread opposition develops.

Social discrimination has been a very sensitive point with Jews. Restrictions on residence, hotel and vacation accommodations, country clubs, fraternities in colleges have all been offensive. To the degree that these social-structured groupings affect the acceptance of Jews in other spheres of life, this is an important aspect of discrimination. Where such discrimination has existed or does exist it puts a severe burden on people who both wish to be of the society and retain affectionate aspects of their own heritage.

Where discrimination persists today, and no one denies that it is still real in some dimensions of life, and particularly in some places, it is usually subtle and hard to document. It is also true that some Jews, because of their history, are hypersensitive to *any* definition of themselves by non-Jews, seeing any recognition of difference as potentially or actually anti-Semitic. In large cities where residents are accustomed to contact with many different kinds of people these definitions may carry no derogation, but are simply part of the present urban drift to acceptance of America as a pluralistic society.[44]

ANTI-SEMITISM IN THE UNITED STATES

Anti-Semitism as a public issue in the United States is usually dated from 1887. There had been hostile incidents against Jews in various localities from time to time but these were brief local affairs. But in 1877 when the New York banker Joseph Seligman wrote for reservations at the Grand Union Hotel in Saratoga Springs, New York—a fashionable resort hotel where he and his family had often stayed before—he was informed that the hotel had adopted a new policy and "did not accept Israelites." Seligman's had been one of the banking houses that had floated the United States government bond issue of 1870–1871 which, in the words of President Grant, "established American credit abroad,"[45] after the financial drain of the Civil War. Joseph Seligman was on the platform at President Grant's inauguration, attended the inaugural ball, and was a frequent guest at the White House. He was

[44] Herbert J. Gans, *The Urban Villagers: Group and Class in the Life of Italian-Americans* (New York: The Free Press of Glencoe, 1962), p. 36.
[45] Birmingham, *Our Crowd*, p. 104.

one of the earliest members of the Union League Club of New York. His refusal at the Grand Union made the national press from coast to coast.[46]

There were many factors in this incident. One was the personal and political animosity between Seligman and the new owner of the Hotel, Judge Hilton. Another was that this hotel was no longer the favorite of the most elite families who had been fellow guests in earlier days with the Seligmans, and the question has been raised as to whether or not Hilton was attempting to recruit a new clientele that was less secure, more *arriviste*, and therefore more anxious to prove their exclusiveness. Whatever the weight of these various factors, the incident and its publicity precipitated a polarization and brought to the surface much latent anti-Semitism. Birmingham thinks the results of the Saratoga Springs incident, in bringing into the open anti-Jewish attitudes, broke Joseph Seligman's spirit. He died within a year.[47]

Anti-Semitism rose in the ensuing decades, probably reaching its peak in the first half of the 1920s, but persisting in organized efforts till World War II. Baltzell, in *The Protestant Establishment*, has traced the role of intellectual and social forces in its development. He delineates the anti-Semitism of the aging Henry Adams who saw the Jews as epitomizing all the evil of industrial America, in which people of his own stratum (the old Protestant leadership of the New England merchant and scholarly occupations) had lost power and took refuge in caste-like exclusiveness.[48] Early American social scientists at the beginning of the twentieth century reflected both the influence of European racist thought and the mistrust of growing urbanism and "business ethic," which they linked to industrialization and immigration.[49]

The Populist movement, extolling the virtues of homogeneous rural life, viewed the declining importance of the rural segment of America as due to the manipulations of urban financial power, and the stereotype of the Jewish international financier, involving a conspiracy of power (and usury), emerged.[50] Anti-Semitism was a factor in many pressures to restrict immigration.[51] The fact that anti-Semitism increased concurrently with the large migration of

[46]*Ibid.*, Ch. 18, "The Seligman-Hilton Affair," pp. 141–150.
[47]*Ibid.*, p. 148.
[48]E. Digby Baltzell, *The Protestant Establishment: Aristocracy and Caste in America* (New York: Random House, 1964), pp. 87–93.
[49]*Ibid.*, pp. 104–108.
[50]Richard Hofstadter, *The Age of Reform, From Bryan to F.D.R.* (New York: Alfred A. Knopf, 1955), pp. 70–83.
[51]Baltzell, *The Protestant Establishment*, pp. 204–206.

Eastern European Jews after 1880 led many people, Gentiles and established Jews, to see the migration as the *cause* of anti-Semitism. Whereas this rationalization may have been important in the minds of some who saw the Eastern Jews as more strange and even "unassimilable,"[52] as we have seen, anti-Semitism had emerged before this migration began and was rooted in other problems and anxieties associated with social change.

Perhaps the most dramatic example of this is the mob hysteria stirred up by a Southern Populist leader against Leo Frank, a young Jewish factory manager in Georgia, which culminated in his being lynched (August 17, 1915).[53] Mr. Frank came from New York City. He was a graduate of Cornell University. He married into an established circle of Jewish business and banking in Atlanta, and symbolized the alien world of big business and big city.

It is a commonplace that when anti-minority feeling is running high, sexual charges are part of the picture. (This was true of anti-Catholic charges of the immorality of priests and nuns.) Leo Frank was charged with the murder of a very young girl who was employed in his factory. The evidence was of the flimsiest and the trial conducted with a mob milling about outside. Frank was convicted. His case was brought to the Supreme Court where the conviction was upheld, Mr. Justice Holmes writing the dissenting opinion. The Governor of Georgia ruined his political career by commuting the sentence. A day later a mob broke into the jail and transported Frank to another part of the state where he was lynched. Oscar and Mary Handlin feel that the commutation of the sentence appeared to the anti-Semites as proof of the influence on the governor of big business and money.[54] Not the least interesting aspect of the whole case was the cautious attitude of many Jews. On the whole, initially, the Jewish community of Atlanta was frightened. There were five prominent Jews on the grand jury that indicted Frank. Only after the case became a national issue were more Atlanta Jews willing to come forward in his defense.[55] The fear was there that the national attention would create anti-Semitism where there had been none. The Georgia Chamber of Commerce, in a letter to the *New York Times* denied any anti-Semitism in Atlanta or any prejudice against industrial employers. The

---

[52]*Ibid.*, p. 106.
[53]Harry Golden, *A Little Girl Is Dead* (New York: Alfred A. Knopf, 1965). See also "Why Frank was Lynched," *Forum Magazine*, Dec., 1916, p. 678.
[54]Oscar and Mary F. Handlin, *Danger in Discord: Origins of Anti-Semitism in the United States* (New York: Anti-Defamation League of B'nai B'rith, 1959).
[55]Golden, *A Little Girl Is Dead*, p. 224; *New York Times*, Aug. 19, 1915, p. 4.

Times, in an editorial, pointed out that Atlanta was no different from any other American city.[56]

In considering the Leo Frank case it is important to compare the caution of established Jews of Atlanta (and to a degree elsewhere) with the fact that the great Negro leader of the same period, Booker T. Washington, refused to join the newly created NAACP, for he feared for the ultimate result of a militant Negro organization. In thinking of the mob of people involved in violence, displaced or fearing displacement, or subject to frustrated personality needs, it might be useful to compare the action against Mexican Americans in the Los Angeles riots of 1943 (Chapter 11).

Anti-Semitism similar to that known in Europe, political in its implications, more organized, and more vitriolic in its propaganda, began to arise about 1917. In the few years following the close of World War I, large quantities of anti-Semitic literature identifying Jews with the rising European revolutionary ideology appeared; the new Ku Klux Klan arose in the North, with its generally antiforeign orientation including anti-Semitism; the Fellowship Forum distributed widely copies of the forged Protocols of the Elders of Zion; and Henry Ford commenced his anti-Semitic campaign through the publication of the *Dearborn Independent.*[57]

That these new anti-Semitic activities had an effect is indicated by an increase in various incidents of which the following are illustrative.

The board of directors of a Milwaukee golf club asked eight Jewish charter members to resign.

The secretary of the Chamber of Commerce in St. Petersburg, Florida, announced that the time had come to make St. Petersburg "a 100 per cent American gentile City."

Several large real estate concerns in New Jersey, New York, Georgia, and Florida were found to have restricted new subdivisions against Jewish occupancy.

Of more than passing interest in this period was President Lowell's graduation address at Harvard in June 1922, in which he advocated quotas against Jews. While the trustees of Harvard later rejected this suggestion, it was painfully apparent that the quota system was spreading.[58]

[56]*The New York Times,* March 5, 1914, p. 1; March 6, 1914, p. 10.
[57]Donald S. Strong, *Organized Anti-Semitism in America* (Washington, D.C.: American Council on Public Affairs, 1941), p. 15.
[58]McWilliams, *A Mask for Privilege,* pp. 38–39. By permission of the publisher Little, Brown & Co.

Abating somewhat during the late 1920s, anti-Semitism rose again in the early 1930s as the Depression intensified. Strong has indicated that there were 121 organizations actively spreading anti-Semitic propaganda in the period 1933–1940.[59] In the late 1930s anti-Semitism began to be used for the first time openly in political campaigns. The manager of the nativist third party in the 1936 Presidential election is quoted by McWilliams as stating, "the trouble with this country now is due to the money powers and Jewish politicians."[60]

While the sweeping victory of Franklin D. Roosevelt in 1936 temporarily set back the agitation, it resumed with new intensity in the late 1930s and continued until Pearl Harbor. Involved in this activity were the Christian Front, led by Father Charles Coughlin, and the Silver Shirts, directed by William Pelley. In a period of nineteen months before July 31, 1938, Pelley mailed approximately three and a half tons of anti-Semitic propaganda from his headquarters. All of this organization and propaganda obviously cost a good deal of money, and though the program was conducted by relatively unimportant people, it occasionally received support in high places. For example, McWilliams quotes Congressman John Rankin as stating to Congress that "Wall Street and a little group of our international Jewish brethren are still attempting to harass the President and Congress into plunging us into the European War."[61] It is interesting to note that this new crescendo in anti-Semitic propaganda was correlated with the increasing strength of the Nazi movement in Europe.

During World War II overt manifestations of anti-Semitism disappeared. They were considered inimical to the war effort and were discouraged by the government. Furthermore, the ideological inconsistency of supporting anti-Semitism while fighting the arch Jew-hater, Adolph Hitler, had some deterrent effect. In the few months following the end of World War II, however, the Fair Employment Practices Committee noted an increase in discrimination against Jews in employment. However, a *Fortune* Survey, which had found the incidence of anti-Semitism in the adult population to be about 9.3 per cent in 1943, found it to be 8.8 per cent in 1946.[62] Organized anti-Semitic activity failed to resume its prewar intensity, although it was far from dormant. The *American Jewish*

[59]Strong, *Organized Anti-Semitism in America*, pp. 146–147.
[60]McWilliams, *A Mask for Privilege*, p. 42.
[61]*Ibid.*, p. 46.
[62]*Fortune*, "The Fortune Survey," Feb. 1946, 33:258.

Year Book for 1950 noted a tendency for individual agitators to combine operations and to favor the distribution of inflammatory literature over holding meetings and demonstrations.[63] These trends indicate that the agitators were having a more difficult time.

This fluctuating course of anti-Semitic behavior suggests that it is more responsive to changes in socioeconomic conditions in the national community than to changes in the behavior of Jews. Such conditions are manifold and we can rarely single out one factor as being the sole determinant. At times it may appear that economic changes have a direct bearing. For example, in the first of the periods of marked discrimination, 1910–1914, the competition of increasingly Americanized Jews for employment in white-collar positions began to be felt by Gentile workers. At other times conflicts in ideologies loomed as the more significant factor. Thus the rise in anti-Semitism following World War I seems related to the spread of radical philosophy in this country, which raised anxiety in the middle class. The sharper political orientation of the anti-Semitism of the 1930s occurred at a time when legislation was enacted which made the position of the working class more secure and, in consequence, increased the anxieties of the other economic levels.

Although there has been a decline in anti-Semitism since World War II, not all has been quiescent. The most dramatic instances have been symbolic acts against institutional property. Acts of vandalism against Jewish property or molestation of Jewish persons are not new. They occurred during World War I and again during the late 20s and early 30s.[64] This particular kind of anti-minority behavior in the post-World War II period seems to reflect other and in some degree more subtle pressures in the society than war, depression, and international tension. A significant example of such outbreaks occurred early in 1960. Beginning with an incident in Cologne, Germany, on December 24, 1959, a wave of vandalism and desecration spread through the United States for nine weeks. There were 643 incidents, nearly two-thirds of which involved only the painting of swastikas. About 60 per cent of the incidents occurred in cities with more than 100,000 inhabitants. Not all these acts were directed toward specific Jewish targets. For example, schools and churches were in some instances de-

[63]American Jewish Yearbook, 1950, 51:110.
[64]Charles Wagley and Marvin Harris, *Minorities in the New World* (New York: Columbia University Press, 1958), p. 221.

faced. The larger the community, the higher the proportion of Jewish targets. The pattern was not consistent throughout the United States; Arizona had an unusually high number of incidents in proportion to its population and its Jewish population, whereas some large cities, such as St. Louis, Newark, New Orleans, Buffalo, and Indianapolis, had hardly any. In the South, states which had made some token effort of desegregation had more incidents than those which had not integrated at all or had made considerable progress in integration.[65]

The new pattern of anti-Semitism has continued as an attempt to damage property and especially symbolic property of the Jewish communities. The Anti-Defamation League tabulates 12 dynamite explosions, 2 other explosions, 9 fire bombings, 4 attempted bombings, and 47 bomb threats for the period 1960–1970.[66] These occurred in Maryland, Louisiana, New Jersey, New York, Massachusetts, Washington, D.C. A number of these occurred on High Holy Days, or at Jewish schools. Vandalism and desecration in 1969–1970 occurred in Louisiana, New York, New Jersey, Connecticut, Massachusetts, Indiana, Maine, and California.[67] These are acts of anger, terrorization, and contempt by frightened, confused and therefore angry people—probably most of them young. They *do* terrorize many Jews who can remember by reading or experience the November night in 1938 when almost all the synagogues in Germany were burned and from then on Jews had to wear yellow arm bands to identify themselves. Many of them perished in concentration camps along with the Jews of the conquered countries —6 million altogether. The Jews are neither a major political force or a major economic threat in the society as a whole. On the contrary they have contributed beyond their numbers to the development (and perhaps the civilization) of this country.

Why Does Anti-Semitism Persist?

There are different degrees of intensity of anti-Semitism, different rationalizations for it, and social science is discovering different levels of motivation. Before we indicate these different levels, it is important to point out that the problem of Jewish-Gentile relations can probably never be divorced entirely from the

[65]David Caplovitz and Candace Rogers, *Swastika 1960* (New York: Anti-Defamation League of B'nai B'rith), pp. 28–30, pp. 51–52.
[66]Testimony before the Permanent Subcommittee on Investigations of the Committee on Government Operations. U.S. Senate, Aug. 4, 1970.
[67]*Ibid.*

historical tradition. In our opinion, and contemporary evidence seems to bear this out with regard to the Soviet Union, even a revolutionary reorganization of society will not automatically solve the problem. A literate tradition, unlike the oral tradition of a folk society, can never entirely lose historical attitudes and the awareness of historic problems. This affects Gentile and Jewish thinking alike.

We have already discussed some of the forms in which anti-Semitism expresses itself. We are here interested in the psychological dimension which leads people either spontaneously to express anti-Semitic sentiments, or to be receptive to organized anti-Semitic efforts.

Much of what are popularly considered individual psychological reactions really constitute appropriate behavior within given social-structural situations. All groups with a highly developed sense of identity perceive other groups as different from themselves (ingroup, outgroup relations.) Thus many spontaneous sentiments are construed as anti-Semitic, though they do not necessarily carry with them any inner commitment or virulence. They may, however, lay the base for mobilizable sentiments if a stable situation is in the throes of change.

Another type of anti-Semitism is related to the larger minority problem of competition between those whom the dominant culture favors and the able members of any minority. It is obvious that many less able people are retained in occupational positions by the practice of discrimination. Occupational discrimination furthermore has social concomitants, involving choice of mate, club membership, social admission, and so forth. The local community power structure is reinforced by this web of relationships. The end product is to create an effect on general public policy.

A popular interpretation of anti-Semitism derives from the so-called "scapegoat" theory, which attributes the need to project blame for personal and social difficulties on somebody else. Here the historic position of the Jews makes them particularly vulnerable to being used as scapegoats, although a comparable attitude was not unknown toward the Japanese through World War II among people on the West Coast. There are different levels of insecurity in which this operates, one of which is insecurity of status, such as the threatened loss of middle-class occupation and style of life, where the individuals feel, correctly or incorrectly, that a competitive threat comes from the minority members. Paul

Massing has analyzed this factor with regard to the growth of anti-Semitism before the Nazis took over in Germany and in the subsequent support given the Nazi leadership. A 1956 study of the Nazi leaders demonstrated that in one way or another these were all marginal men in their societies. What we see from this is that organized anti-Semitism can be aroused in a threatened stratum of the society, and that leaders emerge from those who are less well integrated in the society than the general population of their age group.

The prejudiced personality has been studied from the viewpoint of both sociology and psychiatry. The study of the authoritarian personality which we present in Chapter 18 suggests that certain types of upbringing create this personality need, and that children in authoritative situations where they feel helpless are more apt to be prejudiced than children given freedom to express themselves, to be inventive and exploratory. A person brought up in this manner, it appears, attempts to repress fear, weakness, sex impulses, and aggressive feelings in order to be approved of by the punishing parents. He then compensates by attributing these "bad" repressed impulses to others whom society holds in less esteem, whether or not there is any basis for it in their behavior. Wherever the social situation provides a target for derogation, the repressed wishes will be assigned to the derogated person.

The reduction of anti-Semitism, in the light of what we have said, needs to be approached in different ways, depending on the source of the anti-Semitic attitudes. Thus it may involve varying aspects of social integration or it may be a problem at a deep level of personality structure.

Jews and Other Minorities

When Jews were here in relatively small numbers in the nineteenth century with their belief that, after Europe, here really was an open society in which they could take their place, they did not think of other minorities, but followed the established patterns of dominants. It embarrasses some Jews today, if they know, that some of those early Sephardim who helped build the first synagogue in America made a fortune in the slave trade. Jews from Western Europe shared the attitudes of Western Europe, and there were always many "establishment" Jews.

Equally there are Jews who have empathized with others

462 Jewish-Gentile Relations

against whom discrimination, injustice, and violence have been directed. Jews were active, financially and personally, in the Black Civil Rights movement.

Other minorities often don't like Jews, either out of their own imitation of what they "think" is a dominant attitude, or because, as Mario Puzo has said of the Italians, they envy the elder brother who has been more successful. In today's climate, many blacks are anti-Semitic. Part of this stems from the fact that Jews have been merchants to the black community when blacks hadn't the business skills and WASPs didn't seek black business. For some blacks, Jews become the only direct contact they have had with whites and are therefore the target for outbreaks of generalized hostility, or for the specific efforts to have blacks control business in the ghettoes.

Middle-class Jews like other middle-class families have fled the central cities as the proportion of blacks in schools and neighborhoods increased. Sometimes the migration to the suburbs has created what are in effect all-Jewish suburbs, strengthening a pluralistic relationship to the larger society. Though the attitudes of individuals in the Jewish group present a wide spectrum, it is well to remember that no other group, with the exception of Quakers, has so clearly and consistently worked to reduce discrimination for all minorities and to increase intergroup understanding.

Suggested Readings

Birmingham, Stephen. *The Grandees: the Story of America's Sephardic Elite.* New York: Harper and Row, 1971 (Dell Paperback, 1972).
Very readable account of the Spanish-Portuguese Jews before and after migration to America, based on some newly available family archive material.

Birmingham, Stephen. *"Our Crowd": The Great Jewish Families of New York.* New York: Harper and Row, 1967.
A popular book about the great German Jewish families of nineteenth century New York, their descendants and their impact on business, the arts and welfare.

Goldstein, Sidney and Calvin Goldschneider. *Jewish Americans: Three Generations in a Jewish Community.* Englewood Cliffs, N.J.: Prentice-Hall, Inc., 1968.

A careful sociological survey and analysis of the Jewish community in Providence, Rhode Island.

Kramer, Judith and Seymour Leveantman. *Children of the Gilded Ghetto.* New Haven: Yale University Press, 1961.
Three generations of Jews in Minneapolis, with emphasis on the third generation.

Shapiro, Harry L. *The Jewish People: A Biological History.* Paris, France: UNESCO, 1960.

Sklare. Marshall and Joseph Gerenblum. *Jewish Identity on the Suburban Frontier: A Study of Group Survival in the Open Society.* New York: Basic Books, Inc., 1967.
A superb study of an inter-ethnic prestigous suburb of a midwestern metropolitan center.

Teller, Judd L. *Strangers and Natives: The Evolution of the American Jew from 1921 to the Present.* New York: Delacorte Press, 1968 (Dell edition 1970).
Rich and readable presentation of main currents and cross currents in twentieth century American Jewish life.

Zborowski, Mark and Elizabeth Herzog. *Life Is With People.* New York: International Universities Press, 1952.
Two anthropologists reconstruct with great sensitivity and warmth the eastern European Jewish village of the pre-Nazi era as a culture and a way of life.

Part III

Some Problems of Policy and Theory

17   Interpretation and Assessment

In this chapter we shall provide a summary interpretation of the presence of ethnic differentiation on the dominant-minority basis throughout the history of the United States; we will delineate the remaining problem aspects of this phenomenon and consider the broad objectives which social action may undertake. Since minority status is imposed by the dominant segment and change in the status of minorities lies primarily in the dominants' hands, attention will be focused on dominant behavior.

SYNTHESIZED INTERPRETATION OF DOMINANT BEHAVIOR

Two main generalizations stand out: (1) In every situation where Americans of unquestioned dominant status have come in contact with "other" peoples within the boundaries of the United States, the dominant-minority pattern has been established. (2) This pattern has never remained completely stable, but in some instances, as with white-Negro relations, it has been, in broad terms, essentially stable for long periods of time. The long-term trend has been toward modification in the direction of elimination of ethno-racial discrimination. Short term reversals have occurred under conditions of stress, such as depression and war (as in the case of the West Coast Japanese evacuation episode).

First, the American dominant-minority pattern is, in broad terms, similar to that of interpeople relations throughout the modern world, as we found from the comparative section of Chapter One. To briefly restate, the factors involved are group self-interest,[1] ethnocentrism, superior power, and a situation in which their self-interest can best be pursued by establishing dominance. Given these elements, the more powerful establish institutional arrangements which are favorable to them and unfavorable to the other.

Group, in this case a people, self-interest is a universal consequence of the strong sense of identification with and loyalty to their own people. Even the colonial dominants fought much with one another. The United States clashed with the Spanish, the French, and after the revolution, with England. In all the situations which Americans faced either as "invaders" or "hosts" the historical situation involved institutional arrangements to their advantage and to the disadvantage of others.

In all the situations Americans of native status had the power to establish dominance. It is pertinent to recall situations where the power element of superior numbers was most lacking for the WASP invaders. The establishment of dominance was long delayed as with the Indians, and developed in less severe form in New Mexico and in Hawaii.

In no other modern nation have historical circumstances led to so heterogeneous an ethno-racial population as in the United States. This is a significant reason why ethno-racial problems have been so frequent in American history.

The historical situation differed with the North (typified by the New England farm homestead) and with the South (typified by the plantation system). Since Indians were not useful in either case, they were pushed more and more out of the way with the white Northerners expropriating their lands, and the Southerners importing African slaves.[2]

The society established by the original WASP dominants was focused around four main value orientations: (1) the democratic ethos with its stress on equality, freedom, individualism; (2) the belief in private economic enterprise, with the associated traits of activity and work, achievement and success, and material comfort; (3) Judeo-Christian beliefs (with Protestantism dominating) which have developed in the United States, as Williams views them, a somewhat distinctive "moral orientation" not as strongly

[1] Lee Rainwater is bold enough to use the unacademic term "cupidity" for group self-interest. See *The Negro American*, p. 160.
[2] Indentured laborers, white and British, were required to undergo a probationary period of servitude before being accorded dominant status.

present in other Western nations; and (4) secularism with its emphasis on rationality, progress, and scientific achievement.[3]

It should be noted that these main value orientations make no mention of racial orientation. While, in fact, American WASP self-interest led to racist behavior, it was considerably later that racist ideology was articulated. Williams considers that the presence of "racism and race related group-superiority themes" in the value systems was based on an organic "genetic" racist view of mankind, and quotes Myrdal as follows: "The race dogma is nearly the only way out for a people so moralistically equalitarian, if it is not prepared to live up to its faith."[4] The *belief* in some *genetic* determination of racial difference to which Williams refers is a necessary part of racist ideology. Since the behavioral sciences conclude that racial ideology is essentially based on myth and not fact, as we developed in Chapters 4 and 5, racial prejudice can only be reduced when public beliefs are altered.

It is often stated that racism is the main factor in perpetuating dominance. This has much validity if one makes sure to include the *behavioral* aspects of racism, i.e., discrimination, and not define racism solely in terms of prejudiced attitudes and feelings. Once racist beliefs become well established, and continue to be reconditioned in all dominant children with a substantial core of prejudice, it becomes the *normative* way of life of dominants. Not to be racist—that is, conforming—is to be a deviant and looked at askance by one's associates, or to suffer greater penalties. This distinction is further illuminated by the following paradigm by Merton, which we have adapted as follows:

Type I. *The Unprejudiced Nondiscriminator, or All-Weather Liberal.* Since this type of person believes unequivocally in the Democratic Creed, he practices what he believes consistently. Obviously such people are logical leaders for social action in the same direction. However, Merton considers the all-weather liberal prone to accept three fallacies. The first, the fallacy of group soliloquy, refers to the tendency for such like-minded people to gather in small groups and reinforce each other's attitudes and convictions rather than joining other groups and influencing them in the desired direction. Growing closely out of this is the second fallacy, called the fallacy of unanimity, which is the tendency to exag-

[3]Much of our analysis of the value system relies on Robin Williams, Jr., *American Society: A Sociological Interpretation* (New York: Knopf, 1951), Ch. 11, "Value Orientation in American Society."
[4]See Williams, American Society, p. 439. The quotation is from Myrdal, *An American Dilemma*, Vol. 1, p. 89.

gerate the extent to which the rest of the community shares their own viewpoint. A third limitation to effective action by all-weather liberals is their addiction to the fallacy of private solutions to social problems. Since he himself has solved the problem, this liberal may not feel compelled to do anything more. Rightly, he feels no guilt for himself.

Type II. *The Unprejudiced Discriminator, or Fair-Weather Liberal.* This is the type of man who has no prejudices against ethnic groups and on the whole believes in the American Creed. But he is primarily a man of expediency, who tends to support discriminatory practices when it is the easier or more profitable course. He does, however, feel guilty about his discrimination. He is therefore capable of cure, because he really wants to be cured.

Type III. *The Prejudiced Nondiscriminator, or Fair-Weather Illiberal.* This type of man does not believe in ethnic equality. Being, however, also a man of expediency, he conforms in situations in which the group sanctions are against discrimination through fear of the penalties which might otherwise ensue. But whenever the pressure against it is removed, he discriminates.

Type IV. *The Prejudiced Discriminator, or the All-Weather Illiberal.* This type is the true bigot. Since he believes firmly that certain minorities ought to be discriminated against, he can be counted on to discriminate as thoroughly as is permitted by the customs and institutions of the community. This type is obviously hardest to change, although the situation varies in relation to the prevailing mores of the area where he lives. When the mores support his position, he is a conformist, and change means making himself open to community criticism. When the mores in general are against him, he is a social deviant, and here change on his part would draw him closer into the general community structure.[5]

American Institutional Systems and Racism

It is necessary to distinguish between personal racial discrimination and that practiced by the units of an institutional system. For example, whether a corporation does or does not employ minority persons is determined by the decision of its board of directors as to whether it will yield greater profit or not under the given circumstances at hand, more than by their personal feelings.

[5]Robert K. Merton, "Discrimination and the American Creed," in MacIver, *Discrimination and National Welfare* (New York: Harper & Brothers, 1949), pp. 99–126. The terms "liberal" and "illiberal" used by Merton are based on the degree to which the types illustrated accept or do not accept and practice the American Creed—that is, "the right of equitable access to justice, freedom, and opportunity, irrespective of race or religion, or ethnic origin."

Our discussion of the major institutional complexes focuses around two propositions which the examination of each institutional system appears to support: (1) that there are conflicting interests *between* these major complexes on race issues; and (2) that there are also conflicting interests *within* each institutional complex.

THE ECONOMIC SYSTEM   Historically, the economic system has moved from mercantile capitalism to finance capitalism. Its essence, however, is still private enterprise, a system in which all individuals strive by competition and bargaining to gain the most for themselves individually. While the belief has been widely held that the indirect result of this pluralistic striving is to provide the greatest economic welfare possible for the society as a whole, our interest concerns the way the economic system influences dominant behavior.

The employer has gained from the presence of minorities cheaper labor. The lack of sophistication of immigrant laborers, as well as their interethnic rivalries, have often held back the process of unionization. But the employer must have labor, and in times of labor shortages he is likely to break the previous customary dominant practices of discrimination which barred certain minorities from given occupations or prevented their allocation to higher status positions. Sellers may adhere to prevailing prejudices against serving minority status customers, but if competitive pressures prompt one store owner to break the line, others are motivated to follow suit.

Within the economic system certain special interests gain advantage from the discrimination against minorities, as for example, employers of unskilled labor, particularly agricultural entrepreneurs or real estate operators in housing areas largely restricted to minorities, who can charge higher rents because segregation limits minority choice. Ironically, certain minority people themselves stand to gain from segregation patterns.

Once unionization was established, especially in the skilled trades, the pressure to keep the supply of such workers low resulted in the refusal to admit some minorities to apprenticeships. On the other hand, the bargaining strength of a union is increased when unionization is all-inclusive.

POLITICAL SYSTEM   At the ideal level political democracy expresses what Myrdal has called the "American Creed." The institutional complexes set up to implement it include democratic citizenship, democratic government, and public education.

Democratic citizenship involves both equal opportunity to participate in government and equal protection from it. Participation includes the right to vote, to join a political party, to run for office, and to be appointed to a government job. Protection includes the right to trial by jury, equal treatment by law-enforcing officers, and equal protection from physical harm or property damage. Several former minorities have secured all these rights.

The exercise of civic rights provides minority citizens opportunity to vote in their own interest. In areas of minority group concentration they have elected members of their own group to public office and secured appointment to government positions. Since government is the only institution whose membership embraces the entire population, it is constrained to operate for the benefit of all more than other institutions.

In actual operation the democratic political system falls far short of its idealistic value system. Citizens in the democratic society may be divided into "politicians"—those actively interested in achieving political power or occupational position directly in control of elected officials—and those whose political activity is motivated by other self-interests. The politician attempts to make the best judgment of which way the majority of his electorate feels on any issues and tends to act accordingly. In relation to minority problems, this explains the frequent change of position of many politicians, as for example, why politician X appeals to segregationist sentiment to win election, and when faced with the responsibilities of office acts less "racist"-minded.

The emphasis on the "individual" in the American value system has tended to promote unrealistic thinking about the political power of the individual person, as De Gré has analyzed. "A sociological theory of freedom, therefore, must take as its starting point the *socius*, that is, the individual as a member of a group, class, or social type, rather than the abstract individual-as-such that forms the nucleus of Romanticism."[6] He further contends that the greater stability of the pluralist-democratic political structure in comparison with totalitarian and oligarchic regimes lies in the absence of the concentration of sufficient power in any one power bloc to dominate the others. We might note that the current

---

[6]Gerard De Gré, "Freedom and the Social Structure," *American Sociological Review*, October, 1946, p. 53.

"Black Power" movement is quite in line with the normative political processes. It has been precisely in the South, though less today than earlier, that the overwhelming concentration of power in the hands of whites vis-a-vis Negroes has most strongly nullified the democratic process.

In actual practice the administration of law and government often reflects the prejudice of the officials who administer it; even unprejudiced officials tend to consider how the dominant community wants it administered. Our earlier discussion of the highly sensitive area of policing in Negro areas well illustrates this point.

Finally, our governmental system is itself pluralistic in two main ways. First, powers at the federal, state, and local levels often conflict. A governor of a Southern state was quoted as saying in effect, "the federal court has ordered desegregated schools, let it enforce it." Again, within governmental administration, the various branches often conflict with one another, best illustrated in the huge bureaucracy of the federal government. A conspicuous race-related example is the conflict between the Justice Department, concerned with maintaining "law and order," and HEW, concerned with improving health, education, and welfare, especially where it is most needed.

PUBLIC EDUCATION   The right of all children to free public education has had some effect in undermining minority status. Minority valedictorians deflate the myth of categorical minority inferiority. The contact between dominant and minority children in unsegregated schools is formally on a basis of equality, thus giving dominant status students the experience of associating with minority students on a plane of equality. Despite their handicapped background the abler minority students achieve skills and training enabling upward social mobility.

In actual operation, the public-school system, however, has reflected the pervasive community patterns of dominant-minority intergroup relations. The faculties are disproportionately drawn from the dominant population and in varying degrees hold dominant prejudices which bias, often unconsciously, their relations with minority students. The informal relations among students often manifest prejudice in the formation of cliques and the refusal to elect minority students to certain clubs.

Finally, the context of the curriculum as found in textbooks and as taught by teachers indicates considerable prejudice. In this connection, a recent review summarizes as follows:

Our public schools, through the use of racist textbooks written, edited, published, selected, and taught by whites, are inculcating into white children false notions of superiority over people of color by presenting a distorted view of the historical and contemporary roles of whites and nonwhites in the world. In addition, our schools teach children an attitude of optimism toward race relations, a notion that "things aren't really so bad" and "everything will work out" if we just keep on as we have been doing. Our school system, like our society in general, fails to recognize that the ideals of justice and equality for all cannot be achieved without fundamental change in the institutions of white America.[7]

With reference to teachers, the summary reads in part:

It should be remembered that textbooks do not teach children. The well-informed teacher can instil understanding in her students irrespective of biases and prejudices in textbooks, and the poorly informed teacher, especially if she herself has racial prejudices, can undermine even the best text.

Most teachers are between these two extremes. Often they recognize the problem, but have neither the time nor resources to revise their understanding of U.S. history, either in the domestic sphere or in U.S. foreign policies.[8]

While there has been a recent trend toward more attention to racial history and a less prejudiced teaching of it, most adults were taught as above, and, therefore, many are not favorable to this liberal educational policy toward race.

RELIGIOUS INSTITUTIONS   For the purpose of interpreting dominant behavior, we may confine our discussion to Protestantism and Catholicism.[9] In both these Christian institu-

[7]A recent study of the leading textbooks used in social science studies finds some improvement in the treatment of minorities over past reviews but concludes "that a significant number of texts . . . continue to present a principally white, Protestant, Anglo-Saxon view of America past and present, with the nature and problems of minority groups largely neglected." According to Mr. Kane there is not a single textbook which presents "a reasonably complete and undistorted picture of America's many minority groups." See Michael B. Kane, *Minorities in Textbooks* (Chicago: Quadrangle Books, Copyright 1970 by the Anti-Defamation League of B'nai B'rith).

[8]Louis F. Knowles and Kenneth Prewitt, eds. *Institutional Racism in America* © 1969. Reprinted by permission of Prentice-Hall, Inc., Englewood Cliffs, New Jersey.

[9]Up to World War II we might have omitted Catholicism but on the assumption that Catholicism as well as Judaism has now acquired status equality Catholicism must now be considered in the dominant institutional pattern.

tions at least the formal ethical tenets are against racial and ethnic discrimination. In recent years there has been more positive action in both these religious systems to implement their ethical codes in intergroup relations. This positive action has been more unified and manifest by Catholicism than by Protestantism, in part because the authoritative structure of the Roman Catholic church makes it more possible.[10] Currently the ecumenical movement in the major religions may strengthen the efforts of all organized religion in this direction.

In theological aspects Christian institutions have tended to perpetuate prejudice and discrimination indirectly, as indicated in Chapter 3. Glock and Stark found survivals in doctrine and rituals in Protestantism still perpetuating anti-Semitism.[11] More important to our interest is the informal cleavage in Protestantism between Fundamentalists and Liberal churches. The Liberal churches are less race prejudiced than the Fundamentalists, and in increasing numbers are inviting minority membership.

Finally, the "social" aspect of religious institutions cannot realistically be ignored. Church affiliation and activity is in considerable degree a matter of sociability. In the nation at large but more visible at the local community level, there exists a status differentiation between various Protestant denominations, and less strongly, in Catholic church organization. Episcopalians and Presbyterians usually rank higher than Baptists. "Sociability" involves interaction between people of equal status, which partly explains the racial and ethnic segregation seen in local congregations. It has been pointed out that the hour between 11 and 12 on Sunday morning is the most segregated hour of the week.

THE NON-PECUNIARY INTELLECTUAL AND WELFARE COMPLEX   We refer here to a congeries of institutions which while considered in some sociological analyses of American society have not generally been thought of as a broad institutional complex. Specifically we refer to research agencies (academic or

[10]Lenski found in a Detroit research where the major religious groups were asked to indicate their images of one another that the most favorable image of the Catholic group was held by Negro Protestants. He attributes this to the awareness among black Americans of the strong stand taken by the Catholic hierarchy for racial integration. Gerhard Lenski, *The Religious Factor* (New York: Doubleday, 1961), p. 67.

[11]Charles Y. Glock and Rodney Stark, *Christian Beliefs and Anti-Semitism* (New York: Harper & Row, 1966). Chief finding was that one-fourth of those Christians classified as anti-Semitic had a religious basis for their views and only five per cent with prejudice against Jews lacked any evidence of supposed theological self-justification.

otherwise), social work agencies (some of which are, of course, in the governmental structure), and Foundations. The major characteristic of this currently vast network which provides a common denominator is the absence of the pecuniary interests, or, positively stated, the presence of either an intellectual interest, the search for truth for its own sake with the hope that the findings will serve some useful purpose, or a humane interest, improving the welfare of society, or both[12] The research findings in the behavioral field greatly undermine the whole rationale of intergroup prejudice and discrimination; and the work of social agencies alleviates the effects of the underprivilege which discrimination has produced.

What is most crucial is the fact that there are built-in elements in this structure which to a considerable degree, protect the non-pecuniary institutions from the onslaughts of other interests. Neither government itself nor reactionary groups can prevent these truths from publication or humane activities from being pursued. (The McCarthy periods do not last indefinitely.) For example, the devastating criticism of the Boston School System written by an ex-teacher in a ghetto school *was* published, and *was* favorably reviewed by an eminent psychiatrist associated with Harvard University.[13]

THE OPEN-CLASS SYSTEM   Strictly speaking, the class system is not an institutional system. It is, however, interwoven with the entire institutional structure. Sociological thought generally agrees that status distinctions are inherently part of the nature of the modern industrial-urban society, as they have been in earlier societal forms. But relatively the class system of the modern society is an open system where one's eventual position is in substantial measure *achieved* by one's own efforts as distinct from being *ascribed* at birth.

The open-class system is distinguished from the dominant-minority system in that it is not an imposed phenomenon; and categorical barriers to upward social mobility are absent. If, as many social scientists hold, the open-class system is positively

[12]That persons employed within this broad complex manifest often the pecuniary and status-seeking behavior found in pecuniary institutions is true enough. But there are built-in checks which limit this behavior to a secondary level.
[13]Jonathan Kozel, *Death at an Early Age. The Destruction of the Hearts and Minds of Negro Children in the Boston Public Schools.* (Boston: Houghton Mifflin, 1967.) Reviewed by Robert Coles, a research psychiatrist at Harvard, in *The New York Times Book Review*, October 1, 1967, Section 7, p. 1.

functional for the order of modern societies, its value can be greatly increased by the elimination of the ascribed bases of the dominant-minority system.

The flexibility of the open-class system forestalls the development of any such strong class consciousness, as is currently present in several Latin American countries. There is no homogenous mass proletariat on which to build class consciousness. With reference to ethno-racial relations, the "poor" are divided along ethno-racial lines, and the present trend toward reviving subethnicity will probably make them less so, not more.

The Primary Group Structure

When racism has been established, its continuation involves the constant socialization of dominant status children to absorb it without reflection. This process begins in the family and is developed further in restrictive peer associations and community norms.[14] Even though the opportunity to discriminate is lacking for many dominant children, stereotyped derogatory images are established and tend to carry on into adult life. This early racist orientation prepares them to expect and accept dominant-minority personal and institutional role patterns in adult life, unless some intervening circumstances arise.

Summary Comment

The purpose of this analysis of the main institutional systems has been to relate it to racist behavior and prejudice. What we find is that while racism permeates all of the systems, counter influences are also found in all of them. Their survival as institutions does not require racism. This opens the possibility of eliminating racism without fundamentally changing the systems. From the viewpoint of our acknowledged value orientation, this is a hopeful conclusion. We respect the point of view held by some that racism cannot be eliminated without a radical change in the political and economic structure. If they turn out to be right, in our judgment this will postpone the demise of racist behavior in the United States for a long time. There are no clear indications that any substantial number of dominant Americans, or many from

---

[14]It has been observed that at the poorest levels where dominant status children are *originally* brought up in mixed neighborhoods, less ethno-racial prejudice is found.

minority populations, currently want to basically change the American institutional structure, however much they see need for numerous reforms. Take as an illustration voting behavior in presidential elections during this century. The highest percentage of the total votes cast for a Socialist candidate for the Presidency was in 1912 when Eugene Debs received 16 per cent of all the votes cast. Since then the highest percentage of Socialist votes has been 2.2 in 1924 for Norman Thomas.[15]

THE PROBLEM AREAS

Definition of the Situation as a Problem

Whether a situation is a problem or not depends on how people view it. Whenever enough people feel discomfort about a situation—usually brought about by change—they designate the situation a "problem." Once a problem is named, people in Western culture and most particularly the United States expect action to be taken to solve it. But there is considerable variation in the definition of the nature of the problem and therefore variation in ideas as to ways of solving it. In the American scene four major modes of viewing the "problem" are common: (1) those who believe that minorities should remain minorities, that the problem is one of keeping them in that status; (2) those who hold that the welfare of the depressed minorities should be improved within the framework of segregation, a philosophy followed by some moderate Southerners toward Negroes; (3) those who see a problem only when tension and hostility between groups disturb the peace of the community through disorderly violence; (4) those who define the problem in the light of the American Creed.

It is impossible to discuss social policy without choosing a value frame of reference. Having adopted the value frame of reference of the American Creed we define the problem areas of intergroup relations in its terms.

Minority Problems and the American Creed

The value system of the American Creed holds that all members of American society should have equal opportunity without experiencing discrimination based on race, religion, sex, nation-

---

[15]Votes for other radical parties have been inconsequential nationwide.

ality identity, or lineage. Thus the total elimination of discrimination on these grounds is the basic problem, and the primary goal of all social policy should be directed to that end.

A second problem area arises from the integrationist-pluralistic trends in intergroup relations, as we repeatedly raised in our discussion of the various minority situations.[16]

A third problem concerns the welfare of minorities—such matters as employment, higher income, better education, and improved health conditions. These welfare problems require the most immediate attention but should not deflect social policy from the primary goal of eliminating ethno-racial prejudice. These problem areas interrelate, which adds difficulty to discussing each separately.

Assessment of the Current Problem Areas

A broad assessment of the current problem situation of the various ethno-racial peoples, who have had at some time or still possess minority status, is presented in Chart 17-1 with reference to categorical discrimination, cultural pluralism, structural pluralism, and welfare indices. We include the WASPs, English Protestants, and other peoples of European lineage now generally considered a part of this ethnic component. It also seems necessary to deal with Hawaii's peoples in a distinctive way for reasons indicated in Chapter 15.

The chart suggests problems related to discrimination, with a wide degree of salience; to pluralism—most marked in the lower status groups; and to welfare for the lower status groups. The chart also suggests an approximate positive correlation between degrees of discrimination and welfare.

SOCIAL POLICY AND SOCIAL ACTION

The term social policy implies awareness that problems exist and that social action needs to be taken to cope with them. Having defined the nature of the problems and delineated the specific problem areas, let us now discuss social policy and social action to implement it.

[16]Gordon develops this theme cogently in his *Assimilation in American Life* (New York: Oxford University Press, 1964), Ch. 8, "Assessment and Implications for Intergroup Relations," pp. 233–265.

CHART 17-1   SUMMARY ASSESSMENT: SITUATION OF AMERICAN ETHNIC COMPONENTS

Group	Discrimination	Degree of Cultural Pluralism	Degree of Structural Pluralism	Welfare Situation
Caucasian, Protestant, North-West European Immigrants	None	None	None	Normative, skewed upward
Caucasian, Catholic, South-East European, Irish Descendant	Little in urban America; declining	Some, varying with socioeconomic status	More in large cities; in interethnic Catholic subcommunities	Highly varied, skewed downward
Jewish American	Subtle, likely to increase in crisis periods; some ascription by descent	Variable, depending on generation	High	Moderately varied, skewed upward
Japanese American	Rapidly declining	Disappearing with the Sansei	Moderate	Varied, skewed upward
Chinese American	Declining	Considerable	Moderate, generational	Normal for descendants of "new" Chinese, low for "old" but improving
Mexican American	Considerable	High	High	Low, small upper classes excepted
Puerto Rican (Mainland)	Considerable	High	High	Low
Black American	Very high, but declining; ascription by descent	Little. "Are culturally Americans"	Very high, Primarily due to imposed segregation	Improving for upper classes; very low for masses
American Indian	Extensive for tribal Indians; no ascription by descent	High for reservation Indians	High for tribal Indians	Very low
Hawaii's non-Caucasian Peoples	In process of assimilation on a sub-pluralistic basis, less clear for "Hawaiians" and for newcomer Polynesians.			

Social Forces versus Social Action

At many points in preceding chapters reference has been made to broad social forces in the changing society that impinge on minority situations in the absence of any social action directly undertaken. When such a force is working toward the goal desired, direct social action may only be needed to foster it. However, when the social force is operating to impede the goal, social action is needed to cope with it, if possible. For example, the general expanding economy has offered opportunity for the upward mobility of some minority persons, whereas automation has retarded the advance of blacks. Social action groups should guard against strategic moves which may arrest or temporarily reverse the trend of a force favorable to their goal, and conversely work to cope with those against it.

Indirect Social Action

By indirect social action we mean activities aimed at improving the general conditions in society known to breed prejudice and discrimination. Such conditions are economic changes creating downward mobility in one or more segments of the society; the ever-present efforts of special economic groups to cultivate discrimination for profit; and the failure of certain governmental officials to implement vigorously the democratic institutions they are charged with administering. Persons usually interested in reducing minority discrimination are apt to support public policy aimed at the general conditions favorable to nondiscrimination which widely benefit the nation in general.

The Agents of Social Action

While, ideally, resolving the problems of minorities is the task of all citizens, in fact social action generally is undertaken by groups and agencies most concerned. The most important agencies are government—legal, legislative, and administrative; and at all levels—federal, state, and local; private welfare agencies; and social action groups, initiated by dominants primarily or exclusively interested in the problems of minorities. In addition, there are certain agencies whose broader field of interest encompasses the minority problem, for example, the American Civil Liberties Union. Again even individuals can effect social policy by their support of action groups or by exemplary nondiscriminatory behavior. Finally, many minorities themselves initiate social action either in groups including dominant status members or in groups exclusively their own, sometimes in behalf of their own group exclusively, or for other minorities as well as their own.

Reducing Discrimination

Two main lines of approach to reducing discrimination are (1) to alter the social structure and (2) to change prejudicial attitudes. Change in either affects the other. Since World War II there has been a marked shift in social action efforts toward the first line of approach. Altering the social structure to require the integration of minorities into specific associations of the main institutional structure affords a shorter route to change than attempting to change prejudicial attitudes. As the Merton paradigm indicated, the salience of prejudice varies widely.

Various social action groups have worked for at least a quarter of a century to secure the integration of minority status persons into social structures previously denied them. Research studies of such efforts are numerous and have produced substantive knowledge concerning how integration may be accomplished most effectively. A summary of the research findings for the purpose are stated in 27 propositions presented in Dean and Rosen's *A Manual of Intergroup Relations*.[17] Action aimed at new breakthroughs against discrimination may well be guided by the specialized knowledge now available, but often it is not.

These extensive voluntary efforts toward desegregation have demonstrated that increasing contact and interaction between dominant and minority persons can be accomplished without serious social disturbance, and that their continuance tends to produce a lessening of prejudice under certain conditions.[18]

Certain conditions are favorable to successful integration. Among the conditions are that: (1) contact take place in a situation where both are defined as equal; (2) the contact be continuous and intimate enough to challenge the stereotype of mi-

[17]John P. Dean and Alex Rosen, with the assistance of Robert B. Johnson, *A Manual of Intergroup Relations* (Chicago: The University of Chicago Press, First Phoenix Edition, 1963).
[18]Among the earlier studies demonstrating this point were Morton Deutsch and Mary C. Collins, *Interracial Housing* (Minneapolis: University of Minnesota Press, 1951), and Gerhart Saenger and E. Gilbert, "Customer Reaction to the Integration of Negro Sales Personnel," *International Journal of Opinion and Attitude Research*, 4 (1950), pp. 57–76.

norities held by dominant persons; (3) the minority person does not act according to the stereotype; (4) the situation poses no threat to the security of the dominants involved; (5) the situation is one in which the two groups involved have a common interest; and (6) the more the community norms, or the norms of the reference groups most influential for the dominant parties, support the new integration, the more effective the process will be.[19]

Efforts to increase integration, especially of Negro Americans prior to 1954, were few and thus progress was slow. Since the Supreme Court School Desegregation Decision the employment by social action groups of "forced" integration has greatly increased. By "forced" integration we mean integration effected by the order of authoritative agencies or persons with the power to dictate the process without the consent of all the dominants affected by it. Here the social scientist faces the lack of sufficient research to evaluate the results and must rely on broad observations. Some causal connection between protest activities and the effective desegregation of many public sectors of the society is clear. On the other hand, even in political jurisdiction with open-occupancy housing laws, successful resistance to residential integration is still strong; and "forced" integration has increased the articulate expression of prejudice and in some instances prompted counter organized activity on the part of the less liberal-minded dominant public. Nevertheless, the nation is now committed to integration. Social action groups can best attempt to guide this process with strategic expediency toward the ultimate goal.

EDUCATION   In general, social science has found that the educational approach—giving people the facts about dominant-minority relations—has relatively little value in reducing discrimination or prejudice. Furthermore, recent researches have tended to question the previous belief that educated people are less prejudiced than the less educated. While generally on attitude tests the more highly educated people respond verbally with less prejudice, and tend to support legal equality, inner feelings of prejudice and discrimination in primary group relations have been revealed in recent studies.[20] Williams put it this way: "The prejudice of the well educated, when it does exist, may in some

[19]See Robin Williams, *Strangers Next Door*, Ch. 7, "Social Integration and Inter-group Attitudes" for a fuller discussion.
[20]See, for example, Charles H. Stember, *Education and Attitude Change* (New York: The Institute of Human Relations Press, 1961), and Robin Williams, *Strangers Next Door*, pp. 374–375.

ways be harder, colder, more polite and more thoroughly buttressed by rationalizations, but it is less likely to be global, diffuse, and all-or-none in character."[21]

Welfare Problems

All national states have been class differentiated and had a lower class with a level of living usually characterized as "poor." But poverty until the nineteenth century was generally viewed as an inevitable part of social life. In the twentieth century, however, as a consequence of enormous economic and technological development, there has emerged the conviction that poverty, with the associated frustrations of the lower class, constitutes a "problem" that not only should be but can be eliminated. In varying degrees all modern nations have implemented this belief to a degree.

In the American public there are many beliefs concerning the underprivileged population. We shall focus on two contrasting conceptions: (1) the views that the "poor" are poor because they are incapable, either by genetic determination or in consequence of their willful practice of traits considered disorganizing, for example, laziness; and (2) the belief that the causes of this underprivileged condition lie in the malfunctioning of the social order (quite positively beneficial to the welfare of other classes). Both the current effect of social forces, especially as seen in the governmental sectors, and the development of the behavioral sciences have tended to establish wider acceptance of the second viewpoint. The full acceptance of the welfare state is retarded, however, by the influence of those who still hold the self-responsible viewpoint of lower-class behavior. Misunderstanding of the facts (perhaps because the truth is unpalatable) causes certain publics to oppose the expansion of welfare benefits to the "irresponsible poor." As Young puts it:

> Often citizens have curious misconceptions about typical relief recipients and resent paying money to "all those able-bodied men." It should be noted that approximately nine out of every ten persons who receive assistance is either too young or too old to work, is disabled or busy caring for youngsters who are receiving ADC —aid to dependent children. Of the remaining 10 per cent, most want real jobs rather than work relief or welfare subsistence.[22]

[21]Robin Williams, *Strangers Next Door*, p. 375.
[22]Whitney M. Young, Jr., *To Be Equal*, p. 165.

The most immediate way to cope with the current unrest in the black population is to find employment for its unemployed and underemployed, especially males and youth. Since, however, there is widespread lack of skills, effective job rehabilitation requires extensive training, already initiated in various governmental programs, such as those developed under the Office of Economic Opportunity.

REPARATIONS: A NEW SLOGAN   On a broader scale with reference to welfare, from black leadership in the late 1960s the concept of reparations, or redress emerged. It is based on the idea that since for so long black Americans have been so discriminately underprivileged, they deserve special economic redress.[23] A formal presentation of this idea was made in a Black Manifesto addressed to the white Christian churches and Jewish Synagogues in 1969. In this manifesto was a demand for a half million dollars from the white religious organizations with specifications as to how it should be allocated.[24] This particular presentation made by James Farmer was a dramatic document, and the National Black Economic Development Conference was not adequately organized, nor even well enough supported by blacks. By various devices, including a gift of $200,000 by the Episcopal Church to another black organization, Farmer's organization was virtually destroyed. While this spectacular move failed, the broad idea that reparations on a very large scale were due to black Americans has been used by others at various times in an effort to influence white America to give the highest priority to improving the welfare of blacks.

Problems of welfare and those of integration often present a dilemma. Before the nondiscriminatory laws were passed, projects to improve housing in black areas promoted integration. In practice, even with the nondiscriminatory requirements now, an open-housing project may turn into a segregated project. This dilemma has been, at the turn of this decade, highlighted by the school desegregation problem in the North, in particular as related to the need for more extensive bussing to obtain racial balance in school enrollment. Improvement of the quality of schools in ghetto areas might be offered ghetto people, but this reinforces segregation. But when inner city ghettos are so large that bussing across

[23]See Arnold Schuchter, *Reparations: The Black Manifesto and Its Challenge to White America* (Philadelphia: J. B. Lippincott, 1970).
[24]*Ibid.*, p. 191.

municipal lines is required for racial integration, strong resistances have arisen in the white suburban areas involved, and
to some extent by ghetto parents as well.

Finally, one notes the unfortunate tendency to associate welfare problems with minorities, currently with blacks. Gunnar
Myrdal has recently pointed out the serious threat to world peace
posed by emphasizing race in the relations between poor and rich
countries, and similarly the threat to orderly race relations in the
United States if the extension of welfare activities is thought of
as a black problem rather than a problem of Americans of all
ethnic, racial, and religious backgrounds.[25]

Problems of Ethnic Pluralism

As is noted throughout this book, sociological writing places
considerable emphasis upon what is perceived as a trend toward
the retaining of sub-ethnic identity and its revitalization among
non-WASP peoples who already are substantially assimilated.
There is, however, a need to research more precisely the proportion of those qualified for a particular ethnic identity who actually
do so identify themselves; and what proportion identify themselves ethnically as simply "Americans" and are accepted as such
by other Americans. For ethnic groups who are now approaching
equality in status, the problem is largely an internal matter. For
blacks it is also an intragroup problem as discussed in Chapter 9,
but in their case it is more clearly related to their larger problem
of eliminating discrimination.

The Interrelationship Between Minorities

In our treatment of each minority we have focused largely on
a single-paired relationship—that between the particular minority
and those Americans with dominant status. The variation in degrees of discrimination is seen in Chart 17-1, roughly ranked from
top to bottom.

Social science has long noted that as various minorities moved
up the rank order of subordination, they tended to act toward
those below them like the dominants. Stated otherwise, acculturation has involved adopting the normative prejudice of the dominant WASPs. As an increasing number of former minority status

[25]Address delivered before the American Institute of Planners 50th Anniversary
Convention in Washington, D.C., Oct. 3, 1967.

people reach equal status, they find the rules of the game have been changed—that it is now (outside the South) no longer normative to display racial prejudice, openly at least, and that other advantages open to the earlier WASPs, like cheap labor and low taxes, are now not available to them. It is not surprising that such newcomers to dominant status should feel a certain ambivalence between justice and equality on the one hand, and personal competitive advantage on the other. Such people can often be mobilized to do *for* minorities but not *with* minorities, since "with" is a threat to their new and precarious status.

CURRENT TRENDS AND PROSPECTS

Because of their greater numbers, their continued lower status, and the aggressive challenge which they made in the 1960s, discussion of the current trends and prospects in America's ethnoracial situation is bound to center upon black Americans. In fact, it is pertinent to note that the other more subordinated minorities —Mexican Americans, mainland Puerto Ricans, and Indians—have been influenced by the black movement to act in a more militant manner.

The black movement as it moved into the 1970s has, in relative terms, slowed down as indicated by less dramatic spontaneous uprisings and less outward activity on the part of the more militant groups. It seems probable that this partial lull is due in part to the official repression directed especially at the Black Panthers. It is also possible that the black activist groups are assessing the effects of their activities to plan what strategies will be most promising for future gains. Already may be noted a shift in emphasis toward political gains which bring about more association with whites. At the higher levels of politics this was conspicuously seen at the Democratic Convention in July, 1972.

Another notable trend is the increasing pressure to promote the idea that in all political and civic affairs in communities with substantial minority populations, adequate representation of each minority should be included. This has been carried in its extreme form to the idea that representation of minorities should be substantially proportional to the per cent of each minority in each community. There has been in the past few years a substantial move in this direction.

Small increases in the process of integrating blacks into previously all-white economic enterprises are continuing, and in higher ranking positions proceeding beyond "tokenism." There have also been small increases in housing integration as long as it is kept at a small percentage.

With reference to the ghettos, only token improvements are being made, and there is currently little prospect of marked improvements in them. This problem is closely interrelated with urban redevelopment in general. While the recognition of this as a problem has considerable priority, the allocation of vast capital needed for this purpose faces competition with other national priorities: military security needs and environmental anti-pollution needs are examples. Thus, the continued existence of unreconstructed ghettos suggests the continuation of the frustrating conditions likely to lead to sporadic disorder.

On the whole, whites have made adjustment to the right of black equality in public accommodations, and to accept them as co-workers. In the latter case the increase of blacks into new occupational levels has not yet gone far enough to provide much competition. There does not appear to be a marked change in white willingness to associate with blacks on an equal basis in the primary group area involving social acceptance. No perceptible gain in white "positive invitation," as we have labeled it, has been noted.

Suggested Readings

Barbour, Floyd, B., ed. *The Black Seventies.* New York: Porter Sargent, 1970.
Black authors look at the present to reach into the future.

Henderson, William L. and Larry C. Ledebur. *Economic Disparity: Problems and Strategies for Black Americans.* New York: The Free Press, 1970.
Describes and evaluates the programs by government agencies and white private enterprise for the economic improvement of black Americans.

Kane, Michael B. *Minorities in Textbooks.* Chicago: Quadrangle Press, 1970.
A study of the treatment of minorities in social studies textbooks in high schools.

Knowles, Louis and Kenneth Prewitt, eds. *Institutional Racism in America.* Englewood Cliffs, N.J.: Prentice-Hall, 1969.
Examines and interprets racism in the main American institutions and in community life.

Rose, Peter, I., ed. *Nation of Nations: The Ethnic Experience and Racial Crisis.* New York: Random House, 1971.
A collection of essays providing varying perspectives on the American ethnic experience.

Warren, Roland L., ed. *Politics and the Ghettos.* New York: Aldine-Atherton, 1969.
Thirteen specialists examine the structure and process of policy making relevant to the ghettos.

Williams, Robin, Jr. *Strangers Next Door: Ethnic Relations in American Communities.* Englewood Cliffs, N.J.: Prentice-Hall, 1964.
Chapter 7, "Social Integration and Inter Group Attitudes" and Chapter 10, "Structures and Processes in Multigroup Society" are especially pertinent to this chapter.

18 Sociological Theory and Dominant– Minority Relations

WHAT IS THEORY?

Throughout this book there have been references to various theoretical propositions. Indeed, Chapters 9 through 16 roughly examine the validity of the proposition with which we concluded Chapter 2: that dominant-minority relations in the United States are taking the form of structural pluralism rather than the "melting pot" or assimilation expectations of half a century ago. In a sense, therefore, the student has been examining data to test an hypothesis, which is the theoretic task. Students may even be ready to ask pertinent questions that will stimulate further exploration that may refine, correct, or develop the original statement. For example: Is structural pluralism chosen as a mode of adaptation more by young people or by older age groups? Is it more characteristic of affluent or poorer members of a minority? To what extent is it imposed by dominant patterns of exclusion or freely chosen by a minority group? Answering these questions will be theory building.

The social sciences are still very young compared to the natural sciences. There is much more refinement still to come both of theory and of research methods. The Romans developed a crude theory of physical stress that was sufficient for them to be able to build bridges and aqueducts, but they were not advanced to the point of putting a man on the moon. Social science is still largely in the bridge and aqueduct stage.

THE INTERDISCIPLINARY NATURE OF SOCIAL SCIENCE

The "social" or "behavioral" sciences have all been concerned, though with different emphases, with man's interaction with other men and with his physical environment. Psychology, psychiatry, anthropology, sociology, and history have all contributed to our understanding of dominant-minority relations. Usually psychology and psychiatry have been concerned with problems of learning and perceiving as they are related to people's motivation, attitudes toward others, adaptability in the face of change, and reactions to stresses of the environment or the life cycle. Anthropologists have seen man as a "culture building animal" and have focussed on culture (values, beliefs, language, and other symbols as well as social organization) as man's instrument of adaptation to the physical environment. Much of anthropology has concentrated on small societies which can be studied whole through the careful recording of a researcher who has lived, often at recurring intervals, among the people he or she is describing. Sociologists have increasingly concentrated on studying the stabilized forms of social organization and have developed increasingly sophisticated mathematical methods for analyzing large bodies of data. History, of course, gives a comparative dimension essential to the analysis of social change. Today large interdisciplinary teams may work together, each contributing their specific skill, just as in medicine, biology, or astrophysics most research is team research involving people from different but related fields.

In the studies we have cited in this book we have leaned heavily on the related behavioral sciences, though the focus of our analysis has been *sociological*. Minorities exist within the larger social structure and share in the broader social processes. Therefore there is no separate body of theory of dominant-minority relations, though minority groups may be a special focus for research and for the formulation of special segments of theory. In this chapter we will not attempt to review all the theoretical contributions to our understanding of minority situations. Nor are we writing any new integrated theoretical statement of our own. The purpose of the chapter is to show what theory is about, how it grows, and to give students a chance to speculate on and to challenge the illustrations we have selected. It is the nature of science that it is never complete; one theoretical insight builds upon another or is corrected by another and raises new questions to be explored.

In examining theory the proper questions to be asked are: Does it take into account all the facts that are relevant to its theme? Are the assumptions underlying the initial formulation acceptable? What verifying evidence has been submitted, or should be undertaken as research?

The sources of insight that lead to theory building occur in several ways. Some may be arrived at from concern about problems demanding action. Sometimes theory evolves out of the accidental observations of a person thinking about the general relationships which the particular incident makes vivid. It is part of the folklore of science for example, that the observation of an apple falling from a tree crystallized Newton's formulation of the theory of gravity. Much of the advanced development of science is derived from logical, abstract thought, which must then be validated by appropriate testing procedures. Application can be an end product, as well as an initial stimulus of theory building.

Action and theory are not a dichotomy. As action inevitably stimulates speculation, in a scientifically-oriented society theory sooner or later must be tested if it is to survive in the accepted system of knowledge. Part of the task of the behavioral sciences in the twentieth century has been to develop increasingly reliable methods of testing propositions. That great gains have been made in reliability and acceptance of scientific investigation in the behavioral fields is attested by the use of an "expert brief," prepared by social psychologists, sociologists, and anthropologists in the United States Supreme Court Decision (*Brown* v. the *Board of Education*) on school desegregation.

Theory building occurs on several levels. There is the search for more refined and therefore more precise definition of terms on which all researchers may agree. This, in the jargon of professional research, is call "conceptual clarification." It is essential that this process take place so that there can be a common understanding of what terms mean in order to have different studies comparable, widening the range of information from which generalizations can be made. A single study will formulate its conclusions, and this allows for a simple, preliminary level of generalization or leads to new hypotheses. Comparable studies can lead to some even more abstract (therefore more widely applicable) propositions. This has been called "middle range theory." Finally, there are those scholars who by temperament and endowment have concerned themselves with attempts to analyze complex societies as a whole. These writers of "grand theory" rely on the researches of others and segments of their analyses provide hypotheses for new research.

Some theory will be ahead of what is now testable or applicable. Astronomy advanced far beyond its known applications, and much could not be experimentally verified until technology based on other sciences provided the empirical tools. So it is with the social sciences. For a long time to come we will be improving empirical tools and "getting the bugs out" of applied efforts as we are finding must also be done in aerospace efforts or in virus control. This should not detract from the excitement of the theoretical adventure.

THEORY BUILDING: GENERALIZATIONS AND RESEARCH

To open our discussion of theory—how it comes about, and how trustworthy it is—we have chosen two specific "classical" studies that have influenced a generation of research and theory about dominant-minority relations. These illustrate also the relation of research to theory. An important question is: Does some theoretical formulation precede a research investigation, or should one go in cold and just accurately record? Each illustration shows one way of proceeding.

We are more critical of one than of the other. This is a decision made with regard to how much the study's conclusions are still a valid guide to dominant-minority relations today. To an extent the two studies should not be measured against each other as the method of research in each was different: one sought to explore a generalized problem while the other sought to describe a community reality. Nevertheless they are both great pioneer studies which raise important questions.

The Authoritarian Personality[1]

For the last several decades there has been a growing literature bringing together psychological and sociological concepts about personality structure. One of the postulates on which such conceptual integration rests is that the individual's early experi-

[1]T. W. Adorno, Else Frankel-Brunswik, Daniel J. Levinson, R. Nevitt Sanford, *The Authoritarian Personality* (New York: Harper & Brothers, 1950).

ences exert a lasting effect on his personality, what he learns as norms (sociology) and how he reacts emotionally to this learning (psychiatry). There is now a wide range of material to document the different modes of child-rearing in different cultures.[2] Looking toward a crosscultural typology in the field of social structure and personality, one major step has been taken in the formulation of a type: the authoritarian personality. This was first described in the early 1930s by the German philosopher and sociologist Max Horkheimer.[3] The authoritarian personality is one which has been molded by a fear of authority, as for instance in the relationship to a strict patriarchal father whose decisions are binding and often arbitrary, and who punishes for lack of respect. Some cultures, including the Puritan strain in our own, have valued this type of family structure. The child trained in this way responds to all authority as he did to his father, submissively, and as an adult becomes authoritarian in turn. Deeper study of such personalities has shown that obeying arbitrary authority in childhood results in bottled-up fear and resentment. The child who successfully weathers the discipline develops into a man who is frightened by and morally indignant about (and perhaps covertly envious of) people whose behavior is different from the conduct that he has bitterly achieved. His residue of fear and suppressed wish to retaliate can all too easily be mobilized wherever and whenever an appropriate rationalization is supplied.

This is one example of an analytic concept in the social sciences which has been tested, in at least one dimension, by a major field study. Under the auspices of the American Jewish Committee, T. W. Adorno, a colleague of Horkheimer, and several associates set out to test the relationship between authoritarian versus nonauthoritarian upbringing and degree of anti-Semitic prejudice. They derive from their empirical work a summary profile of the prejudiced and the nonprejudiced personality. The prejudiced personality tries to repress from his consciousness unacceptable tendencies or impulses in himself; the unprejudiced person shows more awareness of his faults and is more willing to face up to them. The prejudiced person particularly attempts to repress fear, weakness, sex impulses, and aggressive feelings toward those in authority—for example, his parents. He shows also a tendency to

[2]For examples see Margaret Mead, *Childhood in Contemporary Culture* (New York: Columbia University Press, 1958).
[3]Max Horkheimer, "Authority and the Family," in Bernard Stern, *The Family, Past and Present* (New York: D. Appleton-Century, 1938), p. 428.

compensate for this over-repression by manifesting a drive for power and success along conventional lines. The prejudiced seem to gain less pleasure from emotional experience—companionship, art, or music—than the unprejudiced. Outward conformance to conventions is a marked characteristic of the prejudiced; the unprejudiced are more genuinely concerned with discovering a valid ethical value system for themselves. The prejudiced are more interested in achieving power; the less prejudiced seek love and affection as satisfactory ends in themselves. The high scorers on the prejudice scale are extremely rigid in their standards of behavior, intolerant of any deviation from the conventional codes of morals or manners; in contrast, the low scorers are more flexible in their own adjustments to the mores, more appreciative of the complexities of human behavior, and more sympathetic with those who err.

The basis for these two contrasting personality types was found by these research workers to have been established in the contrasting patterns of family life to which the subjects were exposed in childhood. The prejudiced report rigid discipline, with affection made conditional on the child's approved behavior. In the families of the prejudiced there were clearly defined roles of dominance by parents and submission by children, in contrast with families where equalitarian practices prevailed.

The study we have just presented is an example of an insightful idea in an essay on family structure. This idea was adopted as the hypothesis for a field study. Since this pioneer study, the hypothesis has been further refined and scales of degree of prejudice as related to authoritarianism have been further developed for use in community studies.[4] The deep-rooted nature of prejudice that serves a personality need has, of course, implications for public and educational policy.

Theory is related to research in another way: undertaking research about "a problem" and then proceeding to find out all about the problem without any preliminary hypotheses. Theoretical statements may then emerge in the end from the relationships that the data show. This was the case with Gunnar Myrdal's study of the American Negro which we have cited in Chapters 6 and 7.

As an example of this kind of emergence of theory we are presenting a summary (in our words) of some propositions that were

---

[4]See Robin Williams, Jr., *Strangers Next Door*, pp. 82–110.

distilled out of a large community study of a New England industrial small city. This study was conducted by a team of Harvard anthropologists. Of its five volumes, volume three deals with interethnic relations.

"Yankee City"[5]

A major systematic attempt to delineate the variables in assimilation was made by Warner and Srole. Their criteria of assimilation were the amount and kind of participation permitted the minority ethnic group by the dominant group, as measured by residential mobility, occupational mobility, social class mobility, and membership in formal associations. On the basis of their research they suggest certain variables as determining the rate of assimiliation. In each case the variable mentioned should be read as if preceded with the phrase "other things being equal." They may be summarized as follows:

THE RECENCY FACTOR   The more recently the ethnic group has come into the community, the slower the degree of assimilation.

THE CULTURAL SIMILARITY FACTOR   The more divergent the culture of the ethnic group from the normative culture of the dominant status group, the slower the degree of assimilation.

THE CONCENTRATION FACTOR   The larger the numerical proportion of the ethnic group in relation to the total population of the area, the slower the degree of assimilation.

THE PHYSIOGNOMIC FACTOR   The "darker" the general physical appearance of the group, the slower the degree of assimilation.

THE PERMANENCY FACTOR   The more temporary the ethnic group conceives its residency in the host society, the slower the degree of assimilation.

These variables lend themselves to the following proposition regarding the assimilation of ethnic groups.

[5]W. Lloyd Warner and Leo Srole, *The Social Systems of American Ethnic Groups,* Vol. 3 of the Yankee City Series (New Haven: Yale University Press, 1945).

> The greater the difference between the host and the immigrant cultures, the greater will be the subordination, the greater the strength of the ethnic social systems, and the longer the period necessary for the assimilation of the ethnic group.[6]

Whereas this early study was full of rich data, and the theoretical propositions were good descriptive generalizations of what the team found, at least two criticisms can be made of the study, and to a degree these criticisms reveal the hazard of not clearly defining assumptions and hypotheses at the beginning of research. The first assumption was that all groups seek assimilation in the four areas they defined. *Indeed this may have been true* for this community, but it is an inadequate assumption for any *inclusive* theory of minorities. Second, the researchers reflect the dominant WASP ethnic group's expectation that the burden of change is on the minorities—therefore assimilation is easiest for those most like dominants in values and behavior (provided they aren't dark complected). No cognizance is taken of discrimination as a factor. In the Yankee City analysis, dominant attitudes of acceptance or enforced subordination and distance *depend* upon minority behavior and appearance (these dominant attitudes then constitute the *dependent variable*). Independent variables can vary. Dependent variables can only respond. The Civil Rights movement showed that many dominants can be reckoned with the statistical group that are the independent variable. This is one of the dangers of not only entering the research task without carefully considered hypotheses, but also of the field technique of living in a community long enough to study it widely and richly without taking on its assumptions and values.

THEORY BUILDING: THE REFINEMENT OF CONCEPTS

If we are to analyze dominant-minority relations, sociology must come to some accepted understanding of the meaning of terms describing the ways in which dominants and minorities relate to one another within a structured situation. (This entails understanding the way in which people pitch their expectations of each other—"structure"—as compared with the way in which they might interact as individual persons.)

We are here presenting three illustrations of critical terms

[6]*Ibid.*, p. 285.

that have changed and expanded in their usage from a very simple reference to a more complex one: acculturation, role, marginality.

Acculturation

All contemporary writing on acculturation takes cognizance of the two levels on which cultural characteristics must be acquired when an individual is divesting himself of one culture and accepting another. These have been described by the terms "manifest" versus "intangible," or "behavioral" versus "attitudinal," or "external" and "internal." Whereas these distinctions are commonplace, little attention has been given to the selectivity involved in taking on new cultural traits, whether external or internal. There is very little known about the resistances that may arise at the introduction of a new culture trait or about specific conditions affecting the traits that are accepted or rejected. For example, there will be a difference of behavioral and/or attitudinal acceptance or resistance according to whether culture traits are forced upon a people or are received voluntarily by them. It will make a difference whether or not there is social or political inequality between groups. The analysis of acculturation must be refined to take cognizance of the situations within which acculturation occurs.[7]

Warner and others have claimed that acculturation is apt to occur more quickly when two cultures are similar. Here the differentiation between behavioral and attitudinal needs also to be made, as is pointed out by Broom and Kitsuse.[8] They call attention to the fact that the obvious, external culture traits of a minority may be markedly different from those of the host society, but this does not mean that the attitudinal ones are necessarily different. They cite the example of the Japanese, and account in this way for the relatively rapid acculturation of Japanese Americans despite many different external modes of behavior in Japanese culture.

Broom and Kitsuse also point out that the person who is taking on a new culture must "validate" his acculturation by having *qualified* and been *accepted* in the major institutional patterns of

---

[7]Melville J. Herskovits, *Acculturation: The Study of Culture Contact* (Gloucester, Mass.: Peter Smith, 1958). Appendix, "Outline for the Study of Acculturation," by Robert Redfield, Ralph Linton, and Melville J. Herskovits, p. 133.
[8]Leonard Broom and John Kitsuse, "The Validation of Acculturation," *American Anthropologist*, February, 1955, 57:44 ff.

the dominant society.[9] In order to do this he must also give up any privileged protection or immunities which he has enjoyed by virtue of being a member of a minority. This has been recognized by Frazier and others who have described as "vested interests" the resistances to assimilation of certain status groups within the minority, where incorporation into equal competition with dominants might diminish their advantages. Dominants can equally shut out minorities by patterns of overprotection, by making pets of individual minority members to whom they have some personal tie, or granting disproportionate privilege to those toward whom they feel guility. In this connection, Margaret Mead, as anthropologist consultant to the Israel Ministry of Health, cautions with regard to the Arab minority:

> ... There seemed to be a tendency to demand for the Arab health services far less local contribution than Jewish communities would make and to treat some Arab nomadic groups with a considerable amount of patronage. I fully realize the delicacy of the problem ... but I think the only safe course of action is to accord the Arab population the same type of expectation, privilege, and responsibility accorded other Israeli citizens, for over-privilege can be as discriminatory as under-privilege, even though there are fewer immediate ill effects.[10]

Validation is the point at which the move to ultimate assimilation will or will not be made. If minority members reject participation in some but not all the major institutional forms of the dominant culture, they have made a choice for stabilized pluralism, with the ensuing development of particular established patterns of interaction with dominants.

Roles

There is an increasing interest in sociological theory in role-behavior. A role, as we have seen, is the appropriate behavior associated with a given position in the society. There are socially expected ways of behaving in each society—a father, a student, a priest, a teacher, a chairman, and so on.

The problem of roles in the older theoretical tradition regard-

[9]*Ibid.*
[10]Margaret Mead, "Problems of Cultural Accommodations," in *Assignment in Israel*, ed. Bernard Mandelbaum (New York: The Jewish Theological Seminary of America, Harper & Brothers, 1958), p. 113.

ing dominant-minority relations was perceived as part of the problem of culture conflict. Handlin has written eloquently on the threatened patriarchal role of the immigrant father, which did not fit the role definition of an "American" father.[11] The first concern with roles, then, was with conflicts in definition of institutional roles between the dominant groups and subcultural groups. Often this may involve the necessity for *role relearning.*

Other writing on minorities has dealt with a second problem of roles: that of *learning new roles,* which are associated with structures and positions that do not exist in the society in which the individual grew up, so that he has had no opportunity to acquire this kind of role behavior in his general social learning. Individuals from folk societies have had to learn the roles appropriate to large-scale technological societies, such as behavior in formal organizations.

Role theory has pointed out that many dilemmas for the individual are contained in the *conflict of roles* he must assume in a complex society. Conflict may occur between the roles of citizen (cooperative in emphasis), entrepreneur (competitive in emphasis), and member of a family (authoritative, or supportive, or subordinate).[12]

Role theory is concerned with analyzing roles charactertistic of situations found recurrently in comparable situations. Thus Yankee traders invading the Reconstruction South played roles associated with marginal business and were stereotyped with traits similar to the stereotype some Gentiles have of Jews. This passing insight of Lipset's was picked up and expanded by Rinder, who suggested crosscultural similarities in the role of the stranger-trader.[13] Stryker has carried the delineation further in an article that explores the circumstances under which prejudice will develop against these middlemen traders. He compares attitudes toward three groups of these peoples in the nineteenth century: Jews in Germany, Christian Armenians in Turkey, and Parsis in India. Prejudice developed against Jews and Armenians, but the variable within these two societies, which was absent in the case of the Parsis, was emergent militant nationalism.[14]

This discussion of the minority trader and the way his role is

[11]Oscar Handlin, *The Uprooted* (Boston: Little, Brown & Co., 1951).
[12]Robert K. Merton, *Social Theory and Social Structure,* p. 369.
[13]Lipset, "Changing Social Status and Prejudice," p. 477; Irwin D. Rinder, "Strangers in the Land," *Social Problems, Winter,* 1958–1959, 6: 253 ff.
[14]Sheldon Stryker, "Social Structure and Prejudice," *Social Problems,* Spring, 1959, 6: 340 ff.

perceived by the dominant society not only shows the value of a wider conceptual frame in making evaluations of particular social behavior, but the sequence of the discussion from Lipset, to Rinder, to Stryker is an excellent example of how theory is developed.

Marginality

Park was the first sociologist to be concerned with the concept of marginality. He and his students emphasized the role of culture conflict affecting the marginal individual. Thus marginality, in Park's terms, refers to the situation in which an individual finds himself when he still retains values and behavior from the culture group in which he had his early childhood training and subsequently attempts to incorporate other values and ways of behaving derived from experience outside his own group. Stonequist expanded Park's concept of marginality to show alternative individual modes of adaptation to this conflict.[15] The emphasis of these earlier writers was on the conflict engendered in the personality by the attempt to internalize two differing sets of values.

Merton sees marginality as behavior "in which the individual seeks to abandon one membership group for another to which he is socially forbidden access." For Merton the concept of marginality is a special instance of reference group theory.[16]

The term *reference group* was introduced by Herbert Hyman, and has been expanded by Merton and his associates. In his initial article, Hyman pointed out that many individuals tend to identify themselves with a group to which they do not in fact belong but to whom they accord prestige. This group is their point of reference, whose behavior and attitudes they attempt to adopt.[17] Frazier states that in the post-Civil War South there was an invasion of "New England School marms" setting up schools for Negroes, who were able to create a generation of Negroes with the best culture of New England.[18] These teachers were a reference group for their students. But, as Merton comments, such reference group behavior may be dysfunctional to the person's best interests. If his reference group is a closed group to which he can

[15]E. V. Stonequist, *The Marginal Man* (New York: Scribners, 1937).
[16]Robert K. Merton and Alice Rossi, "Contributions to the Theory of Reference Group Behavior," in Robert K. Merton, *Social Theory and Social Structure*, p. 266.
[17]Herbert H. Hyman, "The Psychology of Status," in *Archives of Psychology*, No. 269, 1942.
[18]Frazier, *Race and Culture Contacts in the Modern World*, p. 309.

never belong—that is, if he is marginal—his newly adopted be-havior may initially lead to confusion.[19] However, if positions in the social structure are open to the person, he will be able to use the new behavior he has learned.

The rigidity or fluidity of the society as a whole will affect how the person is received. If the society has rigid barriers against movement from one group to another, the person adapting to modes of a group other than his own will be rejected and ridi-culed by the outside group, as some Southerners at times speak of educated Negroes as "uppity." If the society is less rigid, a Negro who achieves a good job, good manners, and good speech may, in New York for example, be respected by whites and Negroes alike.

Park and Stonequist's approach to marginality supplied socio-logical dimensions for the explanation of behavior that had pre-viously been viewed as individual deviance and evaluated in moral terms. They wrote at a time when American society was incor-porating large groups of migrants of diverse cultural origins. Under Merton the concept of marginality is enlarged, so that it applies not only to individuals of ethnic or racial subgroups but to any individual who seeks entrance to and is denied admission to a group, a stratum, or a community. Merton stresses the role of the excluding group as a new dimension of Park's original formulation.

THEORY BUILDING: MIDDLE-RANGE THEORY

Robert K. Merton, who coined the term "middle-range theory," has stated that ". . . theory must advance on . . . interconnected planes: through special theories adequate to limited ranges of social data, and the evolution of a more general conceptual scheme adequate to consolidated groups of special theories."[20] We have just dealt with an array of generalizations based on a limited range of data, and in some instances seen how they have modified or amplified one another. Middle-range theory seeks a consolidation of related insights at a more abstract level than those we have considered thus far in the framework of theory building.

Merton envisages theory growing out of empirical data and an inductive process of reasoning, though he himself has largely

[19]Robert K. Merton, *Social Theory and Social Structure*, p. 266 ff.
[20]Merton, *Social Theory and Social Structure*, Introduction, pp. 9–10.

worked deductively. Middle-range theory thus far has not stated a relationship to one or another "grand theory," but many of the assumptions underlying it are so derived. In Merton's own work with its emphasis on structure and function one may see his heritage, though modified and made his own, from Parsons.

Middle-range theory has made significant contributions to problems of dominant-minority relations. It now awaits increased testing on comparative material to define accurately which variables are generic to minority situations. To illustrate this level of theory we present two of Merton's theoretical formulations that are now a recognized part of all thinking about minority situations, and a third illustration.

"The Self-Fulfilling Prophecy"[21]

In this classic essay Merton explores the phenomenon of the *vicious cycle*. We have already seen in Chapter 2 that Myrdal dealt with this concept and saw it as a spiraling process. Merton is more concerned with analyzing how it gets started and what is inherent in its control. Merton's theory has broader applications than just the vicious cycle, and lends itself equally well to an analysis of, for example, outbreaks of violence.

Starting with the theorem of W. I. Thomas, "If men define situations as real, they are real in their consequences," Merton points out that the trouble begins with an incomplete or false definition of the situation. If this false definition is acted on, it brings about a situation which fits the definition. His first illustration is of how a bank can be caused to fail when a rumor starts that it is shaky. The rumor (false definition) brings about a run on the bank (behavior) that precipitates its failure. His second illustration is of unions excluding Negroes because Negroes have been strike breakers; then since they cannot join unions they will obviously have no union loyalty that would keep them from accepting employment in a shop whose workers are on strike. Merton's theory illuminates the nature of stereotypes. The dominant group's beliefs (definitions of situations) result in discriminatory actions that so structure the interacting of dominants and minorities that they force the minority to intensify the derogated behavior and thus give the stereotype validity.

Furthermore, Merton points out that when a minority has

---

[21]*Ibid.*, pp. 421–436.

been enclaved in a stereotype—that is to say, a false definition of character and behavior—the minority individual who behaves in the approved mode of the dominant group is criticized for so doing. The same behavior is defined differently by the dominant group, depending on whether it is displayed by one of their own group or a member of the minority group. What is virtue for the dominant group becomes vice in the eyes of the majority for the stereotyped minority. If, as Merton cites, a Presbyterian rises from rags to riches, he is held up as a model. If a Jew does the same he is condemned as being too acquisitive and too ambitious.

In considering how the circle of self-fulfilling prophesies can be broken, Merton posits that, logically and ideally, one should begin with a redefinition of the situation. This, however, is not a simple act of will or good will, for deep-seated beliefs are themselves the products of social forces. He notes furthermore, the hopelessness of trying to persuade the psychologically disturbed. Similarly, he is less than optimistic about education as the way out. The fact that the educational system is itself part of the normative institutional structure of the dominant society makes it subject to the, at best, "incomplete" definitions that dominants make of minorities.

For this reason, Merton sets his hope for remedy in the deliberate enactment of institutional change. Returning to his initial illustrations of the failure of a bank and action against Negroes, he points out that banking legislation, or the statutory creation of interracial public housing have been effective enacted institutional controls. The original proposition then may be restated in this way: "The self-fulfilling prophecy, whereby fears are translated into reality, operates only in the absence of deliberate institutional controls."[22]

"Social Structure and Anomie"[23]

In this essay Merton shows how the social structure poses problems of adaptation for individuals in the competitive opportunities offered the members of society. He points out that the person who achieves an honored place in the society is expected to pursue goals which society values, using the means of which the society approves. But other patterns of adjustment occur,

[22]*Ibid.*, p. 436.
[23]*Ibid.*, pp. 131–160. *Anomie* is a term used to describe a condition characterized by lack of norms.

depending on opportunity within the society. Some people have incorporated the approved goals into their thinking very early and have been trained appropriately at successive stages in how to pursue them. The boy who goes to a good school, a college of standing, and a recognized school for business or professional training, or becomes associated with a reputable firm may expect, according to his talents, to achieve desirable goals by legitimate means. But the boy who goes to an overcrowded, understaffed school and cannot get into a good college, or any college, will be at a competitive disadvantage in achieving those same goals. He may lower his aspirations but retain the approved means of pursuing such goals as he can attain. He will be good, conscientious, but not so successful. He may on the other hand, retain the goals and abandon the approved means. He may then become a racketeer or robber baron or a canny politician. He may make a fortune, and perhaps his descendants will endow a college or a church. Or if the barriers are too great or too confusing, he may reject both goals and means. He may retreat into reactive movements, cults, daydreams perhaps stimulated by television or other mass escape mechanisms, or opiates.

The final alternative offered in Merton's paradigm is that of rebellion: the attempt to change both the goals and means. This alternative suggests the association with groups supporting "unofficial values" or counter ideologies. (See Chapter 2.)

Merton has prepared a now well-known paradigm[24] which summarizes the choices of adaptation to goals and means.

Modes of Adaptation	Culture Goals	Institutional Means
I. Conformity	+	+
II. Innovation	+	−
III. Ritualism	−	+
IV. Retreatism	−	−
V. Rebellion	±	±

The contribution of this theory is not in labeling the behavior as rebellion or innovation but in providing an explanation of why one might expect to find such behavior more frequently in minority groups than in the dominant group. The explanation, according to Merton, lies in the differential access to the means (education,

[24]*Ibid.*, p. 140. By permission.

capital, and so on) for achieving the goals of the dominant culture. According to this theory, as these minorities achieve equality of opportunity, one would expect a decline in such types of deviant behavior.

In Kluckhon's description of the Navaho as quoted in Chapter 10, p. 290, we can see an almost perfect application of this paradigm. It is interesting that in the first version of Merton's essay he did not include the dimension of rebellion. When it was pointed out that there was a fifth alternative Merton revised his essay, as may be seen from the comparison of his first edition and his revised edition of *Social Theory and Social Structure*. Indeed the whole revised edition includes continuities of former ideas, reflecting not only further research, but also the stimulus of discussion and debate with other critical minds. The productive intellectual life can only flourish in intellectual interaction. Theory building depends upon this as well as on valid research.

Revitalization Movements

Movements which are organized efforts to revitalize "native" culture and sentiments are now generally recognized to be a special phenomenon of social change. The term "nativist" may apply to a movement within any group, dominant or minority.

A special characteristic of a nativist movement is that it seeks to solve the discomforts which its adherents feel by eliminating what is perceived as alien: persons, artifacts, customs, values.[25] As long as there are visible minorities, they are in a vulnerable position as the target of organized nativist sentiment and action from the dominant group.

Some nativist movements seek to revive and reinstate customs, values, and even beliefs which were thought to be part of the culture complex of earlier generations but are not now present. The Nazis did this with their appeal to *Blut und Boden* (blood —German "Aryan"; and soil—homeland).

The definable stages of the growth of nativist movements have been analyzed by Wallace. At the beginning of the movement the emphasis on excluding alien elements is commonly very low, subordinate to other emphases. Over a number of years the movement grows where individuals or some population group (class, religious, or other definable social group) is experiencing stress. There is a continued lessening of the culture's efficiency in satisfy-

[25]Anthony F. C. Wallace, "Revitalization Movements," *American Anthropologist*, 1956, 59: 264 ff.

ing the needs of this group. The type of leader who reformulates a desirable social system for the group tends to be of the charismatic leadership type, the man with strong personal appeal.

After the movement is conceived and leadership established, it must deal with the establishment of communication and with organization. If it is successful through these initial stages, its success or failure rests on the adequate prediction of the outcome of conflict situations. If it is "unrealistic" about the amount of resistance it will engender, about the consequences of its own and its opponent's moves in a power struggle, it will run the risk of early collapse. Whether its ideology or organization will be viable for long beyond its demise in the power struggle will depend on whether its formulations and structure lead to actions which maintain a low level of stress. This would account for the collapse of defeated political nativistic movements which maximize stress, in contrast with the persistence of religious revivalist or sectarian movements which lower the threshold of stress.

We have cited revitalization movements in Chapters 3 and 9, but it might be interesting to take this theoretical schema and examine anti-minority nativist movements in the United States as presented by the historian, John Higham.[26]

THEORY BUILDING: A TASTE OF "GRAND THEORY"

We have chosen four examples of general, overall theoretical positions by sociologists of this century in America who have sought to analyze society as a whole. The first two emphasize interaction as the critical focus of the study of society. The last two emphasize social structure, that is to say, the persistent patterns that ensure stability and continuity.

It is impossible to summarize briefly the rich contributions of these four men. We have selected just enough to demonstrate approaches, and how these approaches can be related to understanding dominant-minority relations.

Robert E. Park

Robert E. Park's systematic analysis of society revolved around three postulated basic modes of human *interaction:* cooperation, competition, and conflict. Race and culture contacts were

[26]John Higham, *Strangers in the Land: Patterns of American Nativism,* (New Brunswick, N.J.: Rutgers University Press), 1955.

subsumed under this system.[27] He attempted to explore the diversity in race and culture contacts, from those of accommodative peace to those of open conflict. His assumptions were the evolutionary beliefs that were the critical intellectual issues of his period—the early part of this century. With this orientation, Park saw relations between dominants and minorities as moving through a definite cycle, with one outcome, the assimilation of the minority into the dominant society. The sequence of competition, conflict, cooperation was a dynamic process in which Park ignored any volitional elements. This makes him the most deterministic of the theorists we are presenting and the least concerned with psychological and motivational dimensions.

Park's work, together with that of his colleague, Louis Wirth, made the first major impact on theory of dominant-minority relations. The work of these two men and others associated with them as colleagues or students comprise what has been called the Park-Wirth school of thought about "race relations." Several of Park's formulations have been incorporated into all subsequent thinking about minorities and have been validated or expanded by subsequent theory and research. One of the most significant of these is the concept of the marginal man. Park also saw that prejudice is to be separated from discrimination, that it cannot be dispelled by knowledge alone, that it rises in periods of social change as individuals and vested interests resist change in the status of minorities, or, otherwise threatened, vent hostility on a vulnerable minority. Park took cognizance of conflict of interest in the dynamics of social interaction, a dimension neglected by some contemporary theorists. He was also interested in the effect of urbanization on conflict between races and nationality groups. He felt that urbanization increased tension between dominants and minorities. Contemporary research in urban patterns of interaction suggests this may not always be so, depending on other variables.[28]

George C. Homans

A contemporary sociologist whose analysis is on the basis of *interaction* is George C. Homans. The fundamental unit in society,

[27]Robert E. Park, *Race and Culture* (Glencoe, Ill.: The Free Press, 1950).
[28]For a re-evaluation of Park by a contemporary sociologist, see Seymour Martin Lipset, "Changing Social Status and Prejudice: The Race Theories of a Pioneering American Sociologist," *Commentary*, May, 1950, pp. 475–479.

for Homans, is the group as a social system. The elements of group behavior are activities, interaction, and sentiment. These three elements in their various interrelations and priorities constitute the social system.[29]

Homans distinguishes between an "external system" of relationships of those elements which relate primarily to survival in the environment and an "internal system" which is related to liking and preferences. External and internal systems are never wholly independent of one another, but a different order of precedence of the three basic factors governs each system. Essentially what Homans is accounting for is the type of interaction related to survival in the larger society as contrasted with the type of interaction which allows the persistence of widely differentiated subgroups within the society.

Homans derives his three basic elements of behavior from a series of empirical case studies of group behavior, ranging from kinship to occupation. Homans develops some speciflc propositions, several of which can be applied to dominant-minority relations.

Proposition 1
. . . persons who interact with one another frequently are more like one another in their activities than they are like other persons with whom they interact less frequently.

Thus, in line with this proposition, which establishes in Homans' scheme the basis for group coherence, one would expect that individuals in a minority group or in the dominant group who associate frequently would develop similarities of activities that would identify them both subjectively and objectively with their group. This might serve as a base for the development of stereotypes; but, equally, if group barriers disappear to permit frequent interaction the differences of activity should disappear also.

Proposition 2
. . . the more frequently persons interact with one another, the stronger their sentiments of friendship for one another are apt to be.

This proposition would be basic to the reduction of intergroup diffidence or antagonism. Antagonism can be dispelled if

[29]George C. Homans, *The Human Group* (New York: Harcourt, Brace, 1950).

there is a structured situation within which dominants and minorities can interact as equals. Out of interaction sentiments of friendship will develop as, ideally, with school integration.

> Proposition 3
> . . . to the degree that the activities of the other individual in a reciprocal role relationship conform to the norms of one's own group, one will like him.

One might interpret this proposition to suggest that where minority group individuals and dominants carry out their roles in relation to one another with the same standards (for example, two civil servants), they are more likely to conceive of each other as individuals to whom one assigns liking and respect, rather than as representatives of their group.

It is hardly necessary to point out that many efforts at improved intergroup relations operate on one or another of these propositions, whether or not the organizers of programs have ever heard of Homans. Homans' analysis has also stimulated a large development in small group research. His concern is with the dynamics of relationship and he gives greater weight to effective sentiments in his basic schema than do many sociologists. Homans' later work moves even closer to psychology.

Robert M. MacIver

Robert M. MacIver must be included in any discussion of general theory particularly relevant to dominant-minority relations for a number of reasons. Perhaps the least significant but most obvious of these is that he has, in addition to general theory, written specifically on dominant-minority relations.[30]

MacIver's contributions to general theory are largely those of precision and emphasis. He is in the tradition of the classical sociologists of continental Europe, England, and America. Like Park, his assumptions are evolutionary; unlike Park, he avoids the value judgment of "progress," nor is he as deterministic as Park in his view of social change. For MacIver, for good or ill, societies evolve from the simple to the complex. Within the broad limits of evolutionary development, however, there is room for voluntar-

---

[30]Robert M. MacIver, *The More Perfect Union* (New York: Macmillan, 1948). For MacIver's general analysis of social structure and change, see Robert M. MacIver and Charles H. Page, *Society* (New York: Holt, 1949).

istic action to determine directions of change and solutions to problems created by change.

The complexity of the evolving modern social world intrigues MacIver. His main concerns are with the analysis of social structure as a mechanism for sustaining an appropriate balance of necessary controls and optimum individual creativity. He has coined the term "the multi-group society." MacIver sees the State in a pre-eminent role in modern society (he is also distinguished for his writings in political science). Nevertheless, he is convinced of the limited effectiveness of the State if it intrudes beyond its proper sphere, which is adjudicator of competing interests.

MacIver makes a distinction between like (competing) interests and common interests. The function of the State is to regulate *like* interests. *Common* (cultural) interests, where the pursuit of the interest by some members of the society does not detract from the total available to others, is a sphere in which the State is ill-suited or incapable of functioning.

MacIver, concerned as he is with the institutional regulatory patterns of society, still emphasizes that the social reality is groups and associations of people. For him culture is the vehicle for creative and spontaneous expression. All compulsion in the cultural sphere is deadening. MacIver in his insistence on the independence of the cultural sphere opens the way to a redefinition of the question of cultural pluralism more in harmony with what current research is finding to be the reality.

Talcott Parsons[31]

The most ambitious attempt at overall formulation of an inclusive theory of society is that of Parsons, and no discussion of theory could omit mention of his work. Here we can only present his basic approach and discuss briefly one of his theoretical contributions that has become a useful tool for analysis. Parsons seeks for as abstract formulations as possible and he often links words in a complicated way to indicate a specific concept as an expression of various related dimensions. He has, therefore a rather special and difficult vocabulary.

Parsons begins with emphasizing three dimensions of human behavior: the social, the cultural, and the motivational. These are not just randomly part of a person's relations to others, but each

[31]Talcott Parsons, *The Social System* (Glencoe, Ill.: The Free Press, 1950).

dimension shows recurring regularities—in short it is a system of behavior. There are motivational systems, cultural systems, and social systems. Consider for example the motivations of Anglo sportsmen and Indian fishers in the controversy described in Chapter 10. Their difference in motivation changes the way they fish, so that net fishing by Indians concerned with preserving their food supply is not as depleting as net fishing might be for sportsmen interested in a competitive size of catch; yet the sportsman responds to a motivation that is part of his personality and that of others who have been brought up in a competitive society. It is not individual greed that motivates him, but an accepted way of being—a system of behavior. In the same way cultural behavior occurs within a systematic set of symbols: "We speak English," "We are a church-going family" are expressions of symbolic behavior.

The social system is made up of the patterns that insure the survival and continuity of the society: kinship, occupation, etc. These three dimensions—motivation, culture, and society—are held together and made coherent by a consensus of central values. Values, as we pointed out in Chapter 2, are defined by Parsons as "beliefs leading to action." Historically in America we have held as values that man should attempt to overcome and control the hazards of the natural environment; that competition and private property are appropriate values on which to build our economic life; that the nuclear family of father, mother, and children has priority over the extended kinship of aunts, uncles, and grandparents. The survival of a particular society with its values makes necessary the creation of specific positions which represent the distribution of functions in the society. These might be occupational positions, such as banker, machinist, farmer, private secretary, and so forth; or within the kinship patterns, father, aunt, stepmother. These positions are statuses, ranked higher or lower in community evaluation according to how central they are to the preservation of the core values and how limited they are in replaceability. East status demands the carrying out of a function in a socially defined way. This is role.

Parsons' chief focus thus far has been on the *social* system. He sees its institutional structure as regulative, defining the legitimate limits of action, and as relational in its establishment of reciprocal role expectations. Institutions for Parsons translate the private acceptance of values into public commitment, through the carrying out of institutionally defined roles. He sees such problems as negative stereotyping as *deviance by the dominant* from his own institutional norms for the entire society. So long as discrimination is accepted and reinforced within the dominant society, no *single individual has to pay the price for deviance of this kind,* as in other circumstances he would through various kinds of social punishments.[32]

Critics of Parsons have charged that he is too limited in his emphasis on institutional integration and socially induced personality stress. It is felt that he overlooks real conflict of interest in his concern for the stabilizing regulative mechanisms of society and individual acceptance of or reaction formation against these structures.

In Parsons' own view his most significant theoretical contribution has been in the development of what are generally called "pattern variables." These are five pairs of alternatives which the individual may choose as a way of relating to others. Clearly the individual does not choose deliberately, but as a person socialized within a culture and within a given social situation with its expectations of role and status behavior. On a very simple level the pattern variables can delineate dichotomies in expectations as between one culture and another, or a village society and a cosmopolitan society. Some of the variables in their original formulation[33] were:

(1) Particularism versus universalism—that is, in a particularistic pattern a person or object is significant, whereas in universalism a precept is significant. For example, Puerto Ricans today, like older ethnic groups in the past, may see employment in terms of getting a relative a job (if they have one and know of another in the same shop). This is particularism. The union, however, is interested in general hiring policies, and seniority privileges regardless of personal or ethnic ties (ideally). This is universalism.

(2) The second pair of variables is affect positive versus affect neutrality. Affect positive means the willingness to risk the expression of feeling in the expectation of a rewarding response. This is characteristic of small groups with frequent interaction of the members, or with very stable small subsocieties. In urban society with its many daily contacts and its multigroup character, it is impossible to risk the psychic burden of affective relationships in all contacts, and a pattern of viable choice develops in which

[32]*Ibid.,* p. 290.
[33]*Ibid.,* p. 67.

the individual is restrained, cautious, and uninvolved (affect neutral).

Others of the variables need not be elaborated: they are self-interest (individualism) versus collective interest; achievement versus ascription (performance as contrasted with known quality); specificity versus diffuseness (specialization of roles and/or contractually defined limits of obligation versus commitment beyond any defined limit, or roles so loosely defined that they encompass many diverse interactions with varying obligation and response patterns depending on the interaction and not on the role definition.)

Parsons has somewhat revised this earliest formulation to make the variables more abstractly stated in the hope of making them more flexible tools for many levels of analysis. In this earliest formulation, however, they already add a considerable dimension for our view of areas of conflict in behavioral expectations as between dominants and cultural minorities, or as between rural and urban patterns of living and evaluating. For example: A small homogeneous village society will not be able to offer wide choices of roles, therefore role specialization is not a realistic choice; or collective interest may be made by the pressure of social norms to take priority over individual self interest. The student might attempt to apply these to the five communities of Rimrock as discussed in Chapters 3 and 11.

The three contemporary theorists we have just presented have taken cognizance, by their respective designations of "like," "external," and "social," of the separation of the secular systems of relationship and the cultural systems of relations. These latter allow, in MacIver's terms, more creative spontaneity; in Homan's terms, more sentiment-engendered interaction; in Parsons' terms, more particularistic values; and in keeping with all three, the possibility of great variety of group life. The cultural sphere is, as it were, terrain for abundant variant flowering, flourishing from a root of common interest, common norms, and established position in the secular order. All three theorists recognize the interdependence of the social and cultural, but all recognize that the spheres are of a different order. Thus the base is laid for the role of culture in our pluralistic society.

Only the experience of America could produce such a theory. Heretofore cultural pluralism has been discussed as if whole cultures, with their sacred and secular systems intact, were to be incorporated in a quasi-federal fashion. The risks of fragmentation, separation, loss of benefit, and eventual instability of the nation-state have been apparent in this older theory, and aroused grave doubts about the support of that kind of pluralistic society. The solution here presented suggests the appropriateness of separating those functions which are uniquely cultural from the totality, allowing their voluntary development in a variety of patterns and strengthening unity in areas of secular public interest. MacIver feels strongly that such a possibility is inherent in the democratic state. It is in the light of these theories that we can then understand Frazier's vision of cosmopolitan urban societies of the future, in which the interaction of people of varying racial and ethnic identification on the basis of equality will lead to a new flow of human creativity.[34]

Suggested Readings

Dahlke, H. Otto, "Race and Minority Riots—A Study in the Typology of Violence," *Social Forces,* May, 1952.
  In this article Dahlke extrapolates the common elements in disparate situations in which riots have occurred. It is a good example of how theoretical hypotheses are developed.

Hughes, Everett C. "Social Change and Status Protest," *Phylon,* Vol. X, First Quarter, 1949.
  The author, who has richly contributed to the literature on minorities, anticipates here by nearly two decades some of the phenomena we are now witnessing in the Negro revolt.
  (This article is available in a Bobbs-Merrill reprint.)

MacIver, Robert M. *The Web of Government.* New York: The Macmillan Co., 1947.
  The entire argument is an elaboration of MacIver's theory of the state, and the last chapter on the "multi-group" society is especially relevant.

Merton, Robert K. *Social Theory and Social Structure,* rev. ed. Glencoe, Ill.: The Free Press, 1957.
  Merton's principal contributions to middle-range theory, including elaborations and further thoughts on the self-fulfilling prophecy, social structure and anomie, and reference groups.

Parsons, Talcott. *The Social System.* Glencoe, Ill.: The Free Press, 1950.
  Parsons' elaboration of the structure of the social system. Chapter 3 discusses the various combinations of particularistic and universalistic values found in different cultures.

[34]E. Franklin Frazier, *Race and Culture Contacts in the Modern World.* (New York: Knopf, 1957.)

Index of Authors

Index of Subjects